the Unofficial Guide® to Walt Disney World®

1999

the Unofficial Guide® to Walt Disney World® 1999

Bob Sehlinger

Macmillan • USA

For George, the comeback kid

Macmillan Travel
A Simon & Schuster Macmillan Company
1633 Broadway
New York, New York 10019-6785

Produced by Menasha Ridge Press
Design by Barbara E. Williams

MACMILLAN is a registered trademark of Macmillan, Inc.
UNOFFICIAL GUIDE is a registered trademark of Simon & Schuster, Inc.

ISBN 0-02-862616-8

ISSN 1059-3578

Manufactured in the United States of America

10 9 8 7 6 5 4 3 2 1

Contents

LIST OF MAPS

ACKNOWLEDGMENTS

Special thanks to our field research team who rendered a Herculean effort in what must have seemed like a fantasy version of Sartre's *No Exit* to the tune of "It's a Small World." We hope you all recover to tour another day.

Betsy Amster	Shelley DeLuca
Lynne Bachleda	Allison Grizzle
Caroline Blondy	Madeline O'Bryan
Molly Burns	Taylor O'Bryan (the Human Probe)
Holly Cross	Grace Walton
Leslie Cummins	Barbara Williams

Peals of laughter and much appreciation to nationally renowned cartoonist Tami Knight for her brilliant and insightful work.

Mike Jones, Marie Hillin, Patt Palmer, and Robert Clay White all energetically contributed to shaping this latest edition. Betsy Amster provided invaluable counsel regarding the organization of the guide. Psychologists Dr. Karen Turnbow, Dr. Gayle Janzen, and Dr. Joan Burns provided much insight concerning the experiences of young children at Walt Disney World. "Hotel Women" Grace Walton and Shelley DeLuca inspected many dozens of hotels.

Many thanks also to B. Williams & Associates for design, to Holly Cross and Laura Poole for production, and to Carolyn Hassett for editorial work on this book. Caroline Carr earned our appreciation for her fine work and for keeping tight deadlines in providing the typography. Cartography was provided by Tim Krasnansky and Brian Taylor, and the index was prepared by Ann Cassar.

Introduction

How Come "Unofficial"?

DECLARATION OF INDEPENDENCE

The author and researchers of this guide specifically and categorically declare that they are and always have been totally independent of the Walt Disney Company, Inc.; of Disneyland, Inc.; of Walt Disney World, Inc.; and of any and all other members of the Disney corporate family not listed.

The material in this guide originated with the author and researchers and has not been reviewed, edited, or in any way approved by the Walt Disney Company, Inc.; Disneyland, Inc.; or Walt Disney World, Inc.

This guidebook represents the first comprehensive *critical* appraisal of Walt Disney World. Its purpose is to provide the reader with the information necessary to tour Walt Disney World with the greatest efficiency and economy, and with the least hassle and standing in line. The authors believe in the wondrous variety, joy, and excitement of the Disney attractions. At the same time, we recognize that Walt Disney World is a business, with the same profit motivations as businesses the world over.

In this guide we represent and serve you, the consumer. If a restaurant serves bad food, or a gift item is overpriced, or a certain ride isn't worth the wait, we can say so, and in the process we hope to make your visit more fun, efficient, and economical.

THE IMPORTANCE OF BEING GOOFY

A group of Disney executives, clean-shaven (because company policy bans beards and mustaches) and impeccably attired in dark suits, gather around a polished black walnut table. There is an almost palpable tension. Everyone speaks in hushed tones, carefully measuring their words:

"I don't want to be blindsided by this at the shareholders' meeting."

"No one's raised the issue yet. Let's just sit on it. The last thing we want is to stir something up."

"Too late; I've heard the *Post* is working on a story. There are even rumors about a paternity suit."

"What's Donald saying?"

"He's stonewalling. Won't return my calls."

"Well, he's going to have to come clean. Our people need to know what to tell the press."

"Right. And we need to know, too. If he doesn't have a brother and he doesn't have a sister, where *did* Huey, Dewey, and Louie come from?"

And so it goes. . . .

What really makes writing about Walt Disney World fun is that the Disney people take everything so seriously. Day to day, they debate momentous decisions with far-ranging consequences: Will Goofy look swishy in a silver cape? Have we gone too far with the Little Mermaid's cleavage? At a time when the nation is concerned about the drug problem, can we afford to have a dwarf named "Dopey"?

Unofficially, we think having a sense of humor is important. This guidebook has one, and it's probably necessary that you do, too—not to use this book but, more significantly, to have fun at Walt Disney World. Disney World (in the popular phrasing) is the mother of all tourist attractions. A certain amount of levity is required simply to survive. Think of the *Unofficial Guide* as a private trainer to help get your sense of humor in shape. It will help you understand the importance of being Goofy.

HONEY, I BLEW UP THE BOOK!

The first edition of *The Unofficial Guide to Walt Disney World* was considerably less than 200 pages, a mere shadow of its present size. In the years since that edition, Disney World has grown tremendously, adding Disney-MGM Studios, Downtown Disney, the BoardWalk, Typhoon Lagoon, Blizzard Beach, several new attractions in Epcot and the Magic Kingdom, about 20,500 new hotel rooms and, in summer 1998, the Animal Kingdom, Walt Disney World's fourth theme park. The *Unofficial Guide* has grown to match this expansion (and the author has put on a little weight himself).

We have no idea where it all will end. In 30 years we may be selling an alphabetized, 26-volume edition, handsomely packaged in its own imitation-oak bookcase. In the meantime, we offer a qualified apology for the bulk of this edition. We know it may be too heavy to be carried comfortably without the assistance of a handcart, llama, or Sherpa, but we defend the inclusion of all the information presented. Not every diner uses catsup, A-1 Sauce, and Tabasco, but it's nice to have all three on the table.

Because the *Unofficial Guide* is so hefty, and because there's just no room for fun, anecdotal information, we have created two new *Unofficial Guides:*

Mini-Mickey: The Pocket-Sized Unofficial Guide to
   Walt Disney World
   by Bob Sehlinger; 320 pages; $10.95

The Unofficial Disney Companion: The Inside Story of
   Walt Disney World and the Man Behind the Mouse
   by Eve Zibart; 225 pages; $11.95

Mini-Mickey is a nice, portable, *"Cliff Notes"* version of *The Unofficial Guide to Walt Disney World.* Updated annually, it distills information from this comprehensive guide to help short-stay or last-minute visitors decide quickly how to plan their limited hours at Disney World. *The Unofficial Disney Companion* is a behind-the-scenes unauthorized history of Walt Disney World, and it is loaded with all the amazing facts and great stories that we can't squeeze into this book. Both books are available from Macmillan Travel and at most bookstores.

The Death of Spontaneity

One of our all-time favorite letters came from a man in Chapel Hill, North Carolina:

> *Your book reads like the operations plan for an amphibious landing. . . . Go here, do this, proceed to Step 15. . . . You must think that everyone [who visits Walt Disney World] is a hyperactive, Type-A, theme-park-commando. Whatever happened to the satisfaction of self-discovery or the joy of spontaneity? Next you will be telling us when to empty our bladders.*

As it happens, *Unofficial Guide* researchers are a pretty existential crew. We are big on self-discovery if the activity is walking in the woods or watching birds. Some of us are able to improvise jazz without reading music, and others can whip up a mean pot of chili without a recipe. When it comes to Walt Disney World, however, we all agree that you either need a good plan or a frontal lobotomy. The operational definition of self-discovery and spontaneity at Walt Disney World is the "pleasure" of heat prostration and the "joy" of standing in line.

It's easy to spot the free spirits at Walt Disney World, particularly at opening time. While everybody else is stampeding to Space Mountain, they are standing in a cloud of dust, puzzling over the park map. Later, they are the people running around like chickens in a thunderstorm, trying to find an attraction with less than a 40-minute wait. Face it, Walt Disney World is not a very existential place. In many ways it's the quintessential system, the ultimate in mass-produced entertainment, the most planned and programmed environment anywhere. Spontaneity and self-discovery work about as well at Walt Disney World as they do on your tax return.

We aren't saying that you can't have a great time at Walt Disney World. What we *are* saying is that you need a plan. You don't have to be compulsive or inflexible; just think about what you want to do before you go. Don't delude yourself by rationalizing that the information in this guide is only for the pathological and the superorganized. Ask not for whom the tome tells, Bubba—it tells for thee.

The Attraction That Ate Florida

Before Walt Disney World, Florida was a happy peninsula of many more-or-less equal tourist attractions. Distributed around the state in great profusion, they constituted the nation's most perennially appealing vacation opportunity. There were the Monkey Jungle, the Orchid Jungle, venerable Marineland, the St. Augustine Alligator Farm, Silver Springs, the Miami Wax Museum, the Sunken Gardens, the Coral Castle, and the Conch Train

Tour. These, along with Cypress Gardens, Busch Gardens, and others, were the attractions that ruled Florida. Now, like so many dinosaurs, those remaining survive precariously on the droppings of the greatest beast of them all, Walt Disney World. Old standbys continue to welcome tourists, but when was the last time you planned your vacation around a visit to Jungle Larry's Safari Park?

When Walt Disney World arrived on the scene, Florida tourism changed forever. Before Disney (B.D.), southern Florida was the state's and the nation's foremost tourist destination. Throngs sunned on the beaches of Miami, Hollywood, and Fort Lauderdale and patronized such nearby attractions as the Miami Serpentarium and the Parrot Jungle. Attractions in the Ocala and St. Augustine area upstate hosted road travelers in great waves as they journeyed to and from southern Florida. At the time, Orlando was a sleepy little central Florida town an hour's drive from Cypress Gardens, with practically no tourist appeal whatsoever.

Then came Disney, snapping up acres of farm and swampland before anyone even knew who the purchaser was. Bargaining hard, Walt demanded improved highways, tax concessions, bargain financing, and community support. So successful had been his California Disneyland that whatever he requested, he received.

Generally approving, and hoping for a larger aggregate market, the existing Florida attractions failed to discern the cloud on the horizon. Walt had tipped his hand early, however, and all the cards were on the table. When Disney bought 27,500 central Florida acres, it was evident he didn't intend to raise cattle.

The Magic Kingdom opened on October 1, 1971, and was immediately successful. Hotel construction boomed in Orlando and Kissimmee and around Walt Disney World. Major new attractions popped up along recently completed Interstate 4 to cash in on the tide of tourists arriving at Disney's latest wonder. Walt Disney World became a destination, and suddenly nobody cared as much about going to the beach. The Magic Kingdom was good for two days, and then you could enjoy the rest of the week at Sea World, Cypress Gardens, Circus World, Gatorland Zoo, Busch Gardens, the Stars Hall of Fame Wax Museum, and the Kennedy Space Center.

These attractions, all practically new and stretching from Florida's east coast to west coast, formed what would come to be called the Orlando Wall. Tourists no longer poured into Miami and Fort Lauderdale. Instead they stopped at the Orlando Wall and exhausted themselves and their dollars in the shiny attractions arrayed between Cape Canaveral and Tampa. In southern Florida, venerable attractions held on by a parrot feather and more than a few closed their doors. Flagship hotels on the fabled Gold Coast went bust or were converted into condominiums.

When Walt Disney World opened, the very definition of a tourist attraction changed. Setting standards for cleanliness, size, scope, grandeur, variety, and attention to detail, Disney World overnight relegated the majority of Florida's headliner attractions to comparative insignificance. Newer attractions such as Sea World and the vastly enlarged Busch Gardens successfully achieved the new standard. Cypress Gardens, Weeki Wachi, and Silver Springs expanded and modernized. Most other attractions, however, slipped into a limbo of diminished status. Far from being headliners or tourist destinations, they plugged along as local diversions, pulling in the curious, the bored, and the sunburned for two-hour excursions.

Many of the affected attractions were and are wonderful places to spend a day, but even collectively they don't command sufficient appeal to lure many tourists beyond the Wall. We recommend them, however, not only for their variety of high-quality offerings, but as a glimpse of Florida's golden age, a time of less sophisticated, less plastic pleasures before the Mouse. Take a day or two and drive three-and-a-half hours south of Orlando. Visit the Miami Seaquarium or Ocean World. Try Vizcaya, Fairchild Tropical Gardens, and Lion Country Safari. Drive Collins Avenue along the Gold Coast. You'll be glad you did.

When Epcot opened in Walt Disney World on October 1, 1982, another seismic shock reverberated throughout the Florida attractions industry. This time it wasn't only the smaller and more vulnerable attractions that were affected, but the newer large-scale attractions along the Orlando Wall. Suddenly, Disney World swallowed up another one or two days of each tourist's vacation week. When the Magic Kingdom stood alone, most visitors had three or four days remaining to sample other attractions. With the addition of Epcot, that time was cut to one or two days.

Disney ensured its market share by creating multiday admission passes, which allowed unlimited access to both the Magic Kingdom and Epcot. More cost-efficient than a one-day pass to a single park, these passes kept the guest on Disney turf for three to five days.

Kennedy Space Center and Sea World, by virtue of their very specialized products, continued to prosper after Epcot opened. Most other attractions were forced to focus on local markets. Some, like Busch Gardens, did very well, with increased local support replacing the decreased numbers of Walt Disney World–destination tourists coming over for the day. Others, like Cypress Gardens, suffered badly but worked diligently to improve their product. Some, like Circus World and the Hall of Fame Wax Museum, passed into history.

Though long an innovator, Disney turned in the mid-'80s to copying existing successful competitors. Except, copying is not exactly the right word. What Disney did was to take a competitor's concept, improve it, and reproduce it, in Disney style on a grand scale.

The first competitor to feel the heat was Sea World when Disney added The Living Seas pavilion to the Future World section of Epcot. Sea World, however, had killer whales, the Shark Encounter, and sufficient corporate resources to remain preeminent among marine exhibits. Still, many Disney patrons willingly substituted a visit to The Living Seas for a visit to Sea World.

One of Disney's own products was threatened when the Wet 'n Wild water theme park took aim at the older and smaller but more aesthetically pleasing River Country. Never one to take a challenge sitting down, Disney responded in 1989 with the opening of Typhoon Lagoon, then the world's largest swimming theme park.

Also in 1989, Disney opened Pleasure Island, a one-admission, multi-nightclub entertainment complex patterned on Orlando's successful Church Street Station. In the years it has operated, Pleasure Island has robbed Church Street Station of much of its tourist traffic.

In the same year, Walt Disney World opened Disney-MGM Studios, a combination working motion picture and television production complex and theme park. Copying the long-lauded Universal Studios tour in southern California, Disney-MGM Studios was speeded into operation after Universal announced its plans for a central Florida park.

Disney-MGM Studios, however, affected much more than Universal's plans. With the opening of Disney-MGM, the 3-Day World Passport was discontinued. Instead, Disney patrons were offered a single-day pass or the more economical multiday passports, good for either four or five days. With three theme parks on a multiday pass, plus two swimming parks, several golf courses, various lakes, and a nighttime entertainment complex, Disney effectively swallowed up the average family's entire vacation. Break away to Sea World or the Kennedy Space Center for the day? How about a day at the ocean (remember the ocean)? Fat chance.

In 1995, Disney opened Blizzard Beach, a third swimming park, and began plans for a fourth major theme park, the Animal Kingdom, designed to compete directly with Busch Gardens. During the same year, the first phase of Disney's All-Star resorts came on-line, featuring (by Disney standards) budget accommodations. The location and rates of the All-Star resorts were intended to capture the market of the smaller independent and chain hotels along US 192. Disney even discussed constructing a monorail to the airport so that visitors won't have to set foot in Orlando.

As time passes, Disney continues to consolidate its hold. With the opening of Disney's BoardWalk, Fantasia Gardens miniature golf, the Walt Disney World Speedway in 1996, Disney's Wide World of Sports, Disney's

West Side shopping and entertainment district, and a new convention center in 1997, Disney now attracts armies of central Floridians to compensate for decreased tourist traffic during off-season. And for people who can never get enough, there is the town of Celebration, a Disney residential land development project where homebuyers can live in Disney-designed houses in Disney-designed neighborhoods, protected by Disney-designed security.

Finally (for now), Disney's fourth major theme park, the Animal Kingdom, opened in summer 1998. More than twice the size of any existing Disney park, the Animal Kingdom borrows from the Busch Gardens' model of integrating live zoological exhibits with theme park rides, shows, and attractions. Disney's version, of course, is bigger and better. More to the point, the Animal Kingdom again changes the destination-tourist equation. Moving beyond preempting the competition and monopolizing the tourist's vacation, Walt Disney World is now so huge that it can't be experienced in a single vacation. Never mind, muses the Mouse, that we've got you sewn up for this year's vacation; we've got you for next year's as well.

I regret the passing of an era in Florida tourism. The old attractions were more intimate, more personal, more human. Each modest attraction was the realization of some maverick's dream, one he longed to share with anyone who passed through the turnstile. But dreams are only as grand as the people who create them, and only the truly visionary endure. Such was the dream of Walt Disney, modified by corporate Disney and come to fruition in Walt Disney World. Its product is testimony to careful planning, harboring of resources, precise timing, and adherence to a standard of quality unprecedented in the entertainment industry. Walt Disney World presents a show that amazes and delights, one that exceeds the expectations of almost every visitor.

From an entrepreneurial seed, a cartoon mouse, and a California amusement park years ahead of its time has risen an entertainment giant, one that moves sometimes clumsily and sometimes with cold determination but always with a commitment to excellence. Although I am uncomfortable with the Disney Company's stranglehold on Florida tourism, and its plastic, idealized vision of life, I bow to the reality. And there is this: A tourist could do a lot worse.

How This Guide Was Researched and Written

While much has been written about Walt Disney World, very little has been comparative or evaluative. Most guides parrot Disney World's own promotional material. In preparing this guide, however, nothing was taken for granted. Each theme park was visited at different times throughout the year by trained observers. They conducted detailed evaluations and rated each theme park, with all its component rides, shows, exhibits, services, and concessions, according to a formal, pretested rating instrument. Patrons were interviewed to determine what tourists of all age groups enjoyed most and least during their Disney World visit.

While our observers were independent and impartial, we don't claim special expertise or scientific backgrounds relative to the types of exhibits, performances, or attractions. Like you, we visit Walt Disney World as tourists, noting our satisfaction or dissatisfaction. We don't believe it's necessary to be an agronomist to know whether we enjoyed the agricultural exhibits in the Epcot Land pavilion. Disney offerings are marketed to the touring public, and it is as the public that we have experienced them.

The primary difference between the average tourist and the trained evaluator is in the evaluator's professional skills in organization, preparation, and observation. The trained evaluator is responsible for much more than simply observing and cataloging. While the tourist seated next to the evaluator is being entertained by the *Tropical Serenade (Enchanted Tiki Birds)* in the Magic Kingdom, the professional is rating the performance in terms of theme, pace, continuity, and originality. He or she is also checking the physical arrangements: Is the sound system clear and audible without being overpowering; is the audience shielded from the sun or rain; is seating adequate; can everyone in the audience clearly see the staging area? And what about guides and/or performers: Are they knowledgeable, articulate, and professional; are they friendly and engaging? Does the performance begin and end on time; does the show contain the features described in promotional literature? These and many other considerations figure prominently in the rating of any performance. Similarly, detailed and relevant checklists were prepared and applied by observer teams to rides, exhibits, concessions, and the theme parks in general. Finally, observations and ratings were integrated with audience reactions and the opinions of patrons to compile a comprehensive quality profile of each feature and service.

In compiling this guide, we recognize that a tourist's age, sex, background, and interests will strongly influence his or her taste in Disney World offerings and will account for a preference of one ride or feature over another. Given this, we make no attempt to compare apples with oranges. How, indeed, could a meaningful comparison be made between the priceless historic artifacts in Epcot's Mexican pavilion and the wild roller coaster ride of the Magic Kingdom's Space Mountain? Instead, our objective is to provide the reader with sufficient description, critical evaluation, and pertinent data to make knowledgeable decisions according to individual tastes.

The essence of this guide, therefore, consists of individual critiques and descriptions of each feature of the Magic Kingdom, Epcot, Disney-MGM Studios, and the Animal Kingdom, along with detailed touring plans to help you avoid bottlenecks and crowds. Also included are in-depth descriptions for Typhoon Lagoon, Blizzard Beach, Pleasure Island, and nearby Universal Studios Florida.

A WORD TO OUR READERS ABOUT ANNUAL REVISIONS

Some of you who purchase each new edition of the *Unofficial Guide* have chastised us for retaining examples, comments, and descriptions from previous years' editions. This letter from a Grand Rapids, Michigan, reader is typical:

Your guidebook still has the same little example stories since at least 1995. When I got my 1998 book I expected a true update and new stuff, not the same-old, same-old!

First, the *Unofficial Guide* is a reference work. Though we are flattered that some readers read the guide from cover to cover, and that some of you find it entertaining, our objective is fairly straightforward: to provide information that will enable you to have the best possible Walt Disney World vacation.

Each year during our revision research, we check every theme park, water park, attraction, hotel, restaurant, nightspot, shop, and entertainment offering. While there are many changes (most attributable to Disney World's exponential growth), much remains the same from year to year. When we profile and critique an attraction, we try to provide the reader with the most insightful, relevant, and useful information, written in the clearest possible language. It is our opinion that if an attraction does not change, then it makes little sense to risk clarity and content for the sake of freshening up the prose. WDW guests who try the Mad Tea Party, the Haunted Mansion, or the Country Bear Jamboree today, for example, experience exactly the same presentation as guests who visited Disney World in 1997, 1990, or 1986. Moreover, according to our extensive patron surveys (about 3,000 each year), today's guests respond to these attractions in the same way as prior-year patrons.

The bottom line: we believe our readers are better served if we devote our time to that which is changing and new as opposed to that which remains the same. The success or failure of the *Unofficial Guide* is determined not by the style of the writing but by the accuracy of the information and, ultimately, whether you have a positive experience at Walt Disney World. Every change to the guide we make (or don't make) is evaluated in this context.

LETTERS AND COMMENTS FROM READERS

Many of those who use *The Unofficial Guide to Walt Disney World* write us to make comments or share their own strategies for visiting Walt Disney World. We appreciate all such input, both positive and critical, and encourage our readers to continue writing. Readers' comments and observations are frequently incorporated into revised editions of the *Unofficial Guide* and have contributed immeasurably to its improvement. If you write us or return our reader survey form, you can rest assured that we won't release your name and address to any mailing list companies, direct mail advertisers, or other third party.

Reader Questionnaire and Restaurant Survey

At the back of this guide is a short questionnaire you can use to express opinions about your Walt Disney World visit. The questionnaire is designed to allow every member of your party, regardless of age, to tell us what they think. There is also a separate restaurant survey that you can use to describe your Disney World dining experiences. Clip the questionnaire and the restaurant survey on the dotted lines and mail them to:

> Reader Survey
> The *Unofficial Guide* Series
> P.O. Box 43059
> Birmingham, AL 35243

How to Write the Author

> Bob Sehlinger
> *The Unofficial Guide to Walt Disney World*
> P.O. Box 43059
> Birmingham, AL 35243

When you write, put your address on both your letter and envelope. Sometimes the two get separated. It is also a good idea to include your phone number. And remember, as travel writers, we're often out of the office for long periods of time, so forgive us if our response is slow.

Questions from Readers

Questions frequently asked the author by readers are answered in an appendix at the end of the *Unofficial Guide*.

Walt Disney World: An Overview

If you're choosing among tourist attractions in Florida, the question is not whether to visit Walt Disney World but how to see the best of the Disney offerings with some economy of time, effort, and finances.

Make no mistake, there is nothing on earth like Walt Disney World. Incredible in its scope, genius, beauty, and imagination, it's a joy and wonder for people of all ages. A fantasy, a dream, and a vision all rolled into one, it transcends simple entertainment, making us children and adventurers, freeing us to live the dreams of our past, present, and future.

We are critics, but it is the responsibility of critics to credit what is done well as surely as it is to point out what is done poorly. Disney attractions are special, a quantum leap beyond most man-made entertainment offerings.

WHAT WALT DISNEY WORLD ENCOMPASSES

Walt Disney World encompasses 43 square miles, an area twice as large as Manhattan island, or roughly the size of Boston. Situated strategically in this vast expanse are the Magic Kingdom, Epcot, Disney-MGM Studios, and the Animal Kingdom theme parks; three swimming theme parks; a botanical and zoological park; two nighttime entertainment areas; a sports complex; several golf courses, hotels, and campgrounds; almost 100 restaurants; four large interconnected lakes; a shopping complex; three convention venues; a nature preserve; and a complete transportation system consisting of four-lane highways, elevated monorails, and a system of canals.

THE MAJOR THEME PARKS

The Magic Kingdom

When people think of Walt Disney World, most think of the Magic Kingdom. It's comprised of the collection of adventures, rides, and shows symbolizing the Disney cartoon characters, and Cinderella Castle. Although the Magic Kingdom is only one element of Disney World, it remains its heart. The Magic Kingdom is divided into seven subareas or "lands," six of which are arranged around a central hub. First encountered is Main Street, U.S.A., which connects the Magic Kingdom entrance with the central hub. Clockwise around the hub are Adventureland, Frontierland, Liberty Square, Fantasyland, and Tomorrowland. Mickey's Toontown Fair, the first new land in the Magic Kingdom since the park opened (originally named Mickey's Birthdayland), is situated along the Walt Disney Railroad on three acres between Fantasyland and Tomorrowland. Access is through Fantasyland or Tomorrowland, or via the railroad. Main Street and the other six lands will be described in detail later. Three hotels (the Contemporary, Polynesian, and Grand Floridian Beach resorts) are close to the Magic Kingdom and are directly connected to it by monorail and boat. Two additional hotels, Shades of Green (formerly the Disney Inn) and Disney's Wilderness Lodge Resort, are nearby but aren't served by the monorail.

Epcot

Epcot opened in October 1982. Divided into two major areas, Future World and World Showcase, the park is twice as big as the Magic Kingdom and comparable in scope. Future World consists of futuristic pavilions relating to different themes concerning humans' creativity and technological advancement. World Showcase, arranged around a 41-acre lagoon, presents the architectural, social, and cultural heritages of almost a dozen nations,

Walt Disney World

535

535

Osprey Ridge
Golf Course

Bonnet Creek
Golf Club

Live Oak
Lane

Buena Vista Drive

Eagle Pines
Golf Course

Vista Blvd.

535

Community Dr.

Dixie Landings
Resort

Villas at the
Disney Institute

The Crossroads
Shopping Ctr.

Travelodge
Hotel

Port Orleans
Resort

Disney
Institute

DoubleTree
Guest Suites Resort

Buena Vista Palace

Old Key
West

Grosvenor
Resort

Hotel Royal
Plaza

EXIT 27

Lake
Buena Vista
Golf Course

Marketplace

Downtown
Disney

535

Bonnet Creek Rd.

Courtyard by
Marriott

Disney's
West Side

The Hilton
Pleasure Island

Typhoon Lagoon

To Orlando

Caribbean
Beach Resort

EXIT 26

536

4

EXIT 25

To Tampa

Osceola Parkway (toll)

To Kissimmee →

192

with each country represented by replicas of famous landmarks and local settings familiar to world travelers. Epcot is more educationally oriented than the Magic Kingdom and has been repeatedly characterized as a sort of permanent World's Fair.

The five Epcot resort hotels—Disney's Beach Club, Disney's Yacht Club, Disney's BoardWalk Resort, the Walt Disney World Swan and the Walt Disney World Dolphin—are within a 5- to 15-minute walk of the International Gateway entrance to the theme park. The hotels are also linked to the park by canal. Epcot is connected to the Magic Kingdom and its resort hotels by monorail.

Disney-MGM Studios

This $300 million, 100-acre attraction opened in 1989 and is divided into two areas. The first is a theme park focused on the past, present, and future of the motion picture and television industries. This section contains movie-theme rides and shows and covers about half of the Disney-MGM complex. Highlights include a re-creation of Hollywood and Sunset Boulevards from Hollywood's Golden Age, audience-participation shows on TV production and sound effects, movie stunt demonstrations, a children's play area, and three high-tech rides: *The Twilight Zone* Tower of Terror, Star Tours, and The Great Movie Ride.

The second area is a working motion picture and television production facility encompassing three sound stages, a backlot of streets and sets, and creative support services. Public access is limited to studio tours, which take visitors behind the scenes for crash courses on Disney animation and moviemaking, including (on occasion) the opportunity to witness the actual shooting of a feature film, television show, or commercial.

Disney-MGM Studios is connected to other Walt Disney World areas by highway and canal, but not by monorail. Guests can park in the Studios' pay parking lot or commute by bus. Patrons staying in Epcot resort hotels can also reach the Studios by boat.

Disney's Animal Kingdom

More than five times the size of the Magic Kingdom, the Animal Kingdom combines zoological exhibits with rides, shows, and live entertainment. The park is arranged somewhat like the Magic Kingdom, in a hub-and-spoke configuration. A lush tropical rain forest serves as Main Street, funneling visitors to Safari Village at the center of the park. Dominated by the park's central icon, the 14-story-tall, hand-carved Tree of Life, Safari Village is the park's center, with services, shopping, and dining. From Safari Village, guests can access the theme areas: Africa, Asia, DinoLand USA, Camp Minnie-

Mickey, and Mythical Beasts (tentative name). Scheduled to open in phases, Safari Village, Africa, Camp Minnie-Mickey, and DinoLand U.S.A. came on-line in 1998, to be followed by Asia in 1999 and Mythical Beasts over the next couple of years. Africa, the largest theme area at 100 acres, features free-roaming herds in a re-creation of the Serengeti Plain. Guests tour in open-air safari vehicles.

Disney's Animal Kingdom has its own pay parking lot and is connected to other Disney World destinations by the Disney bus system. Although there are no hotels at the Animal Kingdom, the All-Star and Coronado Springs resorts are nearby.

THE WATER THEME PARKS

There are three major swimming theme parks in Walt Disney World: Typhoon Lagoon, River Country, and Blizzard Beach. Typhoon Lagoon is distinguished by a wave pool capable of making six-foot waves. River Country, a pioneer among water theme parks, is much smaller but very well done. Since Typhoon Lagoon opened in 1989, River Country has catered primarily to Disney World campground and resort hotel guests. Blizzard Beach is the newest Disney water park and features more slides than the other two parks combined. All three parks are beautifully landscaped, with great attention to atmosphere and aesthetics. Typhoon Lagoon and Blizzard Beach have their own adjacent parking lots. River Country can be reached on foot by campground guests or on Disney boat or bus by others.

DISCOVERY ISLAND

Discovery Island is a small zoological park on an island in Bay Lake. Featuring birdlife and tropical plants, Discovery Island can be reached by boat from the Magic Kingdom or Fort Wilderness docks. Low-key and quite scenic, the tiny park offers a number of short, circular trails that guests can explore at their own pace. Discovery Island also offers educational shows featuring resident birds and wildlife.

OTHER WALT DISNEY WORLD VENUES

Downtown Disney (Downtown Disney Marketplace, Pleasure Island, and Disney's West Side)

Downtown Disney is a large shopping, dining, and entertainment complex encompassing the Downtown Disney Marketplace on the east, the gated (admission-required) Pleasure Island nighttime entertainment venue in the middle, and Disney's West Side on the west. Downtown Disney Marketplace

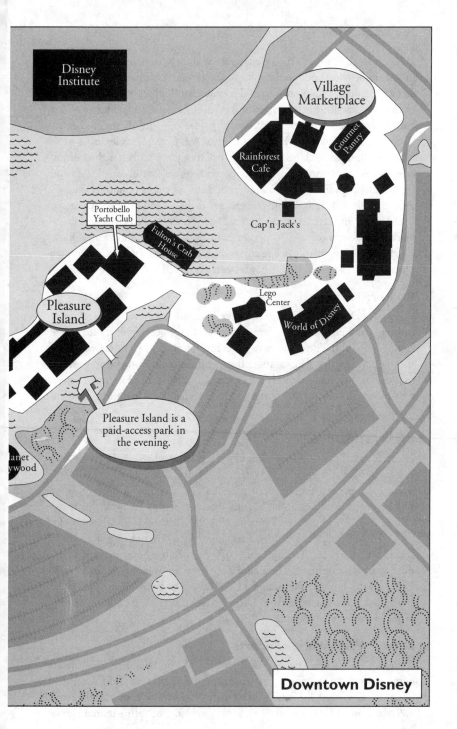

Disney
Institute

Village
Marketplace

Gourmet
Pantry

Rainforest
Cafe

Portobello
Yacht Club

Fulton's Crab
House

Cap'n Jack's

Pleasure
Island

Lego
Center

World of Disney

Pleasure Island is a
paid-access park in
the evening.

Planet
Hollywood

Downtown Disney

is home to the largest Disney character merchandise store in the world, upscale resort-wear and specialty shops, and several restaurants, including the tacky but popular Rainforest Cafe. Pleasure Island, in addition to the gated attractions described below, offers several upscale restaurants. Disney's West Side, which opened in 1997, combines nightlife, shopping, dining, and entertainment. Dan Aykroyd's House of Blues serves Cajun/Creole dishes in its restaurant and electric blues in its music hall. Bongos, a Cuban nightclub and cafe created by Gloria and Emilio Estefan, offers Caribbean flavors and rhythms. Wolfgang Puck Cafe, sandwiched among pricey boutiques (including a three-level Virgin Records megastore) is the West Side's prestige eatery. In the entertainment department are a 24-screen cinema; a permanent showplace for the extraordinary, 70-person cast *Cirque du Soleil;* and DisneyQuest, a high-tech, interactive virtual reality and electronic games venue. Downtown Disney can be accessed via Disney buses from most Disney World locations.

Pleasure Island

Part of the Downtown Disney complex, Pleasure Island is a six-acre nighttime entertainment center where one cover charge gets a visitor into any of eight nightclubs. The clubs have different themes and feature a variety of shows and activities. Music ranges from pop-rock, to country and western, to jazz. For the more sedentary (or exhausted) there is an adjacent 24-screen movie complex, or for the hungry, several restaurants, including a much-hyped Planet Hollywood.

Disney's BoardWalk

Located near Epcot, Disney's BoardWalk is an idealized replication of an east coast turn-of-the-century waterfront resort. Open all day, the Board-Walk features upscale restaurants, shops and galleries, a brew pub, an ESPN sports bar, a nightclub with dueling pianos (New Orleans Pat O'Brien's–style), and a swanky dance club. While there is no admission fee for the BoardWalk per se, individual clubs levy a cover charge at night. In addition to the public facilities are a 378-room deluxe hotel and a 532-unit time-share development. The BoardWalk is within walking distance of the Epcot resorts and the International Gateway of the Epcot theme park. Boat transportation is available from Disney-MGM Studios, with buses serving other Disney World locations.

Disney's Wide World of Sports

Covering 200 acres, Disney's Wide World of Sports is a state-of-the-art compe-tition and training facility consisting of a 7,500-seat ballpark, a field house, and venues for baseball, softball, tennis, track and field, beach volleyball, and 27 other sports. In addition to being the spring training home of the Atlanta Braves, the complex hosts a mind-boggling calendar of professional and amateur competitions. Although Walt Disney World guests are welcome at the complex as paid spectators, none of the facilities are available for use by guests unless they are participants in a scheduled competition.

The Disney Institute and Disney University

The Disney Institute offers life-enriching learning experiences to Walt Disney World resort guests, while Disney University conducts professional-development courses for private groups and corporations. Both programs share the campus located near the Downtown Disney Marketplace and are connected to other Disney World locations by Disney bus service.

DISNEY CRUISE LINE

In 1998, Disney launched (literally) its own cruise line with the 2,400-passenger *Disney Magic*. Its twin ship, the *Disney Wonder,* was launched in November 1998. Cruises depart from Port Canaveral (about a 90-minute drive from Walt Disney World) and stop at Nassau in the Bahamas and at Castaway Cay, Disney's own private island. Three- or four-day cruises are available and can be packaged with a stay at Walt Disney World. Although the cruises are family oriented, extensive children's programs and elaborate childcare facilities allow parents plenty of opportunity for time away from the kids. For additional information about the Disney Cruise Line, see *The Unofficial Guide to Cruises,* by Kay Showker and Bob Sehlinger, available at most bookstores.

DISNEYSPEAK POCKET TRANSLATOR

Although it may come as a surprise to many, Walt Disney World has its own somewhat peculiar language. Here are some of terms you are likely to bump into:

DisneySpeak	English Definition
Adventure	Ride
Attraction	Ride or theater show
Attraction Host	Ride operator
Audience	Crowd
Backstage	Behind the scenes, out of view of customers
Bull Pen	Queuing area
Cast Member	Employee

DisneySpeak	English Definition (continued)
Character	Disney cartoon character impersonated by an employee
Costume	Work attire or uniform
Dark Ride	Indoor ride
Day-guest	Any customer not staying at a Disney resort
Face Character	A character that does not wear a head-covering costume (Snow White, Cinderella, Jasmine, etc.)
General Public	Same as day-guest
Greeter	Employee positioned at the entrance of an attraction
Guest	Customer
Hidden Mickeys	Frontal silhouette of Mickey's head worked subtly into the design of buildings, railings, vehicles, golf greens, attractions, and just about anything else
In Rehearsal	Operating though not officially open
Lead	Foreman or manager, the person in charge of an attraction
On Stage	In full view of customers
Preshow	Entertainment at an attraction prior to the feature presentation
Resort Guest	A customer staying at a Disney resort
Role	An employee's job
Security Host	Security guard
Soft Opening	Opening a park or attraction before its stated opening time
Transitional Experience	An element of the queuing area and/or preshow that provides a story line or information essential to understanding the attraction

Readers Speak Out

Walt Disney World patrons, especially *Unofficial Guide* readers, express strong opinions about their Disney vacation experience. The following is a sampling from our readers and survey respondents.

Our readers gripe more about the quality and cost of food at Disney World than about anything else. In truth, however, most readers have a higher opinion of the food than we do. A Charleston, West Virginia, woman let us have it with both barrels, writing:

> *Get a life! It's crazy and unrealistic to be so snobbish about restaurants at a theme park. Considering the number of people Disney feeds each day, I think they do a darn good job. Also, you act so surprised that the food is expensive. Have you ever eaten at an airport? HELLO IN THERE?....Surprise, you're a captive! It's a theme park!*

More typical, however, is this note from a mother of three in Dallas, Texas:

> *Stick to your guns on the food. It was uniformly bad and exorbitantly expensive. For example, a character breakfast at the Polynesian (all family-style, ho-hum fare) was $100 for a family of five. Eating was a downer three times a day in what would have otherwise been a fabulous vacation.*

An Erie, Pennsylvania, woman struck a practical note, writing:

> *Most of the food [at Walt Disney World] is OK. Certainly in our experience, more of it is good than bad. If you pay attention to what other visitors say and what's in the guidebooks, you can avoid the yucky places. It's true that you pay more than you should, but it's more convenient [to eat in Walt Disney World] than to run around trying to find cheaper restaurants somewhere else. When it comes to Disney World, who needs more running around?*

Second on the hit parade of complaints are the crowd levels at the Magic Kingdom. This letter from a Sandy, Utah, man is typical:

> *Anybody who thinks there is an "Off-Season" any more at the Magic Kingdom seriously needs a reality check. We've tried all different times of the year and just about every day of the week. From our experience crowds come in two basic sizes, huge and huger.*

For the record, though some times of year are less crowded than others, the gentleman from Utah is correct. According to *Amusement Business* magazine, the trade magazine of the theme park industry, 17 million people visited the park in 1997, up 23% from 1996. The 1998 figures are not in, but with the opening of the Animal Kingdom, the Magic Kingdom's numbers are expected to increase. Even if attendance holds steady at the 17 million mark, however, that's an average of about 47,000 guests per day.

During the same period, Epcot averaged 32,000 guests per day and Disney-MGM Studios about 27,000 guests per day. If you're looking for a somewhat less congested theme park, consider Sea World, which averages about 13,000 guests per day.

Rude guests, including sometimes unruly teenage tour groups from Brazil, place third among reader complaints. For a couple of months each year (usually October and July) we are inundated at the *Unofficial Guide* with "Brazil mail":

A woman from Durham, North Carolina, writes:

> *July is Brazilian tour group season. Hordes of same-shirted teenage Brazilians invade all the parks. They are ill-behaved, noisy, under-supervised, use flash photography in dark theaters, cut in line, and claim they do not speak English (except in food lines).*

A man from Cincinnati, Ohio, reports his observations:

> *What bothered us most was watching the park employees ignore the line-jumping. When you got in line, some [of the Brazilians] were behind you and others were outside the line maze. By the time your family got to the front of the line, their entire group would be in front of you. This didn't happen once or twice, it was common. We saw park employees watch them go over or under the ropes and not say a word.*

This just in: Walt Disney World has surrendered unconditionally to Brazil.

A Madison, Wisconsin, woman chimed in with the following:

> *Tour groups from hell: [American] middle-school classes. These kids are the most out-of-control, loud, obnoxious, misbehaved animals we've ever seen. But they get away with it because they are on a class trip. My parents would have grounded me for life if I had behaved as those children do in public.*

A mother from Providence, Rhode Island, points out that indecision can be as maddening as outright discourtesy, especially when you're hungry:

> *It's amazing that I didn't go crazy waiting in those lines for 15 minutes only to have the person in front of me waste more time trying to decide if she should get the Mickey bar or the strawberry bar. Tell these people to read the signs in the very long lines and make up their minds ahead of time.*

A woman from Houston, Texas, reports being the victim of a hit-and-run:

> *I think strollers should be outlawed. I got hit on the heels several times. These people tried to run through the crowd to get to another attraction yelling, "Excuse me!"*

Yet another Texan fell victim to the "Mowing Mamas," commenting:

> *You cannot emphasize enough to your readers how many strollers and wheelchairs they will encounter (and the drivers of said strollers and chairs will run you over without a second thought).*

The lady above from Houston also complains about character hogs:

> *One of the worst parts to deal with are the people with movie cameras who take about three minutes filming their child with Mickey, asking everyone else to move. A 35 mm camera takes about two seconds.*

And finally, a complaint that our readers make with regrettable frequency concerns able-bodied guests pretending to be disabled in order to receive preferential treatment. An outraged Stevens Point, Wisconsin, mother writes:

> *As the parent of a handicapped child, I was appalled to see the blatant misuse of wheelchairs. People who loaded them with purchases and hopped in as they came to a ride. One party came in with the father in the wheelchair. At the next ride, one of the kids was in the chair. At the next, the mother was in the chair! This practice is not only unfair to nonhandicapped people [waiting in line], but also is an affront to those who really need [a wheelchair].*

A woman from Crystal City, Virginia, agreed, stating:

> *Wheelchair abuse is out of control! We saw a woman hop out of her wheelchair and vigorously climb Swiss Family Treehouse!*

On the same topic, a woman from Rockford, Illinois, made a well-considered appeal for tolerance and understanding:

> *I read with interest readers' comments about apparently able-bodied people "abusing" wheelchairs at WDW. I am sure there are a few scoundrels, but the vast majority of people are honest. People with lupus or a number of other connective tissue diseases, people with heel spurs, hip or knee problems, heart or kidney disease, and people on chemotherapy can all look perfectly healthy—even though they would never be able to walk through WDW. Readers may ask why so many of these folks would go to Disney World. Where else can you vacation with your healthy, active spouse and young children and still keep up with them? These are families who can't go surfing or skiing or to water parks together.*
>
> *And if readers find themselves resenting the fact that the children of these people don't have to wait, they might consider that these children do wait—51 weeks a year. They wait at doctors' offices, they wait until the next round of chemo's over before they can go to the zoo (if dad feels better), they wait till mom can walk better before they can go to the mall, they wait until next year and maybe dad will be able to coach soccer—they wait, and wait, and wait.*
>
> *Have a heart, healthy people. Just because someone can walk a little bit or get on a ride without help or doesn't look as handicapped as your child, it doesn't mean they don't need special facilities. Limp a mile in my shoes (with the orthotics).*

In fourth place were a deluge of complaints lamenting delays in the opening of the Test Track attraction at Epcot. The ride was more than 16 months late and counting when we went to press.

Complaints about the high volume levels of Disney sound systems hold down fifth place. The following letter from a Sterling, Massachusetts, father is representative:

> *One thing that bothered me about Magic Kingdom and Epcot was the noise level of many of the attractions. Two in particular—the afternoon parade at Magic Kingdom and Food Rocks at Epcot—I found unbelievably loud and disturbing. Our daughter (5½) had her ears covered during much of both events and my ears were ringing for a long time after the parade. And these two attractions are specifically geared to young children. Why does Disney have to inflict on us such intense noise levels? Why push us into hearing loss earlier than necessary?*

Sixth is a laundry list of problems relating to the Walt Disney World transportation system. (For an in-depth discussion, see the chapter "How to Travel around the World" in Part 6.)

In seventh place is an apparently growing trend that relates to Disney's exponential growth and the resultant difficulty that Disney guest relations and information staff are having keeping up. Many complaints, like this one from a Miami, Ohio, woman, center on Disney attractions outside the theme parks:

> *Our concierge didn't have the foggiest notion what was going on at the Disney sports complex [Disney's Wide World of Sports]. He told us the [Atlanta] Braves were practicing (they weren't) and that there was a big soccer tournament going on (there wasn't). We spent about $40 for the privilege of seeing a bunch of empty stadiums and ball fields.*

A Dalton, Georgia, woman reported similar problems:

> *I must have made five different calls to make sure that Typhoon Lagoon would be open during our visit. Each time I was assured it would be. I made my last call three days before we left home and received the same assurances. When we arrived at Disney World and checked into Port Orleans, I found out that Typhoon Lagoon was closed and had been for three weeks!*

Readers also offer compliments, especially on the courtesy, friendliness, and helpfulness of most Disney cast members (employees). A woman from Yucaipa, California, described the attentiveness of cast members to her injured husband:

> *My husband cracked his head open on a mushroom in the Honey, I Shrunk the Kids! playground and the Disney-MGM people were terrific. Seeing us wandering about with blood streaming down my husband's head, one of the cast members took us straight to First Aid. There they dressed the wound, offered to take us to the emergency room in an ambulance (not necessary), gave my husband a place to rest where they could observe him, and finally called a car from the Grand Floridian to return him to the hotel.*

The mother of a two-year-old couldn't have been more surprised at her son's favorite attraction:

> *Kudos to the customer friendly Epcot employee, Jose, who lifted Harry over the fence and let him help water the lawn. Shades of Tom Sawyer, I know, but my kid got a big kick out of it.*

And a Massachusetts couple, battle-weary from the crowds, related this story:

After coming out of the live production of Beauty and the Beast *we must have looked a little shopworn. A Disney cast member came up to us and asked if we were OK and if we were enjoying ourselves. Her concern and reaching out stunned us. Here we were obviously a bit older than the majority of the other park-goers, probably looking somewhat frazzled by then (3:30 p.m.), but she treated us as if we were the most important of guests.*

We get quite a bit of mail about maids at Disney World resort hotels. This letter from a St. Louis family is typical:

> *Each day when we returned to our room, we would find that the maid had arranged our kids' stuffed animals in a different and highly creative manner. For instance, the animals might be all lined up by the window with the snacks we left in the room in the animals' arms. Our kids loved it and looked forward to seeing the arrangement every day. I was impressed that Disney could even get the maids into the entertainment act—cast members, indeed!*

The parks' cleanliness rates second for praise, with many comments about the nice rest rooms, including this from a woman in Austin, Texas:

> *I was in a stall in the rest room one day when I dropped my map. Before I could retrieve it, the hand of a cleaning woman appeared, grabbed the map and had it in the trash before I knew what was happening. As you know, everything there works this way.*

Many readers have applauded Disney's initiatives to make Epcot more fun. This reader from New York is representative, writing:

> *We also like how Epcot, in general, is more kid-friendly than it was 11 years ago, and the KIDS' ZONES at each country are great. However, by the second day our son was only interested in running to the KIDS' ZONE immediately, getting his passport stamped, and dashing on to the next country (that's because he's O.C. just like his dad).*

Disney landscaping and the beauty of the property comes in third for plaudits. Safety and personal security in Walt Disney World in general comes in fourth, with character encounters holding down fifth. Sixth is the quality of rooms at Disney hotels, followed in seventh place by the creative and elaborate Disney hotel swimming areas. Rounding out the list is the quality of special Disney tours and educational programs.

Part One

Planning Before You Leave Home

Visiting Walt Disney World is a bit like childbirth—you never really believe what people tell you, but once you have been through it yourself you know exactly what they were saying!

—Hilary Wolfe, a mother and *Unofficial Guide* reader from Swansea, United Kingdom

Gathering Information

In addition to this guide, we recommend that you obtain:

1. The Walt Disney Travel Company Walt Disney World Vacations Brochure   This full-color booklet describes Walt Disney World in its entirety, lists rates for all Disney resort hotels and campgrounds, and describes Disney World package vacations. It's available from most travel agents or by calling the Walt Disney Travel Company at (800) 327-2996 or (407) 828-3232. Be prepared to hold; you may have a long wait.

2. The Official Map of the Walt Disney World Resort   Also called the Walt Disney World Property Map, this large folding map contains a road map of Walt Disney World on one side and information about the Disney transportation system on the opposite side. The map is available from Walt Disney World Information at (407) 824-4321.

3. Walt Disney World Guidebook for Guests with Disabilities   If members of your party are sight- or hearing-impaired, or partially or wholly nonambulatory, this small guide will be very helpful. For a copy, call (407) 824-4321. Allow 15 business days for delivery.

4. Orlando MagiCard If you're considering lodging outside of Walt Disney World or if you think you might patronize attractions and restaurants outside of Disney World, it's worthwhile to obtain an Orlando MagiCard, a Vacation Planner, and the Orlando Official Accommodations Guide (all free) from the Orlando/Orange County Convention and Visitors Bureau. The MagiCard makes you eligible for discounts at hotels, restaurants, and attractions outside Disney World. To order the accommodations guide, call (800) 255-5786. For additional information and materials, call (407) 363-5874. Phones are manned during weekday business hours. Allow four weeks for delivery.

5. Florida Traveler Discount Guide Another good source of discounts on lodging, restaurants, and attractions throughout the state is the Florida Traveler Discount Guide. Published by Exit Information Guide, the guide is free, but you will be charged $3 ($5 shipped to Canada) for handling. Call (352) 371-3948, 8 a.m. to 8 p.m. EST Monday–Friday. Similar guides to other states are available at the same number. It's sometimes difficult to get through on the phone, however.

6. Kissimmee–St. Cloud Tour & Travel Sales Guide This full-color directory of hotels and attractions is one of the most complete available and is of particular interest to those who intend to book lodging outside of Disney World. In addition to hotels and motels, the directory lists rental houses, time-shares, and condominiums. To receive a copy, call the Kissimmee–St. Cloud Convention and Visitors Bureau at (800) 327-9159.

REQUEST INFORMATION EARLY

Request information as far in advance as possible, and allow four weeks for delivery. Make a checklist of information you have requested and follow up if you haven't received your materials within six weeks. Sometimes, as a Garland, Texas, man notes, persistence is the key:

> *Per your advice, I called WDW to get the "Florida Vacation Guide." They never sent it. Called back two more times and finally got it the week before we left. In fact, got two.*

Another reader threw in the towel:

> *The Official Map of the WDW Resort sounds great. I wish I knew how to get one. I called the number in your guide and requested it; I received a detailed map and information about Fort Wilderness Resort. I called my travel agent and asked her to request one for me; I received a (second) Disney vacation planning video.*

> *Fortunately, we didn't run into the difficulties described regarding getting around the property. We found the basic layout and signs, although not great, manageable. We also got excellent directions from the people manning the booths at the entries to the resorts.*

A woman from Pittsford, New York, adds:

> *We sent away for the official WDW map and Orlando MagiCard about four weeks before the trip. The WDW map never arrived, and the MagiCard arrived while we were gone. Obviously, people need to send for these very early.*

MOUSETALES

Mousetales is a quarterly newsletter of Disney data. Totally independent of Walt Disney World, *Mousetales* costs $13 a year. To subscribe, write *Mousetales,* P.O. Box 383, Columbus, OH 43216.

GATHERING INFORMATION ON THE WORLD WIDE WEB

In planning your Walt Disney World vacation, you will find all of your favorite characters on the World Wide Web. But in addition to Mickey, Minnie, Donald, Pluto, and Goofy, you will also find Delta, American, Hertz, Hyatt, and Hilton.

The advent of the World Wide Web and its immense popularity have brought about a lot of changes in the way we seek out everyday information. Travel information is one of the most popular and useful areas of publishing and access on the Web. In just a few short years we have gone from getting most of our travel information from printed books or magazines and our favorite travel agent to booking entire vacations online. But as wonderful as this sounds, there are pitfalls. It's no small task figuring out how to find the information you need and understanding the tricks that make navigating the Web easy. Finally, even as an accomplished Web user, you may be surprised to find that your most valuable travel resource is still your tried-and-true travel agent.

You may have heard that travel providers like to sell directly to consumers on the Web in order to avoid paying commissions to travel agents, and that the commission savings are passed along to the buyer. While there is some truth in this, discounts (on the Web or anywhere else) have much more to do with time perishability of travel products than with commissions. An empty seat on a jet, for example, cannot be sold once the plane has left the gate. As the point of perishability approaches, the travel provider (hotel, airline, cruise line, etc.) begins cutting deals to fill its rooms, cabins, and seats. Web sites provide a cheap, quick, and efficient way for travel sellers to make these deals known to the public. You should understand, however, that the same deals are usually also communicated to travel agents.

We like the Web as a method of window shopping for travel, for scouting deals, and for obtaining information. We do not believe that the Web is necessarily the best or cheapest way of purchasing travel or that it can be substituted for the services of a good travel agent. The people who get the most out of the Web are those who work in cooperation with their travel agent, using the Web as a tool to help their agent help them. This is because almost any deal you locate on the Web can be purchased through a travel agent, and the more business you give your travel agent, the harder your agent will work for you. It's all about relationships.

It is a bit convoluted to write about the interactive travel experience on paper without the benefit of the very medium we are discussing. We urge you to use your computer or to find a friend with a computer and a Web connection in order to get the most out of these guidelines. We guarantee that you will discover some wonderful things along the way, many things, in all likelihood, that even we haven't seen. Each person's experience on the Web is unique, and you'll find many compelling distractions along the way. But bring your patience to the Web because it can take some getting used to and it is not perfect. Once you know your way around even slightly you will save a lot of time and, occasionally, some money. When you find resources that you like, bookmark them in your browser. The more you use them, the more efficient you will be.

Walt Disney World on the Web

Searching the World Wide Web for Disney information is like navigating an immense maze for a very small piece of cheese. To be sure, there is a lot of information available on the Net, but you may have to wade through list after list until you find the Internet addresses you want and need. Once you have the addresses you want, finding information can also be time consuming.

Disney's official Web page offers much of the same information as the Walt Disney Travel Company's vacation guidebook, and the guidebook has better pictures. However, the Web page is updated daily, contains some other useful information, and offers a few services. You can now purchase theme park admissions and make resort and dining reservations on the Internet. The Web page also offers online shopping, weather forecasts, and information on renovations and special events. Disney's official company home-page address is **http://www.disney.com.** Universal Studios Florida also offers a home page at **http://www.usf.com.**

If you search for additional information, you will find that there are many private individuals who maintain very elaborate Disney-related Web pages. One woman in California maintains a Web page through which you may access everything from official Disney pages to the "Arielholics Anonymous Home Page." Private individuals also maintain Disney chat groups, which can be sources of both information and misinformation, depending on who is chatting. Disneyphile techies from all over the world help to maintain lists. There are lists of hidden Mickeys, lists of attractions ranked and rated by Joe Blow from Kokomo, lists of characters, and more lists of lists. You could explore the Web for weeks on end for myriad information maintained by private individuals. While a lot of this information is fun and interesting, and some is useful, the best way to get specific, detailed information without too long a wait is to call Disney's main information phone number: (407) 824-4321. Alternatively, if you are looking for an evening's entertainment, try the Net.

Information about Walt Disney World is also available at the public library, travel agencies, and AAA, or by calling or writing any of the following:

Important Walt Disney World Addresses
Walt Disney World Info/Guest Letters/Letters to Mickey Mouse P.O. Box 10040 Lake Buena Vista, FL 32830-0040
Walt Disney World Central Reservations P.O. Box 10100 Lake Buena Vista, FL 32830-0100
Convention and Banquet Information Walt Disney World Resort South P.O. Box 10000 Lake Buena Vista, FL 32830-1000
Walt Disney World Educational Programs P.O. Box 10000 Lake Buena Vista, FL 32830-1000
Merchandise Mail Order (Guest Service Mail Order) P.O. Box 10070 Lake Buena Vista, FL 32830-0070

Important Walt Disney World Addresses (continued)

Walt Disney World Ticket Mail Order
P.O. Box 10140
Lake Buena Vista, FL 32830-0140

Compliments, Complaints, and Suggestions
Walt Disney World Guest Communications
P. O. Box 10000
Lake Buena Vista, Florida 32830-1000

IMPORTANT WDW TELEPHONE NUMBERS

When you call the main information number, you will be offered a menu of options for recorded information on theme park operating hours, recreation areas, shopping, entertainment complexes, tickets and admissions, resort reservations, and directions by highway and from the airport. If you are using a rotary telephone, your call will be forwarded to a Disney information representative. If you are using a touchtone phone and have a question not covered by recorded information, press zero (0) at any time to speak to a Disney representative.

Important Phone Numbers	
General Information	(407) 824-4321
Accommodations/Reservations	(407) 934-7639
	or (407) 824-8000
All-Star Resorts	(407) 939-5000
AMC Theaters Pleasure Island	(407) 298-4488
Beach Club Resort	(407) 934-8000
Blizzard Beach	(407) 560-3400
BoardWalk Resort	(407) 939-5100
Business Programs (corporate training)	(407) 824-7997
Caribbean Beach Resort	(407) 934-3400
Celebration Station	
Business Office	(407) 566-4663
Cirque du Soleil	(407) 939-7600

Important Phone Numbers (continued)

Contemporary Resort	(407) 824-1000
Convention Information	(407) 828-3200
Coronado Springs Resort	(407) 939-1000
Dining Priority Seating	(407) 939-3463
Discovery Island Information	(407) 824-3784
Disney Institute Programs	(800) 746-5858
Disney Institute Resort	(407) 827-1100
Disney's Wide World of Sports	(407) 363-6600
Dixie Landings Resort	(407) 934-6000
Downtown Disney Guest Relations	(407) 828-3058
Downtown Disney Marketplace	(407) 828-3800
Fantasia Gardens Miniature Golf	(407) 560-8760
Fort Wilderness Campground	(407) 824-2900
Golf Reservations and Information	(407) WDW-GOLF
Grand Floridian Beach Resort	(407) 824-3000
Guided Tour Information	(407) 939-TOUR
Guided VIP Solo Tours	(407) 560-6233
House of Blues Tickets and Information	(407) 934-2583
Lost and Found for articles lost:	
Yesterday or before	
(All parks)	(407) 824-4245
Today at Magic Kingdom	(407) 824-4521
Today at Epcot	(407) 560-6105
Today at Disney-MGM	(407) 560-3720
Today at Animal Kingdom	(407) 938-2265
Mediclinic, Highway 192, Kissimmee	(407) 239-1195
Merchandise Mail Order	
and Merchandise Return	(407) 363-6200
Ocala Chamber of Commerce	(352) 629-8051
Ocala Disney AAA Travel Center	(352) 854-0770
Old Key West Resort	(407) 827-7700
Outdoor Recreation Reservations	
and Information	(407) 824-2621
Pleasure Island Information	(407) 934-6374
Polynesian Resort	(407) 824-2000
Port Orleans Resort	(407) 934-5000
Resort Dining and Recreational Information	(407) 939-3463
River Country Information	(407) 824-2760
Shades of Green U.S. Armed Forces Hotel	(407) 824-3400

Important Phone Numbers (continued)	
Telecommunication for the Deaf	(407) 939-7670
Tennis Reservations/Lessons	(407) 939-7529
Typhoon Lagoon Information	(407) 560-4141
Walt Disney Travel Company	(407) 828-3232
Walt Disney World Dolphin	(407) 934-4000
Walt Disney World Speedway	(407) 939-0130
Walt Disney World Swan	(407) 934-3000
Weather Information	(407) 824-4104
Wilderness Lodge Resort	(407) 824-3200
Wrecker Service	(407) 352-0842
Yacht Club Resort	(407) 934-7000

When to Go to Walt Disney World

Why do they call it tourist season if we can't shoot them?
— Palatka, Florida outdoorsman

SELECTING THE TIME OF YEAR FOR YOUR VISIT

Walt Disney World is busiest Christmas Day through New Year's Day. Thanksgiving weekend, the week of Washington's birthday, Martin Luther King holiday weekend, spring break for colleges, and the two weeks around Easter are also extremely busy. What does "busy" mean? As many as 92,000 people have toured the Magic Kingdom alone on a single day in these peak times! While this level of attendance isn't typical, it is possible, and only the ignorant or foolish challenge the Disney parks at their peak periods.

The least busy time is from after the Thanksgiving weekend until the week before Christmas. The next slowest times are November through the weekend preceding Thanksgiving, January 4 through the first week of February, and the week after Easter through early June. Late February, March, and early April are dicey. Crowds ebb and flow according to spring break schedules and the timing of Presidents' Day weekend. Though crowds have grown markedly in September and October as a result of special promotions aimed at locals and the international market, these months continue to be good for weekday touring at the Magic Kingdom, Disney-MGM Studios, and the Animal Kingdom, and for weekend visits to Epcot.

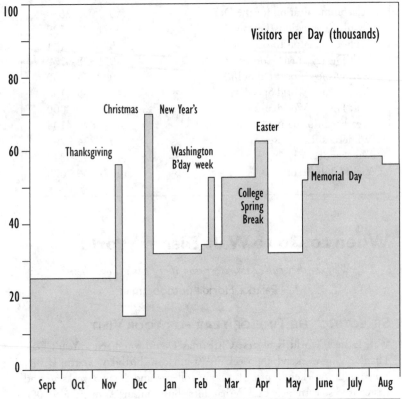

Annual Attendance Patterns at Walt Disney World

(Attendance figures represent weekly averages)

Many readers share their thoughts about the best time to visit Walt Disney World. These letters are representative:

From a Centerville, Ohio, family:

> *Catching on to the "off-season," we took the kids out of school and went to WDW in mid-May. So did a lot of other people. In fact, there were enough people there for me to think crowds must be increasing in the off-season as more people wise up about avoiding the masses. If I'm wrong, and this really was half the summer crowd, "high season" these days must be total and complete gridlock.*

Confirming the Ohio family's experience, a mom from West Plains, Missouri, writes:

> *We have visited WDW three times in the past eight years, each time in the second week of June. Each time the crowds were worse, and this time they were so big that we won't go at this time of year anymore.*

The Downside of Off-Season Touring

Though we strongly recommend going to Walt Disney World in the fall or spring, there are trade-offs. The parks often open late and close early on fall and spring days. When they open as late as 10 a.m., everyone arrives about the same time, making it hard to beat the crowd. A late opening coupled with an early closing drastically reduces the hours available to tour. Even when crowds are small, it's difficult to see a big park like the Magic Kingdom or Epcot between 10 a.m. and 6 p.m. Early closing (before 8 p.m.) also usually means that evening parades or fireworks are eliminated. And, because these are slow times at Disney World, some rides and attractions may be closed for maintenance or renovation. Finally, central Florida temperatures fluctuate wildly during the late fall, winter, and early spring; daytime lows in the 40s are not uncommon.

Given the choice, however, we never would go to Walt Disney World in summer or during a holiday period. To us, small crowds, bargain prices, and stress-free touring are well worth risking a little cold weather or a couple of closed attractions. So much easier is touring in the fall and other "off" periods that our research team, at the risk of being blasphemous, would advise taking children out of school for a week at those times rather than battling the summer crowds.

Most readers who have tried Disney World at various times agree. A gentleman from Ottawa, Ontario, who toured in early December writes:

> *It was the most enjoyable trip [to Walt Disney World] I have ever had, and I can't imagine going [back] to Disney World when it is crowded. Even without the crowds, we were still very tired by afternoon. Fighting crowds certainly would have made a hellish trip. We will never go again at any other time.*

A father of two from Reynoldsburg, Ohio, offers this opinion:

> *Taking your kids out of school. Is it worth it? Yes! Excuse my editorial comment at this point, but it used to be true that missing a week of school would place your child so far behind it could take*

months for him/her to regain that lost week. Not so today. With advance preparations and informing the teachers months before our departure, this was no problem. With less than an hour of homework after dinner, our kids went back to school with assignments completed and no makeup work. But it was all those other hours with no lines and no heat that were the real payoff.

A New Yorker who is accustomed to the vagaries of weather offered this bit of advice about off-season touring:

The weather when we were there was quirky. We were prepared, and brought along umbrellas, ponchos, sweaters, etc. We learned quickly (the hard way) always to have these items with us, because the local weather forecasters were not to be trusted.

Even during the off-season, crowd size can vary enormously. Usually this is the result of a promotion aimed at locals. A mother from Bridgewater, New Jersey, reports:

Although you mentioned the fact that school trips are [common] in Epcot during September and October, we were unprepared for the impact these groups had, especially since the kids are often unsupervised. From what I can see, the park can be enjoyed only on weekends during these months. Our visit was completely destroyed by unsupervised hordes of 10- to 12-year-olds.

A family from Staten Island, New York, found weekdays tranquil, but ran into a mess at the Magic Kingdom on Saturday:

Saturday (at MK) was rather horrifying. There were what seemed to be hordes of "day-trippers" (Scout troops, church groups, the Demolay Temple from Tampa, etc.). Even Tom Sawyer's Island was no idyllic oasis at 11:30 a.m. We left at about 1:30 p.m. for a swim and nap back at our motel and returned at 8 p.m. (the MK was open until midnight that night) to discover that the crowds had not thinned appreciably.

The likelihood of tangling with locals in September and October can be significantly reduced by avoiding the Magic Kingdom on Saturday and Epcot on weekdays. Usually the presence of large groups tapers off in all of the parks by the beginning of November.

SELECTING THE DAY OF THE WEEK FOR YOUR VISIT

Selecting the best day to visit a Walt Disney World theme park requires analyzing several variables. Entering into the equation are:

1. The time of year of your visit (holiday, summer, or off-season).
2. Attendance patterns for each day of the week at the respective parks.
3. Whether you are staying in a Walt Disney World hotel or campground (thereby making yourself eligible for early entry to the theme parks on specified days).
4. Habits of people traveling to Walt Disney World from outside of Florida.

A typical vacation scenario during summer would be for a family to arrive in the Orlando area on Sunday and to visit the Magic Kingdom and the Animal Kingdom on Monday and Tuesday; Epcot and Disney-MGM Studios on Wednesday and Thursday; and Typhoon Lagoon, Blizzard Beach, or a non-Disney area attraction on Friday. For those traveling by car, Friday often is reserved for heading home or to another Florida destination. If this were all we had to consider, we could recommend Fridays and Sundays as the best days all year to avoid crowds at the theme parks.

During the off-season, however, Disney initiates dozens of promotions to attract locals to Walt Disney World. Because these folks aren't on vacation, they tend to visit the theme parks on weekends. During fall, late winter, and spring, crowds might be larger on weekends than weekdays at the Magic Kingdom, the Animal Kingdom, and Disney-MGM Studios.

Crowds at Epcot, however, particularly during September and October, are almost always larger on weekdays. In addition to its promotions, Disney has a cooperative program with local schools that brings tens of thousands of children to Epcot for field trips in March, September, and October. Similarly, in late spring, high school students on "senior days" or prom nights fill the theme parks. Many of these programs are on weekdays.

The most significant shift in daily attendance patterns is the result of an early-entry program for guests staying at Walt Disney World resort hotels and campgrounds (but not for guests at Disney Village Hotel Plaza hotels). Initiated in 1993, the program originally applied only to the Magic Kingdom and operated on four days of the week. In 1994, the program was amended to include Epcot and Disney-MGM Studios. Each day of the week Disney World lodging guests are invited to enter a designated theme park one hour before the general public.

• WALT DISNEY WORLD WEATHER •

		Average Daily Low	Average Daily High	Average Daily Temperature	Average Daily Humidity %	Average Rainfall per Month (inches)	Number of Days of Rain per Month
	January	49°	72°	61°	74	2.1	6
	February	50°	73°	62°	71	2.8	7
	March	55°	78°	67°	71	3.2	8
	April	60°	84°	72°	69	2.2	6
	May	66°	88°	77°	72	3.9	9
	June	71°	91°	81°	77	7.4	14
Hurricane Season	July	73°	92°	82°	79	7.8	17
	August	73°	92°	82°	80	6.3	16
	September	73°	90°	81°	80	5.6	14
	October	65°	84°	75°	77	2.8	9
	November	57°	78°	68°	76	1.8	6
	December	51°	73°	62°	76	1.9	6

During the early-entry hour, Disney resort guests can enjoy attractions opened early for them. At the Magic Kingdom, for example, most attractions in Fantasyland and Tomorrowland are open to the early arrivals. At Epcot, Spaceship Earth, The Living Seas, The Land, and Journey into Imagination open early, and at Disney-MGM Studios, early entrants can enjoy *The Twilight Zone* Tower of Terror, The Great Movie Ride, Star Tours, and *MuppetVision 4-D,* among others. Attractions open for early entry change from time to time. The Animal Kingdom does not participate in the early entry program.

Many guests who try early entry are surprised and disappointed that the entire park is not open. At each park, only specifically designated attractions are operational for early entry. The remainder of the park is shut down (and usually roped off) until the general public is admitted later. Take heart, morning zombies: there will be at least one counter-service restaurant open serving coffee and something to eat.

How Early Entry Affects Attendance at the Theme Parks

Early entry strongly affects attendance at the theme parks, especially during busier times of year. Each day vast numbers of Disney resort guests tour whichever theme park is designated for early entry. If the Magic Kingdom is tapped for early entry on Monday, for example, it will be more crowded that day, and Epcot, the Animal Kingdom, and Disney-MGM Studios will be less crowded. Accordingly, Epcot and Disney-MGM Studios will be more crowded when those parks are respectively slated for early entry.

During holiday periods and summer, when Disney hotels are full, early entry makes a tremendous difference in crowds at the designated park. The program funnels so many people into the early-entry park that it fills by about 10 a.m. and is practically gridlocked by noon. Whatever edge resort guests gain by taking advantage of early entry is completely offset by horrendous crowds later in the day. Our advice during busier times of year, regardless of where you're lodging, is to avoid any park scheduled for early entry.

An alternative strategy for Disney resort guests is to take advantage of early entry, but only until the designated park begins to get crowded. At that time, leave the early-entry park and go to another park. This plan works particularly well at the Magic Kingdom for families with young children who love the attractions in Fantasyland. If you use your early-entry privileges, be among the first early entrants.

A mother of three from Lee Summit, Missouri, writes:

> *Our first full day at WDW, we went to the Magic Kingdom. This was on a Monday, an early-entry day for resort guests. We were there at 7:30 and were able to walk onto all the rides in Fantasyland with no wait. At 8:45 we positioned ourselves at the*

Adventureland rope and ran towards Splash Mountain when the rope dropped. We were able to ride Splash Mountain with no wait (switching off), and then Big Thunder with about a 15-minute wait (switching off). We then went straight to the Jungle Cruise and the wait was already 30 minutes, so we skipped it. The park became incredibly crowded as the day progressed, and we were all exhausted from getting up so early to get there for early entry. We left the park around noon? After that day, I resolved to avoid early-entry days and instead be at a non-early-entry park about a half hour before official opening time. This worked much better for us.

This note from a North Bend, Washington, dad emphasizes the importance of arriving at the beginning of the early-entry period:

We only used early entry once—to [Disney-] MGM. We got there 20 minutes after early entry opened and the wait for the Tower of Terror was already 1½ hours long. We skipped it!

A lady from Ann Arbor, Michigan, who is clearly working overtime trying to figure all this stuff out, says:

We are starting to think that reverse-reverse psychology might work: Disney opens one park earlier for all their guests, so all the guests go to that park, but then, everyone buys your book in which you tell them not to go to that park because all Disney guests are there, so no one goes to that park, therefore we can go to that park because people think it's going to be packed and they avoid it. What do you think?

Because Disney has changed the early-entry program numerous times in the past, we suggest you call Walt Disney Information at (407) 824-4321 before you leave home to verify the early-entry schedule during your stay.

Early-entry changes notwithstanding, we recommend:

Off-Season Touring   If you're a Disney resort or campground guest in the off-season or other less busy time, use your early-entry privileges. You'll get a jump on the general public and add an extra hour to what, in the off-season, is an already short touring day. If you're staying outside of Disney World and aren't eligible for early entry, avoid the park scheduled for early entry and visit one of the other theme parks instead.

A reader from Providence found early admission to be a great advantage during the off-season, writing:

> *During the off-season, the early admission was great. Only on Saturday did the crowd get so large that there were lines and bottlenecks. The mother behind me at Dumbo told me that they had waited three hours to ride Dumbo during their last visit to WDW. She took advantage of early admission to let her kid ride three times in a row with no waiting.*

E-Ticket Express   In 1998, Disney experimented with a program called the E-Ticket Express, where multiday pass holders could (for an extra $10) remain in the Magic Kingdom after official closing time and ride all the biggies with little or no waiting. Offered exclusively in the off-seasons, the E-Ticket Express program is described in detail on pages 418–419. Needless to say, the E-Ticket Express is the best thing since catsup on fries for folks who want to sleep in. Like most Disney programs, it is subject to termination at any time.

Least Crowded Days   From September through May (excluding holidays and spring break), Friday, Saturday, and Sunday are the most crowded days, while during summer the opposite is true (because locals stay home and out-of-state guests use Friday, Saturday, and Sunday for traveling).

Magic Kingdom   At the Magic Kingdom, Sunday and Friday are least crowded in summer, and Tuesday and Wednesday are least crowded during the rest of the year.

Disney-MGM Studios   At Disney-MGM Studios, Monday and Friday are best during summer. During off-season, try Monday and Tuesday.

Epcot   Monday, Wednesday, and Thursday are least crowded from January through May, as well as in November and December. During summer, crowds are smaller on Saturday and Sunday. In September and October, when school groups inundate Epcot, visit on Saturday or Sunday.

Animal Kingdom   High- or low-season, visit the Animal Kingdom on any weekday except Monday.

THE CRUELEST TIMES OF ALL: SUMMER AND HOLIDAYS

A reader from Columbus, Ohio, once observed, "the main thing I learned from your book is not to go during the summer or at holiday times. Once you know that you don't need a guidebook." While we might argue with the reader's conclusion, we certainly agree that avoiding summer and holidays is a strategy worth pursuing. That having been said, we also understand that many folks have no choice concerning the time of year they visit Walt Disney World. Much of this book, in fact, is dedicated to making sure those readers who visit during the busier times of year enjoy their Walt Disney World experience. Sure, off-season touring is preferable, but, armed with a little knowledge and some basic strategy, you can have a great time whenever you visit.

To put it in perspective, early summer (up to about June 15th) and late summer (after August 15th) are not nearly as crowded as the intervening period. And even the crowds of midsummer pale in comparison to the vast hordes that invade during holiday periods. If you visit in midsummer or during a holiday, the first thing you need to know is that the guest capacity of the theme parks is not infinite. In fact, once a park reaches capacity, its parking lot is closed, and only Disney resort guests arriving via the Disney transportation system are allowed to enter. If you are not a Disney resort guest you may find yourself in a situation similar to this dad from Boise, Idaho:

> *This is the worst of it. The Magic Kingdom and the [Disney-]*
> *MGM Studios were so full they closed the parks. For three days we*
> *could not enter those parks so we were forced to go to Epcot and use*
> *up two days of our four-day pass. We decided to pay for another*
> *night at our hotel to see if the crowds would let up, but no luck. All*
> *we could do was just drive around Orlando and sightsee.*

The reader didn't tell us what time he arrived at the Magic Kingdom or the Studios, but we can pretty much assume he wasn't on hand for opening. If you roll out of bed early and get yourself to one of the parks not scheduled for early entry an hour or so prior to official opening time, you are practically certain to be admitted. Regardless of the time of year, if you aren't eligible for early entry, stay clear of the early-entry park.

The thought of teeming, jostling throngs jockeying for position in endless lines under the baking Fourth of July sun is enough to wilt the will and ears of the most ardent Mouseketeer. The Disney folks, however, feeling bad about those long, long lines and the nearly impossible touring conditions on packed holidays, compensate their patrons with a no-less-than-incredible array of first-rate live entertainment and happenings.

Shows, parades, concerts, and pageantry continue throughout the day. In the evening, particularly, so much is going on that you have to make some tough choices. Concerts, parades, light shows, laser shows, fireworks, and dance productions occur almost continually. No question about it, you can go to Walt Disney World on the Fourth of July (or on any other extended-hours, crowded day), never get on a ride, and still have a good time. Admittedly, it isn't the ideal situation for a first-timer who really wants to experience the attractions, but for anyone else it's a great party.

Disney provides colorful holiday decor for most holidays, as well as spe-

cial parades and live entertainment for Christmas, New Year's, Easter, and Fourth of July, among others. Regarding Christmas, our advice is to visit in early December when you can enjoy the decorations and festivities without battling the crowds. A particularly well-known special event is Mickey's Very Merry Christmas Party, for which a separate admission ticket is required. A reader from Pineville, Louisiana, tried the Very Merry Christmas Party during the Christmas–New Year's week and found the guest list too large for her liking, writing:

> *Another thing I will not do again is buy tickets and go to the Very Merry Christmas Party. The event was sold out with 20,000 actually in attendance. We went in December to avoid crowds and were taken by surprise to find wall-to-wall people at the Very Merry Christmas Party. They had some great shows offered, but we could not get to them. The parade at 9 [p.m.] and fireworks at 10 [p.m.], then fighting our way back to the parking lot was all we could muster. We spent 30 minutes on arrival just getting a stroller. We did not ride anything and there were some things that we had wanted to go back and ride. Mickey's Very Merry Christmas Party is not the time for rides!*

Disney monitors the occupancy of hotels in the area in order to project attendance. On days when huge crowds are expected, Disney will often open the parks well in advance of the official opening time. This applies to all the parks, not just the one scheduled for early entry, and it is done to prevent parking toll booths, ticket windows, transportation systems, and entrance plazas from being overwhelmed. When Disney puts its early-opening plan into operation, the parks generally do not discriminate between Disney resort guests and day guests (those not staying at Disney hotels). In other words, when really big crowds are expected, Disney will often open all of the parks early and admit any guest.

Unfortunately, Disney does not disclose in advance that it plans to open the parks early (except the park scheduled for early entry), nor will operators at Disney's main information phone number clue you in. You basically must guess based on the time of year whether implementation of the early-opening procedure is likely. Over major holidays, the probability of Disney opening the parks early is high. For nonholiday periods during the peak summer season, it's a lot iffier.

When we visit during the summer or holidays, we sometimes make a reconnaissance run to one of the Disney transportation system information windows (located at each of the parks and at the Transportation and Ticket Center [TTC]) and ask what time the parks actually opened that morning.

Make it clear that you are not inquiring about the official opening time, but rather that you want to know exactly what time guests were admitted. If the parks opened early on the day in question, there is a great likelihood that the same conditions will prevail for the next couple of days.

If you visit on a nonholiday, midsummer day, arrive an hour to 70 minutes before the stated opening. If you visit during a major holiday period, arrive 90 minutes to 2 hours ahead of the official opening time. In either case, avoid the park that is scheduled for early entry. Hit your favorite rides early using one of our touring plans, and then return to your hotel for lunch, a swim, and perhaps a nap. Don't forget to have your hand stamped for re-entry when you exit. If you are interested in the special parades and shows, return to the park in the late afternoon or early evening. Work under the assumption that early morning will be the only time you can experience the attractions without long waits. Finally, do not wait until the last minute in the evening to leave the park. The exodus at closing is truly mind-boggling.

Epcot is usually the least crowded park during holiday periods unless it's scheduled for early entry. Expect the other parks to be mobbed. To save time in the morning, purchase your admission in advance. Also, consider bringing your own stroller or wheelchair instead of renting one of Disney's. If you are touring Epcot or the Magic Kingdom and plan to spend the day, try exiting the park for lunch at one of the nearby resort hotels. Above all, bring your sense of humor and pay attention to the morale of your party. Bail out when it gets to be more work than fun.

Part Two

Making the Most of Your Time and Money

Allocating Money

Did Walt really intend for it to be so expensive that the average family couldn't afford it?

—*Unofficial Guide* reader and mother of one from Amarillo, Texas

How much you spend depends on how long you stay at Walt Disney World. But even if you only stop by for an afternoon, be prepared to drop a bundle. In Part Three we'll show you how to save money on lodging, and in Part Eight you'll find lots of tips for economizing on meals. This section will give you some sense of what you can expect to pay for admissions, as well as which admission option will best meet your needs.

WALT DISNEY WORLD ADMISSION OPTIONS

Reviewers who complain that prices quoted in guidebooks are out of date should note that Walt Disney World ticket prices change about as often as the prime rate. Prices quoted below are those prevailing at press time. We expect an increase at the end of February 1999. Admission price increases historically have been in the 3–5% range.

There are basically eight Walt Disney World admission options (many with silly names), but several of them are endangered species:

Type of Pass	Adult Price	Child Price
1. 1-Day/One-Park Only Ticket	$45	$36
2. 4-Day Value Pass	$158	$127
3. 5-Day Park-Hopper Pass	$201	$161

4. 6-Day All-in-One Pass	$264	$211
5. 7-Day All-in-One Pass	$291	$233
6. Length of Stay Pass	*Varies according to length of stay*	
7. Annual Passports*	$271–423	$231–360
8. Florida Resident/Seasonal	$169	$144

* More expensive Annual Passports include water parks, Pleasure Island, and Discovery Island.

The **1-Day/One-Park Only Ticket** is good for admission and unlimited use of "attractions and experiences" at the Magic Kingdom, Epcot, the Animal Kingdom, or Disney-MGM Studios but does not provide same-day admission to more than one of the four.

The **4-Day Value Pass** provides four days of separate admissions: a one-day/one-park admission each to the Magic Kingdom, Epcot, the Animal Kingdom, and Disney-MGM Studios. The Magic Kingdom part of the pass can be used only at the Magic Kingdom; Epcot, at Epcot; Disney-MGM Studios, at the Studios; and Animal Kingdom, at the Animal Kingdom. You can visit the parks in any order or on any day of the week you like. A guest who visits the Magic Kingdom in the morning and then goes to Epcot for dinner would have to use two of the pass's four admissions on the same day. You can, however, come and go at the *same* park on a given day as long as you get your hand stamped for re-entry as you leave.

The **5-Day Park-Hopper Pass** provides same-day admission to the Magic Kingdom, the Animal Kingdom, Epcot, and Disney-MGM Studios. You can tour the Studios in the morning, have lunch at the Animal Kingdom and dinner at Epcot, and stop by the Magic Kingdom for the evening parades and fireworks.

The **6-Day** and **7-Day All-in-One Passes** were introduced in the summer of 1997. They provide for unlimited use of the major theme parks as well as Pleasure Island, Blizzard Beach, Typhoon Lagoon, River Country, Wide World of Sports, and Discovery Island for the number of the days stated on the pass. Like the Park-Hopper Pass, All-in-One Passes are good forever and do not have to be used during one stay or on consecutive days.

With the All-in-Ones, admission to any Disney theme park or one of the recreational facilities listed above counts as a "use-day." Let's say you purchase a 6-Day All-in-One and go to the Magic Kingdom on day one, to Disney-MGM Studios on day two, and to Epcot on day three. OK, that's three of your five days used up. On day four you decide to spend the day at Sea World (a non-Disney park), but go clubbing at Pleasure Island in the evening. When you go through the turnstiles at Pleasure Island, you zap another use-day, and you're down to two days left on your 6-Day All-in-One Pass.

With the All-in-One Passes you can visit as many theme parks, swimming parks, etc., as you can cram into a single day. You can swim at Blizzard Beach in the morning, visit Epcot in the afternoon, swing by the Magic Kingdom for dinner, and then head for Pleasure Island at night. It's still just one use-day counted.

The **Length of Stay Pass,** for Walt Disney World lodging and campground guests, provides the same benefits as the Park-Hopper Pass but can be purchased for any length of stay two days or longer. This program is the first time Disney has offered a comprehensive admission option (all major parks) for stays shorter than four days. These passes are incredibly convenient: guests are issued a card that functions as a combination park pass and credit card. The card can be used at restaurants, shops, and other facilities throughout the World, and purchases are charged to the guest's room. Length of Stay Passes may save about 7% over the cost of 4- and 5-Day passes. On the negative side, Length of Stay Passes are good only for the guest's stay.

The **Unlimited Magic Pass** is just like the Length of Stay Pass except that it is sold in advance with a vacation package.

The **Annual Passport** is good for unlimited use of the major theme parks for one year. An add-on is available to provide unlimited use of the minor theme parks. In addition to admission, Annual Pass holders get a number of perks, including complimentary parking and seasonal special offers.

The **Florida Resident's Passport.** In 1995, Walt Disney World expanded the admission options for Florida residents. Florida residents now can select from a menu of choices, including:

Florida Resident's Seasonal Passport. This pass (about $169 for adults) allows unlimited use of the major theme parks during specified (quieter) times of year.

Florida Resident's Epcot After 4 p.m. Passport. About $75 for adults, this pass allows Floridians to visit Epcot any day after 4 p.m.

Florida Resident's Annual Passport. These passports are available to residents at about 12% off the regular price.

Florida Resident's One-Day Discounts. At certain slower times of year, residents are offered discounts on 1-Day/One-Park Only Passes. In 1998, these discounts ran about 20% off the regular price of a 1-Day Pass for those younger than 55, and a whopping 30% off for seniors 55 and older.

While applicants must prove Florida residency to be eligible, it isn't necessary to have a Florida driver's license or to live in Florida year-round. A utility bill in your name for a Florida address will suffice.

WHICH ADMISSION SHOULD YOU BUY?

If you only have one day at Walt Disney World, select the park that most interests you and buy the 1-Day/One-Park Only Ticket. If you have two days and don't plan to return to Florida for a couple of years, buy two 1-Day tickets (or a Length of Stay Pass if you're a Disney lodging guest). If you think you might pass through the area again in the next year or two, spring for a 4-, 5-, 6-, or 7-day pass. Use two days of admission to see as much as you can, and save the remaining days for another trip. Remember that with 5-Day Park-Hopper Passes, admission to Pleasure Island, Blizzard Beach, Typhoon Lagoon, River Country, the Wide World of Sports, and Discovery Island expires within seven days of the first time you use your pass at the Magic Kingdom, Epcot, the Animal Kingdom, or Disney-MGM Studios. Also, remember that you are charged a use-day on the All-in-One Passes at both the major and minor parks.

If you plan to spend three or more days at Walt Disney World, buy a 4- or 5-day pass. If you live in Florida or plan to spend seven or more days in the major theme parks, the Annual Passport (about $285) is a good buy. If you live in Florida and don't mind being restricted to visiting Disney World at designated off-peak times, the Florida Resident's Seasonal Pass should be considered.

If you visit Walt Disney World every year, here's how to save big bucks. Let's say you usually take your vacation during summer. This year, plan your Disney vacation for July and buy an Annual Passport. Next year, go in June. Because Annual Passports start on the date of purchase, those you buy this year will still be good for next year's vacation if you go a month earlier! If you spend four days each year at Disney World (eight days in the two consecutive years), you'll cut your daily admission to about $36 per adult per day. The longer your Disney vacation, of course, the more you save with the Annual Passport. If you visit the theme parks seven days each year, your admission will be less than $21 per day.

DISCOUNTS ON ADMISSION

At Disney World as at Wal-Mart, volume rules. If you buy a 5-day pass, you will pay less per day than if you buy a 1-day or 4-day pass. Admission discounts ranging between 3–5% are available to Magic Kingdom Gold Card holders, AAA members, and Disney time-share owners.

OLD PASSPORTS AND THE ANIMAL KINGDOM

Unused days on multiday passports sold before the Animal Kingdom opened in 1998 are good only for the other three parks. In other words, you can't use them for admission to the Animal Kingdom.

THE BLACK MARKET

Many readers ask if they can use remaining admissions on partially redeemed 4- and 5-day passes brought home by relatives. The facts are:

1. The pass is sold to the purchaser on a nontransferable basis. The pass states on the back, "To be valid this Pass must be used by the same person for all days."
2. On passes sold before February 1994, there is nothing on the pass that identifies the purchaser. On certain multiday, all-park passes sold after that date, the bearer's photograph and/or signature appear.
3. Admission attendants don't request a receipt or other proof of purchase for passes.

A corollary question concerns what to do with unused admissions on 4-, 5-, 6-, or 7-day passes that you purchase legally during your vacation. Our advice is to hang onto the passes. For starters, resale of unused multiday passes is a misdemeanor, and the guy offering you cash for your unused ticket may be a security officer. Second, because Disney raises admission prices almost every year, using an old pass during your next visit will save you money.

WHERE TO BUY YOUR ADMISSION AT WALT DISNEY WORLD

You can purchase passports at the major theme parks and at the resort hotels. If you purchase your passport at the theme parks, the 4-Day Value Pass and the 5-Day Park-Hopper might not be advertised as available. This is because Disney is pushing hard to get guests to accept the new All-in-One Passes. For the time being at least, if you want to buy the Value Pass or the Hopper at the theme parks, you must specifically request it.

WHERE TO BUY YOUR ADMISSION IN ADVANCE

You can buy most multiday passes at a Disney Store before you leave home. The stores also can order 1-Day/One-Park Only tickets (allow three weeks for delivery). If you're driving to Disney World, buy your admission at the

Ocala Disney AAA Travel Center at Exit 68 on I-75. If you fly, buy tickets at the airport Disney Store.

Tickets are also available by mail from the Walt Disney World Ticket Mail Order service (address on page 35) and at most Disney World hotels.

WHERE NOT TO BUY YOUR ADMISSION IN ADVANCE

Because passes to Walt Disney World aren't discounted, offers of free or cut-rate tickets should trigger caution. Anyone offering free tickets to any attraction in the Orlando/Kissimmee area is probably selling real estate or time-share condominiums. You may receive a free ticket, but you will have to endure a lengthy site inspection and/or high-pressure sales pitch.

Many hotels outside of Walt Disney World maintain a desk or kiosk where independent brokers sell tickets to area attractions. These brokers are legitimate, but convenience is the only advantage to buying from them. Expect to pay regular Disney prices or a little more if you buy tickets from an independent broker.

HOW MUCH DOES IT COST PER DAY AT WALT DISNEY WORLD?

A typical day would cost $360.15, excluding lodging and transportation, for a family of four—Mom, Dad, 12-year-old Tim, and 8-year-old

Sandy—driving their own car and staying outside of Disney World. They plan to be in the area for a week, so they buy 5-Day Park-Hopper Passes. Here's a breakdown:

How Much Does a Day Cost?	
Breakfast for four at Denny's with tax & tip	$25.50
Epcot parking fee	5.00
One day's admission on a 4-Day Park-Hopper Pass	
Dad: Adult 5-Day with tax = $201 divided by five (days)	40.20
Mom: Adult 5-Day with tax = $201 divided by five (days)	40.20
Tim: Adult 5-Day with tax = $201 divided by five (days)	40.20
Sandy: Child 5-Day with tax = $161 divided by five (days)	32.20
Morning break (soda or coffee)	7.00
Fast-food lunch (sandwich or burger, fries, soda), no tip	29.00
Afternoon break (soda and popcorn)	14.35
Dinner at Italy (no alcoholic beverages) with tax & tip	88.00
Souvenirs (Mickey T-shirts for Tim and Sandy) with tax*	38.50
One-Day Total	$360.15
(does not include lodging or transportation)	
*Cheer up, you won't have to buy souvenirs every day.	

Allocating Time

During Disney World's first decade, a family with a week's vacation could enjoy the Magic Kingdom and River Country and still have several days for the beach or other area attractions. Since Epcot opened in 1982, however, Disney World has steadily been enlarging to monopolize the family's entire week. Today, with the addition of Blizzard Beach, Typhoon Lagoon, Disney-MGM Studios, the Animal Kingdom, and Downtown Disney, you should allocate six days for a whirlwind tour (or seven to ten days if you're old-fashioned and insist on a little relaxation during your vacation). If you don't have six or more days, or think you might want to venture beyond the edge of "The World," be prepared to make some hard choices.

The theme parks and swimming attractions are huge and require a lot of walking and, sometimes, a lot of waiting in lines. Moving in typically large crowds all day is exhausting. The unrelenting Florida sun often zaps the most hardy traveler, making tempers short. In our many visits to Walt

Disney World we observed, particularly on hot summer days, a dramatic transition from happy, enthusiastic tourists upon arrival to plodding zombies later in the day. Visitors who began their day enjoying the Disney wonders lapsed into an exhausted, production-line mentality ("We've got two more rides in Fantasyland, then we can go back to the hotel.").

We recommend you approach Walt Disney World the same way you would an eight-course Italian dinner: with plenty of time between courses. The best way not to have fun is to cram too much into too little time.

WHICH PARK TO SEE FIRST?

This question is less academic than it appears, especially if there are children or teenagers in your party. Children who see the Magic Kingdom first expect more of the same type of entertainment at the other parks. At Epcot, they're often disappointed by the educational orientation and more serious tone (many adults react the same way). Disney-MGM offers some pretty wild action, but the general presentation is educational and more adult. Though most children enjoy zoos, animals can't be programmed to entertain. Thus, children may not find the Animal Kingdom as exciting as the Magic Kingdom or Disney-MGM.

First-time visitors especially should see Epcot first; you will be able to enjoy it fully without having been preconditioned to think of Disney entertainment as solely fantasy or adventure. Parties with children definitely should see Epcot first. Children will be more likely to enjoy Epcot on its own merits if they see it first, and they will be more relaxed and patient in their touring.

See the Animal Kingdom second. Like Epcot, it has an educational thrust, but it provides a change of pace because it features live animals.

Next, see Disney-MGM Studios, which helps all ages make a fluid transition from the educational Epcot and Animal Kingdom to the fanciful Magic Kingdom. Also, because Disney-MGM Studios is smaller, you won't walk as much or stay as long.

Save the Magic Kingdom for last.

OPERATING HOURS

Disney can't be accused of being inflexible regarding operating hours at the parks. They run a dozen or more schedules each year, making it advisable to call (407) 824-4321 for the *exact* hours before you arrive. In the off-season, parks may be open for as few as eight hours (from 10 a.m. to 6 p.m.). By contrast, at busy times (particularly holidays), they may be open from 8 a.m. until 2 a.m. the next morning.

Usually hours approximate the following: from September through mid-March, excluding holiday periods, the Magic Kingdom is open from 9 a.m. to 7, 8, or 9 p.m. During the same period, Epcot is open from 9 a.m. to 9 p.m., and Disney-MGM Studios is open from 9 a.m. to 7 or 8 p.m. The Animal Kingdom is open from 7 a.m. until 7 or 8 p.m.

During summer, expect the Animal Kingdom to remain open until 8 p.m. Epcot and Disney-MGM Studios are normally open until 9 or 10 p.m., with the Magic Kingdom sometimes open as late as 1 a.m.

OFFICIAL OPENING VS. REAL OPENING

Operating hours you're quoted when you call are "official hours." The parks actually open earlier. Many visitors, relying on information disseminated by Disney Guest Relations, arrive at the official opening time and find the park packed with people. If the official hours are 9 a.m. to 9 p.m., for example, Main Street in the Magic Kingdom will open at 8 or 8:30 a.m. and the remainder of the park will open at 8:30 or 9 a.m. If the official opening for the Magic Kingdom is 8 a.m. and you're eligible for early entry, you will be able to enter the park at 6:30 a.m.

Disney publishes hours of operation well in advance but allows the flexibility to react daily to gate conditions. Disney traffic controllers survey local hotel reservations, estimate how many visitors to expect on a given day, and open the theme parks early to avoid bottlenecks at parking facilities and ticket windows and to absorb the crowds as they arrive.

If you don't have early-entry privileges, tour a park where early entry *isn't* in effect, arriving 50 minutes before the official opening time during the off-season. In mid-summer arrive 70 minutes before official opening. If you visit on a major holiday, arrive 1 hour and 20 minutes before the official opening.

If you're a Disney resort guest and want to take advantage of early entry, arrive 1 hour and 40 minutes before the early-entry park is scheduled to open to the general public. Buses, boats, and monorails will initiate service to the early-entry park about two hours before it opens to the general public.

At day's end, rides and attractions shut down at approximately the official closing time. Main Street in the Magic Kingdom remains open 30 minutes to 1 hour after the rest of the park has closed.

THE VACATION THAT FIGHTS BACK

A vacation is what you make it, but visiting Walt Disney World requires levels of industry and stamina more often associated with running marathons. A mother from Middletown, New York, spells it out:

A vacation at WDW is not a vacation in the usual sense—sleeping late, total relaxation, leisurely meals, etc. It is a doing vacation that's frankly exhausting, but definitely worth doing. It's a magical place, where the visitor feels welcomed from the minute they arrive at their accommodations to the last second before boarding the shuttle bus back to the airport.

A mother of two from Indianapolis, Indiana, adds:

My main thought throughout our time at WDW was, "It's so much work to have so much fun!" I can't imagine going without your touring plans in hand—I'm sure we'd have only seen half as much and we'd have become so angry with each other over trying to decide what to see next. Even with generally careful following of the one-day plans and arriving an hour early, we missed at least one "not to be missed" feature per [theme park], mostly due to brain death in the heat.

The point is: At Walt Disney World, *less is more.* Take the World in small doses, with plenty of swimming, napping, reading, and relaxing in between. And here's some comforting news: Disney World *won't* be packed up and shipped to Tibet next year. If you don't see everything this trip, you can come back!

Hitting the Wall

As you plan your time at Walt Disney World, consider your physical limitations. It is extremely exhausting to rise at the crack of dawn and run around a theme park for 8–12 hours, day after day. Sooner or later (usually sooner), you're going to hit the wall. Every Disney World vacation itinerary should include break days (when you don't go to a theme park) and sleeping-in days (when you take the morning off). Plan your break days and sleeping-in days to follow unusually long and arduous days, particularly after days at the Magic Kingdom and Epcot when you stay to see the evening parades or fireworks. Keep telling yourself over and over that you'll enjoy your vacation more if you are well rested.

A mom from LaGrange, Illinois, tried to sidestep our advice to stay rested, writing:

As I was planning, I was very sure we would not be taking a swim/nap break in the middle of the day. "No Way!" On the very first day of touring (at the Magic Kingdom) my seven-year-old said (at 9:30 a.m.—after only two hours at the park), "I'm hot—when can we go back to the hotel and swim?" Needless to say, we took that little break every day.

If you neglect this all-important element of self-preservation and pacing, you'll be writing us letters like this one from a father of three from Unionville, Connecticut:

It's really difficult to follow your [touring plans] for more than one day in a row. The kids are just too exhausted to last through the fireworks and there isn't time to return to the hotel because of the crowdedness of the [parks].

OPTIMUM TOURING SITUATION

We don't believe there is one ideal itinerary. Tastes, energy levels, and perspectives on what constitutes entertainment and relaxation vary. This understood, here are some considerations for developing your own ideal itinerary.

Optimum touring at Disney World requires a good itinerary, a minimum of six days on-site (excluding travel time), and a fair amount of money. It also requires a prodigious appetite for Disney entertainment. The essence of optimum touring is to see the attractions in a series of shorter, less exhausting visits during the cooler, less crowded times of day, with plenty of rest and relaxation between excursions.

Since optimum touring calls for leaving and returning to the theme parks on most days, it makes sense to stay in one of the Walt Disney World resort hotels. Also, if you stay in the World, you have early-entry privileges at designated parks and the option of advance reservations for the *Hoop-Dee-Doo Revue* and dinner shows performed at the hotels. Disney lodging guests also have freer use of the bus, boat, and monorail systems and have more choices for babysitting and children's programs. Sound good? It is, but be prepared to pay.

If you visit Walt Disney World during busy times (see pages 37–38), you need to get up early to beat the crowds. Short lines and stress-free touring are incompatible with sleeping in. If you want to sleep late *and* enjoy your touring, visit Disney World when attendance is lighter.

SEEING WALT DISNEY WORLD ON A TIGHT SCHEDULE

Many visitors don't have six days to devote to Disney. Some are en route to other destinations or may wish to sample additional attractions of Orlando and central Florida. For these visitors, efficient touring is a must.

Even the most time-effective touring plan won't allow you to cover two or more major theme parks in one day. Plan to allocate at least an entire day to each park (an exception to this rule is when the parks close at different times, allowing you to tour one park until closing and then proceed to another park). If your schedule permits only one day of touring, concentrate on one theme park and save the others for another visit.

One-Day Touring

A comprehensive, one-day tour of the Magic Kingdom, the Animal Kingdom, Epcot, or Disney-MGM Studios is possible but requires knowledge of the park, good planning, and plenty of energy and endurance. One-day touring doesn't leave much time for sit-down meals, prolonged browsing in shops, or lengthy breaks. Even so, one-day touring can be fun and rewarding.

Successful one-day touring of the Magic Kingdom, the Animal Kingdom, Epcot, or Disney-MGM Studios hinges on *three rules:*

1. Determine in Advance What You Really Want to See

What rides and attractions appeal most to you? Which additional rides and attractions would you like to experience if you have time left? What are you willing to forgo?

To help you set your touring priorities, we describe the theme parks and every attraction in detail in this book. In each description, we include the author's evaluation of the attraction and the opinions of Walt Disney World guests expressed as star ratings. Five stars is the best possible rating.

Finally, because attractions range from midway-type rides and horse-drawn trolleys to colossal, high-tech extravaganzas, we have developed a hierarchy of categories to pinpoint attractions' magnitude:

Super Headliners The best attractions the theme park has to offer. Mind-boggling in size, scope, and imagination. Represents the cutting edge of modern attraction technology and design.

Headliners Full blown, multimillion-dollar, full-scale, themed adventures and theater presentations. Modern in technology and design and employing a full range of special effects.

Major Attractions Themed adventures on a more modest scale, but incorporating state-of-the-art technologies. Or, larger-scale attractions of older design.

Minor Attractions Midway-type rides, small "dark" rides (cars on a track, zig-zagging through the dark), small theater presentations, transportation rides, and elaborate walk-through attractions.

Diversions Exhibits, both passive and interactive. Includes playgrounds, video arcades, and street theater.

Though not every Walt Disney World attraction fits neatly into these descriptions, the categories provide a comparison of attraction size and scope. Remember that bigger and more elaborate doesn't always mean better. Peter Pan's Flight, a minor attraction in the Magic Kingdom, continues to be one of the park's most beloved rides. Likewise, for many young children, no attraction regardless of size surpasses Dumbo.

2. Arrive Early! Arrive Early! Arrive Early!

This is the single most important key to efficient touring and avoiding long lines. First thing in the morning, there are no lines and fewer people. The same four rides you can experience in one hour in early morning can take as long as three hours to see after 10:30 a.m. Have breakfast before you arrive so you won't waste prime touring time sitting in a restaurant.

The earlier a park opens, the greater your potential advantage. This is because most vacationers won't make the sacrifice to rise early and get to a theme park before it opens. Fewer people are willing to be on-hand for an 8 a.m. opening than for a 9 a.m. opening. On those rare occasions when a park opens at 10 a.m., almost everyone arrives at the same time, so it's almost impossible to get a jump on the crowd. If you're a Disney resort guest and have early-entry privileges, arrive as early as early entry allows (6:30 a.m. if the park opens to the public at 8 a.m., or 7:30 a.m. if the park opens to the public at 9 a.m.). If you are visiting during midsummer, arrive at non-early-entry parks 70 minutes before the official opening time. During holiday periods, arrive at non-early-entry parks 90 minutes to 2 hours before the official opening.

3. Avoid Bottlenecks

Helping you avoid bottlenecks is what this guide is about. Bottlenecks are caused by crowd concentrations and/or faulty crowd management. Avoiding bottlenecks involves being able to predict where, when, and why they occur. Concentrations of hungry people create bottlenecks at restaurants during lunch and dinner; concentrations of people moving toward the exit near closing time create bottlenecks in gift shops en route to the gate; concentrations of visitors at new and popular rides, and at rides slow to load and unload, create bottlenecks and long lines.

We provide touring plans for the Magic Kingdom, the Animal Kingdom, Epcot, Disney-MGM Studios, and Pleasure Island to help you avoid bottlenecks. In addition, we provide detailed information on all rides and performances, enabling you to estimate how long you may have to wait in line and allowing you to compare rides for their capacity to accommodate large crowds. Touring plans for the Magic Kingdom begin on page 413; Epcot,

page 482; the Animal Kingdom, page 523; Disney-MGM Studios, page 555; and Pleasure Island, page 648. We have also included One-Day Touring Plans for the Universal Studios Florida park on page 581 and Universal's Islands of Adventure park on page 595.

In response to reader requests, we have added clip-out versions of the touring plans (except Universal's Islands of Adventure) at the end of this book.

TOURING PLANS: WHAT THEY ARE AND HOW THEY WORK

We followed your plans to the letter—which at times was troublesome to the dad in our party . . . somewhat akin to testing the strength of your marriage by wallpapering together!

—*Unofficial Guide* reader and mother of two from Milford, Connecticut

When we interviewed Walt Disney World visitors who toured the theme parks on slow days, they invariably waxed eloquent about the sheer delight of their experience. When we questioned visitors who toured on moderate or busy days, however, they talked at length about the jostling crowds and how much time they stood in line. What a shame, they said, that so much time and energy are spent fighting crowds in a place as special as Walt Disney World.

Given this complaint, our researchers descended on the World to determine whether a touring plan could be devised that would liberate visitors from the traffic flow and allow them to see any theme park in one day with minimal waiting in line. On some of the busiest days of the year, our team monitored traffic into and through the parks, noting how they filled and how patrons were distributed among the attractions. We also observed which rides and attractions were most popular and where bottlenecks were most likely to occur.

After many days of collecting data, we devised preliminary touring plans, which we tested during one of the busiest weeks of the year. Each day, our researchers would tour the park using one of the preliminary plans, noting how long it took to walk from place to place and how long the wait in line was for each attraction. Combining the information gained on trial runs, we devised a master plan that we retested and fine-tuned. This plan, with very little variance from day to day, allowed us to experience all major rides and attractions and most lesser ones in one day, with an average wait in line of less than five minutes at each.

From this master plan, we developed alternative plans that took into account the varying tastes and personal requirements of different Disney World patrons. Each plan operated with the same logic as the master plan but addressed the special needs and preferences of its intended users.

Finally, after all of the plans were tested by our staff, we selected (using convenience sampling) Walt Disney World visitors to test the plans. The only requisite for being chosen to test the plans was that the guests must be visiting a Disney park for the first time. A second group of patrons was chosen for a "control group." These were first-time visitors who would tour the park according to their own plans but who would make notes about what they did and how much time they spent in lines.

When the two groups were compared, the results were amazing. On days when major theme park attendance exceeded 48,000, visitors touring without our plans *averaged* 3⅔ hours' more waiting in line per day than the patrons touring with our plans, and they experienced 37% fewer rides and attractions.

General Overview of the Touring Plans

Our touring plans are step-by-step guides for seeing as much as possible with a minimum of standing in line. They're designed to help you avoid crowds and bottlenecks on days of moderate-to-heavy attendance. On days of lighter attendance (see "Selecting the Time of Year for Your Visit," page 37), the plans will still save time but won't be as critical to successful touring.

What You Can Realistically Expect from the Touring Plans

Though we present one-day touring plans for each of the theme parks, you should understand that the Magic Kingdom and Epcot have more attractions than you can see in one day, even if you never wait in line. If you must cram your visit into a single day, the one-day touring plans will allow you to see as much as is humanly possible. Under certain circumstances you may not complete the plan, and you definitely won't be able to see everything. For the Magic Kingdom and Epcot, the most comprehensive, efficient, and relaxing touring plans are by far the two-day plans. Although Disney-MGM Studios has grown considerably since its 1989 debut, you should have no problem seeing everything in one day. The Animal Kingdom likewise is a one-day outing.

Variables That Will Affect the Success of the Touring Plans

How quickly you move from one ride to another; when and how many refreshment and rest room breaks you take; when, where, and how you eat meals; and your ability (or lack thereof) to find your way around will all have an impact on the success of the plans. Smaller groups almost always move faster than larger groups, and parties of adults generally can cover more ground than families with young children. Switching off (see pages

165–167), among other things, prohibits families with little ones from moving expeditiously among attractions. Plus, some children simply cannot conform to the "early-to-rise" conditions of the touring plans.

A mom from Nutley, New Jersey, writes:

> [Although] the touring plans all advise getting to parks at opening, we just couldn't burn the candle at both ends. Our kids (10, 7, and 4) would not go to sleep early and couldn't be up at dawn and still stay relatively sane. It worked well for us to let them sleep a little later, go out and bring breakfast back to the room while they slept, and still get a relatively early start by not spending time on eating breakfast out. We managed to avoid long lines with an occasional early morning, and hitting popular attractions during parades, mealtimes, and late evenings.

And a family from Centerville, Ohio, says:

> The toughest thing about your tour plans was getting the rest of the family to stay with them, at least to some degree. Getting them to pass by attractions in order to hit something across the park was no easy task (sometimes impossible).

Finally, if you have young children in your party, be prepared for character encounters. The appearance of a Disney character is usually sufficient to stop a touring plan dead in its tracks. What's more, while some characters continue to stroll the parks, it is becoming more the rule to assemble characters in some specific venue (like the Hall of Fame at Mickey's Toontown Fair) where families must queue up for photos and autographs. Meeting characters, posing for photos, and collecting autographs can burn hours of touring time. If your kids are into character autograph collecting, you will need to anticipate these interruptions to the touring plan and negotiate some understanding with your children about when you will follow the plan and when you will collect autographs. Our advice is to either go with the flow or alternatively set aside a certain morning or afternoon for photos and autographs. Be aware, however, that queues for autographs, especially in Toontown at the Magic Kingdom and Camp Minnie-Mickey at the Animal Kingdom, are every bit as long as the queues for major attractions. The only time-efficient way to collect autographs is to line up at the character greeting areas first thing in the morning. Because this is also the best time to experience the more popular attractions, you may have some tough decisions to make.

While we realize that following the touring plans is not always easy, we nevertheless recommend continuous, expeditious touring until around noon. After that hour, breaks and diversions won't affect the plans significantly.

Some variables that can profoundly affect the touring plans are beyond your control. Chief among these are the manner and timing of bringing a particular ride to capacity. For example, Big Thunder Mountain Railroad, a roller coaster in the Magic Kingdom, has five trains. On a given morning it may begin operation with two of the five, then add the other three if and when needed. If the waiting line builds rapidly before operators decide to go to full capacity, you could have a long wait, even in early morning.

Another variable relates to the time you arrive for a theater performance. Usually, your wait will be the length of time from your arrival to the end of the presentation in progress. Thus, if *Country Bear Jamboree* is 15 minutes long and you arrive one minute after a show has begun, your wait for the next show will be 14 minutes. Conversely, if you arrive as the show is wrapping up, your wait will be only a minute or two.

What to Do If You Lose the Thread

Anything from a blister to a broken attraction can throw off a touring plan. If unforeseen events interrupt a touring plan:

1. Skip one step on the plan for every 20 minutes you're delayed. If you lose your billfold, for example, and spend an hour finding it, skip three steps and pick up from there.
2. Forget the touring plan and organize the remainder of your day using the *Optimum Touring Times* clip-out charts at the back of this guide. These charts summarize the best times to visit each attraction.

Touring Plan Clip-Out Pocket Outlines

For your convenience, we have prepared outlines of all the touring plans in this guide. These pocket versions present the same itineraries as the detailed plans, but with vastly abbreviated directions. Select the plan appropriate for your party, then familiarize yourself with the detailed version. Once you understand how the plan works, clip the pocket version from the back of this guide and carry it with you as a quick reference at the theme park.

Will the Plans Continue to Work Once the Secret Is Out?

Yes! First, all of the plans require that a patron be there when the theme parks open. Many Walt Disney World patrons simply refuse to get up early while on vacation. Second, less than 1% of any day's attendance has been exposed to the plans, too little to affect results. Last, most groups tailor the plans, skipping rides or shows according to personal taste.

How Frequently Are the Touring Plans Revised?

Because Disney is always adding new attractions and changing operations, we revise the touring plans every year. Most complaints we receive about them come from readers who are using out-of-date editions of the *Unofficial Guide.* Be prepared, however, for surprises. Opening procedures and show times, for example, may change, and you never know when an attraction might break down.

A Word about Early Entry and the Touring Plans

If you're a Disney resort guest and use your early-entry privileges, complete your early-entry touring *before* the general public is admitted and position yourself to follow the touring plan. Usually at Epcot, Disney-MGM Studios, and sometimes at the Magic Kingdom, the general public is admitted a half hour before the published opening time. When the general public is admitted, the park will suddenly swarm. Be prepared, a mother from Wilmington, Delaware, advises:

> *The early-entry times went like clockwork. We were finishing up The Great Movie Ride when Disney-MGM opened [to the public], and [we] had to wait in line quite awhile for* Voyage of the Little Mermaid, *which sort of screwed up everything thereafter. Early-opening attractions should be finished up well before regular opening time so you can be at the plan's first stop as early as possible.*

In the Magic Kingdom, the attractions open during early entry are in Fantasyland and Tomorrowland. At Epcot, early-entry attractions are on the right side of the park's Future World section. At Disney-MGM Studios, they're dispersed. Practically, see any attractions on the touring plan that are open for early entry, crossing them off as you do. If you finish all early-entry attractions that are on the touring plan and still have time left before the general public is admitted, sample early-entry attractions not included in the plan. Stop touring about ten minutes before the public is admitted and position yourself for the first attraction on the touring plan that wasn't open for early entry. In the Magic Kingdom, for example, you usually can experience Peter Pan's Flight and It's a Small World in Fantasyland, as well as Space Mountain and *Alien Encounter* in Tomorrowland, during early entry. As official opening time approaches, go to the boundary between Fantasyland and Liberty Square and be ready to blitz to Splash Mountain and Big Thunder Mountain Railroad according to the touring plan when the rest of the park opens.

Tour Groups from Hell

We have discovered that tour groups of up to 200 people sometimes use our plans. A lady from Memphis writes:

> *When we arrived at The Land [pavilion at Epcot], a tour guide was holding your book and shouting into a bullhorn, "Step 7. Proceed to*

*Journey into Imagination." With this, about 65 Japanese tourists in red
T-shirts ran out the door.*

Unless your party is as large as that tour group, this development
shouldn't alarm you. Because tour groups are big, they move slowly and
have to stop periodically to collect stragglers. The tour guide also has to
accommodate the unpredictability of five dozen or so bladders. In short,
you should have no problem passing a group after the initial encounter.

"Bouncing Around"

Many readers object to crisscrossing a theme park as our touring plans
sometimes require. A lady from Decatur, Georgia, said she "got dizzy from
all the bouncing around" and that the "running back and forth reminded
[her] of a scavenger hunt." We empathize, but here's the rub, park by park.

In the Magic Kingdom, the most popular attractions are positioned
across the park from one another. This is no accident. It's good planning, a
method of more equally distributing guests throughout the park. If you
want to experience the most popular attractions in one day without long
waits, you can arrive before the park fills and see those attractions first
thing (requires crisscrossing the park), or you can enjoy the main attractions on one side of the park first thing in the morning then try the popular attractions on the other side during the hour or so before closing when
crowds presumably have thinned. All other approaches will subject you to
awesome waits at some attractions if you tour during busy times of year.

The best way to minimize "bouncing around" at the Magic Kingdom is
to use the Magic Kingdom Two-Day Touring Plan, which spreads the more
popular attractions over two mornings and works beautifully even when
the park closes at 8 p.m. or earlier.

We have revised the Epcot touring plans to eliminate most of the
"bouncing around" and have added special instructions to even further
minimize walking.

Disney-MGM Studios is configured in a way that precludes an orderly
approach to touring, or to a clockwise or counterclockwise rotation. Orderly
touring is further confounded by live entertainment that prompts guests to
intermittently interrupt their touring to head to whichever theater is about
to crank up. At the Studios, therefore, you're stuck with "bouncing around"
whether you use the touring plan or not. In our opinion, when it comes to
Disney theme parks, it's best to have a plan.

The Animal Kingdom is arranged in a spoke-and-hub configuration
like the Magic Kingdom, simplifying crisscrossing the park.

Touring Plans and the Obsessive-Compulsive Reader

We suggest you follow the touring plans religiously, especially in the mornings if you're visiting Disney World during busy, more-crowded times. The consequence of touring spontaneity in peak season is hours of otherwise-avoidable standing in line. During quieter times of year, there's no need to be compulsive about following the plans.

A mom in Atlanta, Georgia, suggests:

> *Emphasize perhaps not following [the touring plans] in off-season. There is no reason to crisscross the park when there are no lines.*

A father from Marlboro, New Jersey, writes:

> *The time we went in November, the longest line was about a five-minute wait. [At this time of year], your readers do not have to be so neurotic about running into the park and then to various attractions.*

Max is annoyed because he can't find a touring plan for cross-dressing unicyclists.

A mother in Minneapolis expresses her opinion:

> *I feel you should let your readers know to stop along the way to vari-
> ous attractions to appreciate what else may be going on around them.
> We encountered many families using the* Unofficial Guide *[who]
> became too serious about getting from one place to the next, missing the
> fun in between.*

We realize the touring plans can contribute to some stress and fatigue.
A mother from Stillwater, Maine, writes:

> *We were thankful for the touring plan and were able to get through
> the most popular rides early before the lines got long. One drawback
> was all the bouncing around we did backtracking through different
> parts of the Magic Kingdom in order to follow the touring plan. It was
> tiring and a bit hectic at times.*

What can we say? It's a lesser-of-two-evils situation. If you visit Walt
Disney World at a busy time, you can either get up early and hustle
around, or you can sleep in and see less, spending a lot of time in lines.

When using the touring plans, however, relax and always be prepared
for surprises and possible setbacks. When your blood pressure rises and
your Type-A brain does cartwheels, reflect on the advice of a woman from
Trappe, Pennsylvania:

> *You cannot emphasize enough the dangers of using your touring
> plans that were printed in the back of the book, especially if the per-
> son using them has a compulsive personality. I have a compulsive per-
> sonality. I planned for this trip for two years, researched it by use of
> guidebooks, computer programs, video tapes, and information
> received from WDW. I had a two-page itinerary for our one-week trip
> in addition to your touring plans of the theme parks. On night three
> of our trip, I ended up taking a non-scheduled trip to the emergency
> room of Sand Lake Hospital in Lake Buena Vista. When the doctor
> asked what seemed to be the problem, I responded with "I don't know,
> but I can't stop shaking, and I can't stay here very long because I have
> to get up in a couple hours to go to MGM according to my itinerary."
> Diagnosis: an anxiety attack caused by my excessive itinerary. He gave
> me a shot of something, and I slept through the first four attractions
> the next morning. This was our third trip to WDW (not including
> one trip to Disneyland); on all previous trips I used only the Steve
> Birnbaum book, and I suffered no ill effects. I am not saying your*

book was not good. It was excellent! However, it should come with a
warning label for people with compulsive personalities.

Tour Plan Rejection

We have discovered you can't implant a touring plan in certain personalities without fast and often vehement rejection. Some folks just do not respond well to the regimentation. If you bump into this problem with someone in your party, it's best to roll with the punches as this couple from Maryland did:

> *The rest of the group was not receptive to the use of the touring*
> *plans. I think they all thought I was being a little too regimented about*
> *planning this vacation. Rather than argue, I left the touring plans*
> *behind as we ventured off for the parks. You can guess the outcome. We*
> *took our camcorder with us and watched the movies when we returned*
> *home. About every five minutes or so there is a shot of us all gathered*
> *around a park map trying to decide what to do next.*

Finally, as a Connecticut woman alleges, the touring plans are incompatible with some readers' bladders as well as their personalities:

> *I want to know if next year when you write those "day" schedules if*
> *you could schedule bathroom breaks in there too. You expect us to be at*
> *a certain ride at a certain time and with no stops in between. Like one*
> *of the letters in your book a guy writes, "You expect everyone to be*
> *theme park commandos." When I read that I thought, there is a man*
> *who really knows what a problem the schedules are if you are a laid-*
> *back, slow-moving, careful detail noticer. What were you thinking*
> *when you made these schedules?*

A Clamor for Customized Touring Plans

We're inundated by letters urging us to create additional touring plans. These include a plan for ninth- and tenth-graders, a plan for rainy days, a senior's plan, a plan for folks who sleep late, a plan omitting rides that "bump, jerk, and clonk," a plan for gardening enthusiasts, and a plan for single women.

The touring plans in this book are intended to be flexible. Adapt them to your preferences. If you don't like rides that bump and jerk, skip them when they come up in a touring plan. If you want to sleep in and go to the park at noon, use the afternoon part of a plan. If you're a ninth-grader and want to ride Space Mountain three times in a row, do it. Will it decrease the touring plan's effectiveness? Sure, but the plan was created only to help you have fun. It's your day. Don't let the tail wag the dog.

Understanding Walt Disney World Attractions

Walt Disney World's primary appeal is in its rides and shows. Understanding how these are engineered to accommodate guests provides information that is not only interesting but invaluable to developing an efficient itinerary.

All attractions at Disney World, regardless of location, are affected by two overriding elements: capacity and popularity. Capacity is how many guests the attraction can serve at one time, in an hour, or in a day. Popularity shows how well visitors like an attraction. Capacity can be adjusted at some attractions. It's possible, for example, to add additional trams at the Disney-MGM Studios Backlot Tour or to put extra boats on the water at the Magic Kingdom's Jungle Cruise. Generally, however, capacity remains relatively fixed.

From a designer's perspective, the idea is to match capacity and popularity as closely as possible. A high-capacity ride that isn't very popular is a failure of sorts. Lots of money, space, and equipment have been poured into the attraction, yet there are empty seats. El Río del Tiempo, a ride in Epcot, comes closest to fitting this profile.

While it's extremely unusual for a new attraction not to measure up, it is fairly common for an older ride to lose its appeal. The Magic Kingdom's *Tropical Serenade (Enchanted Tiki Birds),* for example, played to half-capacity audiences until its 1998 renovation.

In general, attractions are immensely popular when they're new. Some, like Space Mountain (Magic Kingdom), have sustained great appeal years beyond their debut, while others, like Epcot's The Living Seas and El Río del Tiempo, have declined in popularity after just a few years. Most attractions, however, work through the honeymoon and then settle down to handle the level of demand for which they were designed. When this happens, there are enough interested guests during peak hours to fill almost every seat, but not so many that prohibitively long lines develop.

Sometimes Disney correctly estimates an attraction's popularity but fouls the equation by mixing in a third variable such as location. Spaceship Earth, the ride inside the geosphere at Epcot, is a good example. Placing the ride squarely in the path of every person entering the park assures that it will be inundated during morning hours when the park is filling up. On the flip side, *The American Adventure,* at the extreme op posite end of Epcot, has a huge capacity but plays to a partially filled theater until about noon, when guests finally work their way into that part of the park.

If demand is high and capacity is low, large lines materialize. Dumbo the Flying Elephant in the Magic Kingdom has the smallest capacity of almost any Disney World attraction, yet it probably is the most popular ride among young children. The result of this mismatch is that children and parents often suffer long, long waits for a one-and-a-half-minute ride. Dumbo is a simple yet visually appealing midway ride. Its capacity (and that of many other attractions, including Space Mountain) is limited by the very characteristics that make it popular.

Capacity design is predicated on averages: the average number of peo- ple in the park, the normal distribution of traffic to specific areas within the park, and the average number of staff needed to operate the ride. On a holiday weekend, when all the averages are exceeded, all but a few attractions operate at maximum capacity, and even then they are over- whelmed by the huge crowds. On low-attendance autumn days, full capacity is often not even approximated and guests can walk onto most rides without any wait.

The Magic Kingdom offers the greatest variety in capacity and popu- larity, offering vastly differing rides and shows. Only the Magic Kingdom offers low-capacity midway rides, spook-house genre "dark" rides, and roller coasters. Technologically, the mix ranges from state-of-the art to antiquated. This diversity makes efficient touring of the Magic Kingdom much more challenging. If guests don't understand the capacity/popular- ity relationship and plan accordingly, they might spend most of the day waiting in line.

While Epcot, the Animal Kingdom, and Disney-MGM Studios have fewer rides and shows than the Magic Kingdom, almost all of their attrac- tions are major features and rank on a par with the Magic Kingdom's Pirates of the Caribbean and The Haunted Mansion in scope, detail, imagination, and spectacle. All but one or two of the Epcot, Animal Kingdom, and Disney-MGM Studios rides are fast loading, and most have large capacities. Because Epcot, the Animal Kingdom, and Disney- MGM Studios attractions are on average well engineered and very effi- cient, lines may appear longer than those in the Magic Kingdom but usu- ally move more quickly. There are no midway rides at Epcot, the Animal Kingdom, or Disney-MGM Studios and fewer attractions specifically intended for children.

In the Magic Kingdom, crowds are more a function of the popularity and engineering of individual attractions. At Epcot and the Animal Kingdom, traffic flow and crowding is much more affected by park layout. For touring efficiency, it's important to understand how Magic Kingdom rides and shows operate. At Epcot and the Animal Kingdom, this knowledge is decidedly less important.

Crowds at Disney-MGM Studios have been larger than anticipated since the park opened. Unexpectedly large attendance coupled with relatively few attractions has resulted in long lines and frustrated guests. Though Disney has added new attractions, a well-considered touring plan is essential. Likewise, the Animal Kingdom opened in summer 1998 with only four of its six planned theme areas operational. Lack of capacity plus the allure of a new park translates into lengthy queues.

It's necessary to understand how rides and shows are designed and function to develop an efficient touring plan. We will examine both.

A WORD ABOUT DISNEY THRILL RIDES

Readers of all ages should attempt to be open-minded about the so-called Disney "thrill rides." In comparison with rides at other theme parks, the Disney thrill attractions are quite tame, with more emphasis on sights, atmosphere, and special effects than on the motion, speed, or feel of the ride itself. While we suggest you take Disney's preride warnings seriously, we can tell you that guests of all ages report enjoying rides such as Tower of Terror, Big Thunder Mountain, and Splash Mountain. The biggest, baddest thrill ride in Florida is the Montu inverted roller coaster at Busch Gardens. For the record, Busch Gardens also has the second- and third-baddest roller coasters in Florida (but maybe not for long).

A reader from Washington sums up the situation well:

> Our boys and I are used to imagining typical amusement park rides when it comes to roller coasters. So, when we thought of Big Thunder Mountain and Space Mountain, what came to mind was gigantic hills, upside down loops, huge vertical drops, etc. I actually hate roller coasters, especially the unpleasant sensation of a long drop, and I have never taken a ride that loops you upside down.
>
> In fact, the Disney [thrill rides] are all tame in comparison. There are never any long and steep hills (except Splash Mountain, and it is there for anyone to see, so you have informed consent going on the ride). I was able to build up courage to go on all of them, and the more I rode them the more I enjoyed them—the less you tense up expecting a big

long drop, the more you enjoy the special effects and even swinging
around curves. Swinging around curves is really the primary motion
challenge of Disney roller coasters.

Seniors who experience Disney thrill rides generally enjoy the smoother
rides like Splash Mountain, Big Thunder Mountain, and Tower of Terror,
and tend to dislike more jerky attractions. This letter from a Gig Harbor,
Washington, woman is typical:

> *I am a senior woman of small stature and good health. I am writ-*
> *ing my comments on Space Mountain, Splash Mountain, Big Thunder*
> *Mountain, and Star Tours. My experience [is that] all of the rides, with*
> *the exception of Star Tours, were wonderful rides. Star Tours is too jerky*
> *and fast, the music is too loud and I found it to be unacceptable.*

Not withstanding the reader's comment, we receive mostly positive
comments from seniors concerning Star Tours. Body Wars and Test Track,
however, are different stories.

Disney, recognizing that it needs more attractions that appeal to the
youth and young adult markets, is in the process of adding some roller
coasters to its parks. Curiously, the first coaster to go on-line will be a traditional wooden coaster purchased by Disney from the now defunct Circus
World theme park. To be installed on the left side of Sunset Boulevard in
Disney-MGM Studios, the coaster will fit in nicely with the period setting.
And while there are no loops, spirals, inverted corkscrews, or other elements of torture common to modern steel coasters, the wooden coaster is a
very good roller coaster indeed. In addition to the coaster for the Studios,
Disney is planning for one or more coasters at the Animal Kingdom. These
will probably be badder.

CUTTING DOWN YOUR TIME IN LINE
BY UNDERSTANDING THE RIDES

There are many types of rides at Walt Disney World. Some, like The Great
Movie Ride at Disney-MGM Studios, are engineered to carry more than
3,000 people every hour. At the other extreme, such rides as Dumbo the
Flying Elephant can only accommodate around 400 people an hour. Most
rides fall somewhere in between. Many factors figure into how long you
will wait to experience a ride: its popularity; how it loads and unloads; how
many persons can ride at one time; how many units (cars, rockets, boats,
flying elephants, etc.) are in service at a time; and how many staff are available to operate the ride. Let's take each factor one by one.

1. How Popular Is the Ride?

Newer rides like the Tower of Terror at Disney-MGM Studios and Test Track at Epcot attract a lot of people, as do such longtime favorites as the Jungle Cruise in the Magic Kingdom. If you know a ride is popular, you need to know how it operates in order to determine the best time to ride. But a ride need not be especially popular to form long lines; the lines can result from weak traffic engineering (i.e., it takes so long to load and unload that a line builds regardless). This is the case at the Mad Tea Party and Cinderella's Golden Carrousel in Fantasyland. Since mostly children and teens ride the Mad Tea Party, it serves only a small percentage of any day's attendance at the Magic Kingdom. Yet, because it takes so long to load and unload, long waiting lines form.

2. How Does the Ride Load and Unload?

Some rides never stop. They are like circular conveyor belts that go around and around. These are "continuous loaders." The Magic Kingdom's The Haunted Mansion and Epcot's Spaceship Earth are continuous loaders. The number of people that can be moved through in an hour depends on how many cars, "doom buggies," or whatever are on the conveyor. The Haunted Mansion and Spaceship Earth have lots of cars on the conveyor belt and consequently can each move more than 2,000 people an hour.

Other rides are "interval loaders." Cars are unloaded, loaded, and dispatched at set intervals (sometimes controlled manually, sometimes by computer). Space Mountain in Tomorrowland is an interval loader. It has two tracks (the ride has been duplicated in the same facility). Each track can run as many as 14 space capsules, released at 36-, 26-, or 21-second intervals. (The bigger the crowd, the shorter the interval.)

In one kind of interval loader (Space Mountain), empty cars (space capsules) are returned to where they line up for reloading. In a second type, one group of riders enters the vehicle while the previous group departs. These are "in-and-out" interval loaders. Splash Mountain is a good example of an in-and-out loader. As a boat docks, those who have just completed their ride exit to the left. At almost the same time, those waiting to ride enter the boat from the right. The reloaded boat is released to the dispatch point a few yards down the line where it is launched according to the interval being used.

Interval loaders of both types can be very efficient at moving people if (1) the dispatch (launch) interval is relatively short and (2) the ride can accommodate a large number of vehicles at one time. Since many boats can be floating through Pirates of the Caribbean at one time, and since the dispatch interval is short, almost 3,000 people an hour can see this attraction.

The least efficient rides, in terms of traffic engineering, are "cycle rides," also called "stop-and-go" rides. On cycle rides those waiting to ride exchange places with those who have just ridden. Unlike in-and-out interval rides, cycle rides shut down during loading and unloading. While one boat is loading and unloading in It's a Small World (an interval loader), many other boats are advancing through the ride. But when Dumbo the Flying Elephant touches down, the whole ride is at a standstill until the next flight is launched. Likewise, with Cinderella's Golden Carrousel all riders dismount and the Carrousel stands idle until the next group is ready to ride.

In cycle rides, the time the ride is in motion is "ride time." The time the ride idles while loading and unloading is "load time." Load time plus ride time equals "cycle time," or the time from the start of one run of the ride until the start of the next.

The only cycle rides in Disney World are in the Magic Kingdom.

3. How Many Persons Can Ride at One Time?

This figure expresses "per-ride capacity" or "system capacity." Either way, it's the number of people who can ride at one time. The greater the carrying capacity of a ride (all other things being equal), the more visitors it can accommodate in an hour. Some rides can add extra units (cars, boats, etc.) as crowds build to increase capacity, while others, like the Astro Orbiter in Tomorrowland, have a fixed capacity (it's impossible to add rockets).

4. How Many "Units" Are in Service at a Given Time?

"Unit" is our term for the vehicle in which you ride. At the Mad Tea Party the unit is a tea cup; at Peter Pan's Flight it's a pirate ship. On some rides (mostly cycle rides), the number of units operating at a given time is fixed. Thus, there are always 16 flying elephants on the Dumbo ride and 90 horses on Cinderella's Golden Carrousel. There is no way to increase the capacity of such rides by adding more units. On a busy day, therefore, the only way to carry more people each hour on a fixed-unit cycle ride is to shorten the loading time or decrease the actual time the ride is in motion. The bottom line on a busy day for a cycle ride is that you will wait longer and possibly be rewarded with a shorter ride. This is why we steer you away from cycle rides unless you're willing to ride them early in the morning or late at night. The following are cycle rides, all in the Magic Kingdom:

Fantasyland	Dumbo the Flying Elephant
	Cinderella's Golden Carrousel
	Mad Tea Party
Tomorrowland	Astro Orbiter

Many other rides throughout Walt Disney World can increase their capacity by adding units as crowds build. Big Thunder Mountain Railroad in Frontierland is a good example. If attendance is light, Big Thunder can start the day by running only one of its five mine trains from one of two available loading platforms. If lines build, the other loading platform is opened and more mine trains are placed into operation. At full capacity, the five trains can carry about 2,400 persons an hour. Likewise, Star Tours at Disney-MGM Studios can increase its capacity by using all of its simulators, and the Maelstrom boat ride at Epcot can add more Viking ships. Sometimes a long queue will disappear almost instantly when new units are brought on-line. When an interval loader places more units into operation, it usually shortens the dispatch intervals, allowing more units to be dispatched more often.

5. How Many Staff Are Available to Operate the Ride?

Allocating additional staff to a ride can allow more units to operate or additional loading or holding areas to open. In the Magic Kingdom, Pirates of the Caribbean and It's a Small World can run two separate waiting lines and loading zones. The Haunted Mansion has a one-and-a-half-minute preshow that is staged in a "stretch room." On busy days, a second stretch room can be activated, permitting a more continuous flow of visitors to the actual loading area.

Additional staff make a world of difference to some cycle rides. Often, the Mad Tea Party has only one attendant. This person alone must clear visitors from the ride just completed, admit and seat visitors for the upcoming ride, check that each tea cup is properly secured, return to the control panel, issue instructions to the riders, and finally activate the ride (whew!). A second attendant divides these responsibilities and cuts loading time by 25 to 50%.

By knowing the way a ride loads, its approximate hourly capacity, and its relative popularity, we can anticipate which rides are likely to develop long lines and, more important, how long we will have to wait to ride at any given time of day.

CUTTING YOUR TIME IN LINE BY UNDERSTANDING THE SHOWS

Many featured attractions at Walt Disney World are theater presentations. While they aren't as complex as rides from a traffic engineering standpoint, understanding their operation may save touring time.

Most theater attractions operate in three phases:

1. Guests are in the theater viewing the presentation.

2. Guests who have passed through the turnstile wait in a holding area or lobby. These people will be admitted to the theater as soon as the show in progress concludes. Several attractions offer a preshow in their lobby to entertain guests until they're admitted to the main show. Examples include *Tropical Serenade (Enchanted Tiki Birds)* and *Alien Encounter* in the Magic Kingdom; The Living Seas and *Honey, I Shrunk the Audience* at Epcot; and *ABC Sound Studio* and *MuppetVision 4D* at Disney-MGM Studios.

3. A line waits outside. Guests in line will enter the lobby when there is room, and will ultimately move into the theater.

Theater capacity, the presentation's popularity, and attendance level in the park determine how long lines will be at a theater attraction. Except for holidays and other days of heavy attendance, the longest wait for a show usually doesn't exceed the length of one complete performance.

Since almost all theater attractions run continuously, stopping only long enough for the previous audience to leave and the waiting audience to enter, a performance will be in progress when you arrive. *Impressions de France* in the French pavilion at Epcot is 18 minutes in duration; your longest wait under normal circumstances is about 18 minutes if you arrive just after the show has begun.

All theaters (except the Main Street Cinema in the Magic Kingdom and various amphitheater productions) are very strict about access. Unlike a movie theater at home, you can't enter during a performance. This being the case, you will always have at least a short wait.

Most theaters hold a lot of people. When a new audience is admitted, the outside line (if there is one) usually will disappear. Exceptions are *Country Bear Jamboree* in the Magic Kingdom; *The Making of Me* in the Wonders of Life pavilion and *Honey, I Shrunk the Audience* in the Imagination pavilion at Epcot; and *Voyage of the Little Mermaid* and *MuppetVision 4D* at Disney-MGM Studios. Because these shows are so popular (or have a small capacity like *The Making of Me*), you may have to wait through two or more shows before you're admitted (unless you go early in the morning).

HOW TO DEAL WITH OBNOXIOUS PEOPLE

At every theater presentation at Walt Disney World, visitors in the preshow area elbow, nudge, and crowd one another in order to make sure they're admitted to the performance. It's unnecessary. If you are admitted through

1 THERE IS THE OUTSIDE LINE.

2 THEN PEOPLE ARE ADMITTED TO THE "HOLDING PEN" PENDING ENTRY TO THE THEATRE.

3 THE NUMBER OF PEOPLE IN THE HOLDING PEN IS EXACTLY THE SEATING CAPACITY OF THE THEATRE.

4 SO DON'T JOIN IN THE STAMPEDE, CRUSH & JOSTLE TO ENTER THE THEATRE.

5 WAIT..... ....ENTER AFTER THE RUSH....... AND SCORE YOUR SEATS....

6 EVERY SEAT HAS A NEAR PERFECT VIEW...

the turnstile into the preshow area, a seat has automatically been allocated for you in the theater. When it's time to enter the theater, don't rush. Relax and let other people jam the doorways. When the congestion eases, stroll in and take a seat.

Attendants at many theaters will instruct you to enter a row of seats and move completely to the far side, filling every seat. Invariably, some inconsiderate yahoo will plop down in the middle of the row, stopping traffic or forcing other visitors to climb over him. Take our word for it: There is no such thing as a bad seat. All Disney theaters are designed to provide a near-perfect view from every seat. Our recommendation is to follow instructions and move to the far end of the row.

Visitors are also asked not to use flash photography in the theaters (the theaters are too dark for the pictures to turn out, and the flash disturbs other viewers). This admonition is routinely ignored. Flashers are more difficult to deal with than row-blockers. Options: Threaten to turn the offender over to Disney security or, better, hold your hand over the lens (you have to be quick) when they raise their camera.

Part Three

Selecting Your Hotel

The Basic Considerations

Locating a suitable hotel or condo is critical to planning any Walt Disney World vacation. The basic question is whether to stay in the World. Luxury lodging can be found both in and out of Disney World. Budget lodging is another story. Room rates start at about $90 a night in the World and range to more than $500. Outside Disney World, rooms are as low as $35 a night at some independent motels.

Beyond affordability is the convenience issue. We've lodged both in and out of Walt Disney World, and there is special magic and peace of mind associated with staying inside Disney World. "I feel more a part of everything and less like a visitor," one guest writes.

There's no real hardship in staying outside Disney World and driving (or taking a hotel shuttle) to the theme parks. Meals can be less expensive, and rooming outside the World makes you more receptive toward other Orlando-area attractions and eating establishments. Universal Studios, Kennedy Space Center, Sea World, and Cypress Gardens, among others, are well worth your attention.

Lodging prices are subject to change, but our researchers lodged in an excellent (though not plush) motel surrounded by beautiful orange groves for half the cost of staying in the least expensive Disney hotel. Our commute to the Magic Kingdom or Epcot parking lots was 17 minutes one way.

If you have young children, read Part 4: Walt Disney World with Kids (pages 140–184) before choosing lodging. Similarly, seniors, couples on a honeymoon or romantic holiday, and disabled guests should read the applicable sections of Part 5: Special Tips for Special People (pages 185–204) before choosing a hotel.

BENEFITS OF STAYING IN THE WORLD

Walt Disney World resort hotel and campground guests have privileges and amenities unavailable to those staying outside the World. Though some of these perks are only advertising gimmicks, others are real and potentially valuable. Here are the benefits and what they mean:

1. Convenience   The commute to the theme parks is short via the Disney Transportation System. This is especially advantageous if you stay in one of the hotels connected by the monorail or boat service. If you have a car, however, there are dozens of hotels outside Disney World that are within 5 to 10 minutes of theme park parking lots.

2. Early Entry at the Theme Parks   Walt Disney World lodging guests (excluding guests at the independent hotels of Disney Village Hotel Plaza) are invited to enter a designated theme park one hour earlier than the general public each day. Disney lodging guests are also offered specials on admission, including a passport good for the exact number of days of their visit and discount tickets to the water theme parks. These benefits are subject to change without notice. The early-entry program, however, is in its seventh year.

Early entry can be quite valuable during peak season when the parks are mobbed. If you're willing to get up before sunrise and arrive at the park as early as 6:30 a.m., you'll be rewarded with the least congested, most stress-free touring of your vacation. Early entry is also handy during off-season when the parks close early. Though crowds are manageable at these times, adding an extra hour and a half to an otherwise short touring day significantly increases the number of attractions you'll be able to see.

Disney has also been experimenting with a program that (for an extra $10) allows resort guests with certain multiday passes to remain in the park two to three hours after official closing time. For more on this program see pages 418–419.

3. Babysitting and Childcare Options   A number of options for baby-sitting, childcare, and children's programs are offered to Disney hotel and campground guests. Each of the resort hotels connected by the monorail, as well as several other Disney hotels, offers "clubs," or themed childcare centers, where potty-trained children ages 3 to 12 can stay while the adults go out.

Though somewhat expensive, the clubs do a great job and are highly regarded by children and parents. On the negative side, they're open only in the evening and not all Disney hotels have them. If you're staying at a

Disney hotel that doesn't have a childcare club, you're better off using one of the private in-room babysitting services such as Fairy Godmother or Kinder-Care (page 183). In-room babysitting is also available at hotels outside Disney World.

4. Guaranteed Theme Park Admissions On days of unusually heavy attendance, Disney resort guests are guaranteed admission to the theme parks. In practice, no guest is ever turned away until a theme park's parking lot is full. When this happens, that park most certainly will be packed to the point of gridlock. Under such conditions, you would have to possess the common sense of an amoeba to exercise your guaranteed-admission privilege. The privilege, by the way, doesn't extend to the swimming parks, Blizzard Beach, Typhoon Lagoon, and River Country.

5. Children Sharing a Room with Their Parents There is no extra charge per night for children younger than 18 sharing a room with their parents. Many hotels outside Disney World also observe this practice.

6. Free Parking Disney resort guests with cars don't have to pay for parking in the theme park lots. This privilege saves about $6 per day.

7. Recreational Privileges Disney resort guests get preferential treatment for tee times at the golf courses.

STAYING IN OR OUT OF THE WORLD: WEIGHING THE PROS AND CONS

1. Cost If cost is a primary consideration, you'll lodge much less expensively outside of Disney World. Our hotel quality and cost ratings (pages 130–139) compare specific hotels both in and out of the World.

2. Ease of Access Even if you stay in Disney World, you're dependent on some mode of transportation. It may be less stressful to use Disney transportation, but with the single exception of commuting to the Magic Kingdom, the fastest, most efficient, and most flexible way to get around usually is a car. If you're at Epcot, for example, and want to take the kids back to Disney's Grand Floridian Beach Resort for a nap, forget the monorail. You'll get back much faster in your own car.

A reader from Raynham, Massachusetts, who stayed at the Caribbean Beach Resort (and liked it very much) writes:

> *Even though the resort is on the Disney bus line, I recommend renting a car if it [fits] one's budget. The buses do not go directly to many destinations and often you have to switch at the*

Transportation and Ticket Center. Getting a [bus] seat in the morning is no problem [because] they allow standees. Getting a bus back to the hotel after a hard day can mean a long wait in line.

It must be said that the Disney transportation system, particularly the bus system, is about as efficient as humanly possible. No matter where you're going, you rarely wait more than 15 to 20 minutes for a bus, monorail, or boat. Although it is only for the use and benefit of Disney guests, it nonetheless *is* public transportation and users must expect the inconveniences inherent in any transportation system: conveyances that arrive and depart on their schedule, not yours; the occasional need to transfer; multiple stops; time lost loading and unloading large numbers of passengers; and, generally, the challenge of understanding and using a large, complex transportation network.

If you plan to have a car, consider this: Walt Disney World is so large that some destinations within the World can be reached more quickly from off-property hotels than from Disney hotels. For example, guests at hotels and motels on US 192 (near the so-called Walt Disney World main entrance) are closer to Disney-MGM Studios, the Animal Kingdom, and Blizzard Beach water park than guests at many hotels inside Disney World.

3. Young Children   Although the hassle of commuting to most outside-World hotels is only slightly (if at all) greater than that of commuting to Disney hotels, a definite peace of mind results from staying in Walt Disney World. The salient point, regardless where you stay, is to make sure you get your young children back to the hotel for a nap each day.

4. Splitting Up   If you're in a party that probably will split up to tour (as frequently happens in families with children of widely varying ages), staying in the World offers more transportation options and, thus, more independence. Mom and Dad can take the car and return to the hotel for a relaxed dinner and early bedtime while the teens remain in the park for evening parades and fireworks.

5. Feeding the Army of the Potomac   If you have a large crew that chows down like cattle on a finishing lot, you may do better staying outside the World, where food is far less expensive.

6. Visiting Other Orlando-Area Attractions   If you plan to visit Sea World, Kennedy Space Center, Universal Studios, or other area attractions, it may be more convenient to stay outside the World.

7. Homesickness   If you get homesick and make a lot of phone calls to Mom, you don't want to be calling from Disney hotels. They charge 75¢

for local calls and tack on a hefty 50% surcharge to direct-dial long distance calls. *Tip:* There's no surcharge if you use a calling card.

HOW TO GET DISCOUNTS ON LODGING AT WALT DISNEY WORLD

There are so many guest rooms in and around Walt Disney World that competition is brisk, and everyone, including Disney, wheels and deals to keep them filled. This has led to a more flexible discount policy for Disney World hotels. Here are tips for getting price breaks:

1. Seasonal Savings   You can save from $15 to $50 per night on a Walt Disney World hotel room by scheduling your visit during the slower times of the year. Disney uses so many adjectives (regular, holiday, peak, value, etc.) to describe its seasonal calendar, however, that it's hard to keep up without a scorecard. To confuse matters more, the dates for each "season" vary from resort to resort. Our advice: if you're set on staying at a Disney resort, obtain a copy of the Walt Disney Travel Company Florida Brochure, described on page 30.

2. Ask about Specials   When you talk to Disney reservationists, inquire specifically about special deals. Ask, for example, "What special rates or discounts are available at Disney hotels during the time of our visit?" Being specific and assertive paid off for an Illinois reader:

> *I called Disney's reservations number and asked for availability and rates. . . . [Because] of the* Unofficial Guide *warning about Disney reservationists answering only the questions posed, I specifically asked, "Are there any special rates or discounts for that room during the month of October?" She replied, "Yes, we have that room available at a special price. . . ." [For] the price of one phone call, I saved $440.*

3. Ocala Disney AAA Travel Center   The Ocala Disney AAA Travel Center off I-75 in Ocala, Florida, routinely books Disney hotel rooms at discounts of up to 43%! The discounts are offered as an incentive to walk-in travelers who may not have considered lodging at a Disney property or even going to Disney World. The number of rooms available varies according to date and season, but you almost always can count on getting a good deal. Because the program is designed to snare uncommitted travelers, you must reserve your room in person at the center. If you call in advance and tell staffers you're on your way down, however, they usually will tell you what's available and at what discount. The phone number is (352) 854-

0770. You can also arrange priority seating for dining. The center is open from 9 a.m. to 6 p.m. daily.

4. Travel Agents   Once ineligible for commissions on Disney bookings, travel agents now are active players and particularly good sources of information on time-limited special programs and discounts.

5. Disney Shareholder Discounts   The discount program for Walt Disney Company shareholders has been effectively dismantled. Disney shareholders are currently offered only a modest discount on the purchase of a Magic Kingdom Club Gold Card, available to the public for about $65. For information, call (800) 49-DISNEY.

6. Magic Kingdom Club Gold Card   The Magic Kingdom Club is offered as a benefit by employers, credit unions, and organizations. Membership provides a 10–30% discount on Disney lodging and a 5–7% discount on theme park tickets, among other things. Almost all state and federal government employees are Magic Kingdom Club members (though many don't know it). Ask your personnel department if this benefit is provided. Persons not signed up through work can buy a two-year individual Magic Kingdom Club Gold Card for about $65. A seniors card is about $50. For information, call (714) 781-1550 or write:

> Magic Kingdom Club Gold Card
> P.O. Box 3850
> Anaheim, CA 92803-9832

A dad from Bay Minette, Alabama, chastised us for not giving the Gold Card its due:

> *You didn't say much about the MK Club Gold Card. We went again in late September. It was really crowded. We bought the MK Club Gold Card and saved $300–400 on our rooms and tickets.*

Another pleased Gold Club card holder wrote, suggesting:

> *Contrive to emphasize the MK Gold Card. Between the vacation package and rental car, I estimate I saved about $600 to $700.*

7. Annual Passports   Walt Disney World Annual Passport holders are offered special discounts on rooms at various times. For details on passports, see pages 51 and 52.

8. Organizations and Auto Clubs   Eager to sell rooms, Disney has developed time-limited programs with some auto clubs and other organizations. Recently, for example, AAA members were offered a 10–20% savings on Disney hotels, preferred parking at the theme parks, and discounts on Disney package vacations. Such deals come and go, but the market suggests there will be more in the next year. If you're a member of AARP, AAA, or any travel or auto club, ask whether the group has a program before shopping elsewhere.

9. Room Upgrades   Sometimes, a room upgrade is as good as a discount. If you're visiting Disney World during a slower time, book the least expensive room your discounts will allow. Checking in, ask very politely about being upgraded to a "water-" or "pool-view" room. A fair percentage of the time, you'll get one at no additional charge.

10. Extra-Night Discounts   During slower times, book your Disney hotel for half the period you intend to stay. Often, the hotel will offer extra nights at a discounted rate to get you to stay longer.

WALT DISNEY WORLD LODGING*

The Grand Floridian, Polynesian, Contemporary, Wilderness Lodge, and Shades of Green resorts are near the Magic Kingdom. The Walt Disney World Swan and Dolphin hotels, the Yacht and Beach Club Resorts, and Disney's BoardWalk Inn and Villas are near Epcot. The Villas at the Disney Institute (formerly the Disney Institute Resort) are on the far northeast side of Walt Disney World. The All-Star and Coronado Springs resorts occupy a similar position on the far southwest side. Centrally located are the Caribbean Beach Resort and, along Bonnet Creek, the Old Key West, Port Orleans, and Dixie Landings resorts.

Choosing a Walt Disney World Hotel

If you want to stay in Walt Disney World but don't know which hotel to choose, consider:

1. Cost   First, look at your budget. Rooms start at about $90 a night at the All-Star resorts and top out near $500 at the Grand Floridian. Suites are more expensive.

The BoardWalk Villas, Old Key West Resort, and Villas at the Disney Institute offer condo-type accommodations with one-, two-, and three-bedroom units complete with kitchens, living rooms, VCRs, and washers and dryers. Prices range from about $295 per night for a one-bedroom townhouse at the Disney Institute to more than $1,250 per night for a three-bedroom

*Rates vary depending on room location (view) and/or season, and are subject to change.

villa at the BoardWalk Villas. Fully equipped cabins and house trailers at Fort Wilderness Campground cost $180–260 per night. A limited number of suites are available at the more expensive Disney resorts, but they don't have kitchens.

Also at Disney World are the seven hotels of the Disney Village Hotel Plaza. Although commodious, rooms in these hotels are sometimes more expensive than at hotels served by the monorail. We find few bargains at the Village Hotel Plaza and feel less of the excitement one has when staying inside the World. While the Village Hotel Plaza is technically part of Disney World, staying there is like visiting a colony rather than the mother country. Early entry and free parking at the theme parks aren't offered, and the hotels operate their own buses rather than use Disney transportation.

Not included in these rankings or in the following discussion is Shades of Green, formerly known as the Disney Inn. Shades of Green was purchased by the U.S. Department of Defense in 1994 for the exclusive use of active-duty and retired servicemen. Rates at Shades of Green, one of the nicest Disney World hotels, are based on the guest's rank: the higher the rank, the greater the cost. All rooms, however, regardless of rank, go for a fraction of what military personnel would pay at other Disney resorts. According to a serviceman from Fort Worth, Texas, Shades of Green is the way to go:

> *Shades of Green is the best-kept secret in Disney. It is actually a [military] resort in the Disney complex with all the benefits of being a Disney resort. It was a great deal, and military members usually look for the best deals. When my wife and I stayed there in May, we paid $58 a night. That is not per person. That was the total price. The price will vary according to your rank. The hotel was very nice. The rooms were huge. It had two double beds and a lot of room to spare. They also had VCRs in the rooms and a movie vending machine on the second floor. The rooms also had a coffee machine with packets of coffee, the drink of the military. Shades of Green is right across the street from the Polynesian Resort. It is about a 10–15 minute walk to the Ticket and Transportation Center. The hotel does have shuttle buses that take you to the TTC and that is about a 2-minute ride. Our overall stay at Shades of Green was wonderful. I would highly recommend this hotel to anyone who is eligible to use it.*

What It Costs to Stay in a Disney Resort Hotel	
Grand Floridian	$330–550
Polynesian Resort	$300–450
Swan (Westin)	$315–400
Dolphin (Sheraton)	$315–400
Beach Club Resort	$295–450
Yacht Club Resort	$295–450
BoardWalk Inn	$295–450
BoardWalk Villas	$295–350 (studio)
Old Key West Resort	$250–290 (studio)
Contemporary Resort	$230–415
Villas at the Disney Institute	$225–265 (bungalow)
Wilderness Lodge	$220–340
Coronado Springs Resort	$130–160
Caribbean Beach Resort	$130–160
Dixie Landings Resort	$130–160
Port Orleans Resort	$130–160
All-Star resorts	$85–100

What It Costs to Stay in the Disney Village Hotel Plaza	
Buena Vista Palace Resort & Spa	$170–400
The Hilton Resort	$165–325
DoubleTree Guest Suites Resort	$150–475
Travelodge Hotel	$125–300
Grosvenor Resort	$125–215
Hotel Royal Plaza	$115–250
Courtyard by Marriott	$115–190

2. Location Once you have determined your budget, think about what you want to do at Walt Disney World. Will you go to all four theme parks, or will you concentrate on one or two?

If you intend to use your own car, the location of your Disney hotel isn't especially important unless you plan to spend most of your time at the Magic Kingdom. (Disney transportation is always more efficient than your car in this case because it bypasses the Transportation and Ticket Center and deposits you at the theme park entrance.) If you haven't decided whether you want a car for your Disney vacation, see "How to Travel around the World" (pages 212–225).

Most convenient to the Magic Kingdom are the three resorts linked by monorail: the Grand Floridian, Contemporary, and Polynesian. Commuting to the Magic Kingdom via monorail is quick and simple, allowing visitors to return to their hotel for a nap, swim, or meal.

The Contemporary Resort, in addition to being on the monorail, is only 10–15 minutes' walk to the Magic Kingdom. Contemporary Resort guests reach Epcot by monorail but must transfer at the Transportation and Ticket Center. Buses connect the Contemporary to Disney-MGM Studios and the Animal Kingdom. No transfer is required, but the bus makes several stops before heading to the Studios.

The Polynesian Resort is served by the Magic Kingdom monorail and is an easy walk from the Transportation and Ticket Center, Disney World's transportation hub. At the transportation center you can catch an express monorail to Epcot. This makes the Polynesian the only Disney resort with direct monorail access to both Epcot and the Magic Kingdom. To minimize your walk to the transportation center, book a room in the Pago Pago, Moorea, or Oahu guest buildings.

Most convenient to Epcot and Disney-MGM Studios are the Board-Walk Inn, BoardWalk Villas, Yacht and Beach Club Resorts, and Swan and Dolphin. Though all are within easy walking distance of Epcot's International Gateway, boat service is also available. Vessels also connect Epcot hotels to Disney-MGM Studios. Epcot hotels are best for guests planning to spend most of their time at Epcot and/or Disney-MGM Studios.

If you plan to use Disney transportation and intend to visit all four major parks and one or more of the swimming theme parks, book a centrally located resort with good transportation connections. The Epcot resorts and the Polynesian, Caribbean Beach, Old Key West, Dixie Landings, and Port Orleans resorts fit the bill.

Though not centrally located, the All-Star and Coronado Springs resorts have very good bus service to all Disney World destinations and are closest to the new Animal Kingdom theme park. Wilderness Lodge and Fort Wilderness Campground have the most convoluted and inconvenient transportation service. The Villas at the Disney Institute and the Old Key West Resort also are transportationally challenged, i.e., buses run less frequently than at other Disney resorts.

If you plan to golf, book the Villas at the Disney Institute or the Old Key West Resort. Both resorts are built around golf courses. Shades of

Green, the armed forces recreation center, is adjacent to two golf courses. Located near but not on a golf course are the Grand Floridian, Polynesian, Dixie Landings, and Port Orleans resorts. For boating and water sports, try the Polynesian, Contemporary, or Grand Floridian resorts or Wilderness Lodge. The Lodge is also the best hotel for hikers, bikers, and joggers.

3. Room Quality   Few Walt Disney World guests spend much time in their hotel rooms, though they're among the best designed and most well appointed anywhere. Plus, they're meticulously maintained. Top of the line are the spacious and luxurious rooms of the Grand Floridian. Bringing up the rear are the small, garish rooms of the All-Star resorts. But even these are sparkling clean and livable.

Here's how the Disney hotels (along with the Swan and the Dolphin, which are Westin and Sheraton hotels, respectively) stack up for quality:

Hotel	Room Quality Rating
1. Grand Floridian Beach Resort	96
2. BoardWalk Villas (studio)	95
3. Old Key West Resort (studio)	94
4. BoardWalk Inn	93
5. Beach Club Resort	92
6. Yacht Club Resort	92
7. Polynesian Resort	90
8. Contemporary Resort	87
9. Villas at the Disney Institute	87
10. Coronado Springs Resort	86
11. Dolphin (Sheraton)	86
12. Swan (Westin)	86
13. Wilderness Lodge	86
14. Caribbean Beach Resort	84
15. Dixie Landings Resort	84
16. Port Orleans Resort	84
17. All-Star resorts	73

4. The Size of Your Group   Larger families and groups may be interested in how many persons can be accommodated in a Disney resort room, but only Lilliputians would be comfortable in a room filled to capacity. Groups requiring two or more guest rooms should consider condo/villa accommodations, either in or out of Walt Disney World. The most cost-efficient lodging in Walt Disney World for groups of five or six persons are the cabins or the wilderness homes at Fort Wilderness Campground. Both sleep six adults plus a child or toddler in a crib. If there are more than six in your party, you will need either two hotel rooms, a suite (see Wilderness Lodge below), or a condo.

Hotel	Maximum Number of Persons per Room
All-Star resorts	4 persons plus child in crib
Beach Club Resort	5 persons plus child in crib
BoardWalk Inn	4 or 5 persons plus child in crib
BoardWalk Villas	8 persons plus child in crib
Caribbean Beach Resort	4 persons plus child in crib
Contemporary Resort	5 persons plus child in crib
Coronado Springs Resort	4 persons plus child in crib
Dixie Landings Resort	4 persons plus child in crib; 5 persons in room with child's trundle bed
Dolphin (Sheraton)	4 persons
Fort Wilderness Homes	6 persons plus child in crib
Grand Floridian Beach Resort	4 or 5 persons plus child in crib
Old Key West Resort	8 persons plus child in crib
Polynesian Resort	5 persons plus child in crib
Port Orleans Resort	4 persons plus child in crib
Swan (Westin)	4 persons
Villas at Disney Institute	8 persons plus child in crib
Wilderness Lodge	4 persons plus child in crib; junior suites with bunk beds accommodate 6 persons
Yacht Club Resort	5 persons plus child in crib

5. Theme   All of the Disney hotels are themed. Each is designed to make you feel you're in a special place or period of history. Here are the themes at Disney resorts:

Hotel	Theme
All-Star resorts	Sports and music
Beach Club Resorts	New England beach club of the 1870s
BoardWalk Inn	East coast boardwalk hotel of the early 1900s
BoardWalk Villas	East coast beach cottage of the early 1900s
Caribbean Beach Resort	Caribbean islands
Contemporary Resort	The future as perceived by past and present generations

Hotel	Theme
Coronado Springs Resort	Northern Mexico and the American Southwest
Dixie Landings Resort	Life on the Mississippi in the antebellum South
Dolphin (Sheraton)	Modern Florida resort
Grand Floridian Beach Resort	Turn-of-the-century luxury hotel
Old Key West Resort	Key West
Polynesian Resort	Hawaii/South Sea islands
Port Orleans	Turn-of-the-century New Orleans and Mardi Gras
Swan (Westin)	Modern Florida resort
Villas at the Disney Institute	Combination rustic villas and country club atmosphere
Wilderness Lodge	National park grand lodge of the early 1900s in the American northwest
Yacht Club Resort	New England seashore hotel of the 1880s

Some resorts carry off their themes better than others, and some themes are more exciting. The Wilderness Lodge, for example, is extraordinary. The lobby opens eight stories to a timbered ceiling supported by giant columns of bundled logs. One look eases you into the Northwest-wilderness theme. Romantic and isolated, the lodge is a great choice for couples and seniors, and is heaven for children.

The Polynesian, likewise dramatic, conveys the feeling of the Pacific islands. It's great for romantics and families. Waterfront rooms in the Moorea building offer a perfect view of Cinderella Castle and the Magic Kingdom fireworks across Seven Seas Lagoon.

Grandeur, nostalgia, and privilege are central to the Grand Floridian and Yacht and Beach Club resorts and the BoardWalk Inn and Villas. Although modeled after eastern-seaboard hotels of different eras, the resorts are amazingly similar. Thematic distinctions are subtle and are lost on many guests.

The Port Orleans Resort lacks the mystery and sultriness of the New Orleans French Quarter, but it's hard to replicate the Big Easy in a sanitized Disney version. Dixie Landings, however, hits the mark with its antebellum Mississippi River theme, as does Old Key West Resort with its Florida Keys theme. The Caribbean Beach Resort's theme is much more effective at night, thanks to creative lighting. By day, the resort looks like a Miami condo development.

Coronado Springs Resort offers several styles of Mexican and Southwestern American architecture. Though the lake setting is lovely and the resort is attractive and inviting, the theme (with the exception of the main swimming area) isn't especially stimulating. Coronado Springs feels more like a Scottsdale, Arizona, country club than a Disney resort.

The All-Star resorts encompass 30 three-story, T-shaped hotels with almost 6,000 guest rooms. There are 15 themed areas: five celebrate sports (surfing, basketball, tennis, football, and baseball), five recall Hollywood movie themes, and five have musical motifs. The resort's design, with entrances shaped like musical notes, film canisters, and footballs, is pretty adolescent, sacrificing grace and beauty for energy and novelty. Guest rooms are small, with decor reminiscent of your teenage son's bedroom. Despite the theme, there are no sports facilities at the All-Star Sports Resort.

Pretense aside, the Contemporary, Swan, and Dolphin are essentially themeless though architecturally interesting. The Contemporary is a 15-story, A-frame building with monorails running through the middle. Views from guest rooms in the Contemporary Tower are among the best at Disney World. The Swan and Dolphin resorts are massive yet whimsical. Designed by Michael Graves, they're excellent examples of "entertainment architecture." Unfortunately, a little too much whimsy and entertainment worked their way into the guest rooms, which are "busy," bordering on garish.

6. Dining   The best resorts for quality and selection in dining are the Epcot resorts: Swan, Dolphin, Yacht and Beach Club resorts, and Board-Walk Inn and Villas. Each has good restaurants and is within easy walking distance of the others and of the ten ethnic restaurants in the World Show-case section of Epcot. If you stay at an Epcot resort, you have 21 of Walt Disney World's finest restaurants within a 5- to 12-minute walk.

The only other place in Disney World where restaurants and hotels are similarly concentrated is at the Disney Village Hotel Plaza. In addition to restaurants in the hotels themselves, the Hilton, Courtyard by Marriott, Grosvenor Resort, and Buena Vista Palace are within walking distance of restaurants at Downtown Disney.

Guests at the Contemporary, Polynesian, and Grand Floridian can eat in their hotel, or they can commute to restaurants in the Magic Kingdom (not recommended) or in other monorail-linked hotels. Riding the monorail to another hotel or to the Magic Kingdom takes about ten minutes each way, not counting the wait for the train.

All of the other Disney resorts are somewhat isolated. This means you're stuck dining at your hotel unless (1) you have a car and can go anywhere you like or (2) you eat your meals at the theme parks.

Here's the deal. Disney transportation works fine for commuting from hotels to the theme parks, but it's hopeless for getting from one hotel to another. If you're staying at Dixie Landings and want to dine at the Swan,

Disney Resort Amenities and Recreation

	Suites	Concierge
Disney's All-Star Sports and Music Resorts		
Disney's BoardWalk Inn		•
Disney's BoardWalk Villas	•	
Disney's Caribbean Beach Resort		
Disney's Contemporary Resort	•	•
Disney's Coronado Springs Resort		
Disney's Dixie Landings Resort		
Disney's Fort Wilderness Homes		
Disney's Grand Floridian Beach Resort	•	•
Disney's Old Key West Resort	•	
Disney's Polynesian Resort	•	•
Disney's Port Orleans Resort		
Disney's Wilderness Lodge	•	
Disney's Yacht and Beach Club Resorts	•	•
Disney Institute Resort	•	
Shades of Green		•
Walt Disney World Dolphin		
Walt Disney World Swan		•

forget it. It will take you up to an hour and a half each way by bus. You could take a bus to the Magic Kingdom and catch a train to one of the monorail-served hotels for dinner. That would take "only" 45 minutes each way. You could also bus to Pleasure Island or Downtown Disney, but that, too, would take 40–50 minutes.

Of the more isolated resorts, the Wilderness Lodge serves the best food and offers the most varied selection. Next in quality are the Villas at the Disney Institute. The Coronado Springs, Port Orleans, Dixie Landings, Old Key West, and Caribbean Beach resorts each have a full-service restaurant of acceptable quality, a food court, and in-room pizza delivery. None of the isolated resorts, however, offer enough variety for the average person to be happy eating in his/her hotel every day. The All-Star resorts, Disney's most isolated hotel, have nearly 6,000 guest rooms but no full-service restaurant. There are three food courts, but you have to get to them before 11 p.m.

7. Amenities and Recreation   Disney resorts offer a staggering variety of amenities and recreational opportunities. All provide elaborate swimming pools, themed shops, restaurants or food courts, bar or lounge, and access to the five Disney golf courses. Predictably, the more you pay for your

Number of Rooms	Room Service	Fitness Center	Water Sports	Marina	Beach	Tennis	Biking
6,000							
378	•	•				•	•
383	•	•				•	•
2,112			•	•	•		
1,043	•	•	•	•	•	•	
1,967	•	•	•	•	•		•
2,048			•	•			•
408			•	•		•	
901	•	•	•	•	•	•	
709		•				•	•
853	•			•	•		
1,008			•	•			•
728	•		•	•			•
1,213	•	•	•	•	•		
587		•	•	•		•	•
287	•	•				•	
1,509	•	•	•	•	•	•	
758	•	•	•	•	•		

lodging, the more amenities and opportunities you have. The Grand Floridian, Yacht and Beach Club resorts, and Swan and Dolphin, for example, offer concierge floors.

For sunning and swimming, the Contemporary, Polynesian, Wilderness Lodge, and Grand Floridian offer both pools and white-sand beaches on Bay Lake or Seven Seas Lagoon. The Caribbean Beach Resort also provides both pools and beaches. Though lacking a beach, the Yacht and Beach Club, Port Orleans, Dixie Landings, and Coronado Springs resorts and the BoardWalk Inn and Villas have exceptionally creative pools.

Bay Lake and the Seven Seas Lagoon are the best venues for boating. Resorts fronting these lakes are the Contemporary, Polynesian, Wilderness Lodge, Grand Floridian, and Fort Wilderness Campground. Though situated on smaller bodies of water, the Caribbean Beach, Old Key West, Port Orleans, Dixie Landings, Coronado Springs, Villas at the Disney Institute, Yacht and Beach Club, and Swan and Dolphin resorts also rent watercraft.

For sports and fitness, the Villas at the Disney Institute are unrivaled. The only Disney resort with a golf course on-site, the Villas also boast one of the nation's largest and most high-tech fitness centers. In addition, swimming, aerobics, weight training, tennis, full-court basketball, and even a climbing wall are available. Other Disney resorts with good fitness and weight-training facilities include Old Key West, BoardWalk Inn and Villas, the Contemporary, Yacht and Beach Club, and Grand Floridian resorts. Tennis is also available at Fort Wilderness Campground and the Swan and Dolphin, Grand Floridian, Yacht and Beach Club, Old Key West, and Contemporary resorts.

While there are many places to bike or jog at Disney World (including golf-cart paths), the best biking and jogging is at the Fort Wilderness Campground and the adjacent Wilderness Lodge. Also good for biking and jogging is the area along Bonnet Creek extending from Dixie Landings through Port Orleans and the Old Key West resorts toward Downtown Disney. Epcot resorts offer several biking and jogging trails, though they aren't as secluded or scenic as the above.

Seven Disney resorts offer evening childcare programs on-site: the Grand Floridian, Yacht and Beach Club, Polynesian, Wilderness Lodge, and BoardWalk Inn and Villas. All others offer in-room babysitting.

In the table nearby, we've outlined the amenities and recreational opportunities at each of the Disney resorts. Note that each resort listed also offers restaurants or snack bars, lounges/bars, pools, children's activities, babysitting, and shopping.

8. Nightlife   The boardwalk at BoardWalk Inn and Villas has an upscale dance club, a New Orleans Pat O'Brien–type club with dueling pianos and sing-alongs, a brew pub, and a sports bar. Boardwalk clubs are within easy walking distance of all the Epcot resorts. Similarly, some of the Villas at the Disney Institute are within walking distance of the nightlife at Downtown Disney. Nightlife at other Disney resorts is limited to lounges that stay open late. The best are Mizner's Lounge at the Grand Floridian and the California Grill Lounge on the 15th floor of the Contemporary Resort. At the California Grill Lounge, you can relax with a drink and watch the fireworks at the nearby Magic Kingdom.

Camping at Walt Disney World

Fort Wilderness Campground is a spacious resort campground for tent and RV camping. Fully equipped, air-conditioned trailers also are available for rent, as are newer prefab log cabins. The log cabins offer essentially the same square footage as the trailers (known as "wilderness homes") but are newer, more aesthetically appealing, and have an elevated outdoor deck. Campsites, "preferred" or "regular," are arranged on loops branching from three thoroughfares. The only difference between a preferred and regular campsite is that preferred sites are closer to the campground amenities (swimming pools, restaurants, and shopping). All sites have a 110- and 220-volt outlet, picnic table, and grill. Most RV sites have sanitary hookups. RV sites are roomy by eastern-U.S. standards, but tent campers will probably feel a little cramped. On any day, about 90% of campers will be RVers.

When booking, tent campers should request a site on Loop 1500, Cottontail Curl, or on Loop 2000, Spanish Moss Lane. The better loops for RVers are Loops 200, 400, 500, and 1400. All loops have a comfort station with showers, toilets, phones, an ice machine, and a coin laundry.

Rental trailers and cabins offer a double bed and two bunk beds in the only bedroom, augmented by a Murphy bed (pulls down from the wall) in the living room. There is one rather small bathroom with shower and tub.

Aside from offering economy accommodations, Fort Wilderness Campground has a group camping area, evening entertainment, horseback riding, bike trails, jogging trails, swimming, and a petting farm. River Country water theme park is nearby. Access to the Magic Kingdom and Discovery Island is by boat from the Fort Wilderness landing on Bay Lake. Access to other destinations is by private car or shuttle bus.

If you rent a cabin or a wilderness home, particularly in the fall or spring, keep abreast of local weather conditions. These accommodations are essentially mobile homes, definitely not the place you want to be if the area is under a tornado warning.

Fort Wilderness Campground

784 campsites	boat/bus service	$35–68 per night
408 wilderness homes and cabins (sleeps 4–6)	boat/bus service	$185–230 per night

WALT DISNEY WORLD HOTEL PROFILES

For those of you who have plowed though the foregoing and remain undecided, we provide profiles of each of the Walt Disney World resorts.

The Magic Kingdom Resorts

Disney's Grand Floridian Beach Resort   Walt Disney World's flagship resort is inspired by the grand Victorian seaside resorts of turn-of-the-century Florida. A complex of four- and five-story white frame buildings, the Grand Floridian integrates verandas, intricate laticework, dormers, and turrets beneath a red shingle roof to capture the most memorable elements of 19th-century ocean-resort architecture. A five-story domed lobby encircled by enameled balustrades and overhung by crystal chandaliers establishes the resort's tone of understated opulence. Covering 40 acres along the Seven Seas Lagoon, the resort offers lovely pools, white-sand beaches, and a multifaceted marina. The spa at the Grand Floridian is equaled only by that of the Disney Institute.

The 901 guest rooms, while luxurious with Victorian wood trim and soft-colored-print wall coverings, are warm and inviting without being stuffy or overly feminine. Armoires, marble-topped sinks, and ceiling fans maintain the Victorian theme. The typical room is 440 square feet (dormer rooms are smaller), large by any standard, and furnished with two queen beds, a daybed, a reading chair, and a table with two side chairs. Many rooms have a balcony.

With a high ratio of staff to guests, service is outstanding. There are several full-service restaurants at the Grand Floridian, with a number of others a short monorail ride away. The resort is connected directly to the Magic Kingdom by monorail and to other Walt Disney World destinations by bus. Walking time to the monorail and bus loading areas from the most remote guest rooms is about seven to ten minutes.

Disney's Polynesian Resort   The tropics of the South Pacific are re-created at this deluxe Walt Disney World resort. The Polynesian is composed of 11 two- and three-story Hawaiian "longhouses" situated around the four-story "Great Ceremonial House." The buildings at the Polynesian feature natural wood tones, with exposed-beam roofs and tribal-inspired geometric inlays in the cornices. The Great Ceremonial House contains restaurants, shops, and a rain-forest atrium lobby. With a rocky waterfall and over 70 species of tropical plants, the lobby reinforces the lush, verdant image of the South Seas. Spread over many acres along the Seven Seas Lagoon, the resort has a white-sand beach with volleyball courts. The Polynesian's two landscaped pools look best at night when they are illuminated with bamboo torches.

Many of the 853 guest rooms at the Polynesian offer views of the Seven Seas Lagoon. Typical rooms measure 409 square feet. While the guest rooms are smaller than most of Disney's deluxe rooms, they are quite comfortable. The rooms are furnished with two queen-size beds, a daybed, an armoire, and a table and chairs. With batik-design bedspreads and curtains and bamboo furniture, guest rooms maintain the island theme and are visually interesting. Bathrooms are somewhat small, although well designed. Many rooms have balconies. Finally, be aware that some of the guest rooms are a bit threadbare and overdue for renovation. Request a recently renovated room when you make your reservations.

A problem unique to the Polynesian is the proximity of the Walt Disney World Speedway. A number of guests have written complaining about the noise of roaring racecars while they were trying to nap. Rooms with parking lot views are most likely to be affected.

Service at the Polynesian is excellent. There are two full-service restaurants with easy access to others in the Magic Kingdom area via monorail.

The Polynesian has a monorail station on-site and is within easy walking distance of the Transportation and Ticket Center. Bus service is available to other Walt Disney World destinations. Walking time to the bus and monorail loading areas from the most remote rooms is 8–11 minutes.

Disney's Wilderness Lodge   This deluxe Walt Disney World resort is inspired by turn-of-the-century national park lodges. The Wilderness Lodge is the most impressively themed and meticulously detailed of the Disney resorts. Situated on Bay Lake, the Lodge features an eight-story central building flanked by two seven-story guest-room wings. The rustic building features exposed timber columns, log cabin–style facades, and dormer windows. The Lodge is surrounded by evergreen pine and pampas grass landscaping. An eight-story lobby boasts an 87-foot stone fireplace and two 55-foot Pacific Northwest totem poles. In addition to these centerpieces, details like timber pillars; giant teepee chandeliers; and stone, wood, and marble-inlaid floors maintain the resort's feeling of rustic luxury. Although the Wilderness Lodge is not situated on vast acreage, it does have a beach and a delightful pool. The pool, with its mountain hot spring atmosphere, is modeled after a stone quarry and offers a waterfall and a geyser.

The 728 guest rooms at the Wilderness Lodge are suited with darkly stained mission-style furniture, which is accented by the primary colors in the decor. The Native American–patterned bedspreads, animal-motif armoires, and faux-calfskin fixtures create a cozy feeling. At 340 square feet, average rooms at the Lodge are the smallest Walt Disney World "deluxe" rooms. Typical rooms have two queen-size beds, and some have one queen-size bed and bunk beds. All rooms have a table and chairs, and a vanity outside the bathroom. Most rooms have balconies.

Service at the Wilderness Lodge is rated as excellent. There are two full-service restaurants, with several more a boat ride away. The resort is connected to the Magic Kingdom by boat and to other Disney theme parks by bus. Walking time to the bus and boat loading areas from the most remote rooms is about five to eight minutes.

Disney's Contemporary Resort   This deluxe resort is the least themed of the Walt Disney World–owned properties. The Contemporary is unique in its A-frame design that permits the Magic Kingdom monorail to pass through the structure's cavernous atrium. The only real source of color in the atrium is a 90-foot mosaic depicting Native American children and nature scenes. The white cement A-frame tower is flanked by two three-story "garden" buildings. The landscaping at the Contemporary is a little bizarre, with trees and shrubs trimmed like overgrown poodles. Situated on Bay Lake, the Contemporary offers a marina and a white-sand beach. Its swimming pool, at 6,500 square feet, is the largest of all Walt Disney World resorts.

The rooms in the Contemporary's tower building enjoy fantastic views of either Bay Lake or the Magic Kingdom. At 436 square feet, the rooms are only slightly smaller than those at the Grand Floridian. All of the rooms are tasteful albeit somewhat dull, with simple lines and neutral colors. The Contemporary is a bit cold in our opinion, and the angular lines of the furnishings make the ambiance somewhat uninviting. Most rooms have two queen-size beds, a daybed, and a table and chair. All tower rooms have balconies.

The Contemporary has a new 6,500-square-foot pool with slides and waterfalls. The resort is home to two full-service restaurants (including the well-known California Grill), a buffet restaurant, and a counter-service restaurant. There are six shops at the Contemporary. This resort is within easy walking distance to the Magic Kingdom, and transportation via monorail is available to both the Magic Kingdom and Epcot. Other Walt Disney World destinations can be accessed by bus or boat. Walking time to transportation loading areas from the most remote rooms is six to nine minutes.

Shades of Green   This deluxe resort is owned and operated by the U.S. Armed Forces and is available only to U.S. military personnel (including the National Guard, reserves, and Department of Defense). Shades of Green consists of one three-story building nestled among three golf courses. Tastefully nondescript, Shades of Green is at the same time pure peace and quiet. There is no beach or lake at Shades of Green, but there are several pools, including one shaped like Mickey's head. Although Shades of Green is open only to the military, the surrounding golf courses are open to all Walt Disney World guests.

At 455 square feet, the 288 guest rooms at Shades of Green are larger than those at the Grand Floridian. The rooms are luxuriously decorated with an English-countryside theme, with light-oak furniture, dust ruffles, and soft colors. Most rooms have two queen-size beds, a daybed, and a table and four chairs, as well as a television in an armoire. All rooms have either a patio or balcony.

Even though Shades of Green is not operated by Disney, the service here is comparable to the deluxe Walt Disney World properties. The single restaurant at Shades of Green offers both buffet and menu service. Transportation to all theme parks is by bus, with a transfer required to almost all destinations. Walking time to the bus loading area from the most remote rooms is about five minutes.

Disney's Fort Wilderness Campground   Walt Disney World's Fort Wilderness consists of 700 wooded acres with 408 Wilderness Homes and Cabins, and 784 traditional campsites. The Wilderness Homes are small mobile homes situated on a series of one-way loops near Bay Lake. The beige and brown aluminum siding on the homes blends nicely with the cypress and pine around them. While the homes are only about 20 feet apart, the vegetation between them is dense enough to provide families with a sense of privacy. Disney's Fort Wilderness area is unique in its recreation offerings; canoeing, trail rides, a petting zoo, and a beach are all within walking distance from the homes. Additionally, the homes share two "swimmin' holes" (actually modern pools).

The wilderness theme is maintained inside the mobile homes, which feature mason-jar glassware, rough-hewn furniture, and reproductions of American landscape masterpieces. However, the Wilderness Homes are not luxurious. Each home has a picnic table, a grill, and a one-car driveway. Inside the 504-square-foot homes, there is one bedroom; one bathroom; and an open living, dining, and full-kitchen area. Most Wilderness Homes sleep six people, with a queen-size bed and a set of bunk beds crammed into the bedroom, and a Murphy bed that folds out of the living room wall. Surprisingly, given the spartan accommodations, daily maid service is provided. Finally, about a dozen specially equipped disabled units are available.

Disney is in the process of replacing the older Wilderness Homes with prefab log cabins. The cabins offer the same square footage as the Wilderness Home trailers but are newer, more appealing to the eye, and offer an elevated wood deck. Inside, the cabins provide the same space division as the trailers, with a slight reconfiguration of the living room and kitchen-dining area. Cabins go for about $20 more a night than the Wilderness Homes and are, in our opinion, worth it.

There are several restaurants at Fort Wilderness, the largest of which is inaccessible by car. The Wilderness Homes are connected to the theme parks by bus and boat. Walking time to the transportation loading areas from the most remote homes and campsites is about eight minutes.

The Epcot Resorts

Disney's Yacht and Beach Club Resorts   These five-story deluxe resorts are similarly themed and adjoin each other. Both resorts have clapboard facades with whitewashed-wood trim. The Yacht Club is painted a subdued gray, while the Beach Club is painted a brighter blue. The Yacht Club has a nautical theme with model ships and antique navigational instruments gracing the public areas. The Beach Club is appointed with beach scenes in foam green and white. Both resorts have themed lobbies, with a giant globe in the Yacht Club and sea horse fixtures in the Beach Club. The resorts face 25-acre Crescent Lake and share an elaborate swimming complex.

There are 630 guest rooms at the Yacht Club and 583 at the Beach Club. Most of the rooms are 381 square feet and contain two queen-size beds, a daybed, and a table and two chairs. Like the Grand Floridian, rooms here have a lot of drawer space. Rooms at the Yacht Club are decorated with navy blue and white, while rooms at the Beach Club offer a more muted, soft-green look. Some rooms have balconies.

As deluxe Walt Disney World resorts, the Yacht and Beach clubs provide excellent service. The resorts house nine restaurants and lounges and are within walking distance of Epcot and Disney's BoardWalk. Transportation to other destinations is by bus or boat. Walking time to the transportation loading areas from the most remote rooms is seven minutes.

Disney's BoardWalk Inn and BoardWalk Villas   Situated on Crescent Lake across from the Yacht and Beach Club resorts, the BoardWalk Inn is the newest of Walt Disney World's deluxe resorts. As viewed from Crescent Lake, the complex is a detailed replica of an early-20th-century Atlantic coast boardwalk. Varied facades of hotels, diners, and shops create a waterfront skyline that is both inviting and exciting. In reality, the BoardWalk Inn and Villas form a single integrated structure behind the varied facades. Restaurants and shops occupy the boardwalk level, while Inn and Villas accommodations rise up to six stories above. Painted bright red and yellow along with weathered pastel greens and blues, the BoardWalk resorts are the only Disney hotels that use neon signage as architectural detail. The Inn and Villas share a single, old-fashioned amusement park–themed swimming pool.

The 378 deluxe rooms of the BoardWalk Inn measure 422 square feet, and most contain two queen-size brass beds, a child's cherrywood daybed, a cherrywood table and two chairs, and ceiling fans. Decorating touches include blue and yellow gingham wallpaper and print curtains with a blue postcard pattern. Rooms at the BoardWalk have more closet space than other deluxe Disney rooms. Most rooms have balconies.

The 383 BoardWalk Villas are decorated with warmer tones and primary colors, with bright tiles in the kitchen and bathrooms. Villas range in size from 422 to 1,071 square feet (studio through three-bedroom), and sleep 4 to 12 people. Many villas have full kitchens, laundry rooms, and whirlpool bathtubs. The BoardWalk Villas tend to be more expensive than similar accommodations at other Disney resorts—you pay for the address.

As the newest deluxe Walt Disney World resort, the BoardWalk Inn and Villas are very well staffed and offer excellent service. Additionally, some of Disney World's finest restaurants and shops are located at the BoardWalk. The Inn and Villas are within walking distance of Epcot and are connected to other destinations by bus and boat. Walking time to transportation loading areas from the most remote rooms is five to six minutes.

The Walt Disney World Swan and Dolphin Although these resorts are inside Walt Disney World and Disney handles their reservations, they are owned by Sheraton (Dolphin) and Westin (Swan). The resorts face each other and are situated on either side of an inlet of Crescent Lake. The Dolphin is a 27-story triangular turquoise building. On its roof are two 56-foot-tall fish balanced with their tails in the air. The Swan has a 12-story main building flanked by two 7-story towers. Two 47-foot-tall swans adorn its roof, staring incredulously at the fish across the way. The Swan and Dolphin have been described as "bizarre" and stylistically disjointed. At the very least they are eclectic in their theming. Disney, for its part, claims that you will step into a "fantasy world." For our part, however, the experience is more akin to a drug-induced hallucination of art deco gone haywire. The giant swans look swanlike enough, but the fish on the Dolphin look like catfish from outer space. The mood at these properties could be described alternately as adventurous or confusing, depending on how much you value the work of a good interior decorator.

The lobby at the Dolphin is the more ornate, themed like a circus big top (after all, big tops and dolphins go together like peanut butter and jelly). At the other end of the spectrum, the lobby of the Swan is so small as to appear an afterthought. Both resorts feature artwork of wildly different styles and eras (from Matisse to Roy Lichtenstein). The resorts each have their own pool. The Dolphin's "Grotto" pool is shaped like a seashell and has a waterfall, while the Swan's pool is of a conventional rectangular configuration.

The rooms at the two properties are decorated similarly, with fine art prints and bold colors. However, the rooms at the Dolphin are slightly larger, with an extra vanity. The 1,509 guest rooms at the Walt Disney World Dolphin are 360 square feet, and the 758 rooms at the Swan are 340 square feet. Both are decorated in bright turquoise and peach. Most rooms have two queen-size beds, a desk, and a reading chair. The furniture is modern, with wood and metal marine-inspired accents. Some rooms at the Dolphin have balconies.

Since the Walt Disney World Swan and Dolphin are not run by Disney, the service at these resorts is less sugar-coated than service at other Disney resorts. The Swan and Dolphin collectively house more than a dozen restaurants and lounges, and more are within easy walking distance at Epcot and the BoardWalk. The resorts are connected to other destinations by bus and boat. Walking time from the most remote rooms to the transportation loading areas is seven to nine minutes.

Disney's Caribbean Beach Resort The Caribbean Beach Resort is situated on 200 acres surrounding a 45-acre lake called Barefoot Bay. This mid-priced Disney resort, modeled after resorts of the Caribbean islands, is comprised of the registration area, called the "Custom House," and five two-story "villages" named after Caribbean islands. Each village has its own pool, laundry room, and beach. The Caribbean motif is maintained with red tile roofs, widow's walks, and wooden railed porches. The atmosphere at this resort is cheerful, with buildings painted blue, lime green, and sherbet orange. In addition to the five village pools, the main swimming pool at the Caribbean Beach is themed as an old Spanish fort, complete with slides and water cannons.

Most of the 2,112 guest rooms at the Caribbean Beach are 340 square feet and contain two double beds and a table and two chairs. Some of the rooms are decorated with bright tropical colors, while others are decorated with neutral beachy tones. All of the rooms are suited with the same light-oak furniture. Rooms do not have balconies. Some rooms at the Caribbean are in need of refurbishment. When you make your reservations, request a recently renovated room. Also, be aware that the Caribbean Beach Resort is not known for its check-in efficiency.

One of the most centrally located of the Disney resorts, transportation to all Walt Disney World destinations is by bus. Though the Caribbean Beach has one full-service restaurant and a food court, food service is woefully inadequate for the size of the resort. Because food service at the Caribbean is limited and because it is immensely time consuming to commute to other resorts by Disney bus, guests at the Caribbean Beach should seriously consider renting a car. Walking time to the bus loading area from the most remote rooms is seven to ten minutes.

The Bonnet Creek Resorts

Disney's Old Key West Resort   This is the first of the Disney Vacation Club properties. Although the resort is a time-share property, units not being used by owners are rented on a nightly basis. Old Key West is a large aggregation of two- to three-story buildings modeled after Caribbean residences and guest houses of the Florida Keys. Arranged subdivision-style around a golf course and along Bonnet Creek, the buildings are situated in small neighborhoodlike clusters. They feature pastel-colored facades, white trim, and shuttered windows. The registration area is housed in the Conch Flats Community Hall, along with a full-service restaurant, modest fitness center, marina, and sundries shop. There is a quiet pool in each cluster of accommodations and a larger pool at the Conch Flats Community Hall.

With standard rooms at 376 square feet, one-bedroom villas at 942 square feet, and two-bedroom villas at 1,333 square feet, this resort offers some of the roomiest accommodations at Walt Disney World. Standard rooms contain two queen-size beds, a table and two chairs, and an extra vanity outside the bathroom. One-bedroom villas contain a king-size bed in the master bedroom, a queen-size sleeper sofa in the living room, a laundry room, and a fully equipped kitchen. Two-bedroom villas include an additional bedroom with two queen-size beds. All of the villas have enough closet space to bring your whole wardrobe.

Each villa at the Old Key West has its own private balcony that opens onto a delightfully landscaped private courtyard. Finally, rooms and villas at the Old Key West are tastefully decorated, with wicker and upholstered furniture, and peach and light-green color schemes.

As a Disney Vacation Club resort, Old Key West's service is very personal. Transportation to other Walt Disney World destinations is by bus. Unfortunately, Old Key West buses run less often than those of most other Disney resorts. Walking time to transportation loading areas from the most remote rooms is about six minutes.

Disney's Port Orleans Resort   This mid-priced resort is a sanitized Disney version of the New Orleans French Quarter. Comprised of seven three-story guest-room buildings situated next to Bonnet Creek, the resort gives you an idea of what New Orleans would look like if its buildings were painted every year and the garbage collectors never went on strike. There are very prim pink and blue guest buildings, with wrought-iron filigree, shuttered windows, and old-fashioned iron lampposts. In keeping with the Crescent City theme, Port Orleans is landscaped with magnolia trees and overgrown vines. The centrally located "Mint" houses the registration area and restaurants, and is a reproduction of a turn-of-the-century building where Mississippi Delta farmers sold their harvests. The registration desk features a vibrant Mardi Gras mural and old-fashioned bank teller windows. "Doubloon Lagoon," the only pool at the Port Orleans, surrounds a colorful fiberglass creation depicting Neptune riding a sea serpent.

The 1,008 guest rooms at the Port Orleans each measure 315 square feet. Most contain two double beds, a table and two chairs, and a vanity outside the bathroom. The gold and deep-green rooms feature hardwood furniture and valances over the curtains. None of the rooms at Port Orleans have private balconies.

With a moderate ratio of staff to guests, service at the Port Orleans is good. There is one full-service restaurant as well as a food court at the resort. Port Orleans is connected to other Walt Disney World destinations by bus. Walking time to the transportation loading areas from the most remote rooms is seven to ten minutes.

Disney's Dixie Landings Resort   This mid-priced Walt Disney World resort draws on the lifestyle and architecture of Mississippi River communities in antebellum Louisiana, though it conveniently ignores any reference to slavery. Spread along Bonnet Creek, which encircles "Old Man Island" (the resort's main swimming area), Dixie Landings is divided into two themed areas: the "mansion" area, which features plantation-style architecture, and the "bayou" area, with tin-roofed rustic (imitation) wooden buildings. The mansions are three stories tall, while the bayou guest houses are a story shorter. The theme is augmented by landscaped groves of azalea and juniper. Southern river life is also depicted at Dixie Landings' food court, which houses a working cotton press powered by a 32-foot waterwheel.

The 2,048 rooms at Dixie Landings each measure 315 square feet. Most provide two double beds, a table and two chairs, and two pedestal sinks outside the bathroom. Some rooms also contain a child's trundle bed. All rooms feature brass bathroom fixtures, hickory-branch bedposts, and quilted bedspreads. The rooms are decorated in tasteful neutrals and blues. None of the rooms have private balconies.

Dixie Landings has one full-service restaurant as well as a food court. The resort is served by the Disney bus system, connecting it to all Walt Disney World destinations. Walking time from the most remote rooms to the transportation loading areas is ten minutes.

The Villas at the Disney Institute

This resort offers a wide variety of accommodations stretching from Downtown Disney to Bonnet Creek. Tucked in clusters fronting the Buena Vista Golf Course and along several streams and canals, the various villas are some of the oldest and most geographically dispersed of all Disney lodging options. The grounds are landscaped with native Florida flora, and the forest surrounding the resort provides a quiet barrier between the Disney Institute and the rest of Walt Disney World. There are five small swimming pools at the Disney Institute as well as Walt Disney World's finest guest fitness center and spa.

Of the 587 units at the Disney Institute, there are five different types of accommodations available. There are 316 one-bedroom Bungalows, which measure 500 square feet and offer separate living rooms. These units contain two queen-size beds, a wetbar with refrigerator and microwave, and a balcony or patio. They are decorated nicely, with turtle lamp fixtures and maps of the world on the print curtains.

There are 60 Treehouse Villas at the Disney Institute. These accommodations are smaller than they look. Each Treehouse has two bedrooms (each with one queen-size bed), two bathrooms, a small kitchen, and a living room with a sleeper sofa. They are decorated in natural tones, with rustic wooden furniture. Though somewhat dated, the Treehouse Villas are the most isolated and quietest of all the villas and offer guests the most serene setting at Walt Disney World. For some guests, including this woman from La Crescent, Minnesota, the Treehouse Villas are a tad more rustic than anticipated:

> *We reserved a Treehouse Villa and I tell you, "it ain't no villa." When we pulled up and had to park half a block away with woods and swamp, my worst nightmare came true! The rustic interior both in furniture and decor was not like any Disney [accommodation] we had ever had. Our children looked at us like, why the camping trip?*

There are 128 one- and two-bedroom Town Houses. These Disney Institute accommodations offer a sleeper sofa in the living room, a queen-size bed in the master bedroom, and a full kitchen. The two-bedroom units offer two twin beds in the second bedroom. While the decor in these units is truly bland, many guests enjoy the walking proximity to Downtown Disney.

The fourth type of accommodation are the 64 Fairway Villas at the Disney Institute. These villas have cathedral ceilings, two bedrooms, a full kitchen, and a separate living room. They are furnished with two double beds in one bedroom, a queen-size bed in the other bedroom, and a sleeper sofa in the living room. These villas also feature modern furniture and large windows.

There are only four Grand Vista Homes at the Disney Institute. Visiting Saudi princes will want to check on the availability of these three-bedroom homes. Amenities include nightly turndown service and stocked refrigerators.

Though the Disney Institute staff caters to those who are participating in classes, our research team ranks housekeeping at the Villas as the poorest Disney has to offer. There is only one full-service restaurant at the Disney Institute, but there are plenty of restaurants nearby at Downtown Disney. Disney bus service to other World destinations is marginal compared to other resorts. If you stay at the Villas, we recommend that you rent a car. Walking time to the transportation loading areas from the most remote rooms is 8–11 minutes.

The Animal Kingdom Resort Area

Disney's Coronado Springs Resort   The new Coronado Springs Resort, located near the Animal Kingdom, is Disney's only mid-priced convention property. Inspired by northern Mexico and the American Southwest, the resort is divided into three separately themed areas. The two- and three-story Ranchos call to mind vast Southwestern cattle ranches, while the two- and three-story Cabanas are modeled after Mexican beach resorts. Finally, the multistoried Casitas embody elements of Spanish architecture found in Mexico's great cities. The lobby is part of the Casitas and features a mosaic ceiling and tiled floor. The vast resort surrounds a 15-acre lake, and there are three small pools as well as one large main swimming complex. The main pool is designed to look like ancient ruins and features a reproduction of an Aztec/Mayan steppe pyramid with a waterfall cascading down its side.

There are 1,967 guest rooms at the Coronado Springs. Most of the rooms measure 315 square feet and contain two double beds, a table and chairs, and a vanity outside the bathroom. They are decorated with the colors of the sunset and feature handpainted Mexican wall hangings. All rooms have coffeemakers. None of the rooms have their own balcony.

The Coronado Springs offers one full-service restaurant as well as the best food court at Walt Disney World. Unfortunately, however, there is not nearly enough food service for a resort this large and remote. If you book the Coronado Springs, we suggest that you rent a car to expand your dining options. The resort is connected to other Walt Disney World destinations by bus only. Walking time from the most remote rooms to the bus stop is eight to ten minutes.

As a convention hotel, the Coronado Springs is somewhat peculiar. Unlike most convention hotels, where everything is centrally located with the guest rooms in close proximity, guest rooms at the Coronado Springs are arrayed around a huge lake. If you are assigned one of the rooms on the opposite side of the lake from the meeting and convention area (and restaurants!) plan on a 11- to 15-minute hike every time you leave your room. If your organization books the Coronado Springs for a meeting, think about having your meals catered. The hotel's restaurants simply do not have the capacity during a large convention to accommodate the morning breakfast rush or to serve a quick lunch between meeting sessions.

Disney's All-Star Sports, All-Star Music, and All-Star Movie Resorts
Disney's version of a budget resort features three distinct themes executed in the same hyperbolistic style. Spread over a vast expanse, the resorts are comprised of almost 35 three-story motel-style guest-room buildings. Although the three resorts are neighbors, each has its own lobby, food court, and registration area. The All-Star Sports Resort features huge sports icons: bright football helmets, tennis rackets, and baseball bats, all taller than the buildings they adorn. Similarly, the All-Star Music Resort features 40-foot guitars, maracas, and saxophones, while the All-Star Movie Resort showcases giant popcorn boxes and film canisters. Lobbies of all three resorts are loud (in both decibels and brightness) and cartoonish, with checkerboard walls and photographs of famous athletes, musicians, and film stars. There's even a photo of Mickey Mouse with Alice Cooper (does Mickey know that Alice is a man who wears sundresses and bites the heads

off bats at rock concerts?). The swimming pool at the Music Resort is shaped like a giant guitar, and the pool at the Sports Resort features plastic replicas of the Disney characters shooting water pistols. At the All-Star Movie Resort, the pool is star shaped.

At 260 square feet, the guest rooms at each of the All-Star resorts are very small. They are so small that a family of four attempting to stay in one room might well redefine family values by the end of the week. Each room has two double beds, a separate vanity area, and a table and chairs. The bedspreads feature famous athletes, movie stars, and musicians, and the light fixtures are star-shaped. None of the rooms at the All-Stars have balconies.

If you are planning to save for years for your grand Disney vacation, save enough money for a bigger room. Also, the prevalence of young children running wild makes the All-Stars the noisiest of the Disney resorts, though the guest rooms are well soundproofed and quiet.

With a very low ratio of staff to guests, service is not the greatest at the All-Star resorts. Additionally, there are no full-service restaurants at the resorts. Because the All-Stars are the most remote of the Walt Disney World resorts, the bus ride to a full-service restaurant at another resort takes about 45 minutes each way. There is, however, a new McDonalds about a quarter of a mile away. Bus service to the theme parks and the water parks is pretty efficient. Walking time to the bus stop from the most remote guest rooms is about eight minutes.

How to Evaluate a Walt Disney World Travel Package

Hundreds of Walt Disney World package vacations are offered each year. Some are created by the Walt Disney Travel Company, others by airline touring companies, independent travel agents, and wholesalers. Almost all include lodging at or near Disney World and theme park admissions. Packages offered by airlines include air transportation.

Prices vary seasonally; mid-February to the end of April and holiday periods are the most expensive. Off-season, forget packages: there are plenty of empty rooms, and you can negotiate great discounts (especially at non-Disney properties). Similarly, airfares and rental cars are cheaper off-peak.

Almost all package ads are headlined "5 Days at Walt Disney World from $605" (or such). The key word is "from." The rock-bottom price includes the least desirable hotels. If you want better or more convenient digs, you'll have to pay more, often much more.

Packages offer a wide selection of hotels. Some, like the Disney resorts, are very dependable. Others run the gamut of quality. If you consider a non-Disney hotel, check its quality as reported in an independent rating such as those offered by the *Unofficial Guides, AAA Directories, Mobil Guides,* or *Frommer's America on Wheels.* Checking two or three independent sources is best. Also, before you book, ask how old the hotel is and when the guest rooms were last refurbished. Locate the hotel on a map to verify its proximity to Disney World. If you won't have a car, make sure the hotel has an adequate shuttle service.

Packages with non-Disney lodging are much less expensive. But guests at Disney-owned properties get free parking and early entry to designated theme parks. These privileges don't apply to guests at the seven independent hotels of the Disney Village Hotel Plaza (Buena Vista Palace Resort & Spa, Grosvenor Resort, DoubleTree Guest Suites Resort, The Hilton Resort, Courtyard by Marriott, Hotel Royal Plaza, and Travelodge Hotel).

Packages should be a win/win proposition for both buyer and seller. The buyer makes only one phone call and deals with one salesperson to set up the whole vacation (transportation, rental car, admissions, lodging, meals, and even golf and tennis). The seller, likewise, deals with the buyer only one time. Some packagers also buy airfares in bulk on contract, like a broker playing the commodities market. By buying a large number of airfares in advance, the packager saves significantly over posted fares. The practice is also applied to hotel rooms. Because selling packages is efficient and because the packager often can buy package components (airfare, lodging, etc.) in bulk at discount, savings in operating expenses realized by the seller are sometimes passed on to the buyer, making the package both convenient and an exceptional value.

In practice, however, the seller may realize all of the economies and pass on no savings to the buyer. In some instances, packages are loaded with extras that cost the packager almost nothing but run the retail price of the package sky high. Not surprisingly, the savings passed on to customers are still somewhere in Fantasyland.

Choose a package that includes features you're sure to use. Whether you use all of the features or not, you will pay for them. If price is more important than convenience, call around to see what the package would cost if you booked its components on your own. If the package price is less than the a la carte cost, the package is a good deal. If costs are about equal, the package probably is worth it for the convenience.

An Example   A popular package offered by the Walt Disney Travel Company is the *Disney Resort Magic* plan, which includes:

1. Three or more nights' accommodation at your choice of any Disney resort. Rates vary with choice of lodging; the Grand Florid-

ian is the most expensive, and Fort Wilderness Resort Homes is the least expensive.

2. Unlimited use of the Walt Disney World transportation system.

3. Admission and unlimited use of all Walt Disney World theme parks during your stay.

4. Admission and unlimited use of Pleasure Island nighttime entertainment complex; River Country, Typhoon Lagoon, and Blizzard Beach swimming parks; and Discovery Island zoological park during your stay. (Admission becomes effective upon check-in and is valid until midnight of your check-out day.)

5. Free parking.

The *Disney Resort Magic* plan also includes a "flex feature," which consists of one of the following per person:

1. A round of golf at *Fantasia Gardens* Miniature Golf course.

2. A round of golf at Disney's *Oak Trail Course* (a 9-hole walking course).

3. *Birnbaum's Walt Disney World, 1999; The Official Guide.*

4. Planet Hollywood or ESPN Club T-shirt.

5. One Official All Star Cafe Burger Platter with souvenir sports bottle.

6. One Mickey 'n You photo session.

7. Disney character breakfast.

8. One of a number of theme park tours, such as Gardens of the World Tour at Epcot or the mystery family tour at Magic Kingdom.

Loaded with benefits and amenities, this is one of Walt Disney World's most popular packages (price varies with hotel and room choice and length of stay). Depending on how you use it, you can come out a winner or a loser.

Our sample analysis is done for a couple from Baltimore, Maryland, on a six-night package, traveling in September and arriving in Orlando by air. The couple's choice of hotels is the Wilderness Lodge, connected to the theme parks by bus. Because check-in time at the Wilderness Lodge is 3 p.m. or later, the couple plans to arrive at Walt Disney World in the late afternoon and begin touring the theme parks the next day. Their itinerary calls for additional touring on their check-out day prior to leaving for the airport. The package costs $958 for each adult (two to a room), or $1,916 for the couple (tax included). Their round-trip airfare from Baltimore and transportation from and to the airport are in addition to the package price.

Six days' use of the transportation system is no big deal. Anyone who buys a regular five- or six-day admission can ride all day on the buses, boats, and monorails.

The package provides six days' admission to the major theme parks as well as River Country, Blizzard Beach, Typhoon Lagoon, Discovery Island, and Pleasure Island. Since it takes at least five days to see the major theme parks, little time is left to visit Typhoon Lagoon, Blizzard Beach, River Country, Discovery Island, and Pleasure Island.

Another problem with the six days' admission is that whatever you don't use, you lose. Admissions are good only for the days of the package, unlike the non-package All-in-One or Hopper Passes. Unused days on the Hopper and All-in-One are good forever. If you come back next month or three years from now, you'll be able to finish using your pass. Not so with the package admission.

The package's "flex features" can all be purchased a la carte. Birnbaum's *Official Guide to Walt Disney World* is available at bookstores, exclusive of the package. And the private photo session with Mickey may be more of a liability than an asset, as a Texas gentleman notes:

> *Included in our vacation package was a photograph session with Mickey at You & Me Kid, a shop in the Downtown Disney Marketplace (aka WDW Village). Two caveats emptor here: First, the procedure for the photo session was very poorly arranged and executed with molasses-like speed (much to the ire of a gaggle of bedraggled parents). Second, we suspect that the delay was at least partially intentional: the more hours you were detained at the Disney Village before your appointment with The Mouse, the more steadily your billfold could be emptied on the relentless parade of Disney merchandise. Indeed, since this shopping center was the only location given for this special photo-op, our hunch is that the whole affair is little more than a lure to draw families off the beaten path to a nice but très expensive Disney Marketplace.*

In the final analysis, the *Disney Resort Magic Plan* is best suited to vacationers who plan to be on the go from dawn until midnight and visit the theme parks every day. And, you may have concluded, it's set up in a way that makes it almost impossible not to waste many of its benefits.

Getting Down to Dollars and Cents   If you exclude the recreational extras, here's how the package compares with going it on your own:

Option A: *Disney Resort Magic Plan* for two people
in September, sharing a room at the Wilderness
Lodge Resort: $958 per person × 2 $1,916

Option B: Creating your own vacation with the same basic features of the *Disney Resort Magic Plan*

The Wilderness Lodge Resort (same room as package) for six nights with tax included for two adults	$1,300
Two 6-Day All-in-One Passes (unlimited admission to four major and five minor parks) with tax	$528
Birnbaum's *Official Guide to Walt Disney World*	$14
Grand total for two people	$1,842
Amount saved by arranging things yourself	$74

Another Example   Most Delta Dream Vacations offer almost the same features as *Disney's Resort Magic Plan,* plus round-trip air transportation. If a couple from St. Louis buys a six-night Delta package for late August at the Port Orleans Resort, they'll pay $2,037 for both people. If they book the same components themselves, the cost will be $1,388 *before* buying airline tickets.

If you subtract the a la carte costs of package components from the package price ($2,037 minus $1,388), the remainder ($649) is what the couple is being charged for airfare, in this case $324.50 per person ($649 divided by two). If they can fly round trip to Orlando from St. Louis for less than $324.50 a person, the package isn't such a great deal. If airfares from St. Louis equal or exceed $324.50 per person, the package makes sense.

If you buy a package from Disney, don't expect reservationists to offer suggestions or help you sort out your options. Generally, they won't volunteer information and will respond only to your specific questions, ducking queries that require an opinion. A reader from North Riverside, Illinois, complains:

> *I have received various pieces of literature from WDW and it is very confusing to try and figure everything out. My wife made two telephone calls, and the representatives from WDW were very courteous. However, they only answered the questions posed and were not very eager to give advice on what might be most cost effective. [The] WDW reps would not say if we would be better off doing one thing over the other. I feel a person could spend eight hours on the telephone with WDW reps and not have any more input than you get from reading the literature.*

If you can't get the information you need from Disney, contact a good travel agent. Chances are the agent can help you sort out your options. A dad from Valley Stream, New York, used the Walt Disney Travel Company, travel wholesalers, and travel agents to comparison-shop successfully:

Nothing pays greater dividends than planning in advance. A year before our vacation we joined the Magic Kingdom Club. Some 8–9 months before our vacation I secured a package price from the Magic Kingdom Club, which I was able to use to negotiate a lower package with my travel agent. Yes, the travel agent packages are negotiable (much to my own surprise). What I now realize is that travel agents get WDW packages from different wholesalers and may not be immediately inclined to give you a package offered through the lowest-priced wholesaler. The first quotes I received were from AAA and Liberty Travel but, unbeknownst to me, both packages were, in fact, purchased through Delta Airlines. It was only after I was able to obtain a lower land package price by booking directly through Disney (as a Magic Kingdom Club member) that I was assured by each agent that they could beat the price I was able to secure—and they did, saving me several hundred dollars. The air package was another reason to book through a travel agent. Our agent reserved seats for us on one airline only to call us three weeks later to tell us of discounts being offered through another airline. We acted quickly and bought the discounted tickets, saving another $200 on our air package.

Information Needed for Evaluation   For quick reference, contact Walt Disney World accommodations reservations at (407) 934-7639 or (407) 824-8000 and ask for a Walt Disney Travel Company Walt Disney World Vacations Brochure, which contains descriptions and room rates for all Disney properties. Ask also for a rate sheet listing admission options and prices for all major and minor parks. These in hand, you're ready to evaluate any vacation package. Remember that all packages are quoted on a per-person basis at two to a room (double occupancy), and there is an 11% combined sales and room tax. For about everything else you buy in Florida (except groceries and prescription medicine), a 6–7% sales tax applies.

SELECTING AND BOOKING A HOTEL OUTSIDE WALT DISNEY WORLD

Lodging costs outside Walt Disney World vary incredibly. If you shop around, you can find a clean motel with a pool within 20 minutes of the World for as low as $35 a night. You also can find luxurious, expensive hotels with all the extras. Because of hot competition, discounts abound, particularly for AAA and AARP members.

There are three primary out-of-the-World areas to consider:

1. International Drive Area   This area, about 15 to 20 minutes east of Walt Disney World, parallels I-4 on its southern side and offers a wide selection of both hotels and restaurants. Accommodations range from $35 to $250 per night. The chief drawbacks of the International Drive area are its terribly congested roads, countless traffic signals, and inadequate access to westbound I-4. While the biggest bottleneck is the intersection with Sand Lake Road, the mile of International Drive between Kirkman Road and Sand Lake Road stays in near-continuous gridlock. It's common to lose 25 to 35 minutes trying to navigate this stretch.

Traffic aside, a gentleman from Ottawa, Canada, extols his International Drive experience:

> *International Drive is the place to stay when going to Disney. Your single paragraph description of this location failed to point out that [there are] several discount stores, boutiques, restaurants and mini-putts, and other entertainment facilities, all within walking distance of remarkably inexpensive accommodations and a short drive away from WDW. Many of the chain motels and hotels are located in this area, and the local merchants have created a mini-resort to cater to the tourists. It is the ideal place to unwind after a hard day visiting WDW. I have recommended this location for years and have never heard anything but raves about the wisdom of this advice.*

Hotels in the International Drive area are listed in the *Orlando Official Accommodations Guide* published by the Orlando/Orange County Convention and Visitors Bureau. For a copy, call (800) 255-5786 or (407) 363-5874.

2. Lake Buena Vista and the I-4 Corridor   A number of hotels are situated along FL 535 and north of I-4 between Walt Disney World and I-4's intersection with the Florida Turnpike. These properties are easily reached from the interstate and are near a large number of restaurants, including those on International Drive. Driving time to Disney World is 5 to 15 minutes. Most hotels in this area are listed in the *Orlando Official Accommodations Guide.*

3. US 192   This is the highway to Kissimmee, southeast of Walt Disney World. In addition to a number of large, full-service hotels are many small, privately owned motels that are a good value. Several dozen properties on US 192 are closer to the Disney theme parks than are the more expensive hotels in Walt Disney World Village and the Disney Village Hotel Plaza. Traffic on US 192 is extremely heavy but usually moves smoothly. The number and variety of restaurants on US 192 has increased markedly in the past year, easing the area's primary shortcoming.

Hotel
Concentrations
Around Orlando

Orlando

Lake Apopka

Winter Garden

Winter Park

Pine Hills

Lake Butler

L. Tibet

Orlando

Conway

L. Conway

Walt Disney World

2

Vineland

L. Buena Vista

Orlando International Airport

1

3

Kissimmee

East Lake Tohopekaliga

Florida Turnpike

Internatl. Dr.

Orange Blossom Trail

Florida Turnpike

Ctl. Florida Greenway

Osceola Pkwy.

A senior citizen from Brookfield, Connecticut, was surprised and pleased with lodging in the US 192/Kissimmee area:

> *We were amazed to find that from our cheaper and superior accommodations in Kissimmee it took only 5 minutes longer to reach the park turnstiles than it did from the Disney accommodations. Kissimmee is the way to go, in our opinion.*

Hotels on US 192 and in Kissimmee are listed in the *Kissimmee–St. Cloud Tour & Travel Sales Guide,* available at (800) 327-9159.

Driving Time to the Theme Parks for Visitors Lodging outside Walt Disney World

For those staying outside Walt Disney World, we've calculated the approximate commuting time to the major theme parks' parking lots from several off-World lodging areas. Add a few minutes to our times to pay your parking fee and park. Once parked at the Transportation and Ticket Center (Magic Kingdom parking lot), it takes an average of 20 to 30 additional minutes to reach the Magic Kingdom. To reach Epcot from its parking lot, add 7 to 10 minutes. At Disney-MGM Studios and the Animal Kingdom, the lot-to-gate transit is 5 to 10 minutes. If you haven't purchased your theme park admission in advance, tack on another 10 to 20 minutes.

	To Magic Kingdom	Epcot	Disney–MGM Studios	Animal Kingdom
Minutes From	**Parking Lot**	**Parking Lot**	**Parking Lot**	**Parking Lot**
Downtown Orlando	35	31	33	37
North International Dr. and Universal Studios	24	21	22	26
Central International Dr.–Sand Lake Road	26	23	24	27
South International Dr. and Sea World	18	15	16	20
FL 535	12	9	10	13
FL 192, north of I-4	10–15	7–12	5–10	5–10
FL 192, south of I-4	10–18	7–15	5–13	5–12

Driving Time to the Theme Parks

GETTING A GOOD DEAL ON A ROOM OUTSIDE WALT DISNEY WORLD

Hotel development at Walt Disney World has sharpened the competition among lodgings throughout the Disney World/Orlando/Kissimmee area. Hotels outside Disney World, in particular, struggle to fill their guest rooms. Unable to compete with Disney resorts for convenience or perks, off-World hotels lure patrons with bargain rates. The extent of the bargain depends on the season, day of the week, and area events. In high season, during holiday periods, and when large conventions are held at the Orange County Convention Center, even the most modest lodging properties are sold out. Here are tips and strategies for getting a good deal on a room outside Disney World.

The following list may seem intimidating and may refer to travel-market players unfamiliar to you, but many tips we provide for getting a good deal at Disney World work equally well almost any other place you need a hotel. Once you understand these strategies, you'll routinely be able to obtain rooms at the best hotels for the lowest possible rates.

1. Orlando MagiCard   Orlando MagiCard is a discount program sponsored by the Orlando/Orange County Convention and Visitors Bureau. Cardholders are eligible for discounts of 10–40% at approximately 75 participating hotels. The MagiCard is also good for discounts at area attractions, including Sea World, Cypress Gardens, Universal Studios, several dinner theaters, Church Street Station, and Disney's Pleasure Island. Valid for up to six persons, the card isn't available for groups or conventions.

To obtain an Orlando MagiCard and a list of participating hotels and attractions, call (800) 255-5786 or (407) 363-5874. Anyone older than 18 years is eligible, and the card is free. If you miss getting a card before you leave home, you can get one at the Convention and Visitors Bureau at 8445 International Drive in Orlando. When you call for a MagiCard, also request the *Orlando Official Accommodations Guide* and the Orlando Vacation Planner.

2. Exit Information Guide   Exit Information Guide publishes a book of discount coupons for bargain rates at hotels statewide. The book is free in many restaurants and motels on main highways leading to Florida. Because most travelers make reservations before leaving home, picking up the coupon book en route doesn't help much. If you call and use a credit card, EIG will send the guide first class for $3 ($5 U.S. for Canadian delivery). Contact:

Exit Information Guide
4205 N.W. 6th Street
Gainesville, FL 32609
(352) 371-3948

3. Special Weekend Rates It's a half-hour drive from Walt Disney World, but downtown Orlando offers great weekend rates on rooms. Hotels that cater weekdays to business, state government, and convention travelers offer weekend discounts of 15–40%. Individual hotels or your travel agent can detail the specials.

4. Corporate Rates Many hotels offer corporate discounts of 5–20%. Usually, you don't need to work for a large company to obtain them. Simply call the hotel of your choice and ask for its corporate rates. Many hotels will guarantee the discounted rate when you make your reservation. Others may make the rate conditional on your providing some sort of *bona fides,* for instance a fax on your company's letterhead requesting the rate or a company credit card or business card when you check in. Generally, screening isn't rigorous.

5. Half-Price Programs Larger discounts on rooms (35–60%), in the Disney World area or anywhere else, are available through half-price hotel programs, often called travel clubs. Program operators contract with hotels to provide rooms at a deep discount, usually 50% off the rack rate, on a space-available basis. Generally, space available means you can reserve a room at the discount whenever the hotel expects occupancy will be less than 80%. To increase your chances for the discount, check the calendar to avoid high-season, big conventions, holidays, and special events.

Most half-price programs charge an annual membership or directory subscription fee of $25–125. Once enrolled, you're mailed a membership card and directory listing participating hotels. There are lots of restrictions and exceptions. Some hotels, for instance, "black out" (exclude) certain times. Others may offer the discount only on certain days of the week or may require you to stay a certain number of nights. Still others may offer a discount much smaller than 50%.

More established programs offer members up to 4,000 hotels in the United States. All of the programs have a heavy concentration of hotels in California and Florida. Offerings elsewhere in the United States vary considerably. The programs with the largest selection of hotels in the Disney World area are Encore, at (800) 638-0930, and Entertainment Publications, at (800) 285-5525.

One problem with half-price programs is that not all hotels offer a full 50% discount. Another is the base rate against which the discount is applied. Some hotels figure the discount on an exaggerated rack rate that virtually no one pays. A few participating hotels may deduct the discount from the rate for a "superior" or "upgraded" room, though the room assigned is the hotel's standard accommodation. The majority of participants base discounts on rates published in the *Hotel & Travel Index* (a quarterly reference journal used by travel agents) and work within the spirit of their agreement with the program operator. As a rule, if you travel several times a year, your savings will more than pay for your program membership.

A footnote to this information is that rooms through half-price programs aren't commissionable to travel agents. This means you usually must make your own inquiries and reservations. If you work frequently with your agent, however, he or she will probably do your legwork, lack of commission notwithstanding.

6. Preferred Rates If you cannot book the hotel of your choice through a half-price program, you and your travel agent may have to search for a lesser discount, often called a preferred rate. A preferred rate could be made available to travel agents to stimulate booking activity or be initiated to attract a certain class of traveler. Most preferred rates are promoted through travel-industry publications and are accessible only through agents.

Sound out your travel agent about deals, but be aware that rates shown on agents' computerized reservations systems aren't always the lowest obtainable. Choose a couple of hotels that meet your needs for location and quality, then have your travel agent call for the latest rates and specials. Hotel personnel are almost always more responsive to agents because they could produce additional business. Hotels disclose some specials *only* to travel agents. When the hotel you want is supposedly full, an appeal from your agent to its director of sales and marketing will get you a room more than half the time.

7. Wholesalers, Consolidators, and Reservation Services Wholesalers and consolidators buy rooms, or options on rooms (room blocks), from hotels at a low, negotiated rate. They then resell the rooms at a profit through travel agents and tour packagers, or directly to the public. Most wholesalers and consolidators make provisions for returning unsold rooms to participating hotels but are disinclined to do so. The wholesaler's or consolidator's relationship with any hotel is tied to volume. If unsold rooms are returned, the hotel might not make as many rooms available the next time. So wholesalers and consolidators often offer rooms at rates from 15 to 50% off rack rate, occasionally sacrificing profit to avoid returning the rooms unsold.

When wholesalers and consolidators deal directly with the public, they frequently represent themselves as "reservation services." When you call, ask for a rate for your chosen hotel or for the best deal in the area where you'd like to stay. Say if there's a maximum amount you're willing to pay. The service likely will find something for you, even if it has to shave off a dollar or two of profit. You may have to pay by credit card when you reserve a room. Other times, you pay when you check out. Here are three services that frequently offer substantial discounts:

Accommodations Express	(800) 444-7666
Hotel Reservations Network	(800) 964-6835

8. If You Make Your Own Reservation Always call the hotel in question, not the hotel chain's national 800 number. Often, reservationists at the 800 number are unaware of local specials. Always ask about specials before you inquire about corporate rates. Don't hesitate to bargain, but do it before you check in. If you're buying a hotel's weekend package, for example, and want to extend your stay, you can often obtain at least the corporate rate for the extra days.

9. Condominium Deals   A large number of condo resorts and time shares in the Kissimmee/Orlando area rent to vacationers for a week or less. Look for bargains, especially during off-peak periods. Reservations and information can be obtained from:

Condolink	(800) 733-4445
Holiday Villas	(800) 251-1112
Hospitality Vacation Homes	(800) 969-7077
Kissimmee–St. Cloud Reservations	(800) 333-5477
Vistana Resort	(800) 877-8787

We frequently receive letters from readers extolling the virtues of renting a condo or vacation home. This endorsement by a family from Glenmont, New York, is typical:

> *I would recommend that you include the Vistana Resort in your hotel section. Such luxury for so little. On two past visits we stayed in Disney's Lake Buena Vista Hotel Village. To have two BR, two baths, kitchen, DR, LR, deck, and Jacuzzi for less money was heaven. The children could go to bed at 8:30, and we could stay up and have some privacy. The full kitchen saved $, too—especially at breakfast time. I highly recommend this for families. So close (five minutes to Epcot, ten to MK, seven to Sea World) and convenient.*

A majority of rental condos are listed with travel agents. Condo owners often pay an enhanced commission to agents who rent the units for reduced consumer rates.

Hotels and Motels: Rated and Ranked

In this section, we compare hotels in three main areas outside Walt Disney World (pages 118–121) with those inside the World.

In addition to Disney properties and the three lodging areas we rate, there are hotels at the intersection of US 27 and I-4, on US 441 (Orange Blossom Trail), and in downtown Orlando. All of these require more than 20 minutes' commuting time to Walt Disney World. We also haven't rated lodging south of Siesta Lago Road on US 192.

WHAT'S IN A ROOM?

Except for cleanliness, state of repair, and decor, travelers pay little attention to hotel rooms. There is, of course, a clear standard of quality and luxury that differentiates Motel 6 from Holiday Inn, Holiday Inn from Marriott, and so on. Many hotel guests, however, fail to appreciate that some rooms are better engineered than others. Making the room usable to its occupants is an art, a planning discipline that combines both form and function.

Decor and taste are important, certainly. No one wants to stay in a room that is dated, garish, or ugly. But beyond decor, how "livable" is the room? In Orlando, for example, we have seen some beautifully appointed rooms that simply aren't well designed for human habitation. The next time you stay in a hotel, note the details and design elements of your room. Even more than decor, these are the things that will make you feel comfortable and at home.

ROOM RATINGS

To evaluate properties for their quality, tastefulness, state of repair, cleanliness, and size of their *standard rooms,* we have grouped the hotels and motels into classifications denoted by stars. Star ratings in this guide apply to Orlando-area properties only and don't necessarily correspond to ratings awarded by Frommer, Mobil, AAA, or other travel critics. Because stars have little relevance when awarded in the absence of recognized standards of comparison, we have tied our ratings to expected levels of quality established by specific American hotel corporations.

Room Star Ratings		
★★★★★	*Superior Rooms*	Tasteful and luxurious by any standard
★★★★	*Extremely Nice Rooms*	What you would expect at a Hyatt Regency or Marriott
★★★	*Nice Rooms*	Holiday Inn or comparable quality
★★	*Adequate Rooms*	Clean, comfortable, and functional without frills—like a Motel 6
★	*Super Budget*	

Star ratings apply *only to room quality* and describe the property's standard accommodations. For most hotels and motels, a standard accommodation is a hotel room with either one king bed or two queen beds. In an all-suite property, the standard accommodation is either a one- or two-room suite. In addition to standard accommodations, many hotels offer luxury rooms and special suites, which aren't rated in this guide. Star ratings for rooms are assigned without regard to whether a property has restaurant(s), recreational facilities, entertainment, or other extras.

In addition to stars (which delineate broad categories), we use a numerical rating system. Our rating scale is 0 to 100, with 100 as the best possible rating and zero (0) as the worst. Numerical ratings are presented to show the difference we perceive between one property and another. Rooms at The Villas at the Disney Institute, Buena Vista Suites, and Courtyard by Marriott (at the Disney Village Hotel Plaza) are all rated as three-and-a-half stars (★★★½). In the supplemental numerical ratings, The Villas are rated an 82, the Buena Vista Suites an 81, and the Courtyard a 76. This means that within the three-and-a-half-star category, The Villas at the Disney Institute and Buena Vista Suites are comparable, and both have slightly nicer rooms than the Courtyard.

The location column identifies the area around Walt Disney World where you will find a particular property. The designation "WDW" means that the property is inside Walt Disney World. A "1" means that the property is on or near International Drive. Properties on US 192 (a.k.a. Irlo Bronson Memorial Highway, Vine Street, and Space Coast Parkway) are indicated by a "3." All others are marked with "2" and for the most part are along the I-4 corridor, though some are in isolated locations that don't meet any other criteria.

Properties along US 192 also carry location designations with their names, such as the Holiday Inn Maingate East. The consensus in Orlando seems to be that the main entrance to Walt Disney World is the broad interstate-type road that runs off of US 192. This is called Maingate. Properties along US 192 call themselves Maingate East or West to differentiate their positions along the highway. So, driving southeast from Clermont or the Florida Turnpike, the properties before you reach the Maingate turnoff are called Maingate West, while the properties after you pass the Maingate turnoff are called Maingate East.

How the Hotels Compare

Cost estimates are based on the hotel's published rack rates for standard rooms. Each "$" represents $50. Thus a cost symbol of "$$$" means a room (or suite) at that hotel will be about $150 a night.

Here's a hit parade of the nicest rooms in town. We've focused strictly on room quality and excluded consideration of location, services, recreation, or amenities. In some instances, a one- or two-room suite is available for the same price or less than that of a hotel room.

If you have used an earlier edition of this guide, you'll notice that new properties have been added and many ratings and rankings have changed, some because of room renovation or improved maintenance and housekeeping. Failure to maintain guest rooms or lax housekeeping can bring down ratings.

Before you shop for a hotel, consider this letter we received from a man in Hot Springs, Arkansas:

> *We canceled our room reservations to follow the advice in your book [and reserved a hotel highly ranked by the* Unofficial Guide]. *We wanted inexpensive, but clean and cheerful. We got inexpensive, but [also] dirty, grim, and depressing. I really felt disappointed in your advice and the room. It was the pits. That was the one real piece of information I needed from your book! The room spoiled the holiday for me aside from our touring.*

This letter was as unsettling to us as the bad room was to our reader. Our integrity as travel journalists is based on the quality of the information we provide our readers. Even with the best of intentions and the most conscientious research, we can't inspect every room in every hotel. What we do, in statistical terms, is take a sample: we check several rooms selected at random in each hotel and base our ratings and rankings on those rooms. The inspections are conducted anonymously and without the knowledge of the property's management. Although unusual, it's certainly possible that the rooms we randomly inspect aren't representative of the majority of rooms. Another possibility is that the rooms we inspect in a hotel are representative, but by bad luck a reader is assigned an inferior room. When rechecking the hotel our reader disliked, we discovered our rating was correctly representative, but that he and his wife had unfortunately been assigned one of a small number of threadbare rooms scheduled for renovation.

The key to avoiding disappointment is to snoop in advance. Ask the hotel to send a photo of its standard guest room before you book, or at least get a copy of the hotel's promotional brochure. Be aware that some hotel chains use the same guest-room photo in promotional literature for *all* hotels in the chain and that the guest room in a specific property may not resemble the photo in the brochure. When your travel agent or you call, ask how old the property is and when the guest room you are being assigned was last renovated. If you arrive and are assigned a room inferior to that which you had been led to expect, demand to be moved.

How the Hotels Compare

Hotel	Location	Room Star Rating	Room Quality Rating	Cost $=$50	Phone (A/C 407)
WDW Grand Floridian Resort	WDW	★★★★★	96	$$$$$$$+	934-7639
WDW BoardWalk Villas	WDW	★★★★½	95	$$$$$$$–	934-7639
WDW Old Key West Resort	WDW	★★★★½	94	$$$$$$–	934-7639
Hotel Royal Plaza (tower rooms)	WDW	★★★★½	93	$$$$$$–	828-2828
Shades of Green	WDW	★★★★½	93	na	824-3400
WDW Boardwalk Inn	WDW	★★★★½	93	$$$$$$$–	934-7639
Marriott Orlando World Center	2	★★★★½	92	$$$$+	239-4200
WDW Beach Club Resort	WDW	★★★★½	92	$$$$$$$–	934-7639
WDW Yacht Club Resort	WDW	★★★★½	92	$$$$$$$–	934-7639
Peabody Orlando	1	★★★★½	91	$$$$$+	352-4000
Hyatt Regency Grand Cypress	2	★★★★½	90	$$$$$+	239-1234
WDW Polynesian Resort	WDW	★★★★½	90	$$$$$$$–	934-7639
Renaissance Orlando Resort	2	★★★★	89	$$$$$–	351-5555
Doubletree Guest Suites	WDW	★★★★	87	$$$$$–	934-1000
Hawthorne Suites Orlando	1	★★★★	87	$$$+	351-6600
WDW Contemporary Resort	WDW	★★★★	87	$$$$$$–	934-7639
Wyndham Royal Safari	2	★★★★	87	$$$	(800)423-3297

How the Hotels Compare (continued)

Hotel	Location	Room Star Rating	Room Quality Rating	Cost $=$50	Phone (A/C 407)
Embassy Suites Orlando International	1	★★★★	86	$$$$	352-1400
The Castle Hotel (Holiday Inn Sun Spree Resort)	1	★★★★	86	$$$$–	345-1511
WDW Coronado Springs Resort	WDW	★★★★	86	$$$+	934-7639
WDW Dolphin Resort	WDW	★★★★	86	$$$$$$$+	934-7639
WDW Swan	WDW	★★★★	86	$$$$$$$+	934-7639
WDW Wilderness Lodge	WDW	★★★★	86	$$$$$+	934-7639
Embassy Suites Resort	2	★★★★	85	$$$$$–	239-1144
Doubletree Orlando Suites & Villas	3	★★★★	84	$$$$$–	397-0555
Hilton Disney Village	WDW	★★★★	84	$$$$$$$–	827-4000
Homewood Suites Maingate	3	★★★★	84	$$$–	396-2229
WDW Caribbean Beach Resort	WDW	★★★★	84	$$$+	934-7639
WDW Dixie Landings Resort	WDW	★★★★	84	$$$+	934-7639
WDW Port Orleans Resort	WDW	★★★★	84	$$$+	934-7639
Buena Vista Palace	WDW	★★★★	83	$$$$	827-2727
Embassy Suites Plaza International	1	★★★★	83	$$$–	345-8250
WDW Villas at the Disney Institute (bungalows)	WDW	★★★½	82	$$$$$+	934-7639

How the Hotels Compare (continued)

Hotel	Location	Room Star Rating	Room Quality Rating	Cost $=$50	Phone (A/C 407)
Buena Vista Suites	1	★★★½	81	$$$+	239-8588
Clarion Plaza Hotel	1	★★★½	81	$$+	352-9700
Summerfield Suites	1	★★★½	81	$$$$$	352-2400
Caribe Royale Resort Suites	3	★★★½	80	$$$$–	238-8000
Holiday Inn Sun Spree Resort	2	★★★½	80	$$$–	239-4500
Omni Rosen Hotel	1	★★★½	80	$$$$$–	354-9840
Radisson Inn Lake Buena Vista	2	★★★½	80	$$$+	239-8400
Residence Inn Lake Cecile	3	★★★½	80	$$$–	396-2056
Radisson Resort Parkway	3	★★★½	79	$$$–	396-7000
Summerfield Suites Lake Buena Vista	2	★★★½	79	$$$$$	238-0777
WDW Fort Wilderness Resort		★★★½	79	$$$$$+	934-7639
Radisson Twin Towers Hotel	1	★★★½	78	$$$+	(800) 327-2110
Orlando Marriott	1	★★★½	77	$$$+	351-2420
Residence Inn Orlando	1	★★★½	77	$$$–	345-0117
RUI Orlando	2	★★★½	77	$$$–	239-8500
Courtyard by Marriott	1	★★★½	76	$$$–	351-2244
Grosvenor Resort	WDW	★★★½	76	$$$–	828-4444
Holiday Inn Suites Maingate East	3	★★★½	76	$$$$$+	396-4488
Radisson Barcelo Inn International	1	★★★½	76	$$+	345-0505
Courtyard Disney Village	WDW	★★★½	75	$$$$–	828-8888
Courtyard Maingate	3	★★★½	75	$$$–	396-4000
Hyatt Orlando	3	★★★	74	$$$+	396-1234
Quality Suites International Drive	1	★★★	74	$$+	363-0332
Ramada Plaza and Inn Gateway (tower rooms)	3	★★★	74	$$$–	396-4400

How the Hotels Compare (continued)

Hotel	Location	Room Star Rating	Room Quality Rating	Cost $=$50	Phone (A/C 407)
Sheraton World Resort	1	★★★	74	$$$+	352-1100
La Quinta Inn Int'l	1	★★★	73	$$–	351-1660
Quality Suites Maingate East	3	★★★	73	$$$+	396-8040
WDW All Star Resort	WDW	★★★	73	$$+	934-7639
Westgate Lakes	2	★★★	73	$$$$$$	352-8051
Enclave Suites	1	★★★	72	$$$$–	351-1155
Nikki Bird Resort	3	★★★	72	$$$–	396-7300
Wellesley Inn	1	★★★	72	$$	345-0026
Country Hearth Inn	1	★★★	71	$$$–	352-0008
Holiday Inn International Resort	1	★★★	71	$$+	351-3500
Travelodge Maingate East	3	★★★	71	$$	396-4222
Days Suites Maingate East	3	★★★	70	$$$+	396-7900
Holiday Inn Express	1	★★★	70	$$$–	351-4430
Holiday Inn Hotel Maingate East	3	★★★	70	$$$$	396-4488
Holiday Inn Universal Studios	1	★★★	70	$$$+	351-3333
The Universal Tower Resort Hotel	1	★★★	70	$$–	351-2100
Travelodge Hotel Disney Village	WDW	★★★	70	$$$+	828-2424
Comfort Suites Orlando	2	★★★	69	$$+	351-5050
Ramada Resort Maingate	3	★★★	69	$$$	396-4466
Travelodge Suites Eastgate	3	★★★	69	$$+	396-7666
Hampton Inn International Drive	1	★★★	68	$$	345-1112
Hampton Inn Maingate	3	★★★	68	$$–	396-8484

How the Hotels Compare (continued)

Hotel	Location	Room Star Rating	Room Quality Rating	Cost $=$50	Phone (A/C 407)
Hampton Inn Sandlake	1	★★★	68	$$	363-7886
Hampton Inn Universal Studios	1	★★★	68	$$–	351-6716
Hotel Royal Plaza (garden rooms)	WDW	★★★	68	$$$$$	828-2828
Sheraton Lakeside Inn	3	★★★	68	$$$	396-2222
Days Inn Lake Buena Vista	2	★★★	67	$$–	239-4441
Ramada Resort Florida Center	1	★★★	67	$$$–	351-4600
Westgate Towers	3	★★★	67	$$$$	396-2500
Days Inn Maingate West	3	★★★	66	$$$–	396-1000
Wilson World Maingate	3	★★★	66	$$	396-6000
Club Hotel by Doubletree	2	★★★	65	$$+	239-4646
Holiday Inn Maingate West	3	★★★	65	$$$–	396-1100
Howard Johnson Park Square	2	★★★	65	$$$–	239-6900
MIC Lakefront Inn	1	★★★	65	$$–	345-5340
Best Western Plaza International	1	★★½	64	$$–	345-8195
Days Inn Orlando Lakeside	1	★★½	64	$$–	351-1900
Delta Orlando Resort	1	★★½	64	$$+	351-3340
Floridian of Orlando	1	★★½	64	$$+	351-5009
Howard Johnson Maingate West	3	★★½	64	$$–	396-9300
Howard Johnson Resort Hotel	3	★★½	64	$$–	396-4343
Quality Inn Lake Cecile	3	★★½	64	$$–	396-4455
Days Inn Eastgate	3	★★½	63	$+	396-7700
Howard Johnson South Int'l Drive	1	★★½	63	$$–	351-5100

How the Hotels Compare (continued)

Hotel	Location	Room Star Rating	Room Quality Rating	Cost $=$50	Phone (A/C 407)
Inns of America International	1	★★½	63	$$–	(800) 826-0778
Best Western Maingate	3	★★½	62	$$–	396-0100
Days Inn	3	★★½	62	$$–	(800) 544-5713
Days Inn Universal Studios	1	★★½	62	$$–	351-3800
Larson's Lodge Maingate	3	★★½	62	$+	396-6100
Quality Inn Plaza	1	★★½	62	$$–	345-8585
Ramada Inn Westgate	3	★★½	62	$$–	(941) 424-2621
Red Roof Inn Kissimmee	3	★★½	62	$$–	396-0065
Wynfield Inn Westwood	1	★★½	62	$$+	(800) 346-1551
Days Inn Sea World/ Convention Center	1	★★½	61	$$	352-8700
Fairfield Inn International	1	★★½	61	$$–	363-1944
Howard Johnson Inn Maingate East	3	★★½	61	$$–	396-1748
Quality Inn International	1	★★½	61	$$–	351-1600
Ramada Limited Universal Maingate	1	★★½	61	$$–	354-3996
Ramada Plaza and Inn Gateway (garden rooms)	3	★★½	61	$$–	396-4400
Best Western Eastgate	3	★★½	60	$$–	396-0707
Comfort Inn at Lake Buena Vista	2	★★½	60	$$–	239-7300
Econo Lodge Maingate Hawaiian	3	★★½	60	$$–	396-2000
Howard Johnson Express Inn and Suites	3	★★½	60	$$–	396-4762
Las Palmas Hotel	1	★★½	60	$$+	351-3900
Quality Inn Maingate West	3	★★½	60	$$–	396-1828
Wynfield Inn Maingate	3	★★½	60	$$+	(800) 346-1551

		Room Star	Room Quality	Cost	Phone
How the Hotels Compare (continued)					
Hotel	Location	Rating	Rating	$=$50	(A/C 407)
Ramada Eastgate Fountain Park	3	★★½	59	$$–	396-1111
Sleep Inn Maingate	3	★★½	59	$$–	396-1600
Super 8 Maingate	3	★★½	59	$$	396-8883
Howard Johnson Lodge	1	★★½	58	$$$+	351-2900
Red Roof Inn Orlando	1	★★½	58	$$–	352-1507
Comfort Inn Maingate	3	★★½	57	$$	396-7500
Econo Lodge International	1	★★½	57	$$–	(800) 327-0750
Magic Castle, The	3	★★½	57	$+	396-2212
Motel 6 Maingate East	3	★★½	57	$–	396-6333
Travelodge Suites	3	★★½	57	$$$$	396-1780
Economy Inns of America	3	★★½	56	$+	396-4020
Inns of America Maingate	3	★★½	56	$+	(800) 826-0778
Kissimmee Super 8 Motel	3	★★½	56	$$	396-1144
Riande Continental Plaza	1	★★½	56	$+	352-8211
Super 8 Universal	1	★★½	56	$+	352-8383
Knights Inn Maingate	3	★★	55	$$+	396-4200
Rodeway Inn International	1	★★	55	$+	351-4444
Golden Link Motel	3	★★	54	$$–	396-0555
Days Inn International Drive	1	★★	53	$$+	351-1200
Days Inn Maingate East	3	★★	53	$$$+	396-7900
La Suite Inn & Suites	1	★★	53	$$	351-4410
Park Inn International	3	★★	53	$$–	396-1376
Knights Inn Maingate East	3	★★	52	$$–	396-8186
Motel 6 Maingate West	3	★★	52	$–	396-6427
Traveler's Inn	3	★★	52	$$+	396-1668
Universal Inn	1	★★	52	$$	351-4100
Central Motel	3	★★	51	$$–	396-2333

How the Hotels Compare (continued)

Hotel	Location	Room Star Rating	Room Quality Rating	Cost $=$50	Phone (A/C 407)
Gateway Inn	1	★★	51	$+	351-2000
Red Carpet Inn East	3	★★	50	$+	396-1133
Motel 6 International Drive	1	★★	49	$−	351-6500
Monte Carlo	3	★★	48	$$−	396-4700
Sun Motel	3	★½	46	$+	396-2673

THE TOP 30 BEST DEALS

Having listed the nicest rooms in town, let's take a look at the best combinations of quality and value in a room. As before, the rankings are made without consideration of location or the availability of restaurant(s), recreational facilities, entertainment, and/or amenities.

A reader recently wrote us to complain that he had booked one of our top-ranked rooms in terms of value and had been very disappointed in the room. We noticed that the room the reader occupied had a quality rating of ★★½. We would remind you that the list of top deals are intended to give you some sense of value received for dollars spent. A ★★½ room at $30 may have the same value as a ★★★★ room at $85, but that does not mean the rooms will be of comparable quality. Regardless of whether it's a good deal or not, a ★★½ room is still a ★★½ room.

You will note the small number of Disney hotels on the best-deal list. This is because our ratings focus exclusively on the quality of the guest room. For most people, however, the guest room is only a small part of what they are buying when they book a Disney hotel. For the sake of consistency, the extra convenience, service, and amenities associated with the Disney resorts are necessarily excluded from our comparison. If you factor in these extras, of course, the rates charged at the Disney hotels appear to many to be a fair value for the money.

Listed below are the top 30 room buys for the money, regardless of location or star classification, based on average rack rates. Note that a suite can sometimes cost less than a hotel room.

The Top 30 Best Deals

Hotel	Location	Room Star Rating	Room Quality Rating	Cost $=$50	Phone (A/C 407)
1. Motel 6 Maingate East	3	★★½	57	$–	396-6333
2. Homewood Suites Maingate	3	★★★★	84	$$$–	396-2229
3. Hampton Inn Universal Studios	1	★★★	68	$$–	351-6716
4. Clarion Plaza Hotel	1	★★★½	81	$$+	352-9700
5. Motel 6 International Drive	1	★★	49	$–	351-6500
6. La Quinta Inn Int'l	1	★★★	73	$$–	351-1660
7. Radisson Barcelo Inn International	1	★★★½	76	$$+	345-0505
8. Motel 6 Maingate West	3	★★	52	$–	396-6427
9. The Universal Tower Resort Hotel	1	★★★	70	$$–	351-2100
10. Economy Inns of America	3	★★½	56	$+	396-4020
11. Days Inn Eastgate	3	★★½	63	$+	396-7700
12. Days Inn Lake Buena Vista	2	★★★	67	$$–	239-4441
13. Larson's Lodge Maingate	3	★★½	62	$+	396-6100
14. Wellesley Inn	1	★★★	72	$$	345-0026
15. RUI Orlando	2	★★★½	77	$$$–	239-8500
16. Residence Inn Lake Cecile	3	★★★½	80	$$$–	396-2056
17. Inns of America Maingate	3	★★½	56	$+	(800) 826-0778
18. Riande Continental Plaza	1	★★½	56	$+	352-8211
19. WDW Coronado Springs Resort	WDW	★★★★	86	$$$+	934-7639
20. WDW All Star Resort	WDW	★★★	73	$$+	934-7639

The Top 30 Best Deals

Hotel	Location	Room Star Rating	Room Quality Rating	Cost $=$50	Phone (A/C 407)
21. Days Inn Orlando Lakeside	1	★★½	64	$$–	351-1900
22. Travelodge Maingate East	3	★★★	71	$$	396-4222
23. Radisson Resort Parkway	3	★★★½	79	$$$–	396-7000
24. Hawthorne Suites Orlando	1	★★★★	87	$$$+	351-6600
25. Hampton Inn Maingate	3	★★★	68	$$–	396-8484
26. WDW Caribbean Beach Resort	WDW	★★★★	84	$$$+	934-7639
27. WDW Dixie Landings Resort	WDW	★★★★	84	$$$+	934-7639
28. WDW Port Orleans Resort	WDW	★★★★	84	$$$+	934-7639
29. Inns of America International	1	★★½	63	$$–	(800) 826-0778
30. Holiday Inn Sun Spree Resort	2	★★★½	80	$$$–	239-4500

Part Four

Walt Disney World with Kids

The Ecstasy and the Agony

So overwhelming is the Disney media and advertising presence that any child who watches TV or shops with Mom is likely to get revved up about going to Walt Disney World. Parents, if anything, are even more susceptible. Almost every parent has brightened with anticipation at the prospect of guiding their children through the wonders of this special place. But the reality of taking a young child (particularly in summer) is usually closer to the agony than the ecstasy.

A mother from Dayton, Ohio, describes taking her five-year-old to Disney World in July:

> I felt so happy and excited before we went. I guess it was all worth it, but when I look back I think I should have had my head examined. The first day we went to [the Magic Kingdom] and it was packed. By 11 in the morning we had walked so far and stood in so many lines that we were all exhausted. Kristy cried about going on anything that looked or even sounded scary and was frightened by all of the Disney characters (they are so big!) except Minnie and Snow White.
>
> We got hungry about the same time as everyone else but the lines for food were too long and my husband said we would have to wait. By one in the afternoon we were just plugging along, not seeing anything we were really interested in, but picking rides because the lines were short, or because whatever it was was air-conditioned. We rode Small World three times in a row and I'll never get that song out of my head (Ha!). At around 2:30 we finally got something to eat, but by then we were so hot and tired that it felt like we had worked in the yard all day. Kristy insisted on being carried and we had 50 fights about not going on rides where the lines were too long. At the end, we were so P.O.'d

and uncomfortable that we weren't having any fun. Mostly by this time we were just trying to get our money's worth.

Before you stiffen in denial, let me assure you that the Ohio family's experience is fairly typical. Most young children are as picky about the rides as they are about what they eat, and more than half of preschoolers are intimidated by the friendly Disney characters. Few humans (of any age) are mentally or physically equipped to march all day in a throng of 50,000 people in the hot Florida sun. And would you be surprised to learn that almost 60% of preschoolers said the thing they liked best about their Disney World vacation was the hotel swimming pool?

Reality Testing—Whose Dream Is It?

Remember when you were little and you got that nifty electric train for Christmas, the one Dad wouldn't let you play with? Did you ever wonder who that train was really for? Ask yourself the same question about your vacation to Walt Disney World. Whose dream are you trying to make come true: yours or your child's?

Young children are adept at reading their parents' emotions. When you ask, "Honey, how would you like to go to Disney World?" your child will respond more to your smile and excitement and the idea of doing something with Mom and Dad than to any notion of what Disney World is all about. The younger the child, the more this is true. For many preschoolers, you could elicit the same enthusiasm by asking, "Honey, how would you like to go to Cambodia on a dogsled?"

So, is your happy fantasy of introducing your child to Disney magic a pipe dream? Not necessarily, but you have to be practical and open to reality testing. For example, would you increase the probability of a happy, successful visit by waiting a couple of years? Is your child adventuresome enough to sample the variety of Disney World? Will your child have sufficient endurance and patience to cope with long lines and large crowds?

RECOMMENDATIONS FOR MAKING THE DREAM COME TRUE

When considering a Disney World vacation with young children, consider:

Age Although the color and festivity of Disney World excite all children and specific attractions delight toddlers and preschoolers, Disney entertainment is generally oriented to older children and adults. Children should be a fairly mature seven years old to *appreciate* the Magic Kingdom and the Animal Kingdom, and a year or two older to get much out of Epcot or Disney-MGM Studios.

Time of Year to Visit Avoid the hot, crowded summer months, especially if you have preschoolers. Go in October, November (except Thanksgiving), early December, January, February, or April (except Easter). If you have children of varied ages and they're good students, take the older ones out of school and visit during the cooler, less-congested off-season. Arrange special assignments relating to the educational aspects of Disney World. If your children can't afford to miss school, take your vacation as soon as the school year ends in late May or early June. Nothing, repeat, nothing will enhance your Walt Disney World vacation as much as avoiding summer and holiday periods.

Build Naps and Rest into Your Itinerary The theme parks are huge; don't try to see everything in one day. Tour in early morning and return to your hotel around 11:30 a.m. for lunch, a swim, and a nap. Even during off-season when the crowds are smaller and the temperature more pleasant, the size of the major theme parks will exhaust most children under age eight by lunchtime. Return to the park in late afternoon or early evening and continue touring. A family from Texas underlines the importance of naps and rest:

Despite not following any of your "tours," we did follow the theme of visiting a specific park in the morning, leaving midafternoon for either a nap back at the room or a trip to the Dixie Landings pool, and then returning to one of the parks in the evening. On the few occasions when we skipped your advice, I was muttering to myself by dinner. I can't tell you what I was muttering. . . .

When it comes to naps, this mom does not mince words:

One last thing for parents of small kids—take the book's advice and get out of the park and take the nap, take the nap, TAKE THE NAP! Never in my life have I seen so many parents screaming at, ridiculing, or slapping their kids. (What a vacation!) WDW is overwhelming for kids and adults. Even though the rental strollers recline for sleeping, we noticed that most of the toddlers and preschoolers didn't give up and sleep until 5 p.m., several hours after the fun had worn off, and right about the time their parents wanted them to be awake and polite in a restaurant.

A mom from Rochester, New York, was equally adamant:

[You] absolutely must rest during the day. Kids went from 8 a.m. to 9 p.m. in the Magic Kingdom. Kids did great that day, but we were all completely worthless the next day. Definitely must pace yourself. Don't ever try to do two full days of park sight-seeing in a row. Rest during the day. Go to a water park or sleep in every other day.

If you plan to return to your hotel in midday and would like your room made up, let housekeeping know.

Where to Stay   The time and hassle involved in commuting to and from the theme parks will be lessened if you can afford to stay in the World. But even if you lodge outside, it's imperative that you take young children out of the parks each day for a few hours of rest. Neglecting to relax is the best way we know to get the whole family in a snit and ruin the day (or the vacation).

If you have young children, you must plan ahead. Make sure your hotel is within 20 minutes of the theme parks. Naps and relief from the frenetic pace of the theme parks, even during off-season, are indispensable. It's true you can revive somewhat by retreating to a Disney hotel for lunch or by finding a quiet restaurant in the theme parks, but there's no substitute for returning to the familiarity and comfort of your own hotel. Regardless of what you have heard, children too large to sleep in a stroller won't relax unless you take them back to your hotel.

Thousands of new rooms have been built in and near Disney World, many of them affordable. With sufficient lead time, you should have no difficulty finding accommodations that meet your requirements.

If you are traveling with children age 12 and younger, we recommend the Polynesian, Grand Floridian, or Wilderness Lodge resorts (in that order) if they fit your budget. For less expensive rooms, try the Dixie Landings, Port Orleans, or Caribbean Beach resorts. Bargain accommodations are available at the All-Star resorts. Fully equipped trailers and pre-fab log cabins at Fort Wilderness Campground are also good economy lodging.

Outside of Walt Disney World, an Atlanta mom recommends the Castle DoubleTree, commenting:

> *This is the perfect place to stay for a great value for kids. Your book glides over it, but it has on-site childcare for $1 an hour, pizza on the premises, a video arcade, a kid's dining room, and kitchens in the rooms, all for $75 a night. More for a kid's suite or breakfast. We'd definitely go back. The room was very spacious and quiet.*

Be in Touch with Your Feelings   When you or your children get tired and irritable, call time out and regroup. Trust your instincts. What would feel best? Another ride, an ice cream break, or going back to the room for a nap?

The way to protect your considerable investment in your Disney vacation is to stay happy and have a good time. You don't have to meet a quota for experiencing attractions. Do what you want.

Least Common Denominators   Somebody is going to run out of steam first, and when they do the whole family will be affected. Sometimes a snack break will revive the flagging member. Sometimes, however, as Marshall Dillon would say: Get out of Dodge. Pushing the tired or discontented beyond their capacity will spoil the day for them—and you. Accept that energy levels vary and be prepared to respond to members of your group who poop out. *Hint:* "We've driven a thousand miles to take you to Walt Disney World and now you're going to ruin everything!" is not an appropriate response.

Building Endurance   Though most children are active, their normal play usually doesn't condition them for the exertion required to tour a Disney theme park. We recommend starting a program of family walks four to six weeks before your trip to get in shape. A mother from Wesconsville, Pennsylvania, reports:

We had our six-year-old begin walking with us a bit every day one month before leaving—when we arrived [at Walt Disney World], her little legs could carry her and she had a lot of stamina.

Setting Limits and Making Plans   Avoid arguments and disappointment by establishing guidelines for each day, and get everybody committed. Include:

1. Wake-up time and breakfast plans.
2. When to depart for the park.
3. What to take with you.
4. A policy for splitting the group or for staying together.
5. What to do if the group gets separated or someone is lost.
6. How long you intend to tour in the morning and what you want to see, including plans in the event an attraction is closed or too crowded.
7. A policy on what you can afford for snacks.
8. A time for returning to the hotel to rest.
9. When you will return to the park and how late you will stay.
10. Dinner plans.
11. A policy for buying souvenirs, including who pays: Mom and Dad or the kids.
12. Determination of bedtimes.

Be Flexible   Any day at Walt Disney World includes some surprises; be prepared to adjust your plan. Listen to your intuition.

About the *Unofficial Guide* Touring Plans   Parents who adopt one of our touring plans are often frustrated by interruptions and delays caused by their young children. Here's what to expect:

1. Character encounters can wreak havoc with the touring plans. Many young children will stop in their tracks whenever they see a Disney character. Attempting to haul your child away before he has satisfied his curiosity is likely to cause anything from whining to a full-scale revolt. Our advice is to either go with the flow or set aside a certain morning or afternoon for photos and autographs. Be aware, however, that queues for autographs, especially in Toontown at the Magic Kingdom and Camp Minnie-Mickey at the Animal Kingdom, are every bit as long as the queues for major attractions.

2. Our touring plans call for visiting attractions in a sequence, often skipping attractions along the way. Children don't like skipping anything! If something attracts them, they want to see it that moment. Some children can be persuaded to skip attractions if parents explain their plans in advance. Other kids flip out at skipping something, particularly in Fantasyland. A mom from Charleston, South Carolina, writes:

> We did not have too much trouble following the touring plans at [Disney-]MGM and at Epcot. The Magic Kingdom plan, on the other hand, turned out to be a train wreck. The main problem with the plan is that it starts in Fantasyland. When we were on Dumbo, my five-year-old saw eight dozen other things in Fantasyland she wanted to see. The long and the short is that after Dumbo, there was no getting her out of there.

A mother of two from Burlington, Vermont, adds:

> I found out that my kids were very curious about the castle because we had read Cinderella at home. Whenever I wanted to leave Fantasyland, I would just say, "Let's go to the castle and see if Cinderella is there." Once we got as far as the front door to the castle, it was no problem going out to the [central] hub and then to another land.

3. Children have an instinct for finding rest rooms. We have seen adults with maps search interminably for a rest room. Young children, on the other hand, including those who can't read, will head for the nearest rest room with the certainty of a homing pigeon. You can be sure your children will ferret out (and want to use) every rest room in the theme park.

4. If you are using a stroller, you won't be able to take it into attractions or onto rides. This applies to rides such as the Walt Disney World Railroad that are included in the touring plans as in-park transportation.

5. You probably won't finish the touring plan. Varying hours of operation, crowd levels, the size of your group, the ages of your children, and your stamina will all affect how much of the plan you will complete. Unless you tailor your expectations to this reality, you're likely to experience the frustration expressed by this mother of two from Nazareth, Pennsylvania:

> We do not understand how anyone could fit everything you have on your plans into the time allotted while attending to small children. We found that long lines, potty stops, diaper changes, stroller searches, and autograph breaks ate huge chunks of time. And we were there during the off-season.

While our touring plans will allow you to make the most of your time at the theme parks, it's impossible to define what "most" will be. It differs from family to family. If you have two young children, you probably won't see as much as will two adults. If you have four children, you probably won't see as much as will a couple with only two children.

Overheating, Sunburn, and Dehydration   These are the most common problems of younger children at Disney World. Carry and use sunscreen. Be sure to put some on children in strollers, even if the stroller has a canopy. Some of the worst cases of sunburn we've seen were on the exposed foreheads and feet of toddlers and infants in strollers. Protect skin from overexposure. To avoid overheating, rest regularly in the shade or in an air-conditioned restaurant or show.

Don't count on keeping young children hydrated with soft drinks and stops at water fountains. Long lines may hamper buying refreshments, and fountains may not be handy. Further, excited children may not realize or tell you that they're thirsty or hot. We recommend renting a stroller for children age six and younger and carrying plastic bottles of water. Plastic squeeze bottles with caps are sold in all major parks for about $3.

Blisters and Sore Feet   Guests of all ages should wear comfortable, well-broken-in shoes and two pairs of thin socks (better than one pair of thick socks). If you or your children are susceptible to blisters, precut Moleskin bandages. They offer the best protection, stick great, and won't sweat off. When you feel a hot spot, stop, air out your foot, and place a Moleskin bandage over the area before a blister forms. Moleskin is available by name at all drug stores. Young children may not tell their parents about a developing blister until it's too late, so inspect the feet of preschoolers two or more times a day.

First Aid   Each major theme park has a first-aid center. In the Magic Kingdom, it's next to the Crystal Palace at the end of Main Street. At Epcot, it's on the World Showcase side of the Odyssey Center. At Disney-MGM, it's in the Guest Relations Building just inside the main entrance. At Animal Kingdom, it's in Safari Village. If you or your children have a medical problem, go to a first-aid center. Disney first-aid centers are warmer and friendlier than most doctor's offices and are accustomed to treating everything from paper cuts to allergic reactions.

Children on Medication   Some parents of hyperactive children on medication discontinue or decrease the child's normal dosage at the end of the school year. If you have such a child, be aware that Disney World might overly stimulate him/her. Consult your physician before altering your child's medication regimen.

Sunglasses   If you want your younger children to wear sunglasses, put a strap or string on the frames so that the glasses will stay on during rides and can hang from the child's neck while indoors.

Things You Forgot or Things You Ran Out Of   Rain gear, diapers, diaper pins, formula, film, aspirin, topical sunburn treatments, and other sundries are sold at all the major theme parks and at Typhoon Lagoon, Blizzard Beach, River Country, and Downtown Disney. Rain gear is a bargain, but most other items are high. A good place to find diapers is at the Baby Centers—two diapers plus ointment are $3.50. Ask for goods you don't see displayed.

Infants and Toddlers at the Theme Parks   The major theme parks have centralized facilities for infant and toddler care. Everything necessary for changing diapers, preparing formulas, and warming bottles and food is available. Baby supplies are for sale, and there are rockers and special chairs for nursing mothers. At the Magic Kingdom, the Baby Center is next to the Crystal Palace at the end of Main Street. At Epcot, Baby Services is near the Odyssey Center, right of the Test Track in Future World. At Disney-MGM Studios, Baby Care is in the Guest Relations Building left of the entrance. At the Animal Kingdom, Baby Changing/Nursing is in Safari Village in the center of the park. Dads in charge of little ones are welcome at the centers and can use most services offered. In addition, many men's rooms in the major theme parks have changing tables.

Infants and toddlers are allowed to experience any attraction that doesn't have minimum height or age restrictions. But as a Minneapolis mother reports, some attractions are better for babies than others:

> Theater and boat rides are easier for babies (ours was almost one year old, not yet walking). Rides where there's a bar that comes down are doable, but harder. Peter Pan was our first encounter with this type, and we had barely gotten situated when I realized he might fall out of my grasp. The standing auditorium films are too intense; the noise level is deafening, and the images unescapable. You don't have a rating system for babies, and I don't expect to see one, but I thought you might want to know what a baby thought (based on his reactions). [At the Magic Kingdom:] Jungle Cruise—Didn't get into it. Pirates— Slept through it. Riverboat—While at Aunt Polly's, the horn made him cry. Aunt Polly's—Ate the chicken while watching the birds in relative quiet. Small World—Wide-eyed, took it all in. Peter Pan— Couldn't really sit on the seat. A bit dangerous. He didn't get into it. Carousel of Progress—Long talks; hard to keep him quiet; danced during song. The Timekeeper—Too loud. Dinosaur at beginning scared him. WDW RR—Liked the motion and scenery. Tiki Birds—Loved it. Danced, clapped, sang along. At Epcot: Honey, I Shrunk the Audience—We skipped due to recommendation of Disney worker that

it got too loud and adults screamed throughout. Journey into Imagination—Loved it. Tried to catch things with his hands. Bounced up and down, chortled. The Land—Watchful, quiet during presentation. Food Rocks—Loved it, danced. El Río del Tiempo—Loved it.

The same mom also advises:

We used a baby sling on our trip and thought it was great when standing in the lines—much better than a stroller, which you have to park before getting in line (and navigate through crowds). The food at WDW [includes] almost nothing a baby can eat. No fruits or vegetables. My baby was still nursing when we went to WDW. The only really great place I found to nurse in MK was a hidden bench in the shade in Adventureland in between the freezee stand (next to Tiki Birds) and the small shops. It is impractical to go to the baby station every time, so a nursing mom better be comfortable about nursing in very public situations.

Strollers are available for a modest daily fee at all four major theme parks. If you rent a stroller at the Magic Kingdom and decide to go to Epcot, the Animal Kingdom, or Disney-MGM Studios, turn in your Magic Kingdom stroller and present your receipt at the next park. You'll be issued another stroller without additional charge.

Strollers at the Magic Kingdom, the Animal Kingdom, and Epcot are large, sturdy models with sun canopies. We have seen families load as many as three children at once in one of these. Strollers at Disney-MGM Studios are the light, collapsible type. Strollers can be obtained to the right of the entrance at the Magic Kingdom, to the left of the Entrance Plaza at Epcot, and at Oscar's Super Service just inside the entrance of Disney-MGM Studios. Stroller rentals at the Animal Kingdom are just inside the entrance and to the right. Rental at all parks is fast and efficient, and returning the stroller is a breeze. Even at Epcot, where as many as 900 strollers are turned in after the evening fireworks, there's almost no wait or hassle. If you don't mind forfeiting your dollar deposit, you can ditch your rental stroller anywhere in the park when you're ready to leave.

When you enter a show or board a ride, you must park your stroller, usually in an open, unprotected area. If it rains before you return, you'll need a cloth, towel, or diaper to dry it.

Strollers are a must for infants and toddlers, but we have observed many sharp parents renting strollers for somewhat older children (up to five or so years old). The stroller prevents parents from having to carry children when they sag and provides a convenient place to carry water and snacks.

If you go to your hotel for a break and intend to return to the park, leave your rental stroller by an attraction near the entrance, marking it with something personal like a bandanna. When you return after your break, your stroller will be waiting for you.

It's permissible to bring your own stroller from home. Remember, however, that only collapsible strollers are permitted on monorails and buses. Your stroller is unlikely to be stolen, but mark it with your name.

Also, be aware that rental strollers are too large for all infants and many toddlers. If you plan to rent a stroller for your infant or toddler, bring along some pillows, cushions, or rolled towels to buttress him in. A mother of two from Falls Church, Virginia, advocates taking your own stroller:

> *I was glad I took my own stroller, because the rented strollers aren't appropriate for infants. (We had a five-year-old and a five-month-old in tow.) No one at the Magic Kingdom said anything about my using a bike lock to secure our brand-new Aprica stroller. However, at [Disney] MGM, an attendent came over and told us not to lock it anywhere, because it's a fire hazard! (Outside?) When I politely asked the attendant if she wanted to be responsible for my $300 stroller, she told me to go ahead and lock it but not tell anyone! I observed the attendants at Magic Kingdom and [Disney-]MGM constantly moving the strollers. This seems very confusing—no wonder people think their strollers are getting ripped off!*

Stroller Wars   Sometimes strollers disappear while you're enjoying a ride or show. Disney cast members (employees) often will rearrange strollers parked outside an attraction. Sometimes this is done to "tidy up." At other times, strollers are moved to clear a walkway. Don't assume your stroller has been stolen because it isn't where you left it. It may be "neatly arranged" a few feet away.

Sometimes, however, strollers are taken by mistake or ripped off by people not wanting to spend time replacing one that's missing. Don't be alarmed if yours disappears. You won't have to buy the missing stroller, and you'll be issued a new one for your continued use. In the Magic Kingdom, replacements are available at Tinker Bell's Treasures in Fantasyland, at Merchant of Venus in Tomorrowland, and at the main rental facility near the park entrance. At Epcot, get replacements at the Entrance Plaza rental headquarters and at the International Gateway (in World Showcase between the United Kingdom and France). Strollers at Disney-MGM can be replaced at Oscar's Super Service and at Endor Vendors near Star Tours. In the Animal Kingdom, stroller replacements are available at Garden Gate Gifts and Mombasa Marketplace.

While replacing a stroller is no big deal, it's inconvenient. A family from Minnesota complained that their stroller had been taken six times in one day at Epcot and five times in a day at Disney-MGM Studios. Even with free replacements, larceny on this scale represents a lot of wasted time. Through our own experiments and readers' suggestions, we have developed techniques for hanging on to a rented stroller: Affix something personal (but expendable) to the handle. Evidently, most strollers are pirated by mistake (they all look alike) or because it's easier to swipe someone else's stroller than to replace one when it disappears. Since most stroller "theft" results from confusion or laziness, the average pram pincher will hesitate to haul off a stroller bearing another person's property. After trying several items, we concluded that a bright, inexpensive scarf or bandanna tied to the handle works well. A sock partially stuffed with rags or paper works even better (the weirder and more personal the object, the greater the deterrent). Best of all might be an Ann Arbor, Michigan, mother's strategy:

> We used a variation on your stroller identification theme. We tied a clear plastic bag with a diaper in it on the stroller. Jon even poured a little root beer on the diaper for effect. Needless to say, no one took our stroller and it was easy to identify.

Strollers As Lethal Weapons   A father of one from Purcellville, Virginia, wrote complaining about how inconsiderate some parents are:

> The biggest problem is surviving the migrating herds of strollers. The drivers of these contraptions appear to believe they have the right-of-way in all situations and use the strollers as battering rams to enforce their perceived right. I know they will not be banned from the parks, but how about putting speed governors on these things?

In fact, you would be amazed at how many people are injured by strollers pushed by parents who are driving aggressively, in a hurry, or in the ozone. Though you may desire to use your stroller as a battering ram or to wedge through crowds like Moses parting the seas, think twice. It's very un-Disney to steamroll other guests.

Lost Children

Although it's amazingly easy to lose a child (or two) in the theme parks, it usually isn't a serious problem. All Disney employees are schooled in handling the situation. If you lose a child in the Magic Kingdom, report it to a Disney employee, then check at the Baby Center and at City Hall where lost-children "logs" are kept. At Epcot, report the loss, then check at Baby Services near the Odyssey Center. At Disney-MGM Studios, report the loss at the Guest Relations Building at the entrance end of Hollywood Boulevard. At Animal Kingdom, go to the Baby Center in Safari Village. Paging isn't used, but in an emergency an "all-points bulletin" can be issued throughout the park(s) via internal communications. If a Disney employee encounters a lost child, he or she will take the child immediately to the park's guest relations center or its baby-care center.

We suggest that children younger than eight be color-coded by dressing them in purple T-shirts or equally distinctive clothes. It's also smart to sew a label into each child's shirt that states his name, your name, and the name of your hotel. The same thing can be accomplished by writing the information on a strip of masking tape. Hotel security professionals suggest the information be printed in small letters and the tape be affixed to the outside of the child's shirt, five inches below the armpit. Also, special name tags can be obtained at the major theme parks.

How Kids Get Lost

Children get separated from their parents every day at Disney parks under remarkably similar (and predictable) circumstances:

1. Preoccupied Solo Parent In this situation, the party's only adult is preoccupied with something like buying refreshments, loading the camera, or using the rest room. Junior is there one second and gone the next.

2. The Hidden Exit Sometimes parents wait on the sidelines while two or more young children experience a ride together. Parents expect the kids to exit in one place and, lo and behold, the youngsters pop out somewhere else. Exits from some attractions are distant from the entrances. Make sure you know exactly where your children will emerge before letting them ride by themselves.

3. After the Show At the end of many shows and rides, a Disney staffer will announce, "Check for personal belongings and take small children by the hand." When dozens, if not hundreds, of people leave an attraction simultaneously, it's easy for parents to lose contact with their children unless they have them directly in tow.

4. Rest Room Problems Mom tells six-year-old Tommy, "I'll be sitting on this bench when you come out of the rest room." Three possibilities: One, Tommy exits through a different door and becomes disoriented (Mom may not know there *is* another door). Two, Mom decides she also will use the rest room, and Tommy emerges to find her gone. Three, Mom pokes around in a shop while keeping an eye on the bench, but misses Tommy when he comes out.

If you can't be with your child in the rest room, make sure there's only one exit. The rest room on a passageway between Frontierland and Adventureland in the Magic Kingdom is the all-time worst for disorienting visitors. Children and adults alike have walked in from the Adventureland side and walked out on the Frontierland side (and vice versa). Adults realize quickly that something is wrong. Young children, however, sometimes fail to recognize the problem. Designate a meeting spot more distinctive than a bench, and be thorough in your instructions: "I'll meet you by this flagpole. If you get out first, stay right here." Have your child repeat the directions back to you.

5. Parades There are many parades and shows at which the audience stands. Children tend to jockey for a better view. By moving a little this way and that, the child quickly puts distance between you and him before either of you notices.

6. Mass Movements   Be on guard when huge crowds disperse after fireworks or a parade, or at park closing. With 20,000 to 40,000 people at once in an area, it's very easy to get separated from a child or others in your party. Use extra caution after the evening parade and fireworks in the Magic Kingdom, *Fantasmic!* at the Disney-MGM Studios, or *IllumiNations* at Epcot. Families should have specific plans for where to meet if they get separated.

7. Character Greetings   Activity and confusion are common when the Disney characters appear, and children can slip out of sight. See "Then Some Confusion Happened" (pages 172–173).

8. Getting Lost at the Animal Kingdom   It's especially easy to lose a child at the Animal Kingdom, particularly in the Oasis entryway, on the Maharaja Jungle Trek, and on the Gorilla Falls Exploration Trail. Mom and Dad will stop to observe an animal. Junior stays close for a minute or so, and then, losing patience, wanders to the other side of the exhibit or to a different exhibit.

Especially in the multipath Oasis, locating a lost child can be maddening, as a mother from Safety Harbor, Florida, describes:

> *Manny wandered off in the paths that lead to the jungle village while we were looking at a bird. It reminded me of losing somebody in the supermarket when you run back and forth looking down each aisle but can't find the person you're looking for because they are running around, too. I was nutso before we even got to the first ride.*

A mother from Flint, Michigan, came up with yet another way to lose a kid: abandonment.

> *From the minute we hit the park it was gripe, whine, pout, cry, beg, scream, pick, pester, and aggravate. When he went to the rest room for the ninth time before 11 a.m., I thought I'M OUTTA HERE . . . let the little snothead walk back to Flint. Unfortunately, I was brought up Catholic with lots of guilt so I didn't follow through.*

Disney, Kids, and Scary Stuff

Disney rides and shows are adventures. They focus on themes of all adventures: good and evil, death, beauty and the grotesque, fellowship and enmity. As you sample the attractions at Walt Disney World, you transcend the spinning and bouncing of midway rides to thought-provoking and emotionally powerful entertainment. All of the endings are happy, but the adventures' impact, given Disney's gift for special effects, often intimidates and occasionally frightens young children.

There are rides with menacing witches, burning towns, and ghouls popping out of their graves, all done with a sense of humor, provided you're old enough to understand the joke. And bones. There are bones everywhere: human bones, cattle bones, dinosaur bones, even whole skeletons. There's a stack of skulls at the headhunter's camp on the Jungle Cruise, a platoon of skeletons sailing ghost ships in Pirates of the Caribbean, and a haunting assemblage of skulls and skeletons in The Haunted Mansion. Skulls, skeletons, and bones punctuate Snow White's Adventures, Peter Pan's Flight, and Big Thunder Mountain Railroad. In the Animal Kingdom, there's an entire children's playground comprised exclusively of giant bones and skeletons.

Monsters and special effects at Disney-MGM Studios are more real and sinister than those in the other theme parks. If your child has difficulty coping with the witch in Snow White's Adventures, think twice about exposing him to machine-gun battles, earthquakes, and the creature from *Alien* at the Studios.

One reader tells of taking his preschool children on Star Tours:

> *We took a four-year-old and a five-year-old, and they had the shit scared out of them at Star Tours. We did this first thing in the morning, and it took hours of Tom Sawyer Island and Small World to get back to normal.*
>
> *Our kids were the youngest by far in Star Tours. I assume that other adults had more sense or were not such avid readers of your book.*
>
> *Preschoolers should start with Dumbo and work up to the Jungle Cruise in late morning, after being revved up and before getting hungry, thirsty, or tired. Pirates of the Caribbean is out for preschoolers. You get the idea.*

Expect the inevitable overload Disney World gives children. Be sensitive, alert, and prepared for almost anything, even behavior that is out of character for your child at home. Most young children take Disney's macabre trappings in stride, and others are easily comforted by an arm around the shoulder or a squeeze of the hand. Parents who know that their children tend to become upset should take it slow and easy, sampling more benign adventures like the Jungle Cruise, gauging reactions, and discussing with the children how they felt about what they saw.

Sometimes young children will rise above their anxiety in an effort to please their parents or siblings. This doesn't necessarily indicate a mastery of fear, much less enjoyment. If children leave a ride in apparently good shape, ask if they would like to go on it again (not necessarily now, but sometime). The response usually will indicate how much they actually enjoyed the experience. There's a big difference between having a good time and mustering the courage to get through something.

Evaluating a child's capacity to handle the visual and tactile effects of Disney World requires patience, understanding, and experimentation. Each of us, after all, has our own demons. If a child balks at or is frightened by a ride, respond constructively. Let your children know that lots of people, adults and children, are scared by what they see and feel. Help them understand that it's okay if they get frightened and that their fear doesn't lessen your love or respect. Take pains not to compound the discomfort by making a child feel inadequate; try not to undermine self-esteem, impugn courage, or ridicule. Most of all, don't induce guilt by suggesting the child's trepidation might be ruining the family's fun. It is also sometimes necessary to restrain older siblings' taunting or teasing.

A visit to Walt Disney World is more than an outing or an adventure for a young child. It's a testing experience, a sort of controlled rite of passage. If you help your little one work through the challenges, the time can be immeasurably rewarding and a bonding experience for you both.

The Fright Factor

While each youngster is different, there are seven attraction elements that alone or combined could push a child's buttons:

1. Name of the Attraction   Young children will naturally be apprehensive about something called "The Haunted Mansion" or "Mr. Toad's Wild Ride."

2. Visual Impact of the Attraction from Outside   Splash Mountain and Big Thunder Mountain Railroad look scary enough to give adults second thoughts, and they terrify many young children.

3. Visual Impact of the Indoor Queuing Area   Pirates of the Caribbean's caves and dungeons and The Haunted Mansion's "stretch rooms" can frighten children even before they board the ride.

4. Intensity of the Attraction   Some attractions are overwhelming, inundating the senses with sights, sounds, movement, and even smell. Epcot's *Honey, I Shrunk the Audience,* for example, combines loud sounds, lasers, lights, and 3-D cinematography to create a total sensory experience. For some preschoolers, this is two or three senses too many.

5. Visual Impact of the Attraction Itself   Sights in various attractions range from falling boulders to lurking buzzards, from grazing dinosaurs to attacking white blood cells. What one child calmly absorbs may scare the bejabbers out of another the same age.

6. Dark   Many Disney World attractions operate indoors in the dark. For some children, this triggers fear. A child who is frightened on one dark ride (Snow White's Adventures, for example) may be unwilling to try other indoor rides.

7. The Ride Itself; the Tactile Experience   Some rides are wild enough to cause motion sickness, to wrench backs, and to discombobulate patrons of any age.

SMALL-CHILD FRIGHT-POTENTIAL CHART

Our "Fright-Potential Chart" is a quick reference to identify attractions to be wary of, and why. The chart represents a generalization, and all kids are different. It relates specifically to kids ages three to seven. On average, children at the younger end of the range are more likely to be frightened than children in their sixth or seventh year.

MAGIC KINGDOM

Main Street, U.S.A.

Walt Disney World Railroad: Not frightening in any respect.
Main Street Cinema: Not frightening in any respect.
Main Street Vehicles: Not frightening in any respect.

Adventureland

Swiss Family Treehouse: Not frightening in any respect.
Jungle Cruise: Moderately intense, some macabre sights. A good test attraction for little ones.
Tropical Serenade: A thunderstorm momentarily surprises very young children.
Pirates of the Caribbean: Slightly intimidating queuing area; intense boat ride with gruesome (though humorously presented) sights and a short, unexpected slide down a flume.

Frontierland

Splash Mountain: Visually intimidating from outside, with moderately intense visual effects. The ride, culminating in a 52-foot plunge down a steep chute, is somewhat hair-raising for all ages. Switching off option provided (pages 165–167).

Frontierland (continued)

Big Thunder Mountain Railroad: Visually intimidating from outside, with moderately intense visual effects. The roller coaster is wild enough to frighten many adults, particularly seniors. Switching off provided (pages 165–167).

Tom Sawyer Island: Some very young children are intimidated by dark, walk-through tunnels that can be easily avoided.

Country Bear Jamboree: Not frightening in any respect.

Frontierland Shootin' Arcade: Not frightening in any respect.

Diamond Horseshoe Saloon Revue: Not frightening in any respect.

Liberty Square

The Hall of Presidents: Not frightening, but boring for young ones.

Liberty Belle Riverboat: Not frightening in any respect.

Mike Fink Keelboats: Not frightening in any respect.

The Haunted Mansion: Name raises anxiety, as do sounds and sights of waiting area. Intense attraction with humorously presented macabre sights. The ride itself is gentle.

Fantasyland

Mad Tea Party: Midway-type ride can induce motion sickness in all ages.

Mr. Toad's Wild Ride: Name intimidates some. Moderately intense spook-house-genre attraction with jerky ride. Frightens only a few preschoolers.

Snow White's Adventures: Moderately intense spook-house-genre attraction with some grim characters. Absolutely terrifies many preschoolers.

Legend of the Lion King: Certain special effects frighten some young children.

Dumbo the Flying Elephant: A tame midway ride; a great favorite of most young children.

Cinderella's Golden Carrousel: Not frightening in any respect.

It's a Small World: Not frightening in any respect.

Peter Pan's Flight: Not frightening in any respect.

Skyway to Tomorrowland: Not frightening, except to people afraid of heights.

Mickey's Toontown Fair

All attractions except roller coaster: Not frightening in any respect.

The Barnstormer at Goofy's Wiseacres Farm (roller coaster): May frighten some young children.

Tomorrowland

Alien Encounter: Extremely intense. Capable of frightening all ages. Not for young children. Switching off provided (pages 165–167).

The Timekeeper: Realistic cinematic technique may frighten some young children.

Buzz Lightyear's Space Ranger Spin: Dark ride with cartoonlike aliens may frighten some preschoolers.

Tomorrowland Transit Authority: Not frightening in any respect.

Skyway to Fantasyland: Not frightening in any respect.

Space Mountain: Very intense roller coaster in the dark; the Magic Kingdom's wildest ride and a scary roller coaster by any standard. Switching off provided (pages 165–167).

Astro Orbiter: Visually intimidating from the waiting area. The ride is relatively tame. See safety warning on page 169.

Walt Disney's Carousel of Progress: Not frightening in any respect.

Tomorrowland Speedway: Noise of waiting area slightly intimidates preschoolers; otherwise, not frightening.

EPCOT

Future World

Spaceship Earth: Dark and imposing presentation intimidates a few preschoolers.

Innoventions East and West: Not frightening in any respect.

Universe of Energy: Dinosaur segment frightens some preschoolers; visually intense, with some intimidating effects.

Wonders of Life—Body Wars: Very intense, with frightening visual effects. Ride causes motion sickness in susceptible riders of all ages. Switching off provided (pages 165–167).

Wonders of Life—Cranium Command: Not frightening in any respect.

Wonders of Life—The Making of Me: Not frightening in any respect.

Horizons: Not frightening in any respect.

Test Track: Intense thrill ride may frighten any age.

Future World (continued)

Journey into Imagination Ride: Contains some sights that frighten a very few preschoolers.

Journey into Imagination—Honey, I Shrunk the Audience: Extremely intense visual effects and loudness frighten many young children.

The Land—Living with the Land: Not frightening in any respect.

The Land—Circle of Life Theater: Not frightening in any respect.

The Land—Food Rocks: Not frightening in any respect, but loud.

World Showcase

Mexico—El Río del Tiempo: Not frightening in any respect.

Norway—Maelstrom: Visually intense in parts. Ride ends with a plunge down a 20-foot flume. A few preschoolers are frightened.

China—Wonders of China: Not frightening in any respect, but audience must stand.

Germany: Not frightening in any respect.

Italy: Not frightening in any respect.

The American Adventure: Not frightening in any respect.

Japan: Not frightening in any respect.

Morocco: Not frightening in any respect.

France—Impressions de France: Not frightening in any respect.

United Kingdom: Not frightening in any respect.

Canada—O Canada!: Not frightening in any respect, but audience must stand.

DISNEY-MGM STUDIOS

The Twilight Zone Tower of Terror: Visually intimidating to young children; contains intense and realistic special effects. The plummeting elevator at the ride's end frightens many adults.

The Great Movie Ride: Intense in parts, with very realistic special effects and some visually intimidating sights.

SuperStar Television: Not frightening in any respect.

ABC Sound Studio: The actual production isn't frightening.

Indiana Jones Epic Stunt Spectacular!: An intense show with powerful special effects, including explosions. Presented in an educational context that young children generally handle well.

Star Tours: Extremely intense visually for all ages; the ride is one of Disney's wildest. Not as likely to cause motion sickness as Body Wars at Epcot. Switching off is provided (pages 165–167).

Disney-MGM Studios Backlot Tour: Sedate and nonintimidating except for "Catastrophe Canyon," where an earthquake and a flash flood are simulated. Prepare younger children for this part of the tour.

Backstage Walking Tours: Not frightening in any respect.

Jim Henson's MuppetVision 4D: Intense and loud, but not frightening.

"Honey, I Shrunk the Kids" Movie Set Adventure Playground: Everything is oversized, but nothing is scary.

Voyage of the Little Mermaid: Not frightening in any respect.

The Magic of Disney Animation: Not frightening in any respect.

ANIMAL KINGDOM

The Boneyard: Not frightening in any respect.

Conservation Station: Not frightening in any respect.

Countdown to Extinction: High-tech thrill ride rattles riders of all ages.

Cretaceous Trail: Not frightening in any respect.

Discovery River Boats: Not frightening in any respect.

Festival of the Lion King: A bit loud, but otherwise not frightening in any respect.

Flights of Wonder: Swooping birds alarm a few small children.

Gorilla Falls Exploration Trail: Not frightening in any respect.

Grandmother Willow's Grove: Not frightening in any respect.

It's Tough to Be a Bug!: Very intense and loud with special effects that startle viewers of all ages and potentially terrify young children.

Kilimanjaro Safaris: A "collapsing" bridge and the proximity of real animals make a few young children anxious.

Maharaja Jungle Trek: Some children may balk at the bat exhibit.

The Oasis: Not frightening in any respect.

Tiger Rapids Run: Potentially frightening and certainly wet for guests of all ages.

Theater in the Wild: Not frightening in any respect.

Wildlife Express Train: Not frightening in any respect.

A Bit of Preparation

We receive many tips from parents telling how they prepared their young children for the Disney experience. A common strategy is to acquaint children with the characters and the stories behind the attractions by reading Disney books and watching Disney videos at home. A more direct approach is to rent Walt Disney World travel videos that show the actual attractions. Of the latter, a father from Arlington, Virginia, reports:

> My kids both loved The Haunted Mansion, with appropriate preparation. We rented a tape before going so they could see it, and then I told them it was all "Mickey Mouse Magic" and that Mickey was just "joking you," to put it in their terms, and that there weren't any real ghosts, and that Mickey wouldn't let anyone actually get hurt.

A mother from Teaneck, New Jersey, adds:

> I rented movies to make my five-year-old more comfortable with rides (Star Wars; Indiana Jones; Honey, I Shrunk the Kids). We thought we might go to Universal, so I rented King Kong, and it is now my kid's favorite. If kids are afraid of rides in dark (like ours), buy a light-up toy and let them take it on the ride.

A mother from Gloucester, Massachusetts, solved the fright problem on the spot:

> The 3-½-year-old liked It's a Small World, [but] was afraid of The Haunted Mansion. We just pulled his hat over his face and quietly talked to him while we enjoyed [the ride].

Attractions That Eat Adults	
Magic Kingdom:	Tomorrowland—Space Mountain
	Tomorrowland—Alien Encounter
	Fantasyland—Mad Tea Party
	Frontierland—Big Thunder Mountain Railroad
	Frontierland—Splash Mountain
Epcot:	Future World—Body Wars
	Future World—Test Track
Disney-MGM Studios:	Star Tours
	The Twilight Zone Tower of Terror
Animal Kingdom	Countdown to Extinction
	Tiger Rapids Run

ATTRACTIONS THAT EAT ADULTS

You may spend so much energy worrying about Junior that you forget to take care of yourself. If the motion of a ride is potentially disturbing, persons of any age may be adversely affected. Several attractions are likely to cause motion sickness or other problems for older children and adults.

Waiting Line Strategies for Adults with Young Children

Children hold up better through the day if you minimize the time they spend in lines. Arriving early and using our touring plans immensely reduces waiting. Here are additional ways to reduce stress for children:

1. Line Games Wise parents anticipate children's getting restless in line and plan activities to reduce the stress and boredom. In the morning, have waiting children discuss what they want to see and do during the day. Later, watch for and count Disney characters or play simple guessing games like "20 Questions." Lines move continuously; games requiring pen and paper are impractical. Waiting in the holding area of a theater attraction, however, is a different story. Here, tic-tac-toe, hangman, drawing, and coloring make the time fly by.

2. Last-Minute Entry If an attraction can accommodate an unusually large number of people at once, it's often unnecessary to stand in line. The Magic Kingdom's *Liberty Belle* Riverboat is a good example. The boat holds

Attractions You Can Usually Enter at the Last Minute	
Magic Kingdom	
Liberty Square	*The Hall of Presidents*
	Liberty Belle Riverboat
Tomorrowland	*The Timekeeper*
Epcot	
Future World	*The Circle of Life* (except during mealtimes)
	Food Rocks (except during mealtimes)
World Showcase	*Wonders of China*
	The American Adventure
	O Canada!
Disney-MGM Studios	*SuperStar Television*

about 450 people, usually more than are waiting in line. Instead of standing uncomfortably in a crowd, grab a snack and sit in the shade until the boat arrives and loading is well under way. After the line is almost gone, join it.

At large-capacity theaters like that for Epcot's *The American Adventure*, ask the entrance greeter how long it will be until guests are admitted for the next show. If it's 15 minutes or more, take a rest room break or get a snack, returning a few minutes before the show starts. You aren't allowed to carry food or drink into the attraction, so make sure you have time to finish your snack before entering.

3. The Hail Mary Pass Certain lines are configured to allow you and your smaller children to pass under the rail to join your partner just before actual boarding or entry. This technique allows children and one adult to rest, snack, cool off, or go potty while another adult or older sibling stands in line. Other guests are very understanding about this strategy when used for young children. You're likely to meet hostile opposition, however, if you try to pass older children or more than one adult under the rail.

Attractions Where You Can Usually Complete a Hail Mary Pass	
Magic Kingdom	
Adventureland	Swiss Family Treehouse
	Jungle Cruise
Frontierland	*Country Bear Jamboree*
Fantasyland	Mad Tea Party
	Mr. Toad's Wild Ride
	Snow White's Adventures
	Dumbo the Flying Elephant
	Cinderella's Golden Carrousel
	Peter Pan's Flight
Tomorrowland	Tomorrowland Speedway
Epcot	
Future World	Spaceship Earth
	Living with the Land
Disney-MGM Studios	*ABC Sound Studio*
	Indiana Jones Epic Stunt Spectacular!

4. Switching Off (a.k.a. The Baby Swap)   Several attractions have minimum height and/or age requirements, usually 3'8" tall to ride with an adult, or age 7 *and* 3'8" to ride alone. Some couples with children too small or too young forgo these attractions, while others take turns to ride. Missing some of Disney's best rides is an unnecessary sacrifice, and waiting in line twice for the same ride is a tremendous waste of time.

Instead, take advantage of the "switching off" option, also called "The Baby Swap." To switch off, there must be at least two adults. Everybody waits in line together, adults and children. When you reach an attendant (called a "greeter"), say you want to switch off. The greeter will allow everyone, including the young children, to enter the attraction. When you reach the loading area, one adult rides while the other stays with the kids. Then the riding adult disembarks and takes charge of the children while the other adult rides. A third adult in the party can ride twice, once with each of the switching off adults, so that the switching off adults don't have to experience the attraction alone.

Most rides with age and height minimums load and unload in the same area, facilitating switching off. An exception is Space Mountain, where the first adult at the conclusion of the ride must also inform the unloading attendant that he or she is switching off. The attendant will admit the first adult to an internal stairway that goes back to the loading area.

Attractions Where Switching Off Is Common	
Magic Kingdom	
Tomorrowland	Space Mountain
	Alien Encounter
Frontierland	Splash Mountain
	Big Thunder Mountain Railroad
Epcot	
Future World	Body Wars
	Test Track
Disney-MGM Studios	Star Tours
	The Twilight Zone Tower of Terror
Animal Kingdom	
DinoLand U.S.A.	Countdown to Extinction
Asia	Tiger Rapids Run

Switching Off

Attractions at which switching off is practiced are oriented to more mature guests. Sometimes it takes a lot of courage for a child just to move through the queue holding Dad's hand. In the boarding area, many children suddenly fear abandonment as one parent leaves to experience the attraction. Unless your children are prepared for switching off, you might have an emotional crisis on your hands. A mom from Edison, New Jersey, advises:

> *Once my son came to understand that the switch-off would not leave him abandoned, he did not seem to mind. I would recommend to your readers that they practice the switch-off on some dry runs at home, so that their child is not concerned that he will be left behind. At the very least, the procedure could be explained in advance so that the little ones know what to expect.*

Finally, a mother from Ada, Michigan, who discovered that the procedure for switching off varies from attraction to attraction, offered this suggestion:

> *Parents need to tell the very first attendant they come to that they would like to switch off. Each attraction has a different procedure for this. Tell every other attendant too because they forget quickly.*

5. How to Ride Twice in a Row without Waiting   Many young children like to ride a favorite attraction two or more times in succession. Riding the second time often gives them a feeling of mastery and accomplishment. Unfortunately, even in early morning, repeat rides can be time consuming. If you ride Dumbo as soon as the Magic Kingdom opens, for instance, you will wait only a minute or two for your first ride. When you come back for your second, the wait will be about 12 minutes. If you want to ride a third time, count on 20 minutes or longer.

The best way to get your child on the ride twice (or more) without blowing your morning is to use the "Chuck Bubba Relay" (named in honor of a Kentucky reader):

a. Mom and little Bubba enter the waiting line.

b. Dad lets a specific number of people go in front of him (24 at Dumbo), then gets in line.

c. As soon as the ride stops, Mom exits with Bubba and passes him to Dad to ride the second time.

d. If everybody is really getting into this, Mom can hop in line again, no fewer than 24 people behind Dad.

The Chuck Bubba Relay won't work on every ride, because waiting areas are configured differently (i.e., it's impossible in some cases to exit the ride and make the pass). For those rides (all in Fantasyland) where the Bubba Relay works, here are the numbers of people to count off:

Mad Tea Party: 53
Mr. Toad's Wild Ride: 22
Snow White's Adventures: 52
Dumbo the Flying Elephant: 24
Cinderella's Golden Carrousel: 75
Peter Pan's Flight: 64

If you're the second adult in the relay, you'll reach a place in line where it's easiest to make the hand-off. This may be where those exiting the ride pass closest to those waiting to board. In any event, you'll know it when you see it. If you reach it and the first parent hasn't arrived with Bubba, let those behind you pass until Bubba shows up.

6. Last-Minute Cold Feet   If your young child gets cold feet just before boarding a ride where there is no age or height requirement, you usually can arrange with the loading attendant for a switch off. This is common at Pirates of the Caribbean, where children lose their courage while winding through the dungeon-like waiting area.

No law says you have to ride. If you reach the boarding area and someone is unhappy, tell an attendant you've changed your mind and you'll be shown the way out.

7. Elevator Shoes for the Short and the Brave   If you have a child who is begging to go on the rides with height requirements but who is a little too short, slip heel lifts into his Nikes before he reaches the measuring point. Be sure to leave the heel lifts in, because he may be measured again before boarding.

8. Throw Yourself on the Grenade, Mildred!   For conscientious parents determined to sacrifice themselves on behalf of their children, we provide a Magic Kingdom One-Day Touring Plan called the "Dumbo-or-Die-in-a-Day Touring Plan, for Parents with Small Children." This plan (pages 429–432) will ensure that you run yourself ragged. Designed to help you forfeit everything of your personal interest for the sake of your children's pleasure, the plan guarantees to send you home battered and exhausted, with extraordinary stories of devotion and perseverance. By the way, the plan really works. Anyone under age eight will love it.

9. Catch-22 at Tomorrowland Speedway   Though Tomorrowland Speedway is a great treat for young children, they're required to be 4'4" tall in order to drive. Few children age six and younger measure up, so the ride is essentially withheld from the very age group that would most enjoy it. To resolve this Catch-22, go on the ride with your small child. The attendants will assume that you will drive. After getting into the car, shift your child over behind the steering wheel. From your position, you will still be able to control the foot pedals. Your child will feel like she is really driving, and because the car travels on a self-guiding track, there's no way she can make a mistake while steering.

10. Astro Orbiter—A Safety Warning Parents often board the rocket before lifting their child aboard. Because the attendant can't see small children beside the vehicle from his control station, the ride may start before a child is safely in the cockpit. If you take a small child on this ride, put the child in the rocket, then get in.

The Disney Characters

The large and friendly costumed versions of Mickey, Minnie, Donald, Goofy, and others—known as "Disney characters"—provide a link between Disney animated films and the theme parks. To people emotionally invested, the characters in Disney films are as real as next-door neighbors, never mind that they're drawings on plastic. In recent years, theme park personifications of the characters also have become real to us. It's not just a person in a mouse costume they see; it is Mickey himself. Similarly, meeting Goofy or Snow White in Fantasyland is an encounter with a celebrity, a memory to be treasured.

While there are hundreds of Disney animated film characters, only about 250 have been brought to life in costume. Of these, a relatively small number (less than a fifth) are "greeters" (characters who mix with patrons). The remaining characters perform in shows or parades. Originally confined to the Magic Kingdom, characters are now found in all the major theme parks and Disney hotels.

Character Watching Character watching has become a pastime. Families once were content to meet a character occasionally. They now pursue them relentlessly, armed with autograph books and cameras. Because some characters are only rarely seen, character watching has become character collecting. (To cash in on character collecting, Disney sells autograph books throughout the World.) Mickey, Minnie, and Goofy are a snap to bag; they seem to be everywhere. But Winnie the Pooh seldom comes out. Other characters appear regularly but only in a location consistent with their starring role. Cinderella, predictably, reigns at Cinderella Castle in

Fantasyland, while Brer Fox and Brer Bear frolic in Frontierland near Splash Mountain.

A dad from Brooklyn thinks the character autograph–hunting craze has gotten out of hand, complaining:

> *Whoever started the practice of collecting autographs from the characters should be subjected to Chinese water torture! We went to WDW eleven years ago, with an eight-year-old and an eleven-year-old. We would bump into characters, take pictures, and that was it. After a while, our children noticed that some of the other children were getting autographs. We managed to avoid joining in during our first day at the Magic Kingdom and our first day at Epcot, but by day three our children were collecting autographs. However, it did not get too out of hand, since it was limited to accidental character meeting.*
>
> *This year when we took our youngest child (who is now eight), he had already seen his siblings' collection, and was determined to outdo them. However, rather than random meetings, the characters are now*

available practically all day long at different locations, according to a printed schedule, which our son was old enough to read. We spent more time standing in line for autographs than we did for the most popular rides!

A family from Birmingham, Alabama, found some benefit in their children's relentless pursuit of characters, writing:

We had no idea we would be caught up in this madness, but after my daughters grabbed your guidebook to get Pocahontas to sign it (we had no blank paper), we quickly bought a Disney autograph book and gave in. It was actually the highlight of their trip, and my son even got into the act by helping get places in line for his sisters. They LOVED looking for characters (I think it has all been planned by Kodak to sell film). The possibility of seeing a new character revived my seven-year-old's energy on many occasions. It was an amazing totally unexpected part of our visit.

Preparing Your Children to Meet the Characters   Almost all characters are quite large, and several, like Brer Bear, are huge! Small children don't expect this, and preschoolers especially can be intimidated.

Discuss the characters with your children before you go. On first encounter, don't thrust your child at the character. Allow the little one to deal with this big thing from whatever distance feels safe. If two adults are present, one should stay near the youngster while the other approaches the character and demonstrates that it's safe and friendly. Some kids warm to the characters immediately; some never do. Most take a little time and several encounters.

There are two kinds of characters: those whose costume includes a face-covering headpiece (animal characters and such humanlike characters as Captain Hook) and "face characters," those who resemble the characters so no mask or headpiece is necessary. Face characters include Mary Poppins, Ariel, Jasmine, Aladdin, Cinderella, Belle, Snow White, Esmarelda, and Prince Charming.

Only face characters speak. Headpiece characters don't make noises of any kind. Because cast members couldn't possibly imitate the distinctive cinema voice of the character, Disney has determined it's more effective to keep them silent. Lack of speech notwithstanding, headpiece characters are very warm and responsive, and communicate very effectively with gestures. Tell children in advance that headpiece characters don't talk.

Some character costumes are cumbersome and give cast members very poor visibility. (Eye holes frequently are in the mouth of the costume or even on the neck or chest.) This means characters are somewhat clumsy and have limited sight. Children who approach the character from the back or side may not be noticed, even if the child touches the character. It's possible in this situation for the character to accidently step on the child or knock him down. It's best for a child to approach a character from the front, but occasionally not even this works. Duck characters (Donald, Daisy, Uncle Scrooge), for example, have to peer around their bills. If a character appears to be ignoring your child, pick up your child and hold her in front of the character until the character responds.

It's okay for your child to touch, pat, or hug the character. Understanding the unpredictability of children, the character will keep his feet very still, particularly refraining from moving backward or sideways. Most characters will sign autographs or pose for pictures. If your child collects autographs, it's a good idea to carry a pen the width of a magic marker. Costumes make it exceedingly difficult for characters to wield a pen, so the bigger the better.

The Big Hurt   Many children expect to meet Mickey the minute they enter the park and are disappointed when he isn't around. If your children can't enjoy things until they see Mickey, ask a cast member where to find him. If the cast member doesn't know, he or she can find out quickly. Cast members have a number they can call to learn exactly where the characters are at any time.

"Then Some Confusion Happened"   Young children sometimes become lost at character encounters. Usually, there's a lot of activity around a character, with both adults and children touching it or posing for pictures. Most commonly, Mom and Dad stay in the crowd while Junior approaches to meet the character. In the excitement and with people milling and the character moving around, Junior heads off in the wrong direction to look for Mom and Dad. In the words of a Salt Lake City mom: "Milo was shaking hands with Dopey one minute, then some confusion happened and [Milo] was gone."

Families with several young children and parents who are busy with cameras can lose a youngster in a heartbeat. Our recommendation for parents with preschoolers is to stay with the kids when they meet characters, stepping back only to take a quick picture.

MEETING CHARACTERS FOR FREE

You can *see* Disney characters in live shows at all the theme parks and in parades at the Magic Kingdom and Disney-MGM Studios. Consult your daily entertainment schedule for times. If you want to *meet* the characters, get autographs, and take photos, pick up a copy of the *Disney Character Greeting Location Guide* available free at each park.

At the Magic Kingdom   Characters are encountered more frequently here than anywhere else in Walt Disney World. There almost always will be a character next to City Hall on Main Street and usually one or more in Town Square or near the railroad station. If it's rainy, look for characters on the veranda of Tony's Town Square Restaurant. Characters appear in all the lands but are more plentiful in Fantasyland and Mickey's Toontown Fair. At Mickey's Toontown Fair, you can meet Mickey privately in his "Judge's Tent." Characters actually work shifts at the Toontown Hall of Fame next to Mickey's Country House. Here, you can line up to meet three different assortments of characters. Each assortment has its own greeting area and, of course, its own line. One group, variously labeled Mickey's Pals or Famous Friends or some such, will include Minnie, Pluto, Goofy, Donald, and sometimes Chip 'n' Dale, Daisy, and Uncle Scrooge. The other two assortments vary and are more ambiguously defined. The 100 Acre Wood Friends are mostly Winnie the Pooh characters, while Fairy Tale Friends include Snow White, assorted dwarfs, Sleeping Beauty, the Beast, Belle, Cinderella, Prince Charming, etc. Sometimes, however, it's Villains (Captain Hook, Cruella DeVil, Jabar, et al.), and Princesses (Sleeping Beauty, Mary Poppins, yadda, yadda, yadda). Cinderella regularly greets diners at Cinderella's Royal Table in the castle. Also look for characters in the central hub and by Splash Mountain in Frontierland.

Characters are featured in afternoon and evening parades and also play a major role in Castle Forecourt shows (at the entrance to the castle on the moat side) and at the Galaxy Palace Theater in Tomorrowland. Find performance times for shows and parades in the park's daily entertainment schedule. Sometimes characters stay to greet the audience after shows.

At Epcot   At first Disney didn't think characters would be appropriate for the more serious, educational style of Epcot. Later, in response to criticism that Epcot lacked warmth and humor, characters were imported. To integrate them thematically, new and often bizarre costumes were created. Goofy roams Future World in a metallic silver cape reminiscent of Buck Rogers. Mickey greets guests at the American Adventure dressed like Ben Franklin.

It's unclear whether there are fewer characters at Epcot or if it just seems that way because the place is so big. In any event, don't expect to encounter either the number or variety of characters at Epcot that you would in the Magic Kingdom. Two Epcot original characters, Dreamfinder and Figment, are found at the Journey into Imagination pavilion in Future World, and assorted characters appear at the Showcase Plaza each morning. Characters are also occasionally found at the American Adventure pavilion and at the United Kingdom in World Showcase. Characters aren't featured in parades at Epcot, but character shows are performed daily at the American Gardens Theater in World Showcase. Check the park's daily entertainment schedule.

Characters may be rarer at Epcot, but they're often easier to meet. A father from Effingham, Illinois, writes:

> *Trying to get autographs and pictures with Disney characters in the Magic Kingdom was a nightmare. Every character we saw was mobbed by kids and adults. Our kids had no chance. But at Epcot and Disney-MGM, things were much better. We got autographs, pictures, and more involvement. Our kids danced with several characters and received a lot of personal attention.*

At Disney-MGM Studios   Characters are likely to turn up anywhere at the Studios but are most frequently found in front of the Animation Building, along Mickey Avenue (leading to the soundstages), and at the end of New York Street on the backlot. Mickey and his "friends" pose for keepsake photos (about $10 each) on Hollywood Boulevard and Sunset Boulevard. Characters are also prominent in shows, with *Voyage of the Little Mermaid* running almost continuously and an abbreviated version of *Beauty and the Beast* performed several times daily at the Theater of the Stars. Check the daily entertainment schedule for show times.

At the Animal Kingdom   Camp Minnie-Mickey in the Animal Kingdom is a special location designed specifically for meeting characters. There are four designated character greeting "trails" where you can meet Mickey, Minnie, and various characters from *The Jungle Book* and *The Lion King*.

Also at Camp Minnie-Mickey are two stage shows featuring characters from *The Lion King* and *Pocahontas.*

Responding to requests, each theme park has added a lot of information about characters to its handout map. The reverse side lists where and when certain characters will be available and provides information on character dining. As mentioned earlier, a handout devoted exclusively to character watching, the *Disney Character Greeting Location Guide,* is now commonly available at all of the theme parks except the Animal Kingdom.

Disney has taken several initiatives intended to satisfy guests' inexhaustible desire to meet the characters. Most important, Disney assigned Mickey and a number of other characters to all-day duty in Mickey's Toontown Fair in the Magic Kingdom and Camp Minnie-Mickey in the Animal Kingdom. While making the characters more available has taken the guesswork out of finding them, it has robbed encounters of much of their spontaneity. Instead of chancing on a character, it's much more common now to wait in line to meet the character. Speaking of which, be aware that lines for face characters move m-u-c-h more slowly than do lines for nonspeaking characters. Because face characters are allowed to talk, they often engage children in lengthy conversations, much to the dismay of families still in the queue.

CHARACTER DINING

Fraternizing with characters has become so popular that Disney offers character breakfasts, brunches, and dinners where families can dine in the presence of Mickey, Minnie, Goofy, and other costumed versions of animated celebrities. Besides grabbing customers from Denny's and Hardee's, character meals provide a familiar, controlled setting in which young children can warm gradually to characters. Though we mention only the featured character(s) in the following descriptions, all meals are attended by several characters. Adult prices apply to persons age 12 or older, children's prices to ages 3 to 11. Little ones under age three eat free. For additional information on character dining, call (407) 939-3463 (WDW-DINE).

Because character dining is very popular, we recommend that you arrange priority seating as far in advance as possible. Make priority seating for dining up to 60 days before arrival by calling (407) 939-3463. If you forget to arrange priority seating in advance and all resort and theme park character meals are sold out, try to book a character meal at the Swan or Dolphin. Because the Swan and Dolphin aren't Disney-owned hotels, their character meals aren't booked through Disney central reservations. Consequently, the Swan and Dolphin often will have seating available when all other character meals are booked.

Priority seating is not a reservation, only a commitment to seat you ahead of walk-in patrons at the scheduled date and time. A reserved table won't await you, but you will be seated ahead of patrons who failed to call ahead. Even with priority seating, expect to wait at least 30 minutes to be seated.

Character Dining: What to Expect

Character meals are bustling affairs, held in hotels' or theme parks' largest full-service restaurants. Character breakfasts offer a fixed menu served family-style or a buffet. The typical family-style breakfast includes scrambled eggs; bacon, sausage, and ham; hash browns; waffles or French toast; biscuits, rolls, or pastries; and fruit. The meal is served in large skillets or platters at your table. If you run out of something, you can order seconds (or thirds) at no additional charge. Buffets offer much the same fare, but you have to fetch it yourself.

Character dinners range from a set menu served family-style to buffets or ordering off the menu. The character dinner at the Liberty Tree Tavern in the Magic Kingdom, for example, is served family-style and consists of turkey, ham, marinated flank steak, salad, mashed potatoes, green vegetables, and, for kids, macaroni and cheese. Dessert is extra. Character dinner buffets, such as those at 1900 Park Fare at the Grand Floridian and Chef Mickey's at the Contemporary Resort, offer separate adults' and children's serving lines. Typically, the children's buffet includes hamburgers, hot dogs, pizza, fish sticks, fried chicken nuggets, macaroni and cheese, and peanut butter and jelly sandwiches. Selections at the adult buffet usually include prime rib or other carved meat, baked or broiled Florida seafood, pasta, chicken, an ethnic dish or two, vegetables, potatoes, and salad.

At both breakfasts and dinners, characters circulate around the room while you eat. During your meal, each of the four or five characters present will visit your table, arriving one at a time to cuddle the kids (and sometimes the adults), pose for photos, and sign autographs. Keep autograph books (with pens) and loaded cameras handy. For the best photos, adults should sit across the table from their children. Always seat the children where characters can reach them most easily. If a table is against a wall, for example, adults should sit with their backs to the wall and children on the aisle.

At some of the larger restaurants, including 'Ohana at the Polynesian Resort and Chef Mickey's at the Contemporary, character meals involve impromptu parades of characters and children around the room, group singing, napkin waving, and other organized mayhem.

Disney people don't rush you to leave after you have eaten. You can get seconds on coffee or juice and stay as long as you wish to enjoy the charac-

"Casting? This is George at the character breakfast. There's been a mistake. We were supposed to get the Assorted Character Package with 1 Mickey, 1 Goofy, 1 Donald, 1 Pluto ..."

ters. Remember, however, that there are lots of eager children and adults waiting not so patiently to be admitted.

When to Go

Though a number of character breakfasts are offered around Walt Disney World, attending them usually prevents you from arriving at the theme parks in time for opening. Because early morning is best for touring the parks and you don't want to burn daylight lingering over breakfast, we suggest:

1. Substitute a character breakfast for lunch. Have juice or coffee and roll or banana from room service or from your cooler first thing in the morning to tide you over. Then tour the theme park for an hour or two before breaking off around 10:15 a.m. to go to the character breakfast of your choice. Make a big brunch of your character breakfast and skip lunch. You should be fueled until dinner.

2. Go on your arrival or departure day. The day you arrive and check in is usually good for a character dinner. Settle in at your hotel, swim, then dine with the characters. This strategy has the added benefit of

exposing your children to the characters before chance encounters at the parks. Some children, moreover, won't settle down to enjoy the parks until they have seen Mickey. Departure days also are good for a character meal. Schedule a character breakfast on your check-out day before you head for the airport or begin your drive home.

3. Go on a rest day. If you plan to stay five or more days, you probably will take a day or a half-day from touring to rest or do something else. These are perfect days for a character meal.

4. Go for dinner instead of breakfast. A character dinner in late afternoon or evening won't conflict with your touring schedule.

Character Breakfasts

If your kids are picky eaters or simply don't like eggs, choose a buffet breakfast. Priority seating is recommended for all character breakfasts. Call (407) 939-3463 for breakfasts at Disney resorts or in theme parks. For non-Disney hotels, call the hotel directly.

Here are character breakfasts, by location:

Disney-MGM Studios: Soundstage Restaurant   This cavernous eatery next to the Animation Building serves an excellent breakfast buffet from 8:30 to 11:15 a.m. daily. Characters are usually from Disney's latest animated feature (this year, *Mulan*). Cost is $14 for adults and $8 for children ages 3 to 11. The price of the character meal is in addition to your admission to the park. Priority seating is highly recommended.

Epcot: The Garden Grill Restaurant   This breakfast is served daily from park opening to 11:10 or 11:40 a.m. The menu is fixed, but seconds are available. Cost is $15 for adults and $9 for children ages 3 to 11. Characters include Mickey, Minnie, and Chip 'n' Dale. The price of the character meal is in addition to your admission to the park.

Magic Kingdom: Cinderella's Royal Table in Cinderella Castle   Served from 8 to 10 a.m. daily, the breakfast features Cinderella and Snow White, plus visiting character friends. The menu is fixed. Cost is $15 for adults and $8 for children ages 3 to 11. The price of the character meal is in addition to your admission to the park. Call early; priority seating is required, and the breakfast is booked year-round. In fact, we recommend that you call 60 days prior to your desired reservation to ensure a table. No walk-ins are accepted.

Magic Kingdom: The Crystal Palace   A Winnie the Pooh buffet breakfast is served from 8 to 10:45 a.m. daily, hosted by Pooh, Tigger, and Eeyore. Cost is $14 for adults and $8 for children ages 3 to 11. Priority seating is recommended.

Disney's Beach Club Resort: Cape May Cafe   This buffet breakfast is served from 7:30 to 11 a.m. daily. The Character in Charge is Goofy, assisted by Chip 'n' Dale. Cost is $15 for adults and $9 for children ages 3 to 11. Softer background music and broader food choices make this a good location for adults who want a taste of characters or for parents who are maxed out on the World's frantic pace.

Wilderness Lodge: Artist Point   Winnie the Pooh, Tigger, and Eeyore hold court at this breakfast served from 7:30 to 11:30 a.m. daily. Cost is $15 for adults and $9 for children ages 3 to 11. The menu is all-you-can-eat, with family-style service. This breakfast is one of the quieter of the species.

Contemporary Resort: Chef Mickey's   Mickey, Goofy, and Chip 'n' Dale host this buffet from 7 to 11:30 a.m. daily. Cost is $15 for adults and $8 for children ages 3 to 11. *Note:* Chef Mickey's was moved from the Downtown Disney Marketplace to the Contemporary Resort in 1995.

Polynesian Resort: 'Ohana   This tropical-theme breakfast is named Minnie's Menehune (difficult to pronounce at any time, but especially first thing in the morning). It's served from 7:30 to 11 a.m. daily. Cost is $15 for adults and $9 for children ages 3 to 11. Minnie reigns, in a grass skirt no less, assisted by Goofy and Chip 'n' Dale. Service is family-style.

Grand Floridian Beach Resort: 1900 Park Fare   Mary Poppins hosts this buffet breakfast from 7:30 to 11:30 a.m. daily. Cost is $16 for adults and $10 for children ages 3 to 11. Maddening calliope music plays throughout the meal.

Walt Disney World Swan: Garden Grove Cafe   Held only on Saturdays from 8 to 11 a.m., the Garden Grove character breakfast offers a choice of buffet or menu selection. Pluto and Goofy usually are the characters present. Cost is about $13 for adults and $8 for children ages 3 to 11. Priority seating is not accepted. For details, call (407) 934-3000 or (407) 934-1618.

Old Key West Resort: Olivia's Cafe   Winnie the Pooh, Tigger, and Eeyore host this breakfast from 7:30 to 11 a.m. on Sundays, Mondays, and Wednesdays. Cost is $15 for adults and $8 for children ages 3 to 11.

Pleasure Island: Fulton's Crab House   Two seatings are available at 8:30 and 10 a.m. daily for this buffet hosted by Mickey, Minnie, Goofy, and Pluto. The menu is all-you-can-eat. Cost is $13 for adults and $8 for children ages 3 to 11. Priority seating is recommended.

Character Brunches and Lunches

Walt Disney World Dolphin: Harry's Safari Bar & Grill   This buffet brunch is served only on Sundays from 8:30 to 11:30 a.m. Hosts are Chip 'n' Dale, Pluto, and Goofy. Cost is $20 for adults and $15 for children ages 3 to 12. For priority seating, call (407) 934-4000.

Disney-MGM Studios: Soundstage Restaurant   Buffet lunch is served from 11:30 a.m. to 3:30 p.m. daily. Cost is $15 for adults and $8 for children ages 3 to 11. Hosts include Pocahontas (upstairs) and Genie from *Aladdin,* and various other characters circulating throughout the restaurant. Priority seating is recommended.

Epcot: The Garden Grill Restaurant   This lunch is held from 11:30 a.m. to 4:30 p.m. daily. The menu includes several selections, and seconds are available. Cost is $17 for adults and $10 for children ages 3 to 11. Characters include Mickey and Minnie.

Magic Kingdom: The Crystal Palace   A Winnie the Pooh buffet lunch is served from 11:30 a.m. to 2:45 p.m. daily. Hosts are Pooh, Tigger, and Eeyore. Cost is $15 for adults and $8 for children ages 3 to 11. Priority seating is recommended.

Character Dinners

Magic Kingdom: The Crystal Palace   Winnie the Pooh, Tigger, and Eeyore host this buffet served from 4 p.m. until park closing. Cost is $20 for adults and $10 for children ages 3 to 11. Priority seating is recommended.

Magic Kingdom: Liberty Tree Tavern   A fixed menu is served family-style from 4 p.m. until park closing. Characters on-hand are Minnie, Goofy, Pluto, Meeko, and Chip 'n' Dale. Cost is $20 for adults and $10 for children. Priority seating is recommended.

Walt Disney World Swan: Gullivers   Held daily except for Tuesdays and Saturdays from 5:30 to 10 p.m., the dinner features Timon and Rafiki from *The Lion King* on Monday and Friday, Pooh and Tigger on Thursday, and Goofy and Pluto on Sunday and Wednesday. Diners order from the regular dinner menu. The entree range is $18.50–29.95; kids can eat for $6. An early-bird special is offered before 7 p.m. Reservations are accepted for dinner only.

Grand Floridian Beach Resort: 1900 Park Fare   Mickey and Minnie host a buffet from 5:30 to 9 p.m. daily. Cost is $22 for adults and $12 for children ages 3 to 11. Be prepared for nonstop calliope music.

Polynesian Resort: Mickey's Tropical Luau   This is a dinner show featuring Pacific-island dancing and Disney characters. Staged outdoors at 4:30 p.m. daily, rain or shine, the show is fun (1) if you are hungry that early and (2) if you go during a cooler month of the year. Regardless of when you go, be prepared for lackluster food. Cost is $33 for adults and $16 for children ages 3 to 11. If you're planning ahead, we recommend that you try to book this dinner two years in advance.

Contemporary Resort: Chef Mickey's   This buffet is from 5 to 9:30 p.m. daily. Chef Mickey appears, along with Goofy, Chip 'n' Dale, Pluto, and Minnie. Cost is $20 for adults and $10 for children ages 3 to 11.

Epcot: The Garden Grill   Mickey, Minnie, and Chip 'n' Dale host dinner daily from 4:30 p.m. until park closing. The menu includes several selections, served family-style, with all-you-can-eat portions. The cost is $18 for adults and $10 for children ages 3 to 11.

Character Campfire

A campfire and sing-along are held nightly at 7 or 8 p.m. (depending on the season) near the Meadow Trading Post and Bike Barn at Fort Wilderness Campground. Chip 'n' Dale lead the songs, and a full-length Disney film is shown afterward. The program is free and open to resort guests. For a schedule, call (407) 824-2788.

Babysitting

Childcare Centers   Childcare isn't available within the theme parks, but each Magic Kingdom resort connected by the monorail and each Epcot resort (BoardWalk Inn and Villas, Yacht and Beach Club resorts) has a childcare center for potty-trained children older than three. Services vary, but children generally can be left between 4 p.m. and midnight. Milk and cookies and blankets and pillows are provided at all childcare centers. Play is supervised but not organized, and toys, videos, and games are plentiful. Guests at any Disney resort or campground may use the childcare services.

The most elaborate of the childcare centers (variously called "clubs" or "camps") is Neverland Club at the Polynesian Resort. This and the one at the Wilderness Lodge are the only centers that include a buffet dinner at the club, though at the other locations you can arrange for room service to provide your children's meals. A Disney character (usually Goofy) even visits the children each night at the Neverland Club. The rates for children ages 4–12 are $8 per hour for the first child and $6 per hour for each additional child.

Childcare Clubs*

Hotel	Name of Program	Ages	Phone
Buena Vista Palace	All about Kids	All	(407) 827-2727
BoardWalk Inn & Villas	Harbor Club	4–12	(407) 939-5100
Contemporary Resort	Mouseketeer Clubhouse	4–12	(407) 824-1000
Grand Floridian Beach Resort	Mouseketeer Club	4–12	(407) 824-3000
The Hilton	Vacation Station	4–12	(407) 827-4000
Polynesian Resort	Neverland Club	4–12	(407) 824-2170
Wilderness Lodge Resort	Cub's Den	4–12	(407) 824-1083
Yacht and Beach Club resorts	Sandcastle Club	4–12	(407) 934-7000

*Childcare clubs operate afternoons and evenings. All require reservations.

We get a lot of mail praising the Neverland Club. A dad from Snohomish, Washington, writes:

> The boys loved it! They got a good choice of food to eat in buffet style. It was educational—someone from Discovery Island brought some animals in—and it was fun. There was something for every age—appropriate toys, games, and a game room with free video games. The boys also had a Polaroid picture taken with Goofy, and the boys' smiles showed how good a time they were having. The supervisors seemed very pleasant and caring. As you might expect, it was all very professional and well done, and the beepers they had us carry made us feel extra secure.

A Houston dad adds:

> There were some outstanding surprises during our visit. One was the babysitting club at the Polynesian Hotel, the Neverland Club. I can tell you that our children enjoyed the Neverland Club as much as anything at WDW. It is somewhat expensive, but that includes dinner, free video games, Disney movies, group games and activities, and a visit by an expert from Discovery Island with several birds and animals. A woman registering her child told my wife that her daughter had stayed at the Neverland Club on a visit two years ago and considered it her favorite attraction at WDW!

If you're staying in a Disney resort that doesn't offer a childcare club and you *don't* have a car, you're better off using in-room babysitting. Trying to take your child to a club in another hotel via Disney bus requires a 50- to 90-minute trip each way. By the time you have deposited your little one, it will almost be time to pick him up again. Be aware that the childcare clubs shut down at or before midnight. If you intend to make a late night of it, in-room babysitting is your best bet.

Kinder-Care Learning Centers also operate childcare facilities at Disney World. Originally developed for use by Disney employees, the centers now also take guests' children on a space-available basis. Kinder-Care provides basically the same services as a hotel club, except that the daytime *Learning While Playing Development Program* is more structured and educational. For childcare in the morning and early afternoon, Kinder-Care is the only game in town, but the service is closed on Saturdays and Sundays. Accepted are children ages 1 (provided they're walking and can eat table food) through 12. For reservations, call (407) 827-5437 or (407) 824-3290.

In-Room Babysitting   For those staying in the World, in-room baby-sitting is offered by Kinder-Care (phone (407) 827-5444) and the Fairy Godmothers (no kidding) service described below. Base rates for Kinder-Care are $11 an hour.

Outside of Walt Disney World, childcare services and in-room sitting can be arranged through most larger hotels and motels or by calling the Fairy Godmothers. Godmothers are on-call 24 hours a day (you never get an answering machine) and offer the most flexible and diversified service in town. They will come to any hotel at any hour. If you pay, they will take your children to the theme parks. No child is too young or too old, and Godmothers also care for the elderly and pets. All sitters are female non-smokers. Base rates are $9 an hour for up to three children (in the same family), with a four-hour minimum and a $5 travel fee. For additional children in the same family, add $1 per child per hour. Godmothers will also tend a group of four or fewer children from different families for $6 an hour per family. For each additional child in excess of four, add $1 per child per hour to the base rate. Wishing won't get you a Godmother; you have to call (407) 277-3724 or (407) 275-7326.

WALT DISNEY WORLD LEARNING PROGRAMS FOR CHILDREN

Developed in coordination with leading educators, five learning programs are available at Disney World for persons age 15 and younger. The well-presented and enjoyable programs include admission to any theme park visited, classroom materials, and lunch. All classes are limited in size, so make reservations well in advance.

Courses are expensive, but they provide an interesting and educational glimpse behind the scenes at Walt Disney World. They also offer (if you hadn't thought of it) time for parents to be alone. If you are considering taking your children out of school to visit the World, enrolling them in one of these programs sometimes helps secure teacher approval.

Kidventure Program

This four-hour program at Discovery Island zoological park focuses on identifying plants and wildlife. Offered from 8:30 a.m. to 5:30 p.m. Monday through Friday, the course costs $32 per person and is restricted to students ages 8 to 14. Boat transportation to the island is included. For reservations, call (407) 939-TOUR

Wonders of Walt Disney World

Art Magic: Bringing Illusion to Life   Participants are introduced to animation and look at how costuming, set design, and landscaping are used in movies, stage shows, and theme parks. Tuition for the six-hour program, open to students ages 11 to 15, is $80. For reservations, call (407) 354-1855.

Show Biz Magic: The Walt Disney World of Entertainment   Students look at what goes into a Disney stage show by meeting performers and technicians and observing how timing, music, lighting, and costumes combine to create a show. The six-hour course, open to children ages 11 to 15, costs $80. For reservations or information, call (407) 354-1855.

Disney Day Camp at the Disney Institute

Disney Day Camp offers one or two half-day field trips focusing on art, entertainment, international cultures, and nature for children ages 7 to 10. Morning sessions are 8:30 a.m. until noon; afternoon programs are 1:30 to 5 p.m. Prices vary, and lunch is optional. For information or reservations, call (407) 827-4800 or (800) 746-5858.

Part Five

Special Tips for Special People

Walt Disney World for Singles

Walt Disney World is great for singles. It is safe, clean, and low-pressured. If you're looking for a place to relax without being hit on, Disney World is perfect. Bars, lounges, and nightclubs are the most laid-back and friendly you're likely to find anywhere. In many, you can hang out and not even be asked to buy a drink. Parking lots are well lighted and constantly patrolled. For women alone, safety and comfort are unsurpassed.

With the opening of the BoardWalk and Downtown Disney in 1997, nightlife options increased exponentially. Virtually every type of entertainment performed fully clothed is available at an amazingly reasonable price at a Disney nightspot. If you drink more than you should and are a Disney resort guest, Disney buses will return you safely to your hotel.

If, however, you're looking to meet someone new and exciting, there are better places than Walt Disney World. Most singles at Disney World work there. Even at the Pleasure Island entertainment complex you need to check your dancing partner's wristband to determine whether he or she is old enough to buy a drink.

Far fewer single men vacation at Disney World than do single women. There are men, both single for real and single for the moment, attending meetings and conventions at the resorts, but their schedules rarely permit development of anything meaningful. Filling the void are local single (and married) men who understand that single women on vacation may be vulnerable. Avoid these guys.

The easiest and safest way to meet anyone at Disney World is at the theme parks, including the water theme parks. (Most local cruisers aren't going to shell out the price of admission and hang around the park all day.) Parks give guests something to talk about, and there's no easier place to strike up a conversation than waiting in line for an attraction. A more organized way to meet people is to take a tour for adults or join a program at the Disney Institute (pages 620–622)

Walt Disney World for Couples

So many couples marry or honeymoon at Walt Disney World that a department has been formed to take care of their needs. *Disney's Fairy Tale Weddings & Honeymoons* department offers a range of wedding venues and services, plus honeymoon packages.

Weddings

It takes big bucks to marry at Disney World. Disney's Intimate Wedding (six or fewer guests) includes four nights' lodging for the wedding couple, admission to the parks, a wedding officiant, and one dinner at a Disney "fine-dining" establishment—for $3,400! This price includes a musician, flower bouquet, limousine ride, and a wedding coordinator, as well. For even more, you can arrive at your wedding in Cinderella's glass coach, have Goofy as best man and Minnie as maid of honor, and drive away after the ceremony in a limo chauffeured by Mickey. If you don't have many friends, you can rent additional Disney characters by the half hour to attend your wedding. Volume discounts are available; characters cost $450 for one, $650 for two, $850 for three, and so on. If character prices sound steep, be comforted that they don't eat or drink.

Indoor and outdoor sites are available for weddings at theme parks as well as the Grand Floridian, Yacht Club, Beach Club, BoardWalk Inn and

Villas, Contemporary, Wilderness Lodge, Polynesian, and Disney Village resorts. You can have a nautical wedding aboard the *Kingdom Queen* stern-wheeler on Bay Lake or the riverboat at the Walt Disney World Village. Wedding sites for the nocturnal are at Pleasure Island nightclubs. Disney operates its Fairy Tale Wedding pavilion on a private island near the Grand Floridian. The glass-enclosed pavilion is nondenominational and accommodates 250 guests as well as smaller, more intimate nuptials.

One of the more improbable services available is bachelor parties (obtain information at (407) 828-3074). What goes on at a Disney bachelor party? Stag cartoons or a private showing of *The Making of Me?* Get down!

If you wish to marry at Walt Disney World, you can get a marriage license ($89) at any county courthouse in Florida. Cash, traveler's checks, or money orders are accepted. There's no waiting period; your license is issued when you apply. The ceremony must occur within 60 days. Blood tests aren't required, but you must present identification (driver's license, passport, or birth certificate). If you were divorced within the year, you must produce a copy of your divorce decree. Call the wedding coordinator at (407) 828-3400 for more information.

Honeymoons

Honeymoon packages are adaptations of the regular Walt Disney Travel Company vacations. No special rooms or honeymoon suites are included unless you upgrade. In fact, the only honeymoon features are room service (in one package) and a photo session and keepsake album (in two others).

If you're interested in a Disney wedding or honeymoon, contact:

Disney's Fairy Tale Weddings & Honeymoons
P.O. Box 10020
Lake Buena Vista, FL 32830-0020
(800) 370-6009
www.honeymoondisneyworld.com

Romantic Getaways

Walt Disney World is a favorite getaway for honeymooners and other couples. You don't have to buy a honeymoon package to enjoy a romantic interlude, but not all Disney hotels are equally romantic. Some are too family oriented; others swarm with convention-goers. We recommend these Disney lodgings for romantics:

1. Polynesian Resort
2. Wilderness Lodge Resort
3. Grand Floridian Beach Resort
4. BoardWalk Inn & Villas
5. Yacht and Beach Club resorts
6. Contemporary Resort (tower rooms)

All of these properties are expensive. There are also secluded villas in the Villas at the Disney Institute. Possibly the most romantic Disney accommodation is the Moorea building at the Polynesian Resort. Couples at the Moorea with a waterfront-view room can watch the Magic Kingdom fireworks across the Seven Seas Lagoon. Tower rooms at the Contemporary, especially those on the southwest side, also provide great views.

Quiet, Romantic Places to Eat

Quiet, romantic restaurants with good food are rare in the theme parks. Only the Coral Reef, the terrace at the Rose & Crown, and the San Angel Inn at Epcot satisfy both requirements. Waterfront dining is available at Portobello Yacht Club and Fulton's Crab House at Pleasure Island, Narcoossee's at the Grand Floridian, and Cap'n Jack's Oyster Bar at the Disney Village Marketplace.

The California Grill atop the Contemporary Resort has the best view at Walt Disney World. If window tables aren't available, ask to be served in the adjoining lounge. Victoria & Albert's at the Grand Floridian is the World's showcase gourmet restaurant; expect to pay big bucks. Other good choices for couples include the Yachtsman Steakhouse at the Yacht Club, Kimonos at the Swan and Dolphin resorts, 'Ohana at the Polynesian, and Spoodles and The Flying Fish Cafe at the BoardWalk.

Eating later in the evening and choosing among the restaurants we've mentioned will improve your chances for quiet, intimate dining, but children—well-behaved or otherwise—are everywhere at Walt Disney World, and you won't escape them. Honeymooners from Slidell, Louisiana, write:

> *We made dinner reservations at some of the nicer Disney restaurants. When we made reservations, we made sure they were past the dinner hours and we tried to stress that we were on our honeymoon. [In] every restaurant we went to, we were seated next to large families. The kids were usually tired and cranky. After a whole day in the parks, the kids were not excited about sitting through a long meal. It's very difficult to enjoy a romantic dinner when there are small children crawling around under your table. We looked around the restaurant and always noticed lots of nonchildren couples. Our suggestion is this: Seat couples without children together and families with kids elsewhere. If Disney is such a popular honeymoon destination, then some attempt should be made to keep romantic restaurants romantic.*

A couple from Woodbridge, Virginia, adds:

> *We found it very difficult to find a quiet restaurant for dinner anywhere. We tried a restaurant which you recommended as quiet and pleasant. We even waited until 8:30 p.m. to eat and we were still surrounded by out-of-control children. The waiters were even singing the Barney the Dinosaur theme song. The food was very good, but after a long day in the park, our nerves were shot.*

For complete information about Disney restaurants, as well as recommendations for off-World dining, see Part 8: Dining in and around Walt Disney World (pages 239–347).

Romantic Stuff to Do

Couples, like everyone else, have their own agenda at Disney World. Nonetheless, here are romantic diversions you might not have on your list:

1. *Visit a lounge.* Atop the Contemporary Resort is a nice but pricey lounge. It's great for watching a sunset or viewing night-time fireworks over the nearby Magic Kingdom. If you want to go for the view and not drink, access an outside promenade

through a set of glass doors at the end of the lounge. Also wonderful is Mizner's Lounge on the Alcazar level of the Grand Floridian. It overlooks the hotel grounds and pools and the Seven Seas Lagoon. Each evening a six-piece dance band plays '20s and '30s music on the adjacent landing.

2. *View the Floating Electrical Pageant.* One of Disney's most romantic entertainments, the pageant consists of a train of barges, each with a spectacular light display depicting sea creatures. The show starts after dark to music by Handel played on synthesizers. You see only the lights. The best places to watch are from the piers at the Polynesian, Wilderness Lodge, the Grand Floridian, or Fort Wilderness.

3. *Ride a boat.* Small launches shuttle guests to and from the Grand Floridian, Polynesian, Magic Kingdom, Wilderness Lodge, and Fort Wilderness Campground well into the night. On a summer night, take a tranquil cruise around Bay Lake and the Seven Seas Lagoon. Disney vessels also cruise the canal connecting Disney-MGM Studios and Epcot, stopping at the Swan and Dolphin, Disney's BoardWalk, and the Yacht and Beach Club resorts.

   During daytime at the Fort Wilderness dock, you can rent boats for exploring Bay Lake and the Seven Seas Lagoon. The adjacent Fort Wilderness Campground is honeycombed with footpaths that are lovely for early-morning or early-evening walks.

   If you enjoy hiking and boating, visit Juniper Springs Recreation Area in the Ocala National Forest. About an hour and a half north of Disney World, the forest is extraordinarily beautiful. Trails are well marked, and canoes are available for rent (shuttle included). Paddling down Juniper Springs is like floating through a natural version of the Jungle Cruise. For Juniper Springs information, call (352) 625-2808.

4. *Have a picnic.* During more temperate months, picnic on the beaches of Bay Lake and the Seven Seas Lagoon. Room service at Disney resorts will prepare a carry-along lunch to order. Drinks, including wine and beer, are less expensive at hotel convenience shops. Fort Wilderness Campground also is good for picnics.

5. *Dine and dance on the BoardWalk.* Disney's BoardWalk offers several nice restaurants and an upscale dance club featuring music from the '20s to the '90s. Even if you don't dine or dance, the BoardWalk is romantic and picturesque for strolling.

6. *Go bicycling.* Rent a bike at Wilderness Lodge and explore the paths and roads of nearby Fort Wilderness Campground. Maps are available at the bike-rental shed.

Things to Bring

Once ensconced in your Disney World hideaway, it can be inconvenient to go out for something you've forgotten. Many couples write us to list things they wish they'd remembered to bring. Here are items most often mentioned:

1. Wine (Wine is sold by the bottle at Disney World, but the selection is pretty dismal. The best nearby selection of beer, wine, and champagne is at the Goodings Supermarket in the Crossroads Shopping Center on FL 535, across from the entrance to Disney Village Hotel Plaza.)
2. Corkscrew (Wine glasses are available from room service.)
3. Liquor, aperitifs, and cordials
4. Mixers for fancy drinks such as margaritas, olives for martinis, lemons, and limes
5. Portable tape or disc player and your favorite music
6. Bicycles
7. Picnic basket and blanket or tablecloth
8. Candles and holders
9. Cooler
10. Special snacks such as caviar, chocolates, cheeses (with knife), and fruit

Walt Disney World for Expectant Mothers

It is said that a good shepherd will lay down his life for his sheep. Heaven knows we have tried to be good shepherds for you. We have spun around in teacups and been jostled in simulators until we turned green. We have baked in the sun, flapped in the wind, and come close to drowning in the rain, all while researching this guide. But for expectant mothers we have failed. Try as he might, the author has never become pregnant, and as a consequence, the *Unofficial Guide* has never included good, first-hand information for mothers-to-be. Then, in our darkest hour, to the rescue came Debbie Grubbs, a reader from Colorado in her fifth month of pregnancy. Fearless and undaunted, Debbie waddled all over Walt Disney World, compiling observations and tips for expectant moms. The following is what she had to say.

I was very disappointed to find no information specifically directed to pregnant women, particularly concerning which attractions at the theme parks you can and cannot ride. Generally speaking, there is more that you can do at Walt Disney World than that you can't do. Therefore, I will outline only those rides that are prohibited to pregnant women and the reasons why. There were several rides that I just knew I could ride even though they were restricted, so I sent my husband and friends to ride first and they reported why they thought I could or could not ride.

Magic Kingdom

Splash Mountain is restricted obviously due to the drop, or so I thought. It turns out that the seat configuration in the "logs" has more to do with it than the drop. The seats are made so that your knees are higher than your rear, causing compression on the abdomen (when it is this large). This is potentially harmful to the baby. As always, better safe than sorry. I really hated to miss this one.

Big Thunder Mountain Railroad is restricted for obvious reasons as well. It's just not a good idea to ride roller coasters when you are pregnant.

Mad Tea Party may be okay if you don't spin the cups. We didn't ride this one because I was advised by my doctor not to ride things with centrifugal [or centripetal] force. Dumbo and the Astro Orbiter (Tomorrowland) are okay, but the Mad Tea Party is too fast if you spin the cups.

Space Mountain is restricted. It's one of my favorite rides, but a roller coaster nonetheless.

Tomorrowland Speedway is not recommended due to the amount of rear-ending that always occurs due to overzealous younger drivers.

Epcot Center

Body Wars and **Test Track** are restricted, as are all simulator rides. They are too rough and jerky, much like a roller coaster.

Disney-MGM Studios

Tower of Terror is restricted for the drop alone, and **Star Tours** is restricted because it is a simulator. Although not as rough as Body Wars, Star Tours is still a no-no.

There might be some question about the **Backlot Tour** due to Catastrophe Canyon, where there is a simulated earthquake. It is very tame compared to Earthquake! at Universal Studios and posed no hazard to me. I rode with no problems.

UNIVERSAL STUDIOS

Universal is a colossal bust for pregnant women when it comes to rides. In fact, there's only one a pregnant woman can ride: Hanna-Barbera, in the stationary seats. Here's a summary of the why's:

The **Funtastic World of Hanna-Barbera,** although a simulator, has stationary seats for those who cannot ride in the moving seats. The ride is almost as good without the moving seats.

Kongfrontation is not terribly rough. The problem is the lap bar in the tram that fits very tightly across the abdomen.

Earthquake! has three parts: the film, the demonstration, and the ride. You can stay with your group all the way to the subway ride. Simply exit to the right, and there is a waiting room with chairs for nonriders. Don't miss the first two segments just because of the ride.

Jaws is restricted, though we can't figure out why. The boat ride is smooth; there is no lap bar, and no undue stress on the riders. Are they concerned that the shark or explosions will scare you? In my opinion it's not that scary.

Back to the Future is a very rough simulator ride and is definitely out.

E.T. Adventure was a disappointment. I was sure I could ride, but those pesky lap bars were the culprit again.

At least at Universal there are as many shows as rides.

WATER THEME PARKS

All of the slides are off-limits to pregnant women. You can, however, do Shark Reef at Typhoon Lagoon with an extra-large wetsuit vest. The wave pools and floating creeks are great for getting the weight off your feet.

MORE TIPS

In addition to Debbie's tips, here are a few of our own:

1. Go over your Walt Disney World vacation plans with your obstetrician well in advance of your trip.

2. Be prepared for a lot of walking at Walt Disney World. Get in shape by walking at home, building up endurance and distance gradually.

3. While on vacation get as much rest as you need, even if you have to sacrifice some time at the theme parks. Try to work in an afternoon nap each day.

4. Make sure you eat properly. Drink plenty of water throughout the day, especially if you visit Walt Disney World during the warmer seasons of the year.

5. Use in-park transportation whenever available to cut down on walking.

6. Stay in Walt Disney World if possible. This will make it much easier to separate from your group and return to your hotel for rest.

Walt Disney World for Seniors

Seniors' problems and concerns are common to Disney visitors of all ages. Seniors do, however, often get into predicaments caused by touring with people younger than they are. Run ragged and pressured by grandchildren to endure a frantic pace, many seniors concentrate on surviving Disney World rather than enjoying it. The parks have as much to offer older visitors as they do children, and seniors must either set the pace or dispatch the young folks to tour on their own.

An older reader in Alabaster, Alabama, writes:

> *The main thing I want to say is that being a senior is not for wussies. At Disney World particularly, it requires courage and pluck. Things that used to be easy take a lot of effort, and sometimes your brain has to wait for your body to catch up. Half the time, your grandchildren treat you like a crumbling ruin and then turn around and trick you into getting on a roller coaster in the dark. What you need to tell seniors is that they have to be alert and not trust anyone. Not their children or even the Disney people, and especially not their grandchildren. When your grandchildren want you to go on a ride, don't follow along blindly like a lamb to the slaughter. Make sure you know what the ride is all about. Stand your ground and do not waffle. He who hesitates is launched!*

Most seniors we interview enjoy Disney World much more when they tour with folks their own age. If, however, you're considering going to Disney World with your grandchildren, we recommend an orientation visit without them first. If you know first-hand what to expect, it's much easier to establish limits, maintain control, and set a comfortable pace when you visit with the youngsters.

Doris explains the importance of knowing what you are getting in line for.

If you're determined to take the grandkids, read carefully those sections of this book that discuss family touring. (*Hint:* The Dumbo-or-Die-in-a-Day Touring Plan has been known to bring grown-ups of any age to their knees.)

Because seniors are a varied and willing lot, there aren't any attractions we would suggest they avoid. For seniors, as with other Disney visitors, personal taste is more important than age. We hate to see mature visitors pass an exceptional attraction like Splash Mountain because younger visitors call it a "thrill ride." Splash Mountain is a full-blown adventure that gets its appeal more from music and visual effects than from the thrill of the ride. Because you must choose among those attractions that might interest you, we provide facts to help you make informed decisions.

We know it's easy to get caught up in the spectacle and wonder of Disney World, so much so that you follow a crowd onto something you hadn't fully considered. Here, then, are some of the attractions to know before you enter.

Magic Kingdom

Space Mountain   If you thought the roller coaster at Coney Island was a thrill, this won't be far behind, with dips and pops that pull you through curves and over humps. This ride vibrates a lot. Put your glasses in your fanny pack; we can't guarantee they'll stay in your pocket.

Big Thunder Mountain Railroad   Although sedate compared with Space Mountain, this ride is very jarring. Cars jerk back and forth along the track, though there are few drops. It's the side-to-side shaking that gets to most people.

Splash Mountain   This ride combines the whimsy of Disney with the thrill of a log flume. There's one big drop near the end and some splash (engineered by spray guns and a water cannon, not the drop itself). The enchanting Brer Rabbit story is worth getting wet for.

Swiss Family Treehouse   This isn't a thrill ride, but it does involve lots of stair climbing and a very unsteady pontoon bridge.

Mad Tea Party   An adaptation of a carnival ride, big tea cups spin until riders are nauseated. If you approach this instrument of the devil while it's sitting still, your cunning grandchildren may try to pass it off as an *al fresco* dining patio.

Epcot

Body Wars   This ride jolts more than Star Tours (at Disney-MGM Studios) and is more likely to cause motion sickness than the Mad Hatter's tea cups. It combines a graphic anatomy lesson with the trauma of being chauffeured by a teenager driving his first stick shift.

Test Track   The newest thrill ride in Future World, this attraction simulates test driving a car. The fastest ride in the Disney repertoire, Test Track whizzes you around hairpin turns, over rough road, down straightaways, and up and down steep inclines. Jarring, terrifying, and fun, Test Track provides interesting insight on the life of a crash dummy.

Disney-MGM Studios

Star Tours   Using the plot and characters from *Star Wars,* this flight-simulation ride is a Disney masterpiece. If you're extremely prone to motion sickness, this ride will affect you. Otherwise, it might be the highlight of your Walt Disney World vacation.

The Twilight Zone **Tower of Terror**   Though most of the thrills are visual, the Tower of Terror features a gut-gripping simulation of an elevator in free fall after its cable has broken.

Animal Kingdom

Countdown to Extinction   Fortunately, the name applies to dinosaurs, not those who ride it. The show consists primarily of visual effects, but the ride is pretty jerky.

Tiger Rapids Run   This ride simulates a whitewater raft trip. It's not all that rough, but it's very wet.

Getting Around

Many seniors like to walk, but a seven-hour visit to one of the theme parks normally includes four to eight miles on foot. If you aren't up for that much hiking, let a more athletic member of your party push you in a rented wheelchair. The theme parks also offer fun-to-drive electric carts (convenience vehicles). Don't let your pride get in the way of having a good time. Sure you could march ten miles if you had to, but *you don't have to!*

A big advantage to renting a wheelchair is the boarding privilege granted to guests (and their immediate parties) who use the special entrances for wheelchairs at most attractions. Waiting times at these boarding areas depend on the attraction and the crowd, but you almost always will ride sooner than if you had waited in the regular queue. You must check in with a host or hostess before you board.

Your wheelchair-rental deposit slip is good for a replacement wheelchair in any park during the same day. You can rent a chair at the Magic

Kingdom in the morning, return it, go to Epcot, present your deposit slip, and get another chair at no additional charge.

Timing Your Visit

Retirees should make the most of their flexible schedules and go to Disney World in fall or spring (excluding holiday weeks), when the weather is the nicest and the crowds are the thinnest. Crowds are also sparse from the end of January through the beginning of February, but the weather is unpredictable. If you visit Disney World in winter, bring coats and sweaters, plus warm-weather clothing. Be prepared for anything from near-freezing rain to afternoons in the 80s.

The Price of Admission

Only Florida residents get senior discounts on Disney World admission (page 52). For additional information, see our section on admission options (pages 50–53).

Lodging

If you can afford it, stay in Walt Disney World. If you're concerned about the quality of your accommodations or the availability of transportation, staying inside the Disney complex will ease your mind. The rooms are some of the nicest in the Orlando/Kissimmee area, and are always clean and well maintained. Plus transportation is always available to any destination in Disney World at no additional cost.

Disney hotels reserve rooms closer to restaurants and transportation for guests of any age who can't tolerate much walking. They also provide golf carts to pick up from and deliver guests to their rooms. Cart service can vary dramatically depending on the time of day and the number of guests requesting service. At check-in time (around 3 p.m.), for example, the wait for a ride could be as long as 40 minutes.

There are many quality hotels in the area, but we recommend seniors stay in Walt Disney World because:

1. The quality of the properties is consistently above average.
2. Transportation companies that operate buses for "outside" hotels run only every hour or so. Disney buses run continuously. Staying in Disney World guarantees you can get transportation whenever you need it.
3. You may be eligible for discounts on shows and early entrance to the parks.
4. Boarding pets overnight at the kennels is available only to Disney resort guests.

5. You get free parking in the major theme parks' lots.
6. You get preferential tee times on resort golf courses.

All Disney hotels are large and spread out. While it's easy to avoid most stairs, it is often a long hike to your room from the parking lot, bus stops, or public areas. Seniors intending to spend more time at Epcot and Disney-MGM Studios than at the Magic Kingdom or the Animal Kingdom should consider the Yacht and Beach Club resorts, Swan and Dolphin, or BoardWalk Inn.

The Contemporary Resort is a good choice for mobile seniors who want to be on the monorail system (wheelchairs can't access the monorail platform), as are the Grand Floridian and Polynesian resorts, though both sprawl over many acres, necessitating a lot of walking. For a restful, rustic feeling, choose the Wilderness Lodge. If you want a kitchen and all the comforts of home, book Old Key West Resort or BoardWalk Villas.

RVers will find pleasant surroundings at Disney's Fort Wilderness Campground. There are also several KOA campgrounds within 20 minutes of Walt Disney World. None, however, offer the wilderness setting or amenities that Disney does, but they cost less.

Elderhostels

Elderhostel, an educational travel and study program for seniors, has several programs in the Orlando area that allow time for participants to visit Walt Disney World. Most of the one-week sessions are hosted by educational institutions, though some use private hotels. Subjects range from anthropology to zoology, French to cabinetmaking. Classes last about four-and-a-half hours each day, and most programs don't assign homework, leaving ample opportunity for making friends or taking an afternoon trip to Disney World.

Elderhostel advises participants to arrange their sightseeing before or after their course, but several of the central Florida programs advertise their proximity to Walt Disney World. These include:

- Camp Challenge in Sorrento, 20 miles north of Orlando
- Canterbury Retreat and Conference Center in Oviedo, five miles northeast of Orlando
- Thunderbird Outdoor Center at Wekiva Springs, 20 minutes northwest of Orlando
- Stetson University/Off Campus in De Land, 35 miles north of Orlando
- San Pedro Retreat and Conference Center in Winter Park, 20 minutes from Orlando
- Deerhaven Camp and Conference Center in the Ocala National Forest, 16 miles west of De Land and about 1 hour and 40 minutes from Orlando

For information on Elderhostel, don't contact the camps listed. Instead, contact Elderhostel Monday–Friday, from 9 a.m. to 9 p.m. EST:

Elderhostel
75 Federal Street
Boston, MA 02110
(617) 426-8056

Transportation

Roads in Walt Disney World can be daunting. Armed with a moderate sense of direction and an above-average sense of humor, however, even the most timid driver can learn to get around in the World. If you're easily intimidated, book a hotel on the monorail and stay off the road.

If you drive to limit your walking, parking isn't a problem. Lots are served by trams that link the parking area and the theme park's front gate. For guests with mobility problems, parking spaces for the disabled are available adjacent to each park's entrance. The attendant at the pay booth will give you a special ticket for your dashboard and will direct you to the reserved spaces. Though Disney requires that you be recognized officially as handicapped to use this parking, temporarily disabled or injured persons also are permitted access.

Senior Dining

Eat breakfast at your hotel restaurant or save money by having juice and rolls in your room. Although you aren't allowed to bring food into the parks, fruit, fruit juice, and soft drinks are sold throughout Disney World. Make your lunch priority seating for before noon to avoid the lunch crowds. Follow with an early dinner and be out of the restaurants, rested and ready for evening touring and fireworks, long before the main crowd begins to think about dinner.

We recommend seniors fit dining and rest times into the day. Remember Dad on the Dumbo-or-Die-in-a-Day Touring Plan? He'll be gobbling fast foods as he hauls his toddlers around the park at breakneck speed. Reserve a window table for your early lunch and wave to him as he races by. Plan lunch as your break in the day. Sit back, relax, and enjoy. Then return to your hotel for a nap.

Have a Plan

From planning the time to visit to observing our first rule of touring ("Arrive early! Arrive early! Arrive early!"), seniors generally are the perfect *Unofficial Guide* patrons. Those who can get by on less sleep enjoy the stress-free pleasure of touring the parks in early morning. Late sleepers should visit Disney World during less crowded, off-peak times.

It's imperative to follow our maxim, "Have a plan or get a frontal lobotomy." Select a touring plan. Before you go the park, read the ride and show descriptions and pick what you want to see or skip so that you'll be able to efficiently follow the plan. Arrive at the park's gates at least a half hour before official opening. Move as fast as you can early in the day so that you'll be able to slow down after an hour or so, knowing the most strenuous part of the plan and potential bottlenecks are behind you.

Seniors who ask us whether the touring plans work for folks who want to take things a little slower should take heart:

My mother (age 77) and myself (age 47) visited Disney for the first time. We followed your "Type A" schedule and really enjoyed the challenge of it. We were standing in line for Star Tours and the friendly attendant was advising us on the popular attractions to see. He suggested Tower of Terror, Indiana Jones, Voyage of the Little Mermaid, and Muppet Vision 4D. We said we had already seen them all. He said, "It's only 10 o'clock in the morning and you have seen all of those already?" We said, "Yes," and held up your guidebook.

Every senior should take at least one behind-the-scenes tour, most of which are at Epcot. They offer an in-depth look at the operations of Walt Disney World. Especially worthwhile are Hidden Treasures and Gardens of the World. If you don't have time for these lengthy tours, the shorter Greenhouse Tour at Epcot's The Land pavilion is a "must-see." Backstage Magic visits behind-the-scenes locations at several theme parks, while Keys to the Kingdom provides a glimpse of the history and hidden operations of the Magic Kingdom. Ranging in duration from one to seven hours and in price from $5 to $160 per person, all of the tours require a lot of walking and standing.

Finally, include quiet time in your itinerary. We recommend Disney patrons of all ages return to their hotel during the hot, crowded part of the day for lunch, a nap, and even a swim.

When You Need to Contact the Outside World

Pay telephones are located throughout Walt Disney World. Amplified handsets are available for the hearing-impaired in all four major theme parks. Handset locations are marked on each park's map, provided free when you enter. A Telecommunication Device for the Deaf (TDD) is available at Guest Relations in all theme parks.

Telephones that guests in wheelchairs can reach are scattered throughout all parks except the Magic Kingdom, where they're under the Walt Disney World Railroad Station.

Walt Disney World for Disabled Guests

VISITORS WITH SPECIAL NEEDS

Wholly or Partially Nonambulatory Guests may rent wheelchairs. Most rides, shows, attractions, rest rooms, and restaurants in the World accommodate the nonambulatory disabled. For specific inquiries, call (407) 824-4321. If you're in a theme park and need assistance, go to Guest Relations.

A limited number of electric carts (motorized convenience vehicles) are available for rent. Easy and fun to drive, they give nonambulatory guests a tremendous degree of freedom and mobility. For some reason, vehicles at the Magic Kingdom are much faster than those at other parks.

Close-in parking is available for disabled visitors at all Disney lots. Request directions when you pay your parking fee. All monorails and most rides, shows, rest rooms, and restaurants accommodate wheelchairs. One major exception is the Contemporary Resort monorail station, where passengers must enter or exit on escalators.

An information booklet for disabled guests is available at wheelchair rental locations throughout the World. Theme park maps issued to each guest on admission are symbol-coded to show nonambulatory guests which attractions accommodate wheelchairs.

Even if an attraction doesn't accommodate wheelchairs, nonambulatory guests still may ride if they can transfer from their wheelchair to the ride's vehicle. Disney staff, however, aren't trained or permitted to assist in transfers. Guests must be able to board the ride unassisted or have a member of their party assist them. Either way, members of the nonambulatory guest's party will be permitted to go along on the ride.

Because waiting areas of most attractions won't accommodate wheelchairs, nonambulatory guests and their party should request boarding instructions from a Disney attendant as soon as they arrive at an attraction. Almost always, the entire group will be allowed to board without a lengthy wait.

A woman from New Orleans who traveled with a nonambulatory friend writes:

> The most recent trip is what I really wanted to tell you about. I went with a very dear friend of mine who is a paraplegic, confined to a wheelchair. It was his first trip to WDW, and I knew that it was a handicap-friendly place, but we were still a little apprehensive about how much we would be able to do. The official pamphlet distributed by the WDW staff is helpful, but it implies limitations, such as stating that one must be able to navigate (i.e., walk) the catwalks of Space Mountain in case of emergency. After reading this, Brian and I

thought that we would end up walking around the MK looking at the rides, not riding them. The reality is, nonambulatory visitors are able to do much more—one only has to ask the cast members what is really allowed. Of course, I'm sure the WDW publication is written to cover liability purposes; also, Brian is a very active person, who is able to transfer from his wheelchair without too much difficulty, so we were able to ride almost everything we wanted! We both had a terrific time. The only ride that it seems we should have been able to ride but couldn't was Pirates of the Caribbean, and [this was] only because the railings at the loading site are just a few inches too close together for a wheelchair to pass through. Anyway, my point is that it may be encouraging to disabled readers of the Unofficial Guide *to know that there are options available; of course, with the caveat that it depends on the individual's mobility. I would recommend to anyone to not avoid a ride—ask first.*

Visitors with Dietary Restrictions can be assisted at Guest Relations in the theme parks. For Walt Disney World restaurants outside the theme parks, call the restaurant a day in advance for assistance.

Sight- and/or Hearing-Impaired Guests aren't forgotten. Guest Relations at the theme parks provide complimentary tape cassettes and portable tape players to assist sight-impaired guests (deposit required). At the same locations, TDDs are available for hearing-impaired guests. In addition to TDDs, many pay phones in the major parks are equipped with amplifying headsets. See your Disney map for locations.

In addition, braille guide maps are available. And some rides provide closed captioning, while many theater attractions provide reflective captioning. The theater shows also offer interpreted performances every day at a different park.

Visitors from Other Countries

Foreign visitors are warmly welcomed at Walt Disney World and represent a large percentage of its guests. Most Magic Kingdom and Animal Kingdom attractions are straightforward and easily understood by visitors with limited English. Many attractions at Epcot and Disney-MGM Studios, however, depend heavily on narration. A Scandinavian visitor urges us:

You should write something about how interesting the attractions are to people who don't have English as their mother tongue. We are Norwegians, we all know English fairly well, but we still had problems understanding significant parts of some attractions because the Disney people talk too fast.

That goes especially for Body Wars, which we all thought was boring, but also for the Jungle Cruise and the Backstage Tour.

European guests frequently contrast the Magic Kingdom with Disneyland Paris. This comment from an English gentleman is typical:

The Magic Kingdom was a great disappointment. We all felt it was too crowded whatever the time of day. For European visitors, we recommend they visit Disneyland Paris instead of Magic Kingdom. It is much prettier and far better laid out. Their rides are also better.

The size of the portions in restaurants at Walt Disney World astounds many visitors from abroad, including this man from Surrey, England:

Please warn your readers who are not American about the very big helpings at all of the restaurants. We usually found that a starter alone or a main course shared between two was sufficient (even though at home we consider ourselves to be big eaters). We rarely made it to the dessert menu.

Incidentally, many Walt Disney World restaurants have menus available in French, German, Japanese, and Spanish.

Foreign language assistance is available throughout the World. Call (407) 824-4321 or stop by Guest Relations in the parks. There are also park maps available in German, Spanish, Japanese, Portuguese, and French.

The parks' unabashedly patriotic atmosphere is expressed in flag raisings, attractions that chronicle U.S. history, and entire themed areas inspired by events in America's past (Frontierland and Liberty Square in the Magic Kingdom, for example). While most patriotic fanfare is festive and enjoyable to anyone, *The Hall of Presidents* in the Magic Kingdom and *The American Adventure* at Epcot may be an overdose for some foreign visitors.

Foreign currency of most countries can be exchanged for dollars at the Guest Relations windows of the Ticket and Transportation Center and at the Guest Relations window in the ticketing areas of the theme parks. The amount these locations can exchange is limited. For large transactions, use the American Express office just outside the main entrance to Epcot or the Sun Trust Bank to the left of City Hall in the Magic Kingdom.

Part Six

Arriving and Getting Around

Getting There

DIRECTIONS

Motorists can reach any Walt Disney World destination via World Drive off US 192, or via Epcot Drive off I-4 (see map, pages 210–211).

Warning! I-4, connecting Daytona and Tampa, generally runs east to west but takes a north/south slant through the Orlando/Kissimmee area. This directional change complicates getting oriented in and around Disney World. Logic suggests that highways branching off I-4 should run north and south, but most run east/west here. Until you're somewhat familiar with the area, have a good map at your side.

From I-10   Take I-10 east across Florida to I-75 southbound. Exit I-75 onto the Florida Turnpike. Exit at Clermont and take US 27 south. Turn onto US 192 and follow the signs to Walt Disney World.

From I-75 Southbound   Follow I-75 south to the Florida Turnpike. Exit at Clermont and take US 27 south. Turn onto US 192 and follow the signs to Walt Disney World.

From I-95 Southbound   Follow I-95 south to I-4. Go west on I-4, passing through Orlando. Take Exit 26, marked Epcot/Disney Village, and follow the signs to your Disney destination.

From Daytona or Orlando   Go west on I-4 through Orlando. Take Exit 26, marked Epcot/Disney Village, and follow the signs.

From the Orlando International Airport   Leaving the airport, go southwest on the Central Florida Greenway (FL 417), a toll road. FL 417 will intersect FL 536; keep left. FL 536 will cross over I-4 and become Epcot Drive. From here, follow the signs to your destination. An alternate route is to take FL 528 (Beeline Highway toll road) west for approximately 12 miles to the intersection with I-4. Go west on I-4 to Exit 26, marked Epcot/Disney Village, and follow the signs.

From Miami, Fort Lauderdale, and Southeastern Florida   Head north on the Florida Turnpike to I-4 westbound. Take Exit 26, marked Epcot/Disney Village, and follow the signs.

From Tampa and Southwestern Florida   Take I-75 northbound to I-4. Go east on I-4, take Exit 25 onto US 192 westbound, and then follow the signs.

Walt Disney World Exits Off I-4

Going east to west (in the direction of Orlando to Tampa), three I-4 exits serve Walt Disney World.

Exit 27 (marked FL 535/Lake Buena Vista) primarily serves the Disney Village Hotel Plaza and Downtown Disney, including the Disney Village Marketplace, Pleasure Island, and Disney's West Side. This exit puts you on roads with lots of traffic signals. Avoid it unless you're headed to one of the above destinations.

Exit 26 (marked Epcot/Disney Village) delivers you to a four-lane expressway right into the heart of Disney World. It's the fastest and most convenient way for westbound travelers to access almost all Disney World destinations except the new Animal Kingdom and Disney's Wide World of Sports.

Exit 25 (marked US 192/Magic Kingdom) is the best route for eastbound travelers to all Disney World destinations. For westbound travelers, it's the best exit for accessing the Animal Kingdom and Disney's Wide World of Sports.

GETTING TO WALT DISNEY WORLD FROM THE AIRPORT

If you're flying, buy a package that includes transportation from the airport to your hotel if you don't rent a car. If you aren't purchasing a package, try to find a hotel that offers shuttle service to the airport. Or, try to share transportation to the Disney World area. If you take an independent shuttle (shared with other Disney-bound passengers), expect to pay $20–38 per person round trip. Mears Motor Transportation Service (phone (407) 423-5566) charges $28 per adult and $20 per child ages 3 to 11 round trip (children under age 3 ride free). Mears shuttles depart from the airport every 15–20 minutes; be sure to make a reservation for your return trip. Cabs cost about $32–42 one way.

If there are at least two in your party, you could rent a compact car at the airport at a weekly rate (even if you won't need the car for an entire week). For only a few dollars more than the shuttle fee or cab fare, you will meet your airport transportation needs and have a car at your disposal. Many rental companies, however, require you to keep the car for at least five 24-hour periods to get the weekly rate.

RENTING A CAR

Readers planning to stay in the World frequently ask if they will need a car. If your plans don't include restaurants, attractions, or other destinations outside of Disney World, the answer is a very qualified no. You won't require a car, but, after considering the thoughts of this reader from Snohomish, Washington, you might want one:

> We rented a car and were glad we did. It gave us more options, though we used the [Disney] bus transportation quite extensively. With a car we could drive to the grocery store to restock our snack supply. It also came in handy for our night out. I shudder at how long it might have taken us to get from the Caribbean Beach to the Polynesian to leave our kids [at the childcare facility], then to Pleasure Island, then back to the Polynesian [to get the kids], and then back to the Caribbean Beach. At $8 an hour [for childcare] you don't want to waste time! It was also nice to drive to Typhoon Lagoon with a car full of clothes, lunches, and other paraphernalia. It was also easier to drive to the other hotels for special meals. And, of course, if you plan to travel out of the World during your stay, a car is a must.

A dad from Avon Lake, Ohio, adds:

> It was unbelievable how often we used our rental car. Although we stayed at the Grand Floridian, we found the monorail convenient only for the Magic Kingdom. Of the six nights we stayed, we used our car five days.

For a woman from Derry, New Hampshire, a

> rental car was essential. Considering the price of airport transfers, it doesn't cost much more and the hassle it saves is monumental.

For a grandmother from Allentown, Pennsylvania, however, the rental car was a waste of money:

> *The Disney bus was great, as a matter of fact, excellent! We never waited longer than 10 or 15 minutes, and we traveled everywhere, including resort to resort (the bus driver was very helpful here). I read in your guide that the bus service wasn't that great—we have no complaints. I'm only sorry I rented a car during our stay—it was a waste of money—believe me, I recommend the bus service.*

A family from Erie, Pennsylvania, disagrees:

> *Bus travel at night was ridiculous—1 hour and 15 minutes to get from Port Orleans to the Polynesian for the luau by way of Pleasure Island. There must be a better way; we will rent a car next time.*

A family from Portland, Maine, did just that:

> *We stayed outside of WDW and tried to commute on the bus furnished by our hotel. After two days we gave up and rented a car.*

How the Orlando Rental Car Companies Stack Up

Unofficial Guide readers provide us with a lot of information about the quality of the car and service they receive from Orlando car rental companies. In general, most folks are looking for:

1. Quick, courteous, and efficient processing on pick-up.
2. A nice, well-maintained, late-model automobile.
3. A car that is clean and odor-free.
4. Quick, courteous, and efficient processing on return.
5. If applicable, an efficient shuttle service between the rental agency and the airport.

Most of our readers rent cars from Alamo, Avis, Budget, Dollar, Hertz, or National. On a scale of 0 (worst) to 100 (best), the following table shows how they rate the Orlando operations of each company, based on the five items listed above.

If you would like to participate in our rental car survey, send us your completed *Unofficial Guide* Reader Survey form from the back of this book.

Company	Pick-Up Efficiency	Condition of the Car	Cleanliness of the Car	Return Efficiency	Shuttle Efficiency
Alamo	61	79	82	81	80
Avis	75	93	94	84	96
Budget	80	90	95	89	98
Dollar	79	88	88	88	84
Hertz	78	92	93	92	91
National	82	93	94	92	93

If you rent a car, a 6% sales tax and a $2.05-per-day sta[...]
be heaped onto your rental fee. If you rent from an age[...]
facilities or shuttles, an additional 9% airport tax will be [...]

Remember that you can wait and rent a car at your hotel [...]
actually need it.

Getting Oriented

A GOOD MAP IS HARD TO FIND

Readers frequently complain about signs and maps provided by Disney.
While it's easy to find the major theme parks, it can be quite an odyssey to
locate other Walt Disney World destinations. Many Disney-supplied maps
are stylistic and hard to read, while others provide incomplete information.
Worse, the maps (produced by different Disney divisions) don't always agree.

A good map—the Walt Disney World Property Map—is available by
calling (407) 934-7639. If you forget to get copies before you leave home,
they're available from Guest Relations at any Disney theme park or hotel.

FINDING YOUR WAY AROUND

Walt Disney World is like any big city. It's easy to get lost there. Signs for
the theme parks are excellent, but finding a restaurant or hotel is often confusing, even for Disney World veterans. The easiest way to orient yourself
is to think in terms of five major areas, or clusters:

1. The first major cluster encompasses all the hotels and theme parks
   around the Seven Seas Lagoon. This includes the Magic Kingdom, hotels connected by the monorail, the Shades of Green
   resort, and two golf courses.
2. The second cluster includes developments on and around Bay
   Lake: Wilderness Lodge, Fort Wilderness Campground, Discovery Island, River Country, and two golf courses.
3. Cluster three contains Epcot, Disney-MGM Studios, Disney's
   BoardWalk, Disney's Wide World of Sports, the so-called Epcot
   resort hotels, and the Caribbean Beach Resort.
4. The fourth cluster encompasses Walt Disney World Village; the
   Disney Institute; Downtown Disney (including the Disney Village Marketplace, Pleasure Island, and Disney's West Side);
   Typhoon Lagoon; a golf course; Disney Village Hotel Plaza; and
   the Port Orleans, Dixie Landings, and Old Key West resorts.
5. The fifth and newest cluster contains the Animal Kingdom, Blizzard Beach, and the Disney All-Star and Coronado Springs
   resorts.

Walt Disney World Touring and Hotel Clusters

535

535

Osprey Ridge Golf Course

Bonnet Creek Golf Club

Live Oak Lane

Buena Vista Drive

Eagle Pines Golf Course

Vista Blvd.

Dixie Landings Resort

Community Dr.

Port Orleans Resort

4

Villas at the Disney Institute

Disney Institute

Old Key West

Lake Buena Vista Golf Course

Downtown Disney

Marketplace

Bonnet Creek Rd.

Buena Vista Palace

Grosvenor Resort

The Hilton

Courtyard by Marriott

Disney's West Side

Pleasure Island

3

Typhoon Lagoon

To Orlando

The Crossroads Shopping Ctr.

Travelodge Hotel

DoubleTree Guest Suites Resort

EXIT 27

Hotel Royal Plaza

535

Caribbean Beach Resort

EXIT 26

4

536

EXIT 25

To Tampa

Osceola Parkway (toll)

To Kissimmee ➡

192

How to Travel around the World (or the *Real* Mr. Toad's Wild Ride)

Trying to commute around Walt Disney World can be frustrating. A Magic Kingdom street vendor, telling me how to get to Epcot, proposed, "You can take the ferry or the monorail to the Transportation and Ticket Center. Then you can get another monorail, or you can catch the bus, or you can take a tram out to your car and drive over there yourself." What he didn't say was that it would be easier to ride a mule than to take any conceivable combination from this transportation smorgasbord.

There's no simple way to travel around the World, but there are ways to make it easier. Just don't wait to get moving until ten minutes before you're due somewhere.

TRANSPORTATION TRADE-OFFS FOR GUESTS

Lodging outside Walt Disney World

Disney day guests (those not staying inside Disney World) can use the monorail system, most of the bus system, and some of the boat system. If, for example, you go to Disney-MGM Studios in the morning, then decide to go to Epcot for lunch, you can take a bus directly there. The most important advice we can give day guests is to park your car in the lot of the theme park (or other Disney destination) where you plan to finish your day. This is critical if you stay at a park until closing time.

Driving to the Magic Kingdom

Most Magic Kingdom day guests park in the Transportation and Ticket Center lot, an expanse about the size of Vermont. Sections are named for Disney characters. When you pay your parking fee, you'll get a receipt with aisle numbers and names of sections listed on the reverse. Mark where you have parked and write the aisle number in the space provided. Carry the receipt in a safe place and refer to it when you return to your car. (Failure to do this may result in a long search for your car at a time when you're tuckered out.) If you have a disabled person in your party, you'll be directed to close-in parking.

After parking and marking your space's location on your receipt, walk a short distance to a loading station and catch a tram to the Transportation and Ticket Center (TTC) where you can buy admission to the theme parks. If you're going to the Magic Kingdom, ride the ferryboat across Seven Seas Lagoon or catch the monorail. If the line for the monorail extends down the ramp from the loading platform, take the ferry. (One ferry holds almost as many passengers as three monorail trains.) The trip to the Magic Kingdom takes the monorail about three-and-a-half to five minutes. The ferry crosses in six-and-a-half minutes.

At all theme parks, if you leave and intend to return to that park or visit another on the same day, have your hand stamped for free re-entry.

Going to Epcot from the Magic Kingdom   In the morning, take the monorail to the TTC and transfer to the Epcot monorail. In the afternoon, take the ferry to the TTC. If you plan to remain at Epcot until closing and your car is in the TTC lot, drive your car to Epcot. If you plan to return to the Magic Kingdom or don't have a car at the TTC, take the Epcot monorail.

Going to Disney-MGM Studios from the Magic Kingdom   If you plan to end your day at the Studios, drive. If you intend to return to the Magic Kingdom, take the bus. Incidentally, the loading area for the bus to the Studios is immediately to the left as you leave the Magic Kingdom. You don't have to return to the TTC.

Going to the Animal Kingdom from the Magic Kingdom   If you intend to finish your day at the Animal Kingdom, drive. If you plan to return to the Magic Kingdom, take the bus.

Leaving the Magic Kingdom at the End of the Day   If you need to return to the TTC, try the ferry first. If it's mobbed (usually happens only at closing), take the "express" (doesn't stop at hotels) or "local" monorail.

Sometimes when you reach the TTC, a throng is waiting to board the parking lot trams. Rather than join the crowd, walk to the nearest section in the lot (Chip 'n' Dale) and wait there. When the tram stops and people disembark, board and ride to where your car is parked.

Driving to Epcot

Park at the TTC (Magic Kingdom) lot and commute via monorail, or park in Epcot's lot. Parking at Epcot's lot is best unless you plan to visit the Magic Kingdom later and conclude your day there. Arrangements at Epcot's lot are much like those at the Magic Kingdom: trams shuttle among the parking areas and patrons get a receipt on which to mark their parking place for later reference. At Epcot, sections of the lot are named for pavilions in the park's Future World area. Close-in parking for the disabled is available. The big difference between Magic Kingdom and Epcot parking is that access to the park is direct from the tram at Epcot, whereas to reach the Magic Kingdom you must transfer from the tram to the ferry or monorail at the TTC.

Going to the Magic Kingdom from Epcot   Take the monorail to the TTC, then transfer to the Magic Kingdom express monorail. If you don't plan to return to Epcot and your car is in Epcot's lot, drive to the TTC and take the ferry or monorail as crowd conditions allow.

Going to Disney-MGM Studios from Epcot   You have three choices. If you plan to finish the day at the Studios, drive. If you plan to return to Epcot, exit the park through the main entrance and catch a bus to the Studios or exit through the International Gateway (in World Showcase) and catch a boat. This last option is definitely best if you're returning to Epcot for dinner at one of World Showcase's ethnic restaurants.

Going to the Animal Kingdom from Epcot   If you plan to return to Epcot, take the bus. If you intend to finish your day at the Animal Kingdom, drive.

Driving to Disney-MGM Studios

Disney-MGM Studios has its own pay lot. As at other lots, trams transport you to the park entrance and close-in parking is available for the disabled.

Going to the Magic Kingdom from Disney-MGM Studios   Regardless of where you intend to conclude the day, it is probably easier to take the bus to the Magic Kingdom. Because the bus unloads at the park's entrance rather than the TTC, you bypass the hassle of reparking, taking the tram to the TTC, and catching the monorail or ferry. It's the same story when you return to the Studios.

Going to Epcot from Disney-MGM Studios   Drive to Epcot if you don't intend to return to the Studios. If you plan to return, take a bus or a boat to Epcot. Take the bus if you want to begin your Epcot visit at the main entrance (Future World). If you're headed for World Showcase, take the boat.

Going to the Animal Kingdom from Disney-MGM Studios   If you plan to return to the Studios, take the bus. If you intend to end your day at the Animal Kingdom, drive.

Driving to the Animal Kingdom

The Animal Kingdom has its own pay parking lot. Trams shuttle you to the entrance.

Going to the Other Theme Parks from the Animal Kingdom   Isolated on the west side of Walt Disney World, the Animal Kingdom is accessible only by road. Because it generally closes earlier than the other parks, it's best to commute in your own car. The exception is when you intend to return to the Animal Kingdom from the Magic Kingdom. In this case only, use the bus.

Moving Your Car from Lot to Lot on the Same Day

Once you have paid to park in any major theme park lot, hang on to your receipt. If you visit another park later in the same day, you'll be admitted to that park's lot without additional charge when you show your receipt. Disney lodging guests park free in any theme park lot.

Taking a Shuttle Bus from Your Out-of-the-World Hotel

Many independent hotels and motels near Walt Disney World provide trams and buses. They're fairly carefree, depositing you near theme park entrances and saving you parking fees. The rub is that they might not get you there as early as you desire (a critical point if you take our touring advice) or be available when you wish to return to your lodging. Also, some shuttles go directly to Disney World, while others stop at additional area lodgings. Each service is a bit different; check the particulars before you make reservations.

Warning: Most hotel shuttles don't add vehicles at park opening or closing times. In the mornings, you may not get a seat. At closing or during a hard rain, expect a mass exodus from the park. More people will be waiting for the shuttle than the bus will hold, and some will be left behind. Most (not all) shuttles return for stranded guests, but the guests may wait 20 minutes to over an hour for a ride.

If you're depending on shuttles, leave the park at least 45 minutes before closing. If you stay until closing and lack the energy to hassle with the shuttle, take a cab. Cab stands are near the Bus Information buildings at the Animal Kingdom, Epcot, Disney-MGM Studios, and the Transportation and Ticket Center. If no cabs are on-hand, staff at Bus Information will call one for you. If you're leaving the Magic Kingdom at closing, it's easier to take the monorail to a hotel and catch a cab there (rather than the TTC taxi stand).

TRANSPORTATION TRADE-OFFS FOR GUESTS AT WALT DISNEY WORLD RESORTS AND CAMPGROUND

The most hotly debated topic among Disney resort guests is whether it's more efficient to use a car or Disney transportation to get around the World. These reader comments are representative:

A couple from Woodbridge, Illinois, writes:

> *This time down we rented a car. It really came in handy and turned out to be a good idea. We still took the buses to the major parks, because you just can't beat their system for that, dropping you off right by the gate with only a short walk and no trams, ferries, or monorail required. But the car was great for the water parks, the Marketplace, and going to other hotels for dinner or just to look around. The last two times, we commented [on] how hard and inconvenient it was to get to another hotel by bus. It easily took an hour vs. a five-minute drive by car. You can get around without a car, but it really was nice to have one.*

A man from New Orleans gives us his opinion:

> *We found a car to be an absolute necessity. It added at least two hours each day to our schedule. The monorail system was a bit confusing and slow, not to mention very crowded. The bus stops*

were not particularly convenient to our room, and there were always people waiting. On the other hand, with a car, parking was very easy, traffic was minimal, and once we had our basic orientation, it was easy to get around Disney World.

A dad from Bethel, Connecticut, states:

I have to disagree with your opinion about transportation. Though it may be faster to get from place to place with your own car, we were here to enjoy ourselves. The idea of not having to get behind a wheel for a week was part of the fun of this vacation. With a little patience you could get anywhere you wanted. Why do we have to be in such a hurry? I think Disney's transportation system is fabulous, comfortable, clean, and efficient. It allowed us the freedom of going off in different directions.

A family from Madison, New Jersey, tells us their story:

The second day, we had a problem. We had taken the monorail from the Magic Kingdom to the Contemporary hotel to eat dinner at the cafe, and after dinner we were unsure how to get back to the All-Star resorts. This was about 7 p.m. We asked two different hotel employees and were told to take the bus to the Disney Marketplace and then get another bus to the hotel. After we got on the bus and were on our way, it became obvious this could not have been the best way. It took 40 minutes to get to the Marketplace, then a 20-minute wait for the bus, and another 40 minutes back to the All-Star resorts. The whole time, my husband and I held sleeping children in our arms.

A father of two in Hillsboro, Oregon, writes:

We originally thought that being in a monorail hotel would be convenient. It turned out that it still takes nearly an hour to go to places other than the Magic Kingdom or the TTC. After one day of waiting for the Disney Transportation System, we decided to rent a car. The importance of having your own car in order to reduce the travel times cannot be said enough.

THE DISNEY TRANSPORTATION SYSTEM

The Disney transportation system is large, diversified, and generally efficient, but it sometimes is overwhelmed during peak periods, particularly at park opening and closing times. If you could be assured of getting on a bus, boat, or monorail at these critical times, we would advise you to leave your car at home. However, the reality is that when huge crowds want to go somewhere at the same time, delays are unavoidable. In addition, some destinations are served directly, while many others require one or more transfers. Finally, it's sometimes difficult to figure how the buses, boats, and monorails interconnect.

In the most basic terms, the Disney Transportation system is a "hub and spoke" system. Hubs include the Transportation and Ticket Center, Downtown Disney, and all four major theme parks (from two hours before official opening time to two to three hours after closing). Although there are some exceptions, there is direct service from Disney resorts to the major theme parks and to Downtown Disney, and from park to park. If you want to go from resort to resort, resort to water park, or most anywhere else, you will have to transfer at one of the hubs.

If a hotel offers boat or monorail service, its bus service will be limited, meaning you'll have to transfer at a hub for many Disney World destinations. If you're staying at a Magic Kingdom resort served by monorail (Polynesian, Contemporary, Grand Floridian), you'll be able to commute efficiently to the Magic Kingdom via monorail. If, however, you want to visit Epcot, you must take the monorail to the TTC and transfer to the Epcot monorail. (Guests at the Polynesian can eliminate the transfer by walking five to ten minutes to the TTC and catching the direct monorail to Epcot.)

If you're staying at an Epcot resort (Swan, Dolphin, Yacht and Beach Club resorts, BoardWalk Inn and Villas) you can walk or commute via boat to the International Gateway (back door) entrance of Epcot. Although direct buses link Epcot resorts to the Magic Kingdom and the Animal Kingdom, there's no direct bus to Epcot's main entrance or to Disney-MGM Studios. To reach the Studios from Epcot resorts, you must take a boat.

The Villas of the Disney Institute and the Caribbean Beach, Dixie Landings, Port Orleans, Coronado Springs, Old Key West, and All-Star resorts offer direct buses to all the theme parks. The rub is that guests sometimes must walk a long way to bus stops or endure more than a half-dozen additional pick-ups before actually heading for the park(s). Commuting in the morning from these resorts is generally no sweat, though you may have to ride standing up. Returning in the evening, however, can be a different story.

The hotels of the Disney Village Hotel Plaza terminated their guest-transportation contract with Disney Transportation Operations, so they provide service with another carrier. The substitute, which we feel doesn't measure up, constitutes a real problem for guests at these hotels. Before booking a hotel in the Plaza, check the nature and frequency of shuttles.

Fort Wilderness guests must use the campground's own buses to reach boat landings or the Pioneer Hall bus stop. From these points, respectively, guests can travel directly by boat to the Magic Kingdom or by bus to Disney-MGM Studios, or to other destinations via transfer at the TTC. With the exception of commuting to the Magic Kingdom, the best way for Fort Wilderness guests to commute in Disney World is to drive their own car.

USING THE WALT DISNEY WORLD TRANSPORTATION SYSTEM VS. DRIVING YOUR OWN CAR

To enable you to assess your transportation options, we have developed a chart comparing the approximate commuting times from Disney resorts to various Walt Disney World destinations, using Disney transportation or your own car.

Disney Transportation Times on the chart in the Disney Transportation System (DTS) columns represent a range. For example, if you want to go from the Caribbean Beach Resort to Epcot, the chart indicates a range of 12–45 minutes. The first number (12) is how long your commute will take if everything goes perfectly (your bus is at the stop when you walk up, departs for your destination as soon as you board, and isn't delayed by traffic jams or other problems en route). If you're staying at a resort where the bus makes numerous stops within the complex, the first number assumes that you board at the last embarkation point before the bus heads for its final destination. The second number (45) represents a worst-case scenario. (The bus is pulling away as you arrive at the stop, and you must wait 20 minutes for the next one. When you finally board, the bus makes six more stops in the Caribbean complex before heading for Epcot. Once en route, the bus hits every red light.)

On busier days, buses run every 20 minutes all day. On slower days, some buses (at the Disney Institute and Old Key West, among others) run only once every 45 minutes between noon and 6 p.m. Our worst-case scenario assumes that buses run every 20 minutes. If they're running only every 45 minutes, you must add 25 minutes to the second number to calculate the commute. If buses run from the Caribbean complex to Epcot every 45 minutes, for example, it could take as long as 1 hour and 10 minutes (45 minutes + 25 minutes) to complete the commute. Be sure to ask at your hotel how frequently buses will run during your stay. If your bus makes intermediate stops after leaving your resort, the time spent making the stops is figured into both the best and worst times, because the stops are unavoidable in either case.

Driving Your Own Car The "Your Car" column on the chart indicates the best-case/worst-case situation for driving. To make these times directly comparable to Disney system times, we have added the time it takes to get

Door-to-Door Commuting Times to and from the Disney Resorts and Parks: In Your Car versus the Disney Transportation System†

Time (in minutes) from	To Magic Kingdom		To Epcot		To MGM Studios	
	Your Car	*Disney System*	*Your Car*	*Disney System*	*Your Car*	*Disney System*
All-Star Resorts	26–47	11–31	13–23	8–28	11–20	7–27
Animal Kingdom	15–18	17–37	14–17	14–36	14–17	14–34
Beach Club	25–46	14–34	11–21	5–28*	9–18	16–36
Blizzard Beach	25–46	17–37	13–23	29–62	13–22	30–50
BoardWalk Inn and Villas	25–46	11–31	11–21	5–28*	9–18	16–36
Caribbean Beach	26–47	13–40	13–23	12–45	10–19	6–33
Contemporary	NA	12–23	16–26	13–29	18–27	22–42
Coronado Springs	26–47	11–31	13–23	8–28	11–20	7–27
Disney-MGM Studios	25–46	14–34	14–24	26–59		
Disney Institute	27–48	15–45	13–23	10–37	15–24	8–35
Dixie Landings	27–48	11–36	15–25	9–33	15–24	9–34
Dolphin	24–45	18–38	10–20	10–35*	10–19	12–32
Epcot	25–46	16–35			14–23	21–44
Fort Wilderness	26–47	13–33	13–23	14–60	14–23	17–50
Grand Floridian	NA	4–7	13–23	20–42	15–24	9–29
Magic Kingdom			12–39	13–42	13–29	14–34
Old Key West	25–46	12–40	13–23	7–35	13–22	9–36
Pleasure Island/ Marketplace	27–49	24–58	14–25	21–57	12–22	30–69
Polynesian	NA	7–13	12–22	23–48	14–23	12–32
Port Orleans	26–47	19–39	14–24	15–35	14–23	17–37
Swan	24–45	21–41	10–20	10–35*	10–19	12–32
Typhoon Lagoon	26–47	18–51	13–23	29–62	10–19	38–75
Village Hotel Plaza	30–51	20–74	16–26	12–50	15–24	9–49
Wilderness Lodge	NA	11–41	15–25	18–47	17–26	21–51
Yacht Club	25–46	11–31	11–21	5–28*	9–18	16–36

† Driving time vs. time on the Disney Transportation System (DTS). Driving times include time in your car, stops to pay tolls, time to park, and transfers to Disney trams and monorails where applicable.

* This hotel is within walking distance of Epcot Center; time given includes boat ride

To Animal Kingdom		To Typhoon Lagoon		To Pleasure Island/ Marketplace		To Blizzard Beach	
Your Car	Disney System	Your Car	Disney System	Your Car	Disney System	Your Car	Disney System
9–12	8–25	10–13	9–29	11–14	15–40	4–7	10–28
		15–19	43–57	17–21	33–53	7–13	16–36
15–18	14–33	7–10	22–42	8–11	13–35	10–13	21–41
7–13	8–40	11–14	33–76	12–15	44–77		
15–18	12–30	7–10	24–44	8–11	15–37	10–13	21–41
15–18	15–46	4–7	7–39	5–8	9–43	10–13	23–54
18–21	28–48	15–18	17–40	15–17	28–51	13–16	36–56
9–12	10–31	10–13	9–29	11–14	15–40	4–7	4–26
14–17	14–34	6–9	30–73	7–10	41–74	9–12	30–50
19–22	23–45	7–10	13–37	4–7	5–30	14–17	21–48
18–21	14–43	8–11	9–35	9–12	15–40	13–16	22–49
14–17	20–35	8–11	27–47	9–12	18–40	9–12	8–31
14–17	26–48	10–13	22–43	11–14	30–54	9–12	23–45
22–25	23–56	8–11	18–51	9–12	27–60	17–20	31–56
16–19	16–36	13–16	24–53	14–17	37–64	11–14	24–44
15–18	17–37	15–31	17–53	17–36	30–64	10–13	22–55
17–20	15–43	6–9	9–35	7–10	9–36	12–15	23–49
17–21	33–53	4–7	5–28			12–16	30–50
15–18	18–38	12–15	27–59	13–16	40–70	10–13	24–46
17–20	23–43	7–10	16–36	8–11	24–44	12–15	31–51
14–17	23–38	8–11	30–50	9–12	20–42	9–12	10–32
15–19	43–57			4–7	5–28	11–14	40–57
19–22	30–53	7–10	5–7	4–7	NA	14–17	30–50
18–21	23–51	15–18	23–46	16–19	27–67	13–16	21–48
15–18	16–36	7–10	24–44	8–11	15–37	10–13	21–41

from your parked car to the park's entrance. While Disney buses and monorails deposit guests at the front door, those who drive must sometimes take a tram from their car to the gate, or walk. At the Magic Kingdom, you must take a tram from the parking lot to the TTC, then catch a monorail or ferry to the park's entrance.

WALT DISNEY WORLD TRANSPORTATION SYSTEM FOR TEENAGERS

If you're staying at Walt Disney World and have teens in your party, familiarize yourself with the Disney bus system. Safe, clean, and operating until 1 a.m. on most nights, buses are a great way for teens to get around the World.

WALT DISNEY WORLD BUS SERVICE

Buses in Disney World have an illuminated panel above the front windshield that flashes the bus's destination. Also, theme parks have designated waiting areas for each Disney World destination. To catch the bus to the Caribbean Beach Resort from Disney-MGM Studios, for example, go to the bus stop and wait in the area marked "To the Caribbean Beach Resort." At the resorts, go to any bus stop and wait for the bus with your destination displayed on the illuminated panel. Directions to Disney World destinations are available when you check in or at your hotel's guest relations desk. The clerk at guest relations can also answer your questions about the Disney Transportation System.

Service from the resorts to the major theme parks is fairly direct. You may have to endure intermediate stops, but you won't have to transfer. More problematic, and sometimes requiring transfers, is service to the swimming theme parks and other Disney World hotels.

A dad from Palo Alto, California, describes trying to return to the Disney Inn (now Shades of Green) after dinner at the Beach Club:

> *It took 1½ hours to get back to the Disney Inn by bus, a 10-minute drive by car. Crowds? Breakdowns? Hurricanes? Nope, just waits, connections, and extra stops.*

The fastest way to commute from resort to resort by bus is to take a bus from your resort to one of the major theme parks and from there transfer to your resort destination. This only works, of course, when the major theme parks are open (actually from two hours before opening until two to three hours after closing). If you are attempting to commute to another resort for a late dinner during the off-season when the major parks close early, you will have to transfer at Downtown Disney (Disney Village Marketplace) or at the Transportation and Ticket Center.

Buses begin service to the theme parks at about 7 a.m. on days when the parks' official opening time is 9 a.m. Generally, buses run every 20 minutes. Buses to Disney-MGM Studios, Epcot, or the Animal Kingdom deliver you to the park entrance. Until one hour before the park opens (before 8 a.m. in this example), buses to the Magic Kingdom deliver you to the TTC, where you transfer to the monorail or ferry to complete your commute. Buses take you directly to the Magic Kingdom on early-entry mornings and starting one hour before the park's stated opening on other days.

To be on-hand for the real opening time (when official opening is 9 a.m.), catch direct buses to Epcot, the Animal Kingdom, and Disney-MGM Studios between 7:30 and 8 a.m. Catch direct buses to the Magic Kingdom between 8 and 8:15 a.m. If you must transfer to reach your park, leave 15 to 20 minutes earlier. On days when official opening is 7 or 8 a.m., move up your departure time accordingly.

If you're commuting to a theme park on an early-entry morning, count on the park's opening an hour to an hour and a half before the official opening time for the general public. Buses to the designated early-entry park begin running about two hours before the stated opening time. On an early-entry day when the Magic Kingdom's official opening for the public is 8 a.m., for example, Disney lodging guests can catch a bus to the park as early as 6 a.m. and enter by 6:30 a.m.

For your return bus trip in the evening, leave the park 40 minutes to 1 hour before closing to avoid the rush. If you're caught in the mass exodus, you may be inconvenienced, but you won't be stranded. Buses, boats, and monorails continue to operate for two hours after the parks close.

DISNEY VILLAGE HOTEL PLAZA BUS SERVICE

Although located in Walt Disney World, the hotels of the Disney Village Hotel Plaza provide their own bus service, a service that many, including a family from Prospect, Connecticut, find inferior:

> *We were disappointed in the shuttle bus for the Village hotels. They do not run often enough, and there is no schedule. [The b]us at the parks picks up in [the] middle of busy parking lots. Treats you as second class [compared] to Disney resort guests. Take a cab instead of waiting late at night to get back to [your] hotel. Costs only $9.*

WALT DISNEY WORLD MONORAIL SERVICE

Picture the monorail system as three loops. Loop A is an express route that runs counterclockwise connecting the Magic Kingdom with the Transportation and Ticket Center (TTC). Loop B runs clockwise alongside Loop A, making all stops, with service to (in this order) the TTC, Polynesian Resort, Grand Floridian Beach Resort, Magic Kingdom, and Contemporary Resort. The long Loop C dips southeast like a tail, connecting the TTC with Epcot. The hub for all three loops is the TTC (where you usually park to visit the Magic Kingdom).

The monorail system serving Magic Kingdom resorts usually starts two hours before the official opening time on early-entry days, and an hour and a half before official opening on other days. If you're staying at a Magic Kingdom resort and wish to be among the first in the Magic Kingdom on a non-early-entry morning when official opening is 9 a.m., board the monorail at the times indicated below. On an early-entry morning (when official opening is 9 a.m.), leave 45–60 minutes earlier. If official opening is 8 a.m., bounce everything up yet another hour.

From the Contemporary Resort   7:45–8 a.m.
From the Polynesian Resort   7:50–8:05 a.m.
From the Grand Floridian Beach Resort   8–8:10 a.m.

What's that? You don't have the circadian rhythms of a farmer? Get with the program, Bubba! This is a *Disney* vacation. Haul your buns out of bed and go have fun!

If you're a day guest (no early-entry privileges), you'll be allowed on the monorail at the TTC between 8:15 and 8:30 a.m. on a day when official opening is 9 a.m. If you want to board earlier, walk from the TTC to the Polynesian Resort and board there.

The monorail loop connecting Epcot and the TTC begins operating at 7:30 a.m. on days when Epcot's official opening is 9 a.m. To be at Epcot when the park opens, catch the Epcot monorail at the TTC by 8:05 a.m.

While your multiday pass suggests you can flit at will among parks, actually getting there is more complex. For example, you can't go directly from the Magic Kingdom to Epcot. You must catch the express monorail (Loop A) to the TTC and transfer to the Loop C monorail to Epcot. If lines to board either monorail are short, you can usually reach Epcot in 25–35 minutes. But should you want to go to Epcot for dinner (as many do) and you're departing the Magic Kingdom in late afternoon, you may have to wait 30 minutes or more to board the Loop A monorail. Adding this delay bumps up your commute to 45–55 minutes.

Monorails usually run for two hours after closing to ensure that everyone is served. If a train is too crowded or you need transportation after the monorails have stopped running, catch a bus.

It's great fun to ride in the front cab of the monorail with the conductor. All you have to do is ask, according to a mom from Richmond, Virginia:

> *Speaking of the monorail—don't hesitate to ask about sitting up front—even if you aren't the first ones there. People are somewhat timid about asking, and the monorail attendants won't ever suggest it, so ask! We got to ride up front three times during our stay.*

Major Tip!

Using the Disney transportation system, you can often eliminate a double transfer by commuting to the closest theme park to your destination and transferring there. Works from park opening until an hour after park closing.

Part Seven

Bare Necessities

Credit Cards and Money

CREDIT CARDS

- MasterCard, VISA, and American Express cards are accepted for theme park admission.

- Walt Disney World shops, full-service and counter-service restaurants, and resort hotels will accept only MasterCard, VISA, and American Express.

FINANCIAL MATTERS

Cash Bank service at Epcot, the Animal Kingdom, and Disney-MGM Studios is limited to an automatic teller machine. Branches of Sun Bank are across the street from Downtown Disney Marketplace and at 1675 Buena Vista Drive. Both branches will:

- *Provide cash advances* on MasterCard and VISA (no minimum; maximum equals the patron's credit limit).

- *Cash personal checks* of $200 or less drawn on Sun Bank upon presentation of a driver's license and major credit card.

- *Cash and sell traveler's checks.* The bank cashes the first check up to $100 without charge but levies a $2 service fee for each additional check.

- *Facilitate wiring of money* from the visitor's bank to Sun Bank.

- *Exchange foreign currency* for dollars.

Most VISA and MasterCard cards are accepted at automatic teller machines at Walt Disney World. To use an American Express card, however, you must sign an agreement with American Express before your trip. If your credit card doesn't work in the automatic teller machines, a teller will be able to process your transaction at any Sun Bank full-service location.

A LICENSE TO PRINT MONEY

One of Disney's more sublime ploys for separating you from your money is the printing and issuing of Disney Dollars. Available throughout Disney World in denominations of $1 (Mickey Moolah), $5 (Goofy Greenbacks), and $10 (Minnie Money or Simba Sawbucks), the colorful cash can be used for purchases at Walt Disney World, Disneyland, and Disney Stores nationwide. Disney Dollars can also be exchanged one for one with U.S. currency. Disney money is sometimes included as a perk (for which you're charged dollar for dollar) in Walt Disney Travel Company packages.

While the idea of Disney Dollars seems fun and innocent, it's one of Disney's better moneymakers. Some guests take the money home as souvenirs. Others forget to spend or exchange it before they leave the World, then fail to go to a Disney Store or to exchange the money by mail. Usually, the funny money ends up forgotten in a drawer—exactly as Disney hoped.

THE P.T. BARNUM MEMORIAL WALKWAY

Oh my stars and garters, Mildred, you won't believe what they're doing now! For only $110, you can buy a 10-inch hexagonal brick with your name on it. If you want to go all out, you can purchase a granite brick for $225. Of course, you aren't allowed to take your brick home. Disney is going to use it to build a walkway around a big lake down at Walt Disney World. (They need that walkway really bad in case the monorails and the ferry boats all break down at the same time.) Here's the really good news: It will cost us and our friends who buy bricks only about $9.6 million to build the whole dadgum thing, and we can visit our brick anytime we want . . . if we can find it. Maybe when they get our little sidewalk finished, they'll build another one from Walt Disney World out to Disneyland in California. Those interstate highways are about worn out, you know.

Problems and Unusual Situations

ATTRACTIONS CLOSED FOR REPAIRS

Check in advance with Disney World to see what rides and attractions may be closed for maintenance or repair during your visit. If you're interested in a specific attraction, the call could save you a lot of disappointment. A mother from Dover, Massachusetts, laments:

> *We were disappointed to find Space Mountain, Swiss Family Treehouse, and the* Liberty Belle *Riverboat closed for repairs. We felt that a large chunk of the Magic Kingdom was not working, yet the tickets were still full price and expensive!*

A woman from Pasadena, California, adds:

> *Rides can close without warning. I had called in advance and knew that River Country, Horizons, and 20,000 Leagues would be closed. Our hotel even gave us a list of closed attractions. So, imagine our surprise when we get to the Magic Kingdom and find that Space Mountain is closed with no prior warning. Needless to say, we were disappointed.*

CAR TROUBLE

Security or tow truck patrols will help you if you lock the keys in your parked car or return to find the battery dead. For more serious problems, the closest repair center is Maingate Exxon, US 192 west of I-4, (407) 396-2721. Disney security will help you contact the service station. Arrangements can be made to take you to your Disney World destination or the nearest phone.

LOST AND FOUND

If you lose (or find) something in the Magic Kingdom, go to City Hall. At Epcot, Lost and Found is in the Entrance Plaza. At Disney-MGM Studios, it's at Hollywood Boulevard Guest Relations, and at the Animal Kingdom, it's at Guest Relations at the main entrance. If you discover your loss after you have left the park(s), call (407) 824-4245 (for all parks). See page 36 for the number to call in each park if you're still at the park(s) and discover something is missing.

MEDICAL MATTERS

Relief for a Headache   Aspirin and other sundries are sold at the Emporium on Main Street in the Magic Kingdom (they're kept behind the counter; you must ask), at most retail shops in Epcot's Future World and World Showcase, and in Disney-MGM Studios and the Animal Kingdom.

If You Need a Doctor   Mediclinic provides 24-hour service. Doctors are available for house calls to all area hotels and campgrounds (Disney and non-Disney). House calls are $98 per visit, higher after 10 p.m. If your problem doesn't require a house call, visit the clinic on a walk-in basis (no appointments taken) at 2901 Parkway Boulevard, Suite 3-A in Kissimmee. Minimum charge for a physician consultation at the clinic is $65. The clinic is open from 8 a.m. to 9 p.m. daily, and its main phone is (407) 396-1195.

Center Care walk-in clinic operates two locations that are across the street from one another. The first is at 12500 S. Apopka-Vineland Road and is open 8 a.m. to midnight on weekdays, and 8 a.m. to 8 p.m. on weekends. The second location is at 12139 S. Apopka-Vineland Road and is open 9 a.m. to 9 p.m. on weekdays and 10 a.m. to 10 p.m. on weekends. Call (407) 239-7777 for fees and information. Center Care also operates an "in-room" physician (house call) service. Phone (407) 238-2000.

Prescription Medicine   The closest pharmacy is in Goodings Supermarket on FL 535 in Lake Buena Vista (phone (407) 827-1200). Turner

Drugs (phone (407) 828-8125) charges $5 to deliver a filled prescription to your hotel's front desk. The service is available only to Disney resort guests, and the fee is charged to your hotel account.

SERGEANT BLISTERBLASTER'S GUIDE TO HAPPY FEET AT WALT DISNEY WORLD

1. On Your Feet! Get up, Easy-Boy rider: when you go to Disney World you'll have to walk a lot farther than to the refrigerator. You can log from 5 to 12 miles a day no problem at the Disney parks, so now's the time to get them dogs in shape. Start with some short walks around the neighborhood and increase your distance gradually until you can do 6 miles on weekends without CPR.

2. Attention! During your pre-Disney training program, pay attention when those puppies growl. They will give you a lot of information about your feet and the appropriateness and fit of your shoes. Listen up! No walking in flip-flops, loafers, or sandals. Wear well-constructed, broken-in running or hiking shoes. If you feel a "hot spot," that means a blister is developing. The most common sites for blisters are the heels, the toes, and the balls of your feet. If you note a tendency to develop a hot spot in the same place everytime you walk, cover it prophylactically with Moleskin (available in drugstores without prescription) before you set out. No, sofa bunny, I did not tell you to wear condoms on your feet! *Prophylactically* means to anticipate the problem and treat it in advance. One more thing: keep your toenails cut short and straight across.

3. Sock It Up, Trainee! Good socks are as important as good shoes. When you walk, your feet sweat like a mule in a peat bog, and moisture increases friction. To minimize friction, wear two pairs of socks. The pair next to your feet should ideally be polypropylene thin socks or sock liners. The outer sock can be either a natural fiber like cotton or wool, or a synthetic fiber. To further combat moisture, dust your dogs with some anti-fungal talcum powder.

4. Who Do You Think You Are, John Wayne? Don't be a hero. The time to take care of a foot problem is the minute you notice it. Carry a small foot emergency kit for your platoon. The kit should contain gauze, Betadyne antibiotic ointment, Moleskin or Spenco second skin, scissors, a sewing needle or some such to drain blisters, as well as matches to sterilize the needle. An extra pair of dry socks and some talc is optional.

5. Bite the Bullet! If you develop a hot spot, cover it ASAP with Moleskin or Spenco second skin. Cut the covering large enough to cover the skin surrounding the hot spot. If you develop a blister, air out and dry your foot. Next, drain the fluid but do not remove the top skin. Clean the area with your Betadyne, place a gauze square over the blister, and cover the whole shooting match with Moleskin. If you do not have Moleskin or Spenco second skin, do not try to cover the hot spot or blister with Band-Aids. Band-Aids slip and wad up.

6. Take Care of Your Platoon.   If you have a couple of young green troops in your outfit, they might not sound off when a hot spot comes on. Stop several times a day and check their feet. If you forgot your emergency foot kit and a problem arises, don't be reluctant to call the Disney medics. They have all the stuff you need to keep your command in action.

Okay troops, prepare to move out. Hit the dusty trail and *move* those feet: left, right, left. When you get back old Sarge will teach you how to avoid VD at Walt Disney World.

RAIN

Weather bad? Go to the parks anyway. Crowds are lighter, and most attractions and waiting areas are under cover. Showers, especially during warmer months, are short.

Rain gear is one of the few bargains at the parks. It isn't always displayed in shops; you have to ask for it. Ponchos are available for less than $5; umbrellas go for about $11.

El Niño precipitated (no pun intended) dozens of reader suggestions for dealing with soggy days. Nobody, however, had their act together as well as this mom from Memphis, Tennessee. Here are her tips:

1. Rain gear should include poncho and umbrella. Umbrellas make the rain much more bearable. When rain isn't beating down on your ponchoed head, it's easier to ignore.

2. Buy blue ponchos at Walgreens. We could keep track of each other much easier because we had blue ponchos instead of yellow ones.
[Ponchos sold at Walt Disney World are all yellow. Picking out somebody in your party on a rainy day is like trying to identify a certain, individual bumblebee in a swarm.]

3. ScotchGuard your shoes. The difference is unbelievable.

SUN, HEAT, AND HUMIDITY

Florida's sun, heat, and humidity can be brutal from late April through mid-October. A woman from Durham, North Carolina, advises:

Be prepared for the heat. I am a 24-year-old former aerobics instructor and felt dizzy after a long day in the Magic Kingdom. Carry clear water bottles, as they are the only beverages allowed on rides.

A lady from Ardsley, New York, writes:

I would advise that people carry umbrellas for shelter against the sun. I was the only one with an umbrella, and every time I used it, I would hear people around me say, "She's smart. She brought an umbrella." This came in handy during the wait for the live show [at Disney-MGM Studios]. The show is absolutely the best event in all three parks (and I should know, because I'm a singer and musician), but the wait is absolutely the worst. They line you up on this open piece of pavement for at least 30 minutes. There is absolutely no shade or breeze, and the cement has been baking in the sun all day. If you bring umbrellas and lots of water to throw on the kids, you might make it until show time.

St. Louis Encephalitis

Although contraction occurs very rarely, St. Louis Encephalitis is an ongoing concern for Florida's health officials. The disease is transmitted to humans by mosquito bites, and is often more severe in children and the elderly. In spite of regular warnings by state and county agencies, many people (including Disney cast members) are still unsure how much of a threat the mosquito-borne infection poses. A reader from New York City wrote:

Something very important to keep in mind: our resort's pools were closed by 6 p.m. every night. Why? Mosquitoes. We heard from a cast member that there was an encephalitis scare, so pools were closed early to protect guests from possible exposure. Alternately, we heard it was encephalitis season—implying that this wasn't an isolated scare, but an annual event. We couldn't substantiate this, but either way, you should inform your readers, even if it's not annual. People should know to bring bug spray, and they should plan on possibly not having any late night swims.

Since mosquitoes flourish during periods of summer rain, it can be said that Florida undergoes an annual "encephalitis season." But El Niño rains particularly concerned public health officials since increased ground moisture causes even greater mosquito proliferation.

However, encephalitis is not a common disease in Florida, and most summers see no cases reported. Rather, health officials advise taking precautions during periods of warmth and moisture. Precautions include:

- Avoid outdoor activities between dusk and dawn, when mosquitoes are most active.

- If you must be outside at night, wear long pants and long-sleeved shirts, as well as insect repellent on exposed skin.

- Avoid water, and especially standing water, at night.

There is no vaccine for St. Louis Encephalitis since it occurs in humans so rarely. The good news is that, due to conscientious preventive measures on the part of Florida locals as well as tourists, only a handful of cases were reported in 1997–98, in spite of El Niño.

VISITING MORE THAN ONE PARK IN A SINGLE DAY

If you have a pass that allows you to visit the Magic Kingdom, the Animal Kingdom, Epcot, and Disney-MGM Studios in the same day, it will be validated with the date when you enter your first park. If you decide to go later to another park, you must have your hand stamped for re-entry before you leave. If you start the day at the Magic Kingdom, for example, then go to Epcot for dinner, you must get a re-entry stamp when you leave the Magic Kingdom. At Epcot, you'll have to present your passport and show your hand stamp. The stamp is visible only under ultraviolet light and usually won't come off if you wash your hands or swim.

Services and Shopping

SHOPPING

The *Unofficial Guide* aims to help you see as much as possible, not buy as much as possible. But we acknowledge that for many, a vacation is an extended shopping spree. If you're among these shoppers, you'll love exploring the stores at Walt Disney World. You'll notice that our touring plans keep you on-track to see attractions, dissuading you somewhat from shopping. Because Disney doesn't need our help to keep your wallet flapping, we offer minimal coverage of shopping at Walt Disney World. However, to give you a notion of what it means to an enthusiast, we share this letter from a Los Angeles couple:

> We would like to point out that, although your book discourages it, the shopping is a divine experience at WDW for those who like to shop. One does not shop in WDW for bargains (that's what flea markets, garage sales, and Target are for), but Disney buyers obtain a large selection of above-average to excellent quality merchandise, much of it not

available anywhere else (not even a Disney Store or catalog), and arrange it attractively and imaginatively (at the exit of almost every attraction). They are marketing geniuses! Not even the largest shops have all the merchandise they have to offer, hence, a shopper can make little discoveries in almost every shop—even the smallest hotel gift shops. That, coupled with congenial, helpful Disney staff, and services like complimentary hotel delivery, make shopping its own attraction at WDW.

Cameras and Film

Camera Centers at the major theme parks sell disposable cameras for about $10 ($19 with flash). Film is sold throughout the World. Developing is available at most Disney hotel gift shops and at Camera Centers. For two-hour developing, look for the photo express sign in the theme parks. Drop your film in the container and pick up your pictures at the Camera Center as you leave the park. If you use the express service and intend to stay in the park until closing, pick up your pictures earlier in the evening to avoid the end-of-day rush. The Magic Kingdom Camera Center almost always develops film within the advertised two hours. Camera Centers at the other parks frequently run late.

Photo tips and recommendations for settings and exposures are detailed in the respective maps provided free when you enter the theme parks.

Shopping for Walt Disney World Resort Guests

Disney resort guests who make purchases in a theme park shop can have their merchandise sent directly to their guest rooms.

Disney Souvenirs

Disney souvenirs can be found in any Walt Disney World structure large enough to hold a cash register. Still, readers often ask where to find the greatest variety and best deals.

Disney opened its first character superstore in 1996 at Downtown Disney Marketplace. Called World of Disney, the 50,000-square-foot facility offers the largest selection of Disney merchandise in the world (that's *the* world, Edith, not just Walt Disney World!). It's decidedly less crowded and frenetic than shops in the theme parks, and Downtown Disney Marketplace is accessible by Disney bus or boat. Magic Kingdom Club members get a 10% discount on most merchandise at Downtown Disney Marketplace. For sale are stuffed toys of Disney characters, Disney books and records, character hats, and other items which are difficult, if not impossible, to find outside Disney shops.

Theme Park Shops with the Best Variety of Disney Stuff	
Magic Kingdom	
Main Street	Emporium
	(largest selection at Magic Kingdom)
Tomorrowland	Mickey's Star Traders
Epcot	
Future World	Gateway Gifts
	Centorium
	(largest selection at Epcot)
World Showcase	Disney Traders
	(left side of Showcase Plaza)
Disney-MGM Studios	
Hollywood Boulevard	Mickey's of Hollywood
Sunset Boulevard	Once Upon a Time
Studio Courtyard	Animation Gallery
Animal Kingdom	
Safari Village	Village Merchantile
	Disney Outfitters

Disney T-shirts, the most popular souvenir, are available areawide. Shirts sold at Disney World are expensive ($19–40) but are high-quality, 100% cotton. Those sold outside the World are usually of lesser quality, 50% cotton/ 50% polyester, and sell for $7–18. Many of the same designs of Mickey, Minnie, and Goofy can be found both inside and outside Disney World. The only difference is that shirts sold in Disney shops will say "Walt Disney World" or perhaps "Epcot" or "Disney-MGM Studios" next to the imprint of the character. Shirts sold outside the World usually will say "Florida."

The only retailer selling discounted items from Walt Disney World is the Character Warehouse (phone (407) 345-5285) in Mall Two of the Belz Factory Outlet World at the north end of International Drive. Prices are good, but the selection is generally limited to close-outs and remainders. Don't expect to find the same merchandise that you saw in the parks. The store is open from 10 a.m. to 9 p.m. Monday through Saturday, and 10 a.m. to 6 p.m. on Sunday.

Bargain World (phone (407) 345-8772), with locations at 6454 International Drive (next to Shell World) and 8520 International Drive, offers a good selection of the 50% cotton/50% polyester shirts, as well as Disney beach towels and other character merchandise.

SERVICES

Messages

Messages left at City Hall in the Magic Kingdom, the Guest Relations lobby at Epcot, Hollywood Boulevard Guest Relations at Disney-MGM Studios, or Guest Relations at the Animal Kingdom can be retrieved at any of the four.

Pet Care

Pets aren't allowed in the major or minor theme parks. But never leave an animal in a hot car while you tour; the pet will die. Kennels and holding facilities are provided for temporary care of your pets. They're located adjacent to the Transportation and Ticket Center, left of the Epcot entrance plaza, left of the Disney-MGM Studios entrance plaza, at the outer entrance of the Animal Kingdom, and at Fort Wilderness Campground. If you insist, kennel staff will accept about any type of animal, though owners of exotic and/or potentially vicious pets must place their charge in its assigned cage. Small pets (mice, hamsters, birds, snakes, turtles, alligators, etc.) must arrive in their own escape-proof carrier.

Here are several additional details you may need to know:

- When traveling with your pet in Florida, bring proof of vaccination and immunization, including bordatella for dogs.
- It is against the law in Florida to leave a pet in a closed vehicle.
- Advance reservations for animals aren't accepted.
- Kennels open one hour before the park opens and close one hour after the park closes. The kennels, however, are staffed 24 hours a day.
- Disney resort guests may board a pet overnight for $9 per pet, per night. Other patrons are charged $11 per pet, per night. Day care of pets for all guests costs $6 per day. The kennels aren't really set up for multiday boarding. You must feed and exercise your own pet.
- Guests leaving exotic pets should supply their food.
- Pets are allowed at a limited number of sites at Fort Wilderness Campground.

For more information on pet care, call (407) 824-6568.

Religious Services

On Sundays at the Polynesian Resort, mass for Catholics is celebrated at 8 and 10:15 a.m. For a schedule of services at churches and temples in the Walt Disney World area, inquire at your hotel's front desk.

Excuse Me, but Where Can I Find ...

Someplace to Put All These Packages?   Lockers are available on the ground floor of the Main Street railroad station in the Magic Kingdom, to the right of Spaceship Earth in Epcot, and on the east and west ends of the TTC. At Disney-MGM Studios, lockers are to the right of the entrance on Hollywood Boulevard at Oscar's Super Service. At the Animal Kingdom, lockers are inside the main entrance to the left. Lockers are $3 a day plus a $2 deposit.

Package Pick-up is available at each major theme park. Ask the salesperson to send your purchases to Package Pick-up. When you leave the park, they'll be waiting for you. Epcot has two exits, thus two Package Pick-ups, so specify whether you want your purchases sent to the main entrance or to the International Gateway.

If you're a Disney resort guest, have the salesperson send your purchases from the theme parks directly to your guest room.

A Mixed Drink or a Beer?   Alcoholic beverages aren't sold in the Magic Kingdom; you must leave the park and go to a resort hotel to get one. Everywhere else in Disney World, wine, beer, and mixed drinks are readily available.

Some Chewing Gum?   Sorry, it isn't sold in any theme park. B.Y.O.

A Good Grocery Store?   Stock up on snacks and other edibles at Goodings Supermarket in Crossroads Shopping Center on FL 535 (the shopping center entrance is directly across FL 535 from the entrance to Downtown Disney Marketplace and Village Plaza), or at the Publix Supermarket on the corner of FL 535 and Vineland Road.

Suntan Lotion?   Suntan lotion and other sundries are sold at the Emporium on Main Street in the Magic Kingdom (they're kept behind the counter; you must ask) and in Epcot at many Future World and World Showcase shops. At Disney-MGM Studios and the Animal Kingdom, suntan lotion is sold at almost all shops.

A Smoke?   Cigarettes are sold throughout the Magic Kingdom, the Animal Kingdom, Epcot, and Disney-MGM Studios. But, smoking is prohibited on all attractions, in all attraction waiting areas, and in all shops.

Feminine Hygiene Products?   They're in women's rest rooms throughout Walt Disney World.

Part Eight

Dining in and around Walt Disney World

Dining outside Walt Disney World

Unofficial Guide researchers love good food and invest a fair amount of time scouting new places to eat. And, because food at Walt Disney World is so expensive, we (like you) have an economic incentive for finding palatable meals outside the World. Unfortunately, the area surrounding Disney World is not exactly a culinary nirvana. If you thrive on fast food and the fare at chain restaurants (Denny's, T.G.I. Fridays, Olive Garden, Chi Chi's, etc.), you'll be as happy as an alligator on a chicken farm. If, however, you'd like a superlative dining experience, you'll find the pickings outside the World about the same as those inside, only less expensive.

Some ethnic cuisines aren't represented in Walt Disney World restaurants. If you want Indian, Thai, Greek, or Caribbean, you'll have to forage in surrounding communities. Among specialty restaurants in and out of the World, location and price will determine your choice. There are, for example, decent Italian restaurants in Disney World and adjoining tourist areas. Which one you select depends on how much you want to spend and how convenient the place is. Our recommendations on specialty and ethnic fare served in and out of the World are summarized in the nearby table.

Better restaurants outside Walt Disney World cater primarily to adults and aren't as well equipped to deal with children. If, however, you're looking to escape children or want to eat in peace and quiet, you're more likely to find such an environment outside the World.

DINING IN CELEBRATION

There are currently four full-service restaurants in Disney's community of Celebration. The best is Cafe d'Antonio (691 Front Street, (407) 566-2233,

In or out of the World for Ethnic Cuisine?

Cuisine/Specialty	Recommendations
American	Good selections both in and out of the World.
Barbecue	Better out of the World.
Buffets	This is a toss-up. Disney buffets are expensive but offer excellent quality and extensive selections. Off-World buffets aren't as upscale, but they are a better value.
Chinese	Eat out of the World.
French	Toss-up. Reasonably good but expensive both in and out of the World.
German	Passable, but not great, in or out of the World.
Italian	Tie on quality; better value out of the World.
Japanese	Teppanyaki Dining Room at Epcot is tops for teppan (table grill) dining. For sushi and sashimi, go off-World.
Mexican	We have not been able to find an off-World Mexican restaurant better than San Angel Inn Restaurante at Epcot.
Middle Eastern	More choice and better value out of the World.
Seafood	Toss-up.
Steak & Prime Rib	Though you can get a good piece of meat at many Walt Disney World restaurants, the edge goes to off-World restaurants for both quality and value.

moderate to expensive). This is a sister restaurant to Antonio's La Fiamma, a local favorite in Maitland. The food is authentically Italian, and service is first-rate. A covered patio overlooks the lake at the center of town.

Two restaurants are owned by the same south Florida company. Max's Cafe and Coffee Shop (701 Front Street, (407) 566-1144, inexpensive to moderate), is a little fancier than your basic IHOP. The decor is art deco, and the food is better than you'd find at a greasy spoon. Sandwiches are big, and the meals are substantial. The meatloaf is especially good.

Max's Grille (721 Front Street, (407) 566-1141, moderate to expensive) isn't quite what it should be. While it does some things well, service is spotty; seasonings are uneven; and there is a low quality-to-price ratio.

Now that you know how specialty and ethnic sites compare, here are our recommendations for dining outside Walt Disney World:

American

Cafe Tu Tu Tango: 8625 International Drive, Orlando; inexpensive to moderate; (407) 248-2222

Mediterranean-style tapas in an artist's garret setting.

Chatham's Place: 7575 Dr. Phillips Boulevard, Orlando; moderate to expensive; (407) 345-2992

New American cuisine: the dining room is small and unappealing, but the food and service are some of the best in Orlando.

Manuel's on the 28th: 390 North Orange Avenue, Orlando; expensive; (407) 246-6580

Creative American overlooking downtown Orlando from the 28th floor of the Barnett Bank building.

Pebbles: 12551 FL 535, Crossroads Shopping Center, Lake Buena Vista; moderate to expensive; (407) 827-1111

A casual homegrown chain featuring a Florida version of California cuisine.

Sam Snead's Tavern: 2461 South Hiawassee Road, Orlando; inexpensive to moderate; (407) 295-9999

A golfer's version of the Hard Rock Cafe.

Wild Jack's: 7364 International Drive, Orlando; moderate; (407) 352-4407

Cowboy cuisine in a Rodeo Drive setting.

Barbecue

Bubbalou's Bodacious B-B-Q: 5818 Conroy Road, Orlando (near Universal Studios Florida); inexpensive; (407) 295-1212

Tender smoky barbecue with a tomato-based "killer" sauce.

Beef

Butcher Shop Steakhouse: 8445 International Drive, Mercado Mediterranean Village, Orlando; moderate; (407) 363-9727

High-quality beef you can cook at the open pit.

Charlie's Steak House: 6107 South Orange Blossom Trail, Orlando; moderate; (407) 851-7130

There are other locations for this small chain, including one just south of the I-4 interchange on US 192.

Beef (continued)

Del Frisco's: 729 Lee Road, Orlando (quarter-mile west of I-4);
   expensive; (407) 645-4443
A little pricey but if you're in the mood for a really great steak it's
worth it.

Caribbean

Bahama Breeze: 8849 International Drive, Orlando; moderate; (407)
   248-2499
A creative—and tasty—version of Caribbean cuisine from the owners
   of the Olive Garden and Red Lobster chains.

Chinese

Ming Court: 9188 International Drive, Orlando; expensive; (407)
   351-9988
Ask to see the dim sum menu.

Cuban

Numero Uno: 2499 South Orange Avenue, Orlando; inexpensive;
   (407) 841-3840
No trip to Florida is complete without a sampling of Cuban food.

Rolando's: 870 Semoran Boulevard, Casselberry; inexpensive; (407)
   767-9677
Some of the best Cuban in the area, served by some of the friendliest.

French

Le Coq au Vin: 4800 South Orange Avenue, Orlando; moderate; (407)
   851-6980
A perennial local favorite featuring country French in a not-too-stuffy
atmosphere.

Le Provence: 50 East Pine Street, Orlando; moderate; (407) 843-1320
A more upscale French restaurant, small, intimate, and pricey—but good.

German/Eastern European

Cafe Europa: Church Street Market, 55 W. Church Street, Orlando;
   inexpensive to moderate; (407) 872-3388
The only Eastern European in town; good cabbage rolls.

Old Munich: 5731 South Orange Blossom Trail, Orlando; moderate; (407) 438-8997

Nothing special, but if you've just *got* to have some sauerbraten . . .

Indian

Kohinoor: Ethan Allen Plaza, 249 W. State Road 436, Altamonte Springs; moderate; (407) 788-6004

Try the lamb korma.

Passage to India: 5532 International Drive, Orlando; moderate; (407) 351-3456

A lot of locals brave International Drive just to dine here.

Shamiana: 7040 International Drive, Orlando; inexpensive; (407) 354-1160

Also serves Pakistani cuisine.

Italian

Capriccio: 9801 International Drive, Orlando; moderate to expensive; (407) 345-4450

The Peabody Orlando's casually upscale Italian restaurant serves a good Sunday brunch.

Italianni's: 8148 International Drive, Orlando; inexpensive to moderate; (407) 345-8884

From the T.G.I. Friday's folks, big portions, little prices, and surprisingly good food.

Tarantino's: 917 North Bermuda Avenue, Kissimmee; inexpensive to moderate; (407) 870-2622

An unassuming mom-and-popper owned by some New York transplants.

Japanese/Sushi

Hanamizuki: 8255 International Drive, Orlando; moderate to expensive; (407) 363-7200

Usually filled with Japanese visitors; can be expensive, but very authentic.

Ichiban: 19 South Orange Avenue, Orlando (near Church Street Station); moderate; (407) 423-2688

Sit on the floor or at a table; good sushi and tempura.

Mexican

Amigos: 6036 South Orange Blossom Trail, Orlando; inexpensive;
(407) 857-3144
Tex-Mex with the emphasis on the Tex.

Don Pablo's: 8717 International Drive, Orlando; inexpensive; (407)
354-1345
A pretty good chain that uses fresh ingredients in its Tex-Mex. Can be
a bit noisy.

Middle Eastern

Aladdin's Cafe: 1015 East Semoran Boulevard, Casselberry; moderate;
(407) 331-0488
Call for belly dancer's schedule.

Seafood

Sea Catch Market: 1455 Semoran Boulevard, Casselberry; inexpensive;
(407) 679-5999
Don't be fooled by the unassuming exterior (or interior, for that
matter)—you won't find a better fish for the price anywhere.

Straub's Boatyard: 743 Lee Road, Orlando; moderate; (407) 628-0067
From the owners of Straub's Fine Seafood, which also serves fine
seafood.

Thai

Royal Thai: 1202 North Semoran Boulevard, Orlando; inexpensive to
moderate; (407) 275-0776
If you really like hot Thai food, you'll love this place; have the lemon
fish.

Siam Orchid: 7575 Republic Drive, Orlando; moderate to expensive;
(407) 351-0821
Fancier than most Thais, and a bit pricier, but the best Thai in the
tourist areas.

* Recommended by Scott Joseph, wine and food critic of the *Orlando Sentinel.*

You're better off heading for Cafe d'Antonio or having the meatloaf next door at Max's Cafe.

The most recent addition to Celebration is Columbia (649 Front Street, (407) 566-1505, moderate to expensive), an updated version of the decades-old Columbia in Tampa's Ybor City area. The decor is sumptuous, but the food quality is spotty. Service can be downright poor.

TAKE OUT EXPRESS

If you're staying in a hotel *outside* Disney World, Take Out Express (phone (407) 352-1170) will deliver a meal from your choice among 20 restaurants, including T.G.I. Fridays, Ming Court, Passage to India, Siam Orchid, Bella Roma, Chili's, Ocean Grille, Cafe Tu Tu Tango, Houlihans, and Sizzler. The delivery charge is $3 per restaurant, with a minimum $15 order. Tips aren't included. Cash, traveler's checks, MasterCard, Visa, and American Express are accepted. Hours are 4:30–11 p.m.

ONE MAN'S TREASURE

A man from Richland, Washington, urges:

> *I think that you should in future editions promote the Crossroads of Buena Vista [Shopping Center] a little stronger. There are plenty of non-WDW restaurants at non-WDW prices. The Crossroads is nothing less than a small city that can service all of your needs.*

Crossroads Shopping Center is on FL 535 directly across from the entrance to Walt Disney World Village and Disney Village Hotel Plaza. As the reader suggests, it offers about everything you need. Fast food is sold at McDonald's, Burger King, and Taco Bell. Up a notch are T.G.I. Fridays, Perkins, Jungle Jim's, Pizzeria Uno, and Red Lobster. For a really nice meal, pick Pebbles, featuring fresh Florida seafood. You can fill your coolers and fridge at Goodings Supermarket. Open 24 hours, Goodings also has a deli, bakery, and full-service pharmacy. When you finish eating, shop for sportswear, swimwear, and athletic shoes. Finally, if you lose your *Unofficial Guide,* buy another at the bookstore in Crossroads.

Dining in Walt Disney World

This section aims to help you find good food without going broke or tripping over one of Disney World's many culinary landmines. More than 100 restaurants operate in Walt Disney World, including more than five dozen full-service restaurants, 23 of which are inside the theme parks. Collectively, Disney restaurants offer exceptional variety, serving everything from Cajun to French, Moroccan to Texas barbecue. Most restaurants are expensive, and many serve less than distinguished fare, but the culinary scene at Disney World is generally improving. You can find good deals if you know where to look, and there are ethnic delights rarely found outside of America's largest cities.

Changes on the Culinary Horizon

The success of Planet Hollywood and the Rainforest Cafe have opened the floodgates for a new wave of theme dining. At the Animal Kingdom, the Rainforest Cafe opened a sister restaurant to the one currently operating in the Downtown Disney Marketplace. The Official All-Star Cafe opened in the summer of '98 at Disney's Wide World of Sports. To call it a sports version of Planet Hollywood is most accurate because it comes from Planet Hollywood founder and president Robert Earl.

The Marketplace at Downtown Disney welcomed Walt Disney World's first McDonald's (the second is situated near the All-Star resorts), a Wolfgang Puck California pizza and salad diner, and a Ghirardelli Soda Fountain & Chocolate Shop. Next door at Pleasure Island the Fireworks Factory barbecue restaurant has been replaced with the Wild Horse Saloon, also featuring barbecue but with line dancing on the side to help you work off the calories. At Disney's West Side in Downtown Disney, Dan Aykroyd's House of Blues serves Cajun and Creole dishes with a side of R&B, jazz, and country. Other theme eateries on the West Side include Gloria and Emilio Estefan's Bongos for Cuban fare and Wolfgang Puck's Cafe for California cuisine.

At Disney-MGM Studios, magician David Copperfield has opened a restaurant called Copperfield Magic Underground, where magic and illusion are performed while guests dine. The Copperfield Restaurant, as well as the Rainforest Cafe at the Animal Kingdom, can be accessed without entering the theme park.

There was quite a shake-up in the hotel and theme park restaurant scene. At Epcot, Chefs de France has incorporated the other two smaller restaurants in the France pavilion—Au Petit Café and Bistro de Paris—into one large Chefs de France. Biergarten at Germany has been renovated, and an outdoor cafe is on tap for Italy. Disney is also concentrating on upgrading counter-service eateries. Watch for more new items including fast-service, made-to-order pizzas.

On the hotel side, the Grand Floridian Beach Resort replaced Flagler's, the Italian eatery, with Citricos, which is Spanish for citrus. The new restaurant was supposed to feature dishes flavored with Florida citrus and other fruit, but guests couldn't quite grasp the concept. The current menu offers Mediterranean and American fare. The new Coronado Beach Resort features one full-service restaurant called Maya Grill, with a stylized version of Yucatan region Mexican food. The setting is (get this) a "modern interpretation of a temple."

WALT DISNEY WORLD RESTAURANT CATEGORIES

In general, food and beverage offerings at Walt Disney World are defined by service, price, and convenience:

Full-Service Restaurants Full-service restaurants are in all Disney resorts except the All-Star, and in all major theme parks, Downtown Disney Marketplace, Pleasure Island, and Disney's West Side. Disney operates the restaurants in the theme parks and its hotels. Contractors or franchisees operate the restaurants in hotels of the Disney Village Hotel Plaza, the Swan and Dolphin resorts, Pleasure Island, and Disney's West Side, and some in Downtown Disney Marketplace. Priority seating (explained below), arranged in advance, is recommended for all full-service restaurants except those in Disney Village Hotel Plaza. The restaurants accept VISA, MasterCard, and American Express.

Buffets There has been an explosion of buffets at Disney World during recent years. Many have Disney characters in attendance, and most have a separate children's menu featuring hot dogs, burgers, chicken nuggets, pizza, macaroni and cheese, and spaghetti and meatballs. In addition to the buffets, several restaurants serve a family-style, all-you-can-eat, fixed-price meal. Priority seating arrangements are required for character buffets and recommended for all other buffets and family-style restaurants. Most major credit cards are accepted.

The table below lists buffets (where you can belly up for bulk loading) at Walt Disney World.

Walt Disney World Buffets				
Location	Restaurant	Cuisine	Children's Selections	Disney Characters Present
Magic Kingdom	The Crystal Palace	American	Yes	Yes
Epcot	Biergarten	German	No	No
Epcot	Restaurant Akershus	Scandinavian	No	No
Contemporary Resort	Chef Mickey's	American	Yes	Yes
Beach Club Resort	Cape May Cafe	Clambake	Yes	No
Grand Floridian	1900 Park Fare	American	Yes	Yes

If you want to eat a lot but don't feel like standing in yet another line, consider one of the all-you-can-eat "family-style" restaurants. These feature platters of food that are brought to your table in courses by a server. You can sample everything on the menu and eat as much as you like. You can even go back to a favorite appetizer after you finish the entrees. Food tends to be a little better than you'll find on a buffet line. There is also the sanitation factor—food that doesn't sit on a buffet line isn't exposed to the type of contamination that often affects buffets.

Family-style all-you-can-eat service is available at the Liberty Tree Tavern in the Magic Kingdom (character dining), The Garden Grill Restaurant in the Land pavilion in Epcot (character dining), 'Ohana in the Polynesian Resort (character dining), and Whispering Canyon Cafe in the Wilderness Lodge.

Cafeterias and Food Courts   Cafeterias, in all the major theme parks, offer a middle ground between full-service and counter-service dining. Food courts, featuring a collection of counter-service eateries under one roof, are found at the theme parks as well as at the moderate (Coronado Springs, Caribbean Beach, Dixie Landings, Port Orleans) and budget (All-Star) Disney resorts. No priority seating is required or available at cafeterias or food courts. VISA, MasterCard, and American Express are accepted.

Counter Service   Counter-service fast food is available in all theme parks and at Downtown Disney Marketplace, Pleasure Island, Disney's Board-Walk, and Disney's West Side. The food compares in quality with McDonald's, Captain D's, or Taco Bell but is more expensive, though often served in larger portions. VISA, MasterCard, and American Express are accepted.

Vendor Food   Vendors abound at the theme parks, Downtown Disney Marketplace, Pleasure Island, Disney's West Side, and Disney's BoardWalk. Offerings include popcorn, ice cream bars, churros (Mexican pastry), soft drinks, bottled water, and (in theme parks) fresh fruit. Prices include tax, and payment must be in cash.

Hard Choices

Dining choices will definitely impact your Walt Disney World experience. If you're short on time and you want to see the theme parks, avoid full-service restaurants. Ditto if you're short on funds. If you want to try a Disney full-service restaurant, arrange priority seating in advance. That won't reserve you a table, but it will minimize your wait.

Integrating Meals into the *Unofficial Guide* Touring Plans

Arrive before the park of your choice opens. Tour expeditiously, using your chosen plan (taking as few breaks as possible), until about 11–11:30 a.m.

Once the park becomes crowded around midday, meals and other breaks won't affect the plan's efficiency. If you intend to stay in the park for evening parades, fireworks, or other events, eat dinner early enough to be finished in time for the festivities.

Character Dining

A number of restaurants, primarily those serving all-you-can-eat buffets and family-style meals, offer character dining. At character meals, you pay a fixed price and dine in the presence of three to five Disney characters that circulate throughout the restaurant, hugging children (and sometimes adults), posing for photos, and signing autographs. Character breakfasts, lunches, and dinners are served at restaurants in and out of the theme parks. For an extensive discussion of character dining, see Walt Disney World with Kids (pages 175–181).

FAST FOOD IN THE THEME PARKS

Because most meals during a Disney World vacation are consumed on the run while touring, we'll tackle counter-service and vendor foods first. Plentiful in all theme parks are hot dogs, hamburgers, chicken breast sandwiches, green salads, and pizza. They're augmented by special items that relate to the park's theme or the part of the park you're touring. In Germany at Epcot, for example, counter-service bratwurst and beer are sold. In Frontierland in the Magic Kingdom, vendors sell smoked turkey legs. Counter-service prices are fairly consistent from park to park. Expect to pay the same for your coffee and hot dog at the Animal Kingdom as at Disney-MGM Studios.

The Cost of Counter-Service Food	
To help you develop your dining budget, here are prices of common counter-service items. Sales tax isn't included.	
Food	
Barbecue Chicken Sandwich	$5.95
Barbecue Pork, Beef, or Turkey	$6.75
Brownie	$1.50
Cake or Pie	$2.25
Cheeseburger	$4.65–6.85 (double)
Chicken Breast Sandwich (grilled)	$4.55–6.50
Children's Meals	$3–4
Chips	75¢
Cookies	$1.45
Deli Sandwich	$4.90–6

The Cost of Counter-Service Food (continued)

Food (continued)

Fish Basket (fried)	$5.15
French Fries	$1.50
Fried Chicken (cold)	$4.90
Fried Chicken Nuggets	$5.25
Fruit (whole piece)	$1
Fruit Cup/Fruit Salad	$2.10–4.85
Ham & Cheese, Turkey, or Tuna Sub	$4.65–4.90
Hot Dogs	$2.50–4.75
Ice Cream Bars	$2–2.60
Nachos with Cheese	$2.60
Pasta Salad	$1.35–5.85
Pizza (per slice)	$3.50–5.35
Popcorn	$1.90
Salad (entree)	$5.10–6.95
Salad (side)	$1.75–3.90
Smoked Turkey Leg	$3.99–4.25
Soup/Chili	$2.45–3.50
Taco	$4.45 for two tacos
Taco Salad	$4.85–6.40

Drinks	Small	Large
Beer (not available in the Magic Kingdom)	$3.75	$4.25
Bottled Water	NA	$2
Cappuccino/Espresso	$2.95	
Coffee	$1.25	$1.45
Fruit Juice	$1.30–1.55	NA
Lemonade	$1.55	$2
Milk	$1	NA
Soft Drinks (Coke, etc.)	$1.55	$2
Tea	$1.45	NA

HEALTHFUL FOOD IN THE THEME PARKS

One of the most commendable developments in food service at Walt Disney World has been the introduction of more healthful foods and snacks. Diabetics, vegetarians, weight-watchers, those requiring kosher meals, and guests on restricted diets should have no trouble finding *something* to eat. Ditto for anyone seeking wholesome, nutritious food. Healthful food is available at most fast-food counters and even from vendors. All major theme parks, for example, have fruit stands.

CUTTING YOUR DINING TIME AT THE THEME PARKS

Even if you confine your meals to vendor and counter-service fast food, you lose a lot of time getting food in the theme parks. At Walt Disney World, everything begins with a line and ends with a cash register. When it comes to fast food, "fast" may apply to the time you spend eating it, not the time invested in obtaining it. Here are suggestions for minimizing the time you spend hunting and gathering food:

1. Eat breakfast before arriving. Don't waste touring time eating breakfast at the parks. Besides, restaurants outside the World offer some outstanding breakfast specials. Some hotels furnish small refrigerators in their guest rooms or rent them. If you can get by on cold cereal, rolls, fruit, and juice, having a fridge in your room will save a ton of time.

2. After a good breakfast, buy snacks from vendors in the parks as you tour. This is very important if you're on a tight schedule and can't spend a lot of time waiting in line for food.

3. All theme park restaurants are busiest between 11:30 a.m. and 2:15 p.m. for lunch and 6 and 9 p.m. for dinner. For shorter lines and faster service, avoid eating during these hours.

4. Many counter-service restaurants sell cold sandwiches. Buy a cold lunch (except for drinks) before 11 a.m. and carry it until you're

ready to eat. Ditto for dinner. We met a family that routinely does this, with Mom bringing small plastic bags in which to pack the food. Drinks are purchased at the appropriate time from any convenient vendor.

5. Most fast-food eateries have more than one service window. Regardless of time of day, check the lines at all windows before queuing. Sometimes a window that's manned but out of the way will have a much shorter line or none at all. Note, however, that some windows may offer only some items. For example, some windows may serve only soup and salad, while others serve sandwiches.

6. If you're short on time and the park closes early, stay until closing and eat dinner outside Disney World before returning to your hotel. If the park stays open late, eat dinner about 4 or 4:30 p.m. at the restaurant of your choice. You should miss the last wave of lunchers and sneak in just ahead of the dinner crowd.

BEYOND COUNTER SERVICE: TIPS FOR SAVING MONEY ON FOOD

Though buying food from counter-service restaurants and vendors will save time and money (compared to full-service dining), additional strategies can bolster your budget and maintain your waistline:

1. Go to Disney World during a period of fasting and abstinence. You can save a fortune and save your soul at the same time!

2. Wear clothes that are slightly too small and make you feel like dieting (no spandex allowed!).

3. Whenever you're feeling hungry, ride the Mad Tea Party, Body Wars, or other attractions that induce motion sickness.

4. Leave your cash and credit cards at your hotel. Buy food only with money your children fish out of fountains and wishing wells.

Cost-conscious readers also have volunteered ideas for stretching food dollars. A family from Lee's Summit, Missouri, tells us:

Last year we requested a small refrigerator for our room and were given one for no charge. This year we were charged $5 a day for use of the fridge, but it was definitely worth it for us to be able to eat breakfast in the room to save time and money.

A Missouri mom writes:

I have shared our very successful meal plan with many families. We stayed six nights and arrived at WDW after some days on the beach south of Sarasota. We shopped there and arrived with our steel Coleman cooler well stocked with milk and sandwich fixings. I froze a block of ice in a milk bottle, and we replenished it daily with ice from the resort ice machine. I also froze small packages of deli-type meats for later in the week. We ate cereal, milk, and fruit each morning, with boxed juices. I also had a hot pot to boil water for instant coffee, oatmeal, and soup.

Each child had a belt bag of his own, which he filled from a special box of "goodies" each day. I made a great mystery of filling that box in the weeks before the trip. Some things were actual food, like packages of crackers and cheese, packets of peanuts and raisins. Some were worthless junk, like candy and gum. They grazed from their belt bags at will throughout the day, with no interference from Mom and Dad. Each also had a small, rectangular plastic water bottle that could hang in the belt. We filled these at water fountains before getting into lines and were the envy of many.

We left the park before noon, ate sandwiches, chips, and soda in the room, and napped. We purchased our evening meal in the park, at a counter-service eatery. We budgeted for both morning and evening snacks from a vendor but often did not need them. It made the occasional treat all the more special. Our cooler had been pretty much emptied by the end of the week, but the block of ice was still there.

Note: Disney has a rule against bringing your own food and drink into the park. We interviewed one woman who ignored the rule and brought a huge picnic for her family of five packed in a large diaper/baby paraphernalia bag. She stowed the bag in a locker under the Main Street Station and retrieved it when the family was hungry. A Pennsylvania family adds:

Despite the warning against bringing food into the park, we packed a double picnic lunch in a backpack and a small shoulder bag. Even with a small discount, it cost $195 for the seven of us to tour the park for a day, and I felt that spending another $150 or so on two meals was not in the cards. We froze juice boxes to keep the meat sandwiches cool (it worked fine) and had an extra round of juice boxes and peanut butter sandwiches for a late-afternoon snack. We took raisins and a pack of fig bars for sweets, but didn't carry any other cookies or candy to avoid a "sugar-low" during the day. Fruit would have been nice, but it would have been squashed.

SUGGESTIONS FOR EATING AT THE THEME PARKS

Below are suggestions for dining at each of the major theme parks. If you are interested in trying a theme park full-service restaurant, be aware that the restaurants continue to serve after the park's official closing time. For example, we showed up at The Hollywood Brown Derby just as Disney-MGM Studios closed at 8 p.m. We were seated almost immediately and enjoyed a leisurely dinner while the crowds cleared out. Incidentally, don't worry if you are depending on Disney transportation: buses, boats, and monorails run two to three hours after the parks close.

At the Magic Kingdom

The Magic Kingdom is not now, nor has it ever been, a good place to eat. Although there have been some dramatic improvements in full-service and buffet dining (Cinderella's Royal Table and The Crystal Palace), counter-service restaurants continue to offer the same computerized, homogenized fare that languishes beneath the heat lamps of every fast-food chain restaurant in America. Don't be mistaken, Magic Kingdom food isn't awful. It's merely mediocre and, of course, expensive. Recognizing the challenge of feeding so many people each day, we might be more accepting of the bland fare if (1) we didn't believe Disney could do better and if (2) obtaining food didn't require such an investment of time and effort. The variety found on the numerous menus indicates that somebody once had the right idea.

Here are dining recommendations for your day at the Magic Kingdom:

1. Take the monorail to one of the hotels for lunch. The trip over and back takes very little time, and because most guests have left the hotels for the parks, the resorts' restaurants are often uncrowded. The food is better than in the Magic Kingdom; the service is faster; the atmosphere is more relaxed; and beer, wine, and mixed drinks are available. Decent dinner buffets are served at Chef Mickey's at the Contemporary and at 1900 Park Fare at the Grand Floridian. Both feature characters; don't expect quiet dining. Commuting to the buffets is a snap by monorail. A more adult option is the family-style skillet dinner served at Whispering Canyon Cafe in the Wilderness Lodge. Lunch also is available. To reach Wilderness Lodge, take the boat from the Magic Kingdom docks.

2. If you choose to eat in the Magic Kingdom during the midday rush (11:30 a.m. to 2:15 p.m.) or the evening rush (5 to 8 p.m.), try The Crystal Palace near Adventureland at the central-hub end of Main Street; El Pirata y el Perico in Adventureland, around the corner from Frontierland's Pecos Bill Cafe; or Aunt Polly's Dockside Inn (closes at dusk) on Tom Sawyer Island. These counter-

service eateries offer passable food and usually aren't crowded. Another option is *The Diamond Horseshoe Saloon Revue,* which serves sandwiches between shows. All theme park counter-service restaurants are profiled later in this section.

3. Full-service restaurants that accept priority seating for lunch and/or dinner fill quickly. To obtain priority seating in advance, call (407) 939-3463 or hotfoot to your chosen restaurant as soon as you enter the park. Priority seating is explained and all Magic Kingdom full-service restaurants are profiled later in this section.

4. Of the park's three full-service restaurants, Liberty Tree Tavern in Liberty Square is the best. Tony's Town Square Restaurant on Main Street serves consistently nice salads but is otherwise hit or miss. King Stefan's Banquet Hall in Cinderella Castle has been changed to Cinderella's Royal Table. In addition to the name change, the food has improved. A good rule at any full-service restaurant in the park is to keep it simple. Order sandwiches or basic dishes (roast turkey and mashed potatoes, for example) that are difficult to ruin.

At Epcot

We've been reviewing Epcot's food service since the park opened in 1982 and have seen many changes, most of them for the better. There's more variety now, and guests who don't want to take the time for a full-service, sit-down meal have more options. The fast food is quite good, better than in the other theme parks, and more of the full-service ethnic restaurants now offer sampler platters to showcase their cuisine.

Whereas some World Showcase restaurants were once timid about delivering an honest representation of the host nation's cuisine, you can now enjoy somewhat bolder ethnic foods: mole in Mexico, sushi in Japan, and couscous and bastila in Morocco are examples. Some restaurants, however, still sacrifice ethnic authenticity to please the palates of picky Americans, who ought to welcome a taste challenge or not eat in an ethnic restaurant.

Our researchers find no logical correlation among price, quality, and popularity of World Showcase restaurants. We, for example, found L'Originale Alfredo di Roma Ristorante (Italy) sometimes disappointing despite the fact that it's almost always one of the first restaurants to fill its seatings.

Many Epcot restaurants are overpriced, most conspicuously Nine Dragons Restaurant (China) and the Coral Reef (The Living Seas). Representing relatively good value through the combination of ambiance and well-prepared food are Chefs de France (France), Restaurant Akershus (Norway),

Full Service Restaurants in Epcot	
Future World Full-Service Restaurants	
Coral Reef	The Living Seas
The Garden Grill Restaurant	The Land
World Showcase Full-Service Restaurants	
Biergarten	Germany
Chefs de France	France
L'Originale Alfredo di Roma Ristorante	Italy
Restaurant Akershus	Norway
Restaurant Marrakesh	Morocco
Tempura Kiku	Japan
Teppanyaki Dining Room	Japan
Nine Dragons Restaurant	China
Rose & Crown Dining Room	United Kingdom
San Angel Inn Restaurante	Mexico

Biergarten (Germany), and Restaurant Marrakesh (Morocco). The Biergarten and the Marrakesh also have entertainment.

If cost is an issue, make lunch your main meal. Entrees are similar to those on the dinner menu, but prices are significantly lower.

Epcot has 13 full-service restaurants: 2 in Future World and 11 in World Showcase. With a couple of exceptions, these are among the best restaurants at Disney World, in or out of the theme parks.

Profiles of Epcot full-service restaurants are presented at the end of this section.

While eating at Epcot can be a consummate hassle, an afternoon without priority seating for dinner in World Showcase is like not having a date on the day of the prom. Each pavilion has a beautifully seductive ethnic restaurant, offering the gastronomic delights of the world. To tour these exotic settings and not partake is almost beyond the limits of willpower. And although the fare in some World Showcase restaurants isn't especially compelling, the overall experience is exhilarating. If you fail to dine in World Showcase, you'll miss one of Epcot's more delightful features.

If you follow one of our touring plans, you'll be near the United States (The American Adventure) pavilion at noon. We suggest, therefore, a lunch priority seating for 12:30 or 1 p.m. at nearby Germany or a lighter meal at Tempura Kiku in Japan. For dinner, we recommend priority seating at the San Angel Inn in Mexico or Akershus in Norway. If you plan to eat dinner at the Coral Reef in Future World, wait until afterward to see the attraction.

If you want to sample the ethnic foods of World Showcase without eating in restaurants requiring priority seating, we recommend these counter-service specialties:

Norway	Kringla Bakeri og Kafé, for pastries, open-face sandwiches, and Ringnes beer (our favorite)
Germany	Sommerfest, for bratwurst and Beck's beer
Japan	Matsu No Ma Lounge, for sushi and sashimi
Japan	Yakitori House, for yakitori (meat or vegetables on skewers)
France	Boulangerie Pâtisserie, for French pastries
United Kingdom	Rose & Crown Pub, for Guinness, Harp, and Bass beers and ales

Epcot counter-service restaurants are profiled at the end of this section.

At Disney-MGM Studios

Dining at Disney-MGM Studios is more interesting than in the Magic Kingdom and less ethnic than at Epcot. Disney-MGM has four restaurants where priority seating is recommended: The Hollywood Brown Derby, 50's Prime Time Cafe, Sci-Fi Dine-In Theater Restaurant, and Mama Melrose's Ristorante Italiano. The upscale Brown Derby is by far the best restaurant at the Studios. For simple Italian food, including pizza, Mama Melrose's is fine. Just don't expect anything fancy (except the prices). At the Sci-Fi Dine-In, you eat in little cars at a simulated drive-in movie of the '50s. Though you won't find a more entertaining restaurant in Walt Disney World, the food is quite disappointing. Ditto for the 50's Prime Time Cafe, where you sit in Mom's kitchen of the '50s and scarf down pot roast while watching clips of vintage TV sitcoms. Like the Sci-Fi, the 50's Prime Time Cafe is fun but the food is expensive and lackluster. The best way to experience either restaurant is to stop in for dessert or a drink between 2:30 and 4:30 p.m.

We receive considerable mail from readers recounting their Disney-MGM dining experiences. A man from Sumter, South Carolina, writes:

> *We had lunch at the Sci-Fi Dine-In. In the guide you gave it a terrible review, but I have always felt you guys are too hard on the Disney restaurants, so we went ahead and ate there. Well, on this one you were right on target! While the atmosphere was fun, and the clips were a hoot, the food was lousy . . . and expensive!*

A Menchanicsville, Virginia, family agreed:

You tried to warn us about the Sci-Fi Dine-In, but my four-year old was dying to eat there. The food was even worse than you said—and the cost! $9.50 for a hot dog and fries.

From a Maryland reader:

Prime Time Cafe was a fun experience, but again, the food quality was, at best, mediocre. If my mom really did cook that way, I would have many times run away from home. Our poor reaction to the food quality pushed us quickly into the car and out of WDW. I never thought I would get down on my knees and kiss the sidewalk outside of a Perkins Pancake House.

Finally:

The Brown Derby was a special treat. Sitting in one of the wall booths enveloped by the wood paneling [and listening to] the piano player [in period costume] was a real experience. . . . I think you should mention the Cobb salad. The lettuce was pulverized—not what I expected. I am used to having a salad with lettuce I could recognize. I would not order it again. The oyster-Brie soup, on the other hand, was fabulous! I asked for the recipe, and they very generously brought me a preprinted copy.

Disney-MGM Studios' full-service restaurants are profiled at the end of this section.

If you arrive at Disney-MGM Studios without previously arranging priority seating for meals, do so at the the priority seating kiosk at the corner of Hollywood and Sunset boulevards or at the restaurants.

If you have no priority seating and become hungry during meal times, try the subs at Catalina Eddie's or the franks at Rosie's Red Hot Dogs. Both are by the Tower of Terror and sometimes are overlooked by the teeming hordes. On the park's opposite side, try Toy Story Pizza Planet or the Backlot Express.

Disney-MGM Studios counter-service restaurants are profiled at the end of this section.

At the Animal Kingdom

Because touring the Animal Kingdom takes less than a day, crowds are heaviest from 9:30 a.m. until about 3:30 p.m. Expect a mob at lunch and thinner crowds at dinner. Also, the park will be opened by sections over several years. Thus, during its first year, attractions and facilities, including restaurants, will be strained by the huge crowds anticipated. We recommend you tour early after a good breakfast, then eat a very late lunch or graze on vendor food. If you tour later in the day, eat lunch before you arrive, then enjoy dinner in or out of the theme park.

The Animal Kingdom mostly offers counter-service fast food. Although grilled meats are available, don't expect a broad choice of exotic dishes. Most Animal Kingdom eateries serve up traditional Disney theme park fare: hot dogs, hamburgers, deli sandwiches, and the like. Even so, we found Animal Kingdom fast food to be a cut above the average Disney fare. Flame Tree Barbeque in Safari Village and Tusker House Restaurant in Harambe Village are our picks of the litter, both in terms of food quality and atmosphere. For a quiet refuge away from the crowds, you can't beat Flame Tree Barbeque's waterfront dining pavilions.

The only full-service restaurant is a Rainforest Cafe, with entrances both inside and outside the theme park (you don't have to purchase theme park admission, in other words, to eat at the restaurant). Consistent with the practice of the Rainforest Cafe at the Downtown Disney Marketplace, the Animal Kingdom branch will not accept reservations or priority seatings. Whether you arrive from inside or outside the park, you will be given a time to report for seating. If you arrive from inside the park, you can continue touring the park while waiting for your seating time.

READERS' COMMENTS ABOUT WALT DISNEY WORLD DINING

Eating is a popular topic among *Unofficial Guide* readers. In addition to participating in our annual restaurant survey, many readers share their thoughts. The following comments are representative.

This reader preferred restaurants managed by Disney to those operated by third parties, writing:

> *After a poor experience at the San Angel Inn, perhaps you could identify those restaurants not actually run by Disney in future editions of your guide. I would certainly steer clear of them.*

Interestingly, we received this request the same week:

> *In your next edition, please indicate which restaurants are managed by Disney so we can avoid them.*

A couple from Delaware discovered a good buffet for adults at the Buena Vista Palace:

> *Also, one restaurant we would recommend, especially to those without kids and who are watching their money, is the Laughing*

Kookoobera in the Buena Vista Palace. They have great happy-hour prices and on Wednesday and Friday have a full shrimp and roast beef buffet. A great idea for those looking to save some money!

A mom from Williamsville, New York, also offers a positive report:

We sought out something better and found the lunch buffet at The Crystal Palace restaurant. For $14.95 (adult) we ate a late lunch (1:30 p.m.)—we were thankful for the many hot and cold choices, as well as salad, fresh fruit, fajitas, and dessert. I would definitely recommend this route over the hot dogs and fries fare. We were so full that we did not eat again for the rest of the day—not even our 12-year-old who (until that point) had been requesting a meal every 2–3 hours!

Theme dining comes to Walt Disney World

A woman from Winchester, Virginia, shares this:

> *On another subject—the food. It was horrible. [Counter-]service restaurants did such a poor job on the $7 fast food entrees, that we didn't want to risk spending $22 for entrees in the full-service restaurants. You are on target with your recommendation for Norway's Kringla Bakeri og Kafé. It was the only decent meal we had there. At MK the burger from Pecos Bill's was so cold that I couldn't be sure if it had been sitting for 30 minutes or 3 hours. I had already spent 30 minutes packed shoulder to shoulder waiting to get lunch so I took my chances. And even though we were there during the height of the tomato-picking season, the tomato for my burger was pink. At Epcot, the seagulls at the Cantina de San Angel are so aggressive that one landed on our table during dinner and snatched my daughter's churro right out of her basket.*

A family from Marlborough, Connecticut, however, found Disney food palatable, writing:

> *I was apprehensive about the food, [but] our experiences were very good overall at both the full-service and counter-service restaurants. Face it, you don't go to Disney for the dinner bargains.*

A Greenwood, Indiana, family agrees:

> *The food was certainly expensive, but contrary to many of the views expressed in the* Unofficial Guide, *we all thought the quality was excellent. Everything we had, from chicken strips and hot dogs in the parks to dinner at the Coral Reef, tasted great and seemed very fresh.*

A dad from Couderport, Pennsylvania, chides us:

> *You are tough on all Disney dining. . . . Everyone has to eat while there, so it benefits no one to be this critical. Lighten up a little bit and make your dining recommendations in the same spirit as the rest of the book.*

A family from Youngsville, Louisiana, got a leg up on other guests:

> *The best thing we ate were the smoked turkey legs at Magic Kingdom.*

A mom from Aberdeen, South Dakota, writes:

> *When we want great food we'll be on a different vacation. Who wants to waste fun time with the kids at a sit-down restaurant when you know the food will be mediocre anyway.*

A woman from Verona, Wisconsin, offers this:

We think the character meals are under-rated in all guide books. These meals are in pleasant settings and provide an easy, efficient way for little kids to interact with characters while providing adults with an opportunity to relax. For value and good food, we especially like the breakfasts. Yes, they're a little pricey, but you get more than food. Probably our favorite is at The Garden Grill at The Land at Epcot. This year they even gave us souvenir hats.

A mother of three from Jamaica, New York, waited 2 hours and 40 minutes for a table at the Rainforest Cafe and still had a good time:

The Rainforest Cafe was an absolute delight. Our six-year-old sat right next to a gorilla that ranted every few minutes: our ten-month-old loved the huge fish tanks; and they loved the food. Our wait for a table was two hours, so we went back to the hotel and returned two hours later. We still had to wait 40 minutes but it was worth it. The gorilla room had more of a jungle feel than the elephant room.

An Atlanta family reported:

We had no problems making reservations way ahead of time or a day ahead even though we stayed outside the park.

On the topic of saving money, a woman from Seattle offered the following:

First, for those wanting to save a few bucks (or in some cases several bucks) we would definitely suggest eating outside of WDW for as many meals as possible. To keep down our costs, we would eat a large breakfast before leaving the hotel, have a fast-food lunch in the park, a snack later to hold us over, and then eat a good dinner outside the park. There are several good restaurants in the area that have excellent food at reasonable prices, notably Cafe Tu Tu Tango and Ming [Court], both on International Drive. We also obtained the "Entertainment Book" for Orlando which offers 50% off meals all over town.

A mother from Knoxville, Tennessee, loved Cinderella's Royal Table, commenting:

I love eating at [Cinderella's Royal Table]—we had dinner and breakfast there. It is one spot in Fantasyland where you are not jostled, hurried, and fighting for your life. We have three daughters, and Cinderella's Royal Table is "princess paradise." We met the Fairy Godmother.

Finally, a Pennsylvania reader thinks he understands why Disney thrill rides are so tame:

> *Mickey wouldn't want anyone to get sick on his rides. He wants you to have a good enough appetite for the over-priced food, [but] I think he wants you dizzy so the prices are a little blurry.*

Counter-Service Restaurant Mini-Profiles

To help you find palatable fast-service food that suits your taste, we have developed mini-profiles of Walt Disney World theme park counter-service restaurants. The restaurants are listed alphabetically by theme park.

Counter-service restaurants profiled below are rated for quality and portion size (self-explanatory), as well as for value. The value rating ranges from A to F as follows:

A   =   Exceptional value, a real bargain
B   =   Good value
C   =   Fair value, you get exactly what you pay for
D   =   Somewhat overpriced
F   =   Extremely overpriced

THE MAGIC KINGDOM

Author's Favorite Counter-Service Restaurants

Aunt Polly's Dockside Inn
Columbia Harbour House
The Diamond Horseshoe Saloon Revue
The Plaza Pavilion

Aunt Polly's Dockside Inn   Frontierland, on Tom Sawyer Island

Portion: Medium
Selection: Chilled fried chicken; ham and cheese sandwiches; child's plate with

QUALITY	VALUE
Good	B

chicken or peanut butter and jelly sandwich (includes cookie and a child's beverage); and cookies, ice cream cones and floats, and apple pie.
Comments: Scenic and off the beaten path. One of our great favorites for lunch. Closes at dusk.

Casey's Corner   Main Street

Portion: Medium

Selection: Half-pound hot dogs and fries;
chips; peanuts; and brownies.

QUALITY	VALUE
Good	C

Comments: Restricted menu translates into snappy service.

Columbia Harbour House   Liberty Square

Portion: Medium

Selection: Fried fish and chicken; ham
and cheese, smoked turkey, and tuna

QUALITY	VALUE
Good	C

salad sandwiches; child's plate with bologna and cheese sandwich,
cookie, and child's beverage; New England clam chowder (in bread
bowl) and vegetable chili; cole slaw; chips; fries; seafood pasta salad; and
apple pie.

Comments: Tables usually available upstairs. Quickest service within
spitting distance of Fantasyland.

Cosmic Ray's Starlight Cafe   Tomorrowland

Portion: Large

Selection: Burgers (including vegetarian);
hot dogs; deli sandwiches; cheese steak

QUALITY	VALUE
Fair	B

subs; grilled chicken sandwiches; child's plate with chicken nuggets;
vegetable and cream of chicken soups; chef and chicken Caesar salads;
fries; ice cream bars; and sugar-free cheesecake.

Comments: Big place. Tables usually available. Out-of-this-world
entertainment on stage.

The Diamond Horseshoe Saloon Revue   Liberty Square

Portion: Medium to large

Selection: Ham and cheese, smoked
turkey, and roast beef sandwiches;

QUALITY	VALUE
Fair to Good	C

chicken Caesar and chef salads; child's plates with peanut butter and
jelly sandwich, chips, and a child's beverage; chips; dill pickles; ice cream
cones and floats; and hot fudge sundaes.

Comments: Combine lunch with a show. First come, first served.

El Pirata y el Perico
Adventureland

Portion: Medium

Selection: Tacos; nachos; taco salads; quarter-pound hot dogs with chili,

QUALITY	VALUE
Good	C

cheese, and/or kraut; chili; child's plate with hot dog, cookie, and child's beverage; and ice cream bars and churros.

Comments: Often overlooked. A good bet for lunch.

The Pinocchio Village Haus
Fantasyland

Portion: Medium

Selection: Burgers; double cheeseburger combo meal; turkey sandwiches; hot

QUALITY	VALUE
Fair	C

dogs; pasta salad (vegetarian or with chicken); child's plate with peanut butter and jelly sandwich, chips, and a child's beverage; fruit cup; cupcakes; and cookies.

Comments: Almost always crowded. Try Columbia Harbour House on the border with Liberty Square.

The Plaza Pavilion
Tomorrowland

Portion: Medium to large

Selection: Six-inch pizzas; pizza combo meal with small salad and beverage;

QUALITY	VALUE
Good	B

bread sticks; salads; tuna pasta salad; deli sandwiches; chicken strips; child's plate with peanut butter and jelly sandwiches, chips, and a child's beverage; and ice cream bars.

Comments: Our pick of the Tomorrowland eateries. Try the Italian deli sandwich.

EPCOT
Author's Favorite Counter-Service Restaurants
Kringla Bakeri og Kafé
Pasta Piazza Ristorante
Pure and Simple
Sommerfest
Yakitori House

Boulangerie Pâtisserie

World Showcase, France

Portion: Small to medium
Selection: Coffee, croissants, and pastries.
Comments: Okay for a light meal, better
for a snack. No tables.

QUALITY	VALUE
Good	B

Cantina de San Angel

World Showcase, Mexico

Portion: Medium
Selection: Chips and salsa; beef and
chicken hard and soft tacos; quesadillas;
burritos; ensalada Mexicana; child's plate with burrito, chips, churro,
and child's beverage; churros and flan with caramel sauce; and frozen
margaritas.
Comments: Most meals are served with refried beans and salsa. Tables are
outdoors.

QUALITY	VALUE
Fair	D

Electric Umbrella Restaurant

Future World, Innoventions, Plaza East

Portion: Medium
Selection: Burgers; chicken tenders with
cole slaw and fries; chicken sandwiches
(combo meal available); grilled ham and cheese sandwiches; vegetable
wraps with grapes; child's plates with hot dogs or chicken tenders; hot
dogs; chili; chef, green, and fruit salads; peanut butter pie, chocolate
cake, and apple pie; and Budweiser and Bud Light.
Comments: All items are served with either french fries or an apple.

QUALITY	VALUE
Good	B

Kringla Bakeri og Kafé

World Showcase, Norway

Portion: Small to medium
Selection: Pastries; open-faced sandwiches
(roast beef, smoked turkey, and smoked
salmon); Norwegian cheese platter; sweet pretzels with raisins and
almonds; cinnamon rolls; waffles; and Ringnes beer on tap.
Comments: Good, but pricey.

QUALITY	VALUE
Good to Excellent	D

Liberty Inn

World Showcase, The American Adventure

Portion: Medium

Selection: Burgers and french fries; hot dogs; rotisserie chicken; chicken strips;

QUALITY	VALUE
Fair	C

grilled chicken sandwiches; salads; child's hot dog plate; fruit cups, ice cream cups and drumsticks, apple pie, cheesecake, and chocolate cake; and Budweiser and Bud Light.

Comments: The only place in World Showcase for American fast food. Ample seating.

Lotus Blossom Café

World Showcase, China

Portion: Medium

Selection: Stir-fried beef, chicken, and vegetable dishes; sweet-and-sour chicken;

QUALITY	VALUE
Fair	D

fried-wonton basket; egg rolls; fried rice; egg drop soup with chicken; ginger ice cream, fruit cup with lychee, and fortune cookies; child's plate with sweet-and-sour chicken or eggroll and pork fried rice (includes beverage); and Chinese beer and wine.

Comments: Marginal Chinese at fancy prices.

Pasta Piazza Ristorante

Future World, Innoventions, Plaza West

Portion: Medium

Selection: Eggplant parmigiana; chicken parmigiana with pasta and bread sticks;

QUALITY	VALUE
Good	B

Italian and meatball parmigiana subs; lasagna with bread sticks; pizza by the slice; chicken breast combo meal with pasta salad, bread sticks, and beverage; pasta combo meal with pasta of your choice, bread sticks, and beverage; Caeser salad; Italian cheesecake, cannoli, apple-crisp pizza, and iced cappuccino; and Budweiser and Bud Light.

Comments: Healthy-choice items are available. Good people-watching.

Pure and Simple   Future World, Wonders of Life

Portion: Medium

Selection: Lemon-pepper chicken
sandwiches; tuna salad pitas with chips;

QUALITY	VALUE
Good to Excellent	B

deli sandwiches; vegetable chili in wheat bread bowl; chicken and
vegetable soup; Caesar salads; wonder waffles; child's plate with healthy
hot dog and fruit or chips; fruit cups; smoothies (natural fruit-blend
drinks and papaya juice); and root beer floats.

Comments: A good spot for those seeking low-fat, heart-healthy meals.

Rose & Crown Pub   World Showcase, United Kingdom

Portion: Medium

Selection: Cornish pasties; sausage rolls;
shortbread; and Guinness, Harp, and

QUALITY	VALUE
Fair to Good	C

Bass beers and ales, as well as other spirits.

Comments: The attraction here is the pub atmosphere and the draft beer.

Sommerfest   World Showcase, Germany

Portion: Large

Selection: Bratwurst and frankfurters with
kraut; goulash; soft pretzels; apple

QUALITY	VALUE
Good	B

strudel; sandwiches; and German wine and beer (Beck's).

Comments: Tucked in the entrance to the Biergarten restaurant,
Sommerfest is hard to find from the street. Limited seating.

Sunshine Season Food Fair   Future World, The Land

Portion: Medium

Selection: Potatoes stuffed with beef and
chili, cheese and bacon, and sour cream

QUALITY	VALUE
Good to Excellent	B

and chives; soups and salads; barbecued chicken and ribs, and smoked
sandwiches with corn on the cob, baked beans, cole slaw, and corn
muffins; deli sandwiches such as Italian subs, corned beef, tuna and
chicken salad, ham, and turkey; pastas such as lasagna, tortellini, and
udon noodles with chicken and vegetables; fruit and yogurt cups;

brownies and cookies; ice cream and freshly baked goods; and wine by the glass, beer, and nonalcoholic beer.

Comments: This is a food court with eight different counters. Most of the counters offer adult and child combo meals, and several feature heart-healthy options. Most counters serve beverages, so you don't have to queue up twice. Very crowded at mealtimes. Tables difficult to find.

Yakitori House — World Showcase, Japan

Portion: Small to medium

Selection: Shogun combo meal with beef and chicken teriyaki and rice (adult and child versions); shrimp, chicken, and beef skewers with rice; beef curry; tempura and beef udon; seafood salads; miso soup; ginger, green tea, and red bean ice cream; and Kirin beer, sake, and plum wine.

QUALITY	VALUE
Excellent	B

Comments: A great place for a light meal. Limited seating.

DISNEY-MGM STUDIOS

Author's Favorite Counter-Service Restaurants

Catalina Eddie's
Commissary
Rosie's Red Hot Dogs
Toy Story Pizza Planet

ABC Commissary — Backlot

Portion: Medium to large

Selection: Quarter-pound burgers (combo available); chicken nuggets; chicken sandwich combo; vegetable soup; ham and cheese and turkey subs; French dip; child's chicken nugget plate; chef and pasta salads; fries; and milkshakes.

QUALITY	VALUE
Good	C

Comments: Indoors, centrally located, air-conditioned, and usually not too crowded.

Backlot Express   Backlot

Portion: Medium
Selection: Burgers and french fries;

QUALITY	VALUE
Fair	C

chicken sandwiches with fruit or fries;
chili; hot dog combos; chicken Caesar salad; tuna and meatball subs;
and churros, cookies, and brownies.
Comments: Frequently overlooked.

Catalina Eddie's   Sunset Boulevard

Portion: Medium to large
Selection: Soft-serve yogurt; frozen fruit

QUALITY	VALUE
Good	B

drinks and shakes; and ice cream bars,
cones, and sundaes.
Comments: Seldom crowded.

Min and Bill's Dockside Diner   Echo Lake

Portion: Medium
Selection: Beef or chicken taco salads; soft

QUALITY	VALUE
Fair	C

tacos; nachos; and ice cream cones and
floats.
Comments: Limited outdoor seating.

Rosie's Red Hot Dogs   Sunset Boulevard

Portion: Large
Selection: All manner of hot dogs and

QUALITY	VALUE
Good	B

sausages; barbeque beef sandwiches;
soup; nachos; chili; side salads; turkey or ham subs; brownies; and
cookies.
Comments: Best hot dog stand at Walt Disney World. We like it.

Starring Rolls Bakery

Sunset Boulevard

Portion: Small to medium

Selection: Ham and turkey sandwiches; fruit cups, pastries, pies, cookies, doughnuts, and rolls.

QUALITY	VALUE
Fair to Good	C

Comments: Open for breakfast on early-entry mornings.

Studio Catering Co.

Backlot

Portion: Medium

Selection: Barbecue pork, beef, and chicken sandwiches; turkey subs with cheese; pretzels; popcorn; and ice cream bars.

QUALITY	VALUE
Fair	C

Comments: Ice cream has separate service lines. Good place for a break while your kids enjoy the *Honey, I Shrunk the Kids* playground.

THE ANIMAL KINGDOM
Author's Favorite Counter-Service Restaurants
Flame Tree Barbecue Tuskers House Restaurant

Dino Diner

Dinoland USA

Portion: Medium

Selection: Smoked turkey legs; fresh fruit; breakfast breads in the morning.

QUALITY	VALUE
Good	C

Comments: Often overlooked. Good for a quick snack.

Flame Tree Barbecue

Safari Village

Portion: Large

Selection: Smoked beef brisket, pork shoulder, and turkey; barbecue ribs; combination barbecue platters; vegetarian wraps; and child's plate with turkey sandwich, chips, and cookie.

QUALITY	VALUE
Good	C

Side items include baked beans, chili, steak fries, and apple pie.

Comments: Queues very long at lunch time, but seating is ample and well
  shaded. One of our favorites for lunch.

Mr. Kamel's Burger Grill   Asia

Portion: Medium

Selection: Cheeseburgers.

QUALITY	VALUE
Fair	D

Comments: Not a very good reason to
  walk to Asia.

Pizzafari   Safari Village

Portion: Medium

Selection: Personal pizzas with cheese
  only, pepperoni, or sausage, ham, pep-

QUALITY	VALUE
Good	C

  peroni, peppers, and onions; mesquite
  chicken Caesar salad; Italian deli sandwiches; roasted vegetable calzone;
  chocolate mousse cake and frozen lemonade.

Comments: A favorite with children. Hectic at peak mealtimes, but the
  pizza is good.

Restaurantosaurus   Dinoland USA

Portion: Medium

Selection: Cheeseburgers and hot dogs;
  McDonald's Chicken McNuggets and
  Happy Meals; mesquite-grilled chicken

QUALITY	VALUE
Fair to Good	D

  salad and vegetarian platter; fries, brownies, and cookies.

Comments: Picky children might enjoy Restaurantosaurus. Others will do
  better at another eaterie.

Tamu Tamu   Africa

Portion: Large

Selection: Various flavors of yogurt or ice
  cream, available in cones or as sundaes.

QUALITY	VALUE
Good	C

Comments: Seating is behind building and could easily be overlooked.

Tusker House Restaurant   Africa

Portion: Large

QUALITY	VALUE
Good	C

Selection: Grilled chicken breast with portobello mushrooms; half rotisserie chicken; fried chicken dinner; spit-roasted prime rib; baked lasagna; grilled chicken salad; roasted vegetable sandwich with tabouli; child's plate with macaroni and cheese; garlic mashed potatoes and fresh vegetables; cinnamon rolls and cookies.

Comments: Excellent selections for health-conscious diners. Salads are refreshing. Separate line for bakery items.

Full-Service Restaurants of Walt Disney World

More than five dozen full-service restaurants operate in Walt Disney World, with quality and variety of food improving every year. Unfortunately, the restaurants are generally overpriced, and Disney imposes on dining its genius for complication and regimentation. What elsewhere would be a simple dinner out, is at Disney World a maze of busy phone numbers, pseudo-reservations, and waiting.

In the theme parks, variables affecting your odds of getting into a particular restaurant include its popularity and capacity, and the size of the crowd the day you visit. Each restaurant has lunch and dinner seatings. Lunch is 11 a.m. to 4 p.m. Dinner is served from 4 p.m. until one hour before the park closes.

PRIORITY SEATING

Disney ceaselessly tinkers with its restaurant reservations policy. Since 1997, reservations have been replaced with "Priority Seating." When you call, your name and essential information are taken as if you were making a reservation. The Disney representative then says you have priority seating for the restaurant on the date and time you requested and usually explains that priority seating means you will be seated ahead of walk-ins, i.e., those without priority seating.

From Disney's perspective, if restaurants don't have to hold reserved tables, they can run closer to capacity. Priority seating didn't work very well for the first year or so, but now guests are getting used to the process and things are going smoother.

Go Early, Go Late, or Be Prepared to Wait

Call (407) 939-3463 before you leave home and arrange priority seating at the restaurants of your choice. If you schedule an early or late priority seating, your chances of getting a table at the appointed time are good.

If you want to eat at a full-service restaurant during peak hours, you're better off with a priority seating than with nothing. With priority seating, your wait almost always will be less than 40 minutes during peak hours, and sometimes less than 20 minutes. If you just walk in, especially during busier seasons, expect to wait 40 to 75 minutes.

If you haven't arranged priority seating before you leave home:

1. If you're driving, make priority seating arrangements at Ocala Disney AAA Travel Center off I-75 in Ocala, Florida.

2. If you're lodging outside Walt Disney World or at a hotel in the Disney Village Hotel Plaza, call (407) 939-3463 for advance priority seating.

   Note: With no formal announcement, Disney dining representatives recently began accepting advance priority seatings from guests *not* staying in Disney hotels and campgrounds. Should this continue, it will help redress long-standing discrimination against "day guests." If the new practice is abandoned, guests lodging out of the World will have to make priority seating arrangements at the theme park on the day of the meal.

3. If you're a Disney resort guest, you'll find a button on your phone which will dial WDW-DINE directly.

4. In the theme parks, same-day priority seating can be arranged in the morning at the door of the restaurant. While the restaurants don't begin food service until 11 a.m., their front desks are staffed from park opening.

   At Epcot, arrive at the entrance, admission pass in hand, 45 minutes before the park opens. Upon admission, go quickly to the priority seating service at Guest Relations (left of the geosphere). Lunch and dinner priority seating can be made at the same time. Be ready with alternatives for both restaurants and seatings in case your first choices aren't available.

   If you don't arrive early at Epcot, you may have a long wait at Guest Relations, with no guarantee that any priority seatings will be available. On many days, World Showcase restaurants and the Coral Reef (in Future World) book solid for preferred seating within an hour to an hour and a half of the park's opening. Even if you get a seating, you'll have burned your most productive, crowd-free touring time in the process.

At Disney-MGM Studios, a priority seating desk is operated on the corner of Hollywood and Sunset boulevards.

Magic Kingdom restaurants have no central priority seating service. If you want same-day priority seating, go immediately to the restaurant's door after entering the park.

At the Animal Kingdom there is only one full-service restaurant, the Rainforest Cafe. No priority seatings are accepted.

5. If you're spontaneous and prefer to keep your schedule flexible, most full-service restaurants will take you with a minimal wait as a walk-in between 2:30 and 4:30 p.m.

BOOKING WALT DISNEY WORLD CHARACTER MEALS AND DINNER SHOWS

Priority seating is required for character meals. Make arrangements from home as far in advance as possible. Call (407) 939-3463. Dinner shows continue to book actual reservations. Book your dinner show when you reserve your hotel room.

DRESS

Dress is informal at all theme park restaurants. While theme park attire (shorts, T-shirts, sneakers, etc.) is tolerated at hotel restaurants, you probably would feel more comfortable if you dressed up a bit. The only restaurant requesting jackets for men and dressy clothes for women is Victoria & Albert's at the Grand Floridian.

A FEW CAVEATS

Before you commence eating your way through Walt Disney World, you need to know:

1. However creative and enticing the menu descriptions, avoid fancy food, especially at full-service restaurants in the Magic Kingdom and Disney-MGM Studios. Order dishes the kitchen is unlikely to botch. An exception to this caveat is the Brown Derby Restaurant at the Studios.
2. Don't order baked, broiled, poached, or grilled seafood unless the restaurant specializes in seafood or rates at least ★★★★ on our restaurant profile.

3. Theme park restaurants rush their customers in order to make room for the next group of diners. Dining at high speed may appeal to a family with young, restless children, but for people wanting to relax, it's more like *Beat the Clock* than fine dining.

   If you want to linger over your expensive meal, *do not* order your entire dinner at once. Order drinks. Study the menu while you sip, then order appetizers. Tell the waiter you need more time to decide among entrees. Order your main course only after appetizers have been served. Dawdle over coffee and dessert.

4. If you're dining in a theme park and cost is an issue, make lunch your main meal. Entrees are similar to those on the dinner menu, but prices are significantly lower.

FULL-SERVICE DINING FOR FAMILIES WITH YOUNG CHILDREN

Disney restaurants offer an excellent (though expensive) opportunity to introduce young children to the variety and excitement of ethnic food. No matter how formal a restaurant appears, the staff is accustomed to wiggling, impatient, and often boisterous children. Chefs de France at Epcot, for example, may be the nation's only French restaurant where most patrons wear shorts and T-shirts and at least two dozen young diners are attired in basic black . . . mouse ears. Bottom line: Young children are the rule, not the exception, at Disney restaurants.

Almost all Disney restaurants offer children's menus, and all have booster seats and highchairs. They understand how tough it may be for children to sit for an extended period, and waiters will supply little ones with crackers and rolls and serve your dinner much faster than in comparable restaurants elsewhere. Letters from readers suggest that being served too quickly (not having enough time to relax) is much more common than having a long wait.

Good Walt Disney World Theme Park Restaurants for Children

In Epcot, preschoolers most enjoy the Biergarten in Germany, San Angel Inn Restaurante in Mexico, and Coral Reef in The Living Seas pavilion in Future World. The Biergarten combines a rollicking and noisy atmosphere with good basic food, including roast chicken. A German oompah band entertains. Children often have the opportunity to participate in Bavarian dancing. San Angel Inn is in the Mexican village marketplace. From the table, children can watch boats on El Río del Tiempo drift beneath a smoking volcano. With a choice of chips, tacos, and other familiar items, picky children usually have no difficulty finding something to eat. The Coral Reef, with tables beside viewing windows of The Living Seas aquarium, offers a satisfying mealtime diversion for all ages. If your kids don't eat fish, Coral Reef also serves chicken.

The Biergarten and San Angel Inn offer reasonable value, plus good food. The Coral Reef is overpriced, though the food is palatable.

Cinderella's Royal Table in Cinderella Castle is the big draw in the Magic Kingdom. Though the food won't knock you out, it has improved noticeably over the past 18 months. Interestingly, other Magic Kingdom full-service restaurants hold little appeal for children. For the best combination of food and entertainment, book a character meal at the Liberty Tree Tavern or The Crystal Palace.

At Disney-MGM Studios, all ages enjoy the atmosphere and entertainment at the Sci-Fi Dine-In Theater Restaurant and the 50's Prime Time Cafe. Unfortunately, the Sci-Fi's food is close to dismal and the Prime Time's is uneven. Eat only dessert at these restaurants.

The only full-service restaurant at the Animal Kingdom is the Rainforest Cafe, which is a great favorite of children.

DINING DISNEY STYLE
(FORMERLY THE FOOD 'N FUN PLAN)

In each of the past three years, Disney has revamped its prepaid meal plan. In 1998, Disney divided dining and recreation into two separate packages. The new dining plan operates pretty much the same way as the previous iteration, only without any recreational privileges. Disney resort guests can sign up for the Dining Disney Style meal plan for the course of their stay. Cost is determined by the number of people in your party and the number of nights you stay. It's all or nothing: everyone in your group must participate for your entire length of stay. The now separate recreation plan is covered on pages 624–625. The dining plan works as follows:

For each night of your stay, you pay $50 per adult and $22 per child (ages three to nine), and Disney adds a "Bonus Credit" of $5 per adult and $3 per child. Your cost plus the Disney credit equals the amount you have in your "Food Account" to spend on meals at selected Disney restaurants during your stay.

For example, two adults and two children are staying five nights. They pay $500 for the adults (two adults × five days × $50 per adult) and $220 for the children (two children × five days × $22 per child). Their charge for participating in the dining plan is $720 ($500 + $220). Their Bonus Credits total $50 for the adults (two adults × five days × $5 Bonus Credit per adult per day) and $30 for the children (two children × five days × $3 Bonus Credit per child per day), or $80 in Bonus Credits. Add that $80 to the $720 they paid, and that's $800 in the Food Account.

Each guest signing up for the dining plan (including children) is issued a Resort Identification Card that identifies him/her as a participant. The card, when activated, also can be used as a credit card at Disney shops. If you don't want certain members of your party to have charge privileges, say so when you register for the plan.

Once guests are registered, they can commence eating their way across Walt Disney World. They can order whatever they want . . . appetizers, lobster, wine. When the check comes, they present their I.D. card. The meal's cost will be deducted from the balance in their food account. If, using the above example, the family begins with $800 in its account and eats a meal costing $100, including tax and gratuities, $100 will be subtracted from the account, leaving a balance of $700.

If you exceed your balance, you "will be notified immediately and given the option to pay the unpaid balance by cash or credit card or to charge it directly to your room account."

The dining plan can be used at most full-service restaurants in Disney World and at counter-service restaurants in the theme parks. Also covered are drinks in Disney World lounges and nightclubs; dinner shows, including the *Hoop-Dee-Doo Revue* and the Polynesian's luau; room service; and Disney pizza delivery at your resort, where available.

Excluded are restaurants at the Disney Village Hotel Plaza, Swan and Dolphin resorts, and Shades of Green resort. Also not covered are items from guest room mini-bars and from vendor carts.

It doesn't take a CPA to figure the plan's bottom line. From Disney's perspective, the dining plan accomplishes two things. It gets you to spend all of your food dollars at Disney restaurants. And, because you must eat all of your meals at Disney restaurants in order to get your money's worth, you will never leave Walt Disney World. Checkmate.

The plan's psychological side is less obvious. Some participants order more lavishly than they would if they were paying for one meal at a time, and they exceed their balance before their stay ends (necessitating further expenditures). Others, particularly families, draw down their account crumb by crumb, fearing they'll exceed their balance before it's time to go home. And, as it says in the fine print, "any funds remaining in the food account at the end of your stay are non-refundable." Gotcha.

With the dining plan, Disney is essentially paying you some amount in Bonus Credits to eat exclusively in Disney restaurants. By making you pay

$50 per adult per day, they are trading up most guests (getting them to spend more on meals than they ordinarily would). Whether it's a good deal boils down to your alcohol consumption.

The average Disney World visitor spends most of his time in the theme parks or the water parks and eats only one full-service restaurant meal a day. Time is as valuable as money to the guest, and most meals are consumed at counter-service eateries. Even if you eat a big breakfast at your hotel and a hefty fast-food lunch at the park, your total for both meals will average about $18. Though the plan allows you to feast one day and fast the next (gobble your food account any way you want), you will have to eat an average of $37 worth each evening ($55 per day less the $18 for breakfast and lunch). That's a lot of food to put away, even at the more expensive restaurants. If, however, you throw drinks and wine into the equation, spending $37 per adult per night is no challenge at all.

If you consume a few dollars in alcoholic beverages each day, you can come out okay on the dining plan. But you must be comfortable with spending $50 a day on food and eating all your meals at Disney restaurants. If you don't drink much, you may have trouble getting your money's worth. Such a family from Dublin, Ohio, reports:

> We opted for the [dining] card with our package. We paid approximately $750 up front several weeks in advance. Our total for the week was $601 and we did every special show without skimping. The Food card was a rip-off. We recommend using American Express with 10% Disney discount for food buying.

A family from Sioux Falls, South Dakota, related their experience with the Deluxe Magic Plan, a vacation package that offers much the same benefits as the dining plan:

> We used the Deluxe Magic Plan and loved [the] convenience of not being concerned by the cost of meals, recreation, etc. However, I added up our receipts when I got home, and we didn't spend what we paid for the package—it would be extremely hard to make that package save you $$!! We ate like crazy! Used boats, bikes, and Disney Institute—still didn't pay. And especially for first timers, I wouldn't recommend it because we spent a lot of time sitting in restaurants instead of touring the parks.

Finally, if you participate in the plan and lose your Resort Identification Card, report it immediately to the front desk of your Disney hotel. The lost card will be deactivated and replaced.

WALT DISNEY WORLD FULL-SERVICE RESTAURANT PROFILES*

To help you in your dining choices, we have developed profiles of full-service restaurants at Disney World. Each profile allows you to quickly check the restaurant's cuisine, location, star rating, cost range, quality rating, and value rating. *Profiles are listed alphabetically by restaurant and follow the listing by cuisine nearby.*

Star Rating   The star rating represents the entire dining experience: style, service, and ambiance, in addition to taste, presentation, and quality of food. Five stars is the highest rating and indicates that the restaurant offers the best of everything. Four-star restaurants are above average, and three-star restaurants offer good, though not necessarily memorable meals. Two-star restaurants serve mediocre fare, and one-star restaurants are below average. Our star ratings don't correspond to ratings awarded by AAA, Mobil, Zagat, or other restaurant reviewers.

Cost   The next rating tells how much a complete meal will cost. We include a main dish with vegetable or side dish, and a choice of soup or salad. Appetizers, desserts, drinks, and tips aren't included. We've rated the cost as inexpensive, moderate, or expensive.

Inexpensive	=	$12 or less per person
Moderate	=	$13–23 per person
Expensive	=	More than $23 per person

Quality Rating   If you want the best food available and cost isn't an issue, look no further than the quality rating. It's based on a scale of 0 to 100, with 100 as the best possible rating and zero (0) as the worst. The quality rating is based solely on preparation, presentation, taste, freshness of ingredients, and creativity of the food served. There is no consideration of price, service, or atmosphere—just the food.

Value Rating   If you're looking for both quality and a good deal, check the value rating. Each ranges from A to F, as follows:

A	=	Exceptional value, a real bargain
B	=	Good value
C	=	Fair value, you get exactly what you pay for
D	=	Somewhat overpriced
F	=	Extremely overpriced

Payment   We've listed the types of payment accepted at each restaurant using the following codes:

*For additional information on Disney character dining, see pages 175–181

VISA	VISA
AMEX	American Express
MC	MasterCard
D	Discover
CB	Carte Blanche
DC	Diners Club

Readers' Restaurant Survey Responses For each Disney World restaurant profiled, we include the results of last year's readers' survey responses. Results are expressed as a percentage of responding readers who liked the restaurant well enough to eat there again (Thumbs Up), as opposed to the percentage of responding readers who had a bad experience and wouldn't go back (Thumbs Down). (Readers tend to be less critical than our *Unofficial Guide* restaurant reviewers.) If you would like to participate in the 1998 Walt Disney World Restaurant Survey, complete and return the restaurant survey form on the last page of this book.

Walt Disney World Restaurants by Cuisine

Type of Restaurant	Location	Overall Rating	Price	Quality Rating	Value Rating
American					
California Grill	Contemporary	★★★★½	Moderate	96	C
Planet Hollywood	Pleasure Island	★★★½	Moderate	87	C
The Hollywood Brown Derby	Disney-MGM	★★★	Expensive	84	C
Seasons Dining Room	Disney Institute	★★★	Moderate	84	C
Baskervilles	Grosvenor Resort	★★★	Moderate	82	C
Olivia's Cafe	Old Key West	★★★	Moderate	81	C
Yacht Club Galley	Yacht Club	★★★	Moderate	81	C
House of Blues	West Side	★★★	Moderate	80	C
Wolfgang Puck Cafe	West Side	★★★	Expensive	78	C
The Garden Grill Restaurant	Epcot	★★½	Moderate	79	C
Whispering Canyon Cafe	Wilderness Lodge	★★½	Moderate	79	B
Hollywood & Vine	Disney-MGM	★★½	Inexpensive	74	C
Liberty Tree Tavern	Magic Kingdom	★★½	Mod/Exp	74	C
Boatwright's Dining Hall	Dixie Landings	★★½	Moderate	73	D

Walt Disney World Restaurants by Cuisine (continued)

Type of Restaurant	Location	Overall Rating	Price	Quality Rating	Value Rating
Cinderella's Royal Table	Magic Kingdom	★★½	Moderate	73	D
Rainforest Cafe	Downtown Disney/ Animal Kingdom	★★½	Moderate	73	D
ESPN Club	BoardWalk	★★	Moderate	73	C
Official All-Star Cafe	Disney's Wide World of Sports	★★	Moderate	72	C
Big River Grille & Brewing Works	BoardWalk	★★	Moderate	71	D
50's Prime Time Cafe	Disney-MGM	★★	Moderate	69	D
Coral Isle Cafe	Polynesian	★★	Moderate	68	C
Grand Floridian Cafe	Grand Floridian	★★	Moderate	68	D
Pleasure Island Jazz Company	Pleasure Island	★★	Moderate	68	C
Coral Cafe	Dolphin	★★	Moderate	67	D
Gulliver's Grill at Garden Grove	Swan	★★	Expensive	67	D
Sci-Fi Dine-In Theater Restaurant	Disney-MGM	★★	Moderate	67	D
Buffet					
Cape May Cafe	Beach Club	★★★	Moderate	84	B
The Crystal Palace	Magic Kingdom	★★½	Moderate	79	C
Chef Mickey's	Contemporary	★★	Moderate	67	C
Chinese					
Nine Dragons Restaurant	Epcot	★★½	Expensive	74	F
Cuban					
Bongo's Cuban Cafe	West Side	★★	Moderate	74	D
English					
Rose & Crown Dining Room	Epcot	★★★	Moderate	81	D

Walt Disney World Restaurants by Cuisine (continued)

Type of Restaurant	Location	Overall Rating	Price	Quality Rating	Value Rating
French					
Chefs de France	Epcot	★★★★	Moderate	90	C
German					
Biergarten	Epcot	★★½	Moderate	75	C
Gourmet					
Victoria & Albert's	Grand Floridian	★★★★½	Expensive	96	D
Arthur's 27	Buena Vista Palace	★★★★	Expensive	90	C
Italian					
Portobello Yacht Club	Pleasure Island	★★★½	Expensive	88	D
Palio	Swan	★★★	Moderate	81	C
Tony's Town Square Restaurant	Magic Kingdom	★★½	Moderate	78	D
Mama Melrose's Ristorante Italiano	Disney-MGM	★★½	Moderate	74	D
L'Originale Alfredo di Roma Ristorante	Epcot	★★½	Expensive	74	D
Japanese					
Kimonos	Swan	★★★★	Moderate	90	C
Teppanyaki Dining Room	Epcot	★★★½	Expensive	85	C
Tempura Kiku	Epcot	★★★	Moderate	83	C
Benihana— The Japanese Steakhouse	Hilton	★★½	Moderate	75	C
Mediterranean					
Citricos	Grand Floridian	★★★★	Expensive	91	C
Spoodles	BoardWalk	★★★½	Moderate	87	C
Mexican					
San Angel Inn Restaurante	Epcot	★★★	Expensive	84	D

Walt Disney World Restaurants by Cuisine (continued)

Type of Restaurant	Location	Overall Rating	Price	Quality Rating	Value Rating
Juan & Only's Bar and Jail	Dolphin	★★★	Moderate	80	B
Maya Grill	Coronado	★★	Expensive	66	D
Moroccan					
Restaurant Marrakesh	Epcot	★★★	Moderate	81	C
Norwegian					
Restaurant Akershus	Epcot	★★★½	Moderate	89	B
Polynesian					
'Ohana	Polynesian	★★★	Moderate	79	C
Seafood					
Flying Fish Cafe	BoardWalk	★★★★	Expensive	94	C
Fulton's Crab House	Pleasure Island	★★★½	Expensive	89	D
Narcoossee's	Grand Floridian	★★★½	Expensive	88	D
Artist Point	Wilderness Lodge	★★★½	Moderate	86	C
Cap'n Jack's Oyster Bar	Downtown Disney Marketplace	★★★	Moderate	84	D
Coral Reef	Epcot	★★★	Expensive	84	D
Harry's Safari Bar and Grill	Dolphin	★★★	Expensive	81	D
Bonfamille's Cafe	Port Orleans	★★★	Moderate	80	C
Captain's Tavern	Caribbean Beach	★★	Moderate	67	C
Finn's Grill	Hilton	★	Moderate	55	D
Steak					
Harry's Safari Bar and Grill	Dolphin	★★★	Expensive	81	D
Yachtsman Steakhouse	Yacht Club	★★★	Expensive	80	D
Concourse Steakhouse	Contemporary	★★½	Moderate	72	D
Le Cellier Steakhouse	Epcot	★★	Moderate	67	C
The Outback	Buena Vista Palace	★★	Expensive	67	D

ARTHUR'S 27

Gourmet   ★★★★   Expensive

Buena Vista Palace Resort & Spa, Disney Village Hotel Plaza (407) 827-2727

Readers' Survey Responses:	
49% 👍	51% 👎

QUALITY	VALUE
90	C

Customers: Hotel guests and locals
Reservations: Necessary
When to go: Sunset or during fireworks at any of the three parks
Entree range: $18–60
Payment: VISA, MC, AMEX, DC

Service rating: ★★
Friendliness rating: ★★
Parking: Complimentary valet parking
Bar: Full service
Wine selection: Excellent
Dress: Jackets preferred, tie optional
Disabled access: Yes

Dinner: Every day, 6–10 p.m.

Setting & atmosphere: From its perch on the 27th floor of the Buena Vista Palace, Arthur's gives a breathtaking view of the glittering lights of the Downtown Disney Marketplace and the twirling searchlights of Pleasure Island. Diners sit at large booths, all set apart from each other with their own windows.

House specialties: Florida Gulf shrimp; herb-crusted tuna; medallions of veal; breast of duckling.

Other recommendations: Loin of lamb; salmon in strudel leaves; chilled breast of chicken Alexandra.

Entertainment & amenities: Live entertainment in lounge.

Summary & comments: The best values at this overpriced restaurant are the four-, five-, and six-course table d'hôte offerings for $44, $49, and $55. If you're not looking for a lot of food, you'll pay too much for what you get. Still, it is one of the most impressive views in the area, but only if you are facing the Disney side. Otherwise, you'll be looking at the taillights on Interstate 4 and you'll know what all the locals know: Florida is flat.

Honors & awards: DiRoNa winner.

ARTIST POINT

Seafood   ★★★½   Moderate
Disney's Wilderness Lodge (407) 824-3200

Readers' Survey Responses:	
84% 👍	16% 👎

QUALITY	VALUE
86	C

Customers: Hotel guests, some locals
Priority seatings: Recommended for dinner and character breakfasts
When to go: Anytime
Entree range: $14–25
Payment: VISA, MC, AMEX
Service rating: ★★★★

Friendliness rating: ★★★★★
Parking: Hotel lot
Bar: Full service
Wine selection: Features selections from wineries in America's Northwest
Dress: Casual
Disabled access: Yes

Breakfast: Every day, 7:30–11:30 a.m.
Dinner: Every day, 5:30–10 p.m.

Setting & atmosphere: Two-story-high paintings depicting the landscapes of the Pacific Northwest dominate the interior walls of this casually appointed restaurant. Tall windows offer guests a view of the lake or a waterfall that flows off high rocks and past wildflowers. Huge cast-iron chandeliers hold 12 lanterns with milk-glass panes. Tables are uncovered, and each has a bust of an animal native to the Northwest engraved in it.

House specialties: Maple-glazed salmon fillet; grilled tuna loin steak; grilled halibut chop.

Other recommendations: Porterhouse steak; roasted duck chop; smoked prime rib; omelets; duck hash with egg.

Summary & comments: Unlike the other large hotels, the Wilderness Lodge's top-of-the-line restaurant is not an elegant gourmet room. Still, the beauty of the artwork and the room itself make dining here a pleasure. Breakfast is especially nice, as the landscaping can be fully appreciated in the sunlight.

BASKERVILLES

American   ★★★   Moderate
Grosvenor Resort, Disney Village Hotel Plaza   (407) 828-4444

Readers' Survey Responses:	
74% 👍	26% 👎

QUALITY	VALUE
82	C

Customers: Hotel guests
Reservations: Not accepted
When to go: Anytime
Entree range: $6.50–19.95
Payment: VISA, MC, AMEX, DC, D
Service rating: ★★★

Friendliness rating: ★★
Parking: Hotel lot
Bar: Full service
Wine selection: Good
Dress: Casual
Disabled access: Yes

Breakfast: Every day, 7–11:30 a.m.
Lunch: Monday–Friday, 11:30 a.m.–1 p.m.
Dinner: Every day, 5–10 p.m.

Setting & atmosphere: This is a half-hearted attempt to create an English drawing room atmosphere. Unfortunately, it looks way too much like a cafeteria in a college dormitory.

House specialties: Prime rib; specialty buffets.

Other recommendations: Grilled grouper; stir-fried vegetables; Sherlock's breakfast.

Entertainment & amenities: Murder-mystery weekends where guests solve the crime (priority seatings required).

Summary & comments: Elementary fare. If you're having trouble being entertained, try the murder-mystery dinner—it might make the food a little more exciting. Otherwise, the only reason to dine here is if you're just too tired to leave the hotel or you can't get a priority seating anywhere else. Or if you really have your heart set on an average piece of prime rib.

BENIHANA—THE JAPANESE STEAKHOUSE

Japanese   ★★½   Moderate
The Hilton, Disney Village Hotel Plaza (407) 827-4865

Readers' Survey Responses:	
38% 👍	62% 👎

QUALITY	VALUE
75	C

Customers: Hotel guests and
  some locals
Reservations: Recommended
When to go: Anytime
Entree range: $13–29
Payment: VISA, MC, AMEX,
  DC, JCB, B

Service rating: ★★★★
Friendliness rating: ★★★★
Parking: Hotel lot
Bar: Full service
Wine selection: Good
Dress: Casual
Disabled access: Yes

Dinner: Every day, 5:30–10:30 p.m.

Setting & atmosphere: Large tables with built-in grills are crammed into small rooms decorated with rice-paper panels and Japanese lanterns. Lighting is low and focused on the stage—the chef's grill.

House specialties: Teppanyaki service at large tables (where the chef cooks dinner in front of you). Specialties include New York steak; lobster tail; hibachi vegetables.

Other recommendations: Japanese onion soup.

Entertainment & amenities: Dinner is the show at this teppanyaki-service restaurant where the chef does a lot of noisy chopping and grilling.

Summary & comments: If you're looking for a nice, quiet dinner, be aware that diners sit at tables of eight and private conversation is almost impossible.

BIERGARTEN

German   ★★½   Moderate
Germany, World Showcase, Epcot (407) 939-3463

Readers' Survey Responses:	
73% 👍	27% 👎

QUALITY	VALUE
75	C

(Biergarten)

Customers: Theme park guests
Priority seatings: Recommended
When to go: After 6 p.m.
Entree range: $10.95, lunch;
  $15.75, dinner
Payment: VISA, MC, AMEX
Service rating: ★★★

Friendliness rating: ★★★
Parking: Epcot lot
Bar: Full service
Wine selection: German
Dress: Casual
Disabled access: Yes

Lunch: Every day, 11:30 a.m.–3 p.m.
Dinner: Every day, 4–8:30 p.m.

Setting & atmosphere: After Le Cellier, the Biergarten is the second least appealing restaurant at Epcot. That's why it was scheduled for a makeover in late '97. Guests enter the restaurant through the kitchen, and instead of a traditional buffet line diners make all-you-can-eat selections from the windows of various village merchants and food shops. Guests sit at long tables in a tiered dining area that surrounds a sort of town square of a German village, with the exteriors of shops and houses as the backdrop for the bandstand and dance floor. During the evening meal, an oompah-pah band plays on the stage and encourages diners to join them in sing-alongs and dancing. You may even find yourself swept up in a German version of a conga line.

House specialties: Even though it is all-you-can-eat, the pickings at the current buffet are rather meager. There is German potato salad; lentil salad; smallish sausages and wieners; spaetzle with gravy; and hot dogs in sauerkraut. There is also baked chicken, which looks and tastes like the baked chicken you would get at any other country in World Showcase—or in the world, for that matter. The buffet is set up on wooden barrels, and the food is served from vats, which is about as appealing as it sounds.

Other recommendations: Bratwurst; beer.

Entertainment & amenities: Oompah-pah band and German dancers perform after 6 p.m.

Summary & comments: This is not the greatest food at Epcot, and even the service, which for a serve-yourself buffet is already minimal, doesn't meet usual Disney standards. Go if you can't get enough of polka music. Be aware that you may find yourself seated with other guests.

BIG RIVER GRILLE & BREWING WORKS

American   ★★   Moderate
Disney's BoardWalk (407) 560-0253

Readers' Survey Responses:		QUALITY	VALUE
78% 👍	22% 👎	71	D

Customers: Tourists
Priority seatings: Not accepted
When to go: Anytime
Entree range: $6.95–18
Payment: VISA, MC, AMEX
Service rating: ★★
Friendliness rating: ★★★
Parking: BoardWalk lot.

Note: Valet parking is free before 5 p.m., $5 after (for nonresort guests only).
Bar: Full service
Wine selection: Minimal
Dress: Casual
Disabled access: Good

Lunch & Dinner: Every day, 11:30 a.m.–11 p.m.

Setting & atmosphere: Industrial cubist murals of factories, machinist-metal and wood chairs and tables, and a midnight-blue neon river that flows along the ceiling of the restaurant set a working-class atmosphere. The place is small—it seems like the huge copper brewing tanks take up more room than what is allotted to the diners.

House specialties: Breast of chicken sautéed with shiitake mushrooms; pan-seared salmon fillet with citrus salsa; peppercorn pork loin with gorgonzola; babyback ribs.

Summary & comments: Big River is out-sourced to a Tennessee company and is the first brewpub at Walt Disney World. The Brewing Works brews four regular beers and one or two specialty ales. If you're a beer drinker and like trying something new, you should like this. If you're a beer drinker and have a craving for your favorite brew, you're out of luck—the hand-crafted beers are the only beers sold here. The food is okay, though nothing special. It's another good late-night choice. There is outside seating but no table service there. You can order your food at the bar, however, and cart it outside to watch the people on the BoardWalk while you eat.

BOATWRIGHT'S DINING HALL

American/Cajun ★★½ Moderate
Disney's Dixie Landings Resort (407) 934-6000

Readers' Survey Responses:	
79% 👍	21% 👎

QUALITY	VALUE
73	D

Customers: Hotel guests
Priority seatings: Recommended
for dinner
When to go: Early evening
Entree range: $9.95–17.95
Payment: VISA, MC, AMEX
Service rating: ★★

Friendliness rating: ★★★★
Parking: Hotel lot
Bar: Full service
Wine selection: Fair; the beer
selection is better.
Dress: Casual
Disabled access: Good

Breakfast: Every day, 7–11:30 a.m.
Dinner: Every day, 5–10 p.m.

Setting & atmosphere: Diners sit in a large, noisy room under the skeleton of a riverboat under construction that looks sort of like the carcass of a mastodon. Tables are set with a boatwright's tool kit that contains condiments instead of tools. The real tools—the two-handed saws, hatchets, chisels, and a few that are too foreign to identify—hang along the walls.

House specialties: Cajun étouffée; seafood jambalaya; steak; prime rib.

Other recommendations: Pirogue of pasta and seafood (*pirogue* means boat); bayou bouillabaisse with shrimp, mussels, crawfish, catfish fillets, blue crab, and chunks of new potatoes; grilled catfish served with a Cajun butter sauce.

Summary & comments: Servers can get a little caught up in the theme, a working riverboat-building operation, and forget the basics of good service. Long waits gain no apologies. Fans of true Cajun food may be disappointed with this version, which has been toned down to please the masses. There is, however, a fine selection of regional beers, including Dixie Beer, Blackened Voodoo Lager, and Abita Beer. You'll have a chance to decide which is your favorite while you're waiting for your table.

BONFAMILLE'S CAFE

Seafood   ★★★   Moderate
Disney's Port Orleans Resort (407) 934-5000

Readers' Survey Responses:		QUALITY	VALUE
85% 👍	15% 👎	80	C

Customers: Hotel guests
Priority seatings: Accepted for
  dinner only
When to go: Anytime
Entree range: $5.95–23.95
Payment: VISA, MC, AMEX
Service rating: ★★★★

Friendliness rating: ★★★★
Parking: Hotel lot
Bar: Full service
Wine selection: Fair
Dress: Casual
Disabled access: Yes

Breakfast: Every day, 7–11:30 a.m.
Dinner: Every day, 5–10 p.m.

Setting & atmosphere: A casual setting that recalls New Orleans' French Quarter, only cleaner. Paddle fans and exposed bricks set the mood for this family-oriented restaurant.

House specialties: Limited Creole recipes featuring shrimp, oysters, and crawfish; jambalaya, chicken, and andouille sausage Creole in tomato sauce with onions and green peppers; blackened sea scallops.

Other recommendations: T-bone steak maître d'; roast prime rib of beef; center-cut pork chops; seafood kebab.

Summary & comments: The Creole creations aren't very authentic, and most of the food is pretty tame. Even the andouille sausage, which should have some fire in it, just tastes like Polish sausage. The bayou crawfish pasta appetizer, though, is pretty tasty and at $4.95 is a real bargain. It is also available as an entree for $10.95, but the appetizer portion, along with a soup or salad, is plenty. The name Bonfamille means "good family," and the prices are fair enough for a family to eat pretty well. Don't expect anything out of the ordinary.

BONGO'S CUBAN CAFE

Cuban   ★★   Moderate
Downtown Disney West Side (407) 828-0999

Readers' Survey Responses:	
65% 👍	35% 👎

QUALITY	VALUE
74	D

Customers: Gloria Estefan fans; Disney guests
Reservations: Accepted Monday–Thursday for parties of 15 or more
When to go: Anytime
Entree range: $8.95–19.95
Payment: VISA, MC, AMEX, DC, D

Service rating: ★★★
Friendliness rating: ★★★
Parking: Downtown Disney lot; valet parking available
Bar: Full service
Wine selection: Moderate
Dress: Casual
Disabled access: Elevator to second level

Lunch & Dinner: 11 a.m.–midnight

Setting & atmosphere: This multilevel restaurant features an open, airy environment with a tropical theme built around a three-story pineapple. Other tropical touches include a banana leaf roof, banana leaf ceiling fans, and palm tree–shaped columns. You'll expect Carmen Miranda to dance through the restaurant any minute. Hand-painted murals and mosaics lend an artistic air. A wrap-around, open porch provides a pleasant atmosphere for outdoor dining.

House specialties: Cuban cuisine.

Entertainment & amenities: Latin music.

Summary & comments: Miami resident and Latin singer Gloria Estefan and her husband-producer, Emilio, created this large restaurant that marries salsa music with Cuban cuisine, the adopted cuisine of Florida. There are any number of mom-and-pop Cuban restaurants in the area (not that the Estefans aren't mom-and-pop) that do a better and more consistent job with this wonderful cuisine. If you've never had Cuban food, try it somewhere else. Come here to have a drink with an umbrella in it and listen to music. Expect an upbeat but noisy dining experience.

CALIFORNIA GRILL

American ★★★★½ Moderate
Disney's Contemporary Resort (407) 939-3463

Readers' Survey Responses:		QUALITY	VALUE
81% 👍	19% 👎	96	C

Customers: Locals and hotel guests
Priority seatings: Recommended
When to go: During evening fireworks
Entree range: $16.75–28.75
Payment: AMEX, MC, VISA

Service rating: ★★★★
Friendliness rating: ★★★★
Parking: Complimentary valet
Bar: Full service
Wine selection: California wines
Dress: Casual
Disabled access: Yes

Dinner: Every day, 5:30–10 p.m.
Lounge: Every day, noon to midnight

Setting & atmosphere: From the 15th floor of the Contemporary Resort, California Grill commands one of the most impressive panoramas in central Florida. The dining room is inspired by Wolfgang Puck's Spago restaurant and the Rainbow Room in New York. A show kitchen where the chefs prepare all the food is the centerpiece of the dining room.

House specialties: The catchphrase for the menu is "market inspired," which means the menu changes regularly to take advantage of the freshest produce and available meats and fish. The menu is creative, with Pacific Rim accents. The pork tenderloin is quickly becoming a house favorite and is likely to be kept on most menu rotations.

Other recommendations: Spicy rock shrimp and lemongrass soup, similar to the Thai tom ka gai; goat-cheese ravioli; California designer pizzas; pan-seared tuna; chocolate quake dessert.

Entertainment & amenities: The lights are dimmed during the Magic Kingdom fireworks, and the accompanying music is piped in. You can also step outside onto the 15th floor deck for a closer look. Other entertainment includes watching the chefs; instead of begging for a window seat, sit at the counter. The chefs love to slip samples to the people sitting there.

Summary & comments: This restaurant was designed to be adult oriented and medium priced. It is operated under a recent policy that allows the chef and manager to run the restaurant as if it were their own. The result is a classy, well-operated restaurant that is attracting even Disney-reluctant locals. It is considered one of the best restaurants in central Florida.

CAPE MAY CAFE

Buffet   ★★★   Moderate
Disney's Beach Club Resort   (407) 934-3358

Readers' Survey Responses:	
86% 👍	14% 👎

QUALITY	VALUE
84	B

Customers: Theme park and hotel guests
Priority seatings: Accepted and recommended
When to go: Anytime
Entree range: Breakfast: $14.95 adults, $8.50 children; dinner: $19.95 adults, $9.50 children

Payment: VISA, MC, AMEX
Service rating: ★★★★
Friendliness rating: ★★★★
Parking: Hotel lot
Bar: Full service
Wine selection: Limited
Dress: Casual
Disabled access: Yes

Breakfast: Every day, 7:30–11 a.m.
Dinner: Every day, 5:30–9:30 p.m.

Setting & atmosphere: The natural-finish wood furniture and padded booths are in a clean, nautical New England style—bright, airy, and informal.

House specialties: The buffet features peel-and-eat shrimp, tasty (albeit chewy) clams; mussels; baked fish; barbecued ribs; corn-on-the-cob; Caesar salad; and a good dessert bar.

Other recommendations: Lobster can be ordered as a supplement to the buffet.

Summary & comments: This buffet consistently serves some of the best food available at Walt Disney World. While the restaurant is large and tables turn over rapidly, priority seatings are recommended. Because the Cape May is within easy walking distance of the World Showcase entrance to Epcot, it is a perfect and affordable place to dine before *IllumiNations.*

CAP'N JACK'S OYSTER BAR

Seafood	★★★	Moderate
Downtown Disney Marketplace		(407) 828-3870

Readers' Survey Responses:	
67% 👍	33% 👎

QUALITY	VALUE
84	D

Customers: Tourists
Priority seatings: Not accepted
When to go: Anytime
Entree range: $5.95–33.95
Payment: VISA, MC, AMEX
Service rating: ★★★★

Friendliness rating: ★★★★
Parking: Marketplace lot
Bar: Full service
Wine selection: Not a specialty
Dress: Casual
Disabled access: Yes

Lunch & Dinner: Every day, 11:30 a.m.–10:30 p.m.

Setting & atmosphere: An upscale pierhouse on the edge of the Buena Vista Lagoon.

House specialties: Cap'n Jack's has a limited menu, but what it does it does well. New England clam chowder; spicy conch chowder with tomatoes, carrots, and onions; and crabcakes made with lump crabmeat and onions are a few of the cooked items, but peel-and-eat shrimp and oysters and clams on the half-shell are really this restaurant's forte. You can also get a fresh-fish dinner—usually mahimahi, tuna, or grouper—at a fair price and a stuffed Maine lobster that is more than twice the cost of anything else on the menu, but stick with the oyster-bar items.

Entertainment & amenities: The lagoonside setting offers views of amateur boaters, and sunsets are pretty here.

Summary & comments: Most entrees are under $10—only the stuffed lobster climbs higher. But this is really a place for some shrimp or steamed clams and cold beer.

CAPTAIN'S TAVERN

Seafood	★★	Moderate
Disney's Caribbean Beach Resort		(407) 939-3463

Readers' Survey Responses:	
75% 👍	25% 👎

QUALITY	VALUE
67	C

(Captain's Tavern)

Customers: Resort guests
Priority seatings: Recommended
When to go: Anytime
Entree range: $11.95–15.95
Payment: VISA, AMEX, DC
Service rating: ★★★

Friendliness rating: ★★★
Parking: Resort lot
Bar: Full service
Wine selection: Fair
Dress: Casual
Disabled access: Yes

Dinner: Every day, 5–10 p.m.

Setting & atmosphere: A dark area across from the resort's food court outlets. It is nautical to the nth degree, with lots of dark woods, slatted blinds, and ship's wheel chandeliers. This is a restaurant that was never supposed to be, and to prove it there is no kitchen. The food court was supposed to meet all the resort's culinary needs, but management discovered that people wanted to be waited on after a long day in the parks. So the food court's eating area was converted to a restaurant, and servers schlep the trays across the hall from the food court's kitchens.

House specialties: Lightly blackened scallops with fresh herbs and Parmesan cheese; paella (chicken, shrimp, mussels, and sausage in rice); lightly breaded and baked chicken with a salsa of fruit and vegetables. Captain Morgan's rib eye, flavored with brown sugar; tropical pork chop; fresh catch of the day prepared with island spices and lime zest.

Summary & comments: The restaurant that wasn't supposed to be should probably cease to be. The limitations of the kitchen—or lack of a proper kitchen—show in the quality of the food. A cheddar soup served out of a dining room–based pot is a perfect example of what is wrong here. Guests who are too tired to wait in line at the food court should take a nap and then drive to another area restaurant. Guests not staying at the Caribbean Beach Resort may be hassled by the guards at the front gate (they don't believe anyone not staying at the resort would want to come in just to eat).

LE CELLIER STEAKHOUSE

Steak   ★★   Moderate
Canada, World Showcase, Epcot (407) 939-3463

Readers' Survey Responses:	
82% 👍	18% 👎

QUALITY	VALUE
67	C

Customers: Theme park guests

Priority seatings: Accepted

(Le Cellier SteakHouse)

When to go: Before 6 p.m.
Entree range: $11.50–21.95
Payment: VISA, MC, AMEX
Service rating: ★★★
Friendliness rating: ★★★★
Parking: Epcot lot

Bar: Beer and wine only
Wine selection: Canadian wines
  are featured
Dress: Casual
Disabled access: Yes

Lunch: Every day, from noon–3 p.m.
Dinner: Everyday, from 5 p.m. until park closes

Setting & atmosphere: The name means basement, and that's pretty much what you get here. It's dark and depressing, maybe to simulate long, dark winters in the Canadian tundra. To be fair, however, many park visitors enjoy the sensory deprivation in the windowless room. Go figure.

House specialties: Meat.

Other recommendations: Roast turkey breast; Canadian cheddar cheese soup (a lot like Wisconsin cheese soup); smoked beef brisket; chicken and meatball stew.

Summary & comments: A steakhouse had been absent from the theme parks until the folks from Canada decided to try their hand. Previously a cafeteria-style restaurant, Le Cellier is now full-service with a modest menu of steaks and prime rib. When you really get down to it, steaks are the only Canadian food anyway, the penne pasta Vancouver notwithstanding. While the cuisine change is a vast improvement, this is still one of the least impressive restaurants in World Showcase.

CHEF MICKEY'S

American/Buffet   ★★   Moderate
Disney's Contemporary Resort   (407) 939-3463

Readers' Survey Responses:	
89% 👍	11% 👎

QUALITY	VALUE
67	C

Customers: Theme park guests
Priority seatings: Recommended
When to go: Early evening
Entree range: Breakfast: $14.95
  adults, $7.95 children; dinner:
  $18.95 adults, $8.95 children
Payment: VISA, MC, AMEX

Service rating: ★★★
Friendliness rating: ★★★★
Parking: Resort valet or lot
Bar: Full service
Wine selection: Good
Dress: Casual
Disabled access: Yes

(Chef Mickey's)

Breakfast: Every day, 7–11 a.m.
Dinner: Every day, 5–9:30 p.m.

Setting & atmosphere: A futuristic buffet that resembles Disney's idea of how the Jetsons would dine—colorful seatbacks and padded booths, geometric grids, flowing curves, and a buffet line that circles the center of the room. It is a noisy and bustling place, especially when Goofy, Minnie, and Mickey step out of the kitchen to say hello and dance with the diners.

House specialties: Breakfast: Cooked-to-order pancakes; French toast; biscuits and gravy. **Dinner:** Peel-and-eat shrimp; oven-roasted prime rib; ham.

Other recommendations: Salad bar with fresh greens and mixed salads; pasta selections; mashed potatoes and gravy.

Entertainment & amenities: Character visits.

Summary & comments: Mickey moved his pots and pans from his Village location to make room for the new Rainforest Cafe. In the process he changed the concept from a full-service restaurant to an all-you-can-eat buffet—something Disney is emphasizing currently. The "state-of-the-art" buffet does not use chafing dishes but places the food in casseroles and platters on special heated countertops. However, that doesn't make much difference in the quality. You've still got buffet food, chafing dishes or not, and it just isn't the same as something cooked fresh.

CHEFS DE FRANCE

French   ★★★★   Moderate
France, World Showcase, Epcot (407) 939-3463

Readers' Survey Responses:	
87% 👍	13% 👎

QUALITY	VALUE
90	C

Customers: Theme park guests
Priority seatings: Recommended
When to go: Anytime
Entree range: $8.95–15.75, lunch; $16.75–24.95, dinner
Payment: VISA, MC, AMEX
Service rating: ★★★★

Friendliness rating: ★★★★
Parking: Epcot lot
Bar: Full service
Wine selection: Very good
Dress: Casual
Disabled access: Yes

Lunch: Every day, 11:30 a.m.–3:30 p.m.
Dinner: Every day, 4:30 p.m. until park closes

(Chefs de France)

Setting & atmosphere: The smell of buttery croissants is as much a part of the decor here as the carefully placed copies of *Le Monde* and the huge mottled mirrors. White tablecloths and padded banquettes accentuate the classic bistro decor of the main dining room. Another room sits off to the side, this one a more casual sunroom with a better view of what's going on outside, but you're there for the illusion—insist on a seat in the main room. A recent renovation has enclosed the former sidewalk cafe and included that space in the main room. It is brighter than before to reflect a more authentic bistro atmosphere. The second level (the former Bistro de Paris) remains unchanged. Downstairs is a better place to sit.

House specialties: Chefs de France features some of the dishes served at the real restaurants of the three chefs for whom this restaurant is named: Paul Bocuse, Roger Verge, and Gaston LeNotre. You may sample Verge's brochette of prawns from Moulin de Mougins, LeNotre's fillet of orange roughy in a hazelnut butter from Pre Catelan, or Bocuse's beef braised in burgundy wine from his Lyon restaurant.

Other recommendations: Grilled snapper on artichoke and fennel, estouffade de boeuf, pot-au-feu.

Summary & comments: Here is your chance to eat in a restaurant supervised by three of France's best chefs. Paul Bocuse, Roger Verge, and Gaston LeNotre take turns visiting from France and supervising the staff in the preparation of their creations, so you just might get a chance to meet a culinary legend. But don't expect them to actually prepare your meal. And don't think what you're served here is even close to what you'd get at one of their hometown restaurants. In the past, most of the food coming out of the kitchen was cooked elsewhere in Disney's commissary and warmed here. The recent renovation installed an impressive kitchen (perhaps the best cooking facility of any Disney restaurant) that allows more à la minute preparations from executive chef Bruno Vrignon. Many of the same entrees are available at lunchtime for a reduced price (and smaller portion).

CINDERELLA'S ROYAL TABLE

American	★★½	Moderate
Cinderella Castle, Fantasyland, Magic Kingdom		(407) 939-3463

Readers' Survey Responses:	
67% 👍	33% 👎

QUALITY	VALUE
73	D

Customers: Theme park guests   *Priority seatings:* Required

(Cinderella's Royal Table)

When to go: Early
Entree range: $10.95–16.95
  (adults, lunch); $4.75 (chil-
  dren, lunch and dinner);
  $20.95–27.50 (adults, dinner)
Payment: VISA, MC, AMEX
Service rating: ★★★

Friendliness rating: ★★★
Parking: Magic Kingdom lot
Bar: None
Wine selection: None
Dress: Casual
Disabled access: Limited

Lunch: Every day, 11:30 a.m.–2:45 p.m.
Dinner: Every day, 4 p.m. until park closes

Setting & atmosphere: A medieval banquet hall, appointed with the requisite banners and Round Table–like regalia, located on the second floor of Cinderella Castle. Windows look out over the park.

House specialties: Prime rib; steak; seafood.

Other recommendations: Caesar salad; beef barley soup; grilled swordfish with smoked pepper butter and sautéed beans; sea scallops, shrimp, fish, and vegetables sautéed in white wine and tossed with pasta.

Entertainment & amenities: Cinderella makes appearances.

Summary & comments: Formerly known as King Stefan's Banquet Hall and long the butt of jokes and unkind remarks from Disney workers and locals, Cinderella's has come a long way in improving the quality of the food. Preparations are more exact, and presentation is pleasing. The grilled swordfish is as good as any you'll find at other Disney seafood restaurants. This is the fanciest full-service restaurant in the Magic Kingdom—and the priciest. With the name change Disney officials no longer have to try to explain why Sleeping Beauty's father King Stefan had a restaurant in Cinderella's castle.

CITRICOS

Mediterranean   ★★★★   Expensive
Disney's Grand Floridian Resort (407) 824-2496

Readers' Survey Responses:	
63% 👍	37% 👎

QUALITY	VALUE
91	C

Customers: Hotel guests and
  locals
Priority seatings: Required
When to go: Anytime
Entree range: $19–32

Payment: VISA, MC, AMEX
Service rating: ★★★★
Friendliness rating: ★★★★
Parking: Valet; self-parking is
  deceptively far away.

(Citricos)

Bar: Full service
Wine selection: Very good

Dress: Casually dressy
Disabled access: Good

Dinner: Every day, 5:30–10 p.m.; lounge open until 11 p.m.

Setting & atmosphere: This is another interior design by Martin Dorf, who also did the stylish California Grill and Flying Fish Cafe. Like those upscale restaurants, Citricos features a show kitchen. Autumnal colors in the carpeting are complemented by lemon, lime, and orange wall tiles (the restaurant name is Spanish for citrus). White tablecloths and napkins embroidered with the restaurant's name add an elegant touch.

House specialties: Originally the menu was to feature a plethora of citrus-based items, but the new chef, Roland Muller, wisely saw that as a one-note clunker. You may still find a citrus soufflé for dessert (and it's worth looking for), but the main fare features such nonlemons as braised veal shank with orzo, lamb rack with lobster ratatouille, and roasted sea bass in potato crust.

Other recommendations: Grilled foie gras; oyster and bay scallop risotto; grilled tiger shrimp with sweet potato puree.

Summary & comments: Citricos isn't quite as good as California Grill and Flying Fish Cafe, which it tries to emulate in feel and substance, but it's quite good in its own right. Although it doesn't quite live up to its original mission statement—to provide a Florida dining experience by using native citrus—it does a good job with the Mediterranean fare. If you really want something citrusy, order one of the citrus-infused martinis.

CONCOURSE STEAKHOUSE

Steak   ★★½   Moderate

Disney's Contemporary Resort (407) 939-3463

Readers' Survey Responses:		QUALITY	VALUE
85% 👍	15% 👎	72	D

Customers: Hotel guests
Priority seatings: Recommended
When to go: Anytime
Entree range: $6.50–27.95
Payment: VISA, MC, AMEX
Service rating: ★★★

Friendliness rating: ★★★
Parking: Hotel lot
Bar: Full service
Wine selection: Limited
Dress: Casual
Disabled access: Yes

Lunch: Every day, noon–2:30 p.m.

(Concourse Steakhouse)

Dinner: Every day, 5:30–10 p.m.

Setting & atmosphere: The decor is a cross between art deco and *2001: A Space Odyssey*. Large booths sit in the "open air" of the Contemporary's Concourse, with the monorails gliding by overhead on either side.

House specialties: Although the name says steaks, sandwiches, burgers, pizzas, and pasta dishes are also available.

Other recommendations: Besides red meat, roasted double breast of chicken; grilled chicken kebabs; grilled shrimp tossed with pasta, garlic, and fresh herbs; roasted salmon coated with maple syrup and black peppercorns; and Caesar salad are also offered.

Summary & comments: After a poor start over a year ago, the Concourse Steakhouse has done some fine-tuning in service and food preparation. There is still a big gap between quality and value and better restaurants are a short monorail ride away, but this steakhouse is acceptable in a pinch. If there is a wait you will be given a beeper, which reaches as far as the gift shop but not much farther.

CORAL CAFE

American   ★★   Moderate
Walt Disney World Dolphin (407) 934-4000

Readers' Survey Responses:	
61% 👍	39% 👎

QUALITY	VALUE
67	D

Customers: Hotel guests who can't get into any other restaurants
Priority seatings: Not necessary, but recommended for parties of 8 or more
When to go: Anytime
Entree range: $11.95–18.95

Payment: VISA, MC, AMEX
Service rating: ★★
Friendliness rating: ★★
Parking: Hotel lot
Bar: Full service
Wine selection: Modest
Dress: Casual
Disabled access: Good

Lunch: Every day, 11:30 a.m.–2 p.m.
Dinner: Every day, 5–10 p.m.

Setting & atmosphere: The public relations people would like you to think you're dining in an atmosphere akin to a coral reef, but you're actually in a spot that looks like it never should have been a restaurant. It almost looks like someone said, "Hey, we could put some tables in here and sell food," which would be fine if the food were better.

House specialties: Either an all-you-can-stand buffet or an à la carte menu that changes seasonally. The fare looks interesting enough, with such things as duck in plum sauce or chicken with rigatoni. The kitchen just can't seem to pull it off.

Summary & comments: Ever since the hotel's star restaurant, Sum Chows, closed, the Dolphin has been lacking a main dining room. This doesn't even come close to filling that space. In fact, this restaurant would be a lot better as an open space for people to sit and plan where they can go for a real meal.

CORAL ISLE CAFE

American/Polynesian ★★ Moderate
Disney's Polynesian Resort (407) 824-2170

Readers' Survey Responses:		QUALITY	VALUE
69% 👍	31% 👎	68	C

Customers: Hotel guests
Priority seatings: Recommended
When to go: Breakfast or lunch
Entree range: $8.95–19.95
Payment: VISA, MC, AMEX
Service rating: ★★★
Friendliness rating: ★★★

Parking: Hotel lot; Magic Kingdom lot
Bar: Full service
Wine selection: Fair
Dress: Casual
Disabled access: Yes

Breakfast: Monday–Saturday, 7–11:30 a.m.; Sunday, 7 a.m.–noon
Lunch: Every day, noon–4:45 p.m.
Dinner: Every day, 5–10:45 p.m.

Setting & atmosphere: Coffee shop goes Polynesian: bare tabletops and bamboo chairs. Open to the hotel's atrium lobby with views of the rainforest foliage and the sounds of waterfalls, the restaurant is on the second floor of the Great Ceremonial House.

House specialties: Banana-stuffed French toast; Aloha platter with tempura shrimp; barbecued pork ribs.

Other recommendations: Broiled lemon chicken; Neptune tempura; traditional beef stew.

Summary & comments: Have the French toast at breakfast or a sandwich for lunch; save the big bucks for someplace else.

CORAL REEF

Seafood   ★★★   Expensive

The Living Seas, Future World, Epcot   (407) 939-3463

Readers' Survey Responses:	
74% 👍	26% 👎

QUALITY	VALUE
84	D

Customers: Theme park guests
Priority seatings: Highly recommended
When to go: Anytime
Entree range: $12.95–20.95, lunch; $16.50–33.50, dinner
Payment: VISA, MC, AMEX

Service rating: ★★★★
Friendliness rating: ★★★★
Parking: Epcot lot
Bar: Full service
Wine selection: Adequate
Dress: Casual
Disabled access: Yes

Lunch: Every day, 11:30 a.m.–3 p.m.
Dinner: Every day, 4:30 p.m. until park closes

Setting & atmosphere: Plush deep greens and blues complement the linen table service. Tiered rows of tables face the floor-to-ceiling windows that look into the main marine-life tank of The Living Seas. Lighting is subdued, which enhances the deep-sea atmosphere.

House specialties: Pan-seared swordfish with Thai curry lobster sauce; mixed seafood grill with tuna, salmon, and shrimp; seafood Provençal.

Other recommendations: Caribbean tuna grilled with Jamaican jerk spices; fried calamari or stone crab appetizer.

Entertainment & amenities: Viewing live marine life.

Summary & comments: Though it has taken awhile for the Coral Reef to live up to its potential, the restaurant occasionally serves food worthy of its elegant venue. Fresh seafood, competently prepared, nicely presented, and enhanced by delicate (and sometimes exotic) sauces, makes the Coral Reef Epcot's premier seafood restaurant. Because of its atmosphere and creative menu, the Coral Reef is one of the busiest Epcot restaurants. Lunch and dinner menus are pretty much the same.

THE CRYSTAL PALACE

American/Buffet   ★★½   Moderate
Main Street, U.S.A., Magic Kingdom (407) 939-3463

Readers' Survey Responses:		QUALITY	VALUE
87% 👍	13% 👎	79	C

Customers: Magic Kingdom
  guests
Priority seatings: Recommended
When to go: Anytime
Entree range: Adults: $13.95
  breakfast, $14.95 lunch, $19.95
  dinner; children: $7.95 breakfast
  and lunch, $9.95 dinner

Payment: VISA, MC, AMEX
Service rating: ★★
Friendliness rating: ★★★
Parking: Magic Kingdom lot
Bar: None
Wine selection: None
Dress: Casual
Disabled access: Yes

Breakfast: Every day, 7:30–10:30 a.m. (opens later on non–early-entry days)
Lunch: Every day, 11:30 a.m.–2:45 p.m.
Dinner: Every day, 4 p.m. until park closes; last seating is at 7:15 p.m.

Setting & atmosphere: A turn-of-the-century glass pavilion awash with sunlight and decorated with plenty of summer greenery. Seating is comfortable (a pleasant respite), and buffet lines are open and accessible. There is a low buffet area for kids to help themselves.

House specialties: Waffles and pancakes layered with fresh fruit; muesli; jambalaya; fried chicken with hoisin sauce; grilled vegetable platter; penne pasta tossed with romaine lettuce, grilled chicken, and Parmesan cheese; paella; leg of lamb carving station; grilled mahimahi, salmon, catfish, or marlin, served with caramelized onion relish.

Entertainment & amenities: Winnie the Pooh characters dance about and pose with the kids.

Summary & comments: Disney continues its latest emphasis on "new-age buffets" with this latest conversion. The Crystal Palace was a counter-service restaurant but now offers an all-you-can-eat buffet similar to the one found at Chef Mickey's in the Contemporary Resort. This state-of-the-art buffet boasts no steam tables. All the foods are presented in casserole dishes and pans that sit on special heated countertops. The steam may be missing, but this is still mass feeding and the quality is reflected. Still, with such limited dining in the Magic Kingdom, one more restaurant—and one less counter-service eatery—is a step in the right direction.

ESPN CLUB

American/Sandwiches ★★ Moderate
Disney's BoardWalk (407) 939-5100

Readers' Survey Responses:	
68% 👍	32% 👎

QUALITY	VALUE
73	C

Customers: Tourists
Priority seatings: Not accepted
When to go: Anytime
Entree range: $7–15.95
Payment: VISA, MC, AMEX, Disney Card
Service rating: ★★
Friendliness rating: ★★★

Parking: BoardWalk lot.
  Note: Valet parking is free before 5 p.m., $5 after.
Bar: Full service
Wine selection: Minimal
Dress: Casual—helmets not required
Disabled access: Good

Open: Sunday–Thursday, 11:30 a.m.–1 a.m.; Friday and Saturday, 11:30 a.m.–2 a.m.

Setting & atmosphere: This is a sports bar to the nth degree, with basketball-court flooring, sports memorabilia, and more television monitors than a network affiliate. The bar area has satellite sports-trivia video games. A large octagonal room with a wall of TV monitors serves as the main dining room and is nonsmoking. Smoking is permitted in the bar.

House specialties: Red wings (Buffalo-style wings); half-pound burger with cheddar or Swiss cheese; fresh fin tuna salad sandwich; penne pasta with grilled vegetables; marinated grilled chicken breast on a roll.

Entertainment & amenities: Live sports-trivia contests and televised sports.

Summary & comments: Disney is new to the sports bar concept, and it shows here. The first year was a little slow, but things have started to pick up. Service is a little more brusque than at other property restaurants. Portions are large, and the quality is in-line with the price. This is a good choice for late-night dining or when you have to choose between going out for a bite and staying in the room to catch "the big game."

50'S PRIME TIME CAFE

American　　　★★　　　Moderate
Disney-MGM Studios　(407) 939-3463

Readers' Survey Responses:	
71% 👍	29% 👎

QUALITY	VALUE
69	D

Customers: Theme park guests
Priority seatings: Suggested
When to go: Anytime
Entree range: $7–17, lunch;
　$11.95–25, dinner
Payment: VISA, MC, AMEX
Service rating: ★★★★

Friendliness rating: ★★★★
Parking: Disney-MGM lot
Bar: Full service
Wine selection: Limited
Dress: Casual
Disabled access: Yes

Lunch: Every day, 11 a.m.–3:30 p.m.; opens at 10:30 a.m. on Sunday and Wednesday
Dinner: Every day, 4 p.m. until park closes

Setting & atmosphere: A meal at the 50's Prime Time Cafe is like eating a meal in your own kitchen, '50s-style. Pastel formica, gooseneck lamps, and black-and-white televisions that run vintage sitcoms are the rule.
House specialties: Meatloaf, pot roast, chicken, and other homey fare are featured. We get a lot of mail from readers who like the 50's Prime Time Cafe. Most say the food is good, the portions large, and that it is easy to find something the kids like. We, unfortunately, cannot concur in that opinion. By our evaluation the food is bland, more resembling the meals served in an elementary school cafeteria than in someone's home. The pot roast, for instance, is cooked by itself without the usual onions, potatoes, and carrots—it is served with mashed potatoes.
Entertainment & amenities: '50s sitcom clips on television.
Summary & comments: While we enjoy the ambiance of the 50's Prime Time Cafe and particularly like watching the old sitcoms, we cannot recommend having a meal there. Our suggestion for making the scene is to get late-afternoon or evening priority seatings and order only dessert.

FINN'S GRILL

Seafood   ★   Moderate
The Hilton, Disney Village Hotel Plaza (407) 827-4000

Readers' Survey Responses:	
71% 👍	29% 👎

QUALITY	VALUE
55	D

Customers: Unsuspecting hotel guests
Reservations: Not necessary
When to go: Anytime
Entree range: $12.95–24.95
Payment: VISA, MC, AMEX, DC, D

Service rating: ★
Friendliness rating: ★★
Parking: Valet or hotel lot
Bar: Full service
Wine selection: Fair
Dress: Casual
Disabled access: Yes

Dinner: Every day, 5:30–11 p.m.

Setting & atmosphere: Walls are painted with the bright colors of the sea and are decorated with stylized fish fins, sort of abstract abalone. The oyster bar area is decorated with crab and lobster traps. Staff members wear silly fish hats that seem to denote some staffing hierarchy. The menu is fraught with puns on the word Finn, such as finn-omenal, finn-icky, and finn-tastic.

House specialties: Fresh fish, including snapper, salmon, and swordfish depending on availability, prepared blackened or grilled. Other items include shrimp scampi served with herb butter over yellow rice; Finn's gumbo, with shrimp, crabmeat, chicken, and sausage; and a number of pasta dishes.

Other recommendations: Alaskan king crab legs; steamed Maine lobster; fresh oysters; stone crab claws; shrimp.

Summary & comments: Someone spent an awful lot of time coming up with pleasing decor and a nice collection of dishes that accompany some of Florida's finest seafood. Unfortunately the rest of the time was spent on clever puns, leaving no time to train the staff on even the most rudimentary service skills. Most of the food is acceptable, but service this poor at a hotel this large is not. It might not be bad for a bucket of steamers and a few cold beers.

FLYING FISH CAFE

Seafood ★★★★ Expensive
Disney's BoardWalk (407) 939-3463

Readers' Survey Responses:	
91% 👍	9% 👎

QUALITY	VALUE
94	C

Customers: Tourists and locals
Priority seatings: Recommended
When to go: Anytime
Entree range: $18–26
Payment: VISA, MC, AMEX
Service rating: ★★★★
Friendliness rating: ★★★★
Parking: BoardWalk lot.

Note: Valet parking is free
before 5 p.m., $5 after.
Bar: Full service
Wine selection: Excellent but
pricey
Dress: Casual dressy
Disabled access: Good

Dinner: Sunday–Thursday, 5:30–9:45 p.m.; Friday and Saturday,
5:30–10:15 p.m.

Setting & atmosphere: A whimsical remembrance of a circa-1920 Coney
Island roller coaster served as the inspiration for the decor and the name. Actually the coaster was called The Flying Turns, and one of the cars on the ride was
dubbed The Flying Fish. Booth backs resemble the climbs and swoops of a
coaster. On the far wall is a Ferris wheel, and overhead fish fly on a parachute
ride. Diners may choose to sit at the fishscale-covered counter that overlooks
the open kitchen. Children are given a list of "flaws" in the decor to spot, such
as the one fish flying backward on the parachute ride. If the decor is reminiscent of California Grill it's because they were both designed by Martin Dorf.

House specialties: The creative menu changes weekly. Some samplings of
dishes include seared yellowfin tuna with spiced coriander crust, gingered
lentils, and mizuna salad; grilled Atlantic salmon with sun-dried tomatoes,
baby-artichoke risotto, and calamata; and potato-wrapped yellowtail snapper with leek fondue and a cabernet sauvignon reduction (this one is something of a signature dish and is usually available). For dessert, the warm
chocolate lava cake with a liquid chocolate center and citrus ice cream is
incredibly indulgent—a must.

Summary & comments: The design, style, cuisine, and quality are all reminiscent of California Grill at the Contemporary Resort. However, you're more
likely to find children here than at C.G. because of the BoardWalk location.
Still, the fine food will be more appreciated by adults—and the high cost more
respected. If you can't get a table, check on seating availablity at the counter.
The service is just as good there, and the show in the kitchen is entertaining.

FULTON'S CRAB HOUSE

Seafood   ★★★½   Expensive
Empress Lilly, Pleasure Island   (407) 934-2628

Readers' Survey Responses:	
76% 👍	24% 👎

QUALITY	VALUE
89	D

Customers: Locals, Disney guests
Priority seatings: Accepted
When to go: Early evening
Entree range: $14.95–35.95, din-
   ner; $7.95 (children), $12.95
   (adults), breakfast
Payment: VISA, MC, AMEX
Service rating: ★★★

Friendliness rating: ★★★
Parking: Pleasure Island lot
Bar: Full service
Wine selection: Good; mostly
   American wines
Dress: Casual
Disabled access: Yes

Character Breakfast: Every day, seatings at 8:30 and 10 a.m.
Dinner: Every day, 5–11 p.m.

Setting & atmosphere: Fulton's has taken over the entire three decks of the Empress Lilly, which underwent extensive remodeling that removed the rear paddle wheel and the smokestacks (they didn't really work anyway). The third deck is used mainly for banquets. There is a large lounge on the first deck, where you will spend a good deal of time waiting for your table. Separate dining areas include the Market Room, which is a tribute to New York's Fulton Fish Market (for which the restaurant is named); the Constellation Room, a semicircular room with a starlit night sky; and the Industry Room, which is a tribute to the commercial fishing industry.

House specialties: Stone crab; fresh fish flown in daily (the airbills are on display inside the front door); blue crab fingers; fresh oyster selection; Fulton's seafood chowder; cioppino with crab, shrimp, scallops, and fish in a tomato broth; Alaskan king crab; Alaskan Dungeness crab; calamari steak.

Other recommendations: Tuna filet mignon; crab cake and oyster combination; Crab House clam bake; mixed grill of fresh fish.

Summary & comments: The Levy Restaurants of Chicago operates Fulton's along with Portobello Yacht Club, also at Pleasure Island. Fulton's is an immense restaurant with over 700 seats, but service is geared toward the individual diner. There is no fresher fish available in central Florida (and much of it is flown in from waters around the country). Levy executive chef Ron Pollack is a seafood specialist and takes great pride in presenting the best. The menu is printed daily to reflect the fish that are available. Waits can be long—over an hour even on weekday nights. Have an appetizer in the lounge or on the outside deck while you wait for a table.

THE GARDEN GRILL RESTAURANT

American   ★★½   Moderate
The Land, Future World, Epcot (407) 939-3463

Readers' Survey Responses:	
81% 👍	19% 👎

QUALITY	VALUE
79	C

Customers: Theme park guests
Priority seatings: Recommended
When to go: Anytime
Entree range: $14.95–17.50
  (adults); $8.25–9.95 (children)
Payment: VISA, MC, AMEX
Service rating: ★★★

Friendliness rating: ★★★★
Parking: Epcot lot
Bar: Full service
Wine selection: Fair
Dress: Casual
Disabled access: Yes

Breakfast: Every day, 8:40–11:10 a.m.
Lunch & Dinner: Every day, 11:30 a.m. until park closing

Setting & atmosphere: The Garden Grill is a revolving restaurant, but unlike the ones found at the top of high-rise hotels in large cities, this one is found at ground level and it doesn't even have windows. Instead the booths rotate past the various scenes of the Living with the Land boat ride. Although diners can't see the boats, they can see a rain forest and a prairie, among other things. When you're not looking at the scenes of the rain forest, you'll see brightly painted murals of sunflower fields.

House specialties: The restaurant recently switched from an a la carte menu to an all-you-can-eat concept of fried chicken and barbecued ribs, which are brought to the table on large platters and served "family-style." Accompaniments include salad, bread, and potatoes.

Entertainment & amenities: The view.

Summary & comments: You can bet the vegetables are fresh—many of them are grown in the Epcot experimental farms seen on the pavilion's boat ride. And the lettuce is hydroponically grown.

GRAND FLORIDIAN CAFE

American   ★★   Moderate
Disney's Grand Floridian Beach Resort (407) 824-2496

Readers' Survey Responses:		QUALITY	VALUE
81% 👍	19% 👎	68	D

Customers: Hotel guests
Priority seatings: Not required
When to go: Breakfast or late evening
Entree range: $16.95–29.95
Payment: VISA, MC, AMEX
Service rating: ★★

Friendliness rating: ★★★
Parking: Valet; self-parking is deceptively far away.
Bar: Full service
Wine selection: Very good
Dress: Casual
Disabled access: Yes

Breakfast: Every day, 7–11:30 a.m.

Lunch & Dinner: Every day, noon–11 p.m.

Setting & atmosphere: The large dining room, with high ceilings and decorative windows, looks out on the hotel's pool and center courtyard.

House specialties: Breakfast includes eggs prepared just about every way known to mankind, including omelets, frittatas, and huevos rancheros. Dinnertime appetizers are fairly pedestrian, including fried mozzarella cheese and chicken wings. Entrees have a Southern accent with items such as fried chicken (battered and deep-fried) served with mashed potatoes and gravy (of course); roast prime rib of beef with garlic and pan drippings; deep-fried cornmeal-battered catfish; and seafood "waterzooi" stew with fresh fish, scallops, shrimp, and rice.

Other recommendations: If fried Southern cooking and beef with pan drippings aren't on your diet this decade, G.F.C. offers a good selection of nutritional, lighter meals, including a fruit plate; vegetable lasagna; turkey burgers; and a smoked fish platter.

Summary & comments: The impersonal service detracts from the overall quality. Try it for breakfast or for a burger after the parks close.

GULLIVER'S GRILL AT GARDEN GROVE

American ★★ Expensive
Walt Disney World Swan (407) 934-3000

Readers' Survey Responses:	
59% 👍	41% 👎

QUALITY	VALUE
67	D

Customers: Hotel guests
Reservations: Recommended
When to go: Lunch
Entree range: $8.25–9.95, lunch;
$19.95–29.95, dinner
Payment: VISA, MC, AMEX,
DC

Service rating: ★★
Friendliness rating: ★★
Parking: Hotel lot
Bar: Full service
Wine selection: Good
Dress: Casual
Disabled access: Yes

Breakfast: Every day, 6:30–11 a.m.
Lunch: Every day, 11 a.m.–2 p.m.
Dinner: Every day, 5:30–10 p.m.

Setting & atmosphere: A large greenhouselike rotunda with tall palm trees and parrot figures attached to street lamps. Faux-stone tabletops are set with peach placemats and napkins.

House specialties: Lunch sandwiches include an Italian sub, chicken salad, French dip, and grilled salmon BLT. Evening appetizers are uninspired. Entrees include steaks, such as New York strip, filet mignon with béarnaise sauce, and 18-ounce porterhouse. Prime rib, swordfish, salmon, and snapper are also available. Dinners include Caesar salad tossed tableside, Italian bread with herb butter and rice, steak fries, or baked potato. Vegetables are extra.

Entertainment & amenities: Character breakfasts Wednesdays and Saturdays.

Summary & comments: The name has changed because the folks at the hotel believe you can't have a successful restaurant without a gimmick—food apparently doesn't matter. The menu includes a legend of the Gulliver in question (not Jonathan Swift's fictional character but an even more fictionalized "direct descendant" named Peter Miles Gulliver). The names of the dishes are listed in the language of Brobdingnag, the Land of the Giants. The only item on the dinner menu under $21 is the marinated chicken breast with mushrooms, or kluknkro de sokin & sromes. Oh, please.

HARRY'S SAFARI BAR AND GRILL

Steak/Seafood   ★★★   Expensive
Walt Disney World Dolphin (407) 934-4000

Readers' Survey Responses:	
67% 👍	33% 👎

QUALITY	VALUE
81	D

Customers: Hotel guests
Priority seatings: Recommended
When to go: Early dinner
Entree range: $21–35
Payment: VISA, MC, AMEX, DC
Service rating: ★★

Friendliness rating: ★
Parking: Hotel lot
Bar: Full service
Wine selection: Good
Dress: Casual
Disabled access: Yes

Dinner: Five days a week, 6–10 p.m. (off days change weekly!)

Setting & atmosphere: A jungle atmosphere with huge stuffed animals sitting around on the floor. Waiters will often plop a hairy gorilla into an empty seat to fill up a table.

House specialties: The food here is extraordinarily expensive but the quality doesn't warrant the high price. Appetizers include crab cakes; tiger shrimp; spring rolls stuffed with a mixture of alligator and kangaroo meat; and escargots. Entrees feature broiled South American lobster tail and filet mignon; roast duck; and prime rib.

Other recommendations: Mahimahi, salmon, tuna, or swordfish prepared to request: plank-roasted; pan-grilled with pistachios, pecans, and citrus; or jerk-blackened.

Summary & comments: The staff spends more time making the stuffed animals comfortable than making the guests comfortable. The food, though good, is terribly expensive. The prices are given in U.S. dollars and English pounds, ostensibly to fit in with Harry's "legend" (you can't have a restaurant here without a legend), which claims Harry grew up in Great Britain before heading to Africa to become an explorer.

HOLLYWOOD & VINE

American ★★½ Inexpensive
Disney-MGM Studios (407) 939-3463

Readers' Survey Responses:	
82% 👍	18% 👎

QUALITY	VALUE
74	C

Customers: Theme park guests
Priority seatings: Not accepted
When to go: Lunch
Entree range: $7.50–14.75
Payment: AMEX, MC, VISA
Service rating: ★★★

Friendliness rating: ★★★★
Parking: Disney-MGM lot
Bar: Beer and wine only
Wine selection: Limited
Dress: Casual
Disabled access: Yes

Open: Every day, 8:30 a.m. until park closes

Setting & atmosphere: Large art deco–style cafeteria with tile floors and lots of chrome. The walls are decorated with huge murals that resemble old postcards with vintage scenes of old Hollywood and other California landmarks.

House specialties: Grilled chicken; barbecued ribs; pasta stuffed with cheese and a tomato herb sauce; Cahuenga chicken (rotisserie chicken with rice); spaghetti with meatballs; beef tips served over rice with a mushroom gravy.

Other recommendations: Chef salad.

Summary & comments: If you feel the need to stuff yourself after walking around the park all day, try the all-you-can-eat buffet for dinner. Otherwise a piece of chicken for lunch is plenty. Be prepared for lots of noise—with all the glass, tile, and chrome, the noise echoes for days.

THE HOLLYWOOD BROWN DERBY

American ★★★ Expensive
Disney-MGM Studios (407) 939-3463

Readers' Survey Responses:	
82% 👍	18% 👎

QUALITY	VALUE
84	C

Customers: Theme park guests
Priority seatings: Recommended
When to go: Early evening

Entree range: $6.95–14.75,
 lunch; $4.50–$21.50, dinner
Payment: VISA, MC, AMEX

(The Hollywood Brown Derby)

Service rating: ★★★★
Friendliness rating: ★★★★
Parking: Disney-MGM lot
Bar: Full service

Wine selection: Very good
Dress: Casual
Disabled access: Yes

Lunch: Every day, 11:30 a.m.–3:45 p.m.
Dinner: Every day, 4 p.m. until park closes

Setting & atmosphere: A replica of the original Brown Derby restaurant (not the one shaped like a derby) in California, including duplicates of the celebrity caricatures that cover the paneled walls. An elegant sunken dining room with curved booths, tables draped with yards of white linen, and romantic shaded candles. Tall palm trees in huge pots stand in the center of the room and reach for the high ceiling. Waiters wear white jackets and are better dressed than most of the park guests.

House specialties: Cobb salad (a Brown Derby creation named for Bob Cobb, not Lee J.); baked grouper (battered and topped with meunière butter and served over pasta); sautéed veal.

Other recommendations: Fettucine Derby (pasta with parmesan sauce with a choice of shrimp or chicken); grilled steaks; rack of lamb; beef stroganoff; mixed grill.

Summary & comments: The decor is so perfect you'll feel as though you're in 1930s Hollywood. In fact it is so elegant that it is a shame it is located in a theme park full of T-shirted guests. Everyone should really dress in white ties and long chiffon gowns and do their best Fred Astaire and Ginger Rogers impersonations. Don't expect to see any real stars dining in the next booth, however. There is outdoor dining available, but it is much better to sit inside here.

HOUSE OF BLUES

Regional American   ★★★   Moderate
Downtown Disney West Side (407) 939-2623

Readers' Survey Responses:	
77% 👍	23% 👎

QUALITY	VALUE
80	C

Customers: Blues lovers
Priority seatings: Accepted for lunch weekdays 11 a.m.–4 p.m.
When to go: Early evening; Sun-
day gospel brunch
Entree range: $8.50–23.95
Payment: VISA, MC, AMEX
Service rating: ★★★

(House of Blues)

Friendliness rating: ★★
Parking: Downtown Disney lot; valet $6
Bar: Full service

Wine selection: Modest
Dress: Casual
Disabled access: Good

Brunch: 3 seatings on Sunday, 10:45 a.m., 1 p.m., 3:30 p.m.
Lunch & Dinner: Every day, 11 a.m.–2 a.m.

Setting & atmosphere: You'd think it was a ramshackle hut in the bayous of Louisiana if the place weren't bigger than all of Louisiana. Nearly every available inch of wall space displays some type of folk art, which has a voodoo sort of feel to it. The restaurant area is separate from the performance hall, where blues and rock groups perform. There is often a live band in the restaurant as well. Outdoor dining is available overlooking the lagoon. When recorded music is featured, monitors throughout the restaurant give a detailed description of the artist and the selection.

House specialties: The menu features a selection of New Orleans favorites, including étouffée, jambalaya, and po'boy sandwiches with shrimp or catfish.

Other recommendations: Cajun meatloaf; fried chicken; and blackened prime rib.

Summary & comments: What Hard Rock Cafe is to rock music House of Blues is to rhythm and blues. For a themed restaurant, H.O.B. does an impressively good job with the food. If you're planning on taking in one of the acts at the performance space next door, you're better off going there first so you can assure yourself of a good seat and then eating afterwards.

JUAN & ONLY'S BAR AND JAIL

Tex-Mex   ★★★   Moderate
Walt Disney World Dolphin (407) 934-4000

Readers' Survey Responses:	
73% 👍	27% 👎

QUALITY	VALUE
80	B

Customers: Hotel guests
Reservations: Recommended
When to go: Anytime
Entree range: $10.75–19.50
Payment: VISA, MC, AMEX, DC
Service rating: ★★

Friendliness rating: ★★★
Parking: Valet $8, or self-park in hotel lot
Bar: Full service
Wine selection: Fair
Dress: Casual
Disabled access: Yes

(Juan & Only's Bar and Jail)

Dinner: Every day, 6–10 p.m.

Setting & atmosphere: An upscale jail setting with iron bars and the usual stereotypical bric-a-brac that decorates most Tex-Mex restaurants. However, the designer wisely decided not to trash the interior, much of which is left over from the previous Italian tenant.

House specialties: Fajitas; chile rellenos; grilled chicken Yucatan; tortilla soup.

Other recommendations: Juan & Only's sampler, including poblano chile stuffed with chicken, beef taco, and cheese enchilada.

Summary & comments: This restaurant tries a little too hard to theme itself. The menu contains a lengthy description of Juan and his sidekick Only. Still, the food is good, and if you like it hot and spicy, you won't be disappointed.

KIMONOS

Japanese	★★★★	Moderate
Walt Disney World Swan		(407) 934-1621

Readers' Survey Responses:		QUALITY	VALUE
74% 👍	26% 👎	90	C

Customers: Hotel guests, locals

Reservations: Accepted for parties over 10

When to go: Anytime

Entree range: Sushi and rolls a la carte, $3.75–5

Payment: VISA, MC, AMEX, DC, JCB, D

Service rating: ★★★★

Friendliness rating: ★★★★

Parking: Hotel lot

Bar: Full service

Wine selection: Very good

Dress: Casual

Disabled access: Yes

Dinner: Every day, 5:30 p.m.–midnight; bar opens at 5 p.m.

Setting & atmosphere: The decor consists of black lacquered tabletops and counters, tall pillars rising to bamboo rafters with rice-paper lanterns, and elegant kimonos that hang outstretched on the walls and between the dining sections. The chefs will greet you with a friendly welcome, and you'll be offered a hot towel to clean your hands. Even if you're not in the mood for sushi, this is a delightful place to just sit and sip sake.

House specialties: Although sushi and sashimi are the focus, Kimonos also serves a number of hot appetizers, including tempura-battered shrimp, fish, and vegetables; skewered chicken yakitori; beef teriyaki and gyoza; and steamed dumplings stuffed with a pork mixture. The crispy soft-shell crab is wonderful.

Summary & comments: The skill of the sushi artists is as much a joy to watch as is eating the wonderfully fresh creations. There are no full entrees here, just good sushi and appetizers. The Walt Disney World Swan is host to many Japanese tourists, and you'll find many of them here on any given night. Enough said.

LIBERTY TREE TAVERN

American ★★½ Moderate/Expensive
Liberty Square, Magic Kingdom (407) 939-3463

Readers' Survey Responses:	
86% 👍	14% 👎

QUALITY	VALUE
74	C

Customers: Theme park guests
Priority seatings: Suggested
When to go: Anytime
Entree range: Lunch:
$8.50–13.50 (adults),
$4.75–5.50 (children); dinner:
$19.95 (adults), $9.95 (children)

Payment: VISA, MC, AMEX
Service rating: ★★★★
Friendliness rating: ★★★★
Parking: Magic Kingdom lot
Bar: None
Wine selection: None
Dress: Casual
Disabled access: Yes

Lunch: Every day, 11:30 a.m.–3 p.m.
Dinner: Every day, 4 p.m. until park closes

Setting & atmosphere: Low, exposed-beam ceilings in rooms framed by pastel gray chair rails. Colonial-period wall art, much with a nautical theme, accents simple dark wood tables and chairs with woven seats.

House specialties: Prime rib; roast turkey; chicken breast with Virginia ham. Family-style character dining.

Other recommendations: Sandwiches and salads are good here.

Summary & comments: Though the Liberty Tree is the best of the Magic Kingdom's full-service restaurants, it is often overlooked at lunch. A good plan is to make a priority seating at the Liberty Tree for about an hour or so before parade time. After you eat, you can walk right out and watch the parade.

MAMA MELROSE'S RISTORANTE ITALIANO

Italian   ★★½   Moderate
Disney-MGM Studios (407) 939-3463

Readers' Survey Responses:	
81% 👍	19% 👎

QUALITY	VALUE
74	D

Customers: Theme park guests
Priority seatings: Suggested
When to go: Anytime
Entree range: $8.25–14.75,
  lunch; $11.25–21.50, dinner
Payment: VISA, MC, AMEX
Service rating: ★★★★

Friendliness rating: ★★★★
Parking: Disney-MGM lot
Bar: Full service
Wine selection: Limited
Dress: Casual
Disabled access: Yes

Lunch: Every day, 11:30 a.m.–3:50 p.m.
Dinner: Every day, 4 p.m. until park closes

Setting & atmosphere: Mama Melrose's looks like a big-city neighborhood restaurant of the '30s, with bare wooden floors, red-and-white checkered tablecloths, red vinyl booths, and grapevines hanging from the rafters. By far the most relaxing restaurant at Disney-MGM Studios, Mama Melrose's sports a worn, ethnic look that is as comfortable as an old sweatshirt.
House specialties: Pasta and seafood combos are excellent, as are salads and some of the designer pizzas. Bread is served in the traditional style with olive oil.
Other recommendations: Veal parmesan served with pasta; vegetable lasagna; chicken marsala.
Summary & comments: Because of its out-of-the-way location, you can sometimes just walk into Mama Melrose's, especially in the evening.

MAYA GRILL

Mexican   ★★   Expensive
Coronado Springs Resort (407) 939-3463

Readers' Survey Responses:	
67% 👍	33% 👎

QUALITY	VALUE
66	D

(Maya Grill)

Customers: Hotel guests
Priority seatings: Recommended
When to go: Anytime
Entree range: $17–26
Payment: VISA, MC, AMEX
Service rating: ★★★

Friendliness rating: ★★★
Parking: Hotel lot; no valet
Bar: Full service
Wine selection: Fair
Dress: Casual
Disabled access: Good

Breakfast: Every day, 7–11 a.m.
Dinner: Every day, 5–10 p.m.

Setting & atmosphere: The dining room is meant to evoke the ancient world of the Maya with, according to the menu, "a harmony of fire, sun and water." The fire is fake and in the form of "flames" made of fabric that is fan-blown at the top of two large columns. Diners sit around the base of a Mayan pyramid with flecks of gold in it. The kitchen is open to view, but so is the barren and starkly lit walkway outside, which detracts a bit from the atmosphere.

House specialties: Another attempt to create a new cuisine, this time it's nuevo Latino, for a fusion of New and Old World flavors. This is meant to take Latino foods and marry them with the flavors of the Caribbean, Mexico, and South America. Huachinango features snapper in a pumpkin seed crust; swordfish escabeche is sautéed with Yucatan vegetables. Ropa vieja, braised flank steak, is served on a fresh corn tamale.

Summary & comments: Disney's latest hotel was meant to be for those on a budget, but this restaurant certainly doesn't follow that credo. The prices are way too high here for the quality of the food, which, by the way, is offered by the same company that operates San Angel Inn at the Mexico pavilion in Epcot (the same people run the food court at Coronado Springs as well). The fusion cuisine sometimes works and sometimes falls flatter than a tortilla. Overall the quality doesn't come close to matching the prices, so you're better off eating somewhere else.

NARCOOSSEE'S

Seafood   ★★★½   Expensive
Disney's Grand Floridian Beach Resort (407) 939-3463

Readers' Survey Responses:		QUALITY	VALUE
81% 👍	19% 👎	88	D

(Narcoossee's)

Customers: Hotel guests, locals
Priority seatings: Recommended
When to go: Early evening
Entree range: Lunch,
$6.50–$16.75; dinner,
$16.95–26.75
Payment: VISA, MC, AMEX
Service rating: ★★★★

Friendliness rating: ★★★★
Parking: Valet; self-parking is
deceptively far away.
Bar: Full service
Wine selection: Good
Dress: Casual
Disabled access: Yes

Lunch: Every day, noon–3 p.m.
Dinner: Every day, 5–10 p.m.

Setting & atmosphere: Part of the Grand Floridian Beach Resort complex, Narcoossee's is a free-standing octagonal building at the edge of Seven Seas Lagoon. It offers a great view of the Magic Kingdom and the boats that dock nearby to pick guests up and drop them off after a day at the park. The lack of carpeting and tablecloths, and the high noise level, belie the fine-dining aspect.

House specialties: After a short experiment in a creative fusion cuisine (don't worry, no one in the kitchen knew what that was either), Anette Grecchi was hired to revamp the menu. She came up with a list of entrees that make use of local produce and seafood yet still manage to be creative. Appetizers include duo of mushroom soup, shredded duck confit salad, and brick-baked focaccia with duck pastrami. Entrees include rare seared tuna Niçoise; pan-seared fillet of black grouper with spelt pilaf; and grilled shrimp with saffron couscous.

Other recommendations: Grilled filet mignon with mashed red skin potatoes; orrecchiette pasta with forest mushroom ragout; charred chicken breast with Dijon mustard mayonnaise.

Summary & comments: Under Anette Grecchi (one of the only female executive chefs at Disney World), Narcoossee's is back on track in offering some of the best food on the property. Still, prices are extremely high for this atmosphere, which often features children running about delighting in the reverberating acoustics. This is a good choice for a lunchtime escape from the Magic Kingdom with a short ride by boat or Monorail. Prices are more reasonable at lunch.

NINE DRAGONS RESTAURANT

Chinese   ★★½   Expensive
China, World Showcase, Epcot (407) 939-3463

Readers' Survey Responses:		QUALITY	VALUE
47% 👍	53% 👎	74	F

Customers: Theme park guests
Priority seatings: Suggested
When to go: Anytime
Entree range: $8.95–19, lunch;
 $10.95–24.75, dinner
Payment: VISA, MC, AMEX
Service rating: ★★★

Friendliness rating: ★★★★
Parking: Epcot lot
Bar: Full service
Wine selection: Limited
Dress: Casual
Disabled access: Yes

Lunch: Every day, noon–4:30 p.m.
Dinner: Every day, 4:45 p.m. until park closes

Setting & atmosphere: The Nine Dragons is a stunning restaurant, formal, elegant, and bright. Its decor reflects Asian artistry and sophistication, with combinations of bright lacquered colors and natural wood hues—what every Chinese eatery across America seeks to emulate. There are inlaid ceilings, large and elaborate wood sculptures, and a lush, red, floral-patterned carpet.

House specialties: The Nine Dragons' fare, unfortunately, does not live up to its decor. The limited menu features the same tired sweet-and-sour pork, beef with broccoli, and moo goo gai pan that you can buy for one-third the price at your own neighborhood Chinese restaurant.

Summary & comments: This should be one of the best Chinese restaurants in the United States, but it's not. The lack of a creative menu, along with assembly-line preparation and service, makes Nine Dragons a lost opportunity at best, and an overpriced tourist trap at worst.

OFFICIAL ALL-STAR CAFE

American   ★★   Moderate
Disney's Wide World of Sports (407) 827-8326

Readers' Survey Responses:		QUALITY	VALUE
63% 👍	37% 👎	72	C

(Official All-Star Cafe)

Customers: People attending
  sports events at the Disney sta-
  dium; others who are lost
Reservations: Not accepted
When to go: Before 6 p.m. or
  after 10 p.m.
Entree range: $5.95–18.95
Payment: VISA, MC, AMEX
Service rating: ★★

Friendliness rating: ★★
Parking: Free lot, but when there
  are events, parking may be up
  to a mile away
Bar: Full service
Wine selection: Minimal
Dress: Casual
Disabled access: Yes

Lunch & Dinner: Every day, 11 a.m.–11 p.m.

Setting & atmosphere: A sports bar theme done up to the max, with big-
and small-screen televisions, sports memorabilia, and booths shaped like
catchers' mitts. The large room is designed to give the feel of sitting beneath the bleachers of a stadium.

House specialties: Pizza; pasta dishes; sandwiches.

Summary & comments: Another mega-chain in the making from
Orlando resident and Planet Hollywood chief Robert Earl. If you're familiar with Planet Hollywood, you pretty much have an idea of what the food
is like. The decor is similar, too, if you just substitute sports stuff for movie
stuff. But what is different here is that the quality of the food is not as good
as that of Planet Hollywood. Official All-Star Cafe is part of Disney's Wide
World of Sports complex and is located next to the stadium. There is nothing else around for miles, so this isn't the kind of place you just wander into
to check out. You really have to want to come here. If you want to go to see
the sports memorabilia (Tara Lipinski's tutu?), that's one thing. If you want
to have some good food, that's quite another. Be warned: If there is a game
at the stadium, you may be diverted to park nearly a mile away from the
restaurant. That's something to consider when the food really isn't worth
crossing the street for.

'OHANA

Polynesian   ★★★   Moderate
Disney's Polynesian Resort (407) 939-3463

Readers' Survey Responses:	
80% 👍	20% 👎

QUALITY	VALUE
79	C

Customers: Resort guests

Priority seatings: Recommended

('Ohana)

When to go: Anytime
Entree range: $20.95 (adults);
  $9.95 (children)
Payment: VISA, MC, AMEX
Service rating: ★★★
Friendliness rating: ★★★★

Parking: Hotel lot
Bar: Full service
Wine selection: Limited
Dress: Casual
Disabled access: Yes

Dinner: Every day, 5–10 p.m.

Setting & atmosphere: This restaurant replaces the Papeete Bay Verandah. A large open pit is the centerpiece of the room. Here the grilled foods are prepared with a flare—literally. From time to time the chef will pour some liquid on the fire, causing huge flames to shoot up. This is usually in response to something one of the strolling entertainers has said, evoking a sign from the fire gods. At any given moment there may be a hula-hoop contest or a coconut race where the children in the dining room are invited to push coconuts around the dining room with broomsticks.

House specialties: Skewer service is the specialty here. There is no menu. As soon as you are seated, your server will begin to deliver food. First a couple of sausages, which are portioned off from long skewers right onto the diner's plate. These are followed by smoked turkey, beef and spareribs, then huge shrimp. These are accompanied by assorted salads, placed on a lazy Susan in the center of the table, along with pot sticker dumplings and teriyaki noodles.

Entertainment & amenities: Strolling singers; games.

Summary & comments: 'Ohana, which means family, is a fun place. The food is good but not superior. The method of service and the fact that it just keeps coming make it all taste a little better. Insist on being seated in the main dining room, where the fire pit is located. There are tables around the back, but you can't see what's going on from back there.

OLIVIA'S CAFE

American ★★★ Moderate
Old Key West Resort (407) 939-3463

Readers' Survey Responses:	
75% 👍	25% 👎

QUALITY	VALUE
81	C

Customers: Resort guests
Priority seatings: Not required

When to go: Lunch
Entree range: $9.50–18.95

(Olivia's Cafe)

Payment: VISA, MC, AMEX
Service rating: ★★★★
Friendliness rating: ★★★★
Parking: Hotel lot

Bar: Full service
Wine selection: Limited
Dress: Casual
Disabled access: Yes

Breakfast: Every day, 7:30–11 a.m.
Lunch: Every day, noon–5 p.m.
Dinner: Every day, 5–10 p.m.

Setting & atmosphere: This is Disney's idea of Key West, with lots of pastels and rough wood siding on the walls, mosaic tile floors, potted palms and tropical trees in the center of the room, and plenty of nautical gewgaws, including vintage photos of Key West and its inhabitants of long ago. (Key West is nothing like this.) There is some outside seating, which looks out over the waterway. Tile, wood siding, and no tablecloths add up to a very noisy dining room.

House specialties: Appetizers include conch fritters; seafood nachos; and guacamole and chips. Entrees feature prime rib; breaded and deep-fried Gulf shrimp; fresh fish grilled with fresh spices; and fried chicken with mashed potatoes and gravy. Many of the dishes are accompanied by what is referred to as real Cuban-style black beans and rice, but these beans would look pretty Americanized to anyone from Havana.

Other recommendations: Turkey pot pie; fried chicken; country-fried steak.

Summary & comments: Though perhaps not Key West, the charming atmosphere and low-key pace make the food taste even better than it already is. Not wonderful, just nice. The servers are upbeat and move with alarming speed, though food tends to come out of the kitchen at a more Key Westerly pace (slowly).

L'ORIGINALE ALFREDO DI ROMA RISTORANTE

Italian ★★½ Expensive
Italy, World Showcase, Epcot (407) 939-3463

Readers' Survey Responses:	
74% 👍	26% 👎

QUALITY	VALUE
74	D

Customers: Theme park guests
Priority seatings: Required
When to go: Midafternoon

Entree range: Lunch,
$7.75–17.95; dinner,
$9.95–25.75

(L'Originale Alfredo di Roma Ristorante)

Payment: VISA, MC, AMEX
Service rating: ★★★★
Friendliness rating: ★★★★
Parking: Epcot lot

Bar: Beer and wine only
Wine selection: All Italian
Dress: Casual
Disabled access: Yes

Lunch: Every day, noon–4:15 p.m.
Dinner: Every day, 4:30 p.m. until park closes

Setting & atmosphere: The elegant—some would say garish—Roman decor features huge murals of an Italian piazza along the wall behind the upholstered banquettes. Dark woods and latticework on the high ceilings add to a sumptuous atmosphere. It is, however, a noisy dining room, one that is nearly always filled. This is yet another location for the so-called famous restaurant of the inventor of fettucine Alfredo, the favorite dining spot of Mary Pickford and Douglas Fairbanks.

House specialties: Fettucine Alfredo (what else?); pasta e fagioli; linguine al pesto; vitello alla Milanese.

Other recommendations: Pollo alla Milanese; pollo alla parmigiana; roasted lamb chop.

Entertainment & amenities: Strolling opera singers at dinner.

Summary & comments: Although the word "original" appears in the name, the food is a little worn and old. (So what did Mary Pickford and Douglas Fairbanks know about restaurants?) Most of the entrees are heavy and will have you plodding the rest of the way through the park.

THE OUTBACK

Steak   ★★   Expensive
Buena Vista Palace Resort & Spa, Disney Village Hotel Plaza (407) 827-2727

Readers' Survey Responses:	
45% 👍	55% 👎

QUALITY	VALUE
67	D

Customers: Tourists, locals
Reservations: Recommended
When to go: Very early dinner
Entree range: $12.95–35
Payment: VISA, MC, AMEX, DC, D
Service rating: ★

Friendliness rating: ★
Parking: Complimentary valet parking at the rear of the hotel
Bar: Full service
Wine selection: Excellent
Dress: Casual
Disabled access: Yes

Dinner: 5:30–10:45 p.m.

(The Outback)

Setting & atmosphere: A large, open room with a two-story ceiling and a cascading waterfall. Servers are in Australian bush outfits. That and the menu printed on a boomerang are supposed to make it an Australian restaurant, though the bulk of the menu is what you'd find in just about any American restaurant.

House specialties: There aren't many places where you can get kangaroo steak and rattlesnake salad, but you can here if you really want it. Otherwise there is filet mignon with béarnaise sauce; rack of spring lamb; grilled tuna; and prime rib.

Other recommendations: Six-pound live Maine lobster.

Summary & comments: For some reason that no one bothers to explain, dinner rolls are delivered to the table at the end of long poles. Staff members tend to treat guests as though they'll never be back. The food isn't good enough to put up with rude service. *Note:* This is not part of the Outback Steakhouse national chain.

PALIO

Italian	★★★	Moderate

Walt Disney World Swan (407) 934-3000

Readers' Survey Responses:	
81% 👍	19% 👎

QUALITY	VALUE
81	C

Customers: Hotel guests
Reservations: Recommended
When to go: Anytime
Entree range: $20–30
Payment: VISA, MC, AMEX, DC, JCB, D
Service rating: ★★★

Friendliness rating: ★★★
Parking: Hotel lot
Bar: Full service
Wine selection: Very good
Dress: Casual
Disabled access: Yes

Dinner: Every day, 6–11 p.m.

Setting & atmosphere: The name means banner, and they're hanging all over this upscale Italian trattoria and are even draped over the tables. It is a pretty place and bustles with excitement and the sounds of happy diners. Like just about everything else in the hotel, designer Michael Graves had a hand in the decor and design of the restaurant, and it shows. It is a beautiful place.

House specialties: Veal alla limone, a scallopine served with lemon butter and linguine; saltimbocca alla Romana, veal medallions topped with pro-

(Palio)

sciutto and sage, served with risotto; osso buco alla Milanese, veal shank braised in white wine and vegetable stock, served with saffron risotto.

Other recommendations: Veal picante alla marsala; sautéed chicken breast with tomato; red snapper with sautéed fennel.

Summary & comments: The food isn't bad and the experience is satisfying overall, but there are more exciting dining options available. The roasted-garlic spread served with the hot bread is nice. Fill up on that and then order one of the reasonably priced pizzas.

PLANET HOLLYWOOD

American ★★★½ Moderate
Pleasure Island (407) 827-7827

Readers' Survey Responses:	
74% 👍	26% 👎

QUALITY	VALUE
87	C

Customers: Tourists, locals
Priority seatings: Accepted lunch
  and late-night only
When to go: Late lunch
Entree range: $8.95–18.95
Payment: VISA, MC, AMEX,
  DC, D

Service rating: ★★★★
Friendliness rating: ★★
Parking: Pleasure Island lot
Bar: Full service
Wine selection: Limited
Dress: Casual
Disabled access: Yes

Lunch & Dinner: Every day, 11 a.m.–1 a.m.

Setting & atmosphere: A large planet-shaped structure "floating" in the lagoon next to Pleasure Island. Planet Hollywood's decor is something of a movie museum, with memorabilia from famous movies. These items are easy to come by since Sylvester Stallone, Arnold Schwarzenegger, Bruce Willis, and other actors are partners in the restaurant. Orlando is world headquarters for the chain, and the hometown restaurant is really a special structure. Still, the artifacts leave something to be desired. New York's Planet has Judy Garland's ruby slippers; Orlando's has the gilded potty seat from *The Last Emperor.*

House specialties: The menu is all over the place, with pasta dishes; fajitas; burgers; dinner salads; and pizzas. The burgers are huge (the bleu cheese burger is wonderful), and the Creole pizza—with mustard and red sauce topped with blackened shrimp, andouille sausage, and chicken—is delicious. Desserts are incredible, especially the white-chocolate bread pudding.

(Planet Hollywood)

Other recommendations: Chicken fajitas; linguini and sausage; grilled swordfish.

Summary & comments: Because of its star power, Planet Hollywood attracts a lot of people. But even with the never-ending stream of guests, the kitchen doesn't slack off. The food is good and well thought out. And while $7.50 may seem like a lot of money for a burger, you'll get a thick, juicy patty, cooked the way you want it, with fries. And to give you an idea of the restaurant's attention to details, the potatoes for the fries are stored on the premises until the proper amount of sweetness from aging is achieved.

PLEASURE ISLAND JAZZ COMPANY

Regional American ★★ Moderate
Pleasure Island   (407) 934-7781

Readers' Survey Responses:	
77% 👍	23% 👎

QUALITY	VALUE
68	C

Customers: Tourists, locals
Priority seatings: Not accepted
When to go: Early evening to get a good seat for that night's jazz performance
Entree range: $5.95–7.95
Payment: VISA, MC, AMEX

Service rating: ★★
Friendliness rating: ★★
Parking: Pleasure Island lot
Bar: Full service
Wine selection: Moderate
Dress: Casual
Disabled access: Good

Dinner: 7:30 p.m.–1 a.m.

Setting & atmosphere: A large nightclub with tables set up in front of a performance space where jazz musicians play nightly. This is the sort of place where you don't go just to have the food and not stay for the show. However, you'll find plenty of people who come for the music with no intention of having anything to eat.

House specialties: Red beans and rice; spicy Cajun chicken stack; grilled voodoo pork loin; Oriental grilled salmon.

Summary & comments: Although the jazz club has been serving full dinners for a couple of years, it has remained something of a secret, which is surprising since this is one of the few Downtown Disney eating spots that is not operated by an outside concern. The food is simple, and the service tends to be a bit brusque. But the jazz experience is definitely enhanced when you have a bowl of red beans and rice in front of you.

PORTOBELLO YACHT CLUB

Italian ★★★½ Expensive
Pleasure Island (407) 934-8888

Readers' Survey Responses:	
81% 👍	19% 👎

QUALITY	VALUE
88	D

Customers: Tourists, locals
Priority seatings: Recommended
When to go: Anytime
Entree range: $14.95–29.95
Payment: VISA, MC, AMEX
Service rating: ★★★★
Friendliness rating: ★★★★

Parking: Pleasure Island lot
Bar: Full service
Wine selection: Very good; heavy
 on Italian selections
Dress: Casual
Disabled access: Yes

Lunch: Every day, 11 a.m.–4 p.m.
Dinner: Every day, 4 p.m.–midnight

Setting & atmosphere: This restaurant sports an upscale nautical theme with lots of polished brass, dark woods, and canvas window coverings. There is a patio overlooking the lagoon for those days with low humidity.
House specialties: Northern Italian cuisine; breaded veal ribeye; charcoal-grilled shrimp on a rosemary skewer; boneless half chicken marinated in olive oil, garlic, and fresh rosemary.
Other recommendations: Crispy thin-crust pizza appetizers, including a vegetarian pizza with eggplant, zucchini, and mushrooms and a four-cheese pizza with sun-dried tomatoes. The butterfly pasta with fresh asparagus and snow peas is a good inexpensive selection.
Summary & comments: Tends to be overpriced, but one can make a meal of a pizza and pasta selection for under $20. Ask for the patio if it's a cool evening.

RAINFOREST CAFE

American ★★½ Moderate
Downtown Disney Marketplace (407) 827-8500
Animal Kingdom (407) 938-9100

Readers' Survey Responses:	
83% 👍	17% 👎

QUALITY	VALUE
73	D

(Rainforest Cafe)

Customers: Tourists and locals
Priority seatings: Not accepted
When to go: Late afternoon, after lunch crunch and before dinner hour
Entree range: $8–18
Payment: VISA, MC, AMEX, DC, JCB, D

Service rating: ★★
Friendliness rating: ★★★
Parking: Marketplace lot
Bar: Full bar
Wine selection: Limited
Dress: Casual
Disabled access: Good

Open: *Downtown Disney Marketplace:* Sunday–Thursday, 8 a.m.–11 p.m.; Friday and Saturday, 8 a.m.–midnight; *Animal Kingdom:* every day, 7:30 a.m.–10 p.m.

Setting & atmosphere: The Downtown Disney version of the national chain sits beneath a giant volcano that can be seen (and heard) erupting all over the Marketplace. The smoke coming from the volcano is nonpolluting, in accordance with the restaurant's conservation theme. Inside is a huge dining room designed to look like a jungle (imagine all the silk plants in the world tacked to the ceiling), complete with Animatronic elephants, bats, and monkeys (not the most realistic Animatronics you've seen). There is occasional thunder and even some rainfall. Large aquariums connected with glass "swimways" serve as one of several waiting areas. Next to the dining room is a 5,000-square-foot retail shop. The Animal Kingdom version, featuring a huge waterfall, is easier on the eye externally. Once inside, however, you'll find the same food, decor, and retail space as at the Marketplace.

House specialties: "Pieces of ate" eggroll with chicken, red peppers, corn, and black beans wrapped inside wonton skins; seafood Galapagos with fish, zucchini, and shrimp (but no tortoise) served over pasta; Rainforest pita quesadilla with chicken; and chicken monsoon with shrimp and linguine.

Entertainment & amenities: After the wait you endure, a chair and some sustenance is all the entertainment you'll need.

Summary & comments: Let us say up front that while we are not impressed by the Rainforest Cafes, a lot of our readers rave about them. The slogan for Rainforest Cafe is "a wild place to shop and eat." The shopping experience must be the attraction because it certainly isn't the food. Preparations are spotty; spicing is uneven; and the quality is not as high as at other area theme restaurants such as Planet Hollywood and Hard Rock Cafe. Waits can be horrendous. You must first queue up and wait to approach "the rock," where you will be given a passport with your name and approximate waiting time. This could easily be more than an hour. You are expected to shop in the retail space during this time. When your name is called you will be told to report to "the elephant" (seriously), only to be instructed to go wait at another podium. Even cattle in the world's diminishing rain forests aren't moved around this much. By all means visit the gift shop, but dine somewhere else.

RESTAURANT AKERSHUS

Norwegian/Buffet   ★★★½   Moderate
Norway, World Showcase, Epcot   (407) 939-3463

Readers' Survey Responses:		QUALITY	VALUE
89% 👍	11% 👎	89	B

Customers: Theme park guests
Priority seatings: Required
When to go: Anytime
Entree range: Lunch: $11.95
   adults, $5.25 kids; dinner:
   $18.50 adults, $7.95 kids
Payment: VISA, MC, AMEX

Service rating: ★★★
Friendliness rating: ★★★★
Parking: Epcot lot
Bar: Full service
Wine selection: Limited
Dress: Casual
Disabled access: Yes

Lunch: Every day, 11:30 a.m.–4 p.m.
Dinner: Every day, 4:15 p.m. until park closes

Setting & atmosphere: Modeled on a 14th-century fortress, Akershus entertains its guests in a great banquet hall under high A-framed ceilings and massive iron chandeliers. Stone arches divide the dining rooms. A red carpet alternates with patterned hardwood floors.

House specialties: A bountiful hot and cold buffet features salmon; herring; various Norwegian salads and cheeses; hearty stews; and a variety of hot fish and meats. Be sure to try the mashed rutabagas.

Other recommendations: Cold Ringnes beer on tap.

Summary & comments: Akershus offers a unique introduction to delightful Scandinavian cuisines. The dishes may not be familiar, but the quality is superb, and the overall experience is a real adventure in dining. Akershus's popularity grows every year as word of its quality spreads. We think it's one of the better restaurants at Walt Disney World.

RESTAURANT MARRAKESH

Moroccan   ★★★   Moderate
Morocco, World Showcase, Epcot   (407) 939-3463

Readers' Survey Responses:		QUALITY	VALUE
86% 👍	14% 👎	81	C

(Restaurant Marrakesh)

Customers: Theme park guests
Priority seatings: Suggested
When to go: Anytime
Entree range: $9.95–14.95,
  lunch; $12.95–24.95, dinner
Payment: VISA, MC, AMEX
Service rating: ★★★

Friendliness rating: ★★★★
Parking: Epcot lot
Bar: Full service
Wine selection: Limited
Dress: Casual
Disabled access: Yes

Lunch: Every day, 11:30 a.m.–3:45 p.m.
Dinner: Every day, 4 p.m. until park closes

Setting & atmosphere: One of the more exotic World Showcase restaurants, Marrakesh re-creates a Moroccan palace with gleaming tile mosaics, high inlaid-wood ceilings with open beams and brass chandeliers, and red Bukhara carpets.

House specialties: Start with bastilla (a minced chicken pie sprinkled with confectionary sugar), followed by cornish hen, tangine chicken, or roast lamb. Split an order of couscous. For some reason beef kebabs are available, but the more traditional lamb kebabs are not.

Other recommendations: If you are hungry, curious, or both, go for one of the combination platters for two persons.

Entertainment & amenities: Moroccan band and belly dancing.

Summary & comments: Interesting fare that is almost impossible to find except in the largest U.S. cities. Unlike diners at most Moroccan restaurants, those at Marrakesh sit at tables (instead of on the floor) and eat with utensils rather than with their hands. Because Moroccan food is unfamiliar to most visitors, Marrakesh often has tables available for walk-ins.

ROSE & CROWN DINING ROOM

English   ★★★   Moderate
United Kingdom, World Showcase, Epcot (407) 939-3463

Readers' Survey Responses:	
83% 👍	17% 👎

QUALITY	VALUE
81	D

Customers: Theme park guests
Priority seatings: Recommended
When to go: Anytime

Entree range: $9.25–11.50,
  lunch; $10.75–20.75, dinner
Payment: VISA, MC, AMEX

(Rose & Crown Dining Room)

Service rating: ★★★★
Friendliness rating: ★★★★
Parking: Epcot lot
Wine selection: Limited

Bar: Full bar with Bass ale and Guinness and Harp beers on tap
Dress: Casual
Disabled access: Yes

Lunch: Every day, 11:30 a.m.–4:30 p.m.
Dinner: Every day, 4:30 p.m. until park closes

Setting & atmosphere: The Rose & Crown is both a pub and dining establishment. The traditional English pub has a large cozy bar with rich wood appointments and trim, beamed ceilings, and a hardwood floor. The adjoining English country dining room is rustic and simple. Meals are served outdoors overlooking the World Showcase Lagoon when the weather is nice.

House specialties: Hearty but simple food; try fish and chips or the Welsh chicken and leek pie, washed down with Bass ale.

Other recommendations: Steak and kidney pie; cottage pie; sautéed Irish chicken; grilled lamb chop.

Summary & comments: You do not need priority seatings to stop and refresh yourself on a hot (or cold) afternoon at the friendly bar. The waitresses and barmaids are saucy in the best English tradition and add immeasurably to the experience. Unfortunately, the number of selections on the menu has been cut significantly since our last visit. The Rose & Crown is usually more popular at lunch than at dinner. It is about the fifth Epcot restaurant to book its seatings, owing more to its small size than its popularity.

SAN ANGEL INN RESTAURANTE

Mexican   ★★★   Expensive
Mexico, World Showcase, Epcot   (407) 939-3463

Readers' Survey Responses:	
76% 👍	24% 👎

QUALITY	VALUE
84	D

Customers: Theme park guests
Priority seatings: Recommended
When to go: Anytime
Entree range: $8.95–14.95, lunch; $12.50–23.75, dinner
Payment: VISA, MC, AMEX
Service rating: ★★★★

Friendliness rating: ★★★★
Parking: Epcot lot
Bar: Full service
Wine selection: Limited
Dress: Casual
Disabled access: Yes

(San Angel Inn Restaurante)

Lunch: Every day, 11:30 a.m.–4 p.m.
Dinner: Every day, 4:30 p.m. until park closes

Setting & atmosphere: The San Angel Inn is inside the great Aztec pyramid of the Mexican pavilion. A romantically crafted open-air cantina, the restaurant overlooks both El Río del Tiempo (The River of Time) and the bustling plaza of a small Mexican village.

House specialties: In addition to enchiladas, tacos, quesadillas, and other routine Mexican fare, San Angel Inn features mole poblano (chicken with an exotic sauce made from several kinds of peppers and unsweetened Mexican chocolate) and some interesting regional fish preparations.

Other recommendations: Blackened mahimahi or poached red snapper.

Entertainment & amenities: Mariachi or marimba bands in the adjacent courtyard.

Summary & comments: The San Angel Inn serves good, sometimes excellent, Mexican food at prices much higher than you would find at most Mexican restaurants. The shrimp grilled with pepper sauce, for example, is five medium-sized shrimp for the outrageous sum of $22 ($4.50 per shrimp!). The menu goes beyond normal Mexican selections, offering special and regional dishes that are difficult to find in the United States. If you go, we recommend you skip the tacos and try one of these more unique dishes.

SCI-FI DINE-IN THEATER RESTAURANT

American ★★ Moderate
Disney-MGM Studios (407) 939-3463

Readers' Survey Responses:	
67% 👍	33% 👎

QUALITY	VALUE
67	D

Customers: Theme park guests
Priority seatings: Required
When to go: Anytime
Entree range: $7.95–13.25, lunch; $10.25–22.95, dinner
Payment: VISA, MC, AMEX
Service rating: ★★★★★

Friendliness rating: ★★★★★
Parking: Disney-MGM lot
Bar: Full service
Wine selection: Limited
Dress: Casual
Disabled access: Yes

Lunch: Every day, 10:30 a.m.–4 p.m.
Dinner: Every day, 4 p.m. until park closes

(Sci-Fi Dine-In Theater Restaurant)

Setting & atmosphere: You sit in little cars in a large building where it is always night and watch vintage film clips on a drive-in movie screen as you eat.

House specialties: The fare consists of sandwiches; burgers; salads; and shakes, as well as fancier stuff like barbecued ribs; baked chicken; roast turkey; fried shrimp; and linguine with either veggies or seafood. While we think the food quality is way out of line with the cost, you can have an adequate meal at the Sci-Fi if you stick with simple fare.

Entertainment & amenities: Cartoons and clips of vintage horror and sci-fi movies are shown, such as *The Attack of the Fifty-foot Woman, Robot Monster,* and *Son of the Blob.* Also shown are lurid previews, proclaiming, "See a sultry beauty in the clutches of a half-crazed monster!"

Summary & comments: We recommend making a late-afternoon or late-evening priority seating and ordering only dessert. In other words, think of the Sci-Fi as an attraction (which it is) as opposed to a good dining opportunity (which it is not). If you want to try the Sci-Fi Dine-In and do not have priority seatings, try walking in at 11 a.m. or around 3 p.m.

SEASONS DINING ROOM

American/Eclectic ★★★ Moderate
Disney Institute (407) 939-3463

Readers' Survey Responses:		QUALITY	VALUE
56% 👍	44% 👎	84	C

Customers: Institute guests
Priority seatings: Recommended
When to go: Anytime
Entree range: $13.95–23.95
Payment: VISA, MC, AMEX
Service rating: ★★★★

Friendliness rating: ★★★★
Parking: Institute lot
Bar: Full service
Wine selection: Fair
Dress: Casual
Disabled access: Yes

Breakfast: Every day, 7–11:30 a.m.
Lunch: Every day, 11:30 a.m.–2:30 p.m.
Dinner: Every day, 5:30–10 p.m.

Setting & atmosphere: A huge, cavernous room probably meant to resemble an old dormitory dining hall but which looks more like a barn. Tables include a lazy Susan decorated to reflect the theme being featured that day.

House specialties: There is a different menu each night of the week, including Polynesia night with steamed dumpling salad, grilled turkey with pineapple-soy glaze, pan-seared mahimahi, and exotic fruit soup; New Orleans night with blackened pea and andouille sausage salad, blackened red snapper, and crawfish risotto; Mediterranean night with melon and prosciutto salad, broiled cod over sautéed spinach, and tiramisu; and Northwest night with dried-cherry and wild-rice cakes, roast loin of venison, grilled free-range chicken breast, and fruit cobbler.

Summary & comments: Diners can choose to order a la carte from the menu *or* to opt for fixed-price dinners served family-style, which means each course is brought to the table on platters for your party to dole out for themselves. The food is well executed for the most part, with an emphasis on healthful preparations. If you're really hungry, Seasons represents a good value. If you're lucky enough to dine on Northwest night be sure to save plenty of room for the fruit cobbler (if they run out of it, it's because the staff has eaten it all).

SPOODLES

Mediterranean ★★★½ Moderate
Disney's BoardWalk (407) 939-3463

Readers' Survey Responses:	
93% 👍	7% 👎

QUALITY	VALUE
87	C

Customers: Tourists and locals
Priority seatings: Recommended
When to go: Anytime
Entree range: Tapas, $4–9; entrees, $10–22
Payment: VISA, MC, AMEX
Service rating: ★★★★
Friendliness rating: ★★★★

Parking: BoardWalk lot. *Note:* Valet parking is free before 5 p.m., $5 after.
Bar: Full service
Wine selection: Good selection of Mediterranean countries
Dress: Casual
Disabled access: Good

Breakfast: Every day, 7:30–11 a.m.
Lunch: Every day, noon–2 p.m.
Dinner: Every day, 5–9:50 p.m.

Setting & atmosphere: The dining room is designed like a farmhouse you might find in the Mediterranean countryside—a really big farmhouse. Light fixtures of various sizes and styles (no two are alike), Fiestaware plates and cups stacked on the wooden tables along with a container of flatware, and posters of Mediterranean countries reinforce the family-style atmosphere. The open kitchen adds to the noise, which is already extensive because of the size of the room and the sound of people enjoying themselves and passing around plates of tapas.

House specialties: This is a true Mediterranean restaurant and not just an Italian trattoria that passes itself off as one. Any country with a shoreline on the Mediterranean is represented here, and the result is a plethora of exotic dishes with even more exotic spices. There are full entrees available, but the best way to experience Spoodles is to order an array of tapas, small appetizer-sized portions of entrees, and share them with everyone at the table. Try the spicy shrimp with spinach and garbanzo beans; barbecued Moroccan beef skewers with couscous; Portuguese seafood cataplana soup; Spanish lamb pinchos; taramasalata; or chicken pizza with zhoug.

Other recommendations: Potato-crusted salmon with wild mushrooms and truffle oil; oven-roasted snapper with artichokes, fennel, and oven-dried tomatoes; grilled lamb chops with couscous, spinach, and harissa.

Summary & comments: If you only order beef and a baked potato when you dine out, this is not the place for you (though there is a beef and potato selection on the menu if you get out-voted). This is for the adventurous who really wanted to go to Europe for vacation but wound up in Florida instead. The flavors are fresh and vibrant, and most everything is expertly prepared. Don't be intimidated by ingredients you don't recognize—the staff is very helpful and will gladly tell you what zhoug is.

TEMPURA KIKU

Japanese	★★★	Moderate

Japan, World Showcase, Epcot (407) 939-3463

Readers' Survey Responses:		QUALITY	VALUE
81% 👍	19% 👎	83	C

Customers: Theme park guests
Priority seatings: Not accepted
When to go: Lunch
Entree range: $9.50–16.75, lunch; $15–22, dinner
Payment: VISA, MC, AMEX
Service rating: ★★★★

Friendliness rating: ★★★
Parking: Epcot lot
Bar: Full service
Wine selection: Limited
Dress: Casual
Disabled access: Yes

(Tempura Kiku)

Lunch: Every day, noon–3:45 p.m.
Dinner: Every day, 4:30 p.m. until park closes

Setting & atmosphere: Tempura Kiku is a small (25-person) tempura bar where most patrons sit around the outside of a square counter. The setting is intimate, almost cramped, and very communal.

House specialties: Tempura-battered deep-fried foods featuring chicken, shrimp, and vegetables. The menu tells the story of tempura, which apparently came about when some Portuguese sailors were shipwrecked on a Japanese shore. The Catholic Portuguese did not eat meat on the holy days, which came four times a year and were called quattuor tempora. On these days the sailors ate fried shrimp. The Japanese adapted the word tempura to mean fried shrimp, and the rest of the world adapted it to mean all kinds of fried food.

Other recommendations: Kabuki beef; sushi; sashimi.

Summary & comments: Not the most appealing restaurant at Epcot, but the tempura is arguably the best in the Japan pavilion. The sushi and sashimi are not heavily marketed, but you can bet the sanitation—important in any restaurant but crucial where sushi is served—is impeccable.

TEPPANYAKI DINING ROOMS

Japanese ★★★½ Expensive
Japan, World Showcase, Epcot (407) 939-3463

Readers' Survey Responses:	
87% 👍	13% 👎

QUALITY	VALUE
85	C

Customers: Theme park guests
Priority seatings: Required
When to go: Anytime
Entree range: $9.50–19.95, lunch; $14.95–30.25, dinner
Payment: VISA, MC, AMEX
Service rating: ★★★★

Friendliness rating: ★★★★
Parking: Epcot lot
Bar: Full service
Wine selection: Limited
Dress: Casual
Disabled access: Yes, via elevator

Lunch: Every day, noon–3:45 p.m.
Dinner: Every day, 4:30 p.m. until park closes

Setting & atmosphere: The decor is upscale Japanese, only roomier, with light wood-beam ceilings, grass-cloth walls, and lacquered-finish oak chairs. Overall very clean and spare.

(Teppanyaki Dining Rooms)

House specialties: Chicken, shrimp, beef, scallops, and oriental vegetables stir-fried on a teppan grill by a knife-juggling chef. Teppanyaki is a fancy version of the Benihana restaurant chain.

Entertainment & amenities: Watching the teppan chefs.

Summary & comments: While this restaurant offers some of the best teppan dining you will find in the United States, it has missed a wonderful opportunity to introduce the diversity and beauty of authentic Japanese cuisine to the American public. Be aware that diners at the teppan tables (large tables with a grill in the middle) are seated with other parties. Finally, if you would like to try more traditional Japanese fare, consider Tempura Kiku, a small restaurant in the same building.

TONY'S TOWN SQUARE RESTAURANT

Italian   ★★½   Moderate
Main Street, U.S.A., Magic Kingdom (407) 939-3463

Readers' Survey Responses:		QUALITY	VALUE
68% 👍	32% 👎	78	D

Customers: Theme park guests
Priority seatings: Recommended
When to go: Late lunch or early dinner
Entree range: $11.75–22.75, lunch; $16.25–22.75, dinner
Payment: VISA, MC, AMEX

Service rating: ★★★
Friendliness rating: ★★★★
Parking: Magic Kingdom lot
Bar: None
Wine selection: None
Dress: Casual
Disabled access: Yes

Breakfast: Every day, 8:30–10:45 a.m.
Lunch: Every day, noon–2:45 p.m.
Dinner: Every day, 4 p.m. until park closes

Setting & atmosphere: Decorated like a New York Italian eatery, with tile floors, tablecloths, dark woods, and lots of plants. The walls are filled with memorabilia from *Lady and the Tramp*. It is a bright and open place, but it somehow always has a trampled and unkempt appearance.

House specialties: Spaghetti (long noodles for those who want to try that *Lady and the Tramp* kiss technique); lasagna primavera (the kiss technique doesn't work with this one); Joe's fettucine.

Other recommendations: *Lady and the Tramp* waffles; shrimp scampi.

(Tony's Town Square Restaurant)

Summary & comments: It's perhaps the most pleasant place to dine in the Magic Kingdom, but the choices are few. The pace can be hectic, but the atmosphere is light and airy and the pictures and other knickknacks from *Lady and the Tramp* are a lot of fun. Go ahead, share a plate of over-priced spaghetti with someone you love.

VICTORIA & ALBERT'S

Gourmet	★★★★½	Expensive

Disney's Grand Floridian Beach Resort (407) 939-7707

Readers' Survey Responses:	
91% 👍	9% 👎

QUALITY	VALUE
96	D

Customers: Hotel guests, locals
Priority seatings: Mandatory; must be confirmed by noon the day of your priority seating; call at least 60 days in advance to ensure a table.
When to go: Anytime
Entree range: Fixed price: $80 per person or up to $145 with wine pairings

Payment: VISA, MC, AMEX
Service rating: ★★★★
Friendliness rating: ★★★
Parking: Valet parking; self-parking is deceptively far away.
Wine selection: Excellent
Dress: Jacket required
Disabled access: Yes

Dinner: Two seatings nightly at 5:45–6:30 p.m. and 9–9:45 p.m.

Setting & atmosphere: Victoria & Albert's is a small, intimate room under a domed ceiling. It is elegantly appointed, with large floral displays, fine china, crystal, and silver.

House specialties: The menu changes daily but always features selections of fresh game, poultry, fish, and beef.

Entertainment & amenities: A harpist or violinist entertains from the foyer. Guests receive souvenir menus personalized with gold lettering.

Summary & comments: Except for one bit of kitsch—instead of waiters each table is attended by a maid and butler named Victoria and Albert—this is Disney's most elegant restaurant. It also features some of the finest culinary talent in the southeastern United States. Victoria & Albert's dining room is entirely nonsmoking.

For a special treat, book the chef's table. This will put you in the kitchen, where the executive chef will prepare a special meal for you and your guests, as few as one or as many as eight. There is only one seating each evening, and dinner may take as long as four hours. The cost is at least $115 per person ($160 with wine), but for those who truly love fine food, it's a bargain.

Honors & awards: AAA 4-Diamond Award.

WHISPERING CANYON CAFE

American   ★★½   Moderate
Disney's Wilderness Lodge   (407) 939-3463

Readers' Survey Responses:	
84% 👍	16% 👎

QUALITY	VALUE
79	B

Customers: Hotel guests
Priority seatings: Accepted
When to go: Anytime
Entree range: Breakfast: $9.25 adult, $4.95 children; lunch: $12.95 adult, $6.95 children; dinner: $18.95 adult, $6.95 children

Payment: VISA, MC, AMEX
Service rating: ★★
Friendliness rating: ★★★
Parking: Hotel lot
Bar: Full service
Wine selection: Limited
Dress: Casual
Disabled access: Yes

Breakfast: Every day, 7:30–11 a.m.
Lunch: Every day, noon–3 p.m.
Dinner: Every day, 5–10 p.m.

Setting & atmosphere: Located just off the hotel's atrium lobby, the restaurant looks out on the lobby on one side and a mountain prairie, created by the Disney landscapers, on the other. Tables have a barrel-top lazy Susan where the food is placed; diners dish out their own helpings from the platters.

House specialties: Apple-rosemary rotisserie chicken; maple-garlic pork spareribs; braised lamb shank.

Other recommendations: Smoked barbecue beef brisket; smoked barbecue veal ribs.

Summary & comments: The food is served "family-style," meaning it is brought to the table on platters or in crocks and you dish out however much you'd like. The food is pretty good, and if you're looking to stuff yourself silly, this is the place to be.

WOLFGANG PUCK CAFE

Creative Californian   ★★★   Expensive
Downtown Disney West Side   (407) 938-9653

Readers' Survey Responses:	
69% 👍	31% 👎

QUALITY	VALUE
78	C

Customers: Tourists and locals
Reservations: Upstairs only
When to go: Early evening
Entree range: Cafe, $11.95–14.95; upstairs, $24–34
Payment: VISA, MC, AMEX
Service rating: ★★★★
Friendliness rating: ★★★★

Parking: Downtown Disney lot; valet evenings, $6
Bar: Full service
Wine selection: Very good
Dress: Casual in the Cafe; collared shirt for men, no shorts upstairs
Disabled access: Good

Lunch: (Cafe) Every day, 11 a.m.–4 p.m.
Dinner: (Cafe) Every day, 4–11 p.m.; bar open until midnight; (upstairs) Sunday–Thursday, 6–10:30 p.m.; Friday and Saturday, 6–11 p.m.

Setting & atmosphere: This is actually two restaurants in one—four if you count the attached Wolfgang Puck Express (and there's no reason to count it for anything) and the sushi bar that does a freeform flow into the restaurant's lounge area. The downstairs is the actual Cafe, with several open kitchen areas, colorful tile (one designer has called it a tile factory outlet store), and plenty of pictures of Wolfgang Puck hanging around the place. The upstairs is a more formal dining room, but in name only. Both spaces are inordinately loud and conversation is difficult. Throughout the restaurant are TV monitors trained on various culinary stations. One supposes this is so diners can watch their food being prepared (they certainly can't talk to one another), but unless you have excellent vision—and we're talking something along the lines of Superman—you probably won't be able to see anything. The images are like the surveillance cameras in convenience stores.

House specialties: Wolfgang Puck became famous with his Spago restaurant in California and is the father of the gourmet pizza. His "signature pizza" features smoked salmon, red onion, dill cream, and chives (none of his pizzas has traditional red sauce). You'll also find seared ahi tuna, cafe meatloaf, pepper steak, and blackened catfish. The sushi is quite good. The upstairs dining room has fresh pastas, fish soup, free-range chicken, oven-roasted grouper, and Sonoma lamb chops. The Wiener schnitzel, however, is one of the best items on the menu.

(Wolfgang Puck Cafe)

Summary & comments: Puck, one of the original celebrity chefs, is a master at self-promotion. His cafe, which is really just a chain restaurant, is very much a shrine to his image. But many of the items on the menu are very good, and W.P.C. is one of the better dining options in Downtown Disney. To get out without sticker shock at the end of the meal, go with one of the pizzas and Puck's popular Chinois salad. If you're looking for a quiet, relaxing meal, however, this isn't the place for you.

YACHT CLUB GALLEY

American	★★★	Moderate
Disney's Yacht Club Resort		(407) 939-3463

Readers' Survey Responses:			QUALITY	VALUE
85% 👍	15% 👎		81	C

Customers: Hotel guests
Priority seatings: Not necessary
When to go: Breakfast or lunch
Entree range: $10.95–19.95
Payment: VISA, MC, AMEX
Service rating: ★★★★

Friendliness rating: ★★★★
Parking: Hotel lot
Bar: Full service
Wine selection: Good
Dress: Casual
Disabled access: Yes

Breakfast: Every day, 7–11 a.m.
Lunch: Every day, 11:30 a.m.–3 p.m.
Dinner: Every day, 5–10 p.m.

Setting & atmosphere: The Yacht Club Galley features a bright nautical theme with colorful pastels, blue-striped wallpaper, and tablecloths. A moving seascape mural is the focal point of the large and somewhat noisy dining room.

House specialties: Daily fresh-fish specials; barbecued pork ribs; seafood stir-fry with shrimp, scallops, and fish. Breakfast features a buffet or an a la carte menu, with such selections as "the catamaran": a flour tortilla filled with scrambled eggs, onions, and peppers, and topped with salsa, sour cream, and shredded cheddar cheese.

Other recommendations: Chicken commodore, a breast of chicken with prosciutto ham, fontina cheese sauce, and linguine, tossed with green peppers, garlic, and olive oil; roast prime rib with burgundy horseradish sauce; breaded clam strips.

Entertainment & amenities: Strolling band in the evening.

(Yacht Club Galley)

Summary & comments: Stop here for breakfast or lunch; it's a short walk from Epcot and a good escape if you just need to get out of the park and relax for a while.

YACHTSMAN STEAKHOUSE

Steak ★★★ Expensive
Disney's Yacht Club Resort (407) 939-3463

Readers' Survey Responses:	
90% 👍	10% 👎

QUALITY	VALUE
80	D

Customers: Hotel guests, locals
Priority seatings: Required
When to go: Anytime
Entree range: $17–47
Payment: VISA, MC, AMEX
Service rating: ★★★

Friendliness rating: ★★★★
Parking: Hotel lot
Bar: Full service
Wine selection: Very good
Dress: Casual
Disabled access: Yes

Dinner: Every day, 5:30–10 p.m.

Setting & atmosphere: This restaurant is decorated in a country style—lots of knotty pine and chintz tablecloths. A refrigerated display case with big slabs of beef in various stages of the aging process allows you to get acquainted with your steak before you're seated. You can watch it being cooked at the show kitchen, if you wish, and the staff encourages you to ask questions about your meal's preparation. (How about "Is it ready yet?")

House specialties: All steaks are cut and trimmed on the premises daily. The Yacht Club porterhouse, Kansas City strip, and prime rib of beef au jus are just some of the cuts. The mixed grill includes filet, lamb chops, and chicken breast served with three sauces. All entrees include baked potato and bread-board assortment. Béarnaise and bordelaise sauces are available to complement your meat selection.

Other recommendations: Whole Maine lobster stuffed with crabmeat; full rack of lamb; grilled pork chops.

Entertainment & amenities: Strolling musicians (the same ones who stroll through the Yacht Club Galley).

Summary & comments: For die-hard meat lovers who don't mind paying a lot for a good steak. The chintz tablecloths keep it from being a male domain, but women should be offended by the "yachtress" cut of meat. Besides a good wine list, the Yachtsman also has an impressive beer list.

Part Nine

The Magic Kingdom

ARRIVING

On specified days each week, the Magic Kingdom opens an hour early to Walt Disney World hotel and campground guests (excluding guests at the independent hotels of Disney Village Hotel Plaza). If you aren't a Disney resort guest, avoid the Magic Kingdom on early-entry days.

If you stay at a Disney hotel or campground and want to tour the park on a morning when early entry is in effect, arrive 1 hour and 40 minutes before the official opening time. If official opening is 9 a.m., for example, arrive at the park about 7:20 a.m. When you're admitted at 7:30 a.m., you'll be able to enjoy all attractions in Fantasyland except *Legend of the Lion King* and all Tomorrowland attractions except *The Timekeeper* and *Walt Disney's Carousel of Progress*. Sometimes, Space Mountain opens a half hour later than other Tomorrowland attractions (at 8 a.m. in this example).

One year during our research, the official opening time was 8 a.m. Testing the system, we were waiting at the bus stop at Dixie Landings Resort a little after 6 a.m. Sure enough, the bus rolled up a few minutes later, full of sleepy parents and excited children. We were admitted to the Magic Kingdom at 6:30 a.m., about a half hour before sunrise. Though Main Street was lighted, Disney cast members (employees) kept us moving past the closed shops to Fantasyland. There, dads huddled over coffee while moms and children soared on Dumbo to greet the rising sun.

During summer and holiday periods, increased crowds (resulting from Disney resort guests exercising their early-entry option) create nearly unmanageable congestion by around 10 a.m. If you're eligible for early entry, tour one of the other parks where early entry is not in effect or take advantage of early entry for an hour or two first thing in the morning at the Magic Kingdom, then head to another park for the remainder of the day.

Because Disney is always changing things, call Walt Disney World Information at (407) 824-4321 before you leave home to verify the early-entry days during your stay. Visitors ineligible for early entry should not attempt to sneak in with early-entry guests. All Disney hotel and campground guests, including children, are issued dated identification cards upon check-in at their hotel and must present them with valid admission passes in order to enter a park early.

GETTING ORIENTED

If you drive, the Magic Kingdom/Transportation and Ticket Center (TTC) parking lot opens about two hours before the park's official opening. After paying a fee, you are directed to a parking space, then transported by tram to the TTC, where you catch either a monorail or ferry to the park's entrance.

If you're staying at the Contemporary, Polynesian, or Grand Floridian resorts, you can commute directly to the Magic Kingdom by monorail (guests at the Contemporary can walk there more quickly). If you stay at Wilderness Lodge or Fort Wilderness Campground, you will take a boat. Guests at other Disney resorts can reach the park by bus. All Disney lodging guests, whether they arrive by bus, monorail, or boat, are deposited at the park's entrance, bypassing the TTC.

At the Magic Kingdom, stroller and wheelchair rentals are to the right of the train station and lockers are on the station's ground floor. On your left as you enter Main Street is City Hall, the center for information, lost and found, guided tours, and entertainment schedules.

If you don't already have a handout guidemap of the park, get one at City Hall. The guidemap lists all attractions, shops, and eating places; provides helpful information about first aid, baby care, and assistance for the disabled; and gives tips for good photos. It also lists times for the day's special events, live entertainment, Disney character parades, concerts, and other activities. Also available at City Hall is the *Disney Character Greeting Location Guide*, telling when and where to find Disney characters.

Main Street ends at a central hub from which branch the entrances to five other sections of the Magic Kingdom: Adventureland, Frontierland, Liberty Square, Fantasyland, and Tomorrowland. Mickey's Toontown Fair is wedged like a dimple between the cheeks of Fantasyland and Tomorrowland and doesn't connect to the central hub.

Cinderella Castle is the entrance to Fantasyland and the Magic Kingdom's visual center. If you start in Adventureland and go clockwise around the Magic Kingdom, the castle spires will always be roughly on

1. *Alien Encounter*
2. Ariel's Grotto
3. AstroOrbiter
4. Barnstormer
5. Big Thunder Mountain Railroad
6. Buzz Lightyear's Space Ranger Spin
7. Central hub
8. Cinderella Castle
9. Cinderella's Golden Carrousel
10. City Hall
11. *Country Bear Jamboree*
12. *The Diamond Horseshoe Saloon Revue*
13. Donald's Boat
14. Dumbo the Flying Elephant
15. Ferry dock
16. *The Hall of Presidents*
17. The Haunted Mansion
18. It's a Small World
19. Jungle Cruise
20. *Legend of the Lion King*
21. *Liberty Belle* Riverboat
22. Mad Tea Party

Magic Kingdom

your right; if you start in Tomorrowland and go counterclockwise through the park, the spires will always be roughly on your left. Cinderella Castle is an excellent meeting place if your group decides to split up during the day or is separated accidentally. Because the castle is large, designate a very specific meeting spot, like the entrance to Cinderella's Royal Table restaurant at the rear of the castle.

STARTING THE TOUR

Everyone soon finds their favorite and not-so-favorite attractions in the Magic Kingdom. Be open-minded and adventuresome. Our personal experience and research indicate that each visitor differs on which attraction is most enjoyable. Don't dismiss a ride or show until *after* you have tried it.

Take advantage of what Disney does best: the fantasy adventures of Splash Mountain and The Haunted Mansion and the Audio-Animatronics (talking robots) attractions, including *The Hall of Presidents* and Pirates of the Caribbean. Don't burn daylight browsing the shops: except for some Disney souvenirs, most of the goods are available elsewhere. Minimize the time you spend on midway-type rides; you probably have something similar near your hometown. (Don't, however, mistake Space Mountain and Big Thunder Mountain Railroad as amusement park rides. They may be roller coasters, but they're pure Disney genius.) Eat a good breakfast early, and avoid lines at eateries by snacking during the day on food from vendors. Fare at most Magic Kingdom eateries is on a par with Hardee's or McDonald's (nothing special).

Main Street, U.S.A.

You begin and end your Magic Kingdom visit on Main Street, which opens a half hour before, and closes a half hour to an hour after, the rest of the park. The Walt Disney World Railroad stops at the Main Street

Not to Be Missed at the Magic Kingdom	
Adventureland	Pirates of the Caribbean
Frontierland	Big Thunder Mountain Railroad Splash Mountain
Liberty Square	The Haunted Mansion
Tomorrowland	Space Mountain *The Timekeeper*
Special events	Evening Parade

Station; board here for a grand tour of the park or a ride to Frontierland or Mickey's Toontown Fair.

Main Street is a sanitized Disney re-creation of a turn-of-the-century, small-town American street. Its buildings are real, not elaborate props. Attention to detail is exceptional: all interiors, furnishings, and fixtures are true to the period. Along the street are shops and eating places, City Hall, a fire station, and an old-time cinema. Horse-drawn trolleys, double-decker buses, fire engines, and horseless carriages transport visitors along Main Street to the central hub.

Walt Disney World Railroad

What It Is: Scenic railroad ride around perimeter of the Magic Kingdom, and transportation to Frontierland and Mickey's Toontown Fair

Scope & Scale: Minor attraction

When to Go: Anytime

Special Comments: Main Street is usually the least congested station.

Author's Rating: Plenty to see; ★★½ [Critical ratings are based on a scale of zero to five stars. Five stars is the best possible rating.]

Appeal by Age Group:

Pre-school	Grade School	Teens	Young Adults	Over 30	Senior Citizens
★★★★	★★★	★★½	★★★	★★★	★★★

Duration of Ride: About 19 minutes for a complete circuit

Average Wait in Line per 100 People ahead of You: 8 minutes

Assumes: 2 or more trains operating

Loading Speed: Fast

Description and Comments A transportation ride blending an unusual variety of sights and experiences with an energy-saving way to get around the park. The train provides a glimpse of all lands except Adventureland.

Touring Tips Save the train ride until after you have seen the featured attractions, or use it when you need transportation. On busy days, lines form at the Frontierland Station, but rarely at the Main Street and Mickey's Toontown Fair Stations. Strollers aren't allowed on the train. Wheel-chair access is available only at the Frontierland and Mickey's Toontown Fair stations.

Main Street Cinema

What It Is: Old-time movies and vintage Disney cartoons

Scope & Scale: Diversion

When to Go: Whenever you want

Main Street Services

Most park services are centered on Main Street, including:

Wheelchair & Stroller Rental	Right of the main entrance before passing under the railroad station
Banking Services	Automated tellers (ATMs) are underneath the Main Street railroad station
Storage Lockers	Ground floor of the railroad station at the end of Main Street; all lockers are cleaned out each night.
Lost & Found	City Hall at the railroad station end of Main Street
Live Entertainment & Parade Info	City Hall at the railroad station end of Main Street
Lost Persons	City Hall
Walt Disney World & Local Attraction Information	City Hall
First Aid	Next to The Crystal Palace, left around the central hub (toward Adventureland)
Baby Center/ Baby-Care Needs	Next to The Crystal Palace, left around the central hub (toward Adventureland)

Author's Rating: Wonderful selection of flicks; ★★
Appeal by Age Group:

Pre-school	Grade School	Teens	Young Adults	Over 30	Senior Citizens
★★	★★	★★	★★	★★	★★

Duration of Presentation: Runs continuously
Preshow Entertainment: None
Probable Waiting Time: No waiting

Description and Comments Excellent old-time footage, including vintage Disney cartoons. Sometimes showing is a movie about how Mickey got his first acting job. Note the Michael Eisner phone in Mickey's office.

Touring Tips   Good place to escape the sun or rain or to kill time while others in your group shop on Main Street. Something you can afford to miss.

Transportation Rides

Description and Comments   Trolleys, buses, etc., which add color to Main Street.

Touring Tips   Will save you a walk to the central hub. Not worth waiting in line.

Main Street Eateries and Shops

Description and Comments   Some of the Magic Kingdom's better food and specialty/souvenir shopping in a nostalgic, happy setting. The Emporium offers the park's best selection of Disney trademark souvenirs.

Touring Tips   Shops are fun, but the merchandise (except for certain Disney trademark souvenirs) is available elsewhere. If seeing the park attractions is your goal, save Main Street until day's end. If shopping is your objective, avoid the noon hour and near closing time, when crowds are heavy. Remember, Main Street opens a half hour earlier and closes a half hour to an hour later than the rest of the park.

The Crystal Palace, at the central hub end of Main Street (toward Adventureland), offers a character buffet and is often overlooked by lunch-hour (but not dinner-hour) crowds. If you're nearby at noon, try it.

Adventureland

Adventureland is the first land to the left of Main Street. It combines an African safari theme with an old New Orleans/Caribbean atmosphere.

Swiss Family Treehouse

What It Is: Outdoor walk-through treehouse
Scope & Scale: Minor attraction
When to Go: Before 11:30 a.m. and after 5 p.m.
Special Comments: Requires climbing a lot of stairs
Author's Rating: A visual delight; ★★★
Appeal by Age Group:

Pre-school	Grade School	Teens	Young Adults	Over 30	Senior Citizens
★★★½	★★★½	★★★	★★★	★★★	★★★

Duration of Tour: 10–15 minutes

Average Wait in Line per 100 People ahead of You: 7 minutes

Assumes: Normal staffing

Loading Speed: Doesn't apply

Description and Comments A fantastic replica of the shipwrecked family's treehouse home will fire the imaginations of the inventive and the adventurous. This attraction was renovated in 1998.

Touring Tips A self-guided walk-through tour involves a lot of stairs up and down, but no ropes, ladders, or anything fancy. People who stop for extra-long looks or to rest sometimes create bottlenecks that slow crowd flow. Visit in late afternoon or early evening if you're on a one-day tour, or first thing in the morning of your second day.

Jungle Cruise

What It Is: Outdoor safari-themed boat ride adventure

Scope & Scale: Major attraction

When to Go: Before 10 a.m. or two hours before closing

Author's Rating: A long-enduring Disney masterpiece; ★★★

Appeal by Age Group:

Pre-school	Grade School	Teens	Young Adults	Over 30	Senior Citizens
★★★½	★★★½	★★★	★★★	★★★	★★★

Duration of Ride: 8–9 minutes

Average Wait in Line per 100 People ahead of You: 3½ minutes

Assumes: 10 boats operating

Loading Speed: Moderate

Description and Comments A cruise through jungle waterways. Passengers encounter elephants, lions, hostile natives, and a menacing hippo. Boatman's spiel adds to the fun.

Touring Tips Among the park's oldest attractions. Good staff and improved management plan have speeded lines for this ride. But it's very difficult to estimate the length of the wait for the Jungle Cruise. A mother from the Bronx, New York, complains:

> *The line for this ride is extremely deceiving. We got in line towards the early evening; it was long but we really wanted to take this ride.*

Every time the winding line brought us near the loading dock and we thought we were going to get on, we'd discover a whole new section of winding lanes to go through. It was extremely frustrating. We must have waited a good 20–30 minutes before the two of us finally gave up and got out.

Pirates of the Caribbean

What It Is: Indoor pirate-themed adventure boat ride
Scope & Scale: Headliner
When to Go: Before noon or after 5 p.m.
Special Comments: Frightens some young children
Author's Rating: Disney Audio-Animatronics at its best; not to be missed;
★★★★★
Appeal by Age Group:

Pre-school	Grade School	Teens	Young Adults	Over 30	Senior Citizens
★★★	★★★★★	★★★★	★★★★	★★★★½	★★★★½

Duration of Ride: About 7½ minutes
Average Wait in Line per 100 People ahead of You: 1½ minutes
Assumes: Both waiting lines operating
Loading Speed: Fast

Description and Comments Cruise through a series of sets depicting a pirate raid on an island settlement, from bombardment of the fortress to debauchery after the victory. Regarding debauchery, Pirates of the Caribbean is one of several Disney attractions that has been administered a strong dose of political correctness. See if you can spot the changes.

Touring Tips Undoubtedly one of the park's most elaborate and imaginative attractions. Engineered to move large crowds in a hurry, Pirates is a good attraction to see during later afternoon. It has two waiting lines, both covered.

Tropical Serenade (Enchanted Tiki Birds)

What It Is: Audio-Animatronic Pacific island musical theater show
Scope & Scale: Minor attraction
When to Go: Before 11 a.m. and after 3:30 p.m.
Author's Rating: Very, very unusual; ★★½

Appeal by Age Group:

Pre-school	Grade School	Teens	Young Adults	Over 30	Senior Citizens
★★★★	★★★½	★★	★★½	★★½	★★½

Duration of Presentation: 15½ minutes

Preshow Entertainment: Talking birds

Probable Waiting Time: 15 minutes

Description and Comments   Upgraded in 1998, this theater presentation now features two of Disney's most beloved bird characters, Iago from *Aladdin,* and Zazu from *The Lion King.* A new song, "Friend Like Me," and a revamped plotline add some much needed zip, but the production remains (pardon the pun) a featherweight in the Disney galaxy of attractions. Even so, the *Tiki Birds* are a great favorite of the eight-and-under set.

Touring Tips   One of the more bizarre Magic Kingdom entertainments. Usually not too crowded. We go in the late afternoon when we especially appreciate sitting briefly in an air-conditioned theater.

Adventureland Eateries and Shops

Description and Comments   Restaurants tend to be less crowded during lunch than other Magic Kingdom eateries.

The 357th Stroller Squadron: the Mowin' Mamas

Touring Tips El Pirata y el Perico, featuring Mexican fast food and hot dogs, is often overlooked.

Frontierland

Frontierland adjoins Adventureland as you move clockwise around the Magic Kingdom. The focus is on the Old West, with stockade-type structures and pioneer trappings.

Splash Mountain

What It Is: Indoor/outdoor water-flume adventure ride

Scope & Scale: Super headliner

When to Go: As soon as the park opens, during afternoon or evening parades, or just before closing

Special Comments: Children must be 3'8" tall to ride; those younger than 7 must ride with an adult. Switching off option provided (pages 165–167).

Author's Rating: A wet winner; not to be missed; ★★★★★

Appeal by Age Group:

Pre-school	Grade School	Teens	Young Adults	Over 30	Senior Citizens
†	★★★★★	★★★★★	★★★★★	★★★★★	★★★½

† Many preschoolers are too short to meet the height requirement, and others are visually intimidated when they see the ride from the waiting line. Among preschoolers who actually ride, most give the attraction high marks (3–5 stars).

Duration of Ride: About 10 minutes

Average Wait in Line per 100 People ahead of You: 3½ minutes

Assumes: Operating at full capacity

Loading Speed: Moderate

Description and Comments Amusement park flume ride, Disney-style. Bigger than life and more imaginative than anyone thought possible. Combines steep chutes with excellent special effects. Covers over half a mile, splashing through swamps, caves, and backwood bayous before climaxing in a five-story plunge and Brer Rabbit's triumphant return home. More than 100 Audio-Animatronic characters, including Brer Rabbit, Brer Bear, and Brer Fox, regale riders with songs including "Zip-a-Dee-Doo-Dah."

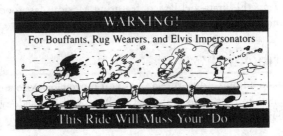

WARNING!

For Bouffants, Rug Wearers, and Elvis Impersonators

This Ride Will Muss Your 'Do

Touring Tips   This happy, exciting, adventuresome ride vies with Space Mountain in Tomorrowland as the park's most popular attraction. Crowds build fast in the morning, and waits of more than two hours can be expected once the park fills. Get in line first thing, certainly no later than 45 minutes after the park opens. Long lines will persist all day.

As occurs with Space Mountain, when the park opens, hundreds are poised to dash to Splash Mountain. The best strategy for this sprint (we call it the Rapid Rampage) is to go to the end of Main Street and turn left to The Crystal Palace restaurant. In front of the restaurant is a bridge that provides a shortcut to Adventureland. Stake out a position at the barrier rope. When the park opens and the rope drops, move as fast as you comfortably can (understanding that the pandemonium unleashed behind you is comparable to a buffalo stampede) and cross the bridge to Adventureland. (While we don't advocate running, we'll tell you candidly that the folks around you aren't down in four-point stance to inspect the pavement.)

Here's another shortcut: Just past the first group of buildings on your right, roughly across from the Swiss Family Treehouse, is a small passageway containing rest rooms and phones. Easy to overlook, it connects Adventureland to Frontierland. Go through the passageway into Frontierland and take a hard left. As you emerge along the waterfront, Splash Mountain is straight ahead. If you miss the passageway, don't fool around looking for it. Continue straight through Adventureland to Splash Mountain.

Less exhausting in the morning is to reach Splash Mountain via the Walt Disney World Railroad. Board at Main Street Station and wait for the park to open. The train will pull out of the station at the same time the rope drops at the central hub end of Main Street. Ride to Frontierland Station (the first stop) and disembark. As you come down the stairs at the station, the entrance to Splash Mountain will be on your right. Because of the time required to unload at the station, train passengers won't arrive at Splash Mountain ahead of sprinters from the central hub. But they'll get there ahead of most other guests.

At Splash Mountain, if you ride in the front seat, you almost certainly will get wet. Riders elsewhere get splashed, but usually not doused. Since you don't know which seat you'll be assigned, go prepared. On a cool day, carry a plastic garbage bag. Tear holes in the bottom and sides to make a water-resistant (not waterproof) sack dress. Be sure to tuck the bag under your bottom. Leave your camera with a nonriding member of your group, or wrap it in plastic.

The scariest part of this adventure ride is the steep chute you see when standing in line, but the drop looks worse than it is. Despite reassurances, however, many children wig out after watching it. A mom from Grand Rapids, Michigan, recalls her kids' rather unique reaction:

> *We discovered after the fact that our children thought they would go underwater after the five-story drop and tried to hold their breath throughout the ride in preparation. They were really too preoccupied to enjoy the clever Brer Rabbit story.*

Another reader thought he was in the clear after his kids took *Alien Encounter* in stride, writing:

> *I'm sure you're going to think our sense of humor is really warped and a sign of the imminent collapse of our civilization, but my ten-year-old son and I found* Alien Encounter *funnier than it was scary, and very well done overall. Just to show, though, that it's often hard to predict what will push somebody's buttons the wrong way, at* Splash Mountain *the drop in the dark and the big final drop terrified both my kids (ages 10 and 13!). And they handled flume rides at other parks without a problem. It will probably be years before they get on a flume ride anywhere again.*

Big Thunder Mountain Railroad

What It Is: Tame, western-mining-themed roller coaster

Scope & Scale: Headliner

When to Go: Before 10 a.m. or in the hour before closing

Special Comments: Children must be 3'4" tall to ride. Those younger than age 7 must ride with an adult. Switching off option provided (pages 165–167).

Author's Rating: Great effects; relatively tame ride; not to be missed; ★★★★

Appeal by Age Group:

Pre-school	Grade School	Teens	Young Adults	Over 30	Senior Citizens
★★★	★★★★	★★★★	★★★★	★★★★	★★★

Duration of Ride: Almost 3½ minutes

Average Wait in Line per 100 People ahead of You: 2½ minutes

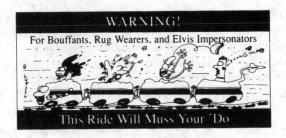

Assumes: 5 trains operating
Loading Speed: Moderate to fast

Description and Comments Roller coaster through and around a Disney "mountain." The idea is that you're on a runaway mine train during the Gold Rush. This roller coaster is about 5 on a "scary scale" of 10. First-rate examples of Disney creativity are showcased: realistic mining town, falling rocks, and an earthquake, all humorously animated.

Touring Tips A superb Disney experience, but not too wild a roller coaster. Emphasis is much more on the sights than on the thrill of the ride.

The opening nearby of Splash Mountain in 1992 forever changed traffic flow to Big Thunder Mountain Railroad. Adventuresome guests ride Splash Mountain first, then go next door to ride Big Thunder. This means much larger crowds in Frontierland all day and longer waits for Big Thunder Mountain. The best way to experience the Magic Kingdom's "mountains" is to ride Space Mountain when the park opens, Splash Mountain immediately afterward, then Big Thunder Mountain.

Guests experience Disney attractions differently. Consider this letter from a lady in Brookline, Massachusetts:

> Being in the senior citizens' category and having limited time, my friend and I confined our activities to those attractions rated as four or five stars for seniors. Because of your recommendation and because you listed it as "not to be missed," we waited for one hour to board the Big Thunder Mountain Railroad, [which you] rated a "5" on a scary scale of "10." After living through three-and-a-half minutes of pure terror, I will rate that attraction a "15" on a scary scale of "10." We were so busy holding on and screaming and even praying for our safety that we did not see any falling rocks, a mining town, or an earthquake. In our opinion, the Big Thunder Mountain Railroad should not be recommended for seniors or preschool children.

Another woman from New England writes:

> *My husband, who is 41, found Big Thunder Mountain too intense for his enjoyment, and feels that anyone who does not like roller coasters would not enjoy this ride.*

Country Bear Jamboree

What It Is: Audio-Animatronic country hoedown theater show

Scope & Scale: Major attraction

When to Go: Before 11:30 a.m., before a parade, or during the two hours before closing

Special Comments: Shows change at Christmas and during summer

Author's Rating: A Disney classic; ★★★

Appeal by Age Group:

Pre-school	Grade School	Teens	Young Adults	Over 30	Senior Citizens
★★★½	★★★	★★½	★★★	★★★	★★★

Duration of Presentation: 15 minutes

Preshow Entertainment: None

Probable Waiting Time: This attraction is very popular but has a comparatively small capacity. Waiting time between noon and 5:30 p.m. on a busy day will average 30–50 minutes.

Description and Comments   A charming cast of Audio-Animatronic (robotic) bears sing and stomp their way through a western-style hoedown. Although one of the Magic Kingdom's most humorous and upbeat shows, *Country Bear Jamboree* hasn't been revised for many moons, disappointing some repeat visitors.

One reader thinks the *Jamboree* is way past its prime, writing:

> Country Bear Jamboree—*"A Disney classic ★★★ "—You cannot be serious!! Although I must admit my ten-year-old daughter enjoyed it and got very angry about all the jokes we made about it for the remainder of the holiday!*

A dad from Cape Coral defends the show:

> *Don't sell the* Country Bear Jamboree *short. It may be boring to repeat visitors, but the look on our three-year-old son's face as he saw the show was priceless. In addition, he was astounded when he left the theater and found the mounted heads on the wall of the restaurant still singing away. It was the best thing we saw for him that day.*

Touring Tips   The *Jamboree* is extremely popular and draws large crowds, even early in the day.

Tom Sawyer Island and Fort Sam Clemens

What It Is: Outdoor walk-through exhibit / rustic playground

Scope & Scale: Minor attraction

When to Go: Midmorning through late afternoon

Special Comments: Closes at dusk

Author's Rating: The place for rambunctious kids; ★★★

Appeal by Age Group:

Pre-school	Grade School	Teens	Young Adults	Over 30	Senior Citizens
★★★★★	★★★★★	★★★	★★	★★	★★

Description and Comments   Tom Sawyer Island is a getaway within the park. It has hills to climb, a cave and windmill to explore, a tipsy barrel bridge to cross, and paths to follow. It's a delight for adults and a godsend for children who have been in tow all day. They love the freedom to explore and the excitement of firing air guns from the walls of Fort Sam Clemens. There even is a "secret" escape tunnel.

Touring Tips   Tom Sawyer Island isn't one of the Magic Kingdom's more celebrated attractions, but it's one of the park's better conceived ones. Attention to detail is excellent, and kids revel in its frontier atmosphere. It's a must for families with children ages 5 through 15. If your group is adults, visit on your second day or stop by on your first day after you've seen the attractions you most wanted to see.

Although children could spend a whole day on the island, plan on at least 20 minutes. Access is by raft from Frontierland; two operate simultaneously and the trip is pretty efficient, though you may have to stand in line to board both coming and going. Despite its limited menu, Aunt Polly's Dockside Inn on Tom Sawyer Island is our favorite place for lunch in the Magic Kingdom.

For a mother from Duncan, South Carolina, Tom Sawyer Island is as much a refuge as an attraction:

> I do have one tip for parents. In the afternoon when the crowds were at their peak, the weather [at] its hottest, and the kids started lagging behind, our organization began to suffer. We then retreated over to Tom Sawyer Island, which proved to be a true haven. My husband and I found a secluded bench and regrouped while sipping iced tea and eating delicious soft ice cream. Meanwhile, the kids were able to run freely

in the shade. Afterward, we were ready to tackle the park again refreshed and with direction once more. (Admittedly, I got this tip from another guidebook.)

According to a dad from Hampton, Connecticut, Tom Sawyer Island was a hit with three generations of his family:

> *Tom Sawyer Island was grandfather's favorite [attraction]—he fell asleep in the rocking chair on Aunt Polly's Landing while the kids explored the islands and mom and dad rested with cool drinks.*

Davy Crockett's Explorer Canoes

What It Is: Outdoor scenic canoe ride
Scope & Scale: Minor attraction
When to Go: Before noon or after 5 p.m.
Special Comments: Skip if the lines are long; closes at dusk
Author's Rating: The most fun way of seeing the Rivers of America; ★★★
Appeal by Age Group:

Pre-school	Grade School	Teens	Young Adults	Over 30	Senior Citizens
★★★★	★★★★	★★★½	★★★½	★★★	★★★

Duration of Ride: 9–15 minutes, depending on how fast you paddle
Average Wait in Line per 100 People ahead of You: 28 minutes
Assumes: 3 canoes operating
Loading Speed: Slow

Description and Comments Paddle-yourself ride around Tom Sawyer Island and Fort Sam Clemens. Same route and same sights as *Liberty Belle* Riverboat and Mike Fink Keelboats. Canoes operate only during the busy times of year.

Touring Tips The canoes represent one of three ways to see the same territory. Since canoes and keelboats are slower loading, we usually ride the riverboat. If you aren't up for a boat ride, walk around Tom Sawyer Island and Fort Sam Clemens for a different view of the same sights.

The Diamond Horseshoe Saloon Revue

What It Is: Live western song and dance show
Scope & Scale: Minor attraction
When to Go: Check the daily entertainment schedule
Special Comments: No Disney characters appear in this show

Author's Rating: Fast-paced and funny; ★★★

Appeal by Age Group:

Pre-school	Grade School	Teens	Young Adults	Over 30	Senior Citizens
★★	★★★	★★	★★★½	★★★½	★★★½

Duration of Show: About 40 minutes

Average Wait in Line per 100 People ahead of You: No wait

Description and Comments *The Diamond Horseshoe Saloon Revue* is a PG-rated version of a cattle-town saloon show, with comedy, song, and sometimes dancing. Audience members are conscripted to join the cast.

Disney World Problem 204: Too Short to Ride

Touring Tips The *Revue* was reservations-only until 1995, when it was reworked. Now, just walk in, have a seat, and wait for the show to begin. Times are listed in the entertainment column of the official guidemap. Sit in the balcony if you want to avoid being part of the show. Sandwiches, chips, cookies, and soft drinks are available at the bar. *The Diamond Horseshoe* is often overlooked by lunch crowds, especially between shows. We like to catch the *Revue* over lunch or after the afternoon parade.

Frontierland Shootin' Arcade

What It Is: Electronic shooting gallery

Scope & Scale: Diversion

When to Go: Whenever convenient

Special Comments: Costs 25¢ per play

Author's Rating: Very nifty shooting gallery; ★½

Appeal by Age Group:

Pre-school	Grade School	Teens	Young Adults	Over 30	Senior Citizens
★★★	★★★	★★★	★★	★★	★★

Description and Comments Very elaborate. One of few attractions not included in Magic Kingdom admission.

Touring Tips Good fun for "them what likes to shoot." Not a place to blow your time if you're on a tight schedule. If time allows, go on your second day.

Walt Disney World Railroad

Description and Comments Stops in Frontierland on its circle tour of the park. See the description under Main Street for additional details regarding sights along the route.

Touring Tips Pleasant, feet-saving link to Main Street and Mickey's Toontown Fair, but the Frontierland Station is usually more congested than those stations. Strollers aren't allowed aboard.

Frontierland Eateries and Shops

Description and Comments Coonskin caps and western-theme shopping. Fast-food eateries usually are very crowded between 11:30 a.m. and 2 p.m. An exception is Aunt Polly's Dockside Inn on Tom Sawyer Island. Under cover but outdoors, Aunt Polly's is a great place to escape the jostling crowds on a busy day. Sit on the veranda and watch riverboats and canoes paddle past on the waterway below. Fare is limited to cold fried chicken served with potato salad and a biscuit; ham and Swiss cheese sandwiches; and peanut butter and jelly sandwiches. Prices are reasonable, and food is good.

Touring Tips Don't waste time shopping unless that's what you came for or you have a very relaxed schedule. If the wait to board the raft to Tom Sawyer Island isn't prohibitive, lunch at Aunt Polly's Dockside Inn. Another time-saver is to eat at the *Diamond Horseshoe* just after a show has concluded.

Liberty Square

Liberty Square re-creates Colonial America at the time of the American Revolution. The architecture is Federal or Colonial. A real, 130-year-old live oak (dubbed the "Liberty Tree") lends dignity and grace to the setting.

The Hall of Presidents

What It Is: Audio-Animatronic historical theater presentation

Scope & Scale: Major attraction

When to Go: Anytime

Author's Rating: Impressive and moving; ★★★

Appeal by Age Group:

Pre-school	Grade School	Teens	Young Adults	Over 30	Senior Citizens
★	★★½	★★★	★★★½	★★★★	★★★★

Duration of Presentation: Almost 23 minutes

Preshow Entertainment: None

Probable Waiting Time: Lines for this attraction look awesome but are usually swallowed up as the theater exchanges audiences. Your wait will probably be the remaining time of the show that's in progress when you arrive. Even during the busiest times of day, waits rarely exceed 40 minutes.

Description and Comments A 23-minute, strongly inspirational and patriotic program highlighting milestones in American history. The performance climaxes with a roll call of presidents from Washington through the present, with a few words of encouragement from Presidents Lincoln and Clinton. A very moving show, coupled with one of Disney's best and most ambitious Audio-Animatronic (robotic) efforts. The production was updated in 1994, and the narration is by Maya Angelou.

Our high opinion notwithstanding, we receive a lot of mail from readers who get more than entertainment from *The Hall of Presidents*. A lady in St. Louis writes:

We always go to The Hall of Presidents *when my husband gets
cranky so he can take a nice nap.*

A young mother in Marion, Ohio, adds:

The Hall of Presidents *is a great place to breast feed.*

Touring Tips Detail and costumes are masterful. If your children fidget during the show, notice the presidents do, too. This attraction is one of the park's
most popular, particularly among older visitors, and draws large crowds from
11 a.m. through about 5 p.m. Don't be put off by long lines. The theater holds
more than 700 people, thus swallowing large lines at a single gulp when visitors are admitted. One show is always in progress while the lobby is being filled
for the next show. At less busy times, you probably will be admitted directly to
the lobby without waiting in line. When the lobby fills, those remaining in
line are held outside until those in the lobby move into the theater for the next
show, at which time another 700 people are admitted into the lobby.

Liberty Belle Riverboat

What It Is: Outdoor scenic boat ride

Scope & Scale: Major attraction

When to Go: Anytime

Author's Rating: Slow, relaxing, and scenic; ★★½

Appeal by Age Group:

Pre-school	Grade School	Teens	Young Adults	Over 30	Senior Citizens
★★★	★★★	★★½	★★★	★★★	★★★

Duration of Ride: About 16 minutes

Average Wait to Board: 10–14 minutes

Assumes: Normal operation

Description and Comments Large-capacity paddle-wheel riverboat navi-
gates the waters around Tom Sawyer Island and Fort Sam Clemens. A
beautiful craft, the riverboat provides a lofty perspective of Frontierland
and Liberty Square.

Touring Tips One of three boat rides that survey the same real estate. Since
Davy Crockett's Explorer Canoes and the Mike Fink Keelboats are slower
loading, we prefer the riverboat. If you don't want to ride, see the same
sights by hiking around Tom Sawyer Island.

The Haunted Mansion

What It Is: Haunted-house track ride

Scope & Scale: Major attraction

When to Go: Before 11:30 a.m. or after 8 p.m.

Special Comments: Frightens some very young children

Author's Rating: Some of Walt Disney World's best special effects; not to be missed; ★★★★

Appeal by Age Group:

Pre-school	Grade School	Teens	Young Adults	Over 30	Senior Citizens
(Varies)	★★★★★	★★★★	★★★★	★★★★	★★★★

Duration of Ride: 7-minute ride plus a 1½-minute preshow

Average Wait in Line per 100 People ahead of You: 2½ minutes

Assumes: Both "stretch rooms" operating

Loading Speed: Fast

Description and Comments More fun than scary, with some of the Magic Kingdom's best special effects. Disney's description—"Come face to face with 999 happy ghosts, ghouls, and goblins in a 'frightfully funny' adventure"—sums it up. Some children become overly anxious about what they think they'll see. Almost nobody is scared by the actual sights.

Touring Tips This attraction would be more at home in Fantasyland, but no matter. It's Disney at its best. Lines here ebb and flow more than those at most other Magic Kingdom high spots because the mansion is near *The Hall of Presidents* and the *Liberty Belle* Riverboat. These two attractions disgorge 700 and 450 people respectively when each show or ride ends, and many of these folks head straight for the mansion. If you can't go before 11:30 a.m. or after 8 p.m., try to slip in between crowds.

Mike Fink Keelboats

What It Is: Outdoor scenic boat ride

Scope & Scale: Minor attraction

When to Go: Before 11:30 a.m. or after 5 p.m.

Special Comments: Don't ride if the lines are long; closes at dusk

Author's Rating: ★★

Appeal by Age Group:

Pre-school	Grade School	Teens	Young Adults	Over 30	Senior Citizens
★★★	★★★	★★★	★★½	★★½	★★½

Duration of Ride: 9½ minutes

Average Wait in Line per 100 People ahead of You: 15 minutes
Assumes: 2 boats operating
Loading Speed: Slow

Description and Comments Small river keelboats circle Tom Sawyer Island and Fort Sam Clemens. The keelboat's top deck is exposed to the elements.

Touring Tips The boats cruise the same circle traveled by Davy Crockett's Explorer Canoes and the *Liberty Belle* Riverboat. Because keelboats and canoes load slowly, we prefer the riverboat. If you don't want to ride, see the same sights by hiking around Tom Sawyer Island.

Liberty Square Eateries and Shops

Description and Comments American crafts and souvenirs in shops. The one full-service restaurant, Liberty Tree Tavern, is often overlooked by lunch crowds.

Touring Tips Liberty Tree Tavern now offers a character dinner with a fixed menu served family-style. Characters aside, the meal may be the best in the Magic Kingdom. Priority seating is required, but it usually isn't hard to come by. Call ahead at (407) 939-3463 or check at the door of the restaurant.

Fantasyland

Fantasyland is the heart of the Magic Kingdom, a truly enchanting place spread gracefully like a miniature Alpine village beneath the lofty towers of Cinderella Castle.

It's a Small World

What It Is: World brotherhood–themed indoor boat ride
Scope & Scale: Major attraction
When to Go: Anytime
Author's Rating: Exponentially "cute"; ★★★
Appeal by Age Group:

Pre-school	Grade School	Teens	Young Adults	Over 30	Senior Citizens
★★★	★★★	★★½	★★½	★★★	★★★

Duration of Ride: Approximately 11 minutes
Average Wait in Line per 100 People ahead of You: 1¾ minutes
Assumes: Busy conditions with 30 or more boats operating

Loading Speed: Fast

Description and Comments   Happy, upbeat attraction with a catchy tune that will replay in your head for weeks. Small boats carry visitors on a tour around the world, with singing and dancing dolls showcasing the dress and culture of each nation. Almost everyone enjoys It's a Small World, but it stands, along with the *Enchanted Tiki Birds,* as an attraction that some could take or leave, while others think it's a masterpiece.

A woman from Holbrook, New York, apparently in the "leave it" camp, suggests that "Small World" would be much better "if each person got three to four softballs on the way in!"

A couple from the Carolinas added this:

> *It's a Small World, Mr. Toad's Wild Ride, and Snow White's Adventures simply don't stack up among the newer, flashier shows and attractions. While they certainly pack a lot of nostalgic value, this is off- set by their blandness and dated feel.*

Touring Tips   Cool off here during the heat of the day. It's a Small World loads fast with two waiting lines and usually is a good bet between 11 a.m. and 5 p.m.

Skyway to Tomorrowland

What It Is: Scenic transportation to Tomorrowland
Scope & Scale: Minor attraction
When to Go: Before noon or during special events
Special Comments: If there's a line, it probably will be quicker to walk
Author's Rating: Nice view; ★★½
Appeal by Age Group:

Pre- school	Grade School	Teens	Young Adults	Over 30	Senior Citizens
★★★★	★★★★	★★★	★★★	★★★	★★★

Duration of Ride: About 5 minutes one way
Average Wait in Line per 100 People ahead of You: 10 minutes
Assumes: 45 or more cars operating
Loading Speed: Moderate to slow

Description and Comments   Part of the Magic Kingdom internal trans- portation system, the Skyway is a chair lift that carries guests high above the park to Tomorrowland. The view is great, and sometimes the Skyway can save a little shoe leather. Usually, however, you can reach Tomorrow- land much faster afoot.

Touring Tips We take this scenic trip in the morning, during the afternoon character parade or evening parade, or just before closing. This ride opens later and closes earlier than other rides in Fantasyland. In other words, ride before crowds build, when they're otherwise occupied, or when they're declining. These times also provide the most dramatic and beautiful vistas. Parents can't take strollers on the Skyway.

Peter Pan's Flight ▷

What It Is: Indoor track ride
Scope & Scale: Minor attraction
When to Go: Before 10 a.m. or after 6 p.m.
Author's Rating: Happy, mellow, and well done; ★★★★
Appeal by Age Group:

Pre-school	Grade School	Teens	Young Adults	Over 30	Senior Citizens
★★★½	★★★½	★★★½	★★★½	★★★½	★★★½

Duration of Ride: A little over 3 minutes
Average Wait in Line per 100 People ahead of You: 5½ minutes
Assumes: Normal operation
Loading Speed: Moderate to slow

Description and Comments Though not considered a major attraction, Peter Pan's Flight is superbly designed and absolutely delightful, with a happy theme uniting unforgettable Disney characters, beautiful effects, and charming music. Because Peter Pan is so well done, it invites comparison with similar Fantasyland attractions. A man from Maryland writes:

> *We agree with the statement that of the three similar rides in Fantasyland (Peter Pan, Snow White, and Mr. Toad), Peter Pan is by far the best. We were able to ride all three in a row due to no lines and feel that Mr. Toad and possibly Snow White can be plowed to make room for new attractions.*

Touring Tips Because Peter Pan's Flight is very popular, count on long lines all day. Ride before 10 a.m., during a parade, or just before the park closes.

Legend of the Lion King ▷

What It Is: Live mixed-media and puppet theater show
Scope & Scale: Major attraction
When to Go: Before 11 a.m. and during parades
Author's Rating: Uplifting and fun; ★★★

Appeal by Age Group:

Pre-school	Grade School	Teens	Young Adults	Over 30	Senior Citizens
★★★	★★★½	★★★	★★★	★★★	★★★

Duration of Presentation: About 16 minutes

Preshow Entertainment: 7-minute preshow

Probable Waiting Time: 12 minutes (before 10:30 a.m.)

Description and Comments   An example of Disney's integrated marketing strategy, the attraction stimulates demand for *The Lion King* video. In production and script, the attraction is a close cousin to *Voyage of the Little Mermaid* at Disney-MGM Studios. The story is poignant and engaging, with some dark moments before it ends on a happy, triumphant note. Imaginative puppetry, animation, and special effects create an effective collage.

A Durham, North Carolina, couple had high praise for the *Lion King* show, writing:

> *We were mesmerized by the* Legend of the Lion King *and the* Voyage of the Little Mermaid *[at Disney-MGM Studios] shows. These represent a level of sophistication in execution and in spectacle that are several orders of magnitude superior to the standard amusement park show (more akin to a good off-Broadway production).*

Touring Tips Popularity of *Legend of the Lion King* has grown as guests have become more familiar with its characters and their story. See this show in early morning or during live events. The audience must stand for the preshow in the waiting area. If you have small children, maneuver them to the front of the room so that they can see. The theater holds about 500 persons, thus most of the line outside disappears each time guests are admitted. Even so, after 10 a.m. budget a 40-minute wait.

Cinderella's Golden Carrousel

What It Is: Merry-go-round
Scope & Scale: Minor attraction
When to Go: Before 11 a.m. or after 8 p.m.
Special Comments: Adults enjoy the beauty and nostalgia of this ride
Author's Rating: A beautiful children's ride; ★★½
Appeal by Age Group:

Pre-school	Grade School	Teens	Young Adults	Over 30	Senior Citizens
★★★★	★★½	★	★★½	★★★	★★★

Duration of Ride: About 2 minutes
Average Wait in Line per 100 People ahead of You: 5 minutes
Assumes: Normal staffing
Loading Speed: Slow

Description and Comments One of the most elaborate and beautiful merry-go-rounds you'll ever see, especially when the lights are on.

Touring Tips Unless young children in your party insist on riding, appreciate this attraction from the sidelines. While lovely to look at, the Carrousel loads and unloads very slowly.

Mr. Toad's Wild Ride

What It Is: Indoor track ride
Scope & Scale: Minor attraction
When to Go: Before 11 a.m. or after 6 p.m.
Author's Rating: Just okay; ★★
Appeal by Age Group:

Pre-school	Grade School	Teens	Young Adults	Over 30	Senior Citizens
★★★	★★★	★★★	★★½	★★½	★★½

Duration of Ride: About 2¼ minutes

Average Wait in Line per 100 People ahead of You: 5½ minutes

Assumes: Both tracks operating

Loading Speed: Slow

Description and Comments   This amusement park spook house doesn't live up to many visitors' expectations or to Disney's reputation for high quality. The facade is intriguing; the size of the building that houses the attraction suggests an elaborate ride. But the building is halved, with a similar version of the same ride in each side. Each half has a separate line. Incidently, plans are afoot to send Mr. Toad on the road and install an attraction based on Winnie the Pooh in his place. Stay tuned.

Touring Tips   We receive lots of letters disagreeing with our criticism of this ride. Clearly, Mr. Toad has his advocates. If you're on a tight schedule, don't wait very long for Mr. Toad. If you have two days allotted for the Magic Kingdom, or just want to add your opinion to the controversy, ride. If you want to be a supertoad, try both sides.

Snow White's Adventures

What It Is: Indoor track ride

Scope & Scale: Minor attraction

When to Go: Before 11 a.m. and after 6 p.m.

Special Comments: Terrifying to many young children

Author's Rating: Worth seeing if the wait isn't long; ★★½

Appeal by Age Group:

Pre-school	Grade School	Teens	Young Adults	Over 30	Senior Citizens
★★	★★★	★★½	★★½	★★½	★★½

Duration of Ride: Almost 2½ minutes

Average Wait in Line per 100 People ahead of You: 6¼ minutes

Assumes: Normal operation

Loading Speed: Moderate to slow

Description and Comments   Mine cars travel through a spook house showing Snow White as she narrowly escapes harm at the hands of the wicked witch. Action and effects are a cut above Mr. Toad's Wild Ride, but not as good as Peter Pan's Flight.

Touring Tips   We get more mail about this ride than any other Disney attraction. It terrifies many children age 6 and younger. Though a 1995

upgrade gave Snow White a larger role, the witch (who is relentless and ubiquitous) continues to be the focal character. Many readers tell us their children have refused to ride any attraction that operates in the dark after having experienced Snow White's Adventures.

A mother from Knoxville, Tennessee, writes:

> *The outside looks cute and fluffy, but inside, the evil witch just keeps coming at you. My five-year-old, who rode Space Mountain three times and took The Great Movie Ride's monster from* Alien *right in stride, was near panic when our car stopped unexpectedly twice during Snow White. [After Snow White] my six-year-old niece spent a lot of time asking "if a witch will jump out at you" before other rides. So I suggest that you explain a little more what this ride is about. It's tough on preschoolers who are expecting forest animals and dwarfs.*

A mom from Long Island, New York, adds:

> *My daughter screamed the whole time and was shot for the day. Grampa kept asking, "Where in the hell is Snow White?"*

Experience Snow White if lines aren't too long, or on a second day at the park.

20,000 Leagues Under the Sea

This submarine ride based on the Disney film of the same name became the subject of a prolonged corporate argument. Closed four years ago for refurbishment, the attraction never reopened. For almost two years, while Disney bigwigs debated 20,000 Leagues' fate, the submarines sat in the water and deteriorated. Finally in 1997, with no decision having been made, the subs were hauled from the lagoon. For now, the former attraction's loading area is being used for character greetings. While there's some agreement that 20,000 Leagues will never reopen, no one is sure what will happen to the lagoon.

Ariel's Grotto

What It Is: Interactive fountain and character greeting area
Scope & Scale: Minor attraction
When to Go: Before 10 a.m. and after 9 p.m.
Author's Rating: One of the most elaborate of the character-greeting venues; ★★★
Appeal by Age Group:

Pre-school	Grade School	Teens	Young Adults	Over 30	Senior Citizens
★★★★★	★★★★	★★	★★	★★	★★

Average Wait in Line per 100 People ahead of You: 30 minutes

Description and Comments   On the submarine-lagoon side of Dumbo, Ariel's Grotto consists of a small children's play area with an interactive fountain and a rock grotto where Ariel, the Little Mermaid, poses for photos and signs autographs. If "interactive fountain" is new to you, it means an opportunity for your children to get ten times wetter than a trout. Can you say "hy-po-ther-mi-a"?

Touring Tips   The Grotto is small, and the wait to meet Ariel is usually long. Because kids in line are fresh from the fountain, it's very difficult for adults to remain dry. A mother from Hagerstown, Maryland, said the experience was "like being packed in a pen with wet cocker spaniels."

If your children spot the Grotto before you do, there's no turning back. Except before 10 a.m., count on a long queue and a 20–40 minute wait to see Ariel. Then there's the fountain. Allow your children to disrobe to the legal limit. (Don't bother with umbrellas or ponchos, because water squirts up from below.) When you're finished meeting Ariel, you will have to navigate an armada of variously aged males plowing upstream through the exit to admire Ariel's cleavage.

Dumbo the Flying Elephant

What It Is: Disneyfied midway ride

Scope & Scale: Minor attraction

When to Go: Before 10 a.m. and after 9 p.m.

Author's Rating: An attractive children's ride; ★★★

Appeal by Age Group:

Pre-school	Grade School	Teens	Young Adults	Over 30	Senior Citizens
★★★★★	★★★★	★★	★½	★½	★½

Duration of Ride: 1½ minutes

Average Wait in Line per 100 People ahead of You: 20 minutes

Assumes: Normal staffing

Loading Speed: Slow

Description and Comments   A tame, happy children's ride based on the lovable flying elephant, Dumbo. Despite being little different from rides at state fairs and amusement parks, Dumbo is the favorite Magic Kingdom attraction of many younger children.

A lot of readers take us to task for lumping Dumbo with carnival rides. A reader from Armdale, Nova Scotia, writes:

> *I think you have acquired a jaded attitude. I know [Dumbo] is not
> for everybody, but when we took our oldest child (then just four), the
> sign at the end of the line said there would be a 90-minute wait. He
> knew and he didn't care, and he and I stood in the hot afternoon sun
> for 90 blissful minutes waiting for his 90-second flight. Anything that a
> four-year-old would wait for that long and that patiently must be
> pretty special.*

Touring Tips   If Dumbo is critical to your child's happiness, make it your
first stop, preferably within 15 minutes of park opening. Also, be aware
that there is an opening-bell race to Dumbo similar to the classic Space
Mountain stampede, only with more strollers than people on foot. And
though the racers are smaller and younger, they are (as a Baltimore woman
discovered) just as tough:

> *I heard a woman say to her husband and small child, "As soon as
> we get to Main Street, we will run, not walk, RUN to ride Dumbo. If
> we stop on Main Street we may as well forget riding the ride." Gulp. I
> didn't realize the competition was so fierce.*

Mad Tea Party

What It Is: Midway-type spinning ride
Scope & Scale: Minor attraction
When to Go: Before 11 a.m. and after 5 p.m.
Special Comments: You can make the tea cups spin faster
   by turning the wheel in the center of the cup
Author's Rating: Fun, but not worth the wait; ★★
Appeal by Age Group:

Pre-school	Grade School	Teens	Young Adults	Over 30	Senior Citizens
★★★★	★★★★	★★★★	★★★	★★	★★

Duration of Ride: 1½ minutes
Average Wait in Line per 100 People ahead of You: 7½ minutes
Assumes: Normal staffing
Loading Speed: Slow

Description and Comments   Riders whirl feverishly in big tea cups. *Alice
in Wonderland*'s Mad Hatter provides the theme. A version of this ride,
without Disney characters, can be found at every local carnival. Teenagers
like to lure adults onto the tea cups, then turn the wheel in the middle,
making the cup spin faster, until the adults are plastered against the side of

the cup and on the verge of throwing up. Unless your life's ambition is to be the test subject in a human centrifuge, don't even consider getting on this ride with anyone younger than 21.

Touring Tips   This ride, well done but not unique, is notoriously slow loading. Skip it on a busy schedule—if the kids will let you. Ride the morning of your second day if your schedule is more relaxed.

Fantasyland Eateries and Shops

Description and Comments   Many of the Magic Kingdom visitors we surveyed wanted to know, "What is in the castle?" or "Can we go up into the castle?" The answer is: You can't see it all, but you can inspect a fair-sized chunk if you eat at Cinderella's Royal Table in the castle.

However, you don't have to eat at Cinderella's Royal Table to see Cinderella. A mother from Stone Mountain, Georgia, reports:

Cinderella greets diners in the waiting area of Cinderella's Royal Table at Cinderella Castle. You can meet her there without the torture of eating at the restaurant. Just enter the area through the left door by the hostess stand. The hostess at the door can tell you when Cinderella is scheduled to appear.

Touring Tips   Priority seating is required at Cinderella's Royal Table. Call (407) 939-3463 before you leave home, preferably 60 days in advance to ensure a table. We don't recommend eating at Cinderella's Royal Table if you're on a tight schedule or are sensitive about paying fancy prices for average food. If you plan to spend two days in the Magic Kingdom and are curious about the castle, try Cinderella's your second day. If there are young children in your party, ask when Cinderella will be present before making your priority seating.

Other Fantasyland lunch options include Lumière's Kitchen (formerly Gurgi's Munchies & Crunchies), where parents can obtain special lunches for children, and The Pinocchio Village Haus, which regrettably no longer serves bratwurst.

Fantasyland offers abundant specialty and souvenir shopping, but don't waste time in the shops unless you have a relaxed schedule or shopping is a priority.

Mickey's Toontown Fair

Mickey's Toontown Fair is the first new "land" to be added to the Magic Kingdom since its opening and the only land that doesn't connect to the central hub. Attractions include an opportunity to meet Mickey Mouse, Mickey's house, Minnie Mouse's house, and a child-sized roller coaster.

Mickey's Toontown Fair is sandwiched between Fantasyland and Tomorrowland, like an afterthought, on about three acres formerly part of the Tomorrowland Speedway. It's the smallest of the lands and more like an attraction than a section of the park. Though you can wander in on a somewhat obscure path from Fantasyland or on a totally obscure path from Tomorrowland, Mickey's Toontown Fair generally receives guests arriving by the Walt Disney World Railroad.

Opened in 1988 and reworked in 1996 with a county fair theme, Mickey's Toontown Fair now serves as the Magic Kingdom's character-greeting headquarters. The Fair provides a place where Disney characters are available to guests on a continuing and reliable schedule. Mickey, in the role of the Fair's chief judge, meets guests for photos and autographs in the Judge's Tent. Other characters appear in the Toontown Hall of Fame. Characters are available throughout the day except during parades.

In general, Mickey's Toontown Fair doesn't handle crowds very well. If your children are into collecting character autographs and want to enjoy the various Toontown attractions without extraordinary waits, we recommend touring first thing in the morning. If you only have one day to visit the Magic Kingdom and hitting the children-oriented attractions is a priority, head first to Fantasyland and ride Dumbo and Peter Pan, then split for Toontown. In Toontown, ride Goofy's Barnstormer first and then tour Mickey's and Minnie's houses. Go next to the Toontown Hall of Fame for character pics and autographs. For adults without children, Toontown is visually interesting but otherwise expendable.

Mickey's Country House & Judge's Tent

What It Is: Walk-through tour of Mickey's house and meeting with
Mickey

Scope & Scale: Minor attraction

When to Go: Before 11:30 a.m. and after 4:30 p.m.

Author's Rating: Well done; ★★½

Appeal by Age Group:

Pre-school	Grade School	Teens	Young Adults	Over 30	Senior Citizens
★★★½	★★★	★★½	★★½	★★½	★★½

Duration of Tour: 15–30 minutes (depending on the crowd)

Average Wait in Line per 100 People ahead of You: 20 minutes

Assumes: Normal staffing

Touring Speed: Slow

Description and Comments   Mickey's Country House is the starting point of a self-guided tour through the famous mouse's house, into his backyard, and past Pluto's doghouse.

Touring Tips   Discerning observers will see immediately that Mickey's Country House is a cleverly devised queuing area for delivering guests to Mickey's Judge's Tent for the Mouse Encounter. It also heightens anticipation by revealing the corporate symbol on a more personal level. Mickey's Country House is well conceived and contains a lot of Disney memorabilia. Children touch *everything* as they proceed through the house, hoping to find some artifact not welded into the set. (An especially tenacious child during one of our visits actually ripped a couple of books from a bookcase.)

Meeting Mickey and touring his house are best done during the first two hours the park is open, or in the evening. If meeting Mickey is your child's priority, take the railroad from Main Street to Mickey's Toontown Fair as soon as you enter the park. Some children are so obsessed with seeing Mickey that they can't enjoy anything else until they have him in the rearview mirror.

Minnie's Country House

What It Is: Walk-through exhibit

Scope & Scale: Minor attraction

When to Go: Before 11:30 a.m. and after 4:30 p.m.

Author's Rating: Great detail; ★★

Appeal by Age Group:

Pre-school	Grade School	Teens	Young Adults	Over 30	Senior Citizens
★★★	★★★	★★½	★★½	★★½	★★½

Duration of Tour: About 10 minutes

Average Wait in Line per 100 People ahead of You: 12 minutes

Touring Speed: Slow

Description and Comments   Minnie's Country House offers a self-guided tour through the rooms and backyard of Mickey's main squeeze. Similar to Mickey's Country House, only predictably more feminine, Minnie's also showcases fun Disney memorabilia. Among highlights of the short tour are the fanciful appliances in Minnie's kitchen.

Touring Tips   The main difference between Mickey's and Minnie's houses is that Mickey is home to receive guests. Minnie was never home during our visits. We did, however, bump into her on the street and in the Toontown Hall of Fame. Minnie's Country House is one of the more accessible attractions in the Fair, but we nonetheless recommend touring early or late in the day.

Toontown Hall of Fame

What It Is: Character-greeting venue

Scope & Scale: Minor attraction

When to Go: Before 10:30 a.m. and after 5:30 p.m.

Author's Rating: You want characters? We got 'em! ★★

Appeal by Age Group:

Pre-school	Grade School	Teens	Young Adults	Over 30	Senior Citizens
★★★★	★★★★	★★	★★	★★	★★

Duration of Greeting: About 7–10 minutes

Average Wait in Line per 100 People ahead of You: 35 minutes

Touring Speed: Slow

Description and Comments   The Toontown Hall of Fame is at the end of a small plaza between Mickey's and Minnie's houses. Just inside to the right are entrances to three queuing areas. Signs over each suggest, somewhat ambiguously, which characters you will meet. Famous Friends include Minnie, Goofy, Donald, Pluto, and sometimes Uncle Scrooge, Chip 'n' Dale, Roger Rabbit, and Daisy. The 100 Acre Wood Friends are mostly Winnie the Pooh characters but may include any character that fits the forest theme. Fairy Tale Friends are Snow White, various dwarfs, Belle, the Beast, Sleeping Beauty, Prince Charming, etc. Other categories we have seen include Mickey's Pals, Disney Princesses, and Disney Villains.

Each category of characters occupies a greeting room where 15–20 guests are admitted at a time. They're allowed to stay 7–10 minutes, long enough for a photo, autograph, and hug with each character.

Touring Tips   If your children want to visit each category, you'll have to queue up three times. Each line is long and slow-moving, and during busier hours you can lose a lot of time here. While Famous Friends are slightly more popular than the other two categories, the longest wait is usually to see the Fairy Tale Friends. The reason is that most Fairy Tale Friends are "face characters," actresses who strongly resemble the character they portray and don't wear any head-covering costume. Face characters are allowed to speak and thus engage children in conversation, prolonging the visit. All characters work in 25-minute shifts, with breaks on the hour and half hour. Because characters in each category change frequently during the day, it's possible to see quite an assortment if you keep recirculating.

A big problem at the Toontown Hall of Fame is that you never know which specific characters in each category you will see. Some kids collecting character autographs wait 35–50 minutes to find characters whose autographs they already have. Before getting in line, ask the Disney greeter which characters are present. If the cast member won't or can't tell you, walk over to the exit and ask departing guests which characters are on duty. Remember that there is some switching of characters on the hour and half hour.

A mother from Winchester, Virginia, reported her solution to seeing characters without waiting in lines:

> *Some of the things that surprised us, both good and bad, were the crowding and lines to see the characters. We stopped to visit a few, especially when we got lucky with a shorter line, but mostly we couldn't justify*

stopping at many because we would have missed so many attractions. The best thing we did with regard to the characters was to have the Winnie the Pooh character dinner at The Crystal Palace. Tigger and Pooh are my kids' favorites, and the characters were VERY attentive; my just-turned three-year-old was in Heaven and did not have to fight crowds.

A thirty-something mother of two comments:

For parents with smaller children at the Magic Kingdom, take the train to Toontown as soon as the park opens—my six-year-old and eight-year-old rode Goofy's Barnstormer roller coaster seven times without getting off. After others wanted on, they moved on to the Toontown Hall of Fame for autographs—No lines!!

A Concord, Massachussets, mom suggests:

Mickey's Toontown was our longest line—should be done RIGHT AT OPENING!

Although time-consuming, the Toontown Hall of Fame offers one of the largest and most dependably available collection of characters in Walt Disney World. If your children (or you) are character hounds, visit the Hall of Fame before 10 a.m. In early morning, you can meet all three categories in less than an hour.

The Barnstormer at Goofy's Wiseacres Farm

What It Is: Small roller coaster

Scope & Scale: Minor attraction

When to Go: Before 10:30 a.m., during parades and in the evening, and just before the park closes

Author's Rating: Great for little ones, but not worth the wait for adults; ★★

Appeal by Age Group:

Pre-school	Grade School	Teens	Young Adults	Over 30	Senior Citizens
★★★★	★★★	★★½	★★½	★★½	★★

Duration of Ride: About 53 seconds

Average Wait in Line per 100 People ahead of You: 7 minutes

Assumes: Normal staffing

Loading Speed: Slow

Description and Comments The Barnstormer is a very small roller coaster.

The ride is zippy but super short. In fact, of the 53 seconds the ride is in motion, 32 seconds are consumed in leaving the loading area, being racheted up the first hill, and braking into the off-loading area. The actual time you spend careering around the track is 21 seconds.

A 42-year-old woman from Westport, Connecticut, warns adults that the Barnstormer may not be as tame as it looks:

> *Goofy's Barnstormer was a nightmare that should have gone in your "Eats Adults" section. It looked so innocent—nothing hidden in the dark, over quickly. . . . It took hours to stop feeling nauseated and my eight-year-old son and I were terrified.*

Touring Tips The cars of this dinky coaster are too small for most adults and whiplash taller people. This plus the limited capacity equal an engineering marvel along the lines of Dumbo. Parties without children should skip the Barnstormer. If you're touring with children, you have a problem. Like Dumbo, the ride is visually appealing. All kids want to ride, subjecting the whole family to slow-moving lines. If the Barnstormer is high on your children's hit parade, try to ride before 9:30 a.m.

Donald's Boat

What It Is: Interactive fountain and playground
Scope & Scale: Diversion
When to Go: Anytime
Special Comments: Children can get wet
Author's Rating: Spontaneous—yeah! ★★½
Appeal by Age Group:

Pre-school	Grade School	Teens	Young Adults	Over 30	Senior Citizens
★★★★	★★½	★	★½	★½	★½

Description and Comments Water spurts randomly from tiny holes in the side of Donald's Boat. The idea is that the boat is springing leaks. Children walk around plugging holes with their hands and trying to guess where the water will squirt next.

Touring Tips Young children love this attraction and will jump around in the spurting water until they're drenched. Our advice: "GET NAKED!" Even on cooler days, bare skin dries faster than wet clothes. Strip your munchkins to the legal limit and toss them into the fray. If you really want to plan ahead, bring extra underwear and a towel.

Tomorrowland

Tomorrowland is a mix of rides and experiences relating to the technological development of man and what life will be like in the future. If this sounds like Epcot's theme, it's because Tomorrowland was a breeding ground for ideas that spawned Epcot. Yet, Tomorrowland and Epcot are very different in more than scale. Epcot is mostly educational. Tomorrowland is more for fun, depicting the future as envisioned in science fiction.

Exhaustive renovation of Tomorrowland was completed in 1995. Before refurbishing, Tomorrowland's 24-year-old buildings resembled 1970s motels more than anyone's vision of the future. The new design is ageless, revealing the future as imagined by dreamers and scientists in the 1920s and '30s. Today's Tomorrowland conjures visions of Buck Rogers, fanciful mechanical rockets, and metallic cities spread beneath towering obelisks. Disney calls the renovated Tomorrowland the "Future That Never Was," while *Newsweek* dubbed it "retro-future."

In the new Tomorrowland, *Alien Encounter* replaced *Mission to Mars* (formerly *Spaceflight to the Moon*). Walt Disney's *Carousel of Progress* has been jazzed up and moved forward in time, and *Transportarium* has been recast as *The Timekeeper*. The StarJets ride, now sporting a campy Jules Verne look, is higher off the ground but still runs in circles. Its new name is Astro Orbiter. The WEDway PeopleMover has become the Tomorrowland Transit Authority. Venerable Space Mountain continues to hold its own, but the Tomorrowland Speedway and Skyway to Fantasyland seem incongruous.

Space Mountain

What It Is: Roller coaster in the dark

Scope & Scale: Super headliner

When to Go: First thing when the park opens, between 6 and 7 p.m., or during the hour before closing

Special Comments: Great fun and action; much wilder than Big Thunder Mountain Railroad. Children must be 3'8" tall to ride, and if younger than age 7, must be accompanied by an adult. Switching off option provided (pages 165–167).

Author's Rating: A great roller coaster with excellent special effects; not to be missed; ★★★★

Appeal by Age Group:

Pre-school	Grade School	Teens	Young Adults	Over 30	Senior Citizens
†	★★★★★	★★★★★	★★★★½	★★★★	†

† Some preschoolers loved Space Mountain; others were frightened. The sample size of senior citizens who experienced this ride was too small to develop an accurate rating.

Duration of Ride: Almost 3 minutes

Average Wait in Line per 100 People ahead of You: 3 minutes

Assumes: Two tracks dispatching at 21-second intervals

Loading Speed: Moderate to fast

A teen from Colchester, Connecticut, wrote us about her bad hair day:

> *WARN Space Mountain riders to take off hair scrunchies. I lost my best one on it and couldn't get it back. This ride was fast, curvy, and very hairdo messing.*

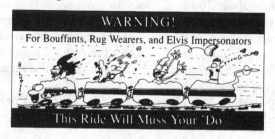

Description and Comments Totally enclosed in a mammoth futuristic structure, Space Mountain is a creative and engineering marvel. The theme is a space flight through dark recesses of the galaxy. Effects are superb, and the ride is the fastest and wildest in the Magic Kingdom. As a roller coaster, Space Mountain is much zippier than Big Thunder Mountain Railroad.

Touring Tips People who can handle a fairly wild roller coaster ride will take Space Mountain in stride. What sets Space Mountain apart is that cars plummet through darkness, with only occasional lighting. Half the fun of Space Mountain is not knowing where the car will go next.

Space Mountain is the favorite attraction of many Magic Kingdom visitors ages 7 to 50. Each morning before opening, particularly during summer and holiday periods, several hundred S.M. "junkies" crowd the rope barriers at the central hub, awaiting the signal to sprint the 250 yards to the ride's entrance. The "Space Mountain Morning Mini Marathon," as our researchers called it, pits parents against offspring, brother against sister, co-eds against truck drivers, nuns against beauticians. If you want to ride Space Mountain without a long wait, you'd better join the marathon, because five minutes after opening, Space Mountain's line is longer than any other in the Magic Kingdom.

There was a time Disney personnel tried to keep guests from running to Space Mountain (they still tell you not to run), but even in the Magic Kingdom reality can't be denied: a dozen Disney security personnel cannot control several hundred stampeding, flipped-out, early-morning space cadets. So here you are, a dental hygienist from Toledo thinking you'd like to ride Space Mountain. Well, Virginia, tie up them Reeboks and get ready to run. You're in the big league now.

But first, a word from the coach. To get ahead of the competition, be one of the first in the park. Proceed to the end of Main Street and cut right past The Plaza Restaurant, stopping under an archway that says:

The Plaza Pavilion Terrace Dining

where a Disney worker will be standing behind a rope barrier. From this point, you're about 100 yards closer to Space Mountain, on a route through The Plaza Pavilion, than your competition waiting to dash from the central hub. From here, middle-aged folks walking fast can beat most teens sprinting from the central hub. And if you're up to some modest jogging, well . . . Another advantage of starting from The Plaza Pavilion entrance: you wait in the shade.

Lest you take the Mini Marathon lightly, heed the words of those who have experienced it. From an Oakland, Tennessee, teen:

We waited for the half hour, made new friends and discussed the "Space Mountain Mini Marathon." I wasn't sure if I believed it or not, but when the announcement came over the loudspeaker and the rope dropped, we all took off. First walking fast, then jogging, then running. What seemed like thousands of people trucking it as fast as their legs could take them over what felt like miles even though no one was sure just how far it actually was because the adrenaline was pumping and no one was stopping to look at the scenery! Well, in that mess I lost my Mom. She quit, figuring she didn't want to ride anything bad enough to fall over with a heart attack. I made it. I don't know how, but I did it. I was also one of the first 25 or 30 people in line. I let some people go on in front of me because I was waiting for my Mom who never showed up. The Mini Marathon is seriously underrated. There are thousands more people involved in this than I ever imagined, and it covers what seems like the same distance as an actual marathon with people running much faster. It really pays to get there early. In updated versions of your book, please stress this. Even though Space Mountain wasn't as great as I had hoped, I wasn't disappointed. I recommend that everyone young or old, no matter who they are, should be in the marathon and ride Space Mountain at least once. It is incredible, and

*no matter where you go in the world, you will never experience any-
thing like the Space Mountain Mini Marathon.*

A family of four from Barre, Vermont, tells us:

> *Running to Space Mountain when the gate opened almost gave us a
> heart attack. Felt I was part of a wildebeest stampede out of* The Lion
> King *movie.*

Couples touring with children too small to ride Space Mountain can
both ride without waiting in line twice by taking advantage of "switching
off." Here's how it works: When you enter the Space Mountain line, tell
the first Disney attendant (Greeter One) that you want to switch off. The
attendant will allow you, your spouse, and your small child (or children) to
continue together, phoning ahead to tell Greeter Two to expect you. When
you reach Greeter Two (at the turnstile near the boarding area), you'll be
given specific directions. One of you will proceed to ride, while the other
stays with the kids. Whoever rides will be admitted by the unloading attendant to stairs leading back up to the boarding area. Here you switch off.
The second parent rides, and the first parent takes the kids down the stairs
to the unloading area where everybody is reunited and exits together.
Switching off is also available at Big Thunder Mountain Railroad and
Splash Mountain.

All riders have their own seat. Parents whose children meet the height
and age requirements for Space Mountain can't sit next to their kids.

If you don't catch Space Mountain early in the morning, try again during the hour before closing. Often, would-be riders are held in line outside
the entrance until all those previously in line have ridden, thus emptying
the attraction. The appearance from the outside is that the line is enormous when, in fact, the only people waiting are those visible. This crowd-
control technique, known as "stacking," discourages visitors from getting
in line. Stacking is used in several Disney rides and attractions during the
hour before closing to ensure that the ride will be able to close on schedule.
It is also used to keep the number of people waiting inside from overwhelming the air conditioning. For those who aren't put off by the apparently long line, the wait is usually no longer than if you had been allowed
to queue inside.

Splash Mountain, which opened in 1992, siphons off some guests who
would have made Space Mountain their first stop. Even so, a mob rushes to
Space Mountain as soon as the park opens. If you especially like the thrill
attractions and have only one day, see *Alien Encounter* first in the morning,
followed by Space Mountain, Big Thunder Mountain Railroad, and Splash
Mountain.

If you're a Disney resort guest eligible for early entry on designated days, you can ride Space Mountain to your heart's content for a half hour to an hour before the general public is admitted.

If you're an early entrant and Big Thunder Mountain Railroad and Splash Mountain also are high on your list, see *Alien Encounter* and ride Space Mountain (as well as Fantasyland attractions) until 10 to 15 minutes before the hour the general public is admitted. At this time, return to Fantasyland and continue to the boundary of Fantasyland and Liberty Square. Wait there for the rest of the park to open. When it does, enter Liberty Square and move quickly along the Liberty Square and Frontierland waterfronts to Big Thunder Mountain Railroad and Splash Mountain.

If you aren't eligible for early entry, visit the Magic Kingdom on a day when the program isn't in effect and make Space Mountain and *Alien Encounter* your first two attractions of the day. If you aren't eligible for early entry but your schedule requires that you visit on an early-entry day, ride Splash Mountain and Big Thunder Mountain Railroad first, then try to catch Space Mountain and *Alien Encounter* during a parade or just before the park closes.

Tomorrowland Speedway

What It Is: Drive-'em-yourself miniature cars

Scope & Scale: Major attraction

When to Go: Before 11 a.m. and after 5 p.m.

Special Comments: Must be 4'4" tall to drive

Author's Rating: Boring for adults (★); great for preschoolers

Appeal by Age Group:

Pre-school	Grade School	Teens	Young Adults	Over 30	Senior Citizens
★★★½	★★★	★	½	½	½

Duration of Ride: About 4¼ minutes

Average Wait in Line per 100 People ahead of You: 4½ minutes

Assumes: 285-car turnover every 20 minutes

Loading Speed: Slow

Description and Comments   An elaborate miniature raceway with gasoline-powered cars that travel up to 7 miles per hour. The raceway, with sleek cars and racing noises, is quite alluring. Unfortunately, the cars poke along on a track, leaving the driver little to do. Pretty ho-hum for most adults and teenagers. The height requirement excludes small children who would enjoy the ride.

Touring Tips   This ride is visually appealing but definitely one adults can skip. Preschoolers, however, love it. If your child is too short to drive, ride along and allow the child to steer the car on its guide rail while you work the foot pedal.

A mom from North Billerica, Massachusetts, writes:

> *I was truly amazed by the number of adults in the line. Please emphasize to your readers that these cars travel on a guided path and are not a whole lot of fun. The only reason I could think of for adults to be in the line would be an insane desire to go on absolutely every ride at Disney World. The other feature about the cars is that they tend to pile up at the end, so it takes almost as long to get off as it did to get on. Parents riding with their preschoolers should keep the car going as slow as [possible] without stalling. This prolongs the preschooler's joy and decreases the time you will have to wait at the end.*

The line for the Tomorrowland Speedway snakes across a pedestrian bridge to the loading areas. For a shorter wait, turn right off the bridge to the first loading area (rather than continuing to the second).

Skyway to Fantasyland

What It Is: Scenic overhead transportation to Fantasyland
Scope & Scale: Minor attraction
When to Go: Before noon and during special events
Special Comments: If there's a line, it's probably quicker to walk
Author's Rating: Nice view; ★★½
Appeal by Age Group:

Pre-school	Grade School	Teens	Young Adults	Over 30	Senior Citizens
★★★★	★★★★	★★★	★★★	★★★	★★★

Duration of Ride: Approximately 5 minutes one way
Average Wait in Line per 100 People ahead of You: 10 minutes
Assumes: 45 or more cars operating
Loading Speed: Moderate

Description and Comments   Chair lift transports you from Tomorrowland to the far corner of Fantasyland near its border with Liberty Square. The view is one of the best in the Magic Kingdom, but walking is usually faster.

Touring Tips   Unless lines are short, Skyway transportation won't save you time. As a ride, however, it affords some incredible views. The Skyway sometimes opens later and closes earlier than other rides in Tomorrowland. Strollers aren't allowed on the ride.

Astro Orbiter

What It Is: Buck Rogers–style rockets revolving around a central axis

Scope & Scale: Minor attraction

When to Go: Before 11 a.m. or after 5 p.m.

Special Comments: This attraction, formerly StarJets, is not as innocuous as it appears

Author's Rating: Not worth the wait; ★★

Appeal by Age Group:

Pre-school	Grade School	Teens	Young Adults	Over 30	Senior Citizens
★★★★	★★★	★★½	★★½	★★	★

Duration of Ride: 1½ minutes

Average Wait in Line per 100 People ahead of You: 13½ minutes

Assumes: Normal staffing

Loading Speed: Slow

Description and Comments Though recently upgraded and visually appealing, the Astro Orbiter is still a slow-loading carnival ride. The fat little rocketships simply fly in circles. The best thing about the Astro Orbiter is the nice view when you're aloft.

Touring Tips Expendable on any schedule. If you ride with preschoolers, seat them first, then board. The Astro Orbiter flies higher and faster than Dumbo and frightens some young children. It also apparently messes with some adults. A mother from Lev Hashomnon, Israel, attests:

> *I think your assessment of [Astro Orbiter] as "very mild" is way off. I was able to sit through all the "Mountains," the "Tours," and the "Wars" without my stomach reacting even a little, but after [Astro Orbiter] I thought I would be finished for the rest of the day. Very quickly I realized that my only chance for survival was to pick a point on the toe of my shoe and stare at it (and certainly not lift my eyes out of the "jet") until the ride was over. My four-year-old was my co-pilot, and she loved the ride (go figure) and she had us up high the whole time. It was a nightmare—people should be forewarned.*

Tomorrowland Transit Authority

What It Is: Scenic tour of Tomorrowland

Scope & Scale: Minor attraction

When to Go: During hot, crowded times of day (11:30 a.m.–4:30 p.m.)

Special Comments: A good way to check out the crowd at Space Mountain

Author's Rating: Scenic, relaxing, informative; ★★★

Appeal by Age Group:

Pre-school	Grade School	Teens	Young Adults	Over 30	Senior Citizens
★★★	★★½	★★½	★★½	★★½	★★★

Duration of Ride: 10 minutes

Average Wait in Line per 100 People ahead of You: 1½ minutes

Assumes: 39 trains operating

Loading Speed: Fast

Description and Comments   A once unique prototype of a linear induction–powered mass-transit system, the Authority's tramlike cars carry riders on a leisurely tour of Tomorrowland, including a peek inside Space Mountain. The attraction was renamed from WEDway PeopleMover.

Touring Tips   A relaxing ride, where lines move quickly and you seldom have to wait. It's good to take during busier times of day, and it can double as a nursery.

A Texas mom writes:

> The [Transit Authority] is an excellent ride for getting a tired infant to fall asleep. You can stay on for several times around. It is also a moderately private and comfortable place for nursing an infant.

Walt Disney's Carousel of Progress

What It Is: Audio-Animatronic theater production

Scope & Scale: Major attraction

When to Go: Anytime

Author's Rating: Nostalgic, warm, and happy; ★★★

Appeal by Age Group:

Pre-school	Grade School	Teens	Young Adults	Over 30	Senior Citizens
★★	★★½	★★½	★★★	★★★	★★★½

Duration of Presentation: 18 minutes

Preshow Entertainment: Documentary on the attraction's long history

Probable Waiting Time: Less than 10 minutes

Description and Comments   Updated and improved during the Tomorrowland renovation, *Walt Disney's Carousel of Progress* offers a delightful look at how technology and electricity have changed the lives of an Audio-Animatronic family over several generations. The family is easy to identify with, and a cheerful, sentimental tune bridges the generations.

Touring Tips   This attraction is a great favorite among repeat visitors and is included on all of our one-day touring plans. The *Carousel* handles big crowds effectively and is a good choice during busier times of day.

Buzz Lightyear's Space Ranger Spin

What It Is: Whimsical space travel–themed indoor ride
Scope & Scale: Minor attraction
When to Go: Anytime
Author's Rating: Not open at press time
Appeal by Age Group: Not open at press time
Duration of Ride: About 6 minutes
Average Wait in Line per 100 People ahead of You: 3 minutes
Assumes: Normal operation
Loading Speed: Fast

Description and Comments   This attraction, based on the space-commando character of Buzz Lightyear from the film *Toy Story,* replaces the Take Flight attraction as the final installment of Tomorrowland's four-year makeover. The marginal story line has you and Buzz Lightyear trying to save the universe from the evil Emperor Zurg. The indoor ride is interactive to the extent that you can spin your car and shoot simulated "laser cannons" at Zurg and his minions.

Touring Tips   Very seldom is there a line. Go during the heat of the day.

The Timekeeper

What It Is: Time-travel movie adventure
Scope & Scale: Major attraction
When to Go: Anytime
Special Comments: Audience must stand throughout presentation
Author's Rating: Outstanding; not to be missed; ★★★★
Appeal by Age Group:

Pre-school	Grade School	Teens	Young Adults	Over 30	Senior Citizens
★★½	★★★½	★★★½	★★★½	★★★★	★★★★

Duration of Presentation: About 20 minutes

Preshow Entertainment: Robots, lasers, and movies

Probable Waiting Time: 8–15 minutes

Description and Comments   Developed as *Le Visionarium* for Disneyland Paris, *The Timekeeper* adds Audio-Animatronic characters and a story line to the long-successful Circle-Vision 360 technology. The preshow introduces Timekeeper (a humanoid) and 9-Eye (a time-traveling robot so named because she has nine cameras that serve as eyes). Afterward, the audience enters the main theater, where Timekeeper places 9-Eye into a time machine and dispatches her on a crazed journey into the past and future. What 9-Eye sees on her odyssey is projected onto huge screens that surround the audience with action. The robot travels to prehistoric Europe and then forward to meet French author and visionary Jules Verne, who hitches a ride into the future. Circle-Vision 360 technology, Disney Audio-Animatronics, and high-tech special effects combine to make *The Timekeeper* one of Tomorrowland's premier attractions.

   The Timekeeper may be the most underrated attraction in the Magic Kingdom, but as this Westport, Connecticut, family attests, it's a "must-see":

> We thought The Timekeeper *was the best [Animatronics] in the whole of Disney World. Robin Williams was brilliant. We saw it twice—5 stars!!*

Touring Tips   *The Timekeeper* draws large crowds from midmorning on. Because the theater accommodates more than 1,000 guests per show, there never is much wait. Go during early afternoon when the park is hot and crowded.

Alien Encounter

What It Is: Theater-in-the-round sci-fi horror show

Scope & Scale: Headliner

When to Go: Before 10 a.m. or after 6 p.m.; try during parades

Special Comments: Frightens children

Author's Rating: ★★★

Appeal by Age Group:

Pre-school	Grade School	Teens	Young Adults	Over 30	Senior Citizens
★★	★★★½	★★★★	★★★★	★★★★	★★★

Duration of Presentation: About 12 minutes

Preshow Entertainment: About 6 minutes

Probable Waiting Time: 12–40 minutes

Description and Comments Heralded as the showpiece of the "new" Tomorrowland, *Alien Encounter* is staged in the building that previously housed *Mission to Mars*. Guests witness a demonstration of "interplanetary teleportation," a technique that converts travelers into electrons for transmission to distant locations. In this case, the demonstration goes awry (of course), and an unsavory alien arrives in the theater. Mayhem ensues.

Alien Encounter is the antithesis of most Disney attractions: there is no uplifting message and no happy ending. There is death in this attraction, and its tone is dark and foreboding. While *The Twilight Zone* Tower of Terror at Disney-MGM Studios is suspenseful and subtle, *Alien Encounter* is uncomfortable and gross. The discomfort begins at the preshow when, in a teleportation experiment, a cuddly Audio-Animatronic character is hideously fried, then vomited, screaming into outer space. Is this someone's idea of entertainment?

Alien Encounter has its advocates, but we consider it mean and twisted. The *coup de grâce,* however, is the hawking of T-shirts (in the adjacent gift shop) decorated with the image of the tortured and maimed Audio-Animatronic creature. Enough already.

Because *Alien Encounter* is such a departure from typical Disney theme park entertainment, we consider it prudent to share the observations of readers.

A St. Louis father of three writes:

> Alien Encounter *in the new Tomorrowland—Outstanding and really scary! Not to be missed! The special effects may be too much for young kids, but ours (ages 10, 8, and 6) did okay.*

A senior from North Charleston, South Carolina, disagrees:

> *Being put in the dark, with a lot of screaming and hollering and having water spritzed in your face, is not scary, nor is it entertaining.*

A woman from Milford, Michigan, has this to say:

> *Warning!!! And I can't stress this enough!* Alien Encounter *is the most intense attraction in any theme park. It is one of those rides I can say I've seen and that I have no intention of ever doing again. In fact, parents who take children under the age of six should be brought up on child abuse.*

A single mom from Phillipsburg, New Jersey, agrees:

> Alien Encounter *was the WORST experience for my 10-year-old (and almost every child in there). It starts out cute enough during the preshow, but the actual show is a disaster for children. My daughter screamed and cried in terror throughout it. I thought the Disney warnings were vague and inaccurate. When we left, there wasn't one child with dry eyes (even sturdy-looking 12-year-old boys were crying). I think an age requirement of 13 or 14 is more appropriate. I talked to a few adults, and we agreed that the special effects were extremely unpleasant even for us. This show isn't a Disney family experience—it's ATROCIOUS!!*

A parent from Laurel, Maryland, shares her experience:

> *The preshow is very deceiving. It kind of lulls you into thinking "this isn't so bad." When the main part came up, I admit the experience gave me the absolute heebie-jeebies. It is INTENSE! I am grateful nothing touched me when we were plunged into the dark (my friend and I sat in the middle row of seats), because I swear I would have either passed out or screamed bloody murder. If someone is the least bit scared of the dark or is the least bit fearful, I do not recommend this attraction. (I am never doing that presentation again—it was way too intense for me, and I'm now 27 years of age!) All sorts of things go running through your mind when it happens. If you don't keep reminding yourself that it's just a theater, you really can get the stuffing scared out of you.*

A mom from Providence, Rhode Island, defends *Alien Encounter*, at least for adults:

> Alien Encounter *was scary in a different way than the other rides. The "theatre of the mind" element really worked. It wasn't just a jarring physical thing. Disney ought to develop more attractions like this one. Although parents of 6–9-year-olds should be forewarned that most of the kids that age were carried out at the end screaming and clinging to their parents. I was in the baby swap holding area (the exit lobby) and was glad I'd ridden before my husband. If I had seen all those kids shrieking before I'd queued, I would have chickened out.*

A Connecticut family with children ages 9 and 12 think the debate over *Alien Encounter* is a tempest in a teapot:

> *Our only disagreement with the book was that [we] almost did not visit* Alien Encounter *because of your write-up. [We] did it twice and*

did not find it gross, nor did it make [the children] scream or cry. They did not know what all the fuss was about.

Ditto for a Johnstown, Pennsylvania, couple:

The effects in Alien Encounter *were fantastic. While certainly not for the very young, any adult who has the common sense to realize that this is pretend (this means you,* Unofficial Guide *authors) can sit back and enjoy it as a wonderful sci-fi experience.*

Joining the chorus "in favor" is an Amarillo, Texas, mother who regrets subjecting her child to the attraction:

My personal favorite was Alien Encounter, *but it literally scared our daughter to pieces. She screamed and cried when ol' Mr. Alien busted loose. We didn't feel like parents of the year, needless to say. I will add that every other little girl I saw under the age of eight was crying also. I think they should have a warning like* Terminator 2 *does at Universal Studios—PG-13.*

A mother from Plum, Pennsylvania, adds this:

You were exactly right about Alien Encounter*—it was far too scary for our nine-year-old—who ended up vomiting as a result of being so very frightened.*

A normally fearless New England teenager decided she was not quite "big enough" for *Alien Encounter*, writing:

Alien Encounter *was very graphic, loud, and frightening. I am going to be 15 and to me it was too much. I love space and alien movies but that went too far. This place is supposed to be for kids and kids at heart. My feelings toward [Disney's] warnings are very negative. They say it may frighten small children but they don't tell you that it may frighten big "children."*

A dad from Greensboro, North Carolina, notes that there is no way possible to comfort your children while the show is in progress, writing:

Alien Encounter *should not be seen by pre-adolescents. You are trapped, alone, isolated, with no way to comfort or explain. Our children could not (or would not) speak for an hour afterward.*

A mother of four from Winchester, Virginia, tells her family's story:

We mistakenly rode Alien Encounter *first. Fortunately the four-year-old and I stayed out. My daughters came out petrified and in tears. Luckily, they recovered quickly. Warn any parents of children seven or younger to ride it first themselves before they subject their kids to it. It's great for adults, though. My vote for best new attraction in the Magic Kingdom.*

A mom from Glenview, Illinois, didn't enjoy it:

> *We saw* Alien Encounter, *and it was horrible! The seats were uncomfortable and we were strapped in with an overhead harness. This was done, no doubt, to keep all the truly terrified children from trying to escape during the show. An eight- or nine-year-old boy next to me was sobbing after the alien escaped. This attraction is pointless, incomprehensible, intense, and no fun at all. It lacked any Disney creativity and whimsy.*

Touring Tips   Disney's most disturbing and frightening attraction, *Alien Encounter* initially was rejected by Walt Disney Company chairman Michael Eisner for not being scary enough. Though reader reaction to *Alien Encounter* is mixed, almost everyone agrees this isn't an attraction for young children. *Alien Encounter* stays busy throughout the day. See it first thing in the morning.

Tomorrowland Eateries and Shops

Description and Comments   Cosmic Ray's Starlight Cafe (formerly Tomorrowland Terrace) is the largest and most efficient Magic Kingdom fast-food restaurant. The Plaza Pavilion, however, serves better food, including a good Italian sub. Several shops provide yet more opportunities to buy souvenirs.

Touring Tips   Unless shopping is your top priority, leave browsing until your second day.

Live Entertainment in the Magic Kingdom

Bands, Disney character appearances, parades, ceremonies, and singing and dancing further enliven the Magic Kingdom. For specific events the day you visit, check the live entertainment schedule in your Disney guidemap (free as you enter the park or at City Hall). Be aware: If you're short on time, it's impossible to see Magic Kingdom featured attractions *and* the live performances. Our one-day touring plans exclude live performances in favor of seeing as much of the park as time permits. This tactical decision is based on the fact that some parades and performances siphon crowds away from the more popular rides, thus shortening lines.

Nonetheless, the color and pageantry of live events are integral to the Magic Kingdom and a persuasive argument for a second day of touring. Here's a list and description of some performances and events presented with regularity that don't require reservations.

Fantasyland Pavilion   Site of various concerts in Fantasyland.

Steel Drum Bands and Luau Dancers   Perform daily at Caribbean Plaza in Adventureland.

Frontierland Stuntmen   Stuntmen stage shootouts in Frontierland; check the daily entertainment schedule.

Kids of the Kingdom   Youthful song-and-dance group performs popular music daily in the Castle Forecourt Stage (front of the castle). Disney characters usually join the fun.

Flag Retreat   At 5 p.m. daily at Town Square (railroad station end of Main Street). Sometimes performed with great fanfare and college marching bands, sometimes with a smaller Disney band.

Sword in the Stone Ceremony   A ceremony based on the Disney animated feature of the same name. Merlin the Magician selects youngsters from the audience to test their courage and strength by removing the sword, Excalibur, from the stone. Staged several times each day behind Cinderella Castle; check the daily entertainment schedule.

Bay Lake and Seven Seas Lagoon Floating Electrical Pageant   This is one of our favorites among the Disney extras, but it's necessary to leave the Magic Kingdom to view it. The pageant is a stunning electric light show afloat on small barges and set to nifty electronic music. It's performed at nightfall (about 9 p.m. most of the year) on Seven Seas Lagoon and Bay Lake. Leave the Magic Kingdom and take the monorail to the Polynesian Resort. Get yourself a drink and walk to the end of the pier to watch the show.

Fantasy in the Sky   A stellar fireworks display unleashed after dark on nights the park is open late. For an uncluttered view and lighter crowds, watch from the terrace of The Plaza Pavilion restaurant in Tomorrowland.

Cosmic Ray's Galaxy Palace Theater   These stages in Tomorrowland feature Top-40 rock music, rap, and jazz, as well as Disney characters and the Kids of the Kingdom.

Disney Character Shows & Appearances   Most days, a character is on duty for photos and autographs from 9 a.m. to 10 p.m. next to City Hall. Mickey and three assortments of other characters are available most of the day at Mickey's Toontown Fair. Shows at the Castle Forecourt Stage and Tomorrowland's Galaxy Palace Theater feature Disney characters several times daily (check the entertainment schedule). In Fantasyland, Ariel can be found in her Grotto daily, while a host of others can be seen at the Character Festival next to Dumbo. Characters also roam the park. For information on character whereabouts on the day you visit, check the *Disney Character Greeting Location Guide* available at City Hall.

Magic Kingdom Bands   Banjo, Dixieland, steel drum, marching, and fife-and-drum bands roam the park daily.

Tinker Bell's Flight   This nice special effect at 10 p.m. in the sky above Cinderella Castle heralds the beginning of Fantasy in the Sky fireworks (when the park is open late).

PARADES

Parades at the Magic Kingdom are full-fledged spectaculars with dozens of Disney characters and amazing special effects. We rate the afternoon parade as outstanding and the evening parade as "not to be missed."

In addition to providing great entertainment, parades lure guests away from the attractions. If getting on rides appeals to you more than watching a parade, you'll find substantially shorter lines just before and during parades. Because the parade route doesn't pass through Adventureland, Tomorrowland, or Fantasyland, attractions in these lands are particularly good bets. Be forewarned: Parades disrupt traffic in the Magic Kingdom. It's nearly impossible, for example, to get to Adventureland from Tomorrowland, or vice versa, during one.

Afternoon Parade

Usually staged at 3 p.m., the parade features bands, floats, and marching Disney characters. A new afternoon parade is introduced every year or two. While some elements, such as Disney characters, remain constant, the theme, music, and float design change. Seasonal parades during major holidays round out the mix.

Evening Parade(s)

The evening parade is a high-tech production employing electroluminescent and fiber-optic technologies, light-spreading thermoplastics (do not try this at home), and clouds of underlit liquid-nitrogen smoke. Don't worry. You won't need a gas mask or an asbestos suit to watch. For those who flunked chemistry and physics, the parade also offers music, Mickey Mouse, and twinkling lights. Depending on closing time, the evening parade is staged either once at 9 p.m. or twice when the park is open late: at 8 and 10 p.m., or at 9 and 11 p.m.

During less busy times of year, the evening parade is held only on weekends, and sometimes not even then. Call (407) 824-4321 before you go to be sure the parade is on.

Parade Route and Vantage Points

Magic Kingdom parades circle Town Square, head down Main Street, go around the central hub and cross the bridge to Liberty Square. In Liberty Square, they follow the waterfront and end in Frontierland. Sometimes they begin in Frontierland, run the route in the opposite direction, and end in Town Square.

Most guests watch from the central hub or from Main Street. One of the best and most popular vantage points is the upper platform of the Walt Disney World Railroad station at the Town Square end of Main Street. This is also a good place for watching the Fantasy in the Sky fireworks, as well as for ducking out of the park ahead of the crowd when the fireworks end. Problem is, you have to stake out your position 30–45 minutes before the events.

Because most spectators pack Main Street and the central hub, we recommend watching from Liberty Square or Frontierland. Great vantage points, frequently overlooked, are:

1. Sleepy Hollow snack and beverage shop, immediately to your right as you cross the bridge into Liberty Square. If you arrive early, buy refreshments and claim a table by the rail. You'll have a perfect view of the parade as it crosses the Liberty Square bridge.

2. The pathway on the Liberty Square side of the moat from Sleepy Hollow snack and beverage shop to Cinderella Castle. Any point along this path offers a clear and unobstructed view as the parade crosses the Liberty Square bridge.

3. The covered walkway between Liberty Tree Tavern and *The Diamond Horseshoe Saloon Revue.* This elevated vantage point is perfect (particularly on rainy days) and usually goes unnoticed until just before the parade starts.

Frontierland

Liberty Square

Adventureland

Main Street

Monorail Station

**Magic Kingdom
Parade Route**

4. Elevated wooden platforms in front of the Frontierland Shootin' Arcade, Frontier Trading Post, and the building with the sign reading "Frontier Merchandise." These spots usually get picked off 10–12 minutes before parade time.

5. Benches on the perimeter of the central hub, between the entrances to Liberty Square and Adventureland. Usually unoccupied until after the parade begins, they offer a comfortable resting place and unobstructed (though somewhat distant) view of the parade as it crosses Liberty Square bridge. What you lose in proximity, you gain in comfort.

6. Liberty Square and Frontierland dockside areas. These spots usually go early.

Assuming it starts on Main Street (evening parades normally do), the parade takes 16–20 minutes to reach Liberty Square or Frontierland.

On evenings when the parade runs twice, the first parade draws a huge crowd, siphoning guests from attractions. Many folks leave the park after the early parade, with many more departing after the fireworks (scheduled on the hour between the two parades). For optimum touring and less congestion, enjoy attractions during the early parade, then break to watch the fireworks. Continue to tour after the fireworks. This is a particularly good time to see *Alien Encounter*, ride Space Mountain, and enjoy attractions in Adventureland. If you're touring Adventureland and the parade begins on Main Street, you won't have to assume your viewing position in Frontierland until 15 minutes after the parade starts (the time it takes the parade to reach Frontierland). If you watch from the Splash Mountain side of the street and head for the attraction as the last float passes, you'll be able to ride with only a couple of minutes' wait. You might even have time to work in a last-minute ride on Big Thunder Mountain Railroad.

Leaving the Park after Evening Parades and Fireworks

Armies of guests leave the Magic Kingdom after evening parades and fireworks. The Disney Transportation System (buses, ferries, and monorail) is overwhelmed, causing long waits in boarding areas.

A mother from Kresgeville, Pennsylvania, pleads:

> *Please stress how terrifying these crowds can be. Our family of five made the mistake of going to the MK the Saturday night before Columbus Day to watch the parade and fireworks. Afterwards, we lingered at The Crystal Palace to wait for the crowds to lessen, but it was no use. We started walking toward the gates and soon became trapped by the throng, not able to go forward or back. There was no way to*

cross the hordes to get to the dock for our hotel's launch. Our group became separated, and it became a living nightmare. We left the park at 10:30 p.m. and didn't get back to the Polynesian (less than a mile away) until after midnight. How dare they expose children to that nightmare! Even if they were to raise Walt Disney himself from cryogenic sleep and parade him down Main Street, I would never go to the MK on a Saturday night again!

Congestion persists from the end of the early evening parade until closing time. Most folks watch the early parade and then the fireworks a few minutes later. If you're parked at the Transportation and Ticket Center and are intent on beating the crowd, view the early parade from the Town Square end of Main Street, leaving the park as soon as the parade ends. Walk (about 12 minutes) or ride the monorail to the Contemporary Resort. Note that the monorail loading platform for the hotels is different from the platform serving the TTC. At the Contemporary Resort, take the elevator to the top floor and go through the lounge (no problem for kids) to the outdoor promenade atop the hotel. There, watch the Magic Kingdom fireworks in a relaxed, uncrowded setting with a perfect, unobstructed view. After the fireworks, return to the TTC on the monorail.

If you're staying at a Disney hotel not served by the monorail and must depend on Disney transportation, watch the early parade and fireworks at the park and then enjoy the attractions until about 20–25 minutes before the late parade is scheduled to begin. At this time, leave the park and catch the Disney bus or boat back to your hotel. Don't cut it too close: Main Street will be so congested that you won't be able to reach the exit.

Here's what happened to a family from Cape Coral, Florida:

We tried to leave the park before the parade began. However, Main Street was already packed and we didn't see any way to get out of the park, so we were stuck. In addition, it was impossible to move across the street, and even the shops were so crowded that it was virtually impossible to maneuver a stroller through them to get close to the entrance.

If you don't have a stroller (or are willing to forgo the $1 return refund for rental strollers), catch the Walt Disney World Railroad in Frontierland or Mickey's Toontown Fair and ride to the park exit at Main Street. Be aware that the railroad shuts down during parades because the floats must cross the tracks when entering or exiting the parade route in Frontierland. If you plan to escape by train, don't cut it too close.

If you're on the Tomorrowland side of the park, it's actually possible for you to exit during a parade. Leaving Tomorrowland, cut through The Plaza

Pavilion Restaurant to Main Street. Before you reach Main Street, bear left into the side door of the corner shop. Once inside, you'll see that Main Street shops have interior doors allowing you to pass from one shop to the next without having to get on Main Street. Work your way from shop to shop until you reach Town Square (easy, because people will be outside watching the parade). At Town Square, bear left and move to the train station and the park exit.

This strategy won't work if you're on the Adventureland side of the park. You can make your way through Casey's Corner restaurant to Main Street, then work your way through the interior of the Main Street shops, but when you pop out of the Emporium at Town Square, you'll be trapped by the parade. As soon the last float passes, however, you can bolt for the exit.

Another strategy for beating the masses out of the park (if your car is at the TTC lot) is to watch the early parade and then leave before the fireworks begin. Line up for the ferry. One will depart about every eight to ten minutes. Try to catch the ferry that will be crossing Seven Seas Lagoon while the fireworks are in progress. The best vantage point is on the top deck to the right of the pilot house as you face the Magic Kingdom, and the sight of fireworks silhouetting the castle and reflecting off Seven Seas Lagoon is unforgettable. While there's no guarantee that a ferry will load and depart within three or four minutes of the fireworks, your chances are about 50/50 of catching it just right. If you're in the front of the line for the ferry and don't want to board the boat that's loading, stop at the gate and let people pass you. You'll be the first to board the next boat.

Shopping in the Magic Kingdom

Shops add realism and atmosphere to Magic Kingdom settings and offer an extensive inventory including souvenirs, clothing, novelties, and decorator items. Much of the merchandise (except Disney trademark souvenir items) is available less expensively elsewhere. We believe shopping isn't one of the main reasons to visit the Magic Kingdom. Bypass the shops if you're on a one-day visit. If you have two or more days in the Magic Kingdom, browse the shops in early afternoon when many of the attractions are crowded. Remember that Main Street and its shops open earlier and close later than the rest of the park. Store your purchases in lockers at the Main Street rail station while you tour. Or, have your packages forwarded from shops to Parcel Pick-up and retrieve them when you leave the park. Disney resort guests can have their purchases delivered to their hotel rooms.

Strollers make nifty shopping carts
(be sure to leave room for the baby!)

We realize that Disney souvenirs and memorabilia are irresistible to many guests. If you have decided you would look good in a Goofy hat with shoulder-length floppy ears, you're in the right place. What's more, you have plenty of company. A reader observes:

> *I've discovered that people have a compelling need to buy Disney stuff when they are at WDW. When you get home you wonder why you ever got a cashmere sweater with Mickey Mouse embroidered on the breast, or a tie with tiny Goofys all over it. Maybe it's something they put in the food.*

Disney trademark merchandise tends to be more expensive at Disney shops than in independent stores outside the World. Quality, however, is better at Disney shops. The best place for quality and value is the Character Warehouse in Mall 2 of the Belz Factory Outlet World on International Drive off I-4. Unfortunately, selection is limited.

If you remember on your flight home that you forgot to buy mouse ears for your nephew, call the Walt Disney Attractions Mail Order Department on weekdays at (407) 363-6200 or the catalog department at (800) 237-5751. Most trademark merchandise sold at Walt Disney World is available.

Behind the Scenes in the Magic Kingdom

Keys to the Kingdom takes guests behind the scenes at the Magic Kingdom. This fascinating guided tour provides an informative and detailed look at the park's logistical, technical, and operational sides. Included are the parade assembly area, the waste treatment plant, and tunnels under the theme park. For additional information, call (407) 939-8687. The program ($45 per person) runs about four to five hours. Advance reservations and payment by credit card are required. Discounts are usually available; ask when you call to book.

For those interested in the tour, a reader from Ludington, Michigan, offers the following advice:

> *People thinking of taking the Keys to the Kingdom tour should know that it is not for the faint of heart. This is a four-hour walking tour with only one 15-minute break plus a few minutes to sit while on Pirates of the Caribbean, the Haunted Mansion, and the Tommorowland Transit Authority. It wore me out, and I am on my feet most of any given working day. If you do this, make it the last day of your visit—it took me three days to recover. Oh, by the way, it is worth every penny!*

Traffic Patterns in the Magic Kingdom

When we research the Magic Kingdom, we study its traffic patterns, asking:

1. Which sections of the park and what attractions do guests visit first? When visitors are admitted to the lands on non-early-entry days during summer and holiday periods, traffic to Tomorrowland and Frontierland is heaviest, followed by Fantasyland, Adventureland, Liberty Square, and Mickey's Toontown Fair. On early-entry days during busier times, Disney hotel and campground guests inundate Fantasyland and Tomorrowland before the general public is admitted. The early-morning crowds of Disney resort guests accelerate the filling of the park by about an hour.

During the school year, when fewer young people are in the park, early-morning traffic is more evenly distributed but remains heaviest in Tomorrowland, Frontierland, and Fantasyland. Our researchers tested the oft-repeated claim that most people turn right into Tomorrowland and tour the Magic Kingdom in a counterclockwise sequence. We found it to be baseless. As the park fills, visitors head for the top attractions they want to ride before lines get long. This, more than any other factor, determines morning traffic patterns.

2. How long does it take for the park to fill up? How are the visitors dispersed in the park? On non-early-entry days, a surge of "early birds" arrives before or around opening time but is quickly dispersed throughout the empty park. After the initial wave is absorbed, there's a lull lasting about an hour after opening. Then the park is inundated for about two hours, peaking between 10 a.m. and noon. Arrivals continue in a steady

Attractions That Are Crowded Early	
Tomorrowland:	Space Mountain *Alien Encounter*
Frontierland:	Splash Mountain Big Thunder Mountain Railroad
Fantasyland:	Dumbo the Flying Elephant
Adventureland:	Jungle Cruise

but diminishing stream until around 2 p.m. Lines we sampled were longest between 1 and 2 p.m., indicating more arrivals than departures into the early afternoon. For touring purposes, most attractions develop long lines between 10 and 11:30 a.m.

On early-entry days, Fantasyland and Tomorrowland fill with early-entry guests who later spill over into Frontierland, Liberty Square, Adventureland, and Mickey's Toontown Fair. The presence of these resort guests slows the touring of day guests who are admitted later. During summer and holidays, the two successive waves of arrivals (first the early-entry resort guests, then the day guests) overwhelm many popular attractions by midmorning. On early-entry days, many rides develop long lines as early as 9:10 a.m. Guests continue to stream into the park throughout the morning and into the afternoon. Though many early-entry guests leave the park between noon and 2 p.m., early entry markedly increases daily attendance. Thus, on early-entry days during busier times, the Magic Kingdom is packed most of the day.

From late morning through early afternoon on both early-entry and non-early-entry days, guests are equally distributed through all of the lands. We found, however, that guests concentrate in Fantasyland, Liberty Square, and Frontierland in late afternoon, with a decrease of visitors in Adventureland and Tomorrowland. Adventureland's Jungle Cruise and Tomorrowland's *Alien Encounter* and Space Mountain continue to be crowded, but most other attractions in those lands are readily accessible.

3. How do most visitors tour the park? Do first-time visitors tour differently from repeat guests? Many first-time visitors are accompanied by friends or relatives familiar with the Magic Kingdom, who guide their tour. These tours may or may not follow an orderly sequence. First-time visitors without personal guides tend to be more orderly in their touring. Many first-time visitors, however, are drawn to Cinderella Castle upon entering the park and thus begin their rotation from Fantasyland. Repeat visitors usually go directly to their favorite attractions. In 1999, expect veterans and first-timers to head directly for Tomorrowland to check out the recent renovation and new attractions.

Early-entry guests go directly to Fantasyland and Tomorrowland. Later, when the remainder of the Magic Kingdom opens, most continue touring Tomorrowland or head for Frontierland and Splash Mountain.

4. How do special events, such as parades and live shows, affect traffic patterns? Parades pull huge numbers of guests away from attractions and provide a window of opportunity for experiencing the more popular attractions with less of a wait. Castle Forecourt Stage shows also attract crowds but only slightly affect lines.

5. What are the traffic patterns near to and at closing time? On our sample days, in busy times and off-season at the park, departures outnumbered arrivals beginning in midafternoon. Many visitors left in late afternoon as the dinner hour approached. When the park closed early, guests departed steadily during the two hours before closing, with a huge exodus at closing time. When the park closed late, a huge exodus began immediately after the early-evening parade and fireworks, with a second mass departure after the late parade, continuing until closing. Because Main Street and the transportation services remain open after the other six lands close, crowds leaving at closing mainly affect conditions on Main Street and at the monorail, ferry, and bus boarding areas. In the hour before closing, the other six lands normally are uncrowded.

6. When there are two or more lines, is the shortest wait always in the left line? We don't recommend the "left-line strategy" because, with the occasional exception of food lines, it doesn't hold up. Disney has techniques for both internal and external crowd control that distribute traffic nearly equally. Placing researchers at the same time in each available line, we could discern no consistent pattern of who was served first. Further, researchers entering the same attraction by different lines almost always would exit the attraction within 30 to 90 seconds of each other.

Occasionally guests ignore a second line that has just opened and stay in the established line. As a rule, if you encounter a waiting area with two lines and no barrier to entry for either, and one line is empty or conspicuously shorter than the other, get in the short line.

Magic Kingdom Touring Plans

Our step-by-step touring plans are field-tested for seeing *as much as possible* in one day with a minimum of time wasted in lines. They're designed to help you avoid crowds and bottlenecks on days of moderate to heavy attendance. Understand, however, that there's more to see in the Magic Kingdom than can be experienced in one day. Since we began covering the Magic Kingdom, four headliner attractions and a new land have been added. Today, even if you could experience every attraction without any wait, you still wouldn't be able to see all of the park in a single day.

On days of lighter attendance (see "Selecting the Time of Year for Your Visit," pages 37–39), our plans will save you time but won't be as critical to successful touring as on busier days. Don't worry that other people will be following the plans and render them useless. Fewer than 1 in every 500 people in the park will have been exposed to this information.

Choosing the Appropriate Touring Plan

We present five Magic Kingdom touring plans:

- Magic Kingdom One-Day Touring Plan for Adults
- Author's Selective Magic Kingdom One-Day Touring Plan for Adults
- Magic Kingdom One-Day Touring Plan for Parents with Young Children
- Magic Kingdom Dumbo-or-Die-in-a-Day Touring Plan for Parents with Young Children
- Magic Kingdom Two-Day Touring Plan

If you have two days (or two mornings) at the Magic Kingdom, the Two-Day Touring Plan is *by far* the most relaxed and efficient. The two-day plan takes advantage of early morning, when lines are short and the park hasn't filled with guests. This plan works well year-round and eliminates much of the extra walking required by the one-day plans. No matter when the park closes, our two-day plan guarantees the most efficient touring and the least time in lines. The plan is perfect for guests who wish to sample both the attractions and the atmosphere of the Magic Kingdom, including parades and fireworks.

If you only have one day but wish to see as much as possible, use the One-Day Touring Plan for Adults. It's exhausting, but it packs in the maximum. If you prefer a more relaxed visit, use the Author's Selective One-Day Touring Plan. It includes the best the park has to offer (in the author's opinion), eliminating some less impressive attractions.

If you have children younger than age eight, adopt the One-Day Touring Plan for Parents with Young Children. It's a compromise, blending the preferences of younger children with those of older siblings and adults. The plan includes many children's rides in Fantasyland but omits roller coaster rides and other attractions that frighten young children or are off-limits because of height requirements. Or, use the One-Day Touring Plan for Adults or the Author's Selective One-Day Touring Plan and take advantage of switching off, a technique where children accompany adults to the loading area of a ride with age and height requirements but don't board (pages 165–167). Switching off allows adults to enjoy the more adventuresome attractions while keeping the group together.

The Dumbo-or-Die-in-a-Day Touring Plan for Parents with Young Children is designed for parents who will withhold no sacrifice for the children. On the Dumbo-or-Die plan, adults generally stand around, sweat, wipe noses, pay for stuff, and watch the children enjoy themselves. It's great.

Two-Day Touring Plans for Families with Young Children

If you have young children and are looking for a two-day itinerary, combine the Magic Kingdom One-Day Touring Plan for Parents with Young Children with the second day of the Magic Kingdom Two-Day Touring Plan.

Touring Plan Clip-out Pocket Outlines

Pocket versions of all touring plans presented in this guide begin on page 685. The outlines present the same itineraries as the detailed plans but with vastly abbreviated directions. Select the touring plan appropriate for your party and familiarize yourself with its detailed version. When you understand how the plan works, clip its pocket outline from the back of this guide and carry it as a quick reference when you visit the theme park.

The Single-Day Touring Conundrum

Touring the Magic Kingdom in a day is complicated by the fact that the premier attractions are at almost opposite ends of the park: Splash Mountain and Big Thunder Mountain Railroad in Frontierland and Space Mountain and *Alien Encounter* in Tomorrowland. It's virtually impossible to ride all four without encountering lines at one or another. If you ride Space Mountain and see *Alien Encounter* immediately after the park opens, you won't have much wait, if any. By the time you leave Tomorrowland and hurry to Frontierland, however, the line for Splash Mountain will be substantial. The same situation prevails if you ride the Frontierland duo first: Splash Mountain and Big Thunder Mountain Railroad, no problem; Space Mountain and *Alien Encounter*, fair-sized lines. From ten minutes after opening until just before closing, lines are long at these headliners.

The only effective way to ride all four without long waits is to tour the Magic Kingdom over two days: Ride Space Mountain and see *Alien Encounter* first thing one morning, and ride Splash Mountain and Big Thunder Mountain first thing on the other. If you have only one day and are unwilling to suffer waits of 45 minutes to 2 hours for these rides, experience one set when the park opens and the other just before closing. Many who attempt this fail because they become too worn out to stay until near closing.

Or, as we recommend in our one-day touring plans, arrive early and rush to *Alien Encounter*. After *Alien Encounter*, ride Space Mountain; then speed to Frontierland and ride Splash Mountain. When you leave Splash Mountain, bear left to Big Thunder Mountain Railroad. If you're fast, your wait should be less than 5 minutes at *Alien Encounter*, about 10–20 minutes at Space Mountain, and about 25–35 minutes each at Splash Mountain and Big Thunder Mountain Railroad. This "bite-the-bullet" strategy requires a lot of hustle, but it probably works best. After riding Big

Thunder Mountain Railroad, take comfort in the knowledge that you have the most popular attractions and the longest lines behind you.

This strategy takes advantage of the 30- to 45-minute morning lull, when guests on-hand at the park's opening have been absorbed and new arrivals are comparatively few. While you're riding Space Mountain and visiting *Alien Encounter,* Big Thunder Mountain Railroad and Splash Mountain are accommodating the early birds who rushed to Frontierland as soon as the park opened. By the time you finish Space Mountain and *Alien Encounter,* most of the first wave will have finished riding Big Thunder and Splash mountains. Because of the lull, crowds at Big Thunder and Splash mountains won't yet have built up again, and waits are tolerable.

Early entry at the Magic Kingdom eliminates any morning lull. If you plan to use the lull in your touring strategy, visit the park on a day when early entry isn't scheduled.

Magic Kingdom Early Entry for Walt Disney World Resort Guests

Walt Disney World hotel and campground guests are eligible to enter the Magic Kingdom one hour before the general public on selected days of the week. Early-entry guests can enjoy all attractions in Fantasyland except *Legend of the Lion King* and all attractions in Tomorrowland except *Walt Disney's Carousel of Progress* and *The Timekeeper.* Space Mountain, the Tomorrowland Transit Authority, and Astro Orbiter, however, sometimes open a half hour later than the other attractions.

Early entry is a mixed blessing during busier times of year. On one hand, the opportunity to get a jump on the general public lures so many Disney resort guests to the park that it fills much earlier than usual. After the general public is admitted, it's packed. If you remain in the Magic Kingdom, you'll have to fight incredible crowds. On the other hand, you have a great opportunity in the hour or so before the general public is admitted, particularly if you're among the first early-entry guests. You can experience the most popular attractions in Fantasyland and Tomorrowland and be poised to head for Splash Mountain and Big Thunder Mountain Railroad when the remainder of the park opens.

By our observation, the earlier the Magic Kingdom's official opening, the better early entry works. During major holiday periods, for example, the park opens to the general public at 8 a.m., with early entrants admitted at 6:30 a.m. Because comparatively few vacationers are willing to get out of bed and go to a theme park at 6 in the morning, those who do make the effort are substantially rewarded. On days when the official opening is 9 or

10 a.m., however, thousands of Disney resort guests are up and at 'em, waiting at the turnstiles to claim their early-entry privileges.

If you're eligible for early entry and visit the Magic Kingdom during the off-season, take advantage of your privileges. You'll get a jump on the general public and add an extra hour to what, in the off-season, is already a short touring day. If you participate in early entry during summer or holiday periods, arrive at the park 1 hour and 40 minutes before its official opening and see everything you can before it fills. At that point, leave the Magic Kingdom and spend the remainder of the day at one of the other parks.

How Early Entry Works

Nothing is simple at Walt Disney World, and everything is subject to tinkering. But here's how early entry usually works:

1. All times are based on the official opening time. If the official opening for day guests (those without early-entry privileges) is 9 a.m., early entry will commence an hour and a half earlier, at 7:30 a.m. If official opening is 8 a.m., the park will open for early entry at 6:30 a.m.

2. Disney transportation to the early-entry park begins about 2 hours and 15 minutes before official opening. If official opening is 8 a.m., Disney buses, monorails, and ferries will start running about 5:45–6 a.m.

3. Disney lodging guests who arrive for early entry can tour for one hour before day guests are admitted. If official opening is 9 a.m., for example, early-entry guests will be admitted at 7:30 a.m., and everybody else will enter at 8:30 a.m. So, you wonder, what happens at 9 a.m.? Who knows? This is Disney; maybe Goofy is in charge of the clocks.

If you're admitted for early entry, you'll encounter little or no congestion at the park's entrance. Be ready to show your Disney guest I.D. and a valid admission pass. Inside the park, you'll be directed down Main Street (everything on the street will be closed) to the central hub, and from there to Fantasyland or Tomorrowland. With early entry, you rarely will experience the crush associated with opening the park to the general public. Proceed leisurely to the attractions of your choice.

Combining Early Entry with the Touring Plans

Here's how to combine early entry with one of our touring plans:

1. Adults touring *without children* should enter when the park opens, experience *Alien Encounter* in Tomorrowland, then go

directly to Space Mountain. Space Mountain sometimes opens a half hour later than *Alien Encounter*. If Space Mountain isn't open when you arrive, plant yourself in line and wait (10 minutes or less). After riding Space Mountain, go to Fantasyland and quiet your nerves on Peter Pan's Flight.

Now, check your watch. Day guests will usually be admitted 30 minutes before official opening time. When their numbers are added to the early-entry throng, the park suddenly becomes stuffed. If you want to continue touring at the Magic Kingdom, and most particularly if you want to ride Splash Mountain and Big Thunder Mountain Railroad without horrendous waits, position yourself on the border of Fantasyland and Liberty Square and hustle to the "mountains" the instant the rest of the park opens. Pick up the touring plan of your choice after you have ridden Big Thunder and Splash mountains, skipping any attractions you experienced during early entry.

2. Adults touring with children should arrive as early as possible and enjoy all attractions of interest in Fantasyland, as well as the Tomorrowland Speedway. About ten minutes before day guests are admitted, position yourself to rush to either Frontierland or Adventureland. When the rest of the park opens, ride Splash Mountain in Frontierland (if your kids are at least 3'8" tall) or the Jungle Cruise in Adventureland. Afterward, return to Fantasyland and see *Legend of the Lion King*. Pick up the touring plan of your choice after *Legend of the Lion King*, bypassing attractions you experienced during early entry.

The E-Ticket Express

In 1998 Disney tested a new program called the E-Ticket Express. As with early entry, only Disney resort guests with multiday passports (and annual and seasonal pass holders) are eligible. For $10 you can purchase a pass that allows you to remain in the Magic Kingdom for three hours after the official closing time and enjoy the following attractions:

Space Mountain	Splash Mountain	Big Thunder Mountain Railroad
Alien Encounter	Astro Orbiter	Pirates of the Caribbean
The Timekeeper	The Haunted Mansion	*Country Bear Jamboree*

Disney limits the number of E-Ticket Express passes sold to 4–5,000 per night, ensuring short to nonexistent waits for most attractions. If you have fantasized about riding Space Mountain ten times in a row with practically no waiting, the E-Ticket Express makes it possible. The E-Ticket Express, however, is not good for admission to the park by itself. It must be used with a multiday admission used at any of the major theme parks on the day in question. In other words, you can spend the day at the Animal Kingdom (have your hand stamped upon exiting) and then head to the Magic Kingdom for after-hours fun. On arriving at the Magic Kingdom, enter the park before official closing time using your multiday pass. Once inside, take your E-Ticket Express voucher to either City Hall, the Tomorrowland Arcade, or Splashdown Photo and exchange it for a wristband that identifies you as eligible to stay in the park. After scheduled park closing, only guests with wristbands are allowed to remain in the park.

Now for the bad news. Thus far, Disney has operated this program only during the slower times of year when the Magic Kingdom closes relatively early (7 or 8 p.m.), and even then on just one day each week. It is unlikely, furthermore, that the E-Ticket Express will ever be operational during the summer or holiday periods when the park closes at 10 p.m. or later. As with all things Disney, this program is subject to change or cancellation at any time.

If You Are Not a Disney Resort Guest

If you aren't eligible for early entry, avoid the Magic Kingdom on early-entry days except as described below. Fantasyland and Tomorrowland will be mobbed even before you're allowed through the turnstiles, and the remainder of the park will be unusually crowded all day.

During major holiday periods Disney frequently opens all theme parks 90 minutes before official opening time, admitting everyone. If you're visiting at such a time, don't worry about early-entry privileges; just show up at the park of your choice, admission in hand, 1 hour and 40 minutes before official opening time.

Preliminary Instructions for All Magic Kingdom Touring Plans

On days of moderate to heavy attendance, follow your chosen touring plan exactly, deviating only:

1. When you aren't interested in an attraction it lists. For example, the plan may tell you to go to Tomorrowland and ride Space Mountain, a roller coaster. If you don't enjoy roller coasters, skip this step and proceed to the next.

2. When you encounter a very long line at an attraction the touring plan calls for. Crowds ebb and flow at the park, and an unusually long line may have gathered at an attraction to which you're directed. For example, you arrive at The Haunted Mansion and find extremely long lines. It's possible that this is a temporary situation caused by several hundred people arriving en masse from a recently concluded performance of *The Hall of Presidents* nearby. If this is the case, skip The Haunted Mansion and go to the next step, returning later to retry The Haunted Mansion.

What to Do If You Get Off Track

If an unexpected interruption or problem throws the touring plan off, consult the "Magic Kingdom: Best Time to Visit Attractions" chart (page 000) for preferred times of day to visit attractions.

Park Opening Procedures

Your success during your first hour of touring will be affected somewhat by the opening procedure Disney uses that day:

A. All guests are held at the turnstiles until the entire park opens (which may or may not be at the official opening time). If this happens on the day you visit, blow past Main Street and head for the first attraction on the touring plan you're following.

B. Guests are admitted to Main Street a half hour to an hour before the remaining lands open. Access to other lands will be blocked by a rope barrier at the central hub end of Main Street. Once admitted, stake out a position at the rope barrier as follows:

If you're going to Frontierland first (Splash Mountain and Big Thunder Mountain Railroad), stand in front of The Crystal Palace restaurant, on the left at the central hub end of Main Street. Wait next to the rope barrier blocking the walkway to Adventureland. When the rope is dropped, move quickly to Frontierland by way of Adventureland. This is also the place to line up if your first stop is Adventureland.

If you're going to *Alien Encounter* and Space Mountain first, turn right at the end of Main Street and wait at the entrance of The Plaza Pavilion restaurant. When the rope drops, dash through The Plaza Pavilion into Tomorrowland.

If you're going to Fantasyland or Liberty Square first, go to the end of Main Street and line up left of center at the rope.

If you're going to Mickey's Toontown Fair first, go to the Main Street Station of the Walt Disney World Railroad and board the first train of the day. Disembark at the second stop. The train pulls out of the Main Street Station at the same time the rope is dropped at the central hub end of Main Street.

Before You Go

1. Call (407) 824-4321 the day before you go to check the official opening time. Also, ask whether early entry will be in effect the day you visit.

2. Purchase admission before you arrive. Order tickets from home by mail or buy them at the Disney Store in your local mall, the Ocala Disney AAA Travel Center off I-75 near Ocala (north of Orlando), the Disney Store in the Orlando airport, or Disney World lodging properties.

3. Familiarize yourself with park opening procedures (above) and reread the touring plan you've chosen so that you know what you're likely to encounter.

Magic Kingdom
One-Day Touring Plan for Adults

For: Adults without young children.
Assumes: Willingness to experience all major rides
(including roller coasters) and shows.

This plan requires considerable walking and some backtracking; this is necessary to avoid long lines. Extra walking plus some morning hustle will spare you two to three hours of standing in line. You might not complete the tour. How far you get depends on how quickly you move from ride to ride, how many times you rest or eat, how quickly the park fills, and what time the park closes.

1. If you're a Disney hotel guest, use Disney transportation to commute to the park, arriving 90 minutes before official opening time *on early-entry days* and 40 minutes before official opening *on non-early-entry days.*

   If you're a day guest, arrive at the Magic Kingdom's parking lot 50 minutes before official opening time *on a non-early-entry day.* Arrive 90 minutes before official opening time if it's a holiday period. Add 15 minutes to the above if you have to buy your admission. These arrivals give you time to park and catch the tram to the Transportation and Ticket Center. At the TTC, transfer to the monorail or ferry to reach the park's entrance. If the line for the monorail is short, take the monorail; otherwise, catch the ferry.

2. At the park, proceed through the turnstiles and have one person go to City Hall for guidemaps containing the daily entertainment schedule.

3. Regroup and move quickly down Main Street to the central hub. Because the Magic Kingdom has two opening procedures, you probably will encounter one of the following:

   a. The entire park will be open. In this case, proceed quickly to *Alien Encounter* in Tomorrowland.

   b. Only Main Street will be open. In this case, turn right at the end of Main Street (before you reach the central hub), pass The Plaza Ice Cream Parlor and The Plaza Restaurant and position your group at the entrance to The Plaza Pavilion. When the rope barrier is dropped at opening time, jog through The Plaza Pavilion and on to *Alien Encounter*. Starting at The Plaza Pavilion entrance will give you a 50-yard advantage over anyone coming from the central hub. Experience *Alien Encounter*.

4. Exit *Alien Encounter*, turn left, and hurry to Space Mountain. Ride.

5. Leave Tomorrowland via the central hub and enter Liberty Square. Turn left and proceed along the waterfront to Splash Mountain. Ride.

6. Exit Splash Mountain to the left and go next door to Big Thunder Mountain Railroad. Ride.

7. Exit Big Thunder Mountain Railroad and bear right to experience the *Country Bear Jamboree*, also in Frontierland.

8. Exit the *Country Bear Jamboree* to your right and, keeping the waterfront on your left, proceed to The Haunted Mansion. Ride.

9. If you're hungry, eat. Fast-food eateries that generally are less crowded include Columbia Harbour House in Liberty Square, Aunt Polly's Dockside Inn on Tom Sawyer Island in Frontierland, El Pirata y el Perico in Adventureland, and The Crystal

Palace at the central hub end of Main Street. As a lunchtime alternative, check your guidemap for the next performance of *The Diamond Horseshoe Saloon Revue*. If the timing is right, eat a sandwich while watching the show.

10. After lunch, enter Adventureland through the passage between the Frontierland Shootin' Arcade and the woodcarving shop. Ride Pirates of the Caribbean.

11. Exit Pirates to the left and proceed to the Frontierland railroad station. Ride the train to Mickey's Toontown Fair.

12. Quickly tour the Fair, exiting via the walkway to Tomorrowland.

13. In Tomorrowland, ride the Tomorrowland Transit Authority.

14. See *Walt Disney's Carousel of Progress*.

15. Ride Buzz Lightyear's Space Ranger Spin.

16. Proceed toward the central hub entrance to Tomorrowland and experience *The Timekeeper*.

17. Via the central hub, return to Liberty Square and check *The Hall of Presidents* and *Liberty Belle* Riverboat. Choose the one with the shorter wait. When you've experienced both, proceed to Step 18.

18. Return to Fantasyland. See *Legend of the Lion King*.

19. Ride It's a Small World.

20. Check the line at Peter Pan's Flight. If the wait is 15 minutes or less, ride. If the wait is longer, skip to Step 21.

21. Exit Fantasyland into Liberty Square and return to Adventureland via the shortcut next to the Frontierland Shootin' Arcade. In Adventureland, ride the Jungle Cruise.

22. After the Cruise, explore Swiss Family Treehouse next door on the right.

23. If you have time left before closing, backtrack to attractions you may have missed or bypassed because lines were too long. View any parades, fireworks, or live performances that interest you. Grab a bite. Save Main Street until last, because it remains open after the rest of the park closes.

24. End your day browsing along Main Street.

Author's Selective Magic Kingdom
One-Day Touring Plan for Adults

For: Adults touring without young children.
Assumes: Willingness to experience all major rides
(including roller coasters) and shows.

This plan includes only those attractions the author believes are the best in the Magic Kingdom. It requires a lot of walking and some backtracking to avoid long lines. Extra walking and morning hustle will spare you two to three hours of standing in line. You might not complete the tour. How far you get depends on how quickly you move from ride to ride, how many times you rest or eat, how quickly the park fills, and what time the park closes.

1. If you're a Disney hotel guest, use Disney transportation to commute to the park, arriving 90 minutes before official opening time *on early-entry days* and 40 minutes before official opening *on non-early-entry days.*

   If you're a day guest, arrive at the parking lot 50 minutes before the Magic Kingdom's official opening time *on a non-early-entry day.* Arrive 90 minutes earlier than official opening if it's a holiday period. Add 15 minutes to the above if you must buy your admission. These arrivals will give you time to park and catch the tram to the Transportation and Ticket Center. At the TTC, transfer to the monorail or ferry to reach the park's entrance. If the line for the monorail is short, take the monorail; otherwise, catch the ferry.

2. At the park, proceed through the turnstiles and have one person go to City Hall for guidemaps containing the daily entertainment schedule.

3. Regroup and move quickly down Main Street to the central hub. Because the Magic Kingdom has two opening procedures, you probably will encounter one of the following:

   a. The entire park will be open. In this case, proceed quickly to *Alien Encounter* in Tomorrowland.

   b. Only Main Street will be open. In this case, turn right at the end of Main Street (before you reach the central hub), pass The Plaza Ice Cream Parlor and The Plaza Restaurant, and stand at the entrance to The Plaza Pavilion. When the rope barrier drops at opening time, jog through The Plaza Pavilion and on to *Alien Encounter*. Starting at the entrance to The Plaza Pavilion will give you a 50-yard advantage over anyone coming from the central hub. Experience *Alien Encounter*.

4. Exit *Alien Encounter*, turn left, and hurry to Space Mountain. Ride.

5. Leave Tomorrowland via the central hub and enter Liberty Square. Turn left and proceed along the waterfront to Splash Mountain. Ride.

6. Exit Splash Mountain to the left and go next door to Big Thunder Mountain Railroad. Ride.

7. Exit Big Thunder Mountain Railroad. Keeping the waterfront on your left, proceed to The Haunted Mansion. Ride.

8. Turn left upon leaving the Mansion and enter Fantasyland. Bear right toward the castle and see *Legend of the Lion King*. The line will appear long, but don't worry. The theater holds 500 people.

9. Retrace your steps to Liberty Square. If you're hungry, eat. Fast-food eateries generally less crowded include the Columbia Harbour House in Liberty Square, Aunt Polly's Dockside Inn on Tom Sawyer Island in Frontierland, El Pirata y el Perico in Adventureland, and The Crystal Palace at the central hub end of Main Street. As a lunchtime alternative, check your guidemap for the next performance of *The Diamond Horseshoe Saloon Revue*. If the timing is right, eat a sandwich while watching the show.

10. After lunch, enter Adventureland through the passage between the Frontierland Shootin' Arcade and the woodcarving shop. Ride Pirates of the Caribbean.

11. Exit Pirates to the left and proceed to the Frontierland railroad station. Ride the train to Mickey's Toontown Fair.

12. Quickly tour the Fair, exiting via the walkway to Tomorrowland.

13. In Tomorrowland, ride the Tomorrowland Transit Authority.

14. See *Walt Disney's Carousel of Progress*.

15. Proceed toward the central hub entrance to Tomorrowland and experience *The Timekeeper*.

16. Return via the central hub to Liberty Square and see *The Hall of Presidents*.

17. Upon exiting *The Hall of Presidents,* turn right and return to Fantasyland. Ride It's a Small World.

18. Check the line at Peter Pan's Flight. If the wait is 15 minutes or less, ride. If the wait is longer, skip to Step 19.

19. Retrace your steps from Fantasyland to Liberty Square and Frontierland. See the *Country Bear Jamboree*.

20. Return to Adventureland via the shortcut next to the Frontierland Shootin' Arcade. Visit the Swiss Family Treehouse.

21. Take the Jungle Cruise, to the left of the Treehouse.

22. If you have time left before closing, backtrack to attractions you may have bypassed because lines were too long. See any parades, fireworks, or live performances that interest you. Grab a bite. Save Main Street until last, because it remains open after the rest of the park closes.

23. End your day browsing along Main Street.

Magic Kingdom One-Day Touring Plan for Parents with Young Children

For: Parents with children younger than age eight.
Assumes: Periodic stops for rest, rest rooms, and refreshments.

This plan represents a compromise between the observed tastes of adults and those of younger children. Included are many amusement park rides that children may have the opportunity to experience at fairs and amusement parks back home. Although these rides are included in the plan, omit them if possible. These cycle-loading rides often have long lines, consuming valuable touring time:

Mad Tea Party	Dumbo the Flying Elephant
Cinderella's Golden Carrousel	Astro Orbiter

This time could be better spent experiencing the many attractions that better demonstrate the Disney creative genius and are found only in the Magic Kingdom. Instead of this plan, try either of the one-day plans for adults and take advantage of "switching off." This allows parents and young children to enter the ride together. At the boarding area, one parent watches the children while the other rides.

Before entering the park, decide whether you will return to your hotel for a midday rest. We strongly recommend that you break from touring and return to your hotel for a swim and a nap (even if you aren't lodging in Walt Disney World). You won't see as much, but everyone will be more relaxed and happy.

**To Convert This One-Day Touring Plan
into a Two-Day Touring Plan**

Skip steps 10 and 11 on the first day. On the second day, arrive 30 minutes prior to opening and take the Walt Disney World Railroad from Main Street to Mickey's Toontown Fair. See Mickey's Toontown Fair in its entirety.

This touring plan requires a lot of walking and some backtracking to avoid long lines. A little extra walking and some morning hustle will spare you two to three hours of standing in line. You probably won't complete the tour. How far you get depends on how quickly you move from ride to ride, how many times you rest or eat, how quickly the park fills, and what time the park closes.

1. If you're a Disney hotel guest, use Disney transportation to commute to the park, arriving 90 minutes before official opening time *on early-entry days* and 40 minutes before official opening *on non-early-entry days*.

   If you're a day guest, arrive at the parking lot 50 minutes before the Magic Kingdom's official opening time *on a non-early-entry day.* Arrive 90 minutes earlier than official opening if it's a holiday period. Add 15 minutes to the above if you must purchase your admission. These arrivals will give you time to park and catch the tram to the Transportation and Ticket Center. At the TTC, transfer to the monorail or ferry to reach the park's entrance. If the line for the monorail is short, take the monorail; otherwise, catch the ferry.

2. At the Magic Kingdom, proceed through the turnstiles and have one person go to City Hall for guidemaps containing the daily entertainment schedule.

3. Rent strollers (if necessary).

4. Move briskly to the end of Main Street. If the entire park is open, go quickly to Fantasyland. Otherwise, position your group by the rope barrier at the central hub. When the park opens and the barrier drops, go through the main door of the castle and ride Dumbo the Flying Elephant in Fantasyland.

5. Ride Peter Pan's Flight.

6. See *Legend of the Lion King*.

7. Exit left from *Lion King* and go to Liberty Square. Turn right at the waterfront and go to The Haunted Mansion. Ride.

8. Enter Frontierland. See the *Country Bear Jamboree*.

9. Go to Adventureland via the passageway between the Frontierland Shootin' Arcade and the woodcarving shop. Ride Pirates of the Caribbean.

10. Turn left out of Pirates and return to Frontierland. At the Frontierland Station, catch the train to Mickey's Toontown Fair. Strollers aren't allowed on the train. Either walk to Mickey's Toontown Fair or leave your stroller at the station, returning by train to retrieve it after visiting the Fair.

11. At the Fair, visit the characters and enjoy Donald's Boat. Ride the roller coaster if the line isn't long.

12. Return to Main Street (walk or take the train) and leave the park for your hotel. Eat lunch and rest. (Have your hand stamped for re-entry as you leave, and keep your parking receipt to show when you return so you won't have to pay again for parking.) Return refreshed to the park between 3:30 and 5 p.m. Once inside, walk or take the train to Frontierland and proceed to Step 13.

13. Take the raft to Tom Sawyer Island. Children could play here all day; set time limits based on the park's closing, your energy, and how many more attractions you wish to experience. If you stayed in the park instead of resting at your hotel, you may want to have lunch at Aunt Polly's Dockside Inn on Tom Sawyer Island. The food is good, and lunchtime crowds are usually lighter than elsewhere.

14. Return to Fantasyland. Ride It's a Small World.

15. Go to Tomorrowland via the castle and central hub. Ride Buzz Lightyear's Space Ranger Spin.

16. Ride the Tommorrowland Transit Authority.

17. Head back toward the central hub entrance to Tomorrowland and try *The Timekeeper*.

18. If you have time or energy left, check the entertainment schedule for parades, fireworks, or live events that interest you. Grab a bite or try any attractions on the plan that you might have missed.

19. End your day browsing Main Street. It stays open later than the rest of the park.

Magic Kingdom Dumbo-or-Die-in-a-Day Touring Plan for Parents with Young Children

For: Adults compelled to devote every waking moment to the pleasure and entertainment of their young children or rich people who are paying someone else to take their children to the theme park.
Prerequisite: This plan is designed for days when the Magic Kingdom doesn't close until 9 p.m. or later.
Assumes: Frequent stops for rest, rest rooms, and refreshment.

Note: Name aside, this touring plan is not a joke. Regardless of whether you're loving, guilty, masochistic, selfless, insane, or saintly, this itinerary will provide a young child with about as perfect a day as is possible at the Magic Kingdom.

To Convert This One-Day Touring Plan into a Two-Day Touring Plan

Skip steps 20 and 21 on the first day. On the second day, arrive 30 minutes prior to opening and take the Walt Disney World Railroad from Main Street to Mickey's Toontown Fair. See Mickey's Toontown Fair in its entirety.

This plan is a concession to adults determined to give their young children the ultimate Magic Kingdom experience. It addresses the preferences, needs, and desires of young children to the virtual exclusion of those of adults or older siblings. If you left the kids with a sitter yesterday or wouldn't let little Marvin eat barbecue for breakfast, this plan will expiate your guilt. It is also a wonderful itinerary if you're paying a sitter, nanny, or chauffeur to take your children to the Magic Kingdom.

1. If you're a Disney hotel guest, use Disney transportation to commute to the park, arriving 90 minutes before official opening time *on early-entry days* and 40 minutes before official opening *on non-early-entry days*.

If you're a day guest, arrive at the parking lot 50 minutes before the Magic Kingdom's official opening time *on a non-early-entry day.* Arrive 90 minutes earlier than official opening if it's a holiday period. Add 15 minutes to the above if you must purchase your admission. These arrivals will give you time to park and catch the tram to the Transportation and Ticket Center. At the TTC, transfer to the monorail or ferry to reach the park's entrance. If the line for the monorail is short, take the monorail; otherwise, catch the ferry.

2. At the Magic Kingdom, proceed through the turnstiles and have one person go to City Hall for guidemaps containing the daily entertainment schedule.

3. Rent a stroller (if needed).

4. Move briskly to the end of Main Street. If the entire park is open, go quickly to Fantasyland. Otherwise, position your group by the rope barrier at the central hub. When the park opens and the barrier is dropped, go through the main door of the castle to Cinderella's Royal Table, on your right as you enter Cinderella Castle.

5. Make a dinner priority seating at the Royal Table for 7 p.m. Eating there will let your kids see the inside of the castle and meet Cinderella. To make your priority seating before you leave home, call (407) 939-3463. If you're a Disney resort guest, dial 55 or 56 to make an advance priority seating.

6. Enter Fantasyland. Ride Dumbo the Flying Elephant.

7. Hey, you're on vacation! Ride again, using the Chuck Bubba Relay if there are two adults in your party (pages 167–168).

8. Experience Mr. Toad's Wild Ride, near Dumbo.

9. Ride Peter Pan's Flight.

10. Ride Cinderella's Golden Carrousel.

11. See *Legend of the Lion King.*

12. Bearing left, go to the Skyway. Ride to Tomorrowland.

    Note: Strollers aren't allowed on the Skyway. If you have a stroller, walk to Tomorrowland.

13. In Tomorrowland, ride the Tomorrowland Speedway. Let your child steer (cars run on a guide rail) while you work the foot pedal.

14. Ride the Astro Orbiter.

    Safety note: Seat your children in the vehicle before you get in. Also, the Astro Orbiter goes higher and faster than Dumbo and may frighten some children.

15. Ride Buzz Lightyear's Space Ranger Spin (near the Astro Orbiter).

16. Return to Main Street via the central hub and leave the park for your hotel. Eat lunch and rest. (Have your hand stamped for re-entry when you leave the park. Keep your parking receipt to show when you return so you won't have to pay again for parking.)

    If you elect not to take a break out of the park, skip to Step 18.

17. Return to the Magic Kingdom refreshed about 4 or 4:30 p.m. Take the Walt Disney World Railroad to Frontierland.

18. Take the raft to Tom Sawyer Island. Stay as long as the kids want. If you're hungry, Aunt Polly's Dockside Inn on Tom Sawyer Island is a winner for both kids and adults.

19. After you return from the island, see the *Country Bear Jamboree.*

20. Return to the Frontierland Station. Ride the train to Mickey's Toontown Fair.

    Note: You'll have to leave your stroller in Frontierland.

21. Walk through Mickey's Country House and Minnie's Country House and play on Donald's Boat (tips for the latter are on page 387). Meet Disney characters at the Toontown Hall of Fame and pose for photos.

22. You should be within an hour of your dinner priority seating at Cinderella's Royal Table. If you left your stroller in Frontierland, take the train back to retrieve it and then walk to Fantasyland. If you don't have a stroller, take the direct path from Mickey's Toontown Fair to Fantasyland. In Fantasyland, if you have 20 minutes or more before your priority seating, ride It's a Small World. Don't forget to sing.

23. Eat; then leave Fantasyland and go to Liberty Square. If your children are up to it, see The Haunted Mansion. If not, skip to Step 24.

24. Evening parades are quite worthwhile. If you're interested, adjust the remainder of the touring plan to allow you to take a

viewing position about 10 minutes before the early parade starts (usually 8 or 9 p.m.). See our recommendations for good vantage points (pages 404–406). If you aren't interested in the parade, enjoy attractions in Adventureland while the parade is in progress. Lines will be vastly diminished.

25. Go to Adventureland by way of Liberty Square, Frontierland, or the central hub. Take the Jungle Cruise if the lines aren't long. If they're prohibitive, try the *Tropical Serenade (Enchanted Tiki Birds)* and/or the Swiss Family Treehouse. If your children can stand a few skeletons, see Pirates of the Caribbean.

26. If you have time or energy left, repeat any attractions the kids especially liked, or try ones on the plan you might have bypassed because of long lines. Buy Goofy hats if that cranks your tractor.

27. If you're parked at the Transportation and Ticket Center, catch the ferry or express monorail. If the express monorail line is long, catch the resort monorail and disembark at the TTC.

Magic Kingdom Two-Day Touring Plan

For: Parties wishing to spread their Magic Kingdom visit over two days.
Assumes: Willingness to experience all major rides (including roller coasters) and shows.

Timing: This two-day touring plan takes advantage of early-morning touring. Each day, you should complete the structured part of the plan by about 4 p.m. This leaves plenty of time for live entertainment. If the park is open late (after 8 p.m.), consider returning to your hotel at midday for a swim and a nap. Eat an early dinner outside Walt Disney World and return refreshed to enjoy the park's nighttime festivities.

Day One

1. If you're a Disney hotel guest, use Disney transportation to commute to the park, arriving 90 minutes before official opening time *on early-entry days* and 40 minutes before official opening *on non-early-entry days*.

   If you're a day guest, arrive at the parking lot 50 minutes before the Magic Kingdom's official opening *on a non-early-*

entry day. Arrive 90 minutes earlier than official opening if it's a holiday period. Add 15 minutes to the above if you must purchase your admission. These arrivals will give you time to park and catch the tram to the Transportation and Ticket Center. At the TTC, transfer to the monorail or ferry to reach the park's entrance. If the line for the monorail is short, take the monorail; otherwise, catch the ferry.

2. At the park, proceed through the turnstiles and have one person go to City Hall for guidemaps containing the daily entertainment schedule.

3. Move as fast as you can down Main Street to the central hub. Because the Magic Kingdom uses two procedures for opening, you probably will encounter one of the following:

    a. The entire park will be open. In this case, proceed quickly to *Alien Encounter* in Tomorrowland.

    b. Only Main Street will be open. In this case, turn right at the end of Main Street (before you reach the central hub), pass The Plaza Ice Cream Parlor and The Plaza Restaurant and position your group at the entrance to The Plaza Pavilion. When the park opens and the rope barrier drops, jog through The Plaza Pavilion and on to *Alien Encounter.* Starting at the entrance to The Plaza Pavilion will give you a 50-yard advantage over anyone coming from the central hub. Experience *Alien Encounter.*

4. Turn left after exiting *Alien Encounter* and move briskly to Space Mountain. Ride.

5. Exit Space Mountain, bear right past the Tomorrowland Speedway, and go to Fantasyland. Ride Peter Pan's Flight.

6. Exit Peter Pan to the right and turn the corner. See *Legend of the Lion King.*

7. Exit *Lion King* to the left, cross the courtyard, and ride It's a Small World.

8. Exit Small World to the right and go to Liberty Square. Experience The Haunted Mansion.

9. See *The Hall of Presidents.*

10. If you're hungry, eat. Fast-food eateries that generally are less crowded include the Columbia Harbour House in Liberty

Square, Aunt Polly's Dockside Inn on Tom Sawyer Island in Frontierland, El Pirata y el Perico in Adventureland, and The Crystal Palace at the central hub end of Main Street. As a lunchtime alternative, check your guidemap for the next performance of *The Diamond Horseshoe Saloon Revue.* If the timing is right, eat a sandwich while watching the show.

11. After lunch, ride the *Liberty Belle* Riverboat.

    Note: At this point, check the entertainment schedule to see if any parades or live performances interest you. Note the times and alter the touring plan accordingly. Since you already have seen all the attractions that cause bottlenecks and have big lines, interrupting the touring plan here won't cause any problems. Simply pick up where you left off before the parade or show.

12. In Frontierland, take a raft to Tom Sawyer Island. Explore.

13. Return from the island and see the *Country Bear Jamboree.*

14. This concludes the touring plan for the day. Enjoy the shops, see some of the live entertainment, or revisit your favorite attractions until you're ready to leave.

Day Two

1. If you're a Disney hotel guest, use Disney transportation to commute to the park, arriving 60 minutes before official opening time *on early-entry days* and 40 minutes before official opening *on non-early-entry days.*

   If you're a day guest, arrive at the parking lot 50 minutes before the Magic Kingdom's official opening time *on a non-early-entry day.* Arrive 90 minutes earlier than official opening if it's a holiday period. Add 15 minutes to the above if you must purchase your admission. These arrivals will give you time to park and catch the tram to the Transportation and Ticket Center. At the TTC, transfer to the monorail or ferry to reach the park's entrance. If the line for the monorail is short, take the monorail; otherwise, catch the ferry.

2. At the park, proceed through the turnstiles. Stop at City Hall for guidemaps containing the day's entertainment schedule.

   Note: If you're a Disney resort guest and enter the park on an early-entry day, revisit your favorite Fantasyland and Tomorrowland attractions. As the time approaches for the park to open to the public, position yourself in Fantasyland at the boundary between Fantasyland and Liberty Square. When the other lands open, head for the Liberty Square waterfront and from there to Splash Mountain. After Splash Mountain, pick up the touring plan at Big Thunder Mountain Railroad (Step 4), skipping steps that direct you to attractions you experienced during your early-entry hour.

3. Proceed to the end of Main Street. If the entire park is open, go immediately to Splash Mountain in Frontierland. Otherwise, turn left past Casey's Corner and position yourself in front of The Crystal Palace, facing the walkway bridge to Adventureland. When the park opens and the rope barrier drops, cross the bridge and turn left into Adventureland. Cut through Adventureland into Frontierland. Go straight to Splash Mountain and ride.

4. Ride Big Thunder Mountain Railroad, next to Splash Mountain.

5. Return to Adventureland. Ride the Jungle Cruise.

6. Across the street, see the *Tropical Serenade (Enchanted Tiki Birds)*.

7. Walk through the Swiss Family Treehouse.

8. Exit the Treehouse to the left. Enjoy Pirates of the Caribbean.

   Note: At this point, check the daily entertainment schedule to see if any parades or live performances interest you. Note the times, and alter the touring plan accordingly. Since you already have seen all the attractions that cause bottlenecks and have big lines, interrupting the touring plan here won't cause any problems. Simply pick up where you left off before the parade or show.

9. If you're hungry, eat. Fast-food eateries that generally are less crowded include the Columbia Harbour House in Liberty Square, Aunt Polly's Dockside Inn on Tom Sawyer Island in Frontierland, El Pirata y el Perico in Adventureland, and The Crystal Palace at the central hub end of Main Street.

10. Exit Adventureland and go to the Frontierland train station between Splash and Big Thunder mountains. Catch the Walt Disney World Railroad. Disembark at Mickey's Toontown Fair (first stop).

11. Tour the Fair and meet the Disney characters.

12. Exit the Fair via the path to Tomorrowland.

13. In Tomorrowland, if you haven't eaten, try Cosmic Ray's Starlight Cafe (okay) or The Plaza Pavilion (better).

14. Ride the Tomorrowland Transit Authority.

15. See *Walt Disney's Carousel of Progress.*

16. Ride Buzz Lightyear's Space Ranger Spin.

17. Proceed toward the central hub entrance of Tomorrowland and experience *The Timekeeper.*

18. This concludes the touring plan. Enjoy the shops, see live entertainment, or revisit your favorite attractions until you are ready to leave.

Part Ten

Epcot

Not to Be Missed at Epcot	
World Showcase	*The American Adventure* *IllumiNations*
Future World	Spaceship Earth Living with the Land *Honey, I Shrunk the Audience* Test Track Body Wars *Cranium Command*

OVERVIEW

Education, inspiration, and corporate imagery are the focus at Epcot, the most adult of the Disney theme parks. What it gains in taking a futuristic, visionary, and technological look at the world, it loses, just a bit, in warmth, happiness, and charm.

Some people find the attempts at education to be superficial; others want more entertainment and less education. Most visitors, however, are in between, finding plenty of entertainment *and* education.

Epcot is more than twice as big as the Magic Kingdom or Disney-MGM Studios and, though smaller than the Animal Kingdom, has more territory to be covered on foot. Epcot rarely sees the congestion so common to the Magic Kingdom, but it has lines every bit as long as those at the Jungle Cruise or Space Mountain. Visitors must come prepared to do considerable walking among attractions and a comparable amount of standing in line.

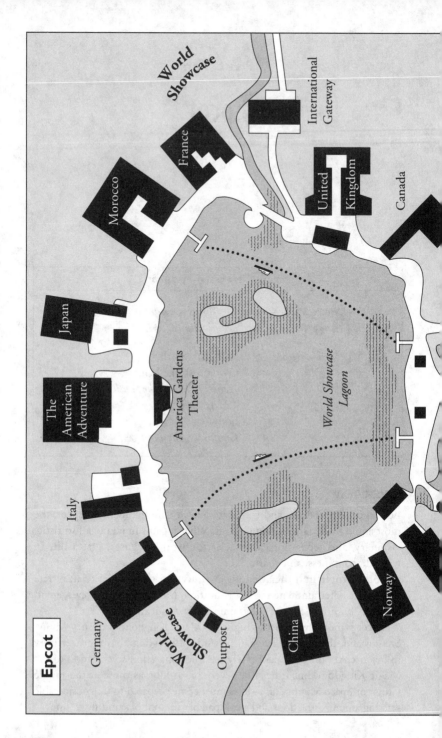

Epcot

World Showcase

International Gateway

France

Morocco

Japan

United Kingdom

Canada

The American Adventure

America Gardens Theater

World Showcase Lagoon

Italy

Germany

World Showcase

Outpost

China

Norway

Epcot's size means you can't see it all in one day without skipping an attraction or two and giving others a cursory glance. A major difference between Epcot and the other parks, however, is that some Epcot attractions can be savored slowly or skimmed, depending on personal interests. For example, the first section of General Motors' Test Track is a thrill ride, the second a collection of walk-through exhibits. Nearly all visitors take the ride, but many people, lacking time or interest, bypass the exhibits.

We have identified several Epcot attractions as "not to be missed." But part of the enjoyment of the park is that there's something for everyone. Ask your group. They're sure to have a variety of opinions as to which attraction is "best."

OPERATING HOURS

Epcot has two theme areas: Future World and World Showcase. Each has its own operating hours. Though schedules change throughout the year, Future World always opens before World Showcase in the morning, and usually closes before World Showcase in the evening. Most of the year, World Showcase opens two hours later than Future World. For exact hours during your visit, call (407) 824-4321.

ARRIVING

Disney resort and campground guests are invited to enter Epcot one hour before official opening on specified days each week. If you have early-entry privileges and want to exercise them, arrive about an hour and a half before the official opening time. For example, if official opening is 9 a.m., arrive by 7:30 a.m.

Visitors lodging outside Walt Disney World must balance the least crowded days of the week (page 45) with an estimation of early entry's impact. We recommend day guests avoid Epcot when it's designated for early entry. It's far better to arrive early and stay ahead of the crowd on non-early-entry days than to tour on an early-entry day when hordes of Disney lodging guests have been allowed into the park ahead of you. The key to efficient touring at any of the parks is to be among the first guests through the turnstiles. If you don't have early-entry privileges, arrive 40 to 50 minutes before official opening on a non-early-entry day and wait to be admitted.

Persons ineligible for early entry shouldn't try sneaking in with early-entry guests. All Disney lodging guests, including children, are issued dated identification cards when they check in at their hotel. These either serve as or must be presented with a valid admission pass in order to enter a park early.

Early-entry days and opening times change. To verify those in effect during your visit, call Walt Disney World Information at (407) 824-4321 before you leave home.

Arriving at the park by private automobile is easy and direct. Epcot has its own parking lot and, unlike at the Magic Kingdom, there's no need to take a monorail or ferry to reach the entrance. Trams serve the parking lot, or you can walk to the front gate. Monorail service connects Epcot with the Transportation and Ticket Center, the Magic Kingdom (transfer required), and Magic Kingdom resorts (transfer required).

GETTING ORIENTED

Epcot's theme areas are distinctly different. Future World combines Disney creativity and major corporations' technological resources to examine where mankind has come from and where it's going. World Showcase features landmarks, cuisine, and culture of almost a dozen nations and is meant to be a sort of permanent World's Fair.

Navigating Epcot is unlike getting around at the Magic Kingdom. The Magic Kingdom is designed so that nearly every location is part of a specific environment—Liberty Square or Main Street, U.S.A., for example. All environments are visually separated to preserve the atmosphere. It wouldn't do for the Jungle Cruise to pass beneath the futuristic spires of Space Mountain, for instance.

Epcot, by contrast, is visually open. And while it seems strange to see a Japanese pagoda and the Eiffel Tower on the same horizon, getting around is fairly simple. An exception is in Future World, where the enormous east and west Innoventions buildings hide everything on the opposite sides.

Cinderella Castle is the central landmark at the Magic Kingdom. At Epcot, the architectural symbol is Spaceship Earth. This shiny, 180-foot geosphere is visible from almost everywhere in the park. Like Cinderella Castle at the Magic Kingdom, Spaceship Earth can help you keep track of where you are in Epcot. But it's in a high-traffic area and isn't centrally located, so it isn't a good meeting place.

Any of the distinctive national pavilions in World Showcase makes a good meeting place, but be specific. "Hey, let's meet in Japan!" sounds fun, but each pavilion is a mini-town with buildings, monuments, gardens, and plazas. You could wander quite awhile "in Japan" without finding your group. Pick a specific place in Japan—the sidewalk side of the pagoda, for example.

THE NEW EPCOT

Correctly assessing that Epcot was getting stale, Disney updated the park beginning in 1994. The Land pavilion and its attractions were renovated.

CommuniCore, at the heart of Future World, was replaced with Innoventions, an ongoing trade show featuring products and technologies of the near future. Spaceship Earth, the attraction inside the huge sphere, was partially redesigned and enhanced, and a new 3-D movie premiered at the Journey into Imagination pavilion. Additional street vendors and entertainers were introduced into World Showcase to make it more lively and give it a sense of community, and two new shows were integrated into the park's live entertainment. Upgrades continued into 1998, when Test Track, a headliner thrill ride, was opened (at least for a while) in Future World.

The EPCOT Acronym

"Epcot" originally was "EPCOT." From when it was envisioned by Walt Disney as a utopian working city of the future until about 1995, EPCOT was the acronym for Experimental Prototype Community Of Tomorrow. When corporate Disney altered Walt's vision and the city became a theme park, the name remained. But because EPCOT was clearly nothing of the sort, the acronym "EPCOT" became the name "Epcot."

Future World

Gleaming, futuristic structures of immense proportions define the first theme area you encounter at Epcot. Broad thoroughfares are punctuated with billowing fountains—all reflected in shining, space-age facades. Everything, including landscaping, is sparkling clean and seems bigger than life. Pavilions dedicated to mankind's past, present, and future technological accomplishments form the perimeter of Future World. Front and center is Spaceship Earth, flanked by Innoventions East and West.

Most Epcot services are concentrated in Future World's Entrance Plaza, near the main gate.

GUEST RELATIONS

Description and Comments   Guest Relations, left of the geodesic sphere, is Epcot's equivalent of the Magic Kingdom's City Hall. It serves as park headquarters and as Epcot's primary information center. Attendants staff information booths, and WorldKey Information Satellite terminals are available just outside.

Touring Tips   If you wish to eat in one of Epcot's sit-down restaurants, you can make your priority seating at Guest Relations through a WorldKey attendant. In the morning, all WorldKey screens outside Guest Relations are tuned to restaurant reservationists. Just march up to the terminal and tell the reservationist where you want to dine.

Spaceship Earth

What It Is: Educational dark ride through past, present, and future
Scope & Scale: Headliner
When to Go: Before 10 a.m. or after 4 p.m.
Special Comments: If lines are long when you arrive, try again after 4 p.m.
Author's Rating: One of Epcot's best; not to be missed; ★★★★
Appeal by Age Group:

Pre-school	Grade School	Teens	Young Adults	Over 30	Senior Citizens
★★★	★★★★	★★★½	★★★★	★★★★	★★★★

Duration of Ride: About 16 minutes
Average Wait in Line per 100 People ahead of You: 3 minutes
Assumes: Normal operation
Loading Speed: Fast

Description and Comments This AT&T ride spirals through the 18-story interior of Epcot's premier landmark, taking visitors past Audio-Animatronic scenes depicting mankind's developments in communications, from cave painting to printing to television to space communications and computer networks. The ride, updated and improved in 1994, is compelling and well done.

Touring Tips Because it's near Epcot's main entrance, Spaceship Earth is inundated with arriving guests throughout the morning. If you're among the first in the park, ride. Otherwise, postpone Spaceship Earth until, say, after 4 p.m.

As you face the entrance to Spaceship Earth, notice that the direct walkway to the entrance runs between two labyrinthine queuing areas. If they're in use, bypass Spaceship Earth for now. If they're nearly empty, hop in line. Spaceship Earth loads continuously and quickly. If the line runs only along the right side of the sphere, you'll board in less than 15 minutes.

Global Neighborhood

What It Is: Interactive communications playground
Scope & Scale: Diversion
When to Go: After riding Spaceship Earth
Special Comments: Spaceship Earth disembarks passengers directly into the Global Neighborhood
Author's Rating: High-tech fun; ★★½

Future World Services

Epcot's service facilities in Future World include:

Wheelchair & Stroller Rental	Inside the main entrance and to the left, toward the rear of the Entrance Plaza.
Banking Services	ATMs are outside the main entrance near the kennels, on the Future World bridge, and in World Showcase at the Germany pavilion.
Storage Lockers	Turn right at Spaceship Earth (lockers are cleaned out nightly).
Lost & Found	Outside the main entrance and to the far right.
Live Entertainment & Parade Information	At Guest Relations, left of Spaceship Earth.
Lost Persons	At Guest Relations and the Baby Center on the World Showcase side of the Odyssey Center.
Dining Priority Seating	At Guest Relations and at World-Key Information Satellites.
Walt Disney World & Local Attraction Information	At Guest Relations.
First Aid	Next to the Baby Center on the World Showcase side of the Odyssey Center.
Baby Center/ Baby-Care Needs	On the World Showcase side of the Odyssey Center.

Appeal by Age Group:

Pre- school	Grade School	Teens	Young Adults	Over 30	Senior Citizens
★★	★★★½	★★★½	★★★½	★★½	★★½

Duration of Attraction: Not limited

Average Wait in Line per 100 People ahead of You: No wait

Description and Comments   Global Neighborhood is at the base of the geosphere. Presented by AT&T, it's a walk-through playground of futuristic, interactive communications devices. Platform simulator rides take two to six guests at a time on a tour of the AT&T Network. A *Storyteller* touch screen allows guests to embellish a story setting by accessing computer-programmed visual and sound effects. The best of the interactive devices is *Communications Breakthrough,* which combines word cues and teamwork with an electronic shooting gallery.

Touring Tips   If Spaceship Earth is busy, the Global Neighborhood will be, too. If you want to spend some time there, go during late afternoon or evening. You don't have to ride Spaceship Earth to enter the Global Neighborhood. Walk directly in from the plaza on the far side of the geosphere.

Innoventions

What It Is: Static and "hands-on" exhibits relating to products and technologies of the near future

Scope & Scale: Major diversion

When to Go: On your second day at Epcot or after you have seen all major attractions

Special Comments: Most exhibits demand time and participation to be rewarding; not much gained here by a quick walk-through

Author's Rating: Vastly improved; ★★★½

Appeal by Age Group:

Pre-school	Grade School	Teens	Young Adults	Over 30	Senior Citizens
★½	★★★½	★★★★	★★★½	★★★	★★★

Description and Comments   Innoventions consists of two huge, crescent-shaped, glass-walled structures separated by a central plaza. Formerly known as CommuniCore, the complex was designed to be the communications and community hub of Epcot, but something was lost in execution. During Epcot's first 12 years, CommuniCore was, at best, a staid museum of science and industry and, at worst, a huge obstacle to circumnavigate when you wanted to cross from one side of Future World to the other.

In 1994, Disney set out to return it to the original concept, this time with a marketplace rather than communications orientation. The result is a huge, busy collection of industry-sponsored, walk-through, hands-on exhibits. Dynamic, interactive, and forward-looking, Innoventions resembles a high-tech trade show. Products preview consumer and industrial goods of the near future. Electronics, communications, and entertainment technology play a prominent role. Exhibits, many of which are changed each year, demonstrate such products as virtual reality games, high-definition TV, voice-activated appliances, and CD-ROM applications. Each of the 15 or so major exhibit areas is sponsored by a different manufacturer or research lab. The emphasis in exhibits is the effect of the product or technology on daily living. The most popular Innoventions attraction is an arcade of video and simulator games. The buildings also house restaurants, gift shops, and the Epcot Discovery Center (described below).

Unofficial Guide reader response to Innoventions is mixed. A family from Port Chester, New York, writes:

> The more unstructured "interactive" parts were incredibly noisy and confusing—rather like a crowded video arcade with games that didn't work very well. Crowd control was poor. The setup leads to pushing and shoving to get to control boards. My kids, being small girls, didn't stand a chance of getting near anything. The display portions of the attraction "Home of the Future," etc., most clearly resembled a trade show at the Javits Center or the fixture displays at Home Depot. Such treats as a booth devoted entirely to faucets hardly suggested the fun and magic one usually associates with WDW. This whole pavilion seemed far more commercial than magical.

We receive a lot of complaints about how difficult it is for children (and even adults) to get a turn on Innoventions' more high-tech gadgets. This comment from a New England woman is typical:

> The virtual reality exhibit was poorly structured [and] there was no time limit. Hence, I was fifth in line and even with two sets of goggles working, I was told I would have to wait at least a half hour to try out the goggles! This was due to a small number of techno-geeks who hogged the attraction and kept going without regard to others in line.

A father of three from Tulsa, Oklahoma, writes:

> The best things at Epcot for my kids were the hands-on exhibits at Innoventions. We bumped into the computer games there as we were passing through en route to something else (I don't remember what, because we never got there).

A mom from Bartlesville, Oklahoma, adds:

> *My 14-year-old son's favorite attraction was Innoventions. He spent*
> *hours there and would have spent more if we'd let him. All those free*
> *Sega games was a teenage boy's idea of heaven.*

Touring Tips   Innoventions East and West provide visitors an opportunity
to preview products of tomorrow in a fun, hands-on manner. Some
exhibits are intriguing, while others are less compelling. We observed a
wide range of reactions by visitors to the exhibits and can suggest only that
you form your own opinion. Regarding touring strategy, spend time at
Innoventions on your second day at Epcot. If you have only one day, visit
during the evening if you have the time and endurance. Many exhibits,
however, are technical and may not be compatible with your mood or
energy toward the end of a long day. Also, you can't get much out of a
walk-through; you have to invest time to understand what's going on.

Epcot Discovery Center

Description and Comments   The Discovery Center offers static displays
illustrating Epcot projects and developments. A library service provides
information on any topic presented in Future World or World Showcase.
Past users should note that the center has been relocated to the far end of
Innoventions East.

Touring Tips   This is where someone will try to answer that question
you've been kicking around all day. If you're an educator with a group,
tour-enhancing handouts are available here.

THE LIVING SEAS 〉

What It Is: Ride beneath a huge saltwater aquarium, plus exhibits on
  oceanography, ocean ecology, and sea life
Scope & Scale: Major attraction
When to Go: Before 10 a.m. or after 3 p.m.
Special Comments: The ride is only a small component of this attraction
Author's Rating: An excellent marine exhibit; ★★★½
Appeal by Age Group:

Pre-school	Grade School	Teens	Young Adults	Over 30	Senior Citizens
★★★	★★★	★★★	★★★★	★★★★	★★★★

Duration of Ride: 3 minutes
Average Wait in Line per 100 People ahead of You: 3½ minutes
Assumes: All elevators in operation

Loading Speed: Fast

Description and Comments The Living Seas is among Future World's most ambitious offerings. Scientists and divers conduct actual marine experiments in a 200-foot-diameter, 27-foot-deep main tank containing fish, mammals, and crustaceans in a simulation of an ocean ecosystem. Visitors can watch the activity through 8-inch-thick windows below the surface (including some in the Coral Reef restaurant) and aboard a three-part adventure ride consisting of a movie dramatizing the link between the ocean and man's survival, a simulated elevator descent to the bottom of the tank, and a three-minute gondola voyage through an underwater viewing tunnel.

The Living Seas' fish population has grown substantially, but the underwater ride is over almost before you're comfortably settled in the gondola. No matter, the strength of this attraction lies in the dozen or so exhibits offered afterward. Visitors can view fish-breeding experiments, watch short films about sea life, and more. The main aquarium, which the ride transits, can also be viewed through huge windows. Stay as long as you wish in the exhibit areas.

The Living Seas is a high-quality marine/aquarium exhibit, but it's no substitute for visiting Sea World, an outstanding marine theme park in Orlando. Sea World is on a par with the Disney theme parks in quality, appeal, educational value, and entertainment.

Touring Tips Exhibits at the end of the ride are the best part of The Living Seas. In the morning, they're often bypassed by guests rushing to stay ahead of the crowd. The Living Seas needs to be lingered over when you aren't in a hurry. Go in late afternoon or evening, or on your second day at Epcot.

THE LAND PAVILION

Description and Comments The Land is a huge pavilion containing three attractions and several restaurants. It was extensively renovated in 1994, and its three attractions were updated and improved. The original emphasis was on farming, but it now focuses on environmental concerns.

Touring Tips This is a good place for a fast-food lunch. If you're there to see the attractions, however, don't go during mealtimes.

Living with the Land

What It Is: Indoor boat-ride adventure through the past, present, and future of U.S. farming and agriculture

Scope & Scale: Major attraction

When to Go: Before 10:30 a.m. or after 7:30 p.m.

Special Comments: Take the ride early in the morning, but save other Land attractions for later in the day. It's located on the pavilion's lower level

Author's Rating: Interesting and fun; not to be missed; ★★★★

Appeal by Age Group:

Pre-school	Grade School	Teens	Young Adults	Over 30	Senior Citizens
★★½	★★★	★★★½	★★★★	★★★★	★★★★

Duration of Ride: About 12 minutes

Average Wait in Line per 100 People ahead of You: 3 minutes

Assumes: 15 boats operating

Loading Speed: Moderate

Description and Comments   Boat ride takes visitors through swamps, past inhospitable environments man has faced as a farmer, and through a futuristic, innovative greenhouse where real crops are grown using the latest agricultural technologies. Inspiring and educational, with excellent effects and good narrative.

Many Epcot guests who read about Living with the Land in guidebooks decide it sounds too dry and educational for their tastes. A woman from Houston, Texas, writes:

> *I had a bad attitude about Living with the Land, as I heard it was an agricultural exhibit. I just didn't think I was up for a movie about wheat farming. Wow, was I surprised. I really wished I had not had a preconceived idea about an exhibit. Living with the Land was truly wonderful.*

Touring Tips   See this attraction before the lunch crowd hits The Land restaurants or after 7:30 p.m.

If you really enjoy this ride or have a special interest in the agricultural techniques demonstrated, take the Behind the Seeds Greenhouse Tour. It's a one-hour guided walk behind the scenes for an in-depth examination of advanced and experimental growing methods. It costs $6 for adults and $4 for children ages three to nine. Reservations are made on a space-available basis at the guided tour waiting area (far right of the restaurants on the lower level).

Food Rocks

What It Is: Audio-Animatronic theater show about food and nutrition

Scope & Scale: Minor attraction

When to Go: Before 11 a.m. or after 2 p.m.

Special Comments: On the lower level of The Land pavilion

Author's Rating: Sugar-coated nutrition lesson; ★★½

Appeal by Age Group:

Pre-school	Grade School	Teens	Young Adults	Over 30	Senior Citizens
★★★	★★★	★★½	★★★	★★★	★★★

Duration of Presentation: About 13 minutes

Preshow Entertainment: None

Probable Waiting Time: Less than 10 minutes

Description and Comments   Audio-Animatronic foods and cooking utensils perform in a marginally educational rock concert. Featured artists include the Peach Boys, Chubby Cheddar, Neil Moussaka, and Pita Gabriel. Little Richard provides the voice of a pineapple singing "Tutti Frutti." Fast-paced and imaginative, *Food Rocks* is better entertainment than its predecessor, *Kitchen Kabaret,* and delivers the proper-diet-and-balanced-nutrition message about as well.

Touring Tips   One of the few light-entertainment offerings at Epcot. Slightly reminiscent of the *Country Bear Jamboree* in the Magic Kingdom (but not as humorous or endearing). The theater isn't large, but we never have encountered long waits, even during mealtimes.

Circle of Life Theater

What It Is: Film exploring man's relationship with his environment

Scope & Scale: Minor attraction

When to Go: Before 11 a.m. and after 2 p.m.

Author's Rating: Highly interesting and enlightening; ★★★½

Appeal by Age Group:

Pre-school	Grade School	Teens	Young Adults	Over 30	Senior Citizens
★★★	★★★	★★★	★★★	★★★	★★★

Duration of Presentation: About 12½ minutes

Preshow Entertainment: None

Probable Waiting Time: 10–15 minutes

Description and Comments   The featured attraction is *The Circle of Life*, starring Simba, Timon, and Pumbaa from Disney's animated feature *The*

Lion King. This superb film spotlights the environmental interdependency of all creatures on earth, demonstrating how easily the ecological balance can be upset. It's sobering, but not too heavy-handed.

Touring Tips Every visitor should see this highly worthwhile film. If you're trying to stay ahead of the crowd, see it in late afternoon. Long lines usually occur at mealtimes.

JOURNEY INTO IMAGINATION PAVILION

Description and Comments Multiattraction pavilion on the west side of Innoventions West and down the walk from The Land. Outside is an "upside-down waterfall" and one of our favorite Future World landmarks, the "jumping water," a fountain that hops over the heads of unsuspecting passersby.

Touring Tips We recommend early-morning or late-evening touring. See the individual attractions for specifics.

Journey into Imagination

What It Is: Dark fantasy-adventure ride
Scope & Scale: Major attraction
When to Go: Before 10:30 a.m. or after 6 p.m.
Author's Rating: Colorful but dull; ★★
Appeal by Age Group:

Pre-school	Grade School	Teens	Young Adults	Over 30	Senior Citizens
★★★½	★★★½	★★½	★★½	★★½	★★½

Duration of Ride: About 13 minutes
Average Wait in Line per 100 People ahead of You: 3 minutes
Assumes: 20 trains operating
Loading Speed: Moderate to fast

Description and Comments This ride stars Figment, an impish purple dragon, and Dreamfinder, a red-bearded adventurer who pilots a contraption designed to search out and capture ideas. This ride, with its happy, humorous orientation, is among Epcot's lighter and more fanciful offerings. It's the favorite ride of some visitors; others find it dull and vacuous.

A mother from Springfield, Missouri, who toured with her husband and children (ages four, seven, and ten), writes:

> *Keep telling people that Journey into Imagination is boring. It is not worth a five-minute wait. We voted it the most boring ride at WDW.*

A couple from Alameda, California, agrees:

> *Journey into Imagination was without question the dumbest, dullest attraction we visited. It did, however, unwittingly provide a moment of high hilarity. The photo that was taken of us toward the end of the ride showed my husband with his eyes shut and me looking sad and profoundly bored. It's a good thing they don't provide copies of those photos.*

A reader from Montreal, Quebec, has this to say:

> *I don't agree with your rating for Journey into Imagination. You claimed it to be dull, but I find it warm, happy, and a great ride. I feel this should be on the "not to be missed" list.*

Touring Tips   This ride, combined with the 3-D movie in the same building, draws large crowds, beginning about 10:30 a.m.

The Image Works

What It Is: Hands-on creative playground

Scope & Scale: Diversion

When to Go: Anytime

Special Comments: You don't have to wait in the long line for the ride in this pavilion to enter The Image Works. Simply go through the open door to the left of where the ride line is entering

Author's Rating: A fun change of pace; be sure to see Dreamfinder's School of Drama; ★★½

Appeal by Age Group:

Pre-school	Grade School	Teens	Young Adults	Over 30	Senior Citizens
★★½	★★★	★★½	★★½	★★½	★★

Probable Waiting Time: None

Description and Comments   This playground for the imagination employs light, color, sound, and electronic devices that visitors can manipulate. The Magic Palette has a video-screen canvas and an electronic paintbrush. Especially fun is the Electronic Philharmonic, which enables visitors to conduct the brass, woodwind, percussion, and string sections of an orchestra by moving their hands. (The secret is raising and lowering your hands over the labeled discs on the console. Don't press the discs as if they were buttons. Pretend you're a conductor—raise a hand away from the disc labeled brass, for example, and you'll get louder brass. Lower your hand toward the disc labeled woodwinds, and you'll get less volume from the woodwinds.)

Dreamfinder's School of Drama is the best offering at The Image Works. Children volunteer to act in a short play augmented by video effects.

A couple touring with their three-year-old writes:

> Another favorite of his [the child] and mine [Mom] was the chance to perform in a Dreamfinder short story at The Image Works. In these stories the players stand in front of a large blue screen and watch themselves get inserted [by video] into a simple story. The process is the same as is used by a local [TV] weatherman, and the acting instructions are clear and easy: "run in place" or "duck down." Video-taping the large [video] screen makes a great souvenir—just don't dress in blue.

Touring Tips   There are many interesting activities here, more than we list. If you have more than one day at Epcot, save The Image Works for the second day. If you're on a one-day schedule, work it in during evening or late afternoon.

Honey, I Shrunk the Audience

What It Is: 3-D film with special effects

Scope & Scale: Headliner

When to Go: Before 10 a.m. or just before Future World closes

Special Comments: Adults should not be put off by the sci-fi theme. The loud, intense show with tactile effects frightens some young children.

Author's Rating: An absolute hoot! Not to be missed; ★★★★½

Appeal by Age Group:

Pre-school	Grade School	Teens	Young Adults	Over 30	Senior Citizens
★★★	★★★★½	★★★★½	★★★★	★★★★	★★★★

Duration of Presentation: About 17 minutes

Preshow Entertainment: 8 minutes

Probable Waiting Time: 12 minutes (at suggested times)

Description and Comments   *Honey, I Shrunk the Audience* is a 3-D off-shoot of Disney's feature film, *Honey, I Shrunk the Kids*. Replacing the long-running *Captain EO* (starring Michael Jackson), *Honey, I Shrunk the Audience* features a similar array of special effects, including simulated explosions, smoke, fiber optics, lights, water spray, and moving seats. Whereas *Captain EO* had a message of brotherly love, *Honey, I Shrunk the Audience* is played strictly for laughs, a commodity in short supply in Epcot entertainment.

Touring Tips   The sound level is earsplitting, frightening some young children. Many adults report that the loud soundtrack is distracting, even uncomfortable. While *Honey, I Shrunk the Audience* is a huge hit, it can be overwhelming for preschoolers. A dad from Lexington, South Carolina, writes:

> Honey, I Shrunk the Audience *is too intense for kids. Our four-year-old took off his [3-D] glasses five minutes into the movie. Because of this experience, he would not wear glasses in the Muppet movie at MGM.*

A New York City dad tells of a similar reaction:

> *One note about* Honey, I Shrunk the Audience: *We all loved it except our four-year-old. He's a brave kid, but this film definitely scared him: specifically, the snake and lion 3-D effects. He refused to see it again, although everyone else in the family wanted to. He loved the Muppet movie at MGM.*

Though launched with very little fanfare, *Honey, I Shrunk the Audience* has become Epcot's most popular attraction. Try to work the production into your touring before 10 a.m. The show is located to the left of the Journey into Imagination ride; it isn't necessary to ride in order to enter the theater. Avoid seats in the first several rows: if you're too close to the screen, the 3-D images don't focus properly.

TEST TRACK

Description and Comments   Test Track, presented by General Motors, contains the Test Track ride and TransCenter, a collection of transportation-themed stationary exhibits and mini theater productions. The pavilion is left of Spaceship Earth when you enter, down toward World Showcase from the Universe of Energy pavilion.

Many readers tell us that Test Track "is one big commercial" for General Motors. We agree that promotional hype is more heavy-handed here than in most other business-sponsored attractions. But Test Track is one of the most creatively conceived and executed attractions in Walt Disney World.

Test Track Ride

What It Is: Automobile test-track simulator ride
Scope & Scale: Super headliner
When to Go: Before 10:15 a.m. and after 6 p.m.

Author's Rating: Not to be missed; ★★★★½

Appeal by Age Group:

Pre-school	Grade School	Teens	Young Adults	Over 30	Senior Citizens
★★★★½	★★★★½	★★★★½	★★★★½	★★★★½	★★★★½

Duration of Ride: About 5 minutes

Average Wait in Line per 100 People ahead of You: 4 minutes

Assumes: Normal operation

Loading Speed: Moderate to fast

Description and Comments Test Track combines roller coaster and simulator technologies. Visitors test a future-model car at high speeds through hairpin turns, up and down steep hills, and over rough terrain. The six-guest vehicle is a motion simulator that rocks and pitches. Unlike simulators at Star Tours, Body Wars, and *Back to the Future,* however, the Test Track model is affixed to a track and actually travels. It accelerates to 45 miles per hour, making it one of the fastest moving attractions developed.

Touring Tips Some great technology is at work here. The attraction is so complex, in fact, that Disney is still trying to work out the kinks. When it's running, it's one of the best attractions in any theme park and deserves its large crowds. We recommend riding first thing in the morning, then high-tailing over to *Honey, I Shrunk the Audience.* Expect crowds most of the day. If you miss Test Track early, try it during the hour before Future World closes.

HORIZONS

What It Is: A look at man's evolving perception of the future

Scope & Scale: Major attraction

When to Go: Before 11 a.m. or after 3:30 p.m.

Author's Rating: Retro-future meets future-future; not to be missed;
★★★½

Appeal by Age Group:

Pre-school	Grade School	Teens	Young Adults	Over 30	Senior Citizens
★★★	★★★	★★★	★★★★	★★★★	★★★★

Duration of Ride: About 15 minutes

Average Wait in Line per 100 People ahead of You: 4 minutes

Assumes: Normal operation

Loading Speed: Fast

Description and Comments   Horizons looks back at yesterday's visions of the future, including Jules Verne's concept of a moon rocket and a 1930s preview of a neon city. Elsewhere, guests visit FuturePort and ride through a family habitat of the next century, with scenes depicting apartment, farm, underwater, and space communities.

Horizons closed in 1994 when its corporate sponsor withdrew but reopened when nearby Test Track was under construction. While the long-term future of Horizons is unclear, it is probable that it will remain open until summer 1999.

Touring Tips   The entire pavilion is devoted to a single, continuously loading, high-capacity ride. If open, this attraction can be enjoyed almost anytime without long waits. Exceptions occur immediately after the conclusion of Universe of Energy performances, when as many as 580 patrons at once troop over and queue up for Horizons. If you encounter this deluge, take a 15-minute break. When you return to Horizons, you'll probably walk right in.

WONDERS OF LIFE PAVILION

Description and Comments   This multifaceted pavilion deals with the human body, health, and medicine. Housed in a 100,000-square-foot, gold-domed structure, Wonders of Life focuses on the capabilities of the human body and the importance of keeping fit.

Body Wars

What It Is: Flight-simulator ride through the human body

Scope & Scale: Headliner

When to Go: Before 10 a.m. or after 6 p.m.

Special Comments: Not recommended for pregnant women or people prone to motion sickness

Motion Sickness

WARNING!

Author's Rating: Anatomy made fun; not to be missed; ★★★★

Appeal by Age Group:

Pre-school	Grade School	Teens	Young Adults	Over 30	Senior Citizens
★★★	★★★★	★★★★	★★★★	★★★½	★★½

Duration of Ride: 5 minutes

Average Wait in Line per 100 People ahead of You: 4 minutes

Assumes: All simulators operating

Loading Speed: Moderate to fast

Description and Comments   This thrill ride through the human body was developed along the lines of Disney-MGM Studios' Star Tours space-simulation ride. The story is that you're a passenger in a miniature capsule injected into a human body to pick up a scientist who has been inspecting a splinter in the patient's finger. The scientist, however, is sucked into the circulatory system, and you rush throughout the body to rescue her. The simulator creates a visually graphic experience as it seems to hurtle at fantastic speeds through human organs. The story is more than a little silly, but we nevertheless rate Body Wars as "not to be missed."

Touring Tips   Epcot's first thrill ride, Body Wars remains popular with all ages. Ride early in the morning after Test Track and *Honey, I Shrunk the Audience,* or during the hour before closing. Be aware that Body Wars makes a lot of people motion sick; it isn't unusual for a simulator to be taken off-line for attendants to clean up a previous rider's mess. If you're at all susceptible to motion sickness, reconsider riding. If you're on Body Wars and become nauseated, fix your gaze on something other than the screen and as far away as possible (the ceiling or side and back walls). Without the visual effects, the ride isn't rough enough to disturb most guests. If you get queasy, rest rooms are nearby as you get off the ride. Star Tours is just as wild but makes very few people sick. Successfully riding Star Tours doesn't necessarily mean you'll tolerate Body Wars. Conversely, if Body Wars makes you ill, you can't assume that Star Tours will, too.

Reader comments on Body Wars cover the spectrum. These are representative:

> *The only thing we won't do on this next trip is go on Body Wars in Epcot. The line is so deceptive. We waited almost two hours and then it was only to get motion sickness and feel awful!*

and:

> *I made the mistake of riding Body Wars first thing in the morning, on an empty stomach, and with a hangover. I thought I was going to throw up. It was very close. Strangely enough, I rode Body Wars again a week later, feeling fine. Guess what? I thought I was going to throw up. It was very close.*

and:

> *Body Wars did not measure up to all the hype and warnings. We expected Space Mountain with visual effects, and it wasn't even close. You weenies!*

and:

> *The ride felt more like the involuntary movements of a hammock.*

and finally:

> *Body Wars at Epcot was great fun. We rode it twice and loved it. A little scary, but exciting. Some of the other things seemed kind of boring after our ride here.*

Motion sickness aside, Body Wars is intense—too intense for some, especially preschoolers and seniors. One elderly gentleman confided, "Feeling sick at my stomach took my mind off being terrified."

Cranium Command

What It Is: Audio-Animatronic theater show about the brain
Scope & Scale: Major attraction
When to Go: Before 11 a.m. or after 3 p.m.
Author's Rating: Funny, outrageous, and educational; not to be missed;
   ★★★★½

Appeal by Age Group:

Pre-school	Grade School	Teens	Young Adults	Over 30	Senior Citizens
★★★	★★★★	★★★★	★★★★½	★★★★½	★★★★½

Duration of Presentation: About 20 minutes
Preshow Entertainment: Explanatory lead-in to feature presentation
Probable Waiting Time: Less than 10 minutes at times suggested

Description and Comments   *Cranium Command* is Epcot's great sleeper attraction. Stuck on the backside of the Wonders of Life pavilion and far less promoted than Body Wars, this most humorous Epcot offering is bypassed by many guests. Characters called "Brain Pilots" are trained to operate human brains. The show consists of a day in the life of one of these Cranium Commanders as he tries to pilot the brain of an adolescent boy. Epcot and Walt Disney World could use a lot more of this type of humor.

Touring Tips   To understand the program, you need to see the preshow cartoon. If you arrive in the waiting area while it's in progress, be sure you see enough to get a sense of the story before you enter the theater. While most preschoolers enjoy *Cranium Command,* many don't really understand it.

The Making of Me

What It Is: Humorous movie about human conception and birth
Scope & Scale: Minor attraction

When to Go: Early in the morning or after 4:30 p.m.

Author's Rating: Sanitized sex education; ★★★

Appeal by Age Group:

Pre-school	Grade School	Teens	Young Adults	Over 30	Senior Citizens
★★½	★★½	★★½	★★★	★★★	★★★

Duration of Presentation: 14 minutes

Preshow Entertainment: None

Probable Waiting Time: 25 minutes or more, unless you go at suggested times

Description and Comments   This lighthearted and very sensitive movie about human conception, gestation, and birth was considered a controversial addition to Wonders of Life, but most viewers agree it's tasteful and creative. The plot's main character goes back in time to watch his parents date, fall in love, marry, and, yes, conceive and give birth to him. Look for the biological error in the film. If you spot it, write us. We'll put all correct answers into a box and draw a winner at the end of the year. The prize? A free salpingoplasty.

Sexual material is well handled, with emphasis on loving relationships, not plumbing. Parents of children younger than age seven tell us the sexual information went over their children's heads for the most part. In older children, however, the film precipitates questions. You be the judge.

A gentleman from Cheshire, England, who believes (correctly, in our view) that Americans are sexually repressed, writes:

> *By the standards of sex education programmes shown to English children of ages eight to nine,* The Making of Me *seemed almost Mary Poppinsish in tone. Certainly other Brits found your warnings over content quite puzzling.*

This reader would have a great time in my hometown (Birmingham, Alabama), where some of the local clergy harangued the city council for months to have Bermuda shorts welded onto the bare buttocks of a large statue depicting Vulcan at his forge.

Touring Tips   *The Making of Me* is excellent and should be moved from its tiny space to a larger theater. Until (and if) it is, expect long lines unless you go at recommended times.

Fitness Fairgrounds

Description and Comments   Participatory exhibits allow guests to test their senses in a fun house, get computer-generated health analyses of their lifestyles, work out on electronically sophisticated exercise equipment, and watch a video called *Goofy about Health* (starring, who else?).

Touring Tips Save the Fitness Fair exhibits for your second day, or the end of your first day at Epcot.

UNIVERSE OF ENERGY: ELLEN'S ENERGY ADVENTURE

What It Is: Combination ride/theater presentation about energy

Scope & Scale: Major attraction

When to Go: Before 10:30 a.m. or after 4:30 p.m.

Special Comments: Don't be dismayed by long lines; 580 people enter the pavilion each time the theater turns over

Author's Rating: The most improved attraction at Walt Disney World; ★★★★

Appeal by Age Group:

Pre-school	Grade School	Teens	Young Adults	Over 30	Senior Citizens
★★★	★★★½	★★★½	★★★★	★★★★	★★★★

Duration of Presentation: About 26½ minutes

Preshow Entertainment: 8 minutes

Probable Waiting Time: 20–40 minutes

Description and Comments Audio-Animatronic dinosaurs and the unique traveling theater make this Exxon pavilion one of Future World's most popular. Because this is a theater with a ride component, the line doesn't move while the show is in progress. When the theater empties, however, a large chunk of the line will disappear as people are admitted for the next show. Visitors are seated in what appears to be an ordinary theater while they watch a film about energy sources. Then the theater seats divide into six 97-passenger traveling cars that glide among the swamps and reptiles of a prehistoric forest. Special effects include the feel of warm, moist air from the swamp, the smell of sulphur from an erupting volcano, and the sight of lava hissing and bubbling toward the passengers.

The original film on energy sources (which many guests characterized as boring) was scrapped in 1996 and replaced with a humorous and upbeat flick starring Ellen DeGeneres. The new film represents a huge improvement for adults, turning a major snoozer into a highly entertaining presentation. For kids, however, Universe of Energy remains a toss-up. The dinosaurs frighten some preschoolers, and kids of all ages lose the thread during the educational segments.

Touring Tips   This attraction draws large crowds beginning early in the morning. Because Universe of Energy can operate more than one show at a time, lines are generally tolerable. If you decide to skip the show, at least see the great dinosaur topiaries outside the pavilion.

THE "MOM, I CAN'T BELIEVE IT'S DISNEY!" FOUNTAIN

What It Is: Combination fountain and shower
When to Go: When it's hot
Scope & Scale: Diversion
Special Comments: Secretly installed by Martians during *IllumiNations*
Author's Rating: Yes!! ★★★★
Appeal by Age Group:

Pre-school	Grade School	Teens	Young Adults	Over 30	Senior Citizens
★★★★★	★★★★★	★★★★	★★★★	★★★★	★★★★★

Duration of Experience: Indefinite
Probable Waiting Time: None

Description and Comments   This simple fountain on the walkway linking Future World to World Showcase isn't much to look at, but it offers a truly spontaneous experience—rare in Walt Disney World, where everything is controlled, from the snow peas in your stir fry to how frequently the crocodile yawns in the Jungle Cruise.

Spouts of water erupt randomly from the sidewalk. You can frolic in the water or let it cascade down on you or blow up your britches. On a broiling Florida day, when you think you might suddenly combust, fling yourself into the fountain and do decidedly un-Disney things. Dance, skip, sing, jump, splash, cavort, roll around, stick your toes down the spouts, or catch the water in your mouth as it descends. You can do all of this with your clothes on or, depending on your age, with your clothes off. It's hard to imagine so much personal freedom at Disney World and almost unthinkable to contemplate soggy people slogging and squishing around the park, but there you have it. Hurrah!

Touring Tips   We don't know how long the fountain will last before its creator is hauled before the Disney Tribunal of People-Who-Sit-on-Sticks, but we hope it's around for a long time. We do know your kids will be right in the middle of this thing before your brain sounds the alert. Our advice: Pack a pair of dry shorts and turn the kids loose. You might even want to bring a spare pair for yourself. Or, maybe not . . . so much advance planning would stifle the spontaneity.

World Showcase

World Showcase, Epcot's second theme area, is an ongoing World's Fair encircling a picturesque, 40-acre lagoon. The cuisine, culture, history, and architecture of almost a dozen countries are permanently displayed in individual national pavilions spaced along a 1.2-mile promenade. Pavilions replicate familiar landmarks and present representative street scenes from the host countries.

World Showcase features some of the most lovely gardens in the United States. Located in Germany, France, England, Canada, and to a lesser extent, China, they are sometimes tucked away and out of sight of pedestrian traffic on the World Showcase promenade. They are best appreciated during daylight hours, as a Clio, Michigan, woman explains:

> *Make sure to visit the World Showcase in the daylight in order to view the beautiful gardens. We were sorry that we did not do this because we were following the guide and riding the rides that we could have done later in the dark.*

Most adults enjoy World Showcase, but many children find it boring. To make it more interesting to children, most Epcot retail shops sell Passport Kits for about $9. Each kit contains a blank passport and stamps for every World Showcase country. As kids accompany their folks to each country, they tear out the appropriate stamp and stick it in the passport. The kit also contains basic information on the nations and a Mickey Mouse button. Disney has built a lot of profit into this little product, but I guess that isn't the issue. More important, parents, including this dad from Birmingham, Alabama, tell us the Passport Kit helps get the kids through World Showcase with a minimum of impatience, whining, and tantrums.

> *Adding stamps from the Epcot countries was the only way I was able to see all the displays with cheerful children.*

Incidentally, if you do not want to spring for the Passport Kit, the Disney folks will be happy to stamp an autograph book or just about anything else (we saw one four-year-old with a stamp from France right in the middle of his forehead).

Children also enjoy "Kidcot Fun Stops," a recent Disney experiment designed to make World Showcase more interesting for the 5-through-12 crowd. So simple and uncomplicated that you can't believe Disney people thought it up, the Fun Stops usually are nothing more than a large table on the sidewalk at each pavilion. Each table is staffed by a Disney cast member who stamps passports and supervises children in modest craft projects relating to the host country. While there's no telling how long the experiment will last, reports from parents about the Fun Stops have been uniformly positive.

Boats ferry the foot-sore and the weary across the lagoon, although it's almost always quicker to walk.

Moving clockwise around the promenade, here are the nations represented and their attractions.

MEXICO PAVILION

Description and Comments   Pre-Columbian pyramids dominate the architecture of this exhibit. One forms the pavilion's facade, and the other overlooks the restaurant and plaza alongside the boat ride, El Río del Tiempo, inside the pavilion.

Touring Tips   Romantic and exciting testimony to Mexico's charms, this installation probably contains more authentic and valuable artifacts and art objects than any other nation's pavilion. Many people zip past these treasures without stopping to look. The village scene inside the pavilion is beautiful and exquisitely detailed. We recommend visiting this pavilion before 11 a.m. or after 6 p.m.

El Río del Tiempo

What It Is: Indoor scenic boat ride
Scope & Scale: Minor attraction
When to Go: Before 11 a.m. or after 3 p.m.
Author's Rating: Light and relaxing; ★★
Appeal by Age Group:

Pre-school	Grade School	Teens	Young Adults	Over 30	Senior Citizens
★★	★★	★½	★★	★★	★★½

Duration of Ride: About 7 minutes (plus 1½-minute wait to disembark)
Average Wait in Line per 100 People ahead of You: 4½ minutes
Assumes: 16 boats in operation
Loading Speed: Moderate

Description and Comments   El Río del Tiempo (The River of Time) cruises among Audio-Animatronic and cinematic scenes depicting the history of Mexico from the ancient cultures of the Maya, Toltec, and Aztec civilizations to modern times. Special effects include fiber-optic projections that simulate fireworks near the ride's end.

The volcano at the entrance suggests great things to come, but the ride disappoints many guests.

A woman from Troy, New York, lambasts El Río del Tiempo:

> *My worst nightmare would be to get stuck in It's a Small World or*
> *El Río del Tiempo. They were both dreadful, boring, and need updat-*
> *ing. I thought El Río was an insult to the Mexico Pavilion—it's a*
> *cheap tourist's version of Mexico and hardly a reflection on the culture,*
> *history, or people.*

We agree. Though tranquil and relaxing, El Río del Tiempo is neither particularly interesting nor compelling, and definitely is not worth a long
wait.

Touring Tips   The ride tends to get crowded during early afternoon.

NORWAY PAVILION

Description and Comments   The Norway pavilion is complex, beautiful,
and architecturally diverse. Surrounding a courtyard is an assortment of
traditional Scandinavian buildings, including a replica of the 14th-century
Akershus Castle, a wooden stave church, red-tiled cottages, and replicas of
historic buildings representing the traditional designs of Bergen, Alesund,
and Oslo. Attractions include an adventure boat ride in the mold of Pirates
of the Caribbean, a movie about Norway, and a gallery of art and artifacts
in the stave church. The pavilion houses Restaurant Akershus, a sit-down
eatery (priority seating required) that serves koldtboard (cold buffet), plus
a variety of hot Norwegian dishes. An open-air cafe and a bakery cater to
those on the run. Shoppers find abundant native handicrafts.

Maelstrom

What It Is: Indoor adventure boat ride

Scope & Scale: Major attraction

When to Go: Before noon or after 4:30 p.m.

Author's Rating: Too short, but has its moments; ★★★

Appeal by Age Group:

Pre-school	Grade School	Teens	Young Adults	Over 30	Senior Citizens
★★★½	★★★½	★★★	★★★	★★★	★★★

Duration of Ride: 4½ minutes, followed by a 5-minute film with a short
wait in between; about 14 minutes for the whole show

Average Wait in Line per 100 People ahead of You: 4 minutes

Assumes: 12 or 13 boats operating

Loading Speed: Fast

Description and Comments In one of Disney World's shorter water rides, guests board dragon-headed ships for a voyage through the fabled rivers and seas of Viking history and legend. They brave trolls, rocky gorges, waterfalls, and a storm at sea. A new-generation Disney water ride, the Viking voyage assembles an impressive array of special effects, combining visual, tactile, and auditory stimuli in a fast-paced and often humorous odyssey. Afterward, guests see a five-minute film on Norway. We don't have any major problems with Maelstrom, but a vocal minority of our readers consider the ride too brief and resent having to sit through what they characterize as a travelogue.

Touring Tips Sometimes, several hundred guests from a recently concluded screening of *Wonders of China* arrive at Maelstrom en masse. Should you encounter this horde, postpone Maelstrom. If you don't want to see the Norway film, try to be one of the first to enter the theater. You can follow the preceding audience right through the exit doors on the far side.

CHINA PAVILION

Description and Comments A half-sized replica of the Temple of Heaven in Beijing identifies this pavilion. Gardens and reflecting ponds simulate those found in Suzhou, and an art gallery features a lotus blossom gate and formal saddle roof line.

Pass through the Hall of Prayer for Good Harvest to view the Circle-Vision 360 film *Wonders of China*. Warm and appealing, it's a brilliant introduction to the people and natural beauty of China. The China pavilion offers two restaurants: a fast-food eatery and a lovely, full-service establishment (priority seating required).

Touring Tips The pavilion is truly beautiful, serene yet exciting. *Wonders of China* plays in a theater where guests must stand, but it can usually be enjoyed anytime without much waiting. If you're touring World Showcase in a counterclockwise rotation and plan next to go to Norway and ride Maelstrom, position yourself on the far left of the theater (as you face the attendant's podium). After the show, be one of the first to exit. Hurry to Maelstrom as fast as you can to arrive ahead of the several hundred other *Wonders of China* patrons who will be right behind you.

Wonders of China

What It Is: Film about the Chinese people and country

Scope & Scale: Major attraction

When to Go: Anytime

Special Comments: Audience stands throughout performance

Author's Rating: Well produced, though film glosses over political unrest and events in Tibet; ★★★

Appeal by Age Group:

Pre-school	Grade School	Teens	Young Adults	Over 30	Senior Citizens
★★	★★½	★★★	★★★½	★★★★	★★★★

Duration of Presentation: About 19 minutes

Preshow Entertainment: None

Probable Waiting Time: 10 minutes

GERMANY PAVILION

Description and Comments   A clock tower, adorned with boy and girl figures, rises above the platz (plaza) marking the Germany pavilion. Dominated by a fountain depicting St. George's victory over the dragon, the platz is encircled by buildings done in traditional German architecture. The main attraction is the Biergarten, a full-service (priority seating required) restaurant serving German food and beer. Yodeling, folk dancing, and oompah band music are included during mealtimes.

New at Germany is a large and elaborate model railroad located just beyond the rest rooms as you walk from Germany toward Italy.

Touring Tips   The pavilion is pleasant and festive. Tour anytime.

ITALY PAVILION

Description and Comments   The entrance to Italy is marked by a 105-foot-tall campanile (bell tower) said to mirror the tower in St. Mark's Square in Venice. Left of the campanile is a replica of the 14th-century Doge's Palace, also in the famous square. Other buildings are composites of Italian architecture. For example, L'Originale Alfredo di Roma Ristorante is Florentine. Visitors can watch pasta being made in this popular restaurant, which specializes in fettucine Alfredo. The pavilion has a waterfront on the lagoon where gondolas are tied to striped moorings.

Touring Tips   Streets and courtyards in the Italy pavilion are among the most realistic in World Showcase. You really feel as if you're in Italy. Because there's no film or ride, tour at any hour.

THE AMERICAN ADVENTURE

What It Is: Patriotic mixed-media and Audio-Animatronic theater presentation on U.S. history

Scope & Scale: Headliner

When to Go: Anytime

Author's Rating: Disney's best historic/patriotic attraction; not to be missed; ★★★★

Appeal by Age Group:

Pre-school	Grade School	Teens	Young Adults	Over 30	Senior Citizens
★★½	★★★	★★★	★★★★	★★★★½	★★★★★

Duration of Presentation: About 29 minutes

Preshow Entertainment: Voices of Liberty chorale singing

Probable Waiting Time: 16 minutes

Description and Comments   The United States pavilion, generally referred to as The American Adventure for the historical production performed there, consists (not surprisingly) of a fast-food restaurant and a patriotic show.

The American Adventure is a composite of everything Disney does best. Located in an imposing brick structure reminiscent of colonial Philadelphia, the production is a stirring, 29-minute sanitized rendition of American history narrated by Audio-Animatronic Mark Twain (who carries a smoking cigar) and Ben Franklin (who climbs a set of stairs to visit Thomas Jefferson). Behind a stage almost half the size of a football field is a 28 × 55–foot rear-projection screen (the largest ever used) on which motion picture images are interwoven with action on stage.

Though the production stimulates patriotic emotion in some viewers, others find it overstated and boring. A man from Fort Lauderdale, Florida, writes:

> *I've always disagreed with you about The American Adventure. I saw it about 10 years ago and snoozed through it. We tried it again since you said it was updated. It was still ponderous. Casey used the time for a nap, and I was checking my watch, waiting for it to be over. I'll try it again in 10 years.*

Touring Tips   Architecturally, The American Adventure isn't as interesting as most other pavilions. But the presentation, our researchers believe, is the very best patriotic attraction in the Disney repertoire. It usually plays to capacity audiences from around noon to 3:30 p.m., but it isn't hard to get into. Because of the theater's large capacity, the wait during busy times of day seldom approaches an hour, and averages 25–40 minutes. Because of its theme, the presentation is decidedly less compelling to non-Americans.

The adjacent Liberty Inn restaurant serves a quick, nonethnic, fast-food meal.

JAPAN PAVILION

Description and Comments   The five-story, blue-roofed pagoda, inspired by a 7th-century shrine in Nara, sets this pavilion apart. A hill garden behind it encompasses waterfalls, rocks, flowers, lanterns, paths, and rustic bridges. The building on the right (as one faces the entrance) was inspired by the ceremonial and coronation hall at the Imperial Palace at Kyoto. It contains restaurants and a large retail store.

Touring Tips   Tasteful and elaborate, the pavilion creatively blends simplicity, architectural grandeur, and natural beauty. Tour anytime.

"I'm sorry, Mister. He thinks you're a Disney character."

Morocco Pavilion

Description and Comments   The bustling market, winding streets, lofty minarets, and stuccoed archways re-create the romance and intrigue of Marrakesh and Casablanca. Attention to detail makes Morocco one of the most exciting World Showcase pavilions. It also has a museum of Moorish art and the Restaurant Marrakesh, which serves some unusual and difficult-to-find North African specialties.

Touring Tips   Morocco has neither a ride nor theater; tour anytime.

France Pavilion

Description and Comments   Naturally, a replica of the Eiffel Tower (a big one) is this pavilion's centerpiece. Beyond it, streets recall La Belle Epoque, France's "beautiful time" between 1870 and 1910. The sidewalk cafe and restaurant are very popular, as is the pastry shop. You won't be the first visitor to buy a croissant to tide you over until your next real meal.

A group from Chicago found the pavilion's realism exceeds what was intended:

> *There were no public rest rooms in the France part of Epcot—just like Paris. We had to go to Morocco to find facilities.*

Impressions de France is an 18-minute movie projected over 200° onto five screens. Unlike at China and Canada, the audience sits to view this well-made film introducing France's people, cities, and natural wonders.

Touring Tips   Detail and the evocation of a bygone era enrich the atmosphere of this pavilion. Streets are small and become quite congested when visitors queue for the film.

Impressions de France

What It Is: Film essay on the French people and country

Scope & Scale: Major attraction

When to Go: Before noon and after 4 p.m.

Author's Rating: Exceedingly beautiful film; not to be missed; ★★★½

Appeal by Age Group:

Pre-school	Grade School	Teens	Young Adults	Over 30	Senior Citizens
★½	★★½	★★★	★★★★	★★★★	★★★★

Duration of Presentation: About 18 minutes

Preshow Entertainment: None

Probable Waiting Time: 12 minutes (at suggested times)

UNITED KINGDOM PAVILION

Description and Comments A variety of period architecture attempts to capture Britain's city, town, and rural atmospheres. One street alone has a thatched-roof cottage, a four-story timber-and-plaster building, a pre-Georgian plaster building, a formal Palladian exterior of dressed stone, and a city square with a Hyde Park bandstand (whew!).

The pavilion is mostly shops. The Rose & Crown Pub and Dining Room is the only World Showcase full-service restaurant with dining on the water side of the promenade.

Touring Tips   No attractions here create congestion; tour anytime. Priority seating isn't required to enjoy the pub section of the Rose & Crown, making it a nice place to stop for a midafternoon beer. In the category of dubious distinctions, the Rose & Crown Pub is the only place at Epcot where smoking is allowed indoors.

CANADA PAVILION

Description and Comments   Canada's cultural, natural, and architectural diversity are reflected in this large and impressive pavilion. Thirty-foot-tall totem poles embellish a Native American village at the foot of a magnificent château-style hotel. Nearby is a rugged stone building said to be modeled after a famous landmark near Niagara Falls and reflecting Britain's influence on Canada. The pavilion also has a fine film extolling the nation's many virtues. *O Canada!* is very enlightening and demonstrates the immense pride Canadians have in their beautiful country. Visitors leave the theater through Victoria Gardens, inspired by the famed Butchart Gardens of British Columbia.

Touring Tips   *O Canada!*, a large-capacity theater attraction (guests must stand), gets fairly heavy late-morning attendance because Canada is the first pavilion encountered as one travels counterclockwise around World Showcase Lagoon. Le Cellier, a steakhouse on the pavilion's lower level, accepts priority seating but also welcomes walk-ins.

O Canada!

What It Is: Film essay on the Canadian people and their country
Scope & Scale: Major attraction
When to Go: Anytime
Special Comments: Audience stands during performance
Author's Rating: Makes you want to catch the first plane to Canada!
   ★★★½
Appeal by Age Group:

Pre-school	Grade School	Teens	Young Adults	Over 30	Senior Citizens
★★	★★½	★★★	★★★½	★★★★	★★★★

Duration of Presentation: About 18 minutes
Preshow Entertainment: None
Probable Waiting Time: 10 minutes

Live Entertainment in Epcot

Live entertainment in Epcot is more diverse than it is in the Magic Kingdom. In World Showcase, it reflects the nations represented. Future World provides a perfect setting for new and experimental offerings. Information about live entertainment on the day you visit is contained in the Epcot guidemap you obtain upon entry or at Guest Relations.

Here are some performers and performances you're apt to encounter:

In Future World   A roving brass band, a musical crew of pseudo janitors, socializing robots (EpBOTS), and gymnasts in *Alien* attire striking statuesque poses work near the front entrance and at Innoventions Plaza (between the two Innoventions buildings and by the fountain) according to the daily entertainment schedule.

Disney Characters   Once believed to be inconsistent with Epcot's educational image, Disney characters have now been imported in significant numbers. They appear for breakfast (from park opening to 11:10 or 11:40 a.m. daily) at The Garden Grill Restaurant at The Land pavilion. The menu is fixed, but seconds are available. Cost is $15 for adults (age 12 and older) and $9 for ages 3 to 11. Characters include Mickey and Minnie (in farm attire) and Chip 'n' Dale. The Garden Grill also offers a character lunch ($17 for adults; $10 for children) and dinner ($18 and $10). The price is in addition to your theme park admission.

Characters now appear throughout the park. If you are looking for one in particular, pick up a copy of the *Disney Character Greeting Location Guide,* available free at Guest Relations.

Characters also join live shows at the American Gardens Theatre and at the Showcase Plaza between Mexico and Canada. Times are listed in the daily entertainment schedule in the Epcot guidemap available upon entry and at Guest Relations.

American Gardens Theatre   The site of Epcot's premier live performances is in a large amphitheater near The American Adventure, facing World Showcase Lagoon. International top talent plays limited engagements there. Many shows spotlight the music, dance, and costumes of the performer's home country. Other programs feature Disney characters.

IllumiNations   An after-dark program of music, fireworks, erupting fountains, special lighting, and laser technology is performed on World Showcase Lagoon (see page 474).

Around World Showcase   Impromptu performances take place in and around the World Showcase pavilions. They include a strolling mariachi group in Mexico; street actors in Italy; a fife-and-drum corps or singing group (The Voices of Liberty) at The American Adventure; traditional songs, drums, and dances in Japan; street comedy in the United Kingdom; white-faced mimes in France; and bagpipes in Canada, among others. Street entertainment occurs about every half hour (though not necessarily *on* the hour or half hour).

Live entertainment in World Showcase exceeded the expectations of a mother from Rhode Island and led her son to develop a new talent:

> *You should stress in the new edition that Epcot's World Showcase is really quite lively now. Street performances are scheduled throughout the day in the different pavilions. The schedules were printed on the daily map we picked up at the ticket booth.*
>
> *My two-year-old was taken with the Chinese acrobats and the Chinese variety performers. We must have watched their shows four times each! As I write this, he's balancing an empty trash can on his feet.*

Dinner & Lunch Shows   Restaurants in World Showcase serve healthy portions of live entertainment to accompany the victuals. Find folk dancing and an oompah-pah band in Germany, singing waiters in Italy and Germany, and belly dancers in Morocco. Shows are performed only at dinner in Italy, but at both lunch and dinner in Germany and Morocco. Priority seating is required.

IllumiNations

IllumiNations is Epcot's great outdoor spectacle, integrating fireworks, laser lights, neon, and music in a stirring tribute to the nations represented at World Showcase. It's the climax of every Epcot day when the park is open late. Don't miss it.

Getting out of Epcot after *IllumiNations* (Read This before Selecting a Viewing Spot)

Decide how quickly you want to leave the park after the show, then pick your vantage point. *IllumiNations* ends the day at Epcot. When it's over, only a couple of gift shops remain open. Because there's nothing to do, everyone leaves at once. This creates a great snarl at Package Pick-up, the Epcot monorail station, and the Disney bus stop. It also pushes to the limit the tram system hauling guests to their cars in the parking lot. Stroller return, however, is extraordinarily efficient and doesn't cause any delay.

If you're staying at an Epcot resort (Swan and Dolphin hotels, Yacht and Beach Club resorts, BoardWalk Inn and Villas), watch *IllumiNations* from somewhere on the southern (The American Adventure) half of World Showcase Lagoon and then leave through the International Gateway between France and the United Kingdom. You can walk or take a boat back to your hotel from the International Gateway. If you have a car and are visiting Epcot in the evening for dinner and *IllumiNations,* park at the Yacht or Beach Club. After the show, duck out the International Gateway and be on the road to your hotel in 15 minutes. If you're staying at any other Disney hotel and don't have a car, the fastest way home is to join the mass exodus through the main gate after *IllumiNations* and catch a bus or the monorail.

Those who have a car in the Epcot lot have a more problematic situation. If you want to beat the crowd, find a viewing spot at the end of World Showcase Lagoon nearest Future World (and the exits). Leave as soon as *IllumiNations* concludes, trying to exit ahead of the crowd. Be forewarned that thousands of people will be doing exactly the same thing. To get a good vantage point anywhere between Mexico and Canada on the northern end of the lagoon, you'll have to stake out your spot 45–90 minutes before the show. Conceivably, you may squander more time holding your spot before IllumiNations than you would if you watched from the less congested southern end of the lagoon and took your chances with the crowd upon departure.

More groups get separated, and more children lost, after *IllumiNations* than at any other time. In summer, you will be walking in a throng of up to 30,000 people. If you're heading for the parking lot, anticipate this congestion and preselect a point in the Epcot entrance area where you can meet in the event that someone gets separated from the group. We recommend the fountain just inside the main entrance. Everyone in your party should be told not to exit through the turnstiles until all noses have been counted. It can be a nightmare if the group gets split up and you don't know whether the others are inside or outside the park.

For those with a car, the main problem is reaching it. Once there, traffic leaves the parking lot pretty well. If you paid close attention to where you parked, consider skipping the tram and walking. If you walk, watch your children closely and hang on to them for all you're worth. The parking lot is pretty wild at this time of night, with hundreds of moving cars.

Good Locations for Viewing *IllumiNations* and Other World Showcase Lagoon Performances

The best place to be for any presentation on World Showcase Lagoon is in a seat on the lakeside veranda of the Cantina de San Angel in Mexico. Come early (*at least* 90 minutes before *IllumiNations)* and relax with a cold drink or snack while you wait for the show.

A woman from Pasadena, California, nailed down the seat but missed the relaxation. She writes:

> *Stake out a prime site for* IllumiNations *at least two hours ahead, and be prepared to defend it. We got a lakeside table at the Cantina de*

San Angel at 6:30 p.m. and had a great view of IllumiNations.
Unfortunately, we had to put up with troops of people asking us to share
our table and trying to wedge themselves between our table and the fence.

The Rose & Crown Pub in the United Kingdom also has lagoonside
seating. Because of a small wall, however, the view isn't quite as good as
from the Cantina. If you want to combine dinner on the Rose & Crown's
veranda with *IllumiNations,* make a dinner priority seating for about 1 hour
and 15 minutes before show time. Report a few minutes early for your seating and tell the Rose & Crown host that you want a table outside where you
can view *IllumiNations* during or after dinner. Our experience is that the
Rose & Crown staff will bend over backward to accommodate you. If you
aren't able to obtain a table outside, eat inside, then hang out until show
time. When the lights dim, indicating the start of *IllumiNations,* you will be
allowed to join the diners on the terrace to watch the show.

Because most guests run for the exits after a presentation, and because
islands in the southern (The American Adventure) half of the lagoon block
the view from some places, the most popular spectator positions are along
the northern waterfront from Norway and Mexico on around to Canada
and the United Kingdom. Although the northern end of the lagoon
unquestionably offers excellent viewing, it's usually necessary to claim a
spot 35–60 minutes before *IllumiNations* begins. For those who are late
finishing dinner or don't want to spend 45 minutes standing by a rail, here
are good viewing spots along the southern perimeter (moving counterclockwise from the United Kingdom to Germany) that often go unnoticed
until 10–20 minutes before show time:

1. The Once-Secret Park. There's a wonderful waterside park, accessible from the United Kingdom, which is known to only a few. To reach it,
walk toward France from the Rose & Crown Pub in the United Kingdom.
As you near the end of the pub, stay on the sidewalk and bear left. You'll
shortly find yourself in an almost private park, complete with benches and
a perfect view of *IllumiNations.* En route to the park, you'll see a roped-off
back entrance to the pub's terrace. This is another good viewing spot (don't
be shy about ducking under the rope).

After earlier editions of the *Unofficial Guide,* the "secret park" became
less secret. A reader from Demotte, Indiana, describes the scene:

We watched the IllumiNations *show from the "Secret Park" behind*
the British pub. It was a very good location and allowed us an easy exit
after the show. On a humorous note, about 10 minutes before the show
was to begin, a lady came hiking down the path to the park with a
copy of your guide in her hand. She became quite agitated when she

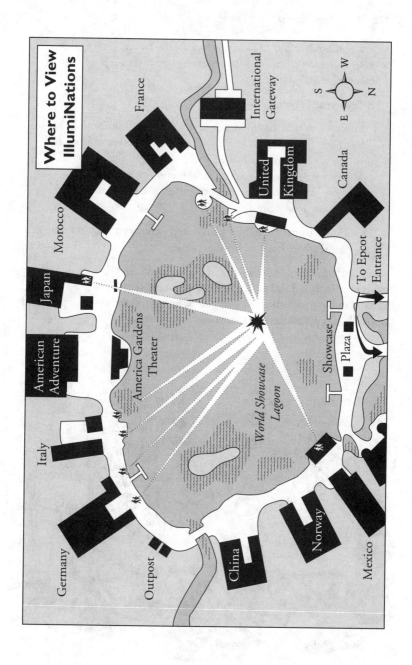

Where to View
IllumiNations

France

International
Gateway

United
Kingdom

Canada

To Epcot
Entrance

Morocco

Japan

American
Adventure

America Gardens
Theater

World Showcase
Lagoon

Showcase
Plaza

Italy

Germany

Outpost

China

Norway

Mexico

N
W ● E
S

477

saw that the area was full and exclaimed quite loudly, "I thought this place was a secret!" About half the people in place for the show held up copies of your book.

A Texas man is more pointed:

> *Which brings us, finally, to the justly renowned* IllumiNations *at Epcot. Since we did not stake out our turf until 30 minutes before the show, we got the vantage point we deserved. Still, by now you should probably concede to your readers that the cover has been thoroughly blown from the so-called "Secret Park"—due, we suspect, to the wide circulation of your guide.*

In addition to the park's not being very secret, you should know that Disney frequently closes it for private parties.

2. International Gateway Island.   The pedestrian bridge across the canal near International Gateway spans an island that offers great viewing. This island is much more obvious to passersby than the secret park and normally fills 30 minutes or more before show time.

The Smith family from East Wimple stakes out their viewing spot for *IllumiNations.*

3. *Second-Floor (Restaurant-Level) Deck of the Mitsukoshi Building in Japan.* An Asian arch slightly blocks your sightline, but this covered deck offers a great vantage point, especially if the weather is iffy. Only the Cantina de San Angel in Mexico is more protected.

4. *Gondola Landing at Italy.* An elaborate waterfront promenade offers excellent viewing positions. Claim your spot at least 30 minutes before show time.

5. *The Boat Dock Opposite Germany.* Another good vantage point, the dock generally fills 30 minutes before *IllumiNations*.

6. *Waterfront Promenade by Germany.* Views are good from the 90-foot-long lagoonside walkway between Germany and China.

Do these suggestions work every time? No. A dad from San Ramon, California, writes:

> *Your recommendations for* IllumiNations *didn't work out in the time frame you mentioned. People had the area staked out two hours ahead of time.*

None of the above viewing locations are reserved for *Unofficial Guide* readers, and on busier nights, good spots go early. But we still won't hold down a slab of concrete for two hours before *IllumiNations* as some people do. Most nights, you can find an acceptable vantage point 15–30 minutes before the show. Because most of the action is significantly above ground level, you don't need to be right on the rail or have an unobstructed view of the water. It's important, however, not to position yourself under a tree, awning, or anything else that blocks your overhead view. If *IllumiNations* is a top priority for you and you want to be absolutely certain of getting a good viewing position, claim your place an hour or more before show time.

A New Yorker who staked out his turf well in advance made this suggestion for staying comfortable until show time:

> *Your excellent guidebook also served as [a] seat cushion while waiting seated on the ground. Make future editions thicker for greater comfort.*

Some American Express package vacations include a VIP viewing spot for *IllumiNations*. For details, call (800) 469-0430.

Shopping in Epcot

Shops in Future World seem out of place. The atmosphere is too visionary and grand to accommodate the pettiness of the bargain table. Similarly, it obviously has been difficult to find merchandise consistent with the surroundings. What is available generally is sold elsewhere, except for Epcot and Disney trademark souvenirs.

The World Showcase shops add realism and atmosphere to the international street scenes, though much of the merchandise is overpriced and readily available elsewhere. Still, some shops really are special. In the United Kingdom, visit The Queen's Table (fine china); in China, Yong Feng Shangdian (crafts, rugs, carvings, furniture); and in Japan, Mitsukoshi Department Store (porcelain, bonsai trees, pearls straight from live oysters). Village Traders, a new shop between China and Germany, sells Kenyan woodcarvings for about the same price you would pay at the carving center in Mombasa where they're made.

Salespersons can forward your purchases to Package Pick-up, where you can retrieve them when you leave the park. Specify whether you'll depart through the main entrance or International Gateway. Allow three hours from the time of purchase for your goods to reach the pick-up facility. If you're a Disney resort guest, packages can be delivered directly to your room.

Behind-the-Scenes Tours in Epcot

Epcot's Gardens of the World offers adults a glimpse of Disney World's gardens, horticulture, and landscaping. The three-hour tour costs $45 plus Epcot admission. Adults (16 and older) can book Hidden Treasures of World Showcase, a tour exploring the architecture of the international pavilions. All countries are covered in the five-hour tour. The cost of $75 includes lunch and admission to Epcot. Also available are two tours that halve World Showcase: Hidden Treasures East explores pavilions of Mexico, Norway, China, Germany, Italy, and the United States. Hidden Treasures West covers Japan, Morocco, France, the United Kingdom, and Canada. Each two-hour tour costs $35 plus Epcot admission.

Readers rave about guided walking tours at Epcot. A couple from Los Angeles writes:

> The best-kept secret is the adult tour, Hidden Treasures of World Showcase in Epcot. The description is misleading and sounds like a real bore, but we got a behind-the-scenes tour with lots of information on everything we ever wanted to know or were curious about. Definitely the best part of our trip. (This is a walking tour and is mostly outside in the heat.)

A gentleman in Houston, Texas, tells us:

> Keep telling people about the Hidden Treasures of World Showcase tour; we finally got to take it, and it was a real highlight. The cast member who took us on the tour (there were only four of us) told us

about a new tour of the Magic Kingdom, called Keys to the Kingdom,
which we took the very next day. It was similar, with backstage touring
and a look at the utilidor system, although it also included going on
several rides. Tell people about this one, too.

Discounts for these tours are available if you charge them on an
American Express card. For reservations, call (407) 939-8687.

The Behind the Seeds Tour is shorter and takes guests behind the scenes
to vegetable gardens in The Land pavilion. It requires same-day reservations; make them on the lower level of The Land (far right of the fast-food
windows). The cost of the hour-long tour is $6 for adults and $4 for children ages three to nine.

Dive Quest

The soggiest behind-the-scenes experience available anywhere is Epcot's
Dive Quest, where open-water scuba-certified divers can swim around
with the fish at The Living Seas. Each tour lasts about 3½ hours, including
a 30-minute dive. The cost is about $140 per diver and includes all gear, a
souvenir T-shirt, a dive log stamp, and refreshments. Reservations are
required and can be made with a credit card by calling (407) WDW-TOUR.
For recorded information, call (407) 560-5590. The experience is for
adults only: no junior certifications are accepted.

Traffic Patterns in Epcot

After long admiring traffic flow in the Magic Kingdom, we were amazed at
Epcot's layout. In the Magic Kingdom, Main Street, U.S.A., with its shops
and eateries, serves as a huge gathering place when the park opens and funnels visitors to the central hub, where entrances branch off to the lands.
Thus, crowds are first welcomed and entertained (on Main Street), then
distributed almost equally to the lands.

At Epcot, by contrast, Spaceship Earth, the park's premier landmark
and one of its headliner attractions, is just inside the main entrance. When
visitors enter the park, they almost irresistibly head for it. Hence, a bottleneck forms less than 75 yards from the turnstiles as soon as the park opens.
Visitors aware of the congestion at Spaceship Earth can take advantage of
the excellent opportunities it provides for escaping waits at other Future
World attractions.

Early-morning crowds form in Future World because most of the park's
rides and shows are there. Except at Test Track, Spaceship Earth, Body
Wars (Wonders of Life pavilion), and *Honey, I Shrunk the Audience*
(Journey into Imagination pavilion), visitors are fairly equally distributed
among Future World attractions.

Between 9 and 11 a.m., crowds build in Future World. Even when World Showcase opens (usually 11 a.m.), more people are entering Future World than are leaving for the Showcase. Attendance continues building in Future World until between noon and 2 p.m. World Showcase attendance builds rapidly as lunch approaches. Exhibits at the far end of World Showcase Lagoon report capacity audiences from about noon through 6:30 or 7:30 p.m.

The Magic Kingdom's premier attractions are situated on the far perimeters of its lands to distribute crowds evenly. Epcot's cluster of attractions in Future World holds the greater part of the throng in the smaller part of the park. World Showcase has only two major draws (Maelstrom in Norway and *The American Adventure*). There is no compelling reason to rush to see them. The bottom line: Crowds build all morning and into early afternoon in Future World. Not until the evening meal approaches do crowds equalize in Future World and World Showcase. Evening crowds in World Showcase, however, don't compare in size to morning and midday crowds in Future World. Attendance throughout Epcot is normally lighter in the evening.

At the Magic Kingdom, repeat visitors make a mad dash for their favorite ride, and preferences are strong and well defined. At Epcot, by contrast, many returning guests say that with the possible exceptions of Test Track and *Honey, I Shrunk the Audience,* they enjoy the major attractions "about the same." The conclusion suggested is that touring at Epcot is more systematic and predictable (by the numbers, clockwise, or counterclockwise) than at the Magic Kingdom.

Some guests leave Epcot in the early evening, but the vast majority exit en masse after *IllumiNations.* Upwards of 30,000 people head for the parking lot and monorail station at once.

Closing time at Epcot doesn't precipitate congestion as it does at the Magic Kingdom. One primary reason for the easier departure from Epcot is that its parking lot is adjacent to the park, not separated from it by a lake as at the Magic Kingdom. At the Magic Kingdom, departing visitors form bottlenecks at the monorail to the Transportation and Ticket Center and main parking lot. At Epcot, they proceed directly to their cars.

Epcot Touring Plans

Our Epcot touring plans are field-tested, step-by-step itineraries for seeing all major attractions at Epcot with a minimum of waiting in line. They're designed to keep you ahead of the crowds while the park is filling in the morning, and to place you at the less crowded attractions during Epcot's busier hours. They assume you would be happier doing a little extra walking rather than a lot of extra standing in line.

Touring Epcot is much more strenuous and demanding than touring the other theme parks. Epcot requires about twice as much walking. And, unlike the Magic Kingdom, Epcot has no effective in-park transportation; wherever you want to go, it's always quicker to walk. Our plans will help you avoid crowds and bottlenecks on days of moderate to heavy attendance, but they can't shorten the distance you have to walk. (Wear comfortable shoes.) On days of lighter attendance, when crowd conditions aren't a critical factor, the plans will help you organize your tour.

We offer four touring plans:

Epcot One-Day Touring Plan This plan packs as much as possible into one long day and requires a lot of hustle and stamina. It can be used on early-entry or non-early-entry days.

Author's Selective Epcot One-Day Touring Plan This plan eliminates some lesser attractions (in the author's opinion) and offers a somewhat more relaxed tour if you have only one day. It can be used on early-entry or non-early-entry days.

Epcot Two-Day Sunrise/Starlight Touring Plan This plan combines the easy touring of early morning on one day with Epcot's festivity and live pageantry at night on the second day. The first day requires some backtracking and hustle but is much more laid-back than either one-day plan. It can be used on early-entry or non-early-entry days.

Epcot Two-Day Early Riser Touring Plan This is the most efficient Epcot touring plan, eliminating 90% of the backtracking and extra walking required by the others while still providing a comprehensive tour. It is designed to be used only on mornings when early entry isn't in effect.

Epcot One-Day Touring Plan

For: Adults and children eight or older.
Assumes: Willingness to experience all major rides and shows.

This plan requires a lot of walking and some backtracking in order to avoid long waits in line. A little extra walking and some early-morning hustle will spare you two to three hours of standing in line. You might not complete the tour. How far you get depends on how quickly you move from attraction to attraction, how many times you rest and eat, how quickly the park fills, and what time it closes.

This plan is not recommended for families with very young children. If you're touring with young children and have only one day, use the Author's Selective Epcot One-Day Touring Plan. Break after lunch and relax at your hotel, returning to the park in late afternoon. If you can allocate two days to Epcot, use one of the Epcot two-day touring plans.

1. If you're a Disney hotel guest, arrive 90 minutes before official opening time *on early-entry days* and 40 minutes before official opening *on non-early-entry days*. If you're a day guest, arrive at the parking lot 45 minutes before Epcot's official opening *on a non-early-entry day*.

2. When admitted, move quickly (jog if you can, but don't run) around the left side of Spaceship Earth to Guest Relations (across the walkway from the geosphere) and make lunch and dinner priority seatings. If you don't wish to do so or have already made them by phone, skip to Step 3.

3. **If only Spaceship Earth and Guest Relations are open** when you're admitted, make your priority seatings and then ride Spaceship Earth. When you exit Spaceship Earth, turn left, and proceed to Innoventions East. When the remainder of Future World opens, pass through Innoventions East and bear right toward Test Track.

    If the entire park is open, make your priority seatings and then head directly to Test Track (bypassing Spaceship Earth) by way of Innoventions East.

    If you're a Disney resort guest taking advantage of early entry, expect only Spaceship Earth, The Living Seas, and attractions in The Land and Journey into Imagination pavilions to be open. Ride Spaceship Earth first, then Living with the Land in The Land pavilion, followed by *Honey, I Shrunk the Audience* at the Journey into Imagination pavilion. Bypass other attractions in The Land and Journey into Imagination pavilions. After *Honey, I Shrunk the Audience,* resume the touring plan at Step 4 (Test Track). Skip any steps directing you to attractions you already experienced.

4. Ride Test Track.

5. Exit Test Track and cross Future World to the Journey into Imagination pavilion. See *Honey, I Shrunk the Audience.*

6. Skip other attractions at Journey into Imagination. Exit and bear left to The Land pavilion. Take the Living with the Land boat ride.

7. Postpone other Land attractions. Backtrack to the other side of the park and ride Body Wars at the Wonders of Life pavilion.

Warning: This ride gives many people motion sickness (see pages 457–459).

8. While at the Wonders of Life pavilion, see *Cranium Command.* Don't miss the cartoon preshow or you may not understand the main presentation.

9. Exit Wonders of Life. Turn right to Universe of Energy and see the show. Don't be dismayed if the line looks long. The large theater gobbles the whole crowd when the audience changes.

10. Turn left out of the Universe of Energy and head back toward Test Track. Take a left past the Wonders of Life pavilion and see Horizons.

11. Bear left after leaving Horizons, passing Test Track. Bear left again on the path that leads to the Odyssey Center. Cut through the Odyssey Center to World Showcase.

    Note: Check your watch. Is your lunch priority seating soon? Suspend touring and go to the restaurant when it's time. After lunch, resume the plan where you left off. You will circle back to Future World to see attractions the touring plan skipped earlier in the day. If you burn a lot of daylight in World Showcase shops, you may not finish the touring plan. If you want to shave time off your World Showcase circuit, skip the boat ride in Mexico and one or more of the three travelogue films (in China, France, and Canada).

12. Turn left and proceed clockwise around World Showcase Lagoon. Experience El Río del Tiempo boat ride in Mexico. The ride is in the far-left corner of the interior courtyard and isn't very well marked. Consign any purchases to Package Pickup for collection when you leave the park.

13. Go left from Mexico to Norway. Ride Maelstrom.

14. Continue left to China. See *Wonders of China.*

15. Continue to Germany and Italy. Enjoy the settings; there are no rides or films. If you don't have a restaurant priority seating, Sommerfest (fast food) at Germany serves tasty bratwurst, soft pretzels, desserts, and Beck's beer on draft.

16. Continue clockwise to The American Adventure. See the show. If you don't have a restaurant priority seating, the Liberty Inn (left side of The American Adventure) serves hamburgers, hot dogs, and chicken breast sandwiches.

17. Visit Japan and Morocco. Consign any purchases to Package Pick-up for collection when you leave the park.

18. Go left from Morocco to France. See *Impressions de France*.

19. Go to the United Kingdom.

20. Continue left; visit Canada. See *O Canada!*

    Note: Attractions in Steps 21 and 22 aren't as compelling as those in Steps 23 and 24. If you're running out of time, The Living Seas and Spaceship Earth (if you didn't see them in the morning) are more worthwhile than the Jouney into Imagination ride and the two theater attractions in The Land pavilion.

21. Return to Future World via the path leading to the Journey into Imagination pavilion. Take the Journey into Imagination ride if the wait is less than 20 minutes.

22. Return to The Land pavilion. See *Food Rocks* and *The Circle of Life*.

23. Exit The Land and turn right to The Living Seas, next door. For maximum efficiency, be one of the last people to enter the theater (where you sit) from the preshow area (where you stand). Sit as near the end of a middle row as possible. This will position you to be first on the ride after the theater presentation. After the ride, enjoy the exhibits of Sea Base Alpha.

24. Exit The Living Seas and turn left, passing through Innoventions West. Ride Spaceship Earth if you missed it earlier.

    Note: Check your watch. Is your dinner priority seating soon? Suspend touring and go to the restaurant when it's time. After dinner, check the daily entertainment schedule for the time of *IllumiNations*. Don't miss it. Give yourself at least a half hour after dinner to find a viewing spot on the perimeter of World Showcase Lagoon. For details on the best viewing spots, read pages 475–479.

25. If there's time before closing, stroll the nations of World Showcase or see the exhibits in Innoventions East and West. Another fun exhibit is The Image Works, upstairs in the Journey into Imagination pavilion.

26. Unless a holiday schedule is in effect, everything at Epcot closes after *IllumiNations* except for a few shops. Thirty thousand people bolt for the exits at once. Suggestions for coping with this exodus are on pages 474–475.

Author's Selective Epcot One-Day Touring Plan

For: All parties.
Assumes: Willingness to experience major rides and shows.

This touring plan includes only what the author believes is the best Epcot has to offer. Exclusion of an attraction doesn't mean it isn't worthwhile.

Families with children younger than eight using this touring plan should review Epcot attractions in the Small-Child Fright-Potential Chart (pages 159–160). Rent a stroller for any child small enough to fit in one, and take your young children back to the hotel for a nap after lunch. If you can allocate two days to see Epcot, try one of the Epcot two-day touring plans.

1. If you're a Disney hotel guest, arrive 90 minutes before official opening time *on early-entry days* and 40 minutes before official opening *on non-early-entry days*. If you're a day guest, arrive at the parking lot 45 minutes before Epcot's official opening *on a non-early-entry day*.

2. When admitted, move quickly (jog if you can, but don't run) around the left side of Spaceship Earth to Guest Relations (across the walkway from the geosphere) and make lunch and dinner priority seatings. If you don't wish to do so or have already made them by phone, skip to Step 3.

3. **If only Spaceship Earth and Guest Relations are open** when you're admitted, make your priority seatings and then ride Spaceship Earth. Exit Spaceship Earth, turn left, and proceed to Innoventions East. When the remainder of the park opens, pass through Innoventions East and bear right toward Test Track.

   If the entire park is open, make your priority seatings and then head directly to Test Track (bypassing Spaceship Earth) by way of Innoventions East.

   If you're a Disney resort guest taking advantage of early entry, expect only Spaceship Earth, The Living Seas, and attractions in The Land and Journey into Imagination pavilions to be open. Ride Spaceship Earth first, then Living with the Land in The Land pavilion, followed by *Honey, I Shrunk the Audience* at the Jouney into Imagination pavilion. Bypass other attractions in The Land and Journey into Imagination pavilions. After *Honey, I Shrunk the Audience,* resume the touring plan at Step 4 (Test Track). Skip any steps directing you to attractions you already experienced.

4. Ride Test Track.

5. Exit Test Track and cross Future World to the Journey into Imagination pavilion. See *Honey, I Shrunk the Audience.*

6. Postpone other attractions at Journey into Imagination. Bear left to The Land pavilion. Take the Living with the Land boat ride.

7. Postpone other Land attractions. Go to the Wonders of Life pavilion. Ride Body Wars. *Warning:* This ride gives many people motion sickness (see pages 457–459).

8. While at Wonders of Life, see *Cranium Command.* Don't miss the cartoon preshow or you may not understand the main presentation.

9. Exit Wonders of Life. Turn right to Universe of Energy and see the show. Don't be dismayed if the line looks long. The large theater gobbles the whole crowd when the audience changes.

10. Exit left from Universe of Energy and head toward Test Track. Go left past Wonders of Life and see Horizons.

11. Exit left from Horizons, passing Test Track. Go left on the path leading to the Odyssey Center. Cut through the Odyssey Center to World Showcase.

12. Turn left and proceed clockwise around World Showcase Lagoon. Visit the courtyard at Mexico, but skip the boat ride. Consign any purchases to Package Pick-up for collection when you leave the park.

13. Continue left to Norway. Ride Maelstrom.

14. Continue left to China. See *Wonders of China.*

   Note: Check your watch. Is your lunch priority seating soon? Suspend touring and go to the restaurant when it's time. After lunch, pick up the plan where you left off. You will circle back to Future World to see attractions the plan skipped earlier. If you burn a lot of daylight shopping, you may not finish the touring plan.

15. Visit Germany and Italy. Enjoy the settings; there are no rides or films. If you don't have a restaurant priority seating, Sommerfest

(fast food) at Germany serves tasty bratwurst, soft pretzels, desserts, and Beck's beer on draft.

16. Continue left to The American Adventure. See the show. If you don't have a restaurant priority seating, the Liberty Inn (left side of The American Adventure) serves hamburgers, hot dogs, and chicken breast sandwiches.

17. Visit Japan and Morocco. Consign any purchases to Package Pick-up for collection when you leave the park.

18. Leave Morocco for France. See *Impressions de France*.

19. Go to the United Kingdom.

20. Continue left to Canada. The film *O Canada!* is quite good, but the audience must stand. Optional.

21. Return to Future World and go to The Living Seas, next to The Land. See the show and take the ride. For maximum efficiency, be one of the last people to enter the theater (where you sit) from the preshow area (where you stand). Sit as close to the right end of a middle row as possible. This positions you to be first on the ride after the theater presentation. Afterward, enjoy the exhibits of Sea Base Alpha.

22. Exit left from The Living Seas and pass through Innoventions West. Ride Spaceship Earth if you missed it earlier.

    Note: Check your watch. Is your dinner priority seating soon? Suspend touring and go to the restaurant when it's time. After dinner, check the daily entertainment schedule for the time of *IllumiNations*. Don't miss it. Give yourself at least a half hour after dinner to find a viewing spot on the perimeter of World Showcase Lagoon. For details on the best viewing spots, see pages 475–479.

23. If you have time before the park closes, consider seeing *The Circle of Life* in The Land pavilion.

24. This concludes the touring plan. Visit attractions you missed or shop until time for dinner and/or *IllumiNations*. Unless a holiday schedule is in effect, everything at Epcot closes after *IllumiNations* except for a few shops. Thirty thousand people bolt for the exits at once. Suggestions for coping with this exodus are on pages 474–475.

Epcot Two-Day Sunrise/Starlight
Touring Plan

For: All parties.

This touring plan is for visitors who want to tour Epcot comprehensively over two days. Day One takes advantage of early-morning touring opportunities. Day Two begins in late afternoon and continues until the park closes.

Many readers spend part of their Disney World arrival day traveling, checking into their hotel, and unpacking. They aren't free to go to the theme parks until afternoon. The second day of the Epcot Two-Day Sunrise/Starlight Touring Plan is ideal for people who want to commence their Epcot visit later in the day.

Families with children younger than eight using this touring plan should review Epcot attractions in the Small-Child Fright-Potential Chart (pages 159–160). Rent a stroller for any child small enough to fit into one. Break off Day One no later than 2:30 p.m. and return to your hotel for rest. If you missed attractions called for in Day One, add them to your itinerary on Day Two.

Day One

1. If you're a Disney hotel guest, arrive 90 minutes before official opening time *on early-entry days* and 40 minutes before official opening *on non-early-entry days*. If you're a day guest, arrive at the parking lot 45 minutes before Epcot's official opening *on a non-early-entry day*.

2. When admitted, move quickly (jog if you can, but don't run) around the left side of Spaceship Earth to Guest Relations (across the walkway from the geosphere) and make lunch and dinner priority seatings. If you don't wish to do so or have already made them by phone, skip to Step 3.

3. **If only Spaceship Earth and Guest Relations are open** when you're admitted, ride Spaceship Earth after making your priority seatings. Exit Spaceship Earth, turn left, and proceed to Innoventions East. When the remainder of the park opens, pass through Innoventions East and bear right toward Test Track.

   If the entire park is open, make your priority seatings and then go directly to Test Track (bypassing Spaceship Earth) by way of Innoventions East.

   If you're a Disney resort guest taking advantage of early entry, expect only Spaceship Earth, The Living Seas, and attractions in The Land and Journey into Imagination pavilions to be open. Ride Spaceship Earth, then Living with the Land in The Land pavilion, followed by *Honey, I Shrunk the Audience* at the Jouney into Imagination pavilion. Bypass other attractions in The Land and Journey into Imagination pavilions. After *Honey, I Shrunk the Audience,* resume the plan at Step 4 (Test Track). Once you're on the plan, skip steps directing you to attractions you already experienced.

4. Ride Test Track.

5. Exit Test Track and cross Future World to the Journey into Imagination pavilion. See *Honey, I Shrunk the Audience.*

6. Skip other attractions at Journey into Imagination and exit left to The Land pavilion. Take the Living with the Land boat ride.

7. Postpone other Land attractions. Go to the Wonders of Life pavilion. Ride Body Wars. *Warning:* This ride gives many people motion sickness (see pages 457–459).

8. While at Wonders of Life, see *Cranium Command.* Don't miss the cartoon preshow or you may not understand the main presentation.

9. Exit Wonders of Life. Turn right to Universe of Energy and see the show. Don't be dismayed if the line looks long. The large theater gobbles the whole crowd when the audience changes.

10. Turn left out of Universe of Energy. Head back toward Test Track. Go left past the Wonders of Life pavilion and see Horizons.

11. Bear left after exiting Horizons, passing Test Track. Go left on the path leading to the Odyssey Center. Cut through the Odyssey Center to World Showcase.

12. Turn left and proceed clockwise around the World Showcase Lagoon. Experience El Río del Tiempo boat ride in Mexico. The ride is in the far-left corner of the interior courtyard and isn't very well marked. Consign any purchases to Package Pickup for collection when you leave the park.

13. Continue left to Norway. Ride Maelstrom.

    Note: Check your watch. Is your lunch priority seating soon? Suspend touring and go to the restaurant when it's time. After lunch, resume the touring plan where you left off.

14. Continue left to China. See *Wonders of China.*

15. Visit Germany and Italy. Enjoy the settings; there are no rides or films. If you don't have a restaurant priority seating, Sommerfest (fast food) at Germany serves tasty bratwurst, soft pretzels, desserts, and Beck's beer on draft.

16. Continue clockwise to The American Adventure. See the show. If you don't have a restaurant priority seating, the Liberty Inn (left side of The American Adventure) serves hamburgers, hot dogs, and chicken breast sandwiches.

17. Visit Japan and Morocco. Consign any purchases to Package Pick-up for collection when you leave the park.

18. This concludes the touring plan for Day One. Attractions and pavilions not included today will be experienced tomorrow. If you're full of energy and wish to continue touring, follow the Epcot One-Day Touring Plan, starting at Step 18. If you've had enough, exit through the International Gateway or leave through the main entrance. To reach the main entrance without walking around the lagoon, catch a boat at the dock near Morocco.

Day Two

1. Enter Epcot about 2 p.m. Get a park guidemap containing the daily entertainment schedule at Guest Relations.

2. While at Guest Relations, make a dinner priority seating, if you haven't done so already. Since it will be well past the usual time for making priority seatings, you may have to summon a reservationist with the WorldKey Information Satellite terminals.

   You can eat your evening meal in any Epcot restaurant without interrupting the sequence and efficiency of the touring plan. We recommend a 7 p.m. priority seating. The timing of the seating is important if you want to see *IllumiNations,* held over the lagoon at 9 p.m.

   If your preferred restaurants and seatings are filled, try for a priority seating at Morocco or Norway. Because these nations' delightful ethnic dishes are little known to most Americans, priority seatings may be available.

3. Ride Spaceship Earth if you missed it on Day One.

4. Pass through Innoventions West and proceed to The Living Seas. For maximum efficiency, be one of the last people to enter the theater (where you sit) from the preshow area (where you stand). Sit as close to the end of a middle row as possible. This will position you to be first on the ride that follows the theater presentation. Afterward, enjoy the exhibits of Sea Base Alpha.

5. Exit right from The Living Seas to The Land. See *Food Rocks* and *The Circle of Life,* featuring characters from *The Lion King.*

6. Turn right from The Land and go to the Journey into Imagination pavilion. Take the ride.

   Note: Check your watch. Is your dinner priority seating soon? Suspend touring and go to the restaurant when it's time. After dinner, check the daily entertainment schedule for the time of *IllumiNations.* Don't miss it. Give yourself at least a half hour after dinner to find a good viewing spot along the perimeter of World Showcase Lagoon. For details on the best spots, see pages 475–479.

7. Leave Future World and walk counterclockwise around World Showcase Lagoon to Canada. See *O Canada!*

8. Turn right and visit the United Kingdom.

9. Turn right and proceed to France. See the film.

10. This concludes the touring plan. Enjoy your dinner and *IllumiNations.* If you have time, shop or revisit your favorite attractions.

11. Unless a holiday schedule is in effect, everything at Epcot closes after *IllumiNations* except for a few shops. Thirty thousand people bolt for the exits at once. Suggestions for coping with this exodus are on pages 474–475.

Epcot Two-Day Early Riser Touring Plan

For: All parties.

The Two-Day Early Riser Touring Plan is the most efficient Epcot touring plan, eliminating much of the backtracking and crisscrossing required by the other plans. It takes advantage of easy touring made possible by morning's light crowds. Most folks will complete each day of the plan by midafternoon. While the plan doesn't include *IllumiNations* or other evening festivities, these activities plus dinner at an Epcot restaurant can be added to the itinerary at your discretion.

The Epcot Two-Day Early Riser Touring Plan is designed to be used on days when early entry isn't in effect.

Families with children younger than eight using this plan should review Epcot attractions in the Small-Child Fright-Potential Chart (pages 159–160). Rent a stroller for any child small enough to fit into one.

Day One

1. Arrive 45 minutes before official opening time on a day when early entry isn't scheduled.

2. When admitted, move quickly (jog if you can, but don't run) around the left side of Spaceship Earth to Guest Relations (across the walkway from the geosphere) and make lunch and dinner priority seatings. If you don't wish to do so or have already made them by phone, skip to Step 3.

3. **If only Spaceship Earth and Guest Relations are open** when you're admitted, ride Spaceship Earth after making your priority seatings. Exit Spaceship Earth, turn left, and proceed to Innoventions West (right of the sphere). When the remainder of the park opens, pass through Innoventions West and bear left to the Journey into Imagination pavilion.

   If the entire park is open, make your priority seatings and then go directly to Journey into Imagination (bypassing Spaceship Earth) by way of Innoventions West.

4. On the left side of the pavilion, see *Honey, I Shrunk the Audience.*

5. Exit left and enjoy the Journey into Imagination ride, on the right side of the same pavilion.

6. Exit left and proceed to The Land. Take the Living with the Land boat ride.

7. In the same pavilion, see *Food Rocks* and *The Circle of Life.* Start with whichever is scheduled to begin first.

8. Exit The Land and bear left to The Living Seas. See the structured part of the presentation, then the exhibits at your leisure.

   Note: Check your watch. Is your priority seating soon? Suspend touring and go to the restaurant if it's time. Resume the plan after you eat.

9. Bear left from The Living Seas and pass through Innoventions West. Cross the plaza behind Spaceship Earth and proceed through Innoventions East to the Universe of Energy. Enjoy the show.

10. From the Universe of Energy, continue past the Wonders of Life pavilion to Horizons. Ride.

11. Departing Horizons, explore attractions of Innoventions East and West.

12. This concludes Day One of the touring plan. If you linger over exhibits at The Living Seas and Innoventions East and West, it may be late in the day when you finish, and you might consider staying for dinner and *IllumiNations*. If you toured more briskly, you probably will complete the plan by about 2:30 p.m., even with a full-service lunch.

Day Two

1. Arrive 45 minutes before official opening time on a day when early entry isn't scheduled.

2. When admitted, move quickly (jog if you can, but don't run) around the left side of Spaceship Earth to Guest Relations (across the walkway from the geosphere) and make lunch and dinner priority seatings. If you don't wish to do so or have already made them by phone, skip to Step 3.

3. **If only Spaceship Earth and Guest Relations are open** when you're admitted, ride Spaceship Earth if you missed it on Day One. After riding (or not), position yourself in Innoventions East (left of the sphere), as close as possible to Test Track. When the remainder of Future World opens, zip directly to Test Track.

   If the entire park is open, make your priority seatings and then head directly to Test Track (bypassing Spaceship Earth) by way of Innoventions East.

4. Ride Test Track.

5. Exit Test Track to the right and proceed to the Wonders of Life pavilion. Ride Body Wars. *Warning:* This ride gives many people motion sickness (see pages 457–459).

6. In the same pavilion, see *The Making of Me*.

7. In the same pavailion, see *Cranium Command*. Afterward, enjoy the exhibits and interactive displays.

8. Exit left from the Wonders of Life pavilion and, passing Horizons, return to Test Track. To the left of Test Track, bear left on the path that leads to the Odyssey Center. Cut through the Odyssey Center to World Showcase.

9. Turn left and proceed clockwise around World Showcase Lagoon. Experience El Río del Tiempo boat ride at Mexico. The ride is in the far-left corner of the interior courtyard and isn't very well marked. Consign any purchases to Package Pick-up for collection when you leave the park.

10. Go left to Norway. Ride Maelstrom.

11. Go left to China. See *Wonders of China*.

12. Visit Germany and Italy. Enjoy the settings; there are no rides or films. If you don't have a restaurant priority seating, Sommerfest (fast food) at Germany serves tasty bratwurst, soft pretzels, desserts, and Beck's beer on draft.

13. Continue clockwise to The American Adventure. See the show. If you don't have a restaurant priority seating, the Liberty Inn (left side of The American Adventure) serves hamburgers, hot dogs, and chicken breast sandwiches.

14. Visit Japan and Morocco. Consign any purchases to Package Pick-up for collection when you leave the park.

15. Continue left to France. See *Impressions de France*.

16. Visit the United Kingdom.

17. Go left to Canada. See *O Canada!*

18. This concludes Day Two of the touring plan. If you futzed around in World Showcase shops and it's late in the day, consider staying for dinner and *IllumiNations*. If you caught *IllumiNations* after Day One, consider exiting Epcot through the International Gateway (between the United Kingdom and France) and exploring the restaurants, shops, and clubs of Disney's BoardWalk. The BoardWalk is an easy five-minute walk from the International Gateway.

Part Eleven

Disney's Animal Kingdom

With its lush flora, winding streams, meandering paths, and exotic setting, the Animal Kingdom is a stunningly beautiful theme park. The landscaping alone conjurs images of rain forest, veldt, and even formal garden. Soothing, mysterious, and exciting all at once, every vista is a feast for the eye. Add to this loveliness a population of more than 1,000 animals, replicas of Africa's and Asia's most intriguing architecture, and a diverse array of singularly original attractions, and you have the most unique of all Disney theme parks. In the Animal Kingdom, Disney has created an environment to savor. And though you will encounter the typical long lines, pricey food, and shops full of Disney merchandise, you will also (with a little effort) experience a day of stimulating private discoveries.

Disney's Animal Kingdom opened in April 1998 amid a storm of controversy. Animal rights activists lambasted Disney, blaming Animal Kingdom zoologists and caretakers for the death of some three dozen various animals. What went largely unreported, however, was that many of these same detractors had for months castigated Disney for pirating away the best zoological talent in the country from America's zoos and research centers. The fact that investigations turned up no evidence of negligence, mistreatment, or neglect did little to satisfy the critics. The Animal Kingdom, for ill or good, is probably destined to be the lightning rod for the ongoing debate concerning the role of zoos and the moral rectitude of confining wild animals in cages (however elaborate) for the pleasure of humans.

At 500 acres, Disney's Animal Kingdom is five times the size of the Magic Kingdom and more than twice the size of Epcot. But like Disney-MGM Studios, most of the Animal Kingdom's vast geography is only accessible on guided tours or as part of attractions. When complete, the Animal Kingdom will feature seven sections or "lands": The Oasis, Safari Village, DinoLand U.S.A., Camp Minnie-Mickey, Africa, Asia, and an as-yet

ASIA

AFRICA

Dinoland U.S.A.

Oasis

Safari Village

Camp Minnie-Mickey

Animal Kingdom

13. Harambe Village
14. Kilimanjaro Safaris
15. Maharaja Jungle Trek
16. Main Entrance
17. Rainforest Cafe
18. Theater in the Wild

19. Ticket Booths
20. Tiger Rapids Run
21. Tree of Life/ *It's Tough to Be a Bug!*
22. Wildlife Express (Train)

unnamed land inspired by mythical beasts. Built in phases, The Oasis, Safari Village, Camp Minnie-Mickey, Africa, and DinoLand U.S.A. were all operational for the park's opening in the summer of 1998. Asia is scheduled to open in late 1998 or early 1999, and "Beastie Land" (our suggestion) will come on-line sometime later, as subsequent phases are completed.

Its size notwithstanding, the Animal Kingdom features a limited number of attractions. To be exact, there are four rides, several walk-through exhibits, an indoor theater, four amphitheaters, a conservation exhibit, and a children's playground. Two of the attractions, however, Countdown to Extinction and Kilimanjaro Safaris, are among the best in the Disney repertoire. When Asia joins the existing lands, a fifth ride and another walk-through exhibit will be added to the lineup.

The evolution of the Animal Kingdom has been interesting in several respects. First, with regard to the Florida theme park market, it is seen to be taking dead aim at the recently resurgent Busch Gardens in Tampa, a theme park known for its exceptional zoological exhibits and numerous thrill rides. Disney has always preferred the neatly controlled movements of Audio-Animatronic animals to the unpredictable behaviors of real critters. Discovery Island, Disney's only previous foray into zoological exhibits, landed the Walt Disney Company in court for exterminating a bunch of indigenous birds that tried to take up residence on the island. When it comes to "rides," Disney won't even dignify the term. In Disney parks there are no rides, you see—only adventures. Attractions such as modern roller coasters, where the thrill of motion dominates visual, audio, and story-line elements, are antithetical to the Imagineering notion of attraction design.

Unfortunately for Disney, however, the creative, natural-habitat zoological exhibits and state-of-the-art thrill rides developed by Busch Gardens are immensely popular, and as any student of the Walt Disney Company can attest, there is nothing like a successful competitor to make the Disney folks change their tune. So, smoke, mirrors, and press releases aside, here's what you'll get when the Animal Kingdom is complete a couple of years from now: natural-habitat zoological exhibits and state-of-the-art thrill rides. Big surprise!

Even if the recipe is tried and true, the Disney version serves up more than its share of innovations, particularly when it comes to the wildlife habitats. In fact, zoologists worldwide are practically salivating at the thought of the Disney Imagineers applying their talent to zoo design. Living up to expectations, the wildlife exhibits at the Animal Kingdom do break some new ground. For starters there's lots of space, thus allowing for the sweeping vistas that Discovery Channel viewers would expect in, say, an African veldt setting. Then there are the enclosures, natural in appearance, with little or no apparent barriers between you and the animals. The operative word, of course, is "apparent." That flimsy stand of bamboo separating you from a gorilla is actually a neatly disguised set of steel rods imbedded in concrete. The Imagineers even take a crack at certain animals' stubborn unwillingness to be on display. A lion that would rather sleep out of sight under a bush, for example, is lured to center stage with nice, cool, climate-controlled artificial rocks.

A second anomaly in the development of the Animal Kingdom has been its erratic course from design to completion. Far from creating a master plan and sticking to it, the Animal Kingdom has been a continuously evolving project with more midstream about-faces than a kindergarten fire drill. Names of lands have changed (the land relating to mythical beasts has had no fewer than five names), as have the number of lands and their premier attractions. Some attraction concepts were half executed and then scrapped. The first attraction designed for the park's architectural icon, the Tree of Life, was discarded as the park entered its final stage of construction. Attractions and lands scheduled for Phase I of development were moved back to Phase II, and so on.

Third, Disney tried to keep the entire development secret. Some of the secrecy, no doubt, stemmed from Disney's obsession with controlling information (even when such control confuses the public and is not in Disney's best interest). Other contributing factors were the frequent conceptual and design changes. It's impossible to publicize a development, after all, when the project is being re-engineered in mid-process. Finally, and most important, Disney worried that making information available would cause travelers to postpone their visits to Walt Disney World until the Animal Kingdom opened. The upshot, of course, is that the secrecy itself became a hot item, drawing more attention to the Animal Kingdom than if Disney had rented every billboard along Interstate 4.

All of this, of course, is in the rearview mirror now—yet another example of Disney's penchant for doing things the hard way. What remains is a new star in Disney's growing galaxy of theme parks.

ARRIVING

The Animal Kingdom is situated off Osceola Parkway in the southwest corner of Walt Disney World, and is not too far from Blizzard Beach, the Coronado Springs Resort, and the All-Star resorts. From I-4, take Exit 25B, US 192, to the so-called Walt Disney World main entrance (World Drive) and follow the signs to the Animal Kingdom. The Animal Kingdom has its own 6,000-car pay parking lot with close-in parking for the disabled. Once parked, you can walk to the entrance or catch a ride on one of Disney's trademark trams. Be sure to mark the location of your car on your parking receipt and tuck it in a safe place (preferably on your person as opposed to in your car).

Though there is some discussion about a monorail loop linking the Animal Kingdom with the Transportation and Ticket Center and Disney-MGM Studios, the new park will be connected to other Walt Disney World destinations by the Disney bus system for the foreseeable future.

A WORD ABOUT ADMISSION

Be forewarned that unused days on multiday "hopper" passports issued prior to the opening of the Animal Kingdom are good only for admission to the Magic Kingdom, Epcot, and Disney-MGM Studios. Thus holders of these older passes must purchase a separate admission for the Animal Kingdom.

OPERATING HOURS AND EARLY ENTRY

The Animal Kingdom, not unexpectedly, hosted tremendous crowds during its first year. Consequently, Disney management has done a fair amount of fiddling and experimenting with operating hours and opening procedures. Generally, the Animal Kingdom opens earlier than the other three parks. In the summer of 1998 it was common practice to advertise 7 a.m. as the official opening time, but to open certain sections of the park as early as 6 a.m. If you are wondering whether any guests are actually on hand at such an ungodly hour, the answer is yes. If you arrive at the Animal Kingdom between 6 and 7 a.m., you will have plenty of company.

The reasoning behind such an early opening is rooted in the basic circadian rhythms of the animals and how the zookeepers take care of them. Most of the Animal Kingdom's 1,000 or so specimens are lodged in buildings or large protected enclosures at night and released into the natural habitat viewing areas during the day. Simply put, almost all are early-to-rise, early-to-bed type critters. The ones that are not, such as lions, cheetahs, and hyenas, who might enjoy a little hunting at night, don't have anything to hunt. So, at the Animal Kingdom, everybody gets plenty of sleep. You, on the other hand, will require a day of recuperation from having stumbled out of bed in the dead of night to go to the theme park. In any event, opening early allows the Animal Kingdom to also close early (usually 8 p.m. or so) and still provide guests with approximately 12–13 hours of touring time.

Because the Animal Kingdom opens so early anyway, there are no designated early-entry days as at the other three parks. This means that everyone has the same opportunity to be among the first to enter the park.

Park opening procedures at the Animal Kingdom vary. Sometimes guests arriving prior to the official opening time are admitted directly into DinoLand U.S.A., where they can experience Countdown to Extinction. When official opening time rolls around, they are admitted to the rest of the park. On other days, early arriving guests are admitted to The Oasis and

Safari Village, where they can see the 3-D movie in the Tree of Life. Once again, the remainder of the park will be roped off until official opening time. On holidays and other days of projected heavy attendance, Disney will open the entire park 30 or 60 minutes early. Our advice is to arrive, admission in hand, an hour before official opening during the summer and holiday periods, and 40 minutes before official opening the rest of the year.

WHEN TO GO

For the time being, expect to encounter large crowds at the Animal Kingdom. The best days of the week to go are Wednesday and Thursday, year-round. Next best are Friday and Tuesday. Avoid Saturday, Sunday, and Monday.

Because the park opens so early, many guests wrap up their tour and leave by 3:30 or 4 p.m. Lines for the major rides and the 3-D movie in the Tree of Life will usually thin appreciably between 4:30 p.m. and closing time. If you arrive at 3 p.m. and take in a couple of stage shows (described later), waits should be tolerable by the time you hit the Tree of Life and the rides. As an added bonus for late-afternoon touring, the animals tend to be more active.

GETTING ORIENTED

At the entrance plaza are ticket kiosks fronting the main entrance. To your right before the turnstiles are the kennel and an ATM. Passing through the turnstiles, wheelchair and stroller rentals are to your right. Guest Relations, the park headquarters for information, handout park maps, entertainment schedules, missing persons, and lost and found, is to the left. Nearby are rest rooms, public phones, and rental lockers. Beyond the entrance plaza you enter The Oasis, a lushly vegetated network of converging pathways winding through a landscape punctuated with streams, waterfalls, and misty glades, and inhabited by what Disney calls "colorful and unusual animals."

The park is arranged somewhat like the Magic Kingdom, in a hub-and-spoke configuration. The lush, tropical Oasis serves as Main Street, funneling visitors to Safari Village on an island at the center of the park. Dominated by the park's central icon, the 14-story-tall, handcarved Tree of Life, Safari Village is the park's retail and dining center. From Safari Village, guests can access the respective theme areas: Africa, Camp Minnie-Mickey, Asia, and DinoLand U.S.A. Safari Village additionally hosts two attractions: a boat ride in the Jungle Cruise tradition and a theater in the Tree of Life.

To help you plan your day, we have profiled all of the Animal Kingdom's major attractions. We suggest, however, that you be open-minded and try everything. Disney rides and shows are rarely what you would anticipate. For the time being, even if you dawdle in the shops and linger over the wildlife exhibits, you should easily be able to take in the Animal Kingdom in one day.

Not to be Missed at the Animal Kingdom	
Safari Village	*It's Tough to Be a Bug!*
Camp Minnie-Mickey	*Festival of the Lion King*
Africa	Kilimanjaro Safaris
DinoLand U.S.A.	Countdown to Extinction

The Oasis

Though the functional purpose of The Oasis is the same as that of Main Street in the Magic Kingdom (i.e., to funnel guests to the center of the park), it also serves as what Disney calls a "transitional experience." In plain English, this means that it sets the stage and gets you into the right mood to enjoy the Animal Kingdom. You will know the minute you pass through the turnstiles that this is not just another Main Street. Where Main Street, Hollywood Boulevard, and the Epcot entrance plaza direct you like an arrow straight into the heart of the respective parks, The Oasis immediately envelops you in an environment that is replete with choices. There is not one broad thoroughfare, but rather multiple paths. Each will deliver you to Safari Village at the center of the park, but which path you choose and what you see along the way is up to you. There is nothing obvious about where you are going, no Cinderella Castle or giant golf ball to beckon you. There is instead a lush, green, canopied landscape with streams, grottos, and waterfalls, an environment that promises adventure without revealing its nature.

The natural-habitat zoological exhibits in The Oasis are representative of those throughout the park. Although extraordinarily lush and beautiful, the exhibits are primarily designed for the comfort and well-being of the animals. This means in essence that you must be patient and look closely if you want to see the animals. A sign will identify the animal(s) in each exhibit, but there's no guarantee the animals will be immediately visible. Because most habitats are large and provide ample terrain for the occupants to hide, you must linger and concentrate, looking for small movements in the vegetation. When you do spot the animal, you may only make out a shadowy figure, or perhaps only a leg or a tail will be visible. In any event, don't expect the animals to stand out like a lump of coal in the snow. Animal-watching Disney-style, requires a sharp eye and a bit of effort.

Touring Tips   The Oasis is a place to linger and appreciate, and although this is exactly what the designers intended, it will be largely lost on Disney-conditioned guests who blitz through at warp speed to queue up for the big attractions. If you are a blitzer in the morning, plan to spend some time in

The Oasis on your way out of the park. The Oasis usually opens 30 minutes before and closes 30–60 minutes after the rest of the park.

Safari Village

Safari Village is an island of tropical greenery and whimsical equatorial African architecture, executed in vibrant hues of teal, yellow, red, and blue. Connected to the other lands by bridges, the island is the hub from which guests can access the park's various theme areas. The village is arrayed in a crescent around the base of the Animal Kingdom's signature landmark, the Tree of Life. Towering 14 stories above the village, the Tree of Life is this park's version of Cinderella Castle or Spaceship Earth. Flanked by pools, meadows, and exotic gardens populated by a diversity of interesting and playful animals, the Tree of Life houses a theater attraction inspired by the Disney/Pixar film, *A Bug's Life*.

Animal Kingdom Services

Most of the park's service facilities are located inside the main entrance and in Safari Village as follows:

Wheelchair & Stroller Rentals	Inside the main entrance to the right.
Banking Services	ATMs are located at the main entrance and at Safari Village.
Storage Lockers	Inside the main entrance to the left.
Lost & Found	Inside the main entrance to the left.
Guest Relations/Information	Inside the main entrance to the left.
Live Entertainment/ Parade Information	Included in the park guidemap available free at Guest Relations.
Lost Persons	Lost persons can be reported at Guest Relations and at Baby Services in Safari Village.
First Aid	In Safari Village, next to the Creature Comforts Shop.
Baby Center/ Baby-Care Needs	In Safari Village, next to the Creature Comforts Shop.
Film & Cameras	Just inside the main entrance at Garden Gate Gifts, in Safari Village at Disney Outfitters, and in Africa at Duka La Filimu.

As you enter Safari Village via the bridge from The Oasis and the main entrance, you will see the Tree of Life directly ahead at the 12 o'clock position, with the village at its base in a rough semicircle. The bridge to Asia is to the left of the tree at the 2 o'clock position, with the bridge to DinoLand U.S.A. at roughly 4 o'clock. The bridge connecting The Oasis to Safari Village is at the 6 o'clock position; the bridge to Camp Minnie-Mickey is at 8 o'clock; and the bridge to Africa is at 11 o'clock.

Safari Village is the park's central shopping, dining, and services headquarters. It is here that you will find the First Aid and Baby-Care Centers. Safari Village is also a transportation hub, with boats transporting guests to and from a dock situated between the Africa and Asia sections of the park. It's a short walk from the dock to the African village of Harambe, where you can transfer to trains for a round trip to Conservation Station on the park's perimeter, or to the Asian village of Anandapur. For the best selection of Disney trademark merchandise, try the Island Mercantile or Disney Outfitters shops. Counter-service food and snacks are available, but there are no full-service restaurants at Safari Village (the only full-service restaurant in the park is the Rainforest Cafe located to the left of the main entrance).

The Tree of Life/It's Tough to Be a Bug!

What It Is: 3-D theater show

Scope & Scale: Major attraction

When to Go: Before 10 a.m. and after 4 p.m.

Special Comments: The theater is inside the tree

Author's Rating: Zany and frenetic; ★★★½

Appeal by Age Group:

Pre-school	Grade School	Teens	Young Adults	Over 30	Senior Citizens
★★½	★★★★★	★★★★★	★★★★	★★★★	★★★★

Duration of Presentation: Approximately 7½ minutes

Probable Waiting Time: 12–30 minutes

Description and Comments The Tree of Life, apart from its size, is quite a work of art. Although from afar it is certainly magnificent and imposing, it is not until you examine the tree at close range that you truly appreciate its rich detail. What appears to be ancient gnarled bark is in fact hundreds of carvings depicting all manner of wildlife, each integrated seamlessly into the trunk, roots, and limbs of the tree. A stunning symbol of the interdependence of all living things, the Tree of Life is the most visually compelling structure to be found in any Disney park.

In sharp contrast to the grandeur of the tree is the subject of the attraction housed within its trunk. Called *It's Tough to Be a Bug!* this humorous 3-D film is about the difficulties of being a very small creature. *It's Tough to Be a Bug!* also contrasts with the relatively serious tone of the Animal Kingdom in general, standing virtually alone in providing some much needed levity and whimsy. *It's Tough To Be A Bug!* is similar to *Honey, I Shrunk the Audience* at Epcot in that it combines a 3-D film with an arsenal of tactile and visual special effects. In our view, the special effects are a bit overdone and the film somewhat anemic. Even so, we rate the bugs as not to be missed.

Another example of Disney's integrated marketing strategy, the 3-D presentation serves to stimulate demand for *A Bug's Life,* a new Disney/Pixar collaboration employing the same computer-animation techniques used in *Toy Story.* In a departure from previous cross-marketing efforts, however, Disney premiered the attraction version first, with the release of the feature film scheduled later.

Touring Tips   Because it's situated in the most eye-popping structure in the park, and also because there aren't that many attractions anyway, you can expect *It's Tough to Be a Bug!* to be mobbed most of the day. We recommend going first thing in the morning and then heading over to the Kilimanjaro Safaris. Safari Village sometimes opens before the rest of the park. If this is the case and the 3-D flick is open, go ahead and see it and then position yourself at the bridge leading to Africa. When the rest of the park opens, zip over to Kilimanjaro Safaris. If you miss the bugs in the morning, try again in the late afternoon.

Be advised that *It's Tough to Be a Bug!* is very intense and that the special effects will do a number on young children as well as anyone who is squeamish about insects.

Discovery River Boats

What It Is: Boat-ride adventure/transportation to Africa and Asia

Scope & Scale: Minor attraction

When to Go: Before 10 a.m. or two hours before closing

Author's Rating: Not worth the wait; ★★

Appeal by Age Group:

Pre-school	Grade School	Teens	Young Adults	Over 30	Senior Citizens
★★★	★★	★½	½	★★	★★

Duration of Ride: 8–9 minutes

Average Wait in Line per 100 People ahead of You: 14 minutes

Assumes: All boats operating

Loading Speed: Slow

Description and Comments A one-way boat ride from Safari Village to the Africa/Asia landing, or from the landing to Safari Village. You must queue up twice if you want to complete a round trip. Most of the sights on the boat ride are visible from the various Safari Village bridges, and in any event are not all that interesting. The cruise provides a scenic alternative to walking to Africa or Asia but is so sluggish loading and unloading that it's not worth the effort.

Touring Tips If the wait for the boat ride is not prohibitive, it's a foot-saving way to access Africa and Asia. If you are in a hurry, you can reach Africa and Asia faster by walking.

Camp Minnie-Mickey

This land is designed to be the Disney characters' Animal Kingdom head-quarters. A small land, Camp Minnie-Mickey is about the size of Mickey's Toontown Fair but has a rustic and woodsy theme like a summer camp. In addition to a character meeting and greeting area, Camp Minnie-Mickey is home to two live stage productions featuring Disney characters.

Situated in a cul-de-sac, Camp Minnie-Mickey is a pedestrian nightmare. Lines for the two stage shows and from the character greeting areas spill out into the congested walkways, making movement almost impossible. To compound the problem, hundreds of parked strollers clog the paths, squeezing the flow of traffic to a trickle.

Character Trails

Description & Comments Characters can be found at the end of each of four "character trails" respectively named Jungle, Forest, Arbor, and Mickey. Each trail has its own private reception area and, of course, its own queue. Jungle Characters features characters from *The Lion King* and *The Jungle Book,* while Forest Characters generally offers characters from *Winnie the Pooh.* The Arbor trail leads to Minnie and the Mickey trail to Mickey. Usually two or three characters are present in the Forest and Jungle greeting areas, while Minnie and Mickey each work solo.

Touring Tips Waiting in line to see the characters can be very time-consuming. We recommend visiting early in the morning or late in the afternoon. Because there are fewer attractions at the Animal Kingdom than at the other parks, expect to find a disproportionate number of guests in Camp Minnie-Mickey. If the place is really mobbed, you may want to consider meeting the characters in one of the other parks. Ditto for the stage shows.

Festival of the Lion King

What It Is: Theater-in-the-round stage show

Scope & Scale: Major attraction

When to Go: Before 11 a.m. or after 4 p.m.

Special Comments: Performance times are listed in the handout park map

Author's Rating: Upbeat and spectacular; ★★★★

Appeal by Age Group:

Pre-school	Grade School	Teens	Young Adults	Over 30	Senior Citizens
★★★★	★★★★½	★★★★	★★★★	★★★★	★★★★

Duration of Presentation: 25 minutes

Preshow Entertainment: None

Probable Waiting Time: 20–35 minutes

Description and Comments This energetic production, inspired by Disney's *Lion King* feature, is part stage show, part parade, and part circus. Guests are seated in four sets of bleachers surrounding the stage and organized into separate cheering sections, which are called on to make elephant, warthog, giraffe, and lion noises. There is a great deal of parading around, some acrobatics, and a lot of singing and dancing. By our count, every tune from *The Lion King* (plus a couple of others) is belted out and reprised several times. No joke, if you don't know the words to all the songs by the end of the show, you must have been asleep.

Touring Tips This show is both popular and difficult to see. Your best bet is to go to the first show in the morning or to one of the last two performances in the evening. To see the show during the more crowded middle of the day, you'll need to queue up at least 35 minutes before show time. There are four separate lines, one for each set of bleachers. The queues fill from left to right and are seated in the same order. To minimize standing in the hot sun, refrain from hopping in line until the Disney people begin directing guests to the far-right queue. If you have small children or short adults in your party, sit higher up in the bleachers. The first five rows in particular have very little rise, making it difficult for those in rows 2–5 to see. Though the theater is covered and air is circulated by fans, there is no air conditioning.

Colors of the Wind, Friends from the Animal Forest at Grandmother Willow's Grove

What It Is: Conservation-theme stage show

Scope & Scale: Major attraction

When to Go: Before 11 a.m. or after 4 p.m.

Special Comments: Performance times are listed in the handout park map

Author's Rating: A little sappy; ★★½

Appeal by Age Group:

Pre-school	Grade School	Teens	Young Adults	Over 30	Senior Citizens
★★★½	★★★½	★★★	★★★½	★★★	★★★

Duration of Presentation: 15 minutes

Preshow Entertainment: None

Probable Waiting Time: 20–30 minutes

Description and Comments   This show featuring Pocahontas addresses the role of man in protecting the natural world. Various live creatures of the forest, including a raccoon, a snake, and a turkey, as well as a couple of Animatronic trees, assist Pocahontas in making the point. The presentation is gushy and overacted but has its moments nonetheless.

Touring Tips   Because the theater is relatively small, and because Camp Minnie-Mickey stays so mobbed, the Pocahontas show is hard to get into. Among other problems, its queuing area adjoins that of *Festival of the Lion King* next door. If you approach when a lot of guests are waiting, which is almost always, it's hard to figure out which show you're lining up for. To avoid the hassle, try to catch the show before 11 a.m. or after 4 p.m. Regardless of time of day, arrive at least 20 minutes before show time and ask a Disney cast member to steer you to the correct line.

Africa

The largest of the Animal Kingdom's lands, guests enter through Harambe, Disney's idealized and immensely sanitized version of a modern, rural African town. There is a market (with modern cash registers), and counter-service food is available. What distinguishes Harambe is its understatement. Far from the stereotypical great-white-hunter image of an African town, Harambe is definitely (and realistically) not exotic. The buildings, while interesting, are quite plain and architecturally simple. Though certainly better maintained and more aseptic than the real McCoy, Disney's Harambe would be a lot more at home in Kenya than the Magic Kingdom's Main Street would be in Missouri.

Harambe serves as the gateway to the African veldt habitat, the Animal Kingdom's largest and most ambitious zoological exhibit. Access to the veldt is via the Kilimanjaro Safaris attraction, located at the end of Harambe's main drag near the fat-trunked baobab tree. Harambe is also the departure point for the train to Conservation Station, the park's veterinary headquarters.

If there is one detail that Disney overlooked in designing the village of Harambe, it's parking. No, not cars—strollers. So many guests are simultaneously experiencing the safari, riding the train, or walking the Gorilla Falls trail, that literally hundreds of empty strollers clog the town square. A crew of Disney cast members are assigned to stack the strollers, sometimes as many as three high, to keep strollerosis of the traffic arteries from shutting Harambe down. It's really pretty amusing until you return to retrieve your stroller. Our advice is to park your stroller along the wall overlooking the river near the African Lounge.

Kilimanjaro Safaris

What It Is: Truck ride through an African wildlife reservation

Scope & Scale: Super headliner

When to Go: Before 9:30 a.m. or in the two hours before closing

Author's Rating: Truly exceptional; ★★★★★

Appeal by Age Group:

Pre-school	Grade School	Teens	Young Adults	Over 30	Senior Citizens
★★★★	★★★★★	★★★★½	★★★★½	★★★★½	★★★★★

Duration of Ride: About 20 minutes

Average Wait in Line per 100 People ahead of You: 4 minutes

Assumes: Full-capacity operation with 18-second dispatch interval

Loading Speed: Fast

Description and Comments The park's premier zoological attraction, Kilimanjaro Safaris offers an exceptionally realistic, albeit brief, imitation of an actual African photo safari. Thirty-two guests at a time board tall, open safari vehicles and are dispatched into a simulated African veldt habitat. Animals such as zebra, wildebeest, impala, Thomson's gazelle, giraffe, and even rhinos roam apparently free, while predators such as lions, as well as potentially dangerous large animals like hippos, are separated from both prey and guests by all-but-invisible, natural-appearing barriers. Although the animals have more than 100 acres of savanna, woodland, streams, and rocky hills to call home, careful placement of water holes, forage, and salt licks ensure that the critters are hanging out by the road when safari vehicles roll by.

A scripted narration provides a story line about finding Big Red and Little Red, a mother elephant and her baby, while an on-board guide points out and identifies the various animals encountered. Toward the end of the ride, the safari chases poachers who have just wounded Big Red. As the vehicle approaches the safari's terminating point, the poachers are seen being taken into custody.

Having traveled in Kenya and Tanzania, I will tell you that Disney has done an amazing job of replicating the sub-Saharan east African landscape. The main difference that an east African would notice is that Disney's version is greener and generally speaking less barren. And, like on a real African safari, what animals you see (and how many) is pretty much a matter of luck. We tried Disney's safari upwards of a dozen times and had a different experience on each trip.

If the attraction has a shortcoming, it is the rather strident story line about the poachers and Big Red, which while thought provoking, is somewhat distracting when you are trying to spot and enjoy the wildlife. Also, because the story is repeated on every trip, it really gets on your nerves after the first couple of times.

Touring Tips   Kilimanjaro Safaris is the park's most popular attraction, drawing large crowds from early morning on. Our recommendation is to experience the safari immediately after the Africa section of the park opens. If Countdown to Extinction in DinoLand U.S.A. and/or *It's Tough to Be a Bug!* in the Tree of Life are open prior to the opening of Africa, by all means take them in and then head to Kilimanjaro Safaris. If you don't make it to the safari before 9:30 a.m., wait until after 4 p.m. and try again. The queue is often short in the late afternoon.

If you want to take photos on your safari, be advised that the vehicle doesn't stop very often, so be prepared to snap while under way. Also, don't worry about the ride itself: it really isn't very rough. Finally, the only thing that a young child might find intimidating is crossing an "old bridge" that pretends to collapse under your truck.

Gorilla Falls Exploration Trail

What it Is: Walk-through zoological exhibit

Scope & Scale: Major attraction

When to Go: Before 9:30 a.m. or in the two hours before closing

Author's Rating: ★★★

Appeal by Age Group:

Pre-school	Grade School	Teens	Young Adults	Over 30	Senior Citizens
★★★½	★★★½	★★½	★★★	★★★	★★★

Duration of Tour: About 20–25 minutes

Description and Comments   Because guests disembark from the safari at the entrance to the Gorilla Falls Exploration Trail, most guests try the trail immediately after the safari. Winding between the domain of two troops of lowland gorillas, it's hard to see what, if anything, separates you from the primates. Also on the trail are a hippo pool with an underwater viewing area, a naked mole rat exhibit (I promise I'm not making this up), and some hyenas. A highlight of the trail is an exotic bird aviary so craftily designed that you can barely tell you're in an enclosure.

Touring Tips The Gorilla Falls Exploration Trail is lush, beautiful, and jammed to the gills with people most of the time. Guests exiting the safari can choose between returning to Harambe or walking the Gorilla Falls Exploration Trail. Not unexpectedly, close to 90% opt for the trail. Thus, when the safari is operating at full tilt, it spews hundreds of guests every couple of minutes onto the Exploration Trail. The one-way trail in turn becomes so clogged that nobody can move or see much of anything. After a minute or two, however, you catch the feel of the mob moving forward in small lurches. From then on you shift, elbow, grunt, and wriggle your way along, every so often coming to an animal exhibit. Here you endeavor to work your way close to the rail but are opposed by people trapped against the rail who are trying to rejoin the forward-surging crowd. The animals, as well as their natural-habitat enclosures, are pretty nifty if you can fight close enough to see them.

   Clearly this attraction is either badly designed, misplaced, or both. Your only real chance for enjoying it is to walk through before 9 a.m. (i.e., before the safari hits full stride) or in the hour or two before closing.

Wildlife Express

What It Is: Scenic railroad ride to Conservation Station
Scope & Scale: Major attraction
When to Go: Before 10:30 a.m. or after 4 p.m.
Special Comments: Most guests will take the train after returning to
   Harambe from the Kilimanjaro Safari
Author's Rating: Ho hum; ★★
Appeal by Age Group:

Pre-school	Grade School	Teens	Young Adults	Over 30	Senior Citizens
★★★	★★★	★½	★★½	★★½	★★½

Duration of Ride: About 5–7 minutes one way
Average Wait in Line per 100 People ahead of You: 9 minutes
Loading Speed: Moderate

Description and Comments A transportation ride that snakes behind the African wildlife reserve as it makes its loop connecting Harambe to Conservation Station. En route to Conservation Station, you see the nighttime enclosures for the animals that populate the Kilimanjaro Safaris. Similarly, returning from Conservation Station to Harambe, you see the backstage areas of Asia. Regardless which direction you're heading, the sights are not especially interesting.

Touring Tips   Most guests will embark for Conservation Station after experiencing the Kilimanjaro Safaris and the Gorilla Falls Exploration Trail. Thus the train begins to get crowded between 10 and 11 a.m. Though you may catch a glimpse of several species from the train, it can't compare to Kilimanjaro Safaris for seeing the animals.

Conservation Station

What It Is: Behind-the-scenes walk-through educational exhibit
Scope & Scale: Minor attraction
When to Go: Anytime
Author's Rating: Evolving; ★★½
Appeal by Age Group:

Pre-school	Grade School	Teens	Young Adults	Over 30	Senior Citizens
★★½	★★	★½	★★½	★★½	★★½

Probable Waiting Time: None

Description and Comments   Conservation Station is the Animal Kingdom's veterinary and conservation headquarters. Located on the perimeter of the African section of the park, Conservation Station is, strictly speaking, a backstage, working facility. Here guests can meet wildlife experts, observe some of the Station's ongoing projects, and learn about the behind-the-scenes operations of the park. The Station includes, among other things, a rehabilitation area for injured animals and a nursery for recently born (or hatched) critters. Vets and other experts are on-hand to answer questions.

While there are several permanent exhibits, including an animal petting area, what you see at Conservation Station will largely depend on what's going on when you arrive. On the days we visited, there wasn't enough happening to warrant waiting in line twice (coming and going) for the train. Hopefully, Conservation Station will improve with age. Ditto for the train ride.

You can access Conservation Station by taking the Wildlife Express train directly from Harambe. To return to the center of the park, continue the loop from Conservation Station back to Harambe.

Touring Tips   Conservation Station is interesting, but you have to invest a little effort and it helps to be inquisitive. Because it's on the far-flung border of the park, you'll never bump into Conservation Station unless you take the train. We recommend seeing the Station after completing the safari. Stay as long as you like.

Asia (Opens Early 1999)

Crossing the Asia Bridge from Safari Village, you enter Asia through the village of Anandapur, a veritable collage of Asian themes inspired by the architecture and ruins of India, Thailand, Indonesia, and Nepal. Situated near the bank of the Chakranadi River (translation: the river that runs in circles) and surrounded by lush vegetation, Anandapur provides access to a gibbon exhibit and to Asia's two feature attractions, the Tiger Rapids Run whitewater raft ride, and the Maharajah Jungle Trek. Also in Asia, and already up and running, is the *Flights of Wonder* show, an educational production about birds.

Tiger Rapids Run (Opens Early 1999)

What It Is: Whitewater raft ride

Scope & Scale: Headliner

When to Go: Before 10 a.m. or after 4:30 p.m.

Special Comments: You are guaranteed to get wet

Author's Rating: Not open at press time

Appeal by Age Group: Not open at press time

Duration of Ride: About 7 minutes

Average Wait in Line per 100 People ahead of You: 5 minutes

Loading Speed: Moderate

Description and Comments   Whitewater raft rides have been a hot-weather favorite of theme park patrons for almost 20 years. The ride itself consists of an unguided trip down a man-made river in a circular rubber raft with a platform seating 12 persons mounted on top. The raft essentially floats free in the current and is washed downstream through rapids and waves. Because the river is fairly wide with numerous currents, eddies, and obstacles, there is no telling exactly where the raft will go. Thus, each trip is different and exciting. At the end of the ride a conveyor belt hauls the raft up to be unloaded and prepared for the next group of guests.

What distinguishes Tiger Rapids Run from other theme park raft rides is Disney's trademark attention to visual detail. Where many raft rides essentially plunge down a concrete ditch, Tiger Rapids Run flows through a dense rain forest, past waterfalls, temple ruins, and bamboo thickets, emerging into a cleared area where greedy loggers have ravaged the forest, and finally drifting back under the tropical canopy as the river cycles back to Anandapur. Along the way your raft runs a gauntlet of raging cataracts, log jams, and other dangers.

Touring Tips   This attraction will be hugely popular, especially on hot summer days. Ride Tiger Rapids Run before 10 a.m. or after 4:30 p.m. You can expect to get wet and possibly drenched on this ride. Our recommendation is to wear shorts to the park and bring along a jumbo size trash bag as well as a smaller plastic bag. Before boarding the raft, take off your socks and punch holes in your jumbo bag for your head. Though you can also cut holes for your arms, you will probably stay dryer with your arms inside the bag. Use the smaller plastic bag to wrap around your shoes. If you are worried about mussing your hairdo, bring a third bag for your head.

Maharaja Jungle Trek (Opens Early 1999)

What It Is: Walk-through zoological exhibit

Scope & Scale: Headliner

When to Go: Before 11 a.m. or in the three hours before closing

Author's Rating: Not open at press time

Appeal by Age Group: Not open at press time

Duration of Tour: About 20–30 minutes

Description and Comments   The Maharaja Jungle Trek is a zoological nature walk similar to the Gorilla Falls Exploration Trail, but with an Asian setting and Asian animals. You start with Komodo dragons and then work up to Malayan tapirs. Next is a cave with fruit bats. Ruins of the maharaja's palace provide the setting for Bengal tigers. From the top of a parapet in the palace you can view a herd of blackbuck antelope and Asian deer. The trek concludes with an aviary.

Labyrinthine, overgrown, and elaborately detailed, the temple ruin would be a compelling attraction even without the animals. Throw in a few bats, bucks, and Bengals and you're in for a treat.

Touring Tips   Most guests will walk the Maharaja Jungle Trek after completing the raft ride. While we don't expect the Trek to be as crowded as the Gorilla Falls Exploration Trail, we nevertheless recommend touring before 11 a.m. and preferably earlier. If the Trek is jammed, try it again after 4 p.m. or so.

Flights of Wonder at the Caravan Stage

What It Is: Open-air show about birds

Scope & Scale: Major attraction

When to Go: Anytime

Special Comments: Performance times are listed in the handout park map

Author's Rating: Unique; ★★★★

Appeal by Age Group:

Pre-school	Grade School	Teens	Young Adults	Over 30	Senior Citizens
★★★★	★★★★	★★★½	★★★★	★★★★	★★★★

Duration of Presentation: 30 minutes

Preshow Entertainment: None

Probable Waiting Time: 20 minutes

Description and Comments This show is about a treasure hunter who bumps into the Disney version of the Birdman of Alcatraz. The Birdman helps the treasure hunter, through a sort of humorous, hard-knocks approach, to appreciate our feathery friends. Both interesting and fun, *Flights of Wonder* is well paced and showcases a surprising number of different bird species.

Touring Tips *Flights of Wonder* plays at the Caravan Stage, located near the Asia Bridge on the walkway connecting Africa and Asia. Because the seating area is in the sun, early-morning and late-afternoon performances are more comfortable. Though we did not have any problem getting a seat for *Flights of Wonder,* we expect the show's attendance to pick up once the rest of Asia opens. To play it safe, arrive about 15–20 minutes before show time.

DinoLand U.S.A.

This most typically Disney of the Animal Kingdom's lands is a cross between an anthropological dig and a quirky roadside attraction. Accessible via the bridge from Safari Village, DinoLand U.S.A. is home to a children's play area, a nature trail, a 1500-seat amphitheater, a couple of natural history exhibits, and Countdown to Extinction, one of the Animal Kingdom's two thrill rides.

Countdown to Extinction

What It Is: Motion-simulator dark ride

Scope & Scale: Super headliner

When to Go: Before 10 a.m. or in the hour before closing

Special Comments: Children must be 3'10" tall to ride (See Switching off on pages 165–167)

Author's Rating: Really good, almost excellent; ★★★★

Appeal by Age Group:

Pre-school	Grade School	Teens	Young Adults	Over 30	Senior Citizens
†	★★★★½	★★★★	★★★★	★★★½	★★★½

† Sample size too small for an accurate rating.

Duration of Ride: 3¹/₃ minutes

Average Wait in Line per 100 People ahead of You: 3 minutes

Assumes: Full-capacity operation with 18-second dispatch interval

Loading Speed: Fast

Description and Comments   Countdown to Extinction is a combination track ride and motion simulator. In addition to moving along a cleverly hidden track, the ride vehicle also bucks and pitches (the simulator part) in sync with the visuals and special effects encountered. The plot has you traveling back in time on a mission of rescue and conservation. Your objective, believe it or not, is to haul back a living dinosaur before the species becomes extinct. Whoever is operating the clock, however, cuts it a little close, and you arrive on the prehistoric scene just as a giant asteroid is hurling toward Earth. General mayhem ensues as you evade carnivorous predators, catch Barney, and make your escape before the asteroid hits.

Countdown to Extinction is a technological clone of the Indiana Jones ride at Disneyland. A good effort, though not as visually interesting as Indiana Jones, Countdown to Extinction serves up nonstop action from beginning to end with brilliant visual effects. Elaborate even by Disney standards, the attraction provides a tense, frenetic ride embellished by the entire Imagineering arsenal of high-tech gimmickry. Although the ride is jerky, it's not too rough for seniors. The menacing dinosaurs, however, along with the intensity of the experience, make Countdown to Extinction a no-go for younger children.

Touring Tips   Disney situated Countdown to Extinction in such a remote corner of the park that it was taking guests awhile to find it. This, in conjunction with the overwhelming popularity of Kilimanjaro Safaris, left Countdown to Extinction (C.T.E. in DisneySpeak) operating at less than capacity. To bump its numbers up, Disney even tried opening the attraction before the rest of the park, providing access to DinoLand through a backstage gate. By the time we went to press, Countdown was doing better but not attracting crowds comparable to Indiana Jones at Disneyland. Despite the slow start, we expect Countdown to turn into a big draw. Thus we continue to recommend that you ride early after experiencing *It's Tough to Be a Bug!*, Kilimanjaro Safaris, and the Gorilla Falls Exploration Trail.

Be forewarned that the technology used in this attraction has been subject to frequent breakdowns at Disneyland. If the ride breaks while you are in line, our suggestion is to stick it out. Usually, it's just a matter of removing a defective ride vehicle, about 15 minutes' worth of work.

Theater in the Wild

What It Is: Open-air venue for live stage shows
Scope & Scale: Major attraction
When to Go: Anytime

Special Comments: Performance times are listed in the handout park map

Author's Rating: ★★★★

Appeal by Age Group:

Pre-school	Grade School	Teens	Young Adults	Over 30	Senior Citizens
★★★★	★★★★	★★★½	★★★★	★★★★	★★★★

Duration of Presentation: 25–35 minutes

Preshow Entertainment: None

Probable Waiting Time: 20–30 minutes

Description and Comments The Theater in the Wild is a 1500-seat, covered amphitheater. The largest stage production facility in the Animal Kingdom, the theater can host just about any type of stage show. *Journey into Jungle Book*, a very solid and colorful adaptation of the *Jungle Book* story, was the opening production for the Theater in the Wild. If it's still playing when you visit, try to catch a show. We rate it as not to be missed.

Touring Tips To get a seat, show up 20–25 minutes in advance for morning and late-afternoon shows, and 25–30 minutes in advance for shows scheduled between noon and 4:30 p.m. Access to the theater is via a relatively narrow pedestrian path. If you arrive as the previous show is letting out, you will feel like a salmon swimming upstream.

The Boneyard

What It Is: Elaborate playground

Scope & Scale: Diversion

When to Go: Anytime

Author's Rating: Stimulating fun for children; ★★★½

Appeal by Age Group:

Pre-school	Grade School	Teens	Young Adults	Over 30	Senior Citizens
★★★★½	★★★★½	†	†	†	†

† Sample sizes too small for accurate ratings.

Duration of Visit: Varies

Waiting Time: None

Description and Comments This attraction is an elaborate playground, particularly appealing to kids age ten and younger, but visually appealing to all ages. Arranged in the form of a rambling open-air dig site, The Boneyard offers plenty of opportunity for exploration and letting off steam. Playground equipment consists of the skeletons of Triceratops, Tyrannosaurus rex, Brachiosaurus, and the like, on which children can swing, slide, and climb. In addition, there are sand pits where little ones can scrounge around for bones and fossils.

Touring Tips   Not the cleanest Disney attraction, but certainly one where younger children will want to spend some time. Aside from getting dirty, or at least sandy, be aware that The Boneyard gets mighty hot in the Florida sun. Keep your kids well hydrated and drag them into the shade from time to time. If your children will let you, save the playground until after you have experienced the main attractions. Because The Boneyard is situated so close to the center of the park, it's easy to stop in whenever your kids get itchy. While the little ones clamber around on giant femurs and ribs, you can sip a tall cool one in the shade (still keeping an eye on them, of course).

Be aware that The Boneyard rambles over about a half-acre and is multistoried. It's pretty easy to lose sight of a small child in the playground. Fortunately, there's only one entrance and exit.

Cretaceous Trail

What It Is: Walk-through floral exhibit
Scope & Scale: Diversion
When to Go: Anytime
Author's Rating: ★★
Appeal by Age Group:

Pre-school	Grade School	Teens	Young Adults	Over 30	Senior Citizens
★★	★★	★★	★★	★★	★★

Duration of Visit: Varies
Waiting Time: None

Description and Comments   The Cretaceous Trail is a footpath through a replica of a primeval forest. Lush and haunting, the trail is enveloped by cycads, ferns, palms, and other flora that thrived in prehistoric forests and swamps. There are a few surprises as well, including a survivor or two from Countdown to Extinction.

Touring Tips   Children will find the trail diverting for awhile but will be ready pretty quickly to move on to something else. Go whenever you are feeling green and shady.

Live Entertainment in the Animal Kingdom

Stage Shows   Stage shows are performed daily at the Theater in the Wild in DinoLand U.S.A., at Grandmother Willow's Grove and at the Lion King Theater in Camp Minnie-Mickey, and at the Caravan Stage in Asia. Presentations at Camp Minnie-Mickey and DinoLand U.S.A. feature the Disney characters.

Street Performers   Street performers can be found most of the time at Safari Village, at Harambe in Africa, and in DinoLand U.S.A.

March of the Animals   During its first year, the Animal Kingdom experimented with a modest parade called the *March of the Animals.* Though not as elaborate as parades at the Magic Kingdom or Disney-MGM Studios, the parade was pleasant enough and allowed management to set up a parade route. Parades in the Animal Kingdom start next to the Creature Comforts shop in Safari Village and cross the Africa Bridge. Turning right, the parade proceeds along the path connecting Africa and Asia before making a right turn over the Asia Bridge back into Safari Village. From here the parade crosses into DinoLand U.S.A. and completes the route at the Theater in the Wild. Sometimes the route is run in reverse.

There are usually two parades each day, both in the afternoon. Check Guest Relations for starting times. If you are a big fan of Disney parades, check it out. Otherwise, for the moment, we don't think that the parade is worth a special effort to see.

Animal Encounters   Throughout the day, knowledgeable Disney staff conduct impromtu short lectures on specific animals at the park. Look for a cast member in safari garb holding a bird, reptile, or small mammal.

Goodwill Ambassadors   A number of Asian and African natives are on-hand throughout the park. Both gracious and knowledgeable, they are delighted to discuss their country and its wildlife. Look for them in Harambe and along the Gorilla Falls Exploration Trail in Africa, and in Anandapur and along the Maharaja Jungle Trek in Asia. They can also be found near the main entrance and at The Oasis.

Shopping in the Animal Kingdom

While most of the shopping at the Animal Kingdom is concentrated in Safari Village, Harambe in Africa, Anandapur in Asia, and DinoLand U.S.A., any nook or hut large enough to house a cash register is likely to sell something. Typical items for sale include wildlife- and conservation-inspired merchandise a la The Nature Company, along with African wood-carving, crafts, and garb, as well as safari attire, dinosaur specialty items, and the inevitable assortment of Disney character goods. The two largest shops, both located in Safari Village, are Island Mercantile and Disney Outfitters.

Frankly, we are disappointed with the selection of merchandise at the Animal Kingdom. There is a surprising scarcity of imported wares from Africa and Asia, and a teeming overabundance of Disney trademark stuff and tacky souvenirs. If you are looking for something interesting and nice, you are much more likely to find it at World Showcase in Epcot, or at Downtown Disney.

Traffic Patterns in the Animal Kingdom

For starters, because the Animal Kingdom is new, expect huge crowds for the foreseeable future, even during the off-season. The three crowd magnets are *It's Tough to Be a Bug!* in the Tree of Life, Kilimanjaro Safaris in Africa, and Countdown to Extinction in DinoLand U.S.A. When it opens in early 1999, add Tiger Rapids Run to the lineup.

Because the park hosts large crowds with only a relative handful of attractions, expect for all the attractions to be extremely busy, and for *It's Tough to Be a Bug!*, Countdown to Extinction, and Kilimanjaro Safaris to be mobbed. Most guests arrive in the morning, with a sizable number on-hand prior to opening and a larger wave arriving between 8 and 9:30 a.m. Guests continue to stream in through the late morning and into the early afternoon, with the crowds peaking at around 2 p.m. From about 2:30 p.m. on, departing guests outnumber arriving guests by a wide margin, as guests who arrived early complete their tour and leave. Crowds thin appreciably by late afternoon and continue to decline into the early evening.

Because the number of attractions, including theater presentations, are limited, most guests complete a fairly comprehensive tour in two-thirds of a day if they arrive early. Thus, generally speaking, your best bet for easy touring is either to be on-hand when the park opens or to arrive at about 3 p.m., when the early birds are heading for the exits. If you decide to visit during the late afternoon, you might have to return on another afternoon to see everything.

How guests tour the Animal Kingdom depends on their prior knowledge of the park and its attractions. Guests arriving without much prior knowledge make their way to Safari Village and depend on their handout park map to decide what to do next. Most experience the attractions at Safari Village and then head off to Africa. A smaller number visit DinoLand U.S.A. first. Those guests who have boned up on the Animal Kingdom make straight for the 3-D movie at Safari Village, Kilimanjaro Safaris in

Africa, and Countdown to Extinction in DinoLand U.S.A. Tiger Rapids Run in Asia will also be an early-morning favorite when it opens.

At the Magic Kingdom you can tour clockwise or counterclockwise without returning to the central hub. To go from land to land at the Animal Kingdom, however, you usually have to pass through Safari Village. Safari Village and its attractions thus draw crowds earlier than the other lands and remain inundated throughout the day. Africa, likewise, draws heavy attendance but is set up to move crowds through in a controlled sequence. Attractions in DinoLand U.S.A., with the exception of Countdown to Extinction, will be easily accessible most of the day. Camp Minnie-Mickey is congested from 9:30 a.m. until about 4 p.m., more because of poor design than popularity.

Animal Kingdom One-Day Touring Plan for Visitors of All Ages

Touring the Animal Kingdom is not as complicated as touring the other parks because it offers a smaller number of attractions. Also, most Animal Kingdom rides, shows, and zoological exhibits are oriented to the entire family, thus eliminating differences of opinion regarding how to spend the day. At the Animal Kingdom the whole family can pretty much see and enjoy everything together.

Since there are fewer attractions than at the other parks, expect the crowds at the Animal Kingdom to be more concentrated. If a line seems unusually long, ask an Animal Kingdom cast member what the estimated wait is. If the wait exceeds your tolerance, try the same attraction again after 3 p.m., while a show is in progress at the Theater in the Wild in DinoLand U.S.A., or while some special event is going on.

The Animal Kingdom One-Day Touring Plan assumes a willingness to experience all major rides and shows. Be forewarned that Countdown to Extinction and Tiger Rapids Run (opens 1999) are sometimes frightening to children under age eight. Similarly, the theater attraction at the Tree of Life might be too intense for some preschoolers. When following the touring plan, simply skip any attraction you do not wish to experience.

Before You Go

1. Call (407) 824-4321 before you go to learn the park's hours of operation.

2. Purchase your admission prior to arrival. You can either order tickets through the mail or buy them at a local Disney Store before

you leave home. You can also buy them at the Ocala Disney AAA Travel Center off I-75, if you are driving. If you arrive by plane, purchase your admission at the Disney Store in the Orlando airport or at a Walt Disney World resort hotel.

At the Animal Kingdom

1. Arrive at the park *one hour* before the official opening time during the summer and holiday periods, and *40 minutes* before the official opening time the rest of the year. At the entrance plaza, pick up a park map. Wait at the entrance turnstiles to be admitted.

2. Depending on operating procedures during your visit, either *It's Tough to Be a Bug!* in Safari Village or Countdown to Extinction in DinoLand U.S.A. will probably be open early. Experience whichever is open.

3. If you experienced Countdown to Extinction early, proceed to Safari Village and see *It's Tough to Be a Bug!* and then skip to Step 5.

4. If you experienced *It's Tough to Be a Bug!* early, proceed directly to Africa.

5. In Africa, experience the Kilimanjaro Safaris.

6. After the Safaris, walk the Gorilla Falls Exploration Trail.

7. Exit Africa on the path connecting Africa and Asia. Proceed to Asia (opens early 1999). If Asia is not yet open, skip to Step 10.

8. In Asia, ride the Tiger Rapids Run.

9. In Asia, walk the Maharaja Jungle Trek.

10. Passing through Safari Village, go to DinoLand U.S.A..

11. In DinoLand U.S.A., ride Countdown to Extinction if you didn't ride it earlier.

12. By now you will have most of the Animal Kingdom's potential bottlenecks behind you. Check your daily entertainment schedule for shows at the Theater in the Wild in DinoLand U.S.A., at the Caravan Stage in Asia, and at Mother Willow's Grove and the Lion King Theater in Camp Minnie-Mickey. Plan the next part of your day around eating lunch and seeing these four shows. During the middle of the day, you will need to queue up as follows:

For the Theater in the Wild:	20 minutes before show time
For the Caravan Stage:	15 minutes before show time
For Mother Willow's Grove:	20–25 minutes before show time
For the Lion King Theater:	25–35 minutes before show time

13. Between shows, check out Cretaceous Trail and The Boneyard in DinoLand U.S.A., and the zoological exhibits around the Tree of Life and in The Oasis. This is also a good time to meet the characters at Camp Minnie-Mickey.

14. Return to Harambe and bear right to the Wildlife Express train station. Take the train to Conservation Station. Once again, take your time.

15. Departing Conservation Station, catch the Wildlife Express train back to Harambe.

16. Shop, snack, or repeat any attractions you especially enjoyed.

17. This concludes the touring plan. Be sure to allocate some time to visit the zoological exhibits in The Oasis on your way out of the park.

They don't have much experience with real animals but i'm sure everything will be fine.

Part Twelve

Disney-MGM Studios, Universal Florida, and Sea World

Disney-MGM Studios vs. Universal Studios Florida

Disney-MGM Studios and Universal Studios Florida are direct competitors. Because both are large and expensive and require at least one day to see, some guests must choose one park over the other. To help you decide, we present a head-to-head comparison of the two parks, followed by a description of each in detail. In the summer of 1999, Universal will launch its second major theme park, Universal's Islands of Adventure, which has no direct Disney competitor. The new park is previewed in detail later in this section. A summary profile of Sea World concludes Part 12.

Both Disney-MGM Studios and Universal Studios Florida draw their theme and inspiration from film and television. Both offer movie- and TV-themed rides and shows, some of which are just for fun, while others provide an educational, behind-the-scenes introduction to the cinematic arts. Both parks include working film and television production studios.

Nearly half of Disney-MGM Studios is off-limits to guests except by guided tour, while virtually all of Universal Studios Florida is open to exploration. Unlike Disney-MGM, Universal Florida's open area includes the entire backlot, where guests can walk at leisure among movie sets.

Universal hammers on the point that it's first a working motion-picture and television studio, and only incidentally a tourist attraction.

Whether this assertion is a point of pride with Universal or an apology to the tourist is unclear. It's true, however, that guests are more likely to see movie or television production in progress at Universal Florida than at Disney-MGM. On any day, production crews will be shooting on the Universal backlot in full view of guests who care to watch.

Universal Studios Florida is about twice as large as Disney-MGM, and because almost all of it is open to the public, most of the crowding and congestion so familiar in the streets and plazas of Disney-MGM is eliminated. Universal Studios Florida has plenty of elbow room.

Attractions are excellent at both parks, though Disney-MGM attractions are on average engineered to move people more efficiently. This disadvantage at Universal is somewhat offset by the fact that Universal offers 18 major rides and shows versus 16 at Disney-MGM.

Each park offers a stellar attraction that breaks new ground, transcending in power, originality, and technology any prior standard for theme park entertainment. Universal offers *Terminator 2: 3-D*, which we consider the most extraordinary attraction in any American theme park. Disney-MGM Studios features *The Twilight Zone* Tower of Terror, our pick for the nation's second best attraction. The next best attractions in each park are also well matched: Back to the Future at Universal in a dead heat with Star Tours at Disney-MGM.

Though Universal Studios must be credited with pioneering a number of innovative and technologically advanced rides, it also must be pointed out that Universal's attractions break down more often than Disney-MGM's. Jaws and Kongfrontation, in particular, are notorious for frequent breakdowns.

A Detroit woman who visited Universal Studios on a particularly bad day writes:

> *Kongfrontation was broken, Earthquake was broken (with us in it for 30 minutes), and E.T. was broken (with us in line for 20 minutes). We got VIP passes for Earthquake, to come later without waiting. It was finally on-line at about 6:45, and when we were just about to get on, it broke again. The rides at this park are really stupendous—very different from WDW, but I think they've bit off more than they can chew.*

A Wisconsin family adds:

> *What happened!??! We arrived at opening and tried to follow the [touring] plan, but the lines were horrendous, and we left at 2:30 after having a baaad day. Kongfrontation was closed down and E.T. broke down several times. I don't think it was the fault of the plan, and I will probably skip Universal when I go back to Orlando.*

But a family from Baltimore, Ohio, reports a totally positive experience:

> *I won't categorize Universal except to say that it was the best. We centered our trip around WDW, but Universal puts Disney to shame. It was not very crowded, the shows are excellent, and the rides are the best we've ever been on as far as entertainment value. We all agreed we could spend two to three days at Universal and not get bored.*

Amazingly, and to the visitor's advantage, each park offers a completely different product mix, so there is little or no redundancy for a person who visits both. Disney-MGM and Universal Florida each provide good exposure to the cinematic arts, though Universal's presentations are generally more informative and comprehensive. Disney-MGM had a distinct edge in educational content until recently, when it turned several of its better tours into infomercials for Disney films. At Universal, you can still learn about post-production, soundstages, set creation, special effects, directing, and cinematography without being bludgeoned by promotional hype.

Stunt shows are similar at both parks. Disney's *Indiana Jones Epic Stunt Spectacular* and Universal's *The Wild, Wild, Wild West Stunt Show* are both staged in 2,000-seat stadiums that allow a good view of the action. The *Dynamite Nights Stuntacular* at Universal is staged in the large lagoon, with patrons taking up viewing positions along the railing. The lagoon provides a realistic setting but is so large that the action sometimes is hard to see or follow. All three shows have their moments, and the two stadium shows are fairly informative. In the final analysis, Disney-MGM wins for drama and intensity, while Universal Studios gets the call for variety.

We recommend you try one of the studios. If you enjoy one, you probably will enjoy the other. If you have to choose between them, consider:

1. Touring Time   If you tour efficiently, it takes about seven to eight hours to see Disney-MGM Studios (including a lunch break). Because Universal Studios Florida is larger and contains more (and often less efficiently engineered) rides and shows, touring, including one meal, takes about 9 to 11 hours.

One reader laments:

> *There is a lot more "standing" at Universal Studios, and it isn't as organized as [Disney-MGM]. Many of the attractions don't open until 10 a.m., and many shows seem to be going at the same time. We were not able to see nearly as many attractions at Universal as we were at [Disney-MGM] during the same amount of time. The one plus here is that there seems to be more property, and things are spaced out better so you have more elbow room.*

2. Convenience If you're lodging along International Drive, I-4's northeast corridor, the Orange Blossom Trail (US 441), or in Orlando, Universal Studios Florida is closer. If you're lodging along US 27 or FL 192 or in Kissimmee or Walt Disney World, Disney-MGM Studios is more convenient.

3. Endurance Universal Studios Florida is larger and requires more walking than Disney-MGM, but it is also much less congested, so the walking is easier. Both parks offer wheelchairs and handicapped access.

4. Cost Both parks cost about the same for one-day admission, food, and incidentals. All attractions are included in the admission price. If you go for two days, however, check to see if Universal is running its Second-Day-Free promotion. This gives you two days at Universal for the price of one.

5. Best Days to Go In order, Tuesdays, Mondays, Thursdays, and Wednesdays are best to visit Universal Studios Florida. At Disney-MGM Studios, visit on a day when early entry isn't in effect.

6. When to Arrive For Disney-MGM, arrive with your ticket in hand 40 minutes before official opening time. For Universal Studios, arrive with your admission already purchased about 50 minutes before official opening time.

7. Young Children Both Disney-MGM Studios and Universal Studios Florida are relatively adult entertainment offerings. By our reckoning, half the rides and shows at Disney-MGM and about two-thirds at Universal Studios have a significant potential for frightening young children.

8. Food Food generally is much better at Universal Studios.

Disney-MGM Studios

Long after Walt Disney's death, corporate Disney decided to make movies for adults. Figuring that Snow White couldn't share the set with Bette Midler mouthing four-letter words, they formed a new production company to handle the adult productions. Results have been impressive: a complete rejuvenation of Disney movies, with new faces, tremendous creativity, and an amazing resurgence at the box office.

How better to showcase and promote this product than with a motion-picture and television entertainment park at Walt Disney World?

THE MGM CONNECTION

To broaden the appeal and to lend additional historical impact, Disney obtained the rights to use the MGM (Metro-Goldwyn-Mayer) name, film library, motion-picture and television titles, excerpts, costumes, music, sets, and even Leo, the MGM lion. Probably the two most recognized names in motion pictures, Disney and MGM represent more than 70 years of movie history.

COMPARING DISNEY-MGM STUDIOS TO THE MAGIC KINGDOM AND EPCOT

The Magic Kingdom entertains, modeling its attractions on Disney movies and TV. Epcot educates, pioneering exhibits and rides that teach. Disney-MGM does both. All three parks rely heavily on Disney special effects and Audio-Animatronics (robotics) in their entertainment mix.

Disney-MGM Studios is about the size of the Magic Kingdom and about half as large as the sprawling Epcot. Unlike the parks, Disney-MGM is a working motion-picture and television production facility. This means, among other things, that about half of it has controlled access, with guests permitted only on guided tours or observation walkways.

When Epcot opened in 1982, Disney patrons expected a futuristic version of the Magic Kingdom. What they got was humanistic inspiration and a creative educational experience. Since then, Disney has tried to inject more magic, excitement, and surprise into Epcot. Remembering the occasional disappointment of those early Epcot guests, Disney fortified the Studios with megadoses of action, suspense, surprise, and, of course, special effects. The formula has proved so successful that it's being trotted out again at the new Animal Kingdom theme park. If you want to learn about the history and technology of movies and television, Disney-MGM Studios will teach you plenty. If you just want to be entertained, you won't leave disappointed.

Self-Promotion Run Amok

While it's true that Disney-MGM Studios educates and entertains, what it does best is promote. Self-promotion of Disney films and products was once subtle and in context. It is now blatant, inescapable, and detracting. The walking segment of the backstage tour, for example, at one time was an informative and masterfully scripted introduction to special effects, set design, and the use of sound stages. The same tour today is no more than an infomercial for the latest Disney feature, with continuity, coherence, and educational content sacrificed for hype. Likewise, segments of The Magic of Disney Animation tour now advertise rather than enlighten. Although most visitors are willing to forgive Disney its excesses, Studios' veterans will lament the changes and remember how good it was when education was the goal instead of the medium.

Not to Be Missed at Disney-MGM Studios
Star Tours Disney-MGM Studios Backlot Tour The Magic of Disney Animation *Indiana Jones Epic Stunt Spectacular* The Great Movie Ride *Jim Henson's MuppetVision 4D* *Fantasmic!* *Voyage of the Little Mermaid* *The Twilight Zone* Tower of Terror

HOW MUCH TIME TO ALLOCATE

It's impossible to see all of Epcot or the Magic Kingdom in one day. Disney-MGM Studios, however, is more manageable. There's much less ground to cover by foot. Trams carry guests through much of the backlot and working areas, and attractions in the open-access parts are concentrated in an area about the size of Main Street, Tomorrowland, and Frontierland combined. Someday, no doubt, as Disney-MGM develops and grows, you'll need more than a day to see everything. For now, the Studios is a nice one-day outing.

Because Disney-MGM is smaller, however, it's more affected by large crowds. Our touring plans will help you stay a step ahead of the mob and minimize waiting in line. Even when the park is crowded, however, you can see almost everything in a day.

DISNEY-MGM STUDIOS IN THE EVENING

Because Disney-MGM Studios can be seen in three-fourths of a day, most guests who arrive early in the morning run out of things to do by 3:30 or 4 p.m. and leave the park. Their departure greatly thins the crowd and makes the Studios ideal for evening touring. Lines for most attractions are manageable, and the park is cooler and more comfortable. The *Indiana Jones Epic Stunt Spectacular* and productions at other outdoor theaters are infinitely more enjoyable during the evening than in the sweltering heat of the day.

One drawback to touring the Studios at night is that there won't be much activity on the production soundstages or in the Animation Building. Another is that you might get stuck eating dinner at the Studios. (If you must eat there, try Mama Melrose's or The Hollywood Brown Derby for full-service dining.)

In 1998, the Studios launched *Fantasmic!* (see pages 543–544), arguably the most spectacular nighttime entertainment event in the Disney

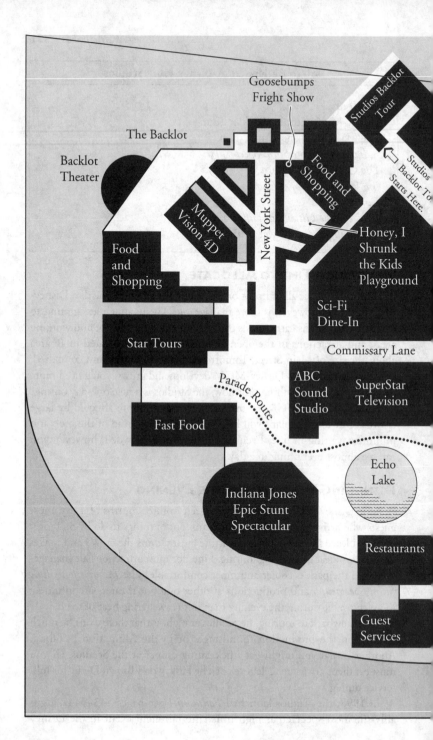

Goosebumps
Fright Show

The Backlot

Backlot
Theater

Studios Backlot
Tour

Studios
Backlot To
Starts Here.

Food and
Shopping

New York Street

Muppet
Vision 4D

Honey, I
Shrunk
the Kids
Playground

Food
and
Shopping

Sci-Fi
Dine-In

Star Tours

Commissary Lane

Parade Route

ABC
Sound
Studio

SuperStar
Television

Fast Food

Echo
Lake

Indiana Jones
Epic Stunt
Spectacular

Restaurants

Guest
Services

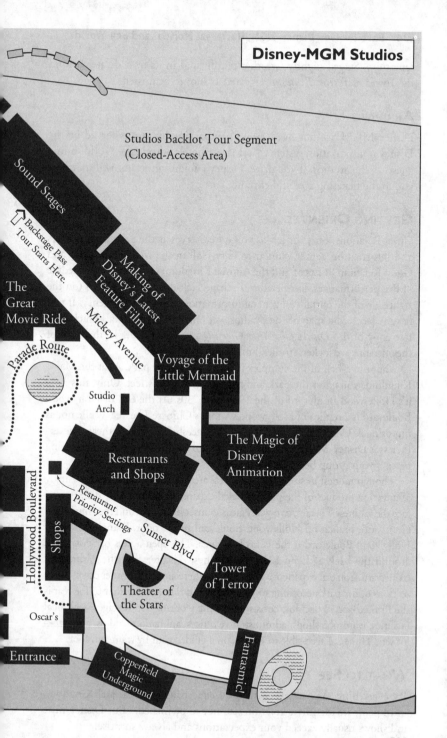

Disney-MGM Studios

Studios Backlot Tour Segment
(Closed-Access Area)

Sound Stages

Backstage Pass Tour Starts Here.

Making of Disney's Latest Feature Film

The Great Movie Ride

Mickey Avenue

Parade Route

Voyage of the Little Mermaid

Studio Arch

The Magic of Disney Animation

Restaurants and Shops

Hollywood Boulevard

Restaurant Priority Seatings

Shops

Sunset Blvd.

Tower of Terror

Theater of the Stars

Oscar's

Fantasmic!

Entrance

Copperfield Magic Underground

repertoire. Staged nightly (weather permitting) in its own theater behind the Tower of Terror, *Fantasmic!* is rated as "not to be missed."

ARRIVING

Disney-MGM Studios has its own pay parking lot and is served by the Disney transportation system. Most larger hotels outside the World shuttle guests to the Studios. If you drive, Disney's ubiquitous trams will transport you to the ticketing area and entrance gate.

GETTING ORIENTED

Guest Relations, on your left as you enter, serves as the park headquarters and information center, similar to City Hall in the Magic Kingdom and Guest Relations at Epcot and the Animal Kingdom. Go there for a schedule of live performances, lost persons, Package Pick-up, lost and found (on the right side of the entrance), general information, or in an emergency. If you haven't received a map of the Studios, get one here. You can also pick up a free copy of the *Disney Character Greeting Location Guide*. To the right of the entrance are locker, stroller, and wheelchair rentals.

About one-half of the complex is set up as a theme park. As at the Magic Kingdom, you enter the park and pass down a main street. Only, this time it's Hollywood Boulevard of the 1920s and '30s. At the end of Hollywood Boulevard is a replica of Hollywood's famous Chinese Theater. While not as imposing as Cinderella Castle or Epcot's Spaceship Earth, the theater nevertheless is Disney-MGM Studios' most central landmark and a good meeting place if your group becomes separated.

Though modest in size, the open-access areas of the Studios are confusingly arranged (a product of the park's hurried expansion in the early '90s). As you face the Chinese Theater, two guest areas, Sunset Boulevard and the Animation Courtyard, branch off Hollywood Boulevard to the right. Branching left off Hollywood Boulevard is the Echo Lake area. The open-access backlot wraps around the back of Echo Lake, the Chinese Theater, and the Animation Courtyard. You can experience all attractions here and in the other open-access sections of the park according to your tastes and time. Still farther to the rear is the limited-access backlot, consisting of the working soundstages, technical facilities, wardrobe shops, administrative offices, animation studios, and backlot sets. These are accessible to visitors on a guided tour by tram and foot.

WHAT TO SEE

Try everything. As we have with the Magic Kingdom, Animal Kingdom, and Epcot, we identify attractions as "not to be missed." But Disney rides and shows usually exceed your expectations and always surprise.

Hollywood Boulevard Services

Most of the park's service facilities are on Hollywood Boulevard, including:

Wheelchair & Stroller Rental Service	Right of the entrance at Oscar's.
Banking Services	An ATM is outside the park to the right of the turnstiles.
Storage Lockers	Rental lockers are right of the main entrance, on the left of Oscar's.
Lost & Found	At Package Pick-up, right of the entrance.
Live Entertainment/ Parade Information	Included in the park guidemap available free at Guest Relations and elsewhere in the park.
Lost Persons	Report lost persons at Guest Relations.
Walt Disney World & Local Attraction Information	At Guest Relations.
First Aid	At Guest Relations.
Baby Center/Baby-Care Needs	At Guest Relations. Oscar's sells baby food and other necessities.
Film	At The Darkroom on the right side of Hollywood Boulevard, just beyond Oscar's.

CHALKBOARD WITH WAITING TIMES

At the corner of Hollywood and Sunset boulevards is a large chalkboard listing current waiting times for all Disney-MGM Studios attractions. It's updated continuously throughout the day. We've found the waiting times listed to be slightly conservative. If the chalkboard says the wait for Star Tours is 45 minutes, for example, you probably will have to wait about 35 to 40 minutes.

Disney-MGM Studios in Detail

Hollywood Boulevard

Hollywood Boulevard is a palm-lined re-creation of Hollywood's main drag during the city's golden age. Architecture is streamlined *moderne* with art deco embellishments. Most service facilities are here, interspersed with eateries and shops. Merchandise includes Disney trademark items, Hollywood and movie-related souvenirs, and one-of-a-kind collectibles obtained from studio auctions and estate sales.

Hollywood characters and roving performers entertain on the boulevard, and daily parades and other happenings pass this way.

Sunset Boulevard

Sunset Boulevard, evoking the 1940s, is a major new addition to Disney-MGM Studios. Intersecting Hollywood Boulevard near The Hollywood Brown Derby restaurant, Sunset Boulevard provides another venue for dining, shopping, and street entertainment.

The Twilight Zone Tower of Terror

What It Is: Sci-fi-theme indoor thrill ride

Scope & Scale: Super headliner

When to Go: Before 10 a.m. and after 5 p.m.

Author's Rating: Walt Disney World's best attraction; not to be missed;
★★★★★

Appeal by Age Group:

Pre-school	Grade School	Teens	Young Adults	Over 30	Senior Citizens
★★★★	★★★★★	★★★★★	★★★★★	★★★★½	★★★★½

Duration of Ride: About 4 minutes plus preshow

Average Wait in Line per 100 People ahead of You: 4 minutes

Assumes: All elevators operating

Loading Speed: Moderate

Description and Comments   The Tower of Terror is a new species of Disney thrill ride, though it borrows elements of The Haunted Mansion at the Magic Kingdom. The story is that you're touring a once-famous Hollywood hotel gone to ruin. As at Star Tours, the queuing area integrates guests into the adventure as they pass through the hotel's once-opulent public rooms. From the lobby, guests are escorted into the hotel's library, where Rod Serling, speaking on an old black-and-white television, greets the guests and introduces the plot.

The Tower of Terror is a whopper, 13-plus-stories tall. Breaking tradition in terms of visually isolating themed areas, you can see the entire Studios from atop the tower, but you have to look quick.

The ride vehicle, one of the hotel's service elevators, takes guests to see the haunted hostelry. The tour begins innocuously, but about the fifth floor things get pretty weird. You have entered the Twilight Zone. Guests are subjected to a full range of special effects as they encounter unexpected horrors and optical illusions. The climax of the adventure occurs when the elevator reaches the top floor (the thirteenth, of course) and the cable snaps.

The Tower of Terror is an experience to savor. Though the final plunge is calculated to thrill, the meat of the attraction is its extraordinary visual and audio effects. There's richness and subtlety here, enough to keep the ride fresh and stimulating after many repetitions.

The Tower has great potential for terrifying young children and rattling more mature visitors. If you have teenagers in your party, use them as experimental probes. If they report back that they really, really liked the Tower of Terror, run as fast as you can in the opposite direction.

Touring Tips   This one ride is worth your admission to Disney-MGM Studios. Because of its height, the Tower is a veritable beacon, visible from outside the park and luring curious guests as soon as they enter. Because of its popularity with school kids, teens, and young adults, you can count on a foot race to the attraction when the park opens. For the foreseeable future, expect the Tower to be mobbed most of the day. Experience it first thing in the morning or in the evening before the park closes.

To save time, when you enter the library waiting area, stand in the far back corner at the opposite end of the long wall from the television set. When the doors to the loading area open, you'll be one of the first admitted.

If you have young children (or anyone) who are apprehensive about this attraction, ask the attendant about switching off (pages 165–167).

The Great Movie Ride

What It Is: Movie-history indoor adventure ride
Scope & Scale: Headliner
When to Go: Before 10 a.m. and after 5 p.m.
Special Comments: Elaborate, with several surprises
Author's Rating: Not to be missed; ★★★½
Appeal by Age Group:

Pre-school	Grade School	Teens	Young Adults	Over 30	Senior Citizens
★★★	★★★½	★★★½	★★★★	★★★★	★★★★

Duration of Ride: About 19 minutes
Average Wait in Line per 100 People ahead of You: 2 minutes
Assumes: All trains operating
Loading Speed: Fast

Description and Comments   Entering through a re-creation of Hollywood's Chinese Theater, guests board vehicles for a fast-paced tour through sound-stage sets from classic films including *Casablanca, Tarzan, The Wizard of Oz, Aliens,* and *Raiders of the Lost Ark.* Each set is populated with new-generation Disney Audio-Animatronic (robot) characters, as well as an occasional human, all augmented by sound and lighting effects. One of Disney's larger and more ambitious dark rides, The Great Movie Ride encompasses 95,000 square feet and showcases some of the most famous scenes in filmmaking. Life-sized Audio-Animatronic sculptures of stars including Gene Kelly, John Wayne, James Cagney, Julie Andrews, and Harrison Ford inhabit some of the largest sets ever constructed for a Disney ride.

Touring Tips   The Great Movie Ride draws large crowds (and lines) from the moment the park opens. As an interval-loading, high-capacity ride, lines disappear quickly. Even so, waits can exceed an hour after midmorning. (Actual waits usually run about one-third shorter than the time posted on the chalkboard. If the chalkboard indicates an hour's wait, your actual time will be around 40 minutes.)

SuperStar Television

What It Is: Audience-participation television production
Scope & Scale: Major attraction
When to Go: After 10 a.m.
Author's Rating: Well-conceived; ★★★

Appeal by Age Group:

Pre-school	Grade School	Teens	Young Adults	Over 30	Senior Citizens
★★★	★★★½	★★★	★★★	★★★	★★★

Duration of Presentation: 30 minutes

Preshow Entertainment: Participants selected from guests waiting in the preshow area

Probable Waiting Time: 10–20 minutes

Description and Comments　Audience volunteers (conscriptees) participate in a television production that uses special effects to integrate the actions of the amateurs with footage of well-known stars of past and current TV shows. The combined result, a sort of video collage where the volunteers miraculously end up in the footage with the stars, is broadcast on large-screen monitors above the set. The outcome, always rated in laughs, depends on how the volunteers respond in their dramatic debut.

As an updated version of *SuperStar Television* plugs shows on the ABC television network, a subsidiary of the Walt Disney Company.

Touring Tips　The theater seats 1,000 people, so it is not usually difficult to get in. If you want to be in the production, however, it is essential that you enter the preshow holding area at least 15 minutes before the next performance. Participants for the show are more or less drafted by a casting director from among guests of both genders and all age groups. Those who stand near the director and those who are distinctively (outlandishly?) attired seem to be selected most often. A woman from New York patted herself on the back, writing: "We were selected to be in *SuperStar Television* when I raised our hands and screamed 'Honeymooners!'" Finally, be aware that Disney sometimes uses this facility to tape game shows, temporarily preempting the usual presentation.

Star Tours

What It Is: Indoor space flight–simulation ride

Scope & Scale: Headliner

When to Go: First hour and a half the park is open

Special Comments: Expectant mothers or anyone prone to motion sickness are advised against riding. The ride is too intense for many children younger than 8

Author's Rating: Not to be missed; ★★★★

Motion Sickness

WARNING!

Appeal by Age Group:

Pre-school	Grade School	Teens	Young Adults	Over 30	Senior Citizens
★★★★	★★★★	★★★★	★★★★	★★★★	★★★★

Duration of Ride: About 7 minutes

Average Wait in Line per 100 People ahead of You: 5 minutes

Assumes: All simulators operating

Loading Speed: Moderate to fast

Description and Comments   This attraction is so real and so much fun that it just makes you grin and giggle. Guests ride in a flight simulator modeled after those used for training pilots and astronauts. You're supposedly on a vacation outing in space, piloted by a droid (android, a.k.a. humanoid, a.k.a. robot) on his first flight with real passengers. Mayhem ensues almost immediately. Scenery flashes by, and the simulator bucks and pitches. You could swear you were moving at the speed of light. After several minutes of this, the droid somehow lands the spacecraft, and you discover you're about ten times happier than you were when you boarded.

Touring Tips   Star Tours hasn't been as popular at Disney-MGM Studios as it has been at Disneyland in California. Except on unusually busy days, waits rarely exceed 35–45 minutes. For the first couple of hours the park is open, expect a wait of 25 minutes or less. Even so, see Star Tours before 11 a.m. If you have young children (or anyone) who are apprehensive about this attraction, ask the attendant about switching off (pages 165-167).

Star Tours is near the exit of the 2,000-seat stadium that houses *Indiana Jones*. When an *Indiana Jones* performance lets out, Star Tours is temporarily inundated. Ditto for *MuppetVision 4D* and *ABC Sound Studio* nearby. If you arrive in the midst of this mayhem, come back later.

ABC Sound Studio

What It Is: Audience-participation show demonstrating sound effects

Scope & Scale: Minor attraction

When to Go: Before 11 a.m. or after 5 p.m.

Author's Rating: Funny and informative; ★★★

Appeal by Age Group:

Pre-school	Grade School	Teens	Young Adults	Over 30	Senior Citizens
★★½	★★★½	★★★	★★★	★★★	★★★★

Duration of Presentation: 12 minutes

Preshow Entertainment: Video introduction to sound effects

Probable Waiting Time: 15–30 minutes

Description and Comments Guests are invited onstage for a crash course in becoming sound-effects technicians. First, guest participants are selected and taught how to use the sound effects equipment. Next the volunteers make a stab at providing the sound effects. The result of their efforts are played back at the end of the show for the audience to enjoy. If the participating guests are duds, the show really tends to suffer.

This show was recently overhauled. Unfortunately the latest iteration is not nearly as clever or interesting as the original version starring Chevy Chase. The new version does, of course, plug Disney programs and products.

Touring Tips Because the theater is relatively small, long waits (partially in the hot sun) are common here. Another thing: *ABC Sound Studio* is periodically inundated by guests coming from a just-concluded performance of *SuperStar Television* or the *Indiana Jones Epic Stunt Spectacular.* This is not the time to get in line. Wait at least 30 minutes and try again.

A reader from Israel suggests that a good time to catch *Sound Studio* is just before the afternoon parade. If the parade starts on Hollywood Boulevard, it takes about 15–18 minutes to wind over to *ABC Sound Studio*—just long enough to catch the show and pop out right in time for the parade.

Indiana Jones Epic Stunt Spectacular

What It Is: Movie-stunt demonstration and action show

Scope & Scale: Headliner

When to Go: First three morning shows or last evening show

Special Comments: Performance times posted on a sign at the entrance to the theater

Author's Rating: Done on a grand scale; ★★★★

Appeal by Age Group:

Pre-school	Grade School	Teens	Young Adults	Over 30	Senior Citizens
★★★	★★★★	★★★★	★★★★	★★★★	★★★★

Duration of Presentation: 30 minutes

Preshow Entertainment: Selection of "extras" from audience

Probable Waiting Time: None

Description and Comments Coherent and educational, though somewhat unevenly paced, the popular production showcases professional stunt men and women who demonstrate dangerous stunts with a behind-the-scenes look at how it's done. Sets, props, and special effects are very elaborate.

While most live shows at Walt Disney World are revised from time to time, the *Stunt Spectacular,* as a Hamden, Connecticut, man laments, has not changed for years:

> *Another bust was the Indy Jones show. The show is the same as it has been since it opened, but the acting grows tired. This is due for a restaging. Its counterpart at Universal,* The Wild [Wild, Wild] West Stunt Show, *was deemed superior by my group.*

Touring Tips   The Stunt Theater holds 2,000 people; capacity audiences are common. The first performance is always the easiest to see. If the first show is at 9:30 a.m. or earlier, you usually can walk in, even if you arrive five minutes late. If the first show is scheduled for 9:45 a.m. or later, arrive 20 or so minutes early. For the second performance, show up about 20–35 minutes ahead of time. For the third and subsequent shows, arrive 30–45 minutes early. If you plan to tour during late afternoon and evening, attend the last scheduled performance. If you want to beat the crowd out of the stadium, sit on the far right (as you face the staging area) and near the top.

To be chosen from the audience to be an "extra" in the stunt show, arrive early, sit down front, and display unmitigated enthusiasm. A woman from Richmond, Virginia, explains:

> Indiana Jones *was far and away the best show—we saw it twice on two different days. After the first performance, I realized the best way to get picked was to stand up, wave my arms, and shout when the "casting director" called for volunteers—sheer enthusiasm wins every time, and sitting towards the front helps, too. We stayed afterwards for autographs of the performers in the obligatory Mickey Mouse autograph book.*

Theater of the Stars

What It Is: Live Hollywood-style musical, usually featuring Disney characters; performed in an open-air theater

Scope & Scale: Major attraction

When to Go: In the evening

Special Comments: Performances are listed in the daily entertainment schedule

Author's Rating: Excellent; ★★★★

Appeal by Age Group:

Pre-school	Grade School	Teens	Young Adults	Over 30	Senior Citizens
★★★★	★★★★	★★★	★★★★	★★★★	★★★½

Duration of Presentation: 25 minutes
Preshow Entertainment: None
Probable Waiting Time: 20–30 minutes

Description and Comments The *Theater of the Stars* combines Disney characters with singers and dancers in upbeat and humorous Hollywood musicals. The *Beauty and the Beast* show, in particular, is outstanding. The theater, which has been in three locations in the park over the years, seems finally to have found a permanent home on Sunset Boulevard. Vastly improved, it now offers a clear field of vision from almost every seat. Best, a canopy protects the audience from the Florida sun (or rain). The theater still gets mighty hot in the summer, but you can make it through a performance now without succumbing to heatstroke.

Touring Tips Unless you visit during the cooler months, see this show in the evening. The production is so popular that you should show up 20–50 minutes early to get a seat.

Fantasmic!

What It Is: Mixed-media nighttime spectacular
Scope & Scale: Super headliner
When to Go: Only staged in the evening
Special Comments: Disney's best nighttime event
Author's Rating: Not to be missed; ★★★★★
Appeal by Age Group:

Pre-school	Grade School	Teens	Young Adults	Over 30	Senior Citizens
★★★★	★★★★★	★★★★½	★★★★½	★★★★½	★★★★½

Duration of Presentation: 25 minutes
Probable Waiting Time: None

Description and Comments *Fantasmic!* is a mixed-media show presented one or more times each evening when the park is open late. Located off Sunset Boulevard behind the Tower of Terror, *Fantasmic!* is staged on a newly created lagoon and island opposite a 6,900-seat amphitheater. By far the largest theater facility ever created by Disney, the amphitheater can accommodate an additional 3,000 standing guests for a total audience of nearly 10,000.

Fantasmic! is far and away the most extraordinary and ambitious outdoor spectacle ever attempted in any theme park. Starring Mickey Mouse in his role as the Sorcerer's Apprentice from *Fantasia,* the production uses lasers, images projected on a shroud of mist, fireworks, lighting effects, and music in combinations so stunning you can scarcely believe what you have seen. The plot is simple: good versus evil. The story gets lost in all the special effects at times, but no matter, it is the spectacle, not the story line, that is so overpowering. While beautiful, stunning, and powerful are words that immediately come to mind, they fail to convey the uniqueness of this presentation. It could be argued, with some validity, that *Fantasmic!* alone is worth the price of the Disney-MGM Studios admission.

Touring Tips   Fantasmic! provides a whole new dimension to nighttime at Disney-MGM Studios. As a day-capping event, it will be to the Studios what *IllumiNations* is to Epcot. While it's hard to imagine running out of space in a 10,000-person stadium, we're sure it will happen during the busier times of year. On evenings when there are two performances, the second show will always be less crowded. If you attend the first (or only) scheduled performance, take your place in the stadium at least 30 minutes in advance. If you opt for the second show, arrive 15 minutes early.

Rain and wind conditions sometimes cause *Fantasmic!* to be cancelled. Unfortunately, Disney officials usually do not make a final decision about whether to proceed or cancel until just before show time. We have seen guests wait stoically for over an hour with no assurance that their patience and sacrifice would be rewarded. We do not recommend arriving more than a few minutes before show time on rainy or especially windy nights. On nights like these, pursue your own agenda until ten minutes or so before show time and then head to the stadium to see what happens.

Finally, make sure to hang on to children after *Fantasmic!* and to give them explicit instructions for regrouping in the event you are separated.

Voyage of the Little Mermaid

What It Is: Musical stage show featuring characters from the Disney
  movie *The Little Mermaid*

Scope & Scale: Major attraction

When to Go: Before 9:30 a.m. or just before closing

Author's Rating: Romantic, lovable, and humorous in the best Disney tradition; not to be missed; ★★★★

Appeal by Age Group:

Pre-school	Grade School	Teens	Young Adults	Over 30	Senior Citizens
★★★★	★★★★	★★★½	★★★★	★★★★	★★★★

Duration of Presentation: 15 minutes

Preshow Entertainment: Taped ramblings about the decor in the preshow
  holding area

Probable Waiting Time: Before 9:30 a.m., 10–30 minutes; after 9:30 a.m., 35–70 minutes

Description and Comments *Voyage of the Little Mermaid* is a winner, appealing to every age. Cute without being silly or saccharine, and infinitely lovable, the *Little Mermaid* show is the most tender and romantic entertainment offered anywhere in Walt Disney World. The story is simple and engaging, the special effects impressive, and the Disney characters memorable.

We receive a lot of mail from Europeans who complain about the "soppy sentimentality" of Americans in general and of Disney attractions in particular. These comments of a man from Bristol, England, are typical:

> *Americans have an ability to think as a child and so enjoy the soppiness of the* Little Mermaid. *English cynicism made it hard for us at times to see Disney stories as anything other than gushing, namby-pamby, and full of stereotypes. Other Brits might also find the sentimentality cloying. Maybe you should prepare them for the need to rethink their wry outlook on life temporarily.*

Touring Tips Because it's well done and located at a busy pedestrian intersection, *Voyage of the Little Mermaid* plays to capacity crowds all day. Unless you make the first or second show, you probably will have to wait an hour or more. If you plan to be in the park all day, see the first *Little Mermaid* show and the evening *Indiana Jones Epic Stunt Spectacular*.

When you enter the preshow lobby, stand near the doors to the theater. When they open, go inside, pick a row of seats, and let six to ten people enter the row ahead of you. The strategy is twofold: to obtain a good seat and be near the exit.

The Making of (Disney's Latest Feature Film)

What It Is: Documentary about the making of Disney's latest feature film
Scope & Scale: Minor attraction
When to Go: Anytime
Author's Rating: Disney infomercial; ★★★
Appeal by Age Group:

Pre-school	Grade School	Teens	Young Adults	Over 30	Senior Citizens
★★½	★★★	★★★½	★★★½	★★★½	★★★½

Duration of Presentation: 17 minutes
Preshow Entertainment: Tour of post-production facilities

Probable Waiting Time: 20 minutes

Description and Comments A short documentary describing casting, art, music, and production of the latest Disney film follows a guided tour through the post-production studios, where combining sound with film animation is explained.

Touring Tips Although this attraction offers an inside perspective on how movies are made, its primary purpose is to lure you to the box office. Transparent self-promotion aside, presentations contribute at least marginally to an enhanced understanding of filmmaking. The presentation usually isn't crowded; see it at your convenience.

Jim Henson's MuppetVision 4D

What It Is: 4-D movie starring the Muppets
Scope & Scale: Major attraction
When to Go: Before 11 a.m. and after 4 p.m.
Author's Rating: Uproarious; not to be missed; ★★★★½
Appeal by Age Group:

Pre-school	Grade School	Teens	Young Adults	Over 30	Senior Citizens
★★★★½	★★★★★	★★★★½	★★★★½	★★★★½	★★★★½

Duration of Presentation: 17 minutes
Preshow Entertainment: Muppets on television
Probable Waiting Time: 12 minutes

Description and Comments *MuppetVision 4D* provides a total sensory experience, with wild 3-D action augmented by auditory, visual, and tactile special effects. If you're tired and hot, this zany presentation will make you feel brand new.

Touring Tips This production has been rising in popularity. Before noon, waits are about 20 minutes. During the hot, busy midday, however, lines are long until about 4 p.m. Also, watch for throngs arriving from just-concluded performances of the *Indiana Jones Epic Stunt Spectacular.* If you encounter a long line, try again later.

Honey, I Shrunk the Kids Movie Set Adventure

What It Is: Small but elaborate playground
Scope & Scale: Diversion
When to Go: Before 10 a.m. or after dark

Author's Rating: Great for young children, optional for adults; ★★½

Appeal by Age Group:

Pre-school	Grade School	Teens	Young Adults	Over 30	Senior Citizens
★★★★½	★★★½	★★	★★½	★★★	★★½

Duration of Presentation: Varies

Average Wait in Line per 100 People ahead of You: 20 minutes

Description and Comments   This elaborate playground appeals particularly to kids age 11 and younger. The story is that you have been "miniaturized" and have to make your way through a yard full of 20-foot-tall blades of grass, giant ants, lawn sprinklers, and other oversized features.

Touring Tips   This imaginative playground has tunnels, slides, rope ladders, and a variety of oversized props. All surface areas are padded, and Disney personnel are on-hand to help keep children in some semblance of control.

While this Movie Set Adventure undoubtedly looked good on paper, the actual attraction has problems that are hard to "miniaturize." First, it isn't nearly large enough to accommodate the children who would like to play. Only 240 people are allowed "on the set" at a time, and many of these are supervising parents or curious adults who hopped in line without knowing what they were waiting for. Frequently by 10:30 or 11 a.m., the playground is full, with dozens waiting outside (some impatiently).

Also, there's no provision for getting people to leave. Kids play as long as parents allow. This creates uneven traffic flow and unpredictable waits. If it weren't for the third flaw, that the attraction is poorly ventilated (as hot and sticky as an Everglades swamp), there's no telling when anyone would leave.

A mom from Shawnee Mission, Kansas, however, disagrees with our assessment:

> *Some of the things your book said to skip were our favorites (at least for the kids). We all thought the playground from* Honey, I Shrunk the Kids *was great—definitely worth seeing.*

If you visit during warmer months and want your children to experience the playground, get them in and out before 11 a.m. (preferably before 10:30 a.m.). By late morning, this attraction is way too hot and crowded for anyone to enjoy. Reach the playground via the New York Backlot, or through the Studio Catering Company fast-food area.

To save time, a couple from Grand Rapids, Michigan, suggests:

> *We staked out a seat at the [fast-food] plaza near the exit of [Honey, I Shrunk the Kids playground] with our children. They then went in to*

play while I got their snacks and beverages. Meanwhile, we had an opportunity to rest and determine our next game plan. When they emerged, they were parched and tired, so the refreshment break was well timed.

New York Street Backlot

What It Is: Walk-through backlot movie set

Scope & Scale: Diversion

When to Go: Anytime

Author's Rating: Interesting, with great detail; ★★★

Appeal by Age Group:

Pre-school	Grade School	Teens	Young Adults	Over 30	Senior Citizens
★★★	★★★	★★★	★★★	★★★	★★★

Duration of Presentation: Varies

Average Wait in Line per 100 People ahead of You: No waiting

Description and Comments This part of the Studios' backlot was previously accessible only on the tram segment of the Backlot Tour. Now guests can stroll the elaborate New York Street set and appreciate its rich detail. Opening this area to pedestrians also relieves some of the congestion in the Hollywood Boulevard and Echo Lake areas.

Touring Tips There's never a wait to enjoy the New York Street Backlot; save it until you've seen those attractions that develop long lines. Mickey Mouse signs autographs and poses for photos on the steps of the hotel in the middle of the block. It has no sign or visible name, but it has flags above the entrance. Consult the daily entertainment schedule for sessions.

Backlot Theater

What It Is: Live Hollywood-style musical, usually based on a Disney film, and performed in an open-air theater

Scope & Scale: Major attraction

When to Go: First show in the morning, or in the evening

Special Comments: Performance times are listed in the daily entertainment schedule

Author's Rating: Excellent; ★★★★

Appeal by Age Group:

Pre-school	Grade School	Teens	Young Adults	Over 30	Senior Citizens
★★★	★★★½	★★★	★★★★	★★★★	★★★★

Duration of Presentation: 25–35 minutes

Preshow Entertainment: None

Probable Waiting Time: 20–30 minutes

Description and Comments The *Backlot Theater,* like *Theater of the Stars,* is an open-air venue for musical theater and concerts. Most productions are based on Disney films or animated features. An excellent show inspired by *The Hunchback of Notre Dame* played through most of 1998. The theater, on the far back side of New York Street, is generally well designed but has several obtrusive support columns. Though protected from the weather, the theater gets terribly hot during warmer months.

A Pennsylvania mom who basically stumbled onto the *Backlot Theater* says:

> *The greatest suprise was* The Hunchback of Notre Dame *performance. I loved the staging, lighting, music, and costuming. It was excellent—a real highlight of our Disney experience.*

Touring Tips Unless you visit during cooler times, see the first morning show or the last evening show. To get to the *Backlot Theater,* walk down New York Street toward the Washington Square monument. At the square, turn left for a short block. Even though the theater's location is obscure, enough guests find it to fill the seats. Arrive early by 25 minutes or more to avoid sitting behind the columns.

Goosebumps Fright Show and Fun House

What It Is: Stage show and "hall-of-mirrors" type fun house

Scope & Scale: Minor attraction

When to Go: At scheduled times for show; anytime for fun house

Author's Rating: ★½

Appeal by Age Group:

Pre-school	Grade School	Teens	Young Adults	Over 30	Senior Citizens
★½	★★	★½	★	★	½

Duration of Presentation: About 10 minutes for stage show

Average Wait in Line per 100 People ahead of You: No waiting for show; waits of up to 30 minutes for fun house

Description and Comments Opened in the fall of 1997 and located at the end of New York Street, this modest stage show and old timey amusement park fun house draw their inspiration from the *Goosebumps* children's book series. The brief stage show features the R. L. Stine characters Amaz-O the magician, Slappy the ventriloquist, Khor-Ru the dummy, and Curly the skeleton. The fun house features a small mirror maze. This show is marginal, and the "fun house" doesn't measure up even to county fair standards. Disney should be embarrassed to have it in the park.

Touring Tips   After the open-air show, during which the audience stands, the *Goosebumps* characters are available for autographs and photos.

The Magic of Disney Animation

What It Is: Walking tour of the Disney Animation Studio

Scope & Scale: Major attraction

When to Go: Before 11 a.m. and after 5 p.m.

Author's Rating: A masterpiece; not to be missed; ★★★★

Appeal by Age Group:

Pre-school	Grade School	Teens	Young Adults	Over 30	Senior Citizens
★★★	★★★	★★★	★★★½	★★★½	★★★½

Duration of Presentation: 36 minutes

Preshow Entertainment: Gallery of animation art in waiting area

Average Wait in Line per 100 People ahead of You: 7 minutes

Description and Comments   The public, for the first time, sees Disney artists at work. Since Disneyland opened in 1955, fans have petitioned Walt Disney Productions to offer an animation studio tour. Finally, after an interminable wait, an admiring public may watch artists create Disney characters.

Revised in 1998, the animation tour exceeds expectations. It's dynamic, fast-paced, educational, and fun. After entering the Animation Building, most guests wait briefly in a gallery of Disney animation art. Use this time to enjoy the combination of art and animation history. From the gallery, guests enter a theater to see an eight-and-a-half minute introductory film on animation. Starring Walter Cronkite and Robin Williams as your tour hosts, it's an absolute delight.

After the film, guests enter the studio and watch artists and technicians through large windows. Starting with story and character development, artists work sequentially through animation (characters are brought to life in rough art); to clean up (rough art is refined to finished line drawings); to effects and backgrounds (backgrounds for the characters are developed); and to photocopying, where drawings are transferred from paper to plastic sheets, called cels, before being finished with ink and paint. The cels are then photographed, assembled, and edited. Finally, the group enters a comfortable theater for a film that melds all the elements of animation production. Clips from Disney animated classics are featured.

The Magic of Disney Animation tour depends on live video and film narration, and only secondarily on the work of animators in the studio. Though animation is well explained, you may be disappointed if you think you'll see a lot of animators working.

Touring Tips Some days, the animation tour doesn't open until 11 a.m., by which time the park is pretty full. Check the entertainment schedule for tour hours, and try to go before noon. The tour is a relatively small-volume attraction, and lines begin to build on busy days by mid- to late morning.

After the introductory film, stay in the studio to watch the artists and technicians as long as you like. You likely will catch up with your group. If you don't, conclude your tour with the next group.

Disney-MGM Studios Backlot Tour

What It Is: Combination tram and walking tour of modern film and video production

Scope & Scale: Headliner

When to Go: Anytime

Author's Rating: Educational and fun; not to be missed; ★★★★

Appeal by Age Group:

Pre-school	Grade School	Teens	Young Adults	Over 30	Senior Citizens
★★★	★★★★	★★★★	★★★★	★★★★	★★★★

Duration of Presentation: About 30 minutes

Special Comments: Can be combined with soundstage tour described below

Preshow Entertainment: A video before the special effects segment and another video in the tram boarding area

Average Wait in Line per 100 People ahead of You: 2 minutes

Assumes: 16 tour departures per hour

Loading Speed: Fast

Description and Comments About two-thirds of Disney-MGM Studios is a working film and television facility, where actors, artists, and technicians work on productions year-round. Everything from TV commercials, specials, and game shows to feature motion pictures are produced. Visitors to

Disney-MGM can take the backstage studio tour to learn production methods and technologies.

Disney periodically changes the name of this tour. At press time, it was called the Disney-MGM Studios Backlot Tour.

The Studios rearranged the tour in 1997. It now begins on the edge of the backlot with the special effects walking segment, then continues with the tram segment. After the tram segment, you can bail out or continue to the soundstage tour. To reach the Disney-MGM Studios Backlot Tour, turn right off Hollywood Boulevard through the Studio Arch into the Animation Courtyard. Bear left at the corner where *Voyage of the Little Mermaid* is situated. Follow the street until you see a red brick warehouse on your right. Go through the door and up the ramp.

The first stop is a special effects water tank where technicians explain the mechanical and optical tricks that "turn the seemingly impossible into on-screen reality." Included are rain effects, a naval battle, and a storm at sea. The waiting area for this part of the tour displays miniature naval vessels used in filming famous war movies.

Next, you enter the special effects workshop, where enlargement, miniaturization, stop-frame photographic animation, and other technical mysteries are demonstrated and explained. Moving to a second workshop, volunteers from the audience are integrated into an action scene using a blue-screen background.

A prop room separates the workshops and the tram tour. Trams depart about once every four minutes on busy days, winding among production and shop buildings before stopping at the wardrobe and crafts shops. Here, costumes, sets, and props are designed, created, and stored. Still seated on the tram, you look through large windows to see craftsmen at work.

The tour continues through the backlot, where western desert canyons and New York City brownstones exist side by side with suburban residential streets. The tour's highlight is Catastrophe Canyon, an elaborate special-effects movie set where a thunderstorm, earthquake, oil-field fire, and flash flood are simulated. The tour's tram portion ends at Backstage Plaza, where you can avail yourself of rest rooms, food, and drink. To reach the start of the soundstage tour, most recently called Backstage Pass to "101 Dalmatians," head back past the entrance of the special effects/tram tour toward the *Little Mermaid*. The soundstage tour begins on the far-left end of the building next to the special effects and tram tour.

Touring Tips Because the Backlot Tour is one of Disney's most efficient attractions, you will rarely wait more than 15–20 minutes (usually less than ten). Take the tour at your convenience, but preferably before 5 p.m., when the workday ends for the various workshops.

Backstage Pass to "101 Dalmatians" Soundstage Tour

What It Is: Walking tour of modern film and video production soundstages

Scope & Scale: Minor attraction

When to Go: Anytime

Author's Rating: Latest version not the best, but still informative; ★★★

Appeal by Age Group:

Pre-school	Grade School	Teens	Young Adults	Over 30	Senior Citizens
★½	★★	★★	★★★	★★★	★★★

Duration of Presentation: About 25 minutes

Special Comments: Can be combined with Disney-MGM Studios Backlot Tour described above

Probable Waiting Time: 10 minutes

Description and Comments   The soundstage tour has had several names. Because it's a thinly disguised promo for a Disney film, the name is usually derived from the movie. Recently, for example, it was called Backstage Pass to "101 Dalmatians." Check your guidemap for the name in use when you visit.

You can take the soundstage tour before the Backlot Tour. In the Disney guidemap, the Backlot Tour and soundstage tours are listed separately. For continuity, start with the Backlot Tour, then tour the soundstages.

On the soundstage tour, soundproofed observation platforms allow unobtrusive viewing of ongoing productions, which are described by a Disney cast member guide. At the next stop, you inspect sets and props used in a Disney film and watch a video explaining how the film was produced.

Touring Tips   While the Backlot Tour is quite worthwhile, the educational value of the soundstage tour is marginal. What once was a compelling educational experience is now little more than a promo for Disney flicks. Waiting time for the tour is usually less than 20 minutes, even during busiest times. The soundstage tour is located roughly next door and to the right of the Backlot Tour on Mickey Avenue.

Live Entertainment at Disney-MGM Studios

When the Studios opened, live entertainment, parades, and special events weren't as fully developed or elaborate as those at the Magic Kingdom or Epcot. With the introduction of an afternoon parade and elaborate shows at *Theater of the Stars,* the Studios joined the big leagues. These outstanding performances, coupled with the Sorcery in the Sky fireworks spectacular, give Disney-MGM live entertainment every bit as compelling as that in the other parks. In the fall of 1998, Disney-MGM premiered a new edition of *Fantasmic!*, a water, fireworks, and laser show that has drawn rave reviews at Disneyland California for years. *Fantasmic!*, staged in its own specially designed 10,000-person amphitheater, makes the Studios the park of choice for spectacular nighttime entertainment. *Fantasmic!* is profiled in detail on pages 543–544.

Sorcery in the Sky Fireworks   An excellent fireworks show based on Mickey Mouse's exploits in his role as the Sorcerer's Apprentice in *Fantasia*. It is held daily at closing time, when the park stays open after dark. During the off-season, the show is staged only on weekends, and sometimes not even then. Watch the fireworks from anywhere along Hollywood Boulevard.

It is conceivable, in the near future, that Sorcery in the Sky will be discontinued, revised, or incorporated into the finale of *Fantasmic!*

Afternoon Parade   Staged one or more times a day, the parade begins near the park's entrance, continues down Hollywood Boulevard, and circles in front of The Great Movie Ride. From there, it passes in front of *SuperStar Television* and *ABC Sound Studio* and ends by Star Tours. An alternate route begins at the far end of Sunset Boulevard and turns right onto Hollywood Boulevard.

The parade features floats and characters from Disney's animated features. Excellent parades based on *Mulan, Aladdin, Toy Story,* and *Hercules* have been produced. Colorful, creative, and totally upbeat, the afternoon parade is great. It does, however, bring pedestrian traffic to a standstill along its route and hampers crossing the park. If you're anywhere on the parade route when the parade begins, your best bet is to stay put and enjoy it. Our favorite vantage point is the steps of *SuperStar Television*.

Theater of the Stars   This covered amphitheater on Sunset Boulevard is the stage for production reviews, usually featuring music from Disney movies and starring Disney characters. Performances are posted in front of the theater and are listed in the daily entertainment schedule in the handout guidemap.

Backlot Theater   This stage is home to musical productions featuring Disney characters and/or based on Disney films. A stage adaptation of *Pocahontas* preceded a musical drawn from *The Hunchback of Notre Dame*. The Backlot Theater is roughly behind the Muppets theater. Walk down New York Street toward the back of the park. At the end of the street, turn left.

Disney Characters Find characters at the *Theater of the Stars* and Backlot Theater, in parades, on New York Street, in the Animation Courtyard, in Backstage Plaza, and along the street running next to the soundstages. Mickey sometimes appears for autographs and photos on Sunset Boulevard. A breakfast with characters from Disney's latest animated film is offered most mornings at the Soundstage Restaurant. To find out where the characters are during your visit, pick up a free copy of the *Disney Character Greeting Location Guide* available at Guest Relations.

Street Entertainment Jugglers and other roving performers appear on Hollywood and Sunset boulevards. The Studios' modest marching band and a brass quartet play Hollywood Boulevard, Sunset Boulevard, Studio Courtyard, and the Echo Lake area. Not exactly street entertainment, a piano player performs daily at The Hollywood Brown Derby.

Shopping at Disney-MGM Studios

Shops throughout the park carry movie-oriented merchandise and numerous Disney trademark souvenirs. Most shopping is concentrated on Hollywood Boulevard and features movie nostalgia items ranging from black-and-white postcards of the stars to JuJubes (if you're over 40, you still probably have some stuck in your teeth).

Unusual shops include Animation Gallery in the Animation Building, which sells reproductions of "cels" from animated features and other animation art. Sid Cahuenga's near the park's entrance sells vintage movie posters and celebrity autographs. Disney collectibles are specialties at Celebrity 5 & 10 on Sunset Boulevard. Planet Hollywood Super Store on Hollywood Boulevard is the place for celebrity memorabilia and Planet Hollywood trademark apparel.

Disney-MGM Studios One-Day Touring Plan
for Visitors of All Ages

Because Disney-MGM offers fewer attractions, touring isn't as complicated as at the Magic Kingdom or Epcot. Most Disney-MGM rides and shows are oriented to the entire family, eliminating disagreements on how to spend the day. Whereas in the Magic Kingdom Mom and Dad want to see *The Hall of Presidents,* Big Sis is revved to ride Space Mountain, and the preschool twins are clamoring for Dumbo the Flying Elephant, at Disney-MGM Studios the whole family can pretty much tour together.

Since there are fewer attractions, crowds are more concentrated at Disney-MGM. If a line seems unusually long, ask an attendant what the estimated wait is. If it exceeds your tolerance, retry the attraction while *Indiana Jones* is in progress or during a parade or special event. These draw people away from the lines.

Our touring plan assumes a willingness to experience all major rides and shows. Be aware that Star Tours, The Great Movie Ride, *The Twilight Zone* Tower of Terror, and the Catastrophe Canyon segment of the tram tour sometimes frighten children younger than eight. Further, Star Tours can upset anyone prone to motion sickness. When following the plan, skip any attraction you don't wish to experience.

Early Entry at Disney-MGM Studios

Two days each week, Disney resort and campground guests are invited to enter Disney-MGM Studios 90 minutes before official opening time. During the early-entry hour, guests usually can enjoy The Great Movie Ride, *MuppetVision 4D,* Star Tours, and *The Twilight Zone* Tower of Terror. (These attractions are subject to change, as are the days early entry is scheduled.)

Early entry at Disney-MGM offers some real advantages. All of the attractions that open early are top of the line and draw huge crowds when the park fills. If you get them in the rearview mirror early, the remainder of the day will run smoothly. If you participate in early entry, be ready to enter the moment the park opens. If official opening is 9 a.m., arrive at the park by 7:30 a.m. Once inside, hurry immediately to the Tower of Terror, then to The Great Movie Ride, then to Star Tours. If you use our touring plan, skip steps that call for seeing attractions you already enjoyed.

If you aren't eligible for early entry, arrive at the Studios 40 minutes before official opening time on a day when early entry is not in effect.

Before You Go

1. Call (407) 824-4321 to determine which days of the week early entry is in effect and to verify the park's hours.

2. Buy your admission before arriving. Order tickets by mail or purchase them at a local Disney Store before you leave home. They're also available at the Ocala Disney AAA Travel Center off I-75 if you're driving. If you arrive by plane, buy them at the Disney Store in the Orlando airport or at a Disney resort hotel.

3. Make lunch and dinner priority seatings (if desired) before you arrive by calling (407) 939-3463. Disney resort guests can dial 55 from their room to make advance lunch and dinner priority seatings.

4. The schedule of live entertainment changes from month to month and even from day to day. Review the examples in the touring plan to get a fairly clear picture of your options.

At Disney-MGM Studios

1. Arrive at the park 1 hour and 40 minutes before official opening time if you're a Disney resort guest taking advantage of early entry. On non-early-entry days, arrive 40 minutes before official opening. Day guests (those without early-entry privileges) should avoid early-entry days.

2. When you're admitted, go to Guest Relations for a guidemap containing the daily entertainment schedule. Then blow down Hollywood Boulevard and turn right at Sunset Boulevard. Proceed to the Tower of Terror and ride. If young children or terrified adults are in your party, take advantage of switching off (pages 165–167).

3. After Tower of Terror, four attractions remain that are tough to see without long waits in line. Two, The Great Movie Ride and Star Tours, are rides. The others, *Voyage of the Little Mermaid* and *Indiana Jones Epic Stunt Spectacular*, are theater presentations.

   Check your guidemap for times of first performances for *Voyage of the Little Mermaid* and *Indiana Jones*. Your mission (should you choose to accept it) is to see the first performance of each show, working in the two rides as you can. Here's what you need to know:

   a. *Before 10 a.m.*, on a day when early entry isn't in effect, it usually takes about 30 minutes to experience The Great Movie Ride and about 15–20 minutes to ride Star Tours. These estimates include your time in line and the time you spend riding. They don't include the time it takes to walk between the attractions.

   b. *Voyage of the Little Mermaid* lasts about 20 minutes, and *Indiana Jones Epic Stunt Spectacular* runs about 35 minutes. When the first performance is scheduled at 9:30 a.m. or earlier, usually neither show plays to a capacity audience. To see the first performance of the *Little Mermaid*, arrive five to ten minutes before show time. You can cut it closer at *Indiana Jones*. Guests are usually allowed to enter *Indiana Jones* three to five minutes *after* the first show has begun (there's nothing you can't afford to miss). If, however, the first performance of *Indiana Jones* begins at 9:45 a.m. or later, arrive at least 20 minutes before show time.

Here's how one family applied this information:

Pete, Marie, and their 12-year-old twins waited outside the entrance of the Studios on a non-early-entry day when official opening time was 9 a.m. The park opened at 8:30 a.m. (as usual). They passed through the turnstiles at 8:35 a.m. and reached the Tower of Terror by 8:40 a.m. It was about 9 a.m. when they finished riding the Tower of Terror. Checking the entertainment schedule in the park guidemap, they saw that the first showing of *Little Mermaid* was at 9:15 a.m. and the first performance of *Indiana Jones* was at 10 a.m.

There wasn't enough time to catch one of the rides, so the family went straight to the *Little Mermaid*, arriving in time to be admitted for the first show. It was 9:35 a.m. when they left the theater. Assuming the 10 a.m. performance of *Indiana Jones* would fill, they proceeded directly to *Indiana Jones*. Taking into consideration that the *Indiana Jones* audience would inundate nearby attractions after the show, they turned right upon entering the *Indiana Jones* stadium and sat high and near the exit. When the show ended, they hurried out ahead of the crowd and arrived at Star Tours at about 10:45. At Star Tours, they had a 20-minute wait. Departing Star Tours at about 11:10, they headed to The Great Movie Ride, arriving at about 11:15. By this time, The Great Movie Ride had a fairly long line, so the family waited 30 minutes before riding. When they completed The Great Movie Ride at 12:05 p.m., the family had experienced all of the park's attractions that cause lengthy waits.

Here's another example:

Jack and Cathy, two adults who can move pretty fast, hit the turnstiles at 8:32 a.m. and were among the first guests at the Tower of Terror. By 8:50, they were back on the street. Postponing the *Little Mermaid*, they figured they could catch both The Great Movie Ride and Star Tours before the first performance of *Indiana Jones* at 10 a.m. They arrived at The Great Movie Ride at 8:55 and were out by 9:20. They arrived at Star Tours at 9:25 and, after riding, were able to reach *Indiana Jones* by 9:42 a.m. This was cutting it close, but they were able to get in. After *Indiana Jones*, Jack and Cathy checked the wait at *Little*

Mermaid and found it prohibitive. They returned during the afternoon parade and were able to see the show after a 25-minute wait.

Some what-ifs:

- *What if you miss the first performance of one of the shows?* After the first show, the *Little Mermaid* runs continuously throughout the day. If you arrive too late for the first show, ask a Disney cast member at the attraction when you'll be admitted if you line up now. If the wait is 30 minutes or less, that probably is the best you can expect all day unless you retry during a parade. *Indiana Jones* is a little easier to catch after the first show. If you arrive 25–35 minutes before the second show, you shouldn't have trouble getting in. Before you queue up, however, ask a cast member how long the wait is.

- *What if the first performances of the* Little Mermaid *and* Indiana Jones *begin at the same time?* See the *Little Mermaid* first, then catch the second show of *Indiana Jones.*

- *What if you're a Disney resort guest taking advantage of early entry?* Arrive 1 hour and 40 minutes before official opening time. When you're admitted, experience Tower of Terror, The Great Movie Ride, and Star Tours, in that order. After Star Tours, check the guidemap for the first performance of the *Little Mermaid.* If show time is within 35 minutes, go to *Little Mermaid* and line up. If you have more than 35 minutes, you might be able to squeeze in *MuppetVision 4D.* Go to *MuppetVision 4D* and ask a cast member when the next show will begin. If it's in less than 10 minutes, see the show, then hurry back to *Little Mermaid.* If you don't think *Little Mermaid* is worth the fuss, go directly from Star Tours to *MuppetVision 4D.*

Here are some time-savers for the *Little Mermaid* and *Indiana Jones:*

- *Little Mermaid.* Once you're admitted to the preshow area, stand next to the doors leading to the theater. When they open, enter the theater and pick a row of seats, allowing about six people to enter the row ahead of you. Your objective is to score seats near the exit doors on the far side, but not get stuck with the four or five seats nearest the exits. This strategy ensures a good view of the stage and puts you in a perfect position to be among the first to exit when the show ends.

- *Indiana Jones.* This production is staged in a 2,000-seat covered outdoor theater. If you want to beat the crowd when the performance ends, sit in the upper rows on the far right (as you face the stage). When the show is over, you'll be perfectly positioned to make a speedy exit.

4. After completing Star Tours, The Great Movie Ride, the *Little Mermaid,* and *Indiana Jones,* see *MuppetVision 4D.*

5. Backtrack through the Studios Arch (past the *Little Mermaid*) and across the square to the Animation Building on the far right. Take The Magic of Disney Animation tour. If you need a rest room, they're at the left rear of the square.

6. Eat lunch if you're hungry.

7. Exiting the Animation Building, take the street alongside the *Little Mermaid* and proceed past the soundstages to the red-brick facade resembling a warehouse. This is the entrance to the special effects / tram segment of the Disney-MGM Studios Backlot Tour. Enjoy the tour. The combined special effects / tram tour takes about 30 minutes.

8. Disembark from the tram and go through the movie artifacts museum. Bear left, circling back past the entrance to the special effects / tram tour. Next door, to the right, is the entrance to the soundstage tour. Like the Backlot Tour, this tour's name changes almost yearly; check your guidemap for the current name.

9. After the walking tour, see *The Making of (Disney's Latest Feature Film)* on Dalmation Avenue between the soundstages and *Voyage of the Little Mermaid.*

10. Check the daily entertainment schedule for parades, live shows, or events that interest you. Musicals at the *Theater of the Stars* and the *Backlot Theater* are outstanding and should be worked into your itinerary.

11. By now you have seen all major attractions except *SuperStar Television* and *ABC Sound Studio.* Check the daily entertainment schedule for *SuperStar Television* performance times. If one is within the next 20–30 minutes, enjoy the show. Otherwise, see *ABC Sound Studio* first. When you check the line at *ABC Sound Studio,* be aware that this attraction is often inundated after a performance of nearby *Indiana Jones.* If *ABC Sound Studio* has a long line when you arrive, retry later.

12. After seeing *ABC Sound Studio* and *SuperStar Television,* bear right and explore the New York Street set.

13. Tour Hollywood and Sunset boulevards. Consult the daily entertainment schedule for parades and special events. Remember that we rate *Fantasmic!,* the nighttime entertainment spectacular, as "not to be missed."

14. This concludes the touring plan. Eat, shop, enjoy live entertainment, or revisit your favorite Disney-MGM attractions. When you're ready to leave the park, walk (the Disney-MGM parking lot isn't that big) or take a tram to your car.

Universal Florida

Universal Florida is well along in the expansion project that will transform the facility into a destination resort with two theme parks; a shopping, dining, and entertainment complex; and two hotels. The second theme park, Islands of Adventure (described later in this section), is scheduled to open in 1999 with five theme areas. Jurassic Park is the centerpiece, with a boat ride similar to one operating at Universal Studios Hollywood. Giving Disney some of its own medicine, other theme areas will feature attractions designed to compete directly with Disney headliners. Superhero Island, inspired by Marvel Comic heroes, will have a free-fall thrill ride to rival Disney's Tower of Terror. Toon Lagoon will be home to Popeye, Olive Oyl, and other cartoon characters. The main attraction will be a flume ride (watch out, Splash Mountain!). Other theme areas will include Seuss Landing, with children's attractions based on the Dr. Seuss books, and Lost Continent, inspired by legends of mythical explorers and places.

A new system of roads and two multistory parking facilities are connected by moving sidewalks to CityWalk, a shopping, dining, and nighttime entertainment complex that will also serve as a gateway to both the current Universal Studios Florida and the new Islands of Adventure theme parks. Opened in the summer of 1998, CityWalk includes the world's largest Hard Rock Cafe, complete with its own concert facility; an Emeril's restaurant; a NASCAR Cafe, with an auto-racing theme; a Pat O'Brien's New Orleans nightclub, with dueling pianos; a Motown Cafe; a Bob Marley restaurant and museum; a multifaceted Jazz Center; an E! Entertainment production studio; Jimmy Buffett's Margaritaville Café; and a 16-screen cinema complex.

The Portofino Bay Resort will open in 1999 with 750 rooms, followed by a Hard Rock Hotel.

ARRIVING

The Universal Florida complex can be accessed via Kirkman Road from I-4 exits 29 or 30B. Driving from the Walt Disney World area, exit I-4 onto Sandlake Road heading north (away from International Drive) and turn right onto Turkey Lake Road. Follow the signs to the Turkey Lake Road entrance.

Once on-site, you will be directed to park in one of two multitiered parking garages. Parking runs $6 for cars and $8 for RVs. Be sure to write down the location of your car before heading for the parks. From the garages, moving sidewalks deliver you to the Universal CityWalk dining, shopping, and entertainment venue described above. From CityWalk you can access the main entrances of both Universal Studios Florida theme park and Universal's Islands of Adventure theme park. Even with the moving walkways it takes about 10–12 minutes to commute from the garages to the entrances of the theme parks.

One-Day and Two-Day Tickets cost about $40 and $64 (including tax), respectively, for adults; $32 and $53 for children (ages three to nine). Annual Passes cost about $75 for adults and $60 for children.

Combination passes are available: A four-park, seven-day pass allows unlimited entry to Universal Studios, Universal's Islands of Adventure (opens summer 1999), Sea World, and Wet 'n Wild and costs about $106 for adults and $88 for children (ages three to nine). A five-park, ten-day pass provides unlimited entry to Universal Studios, Universal's Islands of Adventure (opens summer 1999), Sea World, Wet 'n Wild, and Busch Gardens and costs about $138 for adults, and $115 for children.

Universal Studios frequently runs specials, including "Second-Day-Free" promotions. If you buy a one-day pass during the promotion, you can return for a second day free anytime within seven days of your first visit.

The main Universal Florida information number is (407) 363-8000. Reach Guest Services at (407) 224-6035, schedule a character breakfast at (407) 224-6339, and order tickets by mail at (800) 224-3838.

Universal Studios Florida

Universal City Studios Inc. has run a studios tour and movie-theme tourist attraction for more than 29 years, predating all Disney parks except Disneyland. In the early 1980s, Universal announced plans to build a studios/theme park complex in Florida. While Universal labored over its new project, Disney jumped into high gear and rushed its own studios/theme park onto the market, beating Universal by a year and a half.

Universal Studios Florida opened in June 1990. At that time, it was almost four times the size of Disney-MGM Studios (Disney-MGM has since expanded somewhat), with much more of the facility accessible to visitors. Like its sister facility in Hollywood, Universal Studios Florida is spacious, beautifully landscaped, meticulously clean, and delightfully varied in its entertainment. Rides are exciting and innovative and, as with many Disney rides, focus on familiar and/or beloved movie characters or situations.

On Universal Studios Florida's E.T. ride, you escape the authorities on a flying bike and leave Earth to visit E.T.'s home planet. In Kongfrontation, King Kong tears up a city with you in it. In Jaws, the persistent great white shark makes heart-stopping assaults on your small boat, and in Earthquake—The Big One, special effects create the most realistic earthquake simulation ever produced. The Funtastic World of Hanna-Barbera puts you in a bucking rocket simulator for a high-speed chase with Yogi Bear and the Flintstones. Guests also ride in a Delorean-cum-time machine in yet another chase, this one based on the film *Back to the Future.*

While many of these rides incorporate state-of-the-art technology and live up to their billing in terms of excitement, creativity, uniqueness, and special effects, they lack the capacity to handle the number of guests who frequent major Florida tourist destinations. If a ride has great appeal but can accommodate only a small number of guests per ride or per hour, long lines form. It isn't unusual for the wait to exceed an hour and a quarter for the E.T. ride and 50 minutes for the Hanna-Barbera ride.

Happily, most shows and theater performances at Universal Studios Florida are in theaters that accommodate large numbers of people. Since many shows run continuously, waits usually don't exceed twice the show's performance time (40–50 minutes). At several shows, the audience moves to three or more staging areas as the presentation unfolds.

Universal Studios Florida is laid out in an upside-down **L** configuration. Beyond the main entrance, a wide boulevard stretches past several shows and rides to a New York City backlot set. Branching off this pedestrian thoroughfare to the right are five streets that access other areas of the studios and intersect a promenade circling a large lake.

The park is divided into five sections: the Front Lot/Production Central, New York, Hollywood, San Francisco/Amity, and Expo Center. Where one section begins and another ends is blurry, but no matter. Guests orient themselves by the major rides, sets, and landmarks and refer, for instance, to "New York," "the waterfront," "over by E.T.," or "by Mel's Diner." The area of Universal Studios Florida open to visitors is about the size of Epcot.

The park offers all standard services and amenities, including stroller and wheelchair rental, lockers, diaper-changing and infant-nursing facilities, car assistance, and foreign-language assistance. Most of the park is accessible to disabled guests, and TDDs are available for the hearing impaired. Almost all services are in the Front Lot, just inside the main entrance.

Universal Studios offers a character breakfast on Tuesdays and Thursdays during slow season, and Monday through Friday during high season. Breakfast is hosted by at least four Hanna-Barbera characters at the International Food Bazaar, just inside the park on the right. The cost is $13.50 for adults and $8.75 for children ages three to nine for an all-you-can-eat cafeteria-style breakfast.

UNIVERSAL STUDIOS FLORIDA ATTRACTIONS

Terminator 2: 3-D

What It Is: 3-D thriller mixed-media presentation

Scope & Scale: Super headliner

When to Go: After 3:30 p.m.

Special Comments: The nation's best theme park attraction; very intense for some preschoolers and grade-schoolers

Author's Rating: Furiously paced high-tech experience; not to be missed; ★★★★★

Appeal by Age Group:

Pre-school	Grade School	Teens	Young Adults	Over 30	Senior Citizens
★★★	★★★★★	★★★★★	★★★★★	★★★★★	★★★★

Duration of Presentation: 20 minutes, including an 8-minute preshow

Probable Waiting Time: 20–40 minutes

Description and Comments The Terminator "cop" from *Terminator 2* morphs to life and battles Arnold Schwarzenegger's T-800 cyborg character. If you missed the *Terminator* flicks, here's the plot: A bad robot arrives from the future to kill a nice boy. Another bad robot (who has been reprogrammed to be good) pops up at the same time to save the boy. The bad robot chases the boy and the rehabilitated robot, menacing the audience in the process.

The attraction, like the films, is all action, and you really don't need to understand much. What's interesting is that it uses 3-D film and a theater full of sophisticated technology to integrate the real with the imaginary. Images seem to move in and out of the film, not only in the manner of traditional 3-D, but also in actuality. Remove your 3-D glasses momentarily and you'll see that the guy on the motorcycle is actually onstage.

We've watched this type of presentation evolve, pioneered by Disney's *Captain EO, Honey, I Shrunk the Audience,* and *MuppetVision 4D.* Terminator 2: 3-D, however, goes way beyond lasers, with moving theater seats, blasts of hot air, and spraying mist. It creates a multidimensional space that blurs the boundary between entertainment and reality. Is it seamless? Not quite, but it's close. We rank *Terminator 2: 3-D* as not to be missed and consider it the absolute best theme-park attraction in the United States. If *Terminator 2: 3-D* is the only attraction you see at Universal Studios Florida, you'll have received your money's worth.

Touring Tips   The 700-seat theater changes audiences about every 19 minutes. Even so, because the show is new and hot, expect to wait about 30–45 minutes. The attraction, on Hollywood Boulevard near the park's entrance, receives huge traffic during morning and early afternoon. By about 3 p.m., however, lines diminish somewhat. Though you'll still wait, we recommend holding off on *Terminator 2: 3-D* until then. If you can't stay until late afternoon, see the show first thing in the morning. Families with young children should know that the violence characteristic of the *Terminator* movies is largely absent from the attraction. There's suspense and action but not much blood and guts.

Not to Be Missed at Universal Studios Florida

Back to the Future	*Terminator 2: 3-D*
Earthquake—The Big One	*The Wild, Wild, Wild West*
Hercules and Xena	*Stunt Show*
Jaws	

The Funtastic World of Hanna-Barbera

Motion Sickness WARNING!

What It Is: Flight-simulation ride

Scope & Scale: Major attraction

When to Go: Before 11 a.m.

Special Comments: Very intense for some preschoolers

Author's Rating: A delight for all ages; ★★★½

Appeal by Age Group:

Pre-school	Grade School	Teens	Young Adults	Over 30	Senior Citizens
★★★★	★★★★	★★★½	★★★½	★★★½	★★★½

Duration of Ride: 4½ minutes with a 3½-minute preshow

Loading Speed: Moderate to slow

Description and Comments   A flight-simulation ride in the same family as

Universal Studios Florida

1. Nickelodeon Studios Walking Tour
2. The Funtastic World of
   Hanna-Barbera
3. Lucy, A Tribute
4. "Alfred Hitchcock: The Art
   of Making Movies"
5. *Hercules and Xena*
6. The Boneyard
7. *Twister*
8. Kongfrontation
9. *Bettlejuice's Rock 'n Roll
   Graveyard Revue*
10. Earthquake—The Big One
11. Jaws

12. *The Wild, Wild, Wild West*
    Stunt Show
13. *Dynamite Nights Stuntacular*
14. Back to the Future—The Ride
15. *Animal Actors Stage*
16. *A Day in the Park with Barney*
17. Hard Rock Cafe

18. E.T. Adventure
19. Fievel's Playland
20. *The Gory Gruesome & Grotesque*
    Horror Make-Up Show
21. *Terminator 2: 3-D*

Disney's Star Tours and Body Wars, except that all visuals are cartoons. Guests accompany Yogi Bear in a high-speed chase to rescue a kidnapped child.

Touring Tips   Unfortunately, this wild, funny, and thoroughly delightful attraction is a cycle ride. It must shut down completely during loading and unloading. Consequently, large lines build early and move very slowly. Ride during the first two hours the park is open.

"Alfred Hitchcock: The Art of Making Movies"

What It Is: Mini-course on filming action sequences and a testimonial to the talents of Alfred Hitchcock

Scope & Scale: Major attraction

When to Go: After 3:30 p.m.

Special Comments: May frighten young children

Author's Rating: A little slow-moving, but well done; ★★★½

Appeal by Age Group:

Pre-school	Grade School	Teens	Young Adults	Over 30	Senior Citizens
★★½	★★★	★★★½	★★★½	★★★½	★★★½

Duration of Presentation: 40 minutes

Probable Waiting Time: 22 minutes

Description and Comments   Guests view a film featuring famous scenes from Hitchcock movies (including some unreleased 3-D footage) and then go to an adjoining soundstage where the stabbing scene from *Psycho* is re-created using professional actors and audience volunteers. In a third area, the technology of filming action scenes is explained. The Hitchcock "greatest hits" film is disjointed and confusing unless you have a good recollection of the movies and scenes highlighted. Re-enactment of the scene from *Psycho* is both informative and entertaining, as are sets and techniques demonstrated in the third area.

Touring Tips   The attraction is just beyond the main entrance, and lines build. Usually, however, they disappear quickly. Let morning crowds clear; see the attraction just before you leave in the evening.

Nickelodeon Studios Walking Tour

What It Is: Behind-the-scenes guided tour

Scope & Scale: Minor attraction

When to Go: When Nickelodeon shows are in production (usually weekdays)

Author's Rating: ★★★
Appeal by Age Group:

Pre-school	Grade School	Teens	Young Adults	Over 30	Senior Citizens
★★½	★★★★	★★★	★★★	★★★	★★★

Duration of Tour: 36 minutes
Probable Waiting Time: 30–45 minutes

Description and Comments   The tour examines set construction, soundstages, wardrobe, props, lighting, video production, and special effects. Much of this information is presented more creatively in the "Alfred Hitchcock," *Hercules and Xena,* and *Horror Make-Up Show* productions, but the Nickelodeon tour is tailored for kids. They're made to feel supremely important; their opinions are used to shape future Nickelodeon programming.

Adding some much-needed zip is the Game Lab, where guests preview strange games being tested for possible inclusion on Nickelodeon. Game Lab ends with a lucky child getting "slimed." If you don't understand, consult your children.

Touring Tips   While grade-schoolers, especially, enjoy this tour, it's expendable for everyone else. Go on a second day or second visit at Universal. If Nickelodeon isn't in production, forget it.

Twister

What It Is: Theater presentation featuring special effects from the movie *Twister*
Scope & Scale: Major attraction
When to Go: Should be your first show after experiencing all rides
Special Comments: High potential for frightening young children
Author's Rating: Gusty; ★★★½
Appeal by Age Group:

Pre-school	Grade School	Teens	Young Adults	Over 30	Senior Citizens
★★	★★★★	★★★★	★★★★	★★★★	★★★★

Duration of Presentation: 15 minutes
Probable Waiting Time: 26 minutes

Description and Comments   Replacing the *Ghostbusters* attraction in 1998, *Twister* combines an elaborate set and special effects, climaxing with a five-story-tall simulated tornado created by circulating more than 2 million cubic feet of air per minute.

Touring Tips   The wind, pounding rain, and freight-train sound of the tornado are deafening, and the entire presentation is exceptionally intense. Schoolchildren are mightily impressed, while younger children are terrified and overwhelmed. Unless you want the kids hopping in your bed whenever they hear thunder, try this attraction yourself before taking your kids.

Kongfrontation

What It Is: Indoor adventure ride featuring King Kong
Scope & Scale: Major attraction
When to Go: Before 11 a.m.
Special Comments: May frighten young children
Author's Rating: ★★★★
Appeal by Age Group:

Pre-school	Grade School	Teens	Young Adults	Over 30	Senior Citizens
★★★½	★★★★	★★★½	★★★½	★★★	★★★

Duration of Ride: 4½ minutes
Loading Speed: Moderate

Description and Comments   Guests board an aerial tram to ride from Manhattan to Roosevelt Island. En route, they hear the giant ape has escaped. The tram passes evidence of Kong's path of destruction and encounters the monster himself. In the course of the journey, King Kong demolishes buildings, uproots utility poles, swats helicopters, and hurls your tram car to the ground.

Touring Tips   Truly amazing, when it works. Ride in the morning after Back to the Future, E.T. Adventure, and Jaws.

The Gory Gruesome & Grotesque Horror Make-Up Show

What It Is: Theater presentation on the art of make-up
Scope & Scale: Major attraction
When to Go: After you have experienced all rides
Special Comments: May frighten young children
Author's Rating: A gory knee-slapper; ★★★½
Appeal by Age Group:

Pre-school	Grade School	Teens	Young Adults	Over 30	Senior Citizens
★★★	★★★½	★★★½	★★★½	★★★½	★★★½

Duration of Presentation: 25 minutes

Probable Waiting Time: 20 minutes

Description and Comments   Lively, well-paced look at how make-up artists create film monsters, realistic wounds, severed limbs, and other unmentionables. Funnier and more upbeat than many Universal Studios presentations, the show also presents a wealth of fascinating information. It's excellent and enlightening, if somewhat gory.

Touring Tips   Exceeding most guests' expectations, the *Horror Make-Up Show* is the "sleeper" attraction at Universal. Its humor and tongue-in-cheek style transcend the gruesome effects, and most folks (including preschoolers) take the blood and guts in stride. It usually isn't too hard to get into.

Hercules and Xena

What It Is: A multisequence mini-course on special effects, mechanical and computer-generated creatures, blue-screen applications, and sound effects

Scope & Scale: Major attraction

When to Go: After you have experienced all the rides

Special Comments: A nice air-conditioned break during the hottest part of the day

Author's Rating: Sugar-coated education; ★★★★

Appeal by Age Group:

Pre-school	Grade School	Teens	Young Adults	Over 30	Senior Citizens
★★★½	★★★★	★★★★	★★★★	★★★★	★★★★

Duration of Presentation: 40 minutes

Probable Waiting Time: 20 minutes

Description and Comments   Guests move from theater to theater in this mini-course attraction. The presentation, which replaced the "Murder, She Wrote" Mystery Theater in 1997, begins with a preshow that introduces the characters of Hercules and Xena. Next is the Creature Shop, a theater where members of the audience help to create a scene for a Hercules and Xena film by manipulating the limbs of mechanical critters. In the second theater, computer-created special effects are added to the mechanical critters scene and combined through blue-screen technology with backgrounds and footage of the characters Hercules and Xena. In the last theater, sound effects are added to complete the scene.

Touring Tips   Informative, worthwhile, sometimes hilarious, and consistently high-tech, *Hercules and Xena* does a great job of making several complicated subjects understandable. The show borrows from the truly amazing technology developed for *Terminator 2: 3-D* and is a more lively presentation than "Murder, She Wrote," which covered much of the same territory. We recommend enjoying the show during the heat of the day.

Earthquake—The Big One

What It Is: Combination theater presentation and adventure ride

Scope & Scale: Major attraction

When to Go: In the morning, after Kongfrontation

Special Comments: May frighten young children

Author's Rating: Not to be missed; ★★★★

Appeal by Age Group:

Pre-school	Grade School	Teens	Young Adults	Over 30	Senior Citizens
★★★	★★★★	★★★★	★★★★	★★★★	★★★★

Duration of Presentation: 20 minutes

Loading Speed: Moderate

Description and Comments   Film shows how miniatures are used to create special effects in earthquake movies, followed by a demonstration of how miniatures, blue screen, and matte painting are integrated with live-action stunt sequences (starring audience volunteers) to create a realistic final product. Afterward, guests board a subway from Oakland to San Francisco and experience an earthquake—the big one. Special effects range from fires and runaway trains to exploding tanker trucks and tidal waves. This is Universal's answer to Disney-MGM's Catastrophe Canyon. The special effects are comparable, but the field of vision is better at Catastrophe Canyon. Nonetheless, Earthquake is one of Universal's more compelling efforts.

Touring Tips   Experience Earthquake in the morning, after you ride Back to the Future, E.T., Jaws, and Kongfrontation.

Jaws

What It Is: Adventure boat ride

Scope & Scale: Headliner

When to Go: Before 11 a.m.

Special Comments: Will frighten young children

Author's Rating: Not to be missed; ★★★★
Appeal by Age Group:

Pre-school	Grade School	Teens	Young Adults	Over 30	Senior Citizens
★★½	★★★★	★★★★	★★★★	★★★★	★★★★

Duration of Ride: 5 minutes
Loading Speed: Fast
Probable Waiting Time Per 100 People Ahead of You: 3 minutes
Assumes: All 8 boats are running

Description and Comments The original Jaws ride never operated dependably and was dismantled. Its replacement, in which guests on a boat battle the great white shark, opened in summer 1993. This version, while also mechanically temperamental, runs most of the time. It delivers five minutes of nonstop action, with the huge shark repeatedly attacking. A West Virginia woman, fresh from the Magic Kingdom, told us the shark is "about as pesky as that witch in Snow White." While the story is entirely predictable, the shark is realistic and as big as Rush Limbaugh.

What makes the ride unique is its sense of journey. Jaws builds an amazing degree of suspense. It isn't just a cruise into the middle of a pond where a rubber fish assaults the boat interminably. Add inventive sets and powerful special effects, and you have a first-rate attraction.

A variable at Jaws is the enthusiasm and acting ability of your boat guide. Throughout the ride, the guide must set the tone, elaborate the plot, drive the boat, and fight the shark. Most guides are quite good. They may overact a bit, but you can't fault them for lack of enthusiasm. Consider also that each guide repeats this wrenching ordeal every eight minutes.

Touring Tips Jaws is as well designed to handle crowds as any theme park attraction in Florida. People on the boat's left side tend to get splashed more. If you have young children, consider switching off (pages 165–167).

A mother of two from Williamsville, New York, who believes our warning about getting wet should be more strongly emphasized, has this to say:

> *Your warning about the "Jaws" attraction . . . is woefully understated. Please warn your readers—we were seated on the first row of the boat. My 9-year-old sat at the end of the boat (first person on the far left), and I was seated next to him. We were wary of these seats as I had read your warning, but I felt prepared. NOT!!!! At "that" moment the water came flooding over the left front side of the boat thoroughly drenching the two of us and filling our sneakers with water. Unfortunately for us, this was*

only our third attraction of the day (9:30 a.m.) and we still had a long day ahead of us. It was a rather chilly and windy 62° day. We went to the rest rooms, removed our shorts, and squeezed out as much water as we could, but we were very cold and uncomfortable all day. This will be our most vivid and lasting memory of our day at Universal Studios!!!

A dad from Seattle suggests that getting wet takes a backseat to being terrified:

Our 8-year-old was so frightened by Jaws that we scrapped the rest of the Universal tour and went back to E.T. An employee said she wouldn't recommend it to anyone under 10. Maybe you should change "may frighten small children" to "definitely will scare the pants off most children."

Back to the Future—The Ride

What It Is: Flight-simulator thrill ride

Scope & Scale: Super headliner

When to Go: First thing in the morning

Special Comments: Very rough ride; may induce motion sickness. Must be 3'4" tall to ride. Switching off available (pages 165–167)

Author's Rating: Not to be missed, if you have a strong stomach; ★★★★★

Appeal by Age Group:

Pre-school	Grade School	Teens	Young Adults	Over 30	Senior Citizens
†	★★★★★	★★★★★	★★★★★	★★★★	★★½

† Sample size too small for an accurate rating

Duration of Ride: 4½ minutes

Loading Speed: Moderate

Description and Comments This attraction is to Universal Studios Florida what Space Mountain is to the Magic Kingdom: the most popular thrill ride in the park. Guests in Doc Brown's lab get caught up in a high-speed chase through time that spans a million years. An extremely intense simulator ride, Back to the Future is similar to Star Tours and Body Wars at Walt Disney World but is much rougher and more jerky. Though the story doesn't make much sense, the visual effects are wild and powerful. The vehicles (Delorean time machines) in Back to the Future are much smaller than those of Star Tours and Body Wars, so the ride feels more personal and less like a group experience.

In a survey of 84 tourists who had experienced simulator rides in both Universal Studios and Disney World, riders younger than 35 preferred Back to the Future to the Disney attractions by a seven-to-four margin. Older riders, however, stated a two-to-one preference for Star Tours over Back to the Future or Body Wars. The remarks of a woman from Mount Holly, New Jersey, are typical:

> *Our favorite [overall] attraction was Back to the Future at Universal. Comparing it to Star Tours and Body Wars, it was more realistic because the screen surrounds you.*

Most guests also find Back to the Future wilder than its Disney cousins. A Michigan woman writes:

> *Back to the Future was off the charts on the scary-o-meter. It made Splash and Big Thunder mountains seem like carnival kiddie rides. Even Busch Gardens' Kumba was tame by comparison.*

An English woman from Fleet Hants, who was tired of being jerked around, finally got mad (go girl!):

> *The simulators were fun, but they do seem to go out of their way to jerk you about, and the Back to the Future one was SO jerky that it made me quite angry.*

A man from Evansville, Indiana, reminds us that Back to the Future can humble even the most intrepid:

> *The Back to the Future ride at Universal was very rough and we are members of a roller coaster club. We have seldom experienced such a rough ride and ridden over 300 coasters. If it was too strong for us, we shudder to think about mere mortals.*

Because the height requirement on Back to the Future has been lowered from 3'10" to 3'4", younger children are riding. Many of them require preparation. A Virginia mother suggests:

> *The five-year-old was apprehensive about the ride, but he liked it a lot. We assured him ahead of time that (1) it's only a movie, and (2) the car doesn't actually go anywhere, just shakes around. This seemed to increase his ability to enjoy that ride (rather than taking all the fun out of it).*

Touring Tips   As soon the park opens, guests stampede to Back to the Future. Our recommendation: Be there when the park opens, and join the rush. If you don't ride before 10 a.m., your wait may be exceptionally long. *Note:* Sitting in the rear seat of the car makes the ride more realistic.

E.T. Adventure

What It Is: Indoor adventure ride based on the *E.T.* movie
Scope & Scale: Major attraction
When to Go: Before 10 a.m.
Special Comments: This ride was renovated and greatly improved in 1992
Author's Rating: ★★★★
Appeal by Age Group:

Pre-school	Grade School	Teens	Young Adults	Over 30	Senior Citizens
★★★★	★★★★	★★★½	★★★½	★★★½	★★★½

Duration of Ride: 4½ minutes
Load Speed: Moderate

Description and Comments Guests aboard a bicycle-like conveyance escape with E.T. from earthly law enforcement officials and then journey to E.T.'s home planet. The attraction is similar to Peter Pan's Flight at the Magic Kingdom but is longer and has more elaborate special effects and a wilder ride.

Touring Tips Most preschoolers and grade-school children love E.T. We think it worth a 20- to 30-minute wait, but nothing longer. Lines build quickly after 9:45 a.m., and waits can be more than two hours on busy days. Ride in the morning, right after Back to the Future. Guests who balk at sitting on the bicycle can ride in a comfortable gondola.

A mother from Columbus, Ohio, writes about horrendous lines at E.T.:

> *The line for E.T. took two hours! The rest of the family waiting outside thought that we had gone to E.T.'s planet for real.*

A woman from Richmond, Virginia, objects to how Universal represented the waiting time:

> *We got into E.T. without much wait, but the line is very deceptive. When you see a lot of people waiting outside and the sign says "10 minute wait from this point," it means 10 minutes until you are inside the building. But there's a very long wait inside [before] you get to the moving vehicles.*

Animal Actors Stage

What It Is: Trained-animals stadium performance
Scope & Scale: Major attraction
When to Go: After you have experienced all rides

Author's Rating: Warm and delightful; ★★★½

Appeal by Age Group:

Pre-school	Grade School	Teens	Young Adults	Over 30	Senior Citizens
★★★★½	★★★★	★★★½	★★★½	★★★½	★★★½

Duration of Presentation: 20 minutes

Probable Waiting Time: 25 minutes

Description and Comments Humorous demonstration of how animals are trained for films. Well-paced and informative, the show features cats, dogs, monkeys, birds, and other creatures. Sometimes animals don't behave as expected, but that's half the fun. Often the animal stars are quite famous. In 1998, for example, the pig from the acclaimed movie *Babe* was featured.

Touring Tips We would like this show better if guests could simply walk in and sit down. As it is, everyone must line up to be admitted. Presented six to ten times daily, the program's schedule is in the daily entertainment guide. Go when it's convenient for you; queue about 15 minutes before show time.

Dynamite Nights Stuntacular

What It Is: Simulated stunt-scene filming

Scope & Scale: Major attraction

When to Go: In the evening according to the daily entertainment schedule

Author's Rating: Well done; ★★★★

Appeal by Age Group:

Pre-school	Grade School	Teens	Young Adults	Over 30	Senior Citizens
★★★	★★★★	★★★★	★★★★	★★★½	★★★½

Duration of Presentation: 20 minutes

Probable Waiting Time: None

Description and Comments Each evening on the lagoon, stunt men demonstrate spectacular stunts and special effects. The plot involves lawmen trying to intercept and apprehend drug smugglers. Our main problem with this show is that the lagoon is so large that it's somewhat difficult to follow the action. The production was upgraded in 1994 and 1997.

Touring Tips This version is on a par with Disney-MGM's stunt show. Onlookers watch from the rail encircling the lagoon. There's no waiting in line, but if you want a really good vantage point, stake out your position about 25 minutes before show time. The best viewing spots are along the docks at Lombard's Landing and adjacent areas on the Embarcadero water-front, across the street from Earthquake. Primary viewing spots are identified on the park map with a "PV" icon.

The Wild, Wild, Wild West Stunt Show

What It Is: Stunt show with a western theme

Scope & Scale: Major attraction

When to Go: After you've experienced all rides

Author's Rating: Solid and exciting; ★★★★

Appeal by Age Group:

Pre-school	Grade School	Teens	Young Adults	Over 30	Senior Citizens
★★★★½	★★★★	★★★★	★★★★	★★★★	★★★★

Duration of Presentation: 16 minutes

Probable Waiting Time: None

Description and Comments   The *Wild West* stunt show has shootouts, fist-fights, horse tricks, and high falls, all exciting and well executed. The fast-paced show is staged about ten times daily in a 2,000-seat, covered stadium. Unlike the stunt show on the lagoon, the action is easy to follow.

Touring Tips   Show times are listed in the daily entertainment guide; go at your convenience. During summer, the stadium is more comfortable after dusk.

Fievel's Playland

What It Is: Children's play area with water slide

Scope & Scale: Minor attraction

When to Go: Anytime

Author's Rating: A much-needed attraction for preschoolers; ★★★★

Appeal by Age Group:

Pre-school	Grade School	Teens	Young Adults	Over 30	Senior Citizens
★★★★	★★★★	★★★	★★★	★★★	★★★

Probable Waiting Time: 20–30 minutes for the water slide; otherwise, no waiting

Description and Comments   Imaginative playground features ordinary household items reproduced on a giant scale, as a mouse would experience them. Preschoolers and grade-schoolers can climb nets, walk through a huge boot, splash in a sardine-can fountain, seesaw on huge spoons, and climb onto a cow skull. Most of the playground is reserved for preschoolers, but a water slide/raft ride is open to all ages.

Touring Tips   Walk into Fievel's Playland without waiting, and stay as long as you want. Younger children love the oversized items, and there's enough to keep teens and adults busy while little ones let off steam. The water slide/raft ride is open to everyone but is extremely slow-loading and carries only 300 riders per hour. With the wait an average of 20–30 minutes, we don't think the 16-second ride is worth the trouble. Also, you're highly likely to get soaked.

Lack of shade is a major shortcoming of the entire attraction. Don't go during the heat of the day.

Beetlejuice's Rock 'n Roll Graveyard Revue

What It Is: Rock-and-roll stage show
Scope & Scale: Minor attraction
When to Go: At your convenience
Author's Rating: Outrageous; ★★★½
Appeal by Age Group:

Pre-school	Grade School	Teens	Young Adults	Over 30	Senior Citizens
★★★★	★★★★	★★★★	★★★½	★★★½	★★★½

Duration of Presentation: 16 minutes
Probable Waiting Time: None

Description and Comments   High-powered rock-and-roll stage show stars Beetlejuice, Frankenstein, the Bride of Frankenstein, Wolfman, Dracula, and the Phantom of the Opera. In addition to fine vintage rock, the show features some of the most exuberant choreography found anywhere, plus impressive sets and special effects.

Touring Tips   Mercifully, this attraction has been moved under cover.

A Day in the Park with Barney

What It Is: Live character stage show
Scope & Scale: Major children's attraction
When to Go: Anytime
Author's Rating: A great hit with preschoolers; ★★★★
Appeal by Age Group:

Pre-school	Grade School	Teens	Young Adults	Over 30	Senior Citizens
★★★★½	★★★	★★	★★½	★★★	★★★

Duration of Presentation: 12 minutes plus character greeting
Probable Waiting Time: 15 minutes

Description and Comments   Barney, the purple dinosaur of Public Television fame, leads a sing-along with the help of the audience and side-kicks Baby Bop and BJ. A short preshow gets the kids lathered up before they enter the theater, Barney's Park. Interesting theatrical effects include wind, falling leaves, clouds and stars in the simulated sky, and snow. After the show, Barney exits momentarily to allow parents and children to gather along the stage. He then thunders back and moves from child to child, hugging each and posing for photos.

Touring Tips   If your child likes Barney, this show is a must. It's happy and upbeat, and the character greeting that follows is the best organized we've seen in any theme park. There's no line and no fighting for Barney's attention. Just relax by the rail and await your hug.

Lucy, a Tribute

What It Is: Walk-through tribute to Lucille Ball
Scope & Scale: Diversion
When to Go: Anytime
Author's Rating: A touching remembrance; ★★★
Appeal by Age Group:

Pre-school	Grade School	Teens	Young Adults	Over 30	Senior Citizens
★	★	★★	★★★	★★★	★★★

Probable Waiting Time: None

Description and Comments   The life and career of comedienne Lucille Ball are spotlighted, with emphasis on her role as Lucy Ricardo in the long-running television series *I Love Lucy.* Well designed and informative, the exhibit succeeds admirably in recalling the talent and temperament of the beloved redhead.

Touring Tips   See Lucy during the hot, crowded midafternoon, or on your way out of the park. Adults could easily stay 15–30 minutes. Children, however, get restless after a couple of minutes.

Street Scenes

What It Is: Elaborate outdoor sets for making films
Scope & Scale: Diversion
When to Go: Anytime

Special Comments: You'll see most sets without special effort as you tour the park

Author's Rating: One of the park's great assets; ★★★★★

Appeal by Age Group:

Pre-school	Grade School	Teens	Young Adults	Over 30	Senior Citizens
★★★	★★★★½	★★★★½	★★★★½	★★★★★	★★★★★

Probable Waiting Time: No waiting

Description and Comments   Unlike at Disney-MGM Studios, all Universal Studios Florida's backlot sets are accessible for guest inspection. They include New York City streets, San Francisco's waterfront, a New England coastal town, the house from *Psycho,* Rodeo Drive and Hollywood Boulevard, and a Louisiana bayou.

Touring Tips   You'll see most as you walk through the park.

One-Day Touring Plan for Universal Studios Florida

This plan is for all visitors. If a ride or show is listed that you don't want to experience, skip that step and proceed to the next. Move quickly from attraction to attraction and, if possible, don't stop for lunch until after Step 10.

Buying Admission to Universal Studios Florida

One of our big gripes about Universal Studios is that there never are enough ticket windows open in the morning to accommodate the crowd. You can arrive 45 minutes before official opening time and still be in line to buy your admission when the park opens. Therefore, we strongly recommend you buy your admission in advance. Passes are available by mail from Universal Studios at (800) 224-3838. They are also sold at the concierge desk or attractions box office of many Orlando-area hotels. If your hotel doesn't offer tickets, try Guest Services at the Radisson Twin Towers (407) 351-1000, at the intersection of Major Boulevard and Kirkman Avenue, directly across from the main entrance of Universal Studios.

Many hotels that sell Universal admissions don't issue actual passes. Instead, the purchaser gets a voucher that can be redeemed for a pass at the theme park. Fortunately, the voucher-redemption window is separate from the park's ticket sales operation. You can quickly exchange your voucher for a pass and be on your way with little or no wait.

Touring Plan

1. Call (407) 363-8000 the day before your visit for the official opening time.

2. On the day of your visit, eat breakfast and arrive at Universal Studios Florida 50 minutes before opening time with your admission pass or an admission voucher in hand. If you have a voucher, exchange it for a pass at the voucher-redemption window. Pick up a map and the daily entertainment schedule.

3. Line up at the turnstile. Ask any attendant whether any rides or shows are closed that day. Adjust the touring plan accordingly.

4. When the park opens, take a right on Hollywood Boulevard, pass Mel's Diner (on your left), and (keeping the lagoon on your left) go directly to Back to the Future. Ride.

5. Exit left and pass the International Food Bazaar. Continue bearing left past the *Animal Actors Stage* and go to the E.T. Adventure. Ride.

6. Retrace your steps toward Back to the Future. Keeping the lagoon on your left, cross the bridge to Amity. Ride Jaws.

7. Exit and turn left down The Embarcadero. Postpone Earthquake and head directly to Kongfrontation in the New York set. Go ape.

8. Return to San Francisco. Ride Earthquake—The Big One.

9. Work your way back toward the main entrance and ride The Funtastic World of Hanna-Barbera. Expect to wait 25–40 minutes. If you've had enough simulator rides for now, skip to Step 10.

10. If you're still intact after the Flintstones, a bike ride to another galaxy, a shark attack, an earthquake, and an encounter with King Kong, take on a tornado. Return to the New York set and see *Twister*. The line will appear long but should move quickly as guests are admitted inside.

11. If you haven't already eaten, do so now. Cafe La Bamba in the Hollywood area serves tacos and burgers, and Mel's Diner nearby has decent, machine-made milk shakes. The Inter-national Food Bazaar next to Back to the Future serves gyros, bratwurst, pizza, and other ethnic fare. In the New York area, we like Louie's Italian Restaurant for pizza, calzone, and salads. Outrageous sandwiches and pastries are the specialty of Beverly Hills Boulangerie near the park's main entrance. If you're in the mood for more relaxed,

upscale dining, the park's nicest restaurant is Lombard's Landing on the waterfront (across from Earthquake). In addition to prime rib and creative seafood entrees, Lombard's serves an exceptional hamburger at a fair price.

12. At this point you have eight major attractions yet to see:

> *Terminator 2: 3-D*
> *The Gory Gruesome & Grotesque Horror Make-Up Show*
> *Hercules and Xena*
> *Animal Actors Stage*
> *Dynamite Nights Stuntacular*
> *The Wild, Wild, Wild West Stunt Show*
> "Alfred Hitchcock: The Art of Making Movies"
> *Beetlejuice's Rock 'n Roll Graveyard Revue*

Animal Actors Stage, the *Beetlejuice* show, and the stunt shows are performed several times daily, as listed in the entertainment schedule. Plan the remainder of your itinerary according to the next listed shows for these presentations. The *Horror Make-Up Show* and *Hercules and Xena* (on opposite sides of Mel's Diner) run pretty much continuously and can be worked in as time permits. Try to see *Terminator 2: 3-D* after 3:30 p.m., but whatever you do, don't miss it. Save "Alfred Hitchcock" for your last attraction as you leave the park.

13. Our touring plan doesn't include the Nickelodeon Studios Tour or *A Day in the Park with Barney*. If you have school-age children in your party, consider taking the Nickelodeon tour in late afternoon or on a second day at the park. If you're touring with preschoolers, see Barney after you ride E.T.

14. This concludes the touring plan. Spend the remainder of your day revisiting your favorite attractions or inspecting sets and street scenes you may have missed. Also, check your daily entertainment schedule for live performances that interest you.

Universal's Islands of Adventure Theme Park

When Universal's Islands of Adventure theme park opens in 1999, it will provide Universal with enough critical mass to actually compete with Disney. For the first time, Universal will have on-site hotels, a shopping and entertainment complex, and two major theme parks. Doubly interesting is that the new Universal park will be pretty much just for fun, in other words, a direct competitor to Disney's Magic Kingdom, the most visited theme park in the world.

How direct a competitor is it? Check this out:

Islands of Adventure	Magic Kingdom
Six Islands (includes Port of Entry)	Seven Lands (includes Main Street)
Two roller coaster attractions	Two roller coaster attractions
Two Dumbo-type rides	Two Dumbo-type rides
One flume ride	One flume ride
Toon Lagoon character area	Mickey's Toontown Fair character area

And though it may take central Florida tourists awhile to make the connection, here's what will dawn on them when they finally do: Universal's Islands of Adventure is a brand-new, state-of-the-art park competing with a Disney park that is more than 25 years old and has not added a major new attraction for three years.

Of course, that's only how it looks on paper. The reality, as they say, is still blowing in the wind. The Magic Kingdom, after all, is graceful in its maturity and much beloved. And then there's this: Will all of Universal's Islands of Adventure's innovative, high-tech attractions work this time around? Or will we see a repeat of the disastrous first year that Universal Studios Florida experienced? Signals are mixed. *Terminator 2: 3-D* is ample evidence that Universal knows how to run a hit up the pop charts. On the other hand, the Jurassic Park ride at Universal Studios California has not lived up to its hype. One thing is for sure, however: the clash of the titans is once again hot. Universal is coming on strong with the potential of sucking up three days of a tourist's week (four days, if you include Universal's strategic relationship with Sea World). And that's more time than anyone has spent off the Disney campus for a long, long time.

BEWARE OF THE WET AND WILD

Although we have described Universal's Islands of Adventure as a direct competitor to the Magic Kingdom, there is one major qualification you should be aware of. Whereas most Magic Kingdom attractions are designed to be enjoyed by guests of any age, attractions at Islands of Adventure are largely created for an under-40 population. The roller coasters at Universal are serious with a capital "S," making Space Mountain and

Big Thunder Mountain look about as tough as Dumbo. In fact, seven out of the nine top attractions at Islands are thrill rides, and of these, there are three that not only scare the bejeebers out of you but also drench you with water.

In addition to thrill seekers, families with young children will find a lot to do at Islands of Adventure. There are three interactive playgrounds for little ones, as well as four rides that young children will enjoy. Of the thrill rides, only the two in Toon Lagoon (described later) are marginally appropriate for young children, and even on these rides your child needs to be fairly stalwart.

GETTING ORIENTED

Both Universal theme parks are accessed via the Universal CityWalk entertainment complex. Crossing CityWalk from the parking garages, you can bear right to Universal Studios Florida or left to Universal's Islands of Adventure.

Universal's Islands of Adventure is arranged much like the World Showcase section of Epcot, that is, in a large circle surrounding a lake. Unlike Epcot, however, the Islands of Adventure theme areas evidence the sort of thematic continuity pioneered by Disneyland and the Magic Kingdom. Each land, or island in this case, is self-contained and visually consistent in its theme, though you can see parts of the other islands across the lake.

Passing through the turnstiles, you first encounter the Moroccan-style Port of Entry, where you will find Guest Services, lockers, stroller and wheelchair rentals, ATM banking, lost and found, and, of course, shopping. From the Port of Entry, moving clockwise around the lake, you can access Marvel Super Hero Island, Toon Lagoon, Jurassic Park, Lost Continent, and Seuss Landing. You can crisscross the lake on small boats, but otherwise there is no in-park transportation.

MARVEL SUPER HERO ISLAND

This island, with its futuristic and retro-future design, offers shopping and attractions based on Marvel Comic characters.

The Adventures of Spider-Man

What It Is: Indoor adventure ride based tenuously on Spider-Man
Scope & Scale: Super headliner
When to Go: Before 10:30 a.m.
Author's Rating: Not open at press time

Appeal by Age Group: Not open at press time

Duration of Ride: 4½ minutes

Loading Speed: Fast

Description and Comments   Covering 1½ acres and combining moving ride vehicles, 3-D film, and live action, Spider-Man is widely regarded to be Universal's answer to Disney-MGM's Tower of Terror. The story line is that you are touring the offices of the *Daily Bugle* newspaper (where Peter Parker, a.k.a. Spider-Man works as a mild-mannered reporter), when it's discovered that evil villains have stolen (I promise I'm not making this up) the Statue of Liberty. You are drafted on the spot to join a posse to save Ms. Liberty. After speeding around and being thrust into "a battle between good and evil," you will experience a "sensory drop" of 400 feet into darkness.

Touring Tips   Ride first thing in the morning or two hours before closing.

The Incredible Hulk Coaster

What It Is: Roller coaster

Scope & Scale: Headliner

When to Go: Before 10:30 a.m.

Author's Rating: Not open at press time

Appeal by Age Group: Not open at press time

Duration of Ride: 2½ minutes

Loading Speed: Moderate

Description and Comments   There is as always a story line, but for this attraction it's of no importance whatsoever. What you need to know about this attraction is simple. You will be launched like a cannonball shot from 0 to 40 miles per hour in 2 seconds, and then you will be flung upside down 100 feet off the ground, which will, of course, induce weightlessness. From there it's a mere seven rollovers punctuated by two plunges into holes in the ground before you're allowed to get out and throw up.

Touring Tips   What more is there? Can you say CRAZEE? Ride immediately after Spider-Man.

Dr. Doom's Fearfall

What It Is: Lunch liberator

Scope & Scale: Headliner

When to Go: Before 10:30 a.m.

Author's Rating: Not open at press time

Appeal by Age Group: Not open at press time

Duration of Ride: 1½ minutes
Loading Speed: Slow

Description and Comments Here you are (again) strapped into a seat with your feet dangling and blasted 200 feet up in the air and then allowed to partially free-fall back down. If you are having trouble forming a mental image of this attraction, picture the midway game where a macho guy swings a sledgehammer, propelling a metal sphere up a vertical shaft. At the top of the shaft is a bell. If the macho man drives the sphere high enough to ring the bell, he wins a prize. Got the idea? OK, on this ride you are the metal sphere.

Touring Tips Ride in the morning after Spider-Man and Hulk.

TOON LAGOON

Toon Lagoon is cartoon art translated into real buildings and settings. Whimsical and gaily colored, with rounded and exaggerated lines, Toon Lagoon is Universal's answer to Mickey's Toontown Fair in the Magic Kingdom. The main difference between the two toon lands is that (as you will see) you've about a 60% chance of going into hypothermia at Universal's version.

Dudley Do-Right's Ripsaw Falls

What It Is: Flume ride
Scope & Scale: Headliner
When to Go: Before 10:30 a.m.
Author's Rating: Not open at press time
Appeal by Age Group: Not open at press time
Duration of Ride: 5½ minutes
Loading Speed: Moderate

Description and Comments Inspired by the *Rocky and Bullwinkle* cartoon series, this ride features Canadian Mountie Dudley Do-Right as he attempts to save Nell from evil Snidely Whiplash. Story line aside, it's a flume ride, with the inevitable big drop at the end. Universal claims this is the first flume ride to "send riders plummeting 15 feet below the surface of the water." We're not exactly sure how this works, but it sounds like you better bring your diving gear.

Touring Tips This ride is bound to leave you soggy unless you arrive prepared with a poncho or at least a big garbage bag with holes cut out for your head and arms. Ride after experiencing the Marvel Super Hero rides.

Popeye & Bluto's Bilge-Rat Barges

What It Is: Whitewater raft ride
Scope & Scale: Headliner
When to Go: Before 10:30 a.m.
Author's Rating: Not open at press time
Appeal by Age Group: Not open at press time
Duration of Ride: 4½ minutes
Loading Speed: Moderate

Description and Comments   This sweetly named attraction is a whitewater raft ride that includes an encounter with an 18-foot-tall octopus. Engineered to ensure that everyone gets drenched, the ride even provides water cannons for highly intelligent nonparticipants ashore to fire at those aboard.

Touring Tips   If you didn't drown on Dudley Do-Right, here's a second chance. You'll get a lot wetter from the knees down on this ride, so use your poncho or garbage bag and ride barefoot with your britches rolled up.

Me Ship, The Olive

What It Is: Interactive playground
Scope & Scale: Minor attraction
When to Go: Before 10:30 a.m.
Author's Rating: Not open at press time
Appeal by Age Group: Not open at press time

Description and Comments   *The Olive* is Popeye's three-story boat come to life as an interactive playground. Younger children can scramble around in Swee' Pea's Playpen, while older sibs shoot water cannons at riders trying to survive the adjacent Bilge-Rat raft ride.

Touring Tips   If you are into the big rides, save the playground for later in the day.

Comic Strip Lane

What It Is: Walk-through exhibit and shopping/dining venue
Scope & Scale: Diversion
When to Go: Anytime
Author's Rating: Not open at press time
Appeal by Age Group: Not open at press time

Description and Comments   This is the main street of Toon Lagoon. Here you can visit the domains of Beetle Bailey, Hagar the Horrible, Krazy Kat, the Family Circus, and Blondie and Dagwood, among others. Shops and eateries tie into the cartoon-strip theme.

Touring Tips   This is a great place for photo ops with cartoon characters in their own environment. It's also a great place to drop a few bucks in the diners and shops, but you probably already figured that out.

JURASSIC PARK

Jurassic Park (for anyone who's been asleep for 20 years) is a Steven Spielberg film about a fictitious theme park with real dinosaurs. Jurassic Park at Universal's Islands of Adventure is a real theme park (or at least a section of one) with fictitious dinosaurs.

Jurassic Park River Adventure

What It Is: Indoor/outdoor adventure ride based on the *Jurassic Park* movie

Scope & Scale: Super headliner

When to Go: Before 10:30 a.m.

Author's Rating: Not open at press time

Appeal by Age Group: Not open at press time

Duration of Ride: 6 minutes

Loading Speed: Fast

Description and Comments   Guests board boats for a water tour of Jurassic Park. Everything is tranquil as the tour begins, and the boat floats among large herbivorous dinosaurs such as brontosaurus and stegosaurus. Then, as word is received that some of the carnivores have escaped their enclosure, the tour boat is accidentally diverted into Jurassic Park's maintenance facilities. Here, the boat and its riders are menaced by an assortment of hungry meat eaters led by the ubiquitous T-Rex. At the climactic moment, the boat and its passengers escape by plummeting over an 85-foot drop billed as the "longest, fastest, steepest water descent ever built" (did anyone other than me notice the omission of the word wettest?).

Touring Tips   You can get very wet on this ride. Even before the boat leaves the dock you must sit in the puddles left by previous riders. Once underway there's a little splashing, but nothing major until the big drop at the end of the ride. When you hit the bottom, however, enough water will cascade into the boat to extinguish a three-alarm fire. Our recommendation is to bring along an extra-large plastic garbage bag and (cutting holes for your head and arms) wear it like a sack dress. If you forget to bring a garbage bag, you can purchase a Universal Studios poncho for $7.50.

Young children must endure a double whammy on this ride. First, they are stalked by giant, salivating (sometimes spitting) reptiles, and then they're sent catapulting over the falls. Unless your children are fairly stalwart, wait a year or two before you spring Jurassic Park on them.

Triceratops Encounter

What It Is: Prehistoric petting zoo

Scope & Scale: Major attraction

When to Go: Before 10:30 a.m.

Author's Rating: Not open at press time

Appeal by Age Group: Not open at press time

Duration of Show: 5 minutes

Probable Waiting Time: 15–25 minutes

Description and Comments Guests are ushered in groups into a "feed and control station," where they can view and pet a 24-foot-long, animatronic triceratops dinosaur. While the trainer lectures about the creature's behaviors, habits, and lifestyle, the triceratops breathes, blinks, chews, and flinches at the touch of the guests.

Touring Tips Nothing is for sure, but this may be the only attraction in the park where you won't get wet. Just to be sure, however, stand near the middle of the dinosaur.

Discovery Center

What It Is: Interactive natural history exhibit

Scope & Scale: Minor attraction

When to Go: Anytime

Author's Rating: Not open at press time

Appeal by Age Group: Not open at press time

Description and Comments The Discovery Center is an interactive, educational exhibit that mixes fiction from the movie, such as using fossil DNA to bring dinosaurs to life, with various skeletal remains and other paleontological displays. One exhibit allows guests to watch an animatronic raptor being hatched.

Touring Tips Cycle back after experiencing all the rides. Most folks can digest this exhibit in 10–15 minutes.

Pteranodon Flyers

What It Is: Dinosaur version of Dumbo, the Flying Elephant

Scope & Scale: Minor attraction

When to Go: Before 10:30 a.m.

Author's Rating: Not open at press time

Appeal by Age Group: Not open at press time

Duration of Ride: 1½ minutes

Loading Speed: Slow

Description and Comments This elaborate midway-inspired ride features flying dinosaurs with ten-foot wing spans revolving around a central axis with you on their back. The best thing about this ride is the view overlooking the tropical landscaping of Camp Jurassic. The pteranodons are not quite as cuddly as Dumbo, but they get the job done.

Touring Tips This one is bound to load slowly. Ride early or be prepared to wait.

Camp Jurassic

What It Is: Interactive play area

Scope & Scale: Minor attraction

When to Go: Anytime

Author's Rating: Not open at press time

Appeal by Age Group: Not open at press time

Description and Comments Camp Jurassic is a great place for children to let off steam. Sort of a Jurassic version of Tom Sawyer Island, kids can explore lava pits, caves, mines, and a rain forest inhabited by a few animatronic dinosaurs.

Touring Tips Camp Jurassic will fire the imaginations of the under-13 set. If you don't impose a time limit on the exploration, you'll probably be here awhile.

LOST CONTINENT

This theme area is an exotic mix of Silk Road bazaar and ancient ruins, with Greco-Moroccan accents. And you thought your decorator was nuts. Anyway, this is the land of mythical gods, fabled beasts, and expensive souvenirs.

Poseidon's Fury! Escape from the Lost City

What It Is: High-tech theater attraction
Scope & Scale: Headliner
When to Go: Before 10:30 a.m.
Author's Rating: Not open at press time
Appeal by Age Group: Not open at press time
Duration of Presentation: 15 minutes including preshow
Probable Wait: 25 minutes

Description and Comments   In this megatheater attraction, Poseidon, the Greek god of the sea, dukes it out with Zeus, the supreme deity of the ancient Greeks. All this happens, of course, with you in the middle, but with less subtlety than in the average dysfunctional family quarrel. The operative word in this brawl is special effects. Poseidon fights with water, 350,000 gallons to be specific, while Zeus uses fire.

Touring Tips   If you are still wet from Dudley Do-Right, the Bilge-Rat Barges, and the Jurassic Park River Adventure, you will probably be pulling for Zeus in hopes you might finally dry out. Our money, however, is on Poseidon. It's legal in Florida for theme parks to get you wet, but setting you on fire is somewhat frowned upon.

Dueling Dragons

What It Is: Roller coaster
Scope & Scale: Headliner
When to Go: Before 10:30 a.m.
Author's Rating: Not open at press time
Appeal by Age Group: Not open at press time
Duration of Ride: 2½ minutes
Loading Speed: Moderate

Description and Comments   This high-tech coaster launches two trains at the same time on tracks that are closely intertwined. Each track, however, is differently configured so that you get a different experience on each. Several times a collision with the other train seems imminent, a catastrophe that seems all the more real because the coasters are inverted (i.e., suspended from above so that you sit with your feet dangling). At times, the two trains and their passengers are separated by a mere 12 inches.

Touring Tips   The good news about this ride is that you won't get wet unless you wet yourself. The bad news is that wetting yourself comes pretty naturally.

The Eighth Voyage of Sinbad

What It Is: Theater stunt show
Scope & Scale: Major attraction
When to Go: Before 10:30 a.m.
Author's Rating: Not open at press time
Appeal by Age Group: Not open at press time
Duration of Presentation: 1½ minutes
Probable Waiting Time: 15 minutes

Description and Comments   A story about Sinbad the Sailor is the glue that (loosely) binds this stunt show featuring water explosions, ten-foot-tall circles of flame, and various other daunting eruptions.

Touring Tips   The theater seats 1,700; performance times are listed in the daily entertainment schedule.

SEUSS LANDING

A ten-acre island based on Dr. Seuss's famous children's books.

The Cat in the Hat

What It Is: Indoor adventure ride
Scope & Scale: Major attraction
When to Go: Before 10:30 a.m.
Author's Rating: Not open at press time
Appeal by Age Group: Not open at press time
Duration of Ride: 5 minutes
Loading Speed: Moderate

Description and Comments   Guests ride on "couches" through 18 different sets inhabited by animatronic Seuss characters, including The Cat in the Hat, "Thing 1," "Thing 2," and the beleaguered goldfish who tries to maintain order in the midst of mayhem.

Touring Tips   This should be fun for all ages. Try to ride early.

One Fish, Two Fish, Red Fish, Blue Fish

What It Is: Wet version of Dumbo, the Flying Elephant
Scope & Scale: Minor attraction
When to Go: Before 10:30 a.m.
Author's Rating: Not open at press time

Appeal by Age Group: Not open at press time

Duration of Ride: 2 minutes

Loading Speed: Slow

Description and Comments   Imagine Dumbo with Seuss-style fish instead of elephants and you've got half the story. The other half of the story involves yet another opportunity to drown. Guests steer their fish up or down 15 feet in the air while traveling in circles. At the same time, they try to avoid streams of water projected from "squirt posts."

Touring Tips   We don't know what it is about this theme park and water, but you'll get wetter than at a full-emersion baptism.

Caro-Seuss-El

What It Is: Merry-go-round

Scope & Scale: Minor attraction

When to Go: Before 10:30 a.m.

Author's Rating: Not open at press time

Appeal by Age Group: Not open at press time

Duration of Ride: 2 minutes

Loading Speed: Slow

Description and Comments   Totally outrageous, the Caro-Seuss-El is a full-scale, 57-mount merry-go-round made up exclusively of Dr. Seuss characters.

Touring Tips   Even if you are too old or don't want to ride, this attraction is worth an inspection. Whatever your age, chances are good you'll see some old friends. If you are touring with young children, try to get them on early in the morning.

Sylvester McMonkey McBean's Very Unusual Driving Machines

What It Is: Indoor/outdoor track ride

Scope & Scale: Major attraction

When to Go: Before 10:30 a.m.

Author's Rating: Not open at press time

Appeal by Age Group: Not open at press time

Duration of Ride: 5 minutes

Loading Speed: Slow

Description and Comments   This long-titled ride offers a tour of Seuss Landing on an elevated track, passing in and out of various attractions, shops, and restaurants. The inspiration, a Seuss book about discrimination, is sort of lost in the translation. Guests can, however (within limits), control the speed of their vehicle (conducive to bumping other cars), honk their horns, and shout expletives commonly associated with California freeway driving.

Touring Tips   Visually appealing. You can cover the same territory on foot.

If I Ran the Zoo

What It Is: Interactive playground
Scope & Scale: Minor attraction
When to Go: Before 10:30 a.m.
Author's Rating: Not open at press time
Appeal by Age Group: Not open at press time

Description and Comments   Based on Dr. Seuss's *If I Ran the Zoo,* this playground is divided into three distinct areas, Hedges, Water, and the New Zoo. Each area features various interactive elements, including, of course, another opportunity for a good soaking.

Touring Tips   Visit this playground after you've experienced all the major attractions.

One-Day Touring Plan for
Universal's Islands of Adventure

Because the Islands of Adventure theme park was in the midst of construction when the *Unofficial Guide* went to press, this touring plan represents an educated guess based on our understanding of the attractions and the layout of the park. It should, however, be close enough to save you some time. Be aware that there are an inordinate number of attractions in this park that will get you wet. If you want to experience them, come armed with ponchos, large plastic garbage bags, or some other protective covering. Failure to follow this prescription will make for a potentially squishy, sodden day.

   This plan is for groups of all sizes and ages and includes thrill rides that may induce motion sickness or get you wet. If the plan calls for you to experience an attraction that does not interest you, simply skip that attraction and proceed to the next step. Be aware that the plan calls for some backtracking. If you have young children in your party, customize the plan to fit their needs and take advantage of switching off at thrill rides.

1. Call (407) 363-8000, the main information number, the day before your visit for the official opening time. Try to purchase your admission sometime prior to the day you intend to tour.

2. On the day of your visit, eat breakfast and arrive at Universal Florida 50 minutes before opening time. Park, buy your admission (if you did not purchase it in advance), and wait at the turnstiles to be admitted.

3. While at the turnstile, ask an attendant whether any rides or shows are closed that day. Adjust the touring plan accordingly.

4. When the park opens, go straight through the Port of Entry and take a left, crossing the bridge into Marvel Super Hero Island.

5. Ride The Incredible Hulk Coaster.

6. Also on Super Hero Island, try Dr. Doom's Fearfall.

7. Also on Super Hero Island, experience The Adventures of Spider-Man.

8. Continuing clockwise around the lake, depart Super Hero Island and cross into Toon Lagoon.

9. In Toon Lagoon, ride Dudley Do-Right's Ripsaw Falls.

10. Also in Toon Lagoon, subject yourself to Popeye & Bluto's Bilge-Rat Barges.

11. After the barge ride, either walk or take a boat across the lake to Lost Continent.

12. At Lost Continent, ride both tracks of Dueling Dragons.

13. While at Lost Continent, experience Poseidon's Fury! Escape from the Lost City.

14. Depart Lost Continent, moving counterclockwise around the lake, and enter Jurassic Park.

15. In Jurassic Park, try the Jurassic Park River Adventure.

16. Also in Jurassic Park, check out the Triceratops Encounter.

17. Return to Lost Continent. Check the daily entertainment schedule for the next performance of *The Eighth Voyage of Sinbad* stunt show. If a show is scheduled to begin within 30

minutes or so, go ahead and check it out. Otherwise, skip ahead to Step 18 and work *Sinbad* in later.

18. From Lost Continent, move clockwise around the lake to Seuss Landing. Ride The Cat in the Hat.

19. While in Seuss Landing, ride Sylvester McMonkey.

20. At this point you will have done all the big stuff. Spend the rest of your day experiencing attractions that you bypassed earlier or repeating ones that you especially enjoyed.

About Sea World

Many dozens of readers have written to extol the virtues of Sea World. The following are representative.

An English family writes:

> *The best organized park [is] Sea World. The computer printout we got on arrival had a very useful show schedule, told us which areas were temporarily closed due to construction, and had a readily understandable map. Best of all, there was almost no queuing. Overall, we rated this day so highly that it is the park we would most like to visit again.*

A woman in Alberta, Canada, gives her opinion:

> *We chose Sea World as our fifth day at "The World." What a pleasant surprise! It was every bit as good (and in some ways better) than WDW itself. Well worth the admission, an excellent entertainment value, educational, well run, and better value for the dollar in food services. Perhaps expand your coverage to give them their due!*

A father of two from Winnipeg, Manitoba, gives Sea World's nighttime laser show top marks, commenting:

> *But the absolute topper is the closing laser show, which beats out IllumiNations at Epcot for extravaganza. The Sea World show combines fireworks, lasers, and moving holographic images back-projected on a curtain of water. In the word of our older daughter: awesome! And you watch the whole thing seated in the lakeside arena, instead of jostling for a standing view around the Epcot lagoon.*

A reader from Sylvania, Georgia, believes Disney could learn a thing or two from Sea World:

Star Ratings for Sea World Attractions

★★★★½	Terrors of the Deep (shark and eel exhibit)
★★★★½	Penguin Encounter (penguin and puffin exhibit)
★★★★	Manatees: The Last Generation (manatee exhibit)
★★★★	Wild Arctic (simulation ride and Arctic wildlife polar bears)
★★★★	Shamu Killer Whale Show
★★★★	Sea Lion and Otter Show
★★★★	Atlantis Water Ski Show
★★★★	Journey to Atlantis
★★★★	Pacific Point Preserve (sea lion exhibit)
★★★★	Shamu's Happy Harbor (children's play area)
★★★★	Whale and Dolphin Discovery Show
★★★½	Tropical Reef (reef-fish aquarium exhibit)
★★★	Hawaiian Rhythms (Polynesian dance and music)
★★½	Mermaids, Myths, & Monsters (fireworks and lasers; nights only)
★★½	Sea World Theater (Sea World propaganda and dancing fountains)
★★	Nautilus Theatre (musical revue)

Disney ought to take a look at how well this place is run. I know they don't have the same crowds or the exciting rides, but there is still a lot of entertainment here and never a wait. This allows you to set your pace without worrying about what you'll have to miss. You'll see it all no matter how you do it, you'll come away feeling you got better value for your dollars, you won't feel as tired as a Disney day, and you will probably learn more, too. Only downturn is you'll probably be hungry. Food is not one of the park's assets.

Okay here's what you need to know (for additional information, call (407) 363-2613):

Sea World is a world-class marine-life theme park near the intersection of I-4 and the Bee Line Expressway. Open daily from 9 a.m. to 10 p.m., Sea World charges about $40 admission (plus tax) for adults and $33 (plus tax) for children (ages three to nine). Five-day combination passes, which include admission to Sea World, Universal Studios, Wet 'n Wild, and

Busch Gardens, are also available. Parking is $5 per car, $7 per RV or camper. Discount coupons for Sea World admission are available in the free visitor magazine found in most hotel lobbies. Figure six to nine hours to see everything, but only five or so if you stick to the big deals.

Sea World is about the size of the Magic Kingdom and requires about the same amount of walking. Most attractions are accessible to nonambulatory disabled persons. In terms of size, quality, and creativity, Sea World is unequivocally on a par with Disney's major theme parks. Unlike Walt Disney World, however, Sea World primarily features stadium shows or walk-through exhibits. This means that you will spend about 90% less time waiting in line during eight hours at Sea World than you would for the same-length visit at a Disney park.

Because lines, with one or two exceptions, aren't much of a problem at Sea World, you can tour at almost any time of day. We recommend you start about 3:30 or 4 p.m. (when the park is open until 9 p.m. or later). Many of the day's early guests will have left by this hour, and you'll be able to enjoy the outdoor attractions in the relative cool of late afternoon and evening. If you visit in the morning, arrive early or late. Midmorning arrivals tend to create long waits at the ticket windows.

A daily entertainment schedule is printed conveniently on a placemat-sized map of the park. The four featured shows are:

- Shamu Killer Whale Show
- Sea Lion and Otter Show
- Atlantis Water Ski Show
- Whale and Dolphin Discovery Show

When you arrive, build your itinerary around these shows. You'll notice immediately as you check the performance times that they're scheduled in a way that makes it almost impossible to see them back to back. The Shamu show, for example, might run from 5 to 5:25 p.m. Ideally, you'd like to bop over to the Sea Lion and Otter Show, which begins at 5:30 p.m. Unfortunately, five minutes isn't enough time to exit Shamu Stadium and cross the park to the Sea Lion & Otter Stadium. Sea World, of course, planned it this way so you would stay longer.

It is possible to catch the Shamu show and the Sea Lion and Otter Show in succession by sitting near an exit at Shamu Stadium and leaving a minute or two early (while the performers are taking their bows). Getting a couple of minutes' head start on the crowd and hurrying directly to the Sea Lion & Otter Stadium will get you seated just as the show is beginning.

If you're going to a show in Shamu Stadium or at the Atlantis Water Ski Stadium, don't worry about arriving late. Both stadiums are huge, so you almost certainly will get a seat. Plus, there isn't much in the first few minutes of either show that you can't afford to miss. The same goes for the Whale and Dolphin Discovery Show. The beginning of the Sea Lion and Otter Show, however, is really good; try to be on time.

In early summer 1998, Sea World was set to unveil Journey to Atlantis, the latest entry into the theme park super-attraction competition. Occupying the equivalent of six football fields, Journey to Atlantis is the world's first attraction to combine elements of a high-speed water ride and a roller coaster. Guests are invited to explore the lost city of Atlantis, recently risen from the depths. After boarding a rickety Greek fishing boat, however, they're sucked into the city and "plunged into a swirling vortex." While this obviously is press-release language, this is not a ride to trifle with. If you visit after Journey to Atlantis opens, catch it just after the park opens, or be prepared to wait. By the way, you'll get soaked.

Stand-alone exhibits feature dolphins, stingrays, pelicans, spoonbills, flamingos, and the Anheuser-Busch Clydesdale horses, plus a tidal pool and tropical rain forest.

Part Thirteen

The Water Theme Parks

Disney has three swimming theme parks, and two more independent water parks are in the area. At Disney World, River Country is the oldest and smallest park. Typhoon Lagoon, about five years old, is the most diverse Disney splash pad, while three-year-old Blizzard Beach takes the prize for the most slides and most bizarre theme. Outside the World, find Wet 'n Wild and Water Mania.

At all Disney water parks, the following rules and prices apply: one cooler per family or group is allowed, but no glass and no alcoholic beverages; towels $1, small locker $3, large locker $5 ($2 deposit required for lockers), life jacket $25 refundable deposit.

BLIZZARD BEACH

Blizzard Beach is Disney's most exotic water adventure park and, like Typhoon Lagoon, it arrived with its own legend. This time, the story goes, an entrepreneur tried to open a ski resort in Florida during a particularly savage winter. Alas, the snow melted; the palm trees grew back; and all that remained of the ski resort was its Alpine lodge, the ski lifts, and, of course, the mountain. Plunging off the mountain are ski slopes and bobsled runs transformed into water slides. Visitors to Blizzard Beach catch the thaw: icicles drip and patches of snow remain. The melting snow has formed a lagoon (the wave pool), fed by gushing mountain streams.

Like Typhoon Lagoon, Blizzard Beach is distinguished by its landscaping and the attention paid to executing its theme. As you enter Blizzard Beach, you face the mountain. Coming off the highest peak and bisecting the area at the mountain's base are two long slides. To the left of the slides is the wave pool. To the right are the children's swimming area and the ski lift. Surrounding the layout like a moat is a tranquil stream for floating in tubes. Picnic areas are scattered around the park, as are pleasant places for sunbathing.

On either side of the highest peak are tube, raft, and body slides. Including the two slides coming off the peak, Blizzard Beach has 17 slides.

Captain Nemo surfaces by mistake
at Blizzard Beach.

Among them is Summit Plummet, Disney World's longest speed slide, which begins with a 120-foot free-fall, and the Teamboat Springs water bobsled run, 1,200 feet long.

For our money, the most exciting and interesting slides are the Slush Gusher and Teamboat Springs on the front right of the mountain, and Run-Off Rapids on the back side of the mountain. Slush Gusher is an undulating speed slide that we consider as exciting as the more vertical Summit Plummet without being as bone-jarring. On Teamboat Springs, you ride in a raft that looks like a round, children's blow-up wading pool. The more people you load into the raft, the faster it goes. If you have only a couple in it, the slide is kind of a snore.

Run-Off Rapids is accessible from a path that winds around the far left bottom of the mountain. The Rapids consists of three corkscrew tube slides, one of which is enclosed and dark. As at Teamboat Springs, you'll go much faster on a two- or three-person tube than on a one-person tube. If you lean so that you enter curves high and come out low, you'll really fly. Because we like to steer the tube and go fast, we much prefer the open slides (where we can see) to the dark, enclosed tube. We thought crashing through the pitch-dark tube felt disturbingly like being flushed down a toilet.

The Snow Stormer's mat slides on the front of the mountain are fun but not as fast or interesting as Run-Off Rapids. The Toboggan Racers at front and center on the mountain consists of eight parallel slides where riders are dispatched in heats to race to the bottom. The ride itself is no big deal, and the time needed to get everybody lined up ensures that you'll wait extra long to ride. On one visit, as an added annoyance, we had to line up once to get a mat and again to actually ride.

A ski lift carries guests to the mountaintop (you can also walk up) where they can choose from Summit Plummet, Slush Gusher, or Teamboat Springs. For all other slides at Blizzard Beach, the only way to reach the top is on foot. If you're among the first in the park and don't have to wait to ride, the ski lift is fun and provides a bird's-eye view of the park. After riding once to satisfy your curiosity, however, you're better off taking the stairs to the top.

The wave pool, called Melt-Away Bay, has gentle, bobbing waves. The float creek, Cross Country Creek, circles the park, passing through the mountain. The children's areas, Tike's Peak and Ski Patrol Training Camp, are creatively designed, nicely isolated, and, like the rest of the park, visually interesting.

Like Typhoon Lagoon, Blizzard Beach is a bit convoluted in its layout. With slides on both the front and back of the mountain, it isn't always easy to find a path leading to where you want to go.

At the ski resort's now-converted base area are shops; counter-service food; rest rooms; and tube, towel, and locker rentals. Blizzard Beach has its own parking lot but offers no lodging, though Disney's All-Star resorts are almost within walking distance. Disney resort and campground guests can commute to the park aboard Disney buses.

Because it's new and has popular slides, Blizzard Beach fills early during hotter months. To stake out a nice sunning spot and to enjoy the slides without long waits, arrive at least 35 minutes before the official opening time. Admission is about $28 per day for adults and $22 per day for children ages three to nine. Children younger than three are admitted free. If you're going primarily for the slides, you'll have about two hours in the early morning to enjoy them before the waiting becomes intolerable.

TYPHOON LAGOON

Typhoon Lagoon is comparable in size to Blizzard Beach and about four times larger than River Country. Nine water slides and streams, some as long as 400 feet, drop from the top of a 100-foot-tall, man-made mountain. Landscaping and an "aftermath-of-a-typhoon" theme add adventure to the wet rides.

Entry to Typhoon Lagoon is through a misty rain forest that emerges in a ramshackle tropical town, where concessions and services are situated. Special effects make every ride an odyssey as swimmers encounter bat caves, lagoons and pools, spinning rocks, formations of dinosaur bones, and many other imponderables.

Typhoon Lagoon has its own parking lot but no lodging. Disney resort and campground guests can commute to the park on Disney buses.

Like Blizzard Beach, Typhoon Lagoon is expensive: about $28 a day for adults and $22 a day for children ages three to nine. Children younger than three are admitted free. If you indulge in all features of Typhoon Lagoon, admission is a fair value. If you go primarily for the slides, you will have only two early-morning hours to enjoy them before the wait becomes prohibitive.

Typhoon Lagoon provides water adventure for all ages. Activity pools for young children and families feature geysers, tame slides, bubble jets, and fountains. For the older and more adventurous are two speed slides, three corkscrew body slides, and three tube rapids rides (plus one children's rapids ride) plopping off Mount Mayday. Slower metabolisms will like the scenic, meandering, 2,100-foot-long stream that floats tubers through a hidden grotto and rain forest. And, of course, the sedentary will usually find plenty of sun to sleep in. Typhoon Lagoon's surf pool and Shark Reef are unique, and the wave pool is the world's largest inland surf facility, with waves up to 6 feet in height (enough, so Disney says, to "encompass an oceanliner"). Shark Reef is a saltwater snorkeling pool where guests can swim among real fish.

Shark Reef

Fins, mask, snorkel, and wet-suit vest are provided free in the wooden building beside the diving pool. After you obtain the proper equipment (no forms or money involved), you shower and then report to a snorkeling instructor. After a brief lesson, you swim about 60 feet to the other side of the pool. You aren't allowed to paddle aimlessly, but must traverse the pool more or less directly.

The reef is fun in early morning. Equipment collection, shower, instruction, and the quick swim can be accomplished without much hassle. Also, because few guests are present, attendants are more flexible about your lingering in the pool or making minor departures from the charted course.

Later, as crowds build, it becomes increasingly difficult and time-consuming to provide the necessary instruction. The result is platoons of would-be frogmen restlessly awaiting their snorkeling lesson. Guests are grouped in impromptu classes with the entire class briefed and then launched together. What takes four or five minutes shortly after opening can take more than an hour by 11 a.m.

By far the most prevalent species in the pool are the dual-finned Homo sapiens. Other denizens include small, colorful tropical fish, some diminutive rays, and a few very small leopard and hammerhead sharks. In terms of numbers, it would be unusual to cross the pool and not see some fish. On the other hand, you aren't exactly bumping into them.

It's very important to fit your diving mask on your face so that it seals around the edges. Brush your hair from your forehead and sniff a couple of times once the mask is in place, to create a vacuum. Mustaches often prevent the mask from sealing properly. The first indication that your mask isn't correctly fitted will be saltwater in your nose.

If you don't want to swim with fish early in the morning or fight crowds later in the day, visit the underwater viewing chamber, accessible anytime without waiting, special equipment, showers, instruction, or water in your nose.

Typhoon Lagoon Surf Pool

While Blizzard Beach, Wet 'n Wild, and Water Mania have wave pools, Typhoon Lagoon has a *surf pool*. Most people will encounter larger waves here than they have in the ocean. The surf machine puts out a wave about every 90 seconds (just about how long it takes to get back in position if you caught the previous wave). Perfectly formed and ideal for riding, each wave is about five to six feet from trough to crest. Before you join the fray, watch two or three waves from shore. Since each wave breaks in almost the same spot, you can get a feel for position and timing. Observing other surfers is also helpful.

The best way to ride the waves is to swim about three-fourths of the way to the wall at the wave-machine end of the surf pool. When the wave comes (you will both feel and hear it), swim vigorously toward the beach, attempting to position yourself one-half to three-fourths of a body length below the breaking crest. The waves are so perfectly engineered that they will either carry you forward or bypass you. Unlike an ocean wave, they won't slam you down.

A teenage girl from Urbana, Illinois, notes that the primary hazard in the surf pool is colliding with other surfers and swimmers:

> *The surf pool was nice except that I kept landing on really hairy fat guys whenever the big waves came.*

The best way to avoid collisions while surfing is to paddle out far enough that you will be at the top of the wave as it breaks. This tactic eliminates the possibility of anyone landing on you from above and assures maximum forward visibility. A corollary to this: The worst place to swim is where the wave actually breaks. You will look up to see a six-foot wall of water carrying eight dozen screaming surfers bearing down on you. This is the time to remember every submarine movie you've ever seen . . . Dive! Dive! Dive!

A final warning: The surf pool has a knack for loosening watchbands, stripping jewelry, and sucking stuff out of your pockets. Don't take anything out there except your swimsuit (and hold on to it).

RIVER COUNTRY

River Country is among the most aesthetically pleasing of the water theme parks—it's beautifully landscaped and immaculately manicured, with rocky canyons and waterfalls skillfully blending with white-sand beaches. The park is even positioned to take advantage of the breeze off Bay Lake. The least expensive of Disney's water parks, River Country costs about $17 a day for adults and $14 a day for children ($14 adults, $11 children for Fort Wilderness guests).

For pure and simple swimming and splashing, River Country gets high marks. Its slides, however, don't begin to compete with its big brothers or nearby competitors. Whereas Blizzard Beach and Wet 'n Wild feature more than 16 major slides and tube rides, River Country has 1 tube ride and 2 corkscrew slides. Few slides and many swimmers add up to long lines. If slides are your thing, go elsewhere.

Sunbathers will enjoy River Country, particularly if they lie near the lakefront to take advantage of the cooling breezes. Most chaise lounges are basically flat, with the head slightly elevated, and don't have adjustable backs. They leave a great deal to be desired for a comfortable reading position or for lying on your stomach.

Reaching River Country by car is a hassle. You're directed to a parking lot, where you leave your car, gather your belongings, and wait for a Disney bus to take you to the park. The ride is rather lengthy, and pity the poor soul who left his bathing suit in the car (a round trip to retrieve it will take about 30 minutes). In the morning, the bus from the parking lot to River Country is very crowded. We suggest catching the bus to Pioneer Hall (which loads at the same place in the parking lot), then walking to River Country from there.

There's no lodging at River Country, but it's within walking distance of much of Fort Wilderness Campground. Food is available, or you can pack a lunch to eat in the park's picturesque, shaded, lakeside picnic area. Access is by bus from the Transportation and Ticket Center (junction and transfer point for the Epcot and Magic Kingdom monorails) or from the River Country parking lot at the entrance of Fort Wilderness Campground. River Country can also be reached by boat from the Magic Kingdom and from any hotel on Bay Lake or Seven Seas Lagoon.

DISNEY VS. WET 'N WILD AND WATER MANIA THEME PARKS

Wet 'n Wild, on International Drive in Orlando, is on a par with Blizzard Beach and beats Typhoon Lagoon, River Country, and Water Mania for slides. The headliners at Wet 'n Wild are the Black Hole, the Surge, and the Fuji Flyer. At the Black Hole, guests descend on a two-person tube down a totally enclosed corkscrew slide, sort of a wet version of Space Mountain—only much darker. Our researchers think this is the most exciting slide at any Florida swimming theme park (Water Mania and Blizzard Beach have similar slides). The Surge launches groups of five down a 580-foot twisting, turning course. The Fuji Flyer is a 450-foot water-toboggan course. Another Wet 'n Wild thrill slide is Bomb Bay, which drops guests from a compartment resembling a bomb bay down a chute angled at 79°.

Water Mania, on US 192 south of I-4, edges out Typhoon Lagoon for slides and is less crowded than its competitors. In addition, it's the only water park to offer a stationary surfing wave.

What sets Disney water parks apart is not so much their slides and individual attractions but the Disney attention to detail in creating an integrated adventure environment. Both eye and body are deluged with the strange, the exotic, the humorous, and the beautiful. Wilder slides and rapids rides can be found elsewhere, but other water parks can't compete with Disney in diversity, variety, adventure, and total impact. Water Mania is nicely landscaped, but it doesn't have a theme. Wet 'n Wild, though attractive and clean, is cluttered and not especially appealing to the eye.

In the surf and wave pool department, Typhoon Lagoon wins hands down, with Wet 'n Wild taking second place. All of the parks have an outstanding water activity area for young children, and all except River Country feature unique attractions. Wet 'n Wild has a ride in which guests kneel on water skis, and Blizzard Beach has a 1,200-foot water bobsled. At Typhoon Lagoon, guests can snorkel among live fish, and Water Mania has a surfing wave.

Prices for one-day admission are about the same at Wet 'n Wild, Blizzard Beach, and Typhoon Lagoon, and slightly less at Water Mania. River Country is the least expensive of the water parks. Discount coupons are often available in local visitor magazines for Water Mania and Wet 'n Wild.

Wet 'n Wild is open until 11 p.m. during summer; the Disney swimming parks and Water Mania generally close between 5 and 8 p.m. The late closing is a huge plus for Wet 'n Wild. Warm Florida nights are great for enjoying a water theme park. There's less waiting for slides, and the pavement is cooler under your feet. To top it off, Wet 'n Wild features live music in the evening at its Wave Pool Stage and sells half-price tickets after 4 p.m. on days when the park is open late.

If your primary interest is sunning and swimming, you can't beat River Country. It's beautiful and usually has a nice breeze blowing off Bay Lake. If you're into slides, Blizzard Beach is tops among the Disney water parks, with Wet 'n Wild leading the independents. Typhoon Lagoon offers enough slides to keep most folks happy, has the largest wave pool, and provides the most variety. If you like slides but not crowds and are willing to sacrifice exotic surroundings for more elbow room, Water Mania is a good and cheaper choice. For evening and nighttime swimming fun, Wet 'n Wild is the only game in town.

TYPHOON LAGOON VS. BLIZZARD BEACH

Many Walt Disney World guests aren't interested in leaving the World. For them, the question is which is better, Typhoon Lagoon or Blizzard Beach?

Our readers answer.

A mother of four from Winchester, Virginia, gives her opinion:

> *At Blizzard Beach the family raft ride is great, [but] the kids' area is poorly designed. As a parent, when you walk your child to the top of a slide or the tube ride, they are lost to your vision as they go down because of the fake snow drifts. There are no direct ways down to the end of the slides, so little ones are left standing unsupervised [while] parents scramble down from the top. The Typhoon Lagoon kids' area is far superior in design.*

A couple from Woodridge, Illinois, writes:

> *We liked Blizzard Beach much more. It seems like they took everything from Typhoon Lagoon and made it better and faster. Summit Plummet was awesome—a total rush. Worth the half-hour wait. Toboggan and bobsled rides were really exciting—bobsled really throws you around. Family tube ride was really good—much better and much longer than at Typhoon Lagoon. Tube rides were great, especially in enclosed tube. If you only have time to go to one water park, go to Blizzard Beach.*

But a hungry reader from Aberdeen, New Jersey, complains:

> *At Blizzard Beach, there is only one main place to get food (most of the other spots are more for snacks). At lunchtime, it took almost 45 minutes to get some sandwiches and drinks.*

A couple from Bowie, Maryland, didn't enjoy Summit Plummet:

> *The tallest and fastest slide at Blizzard Beach gave me a bunch of bruises. Even my husband hurt for a few days. It wasn't a fun ride, and we both agree that it wasn't worth waiting in line for. Basically, you drop until you hit the slide and that is why everyone comes off rubbing their butts. They say you go 60 mph on a 120-foot drop. I'll never do it again.*

A man from Lexington, Massachusetts, who felt like a "hen egg in a skillet" reports:

> *Blizzard Beach is not well thought out. No shade from the Florida sun and way too much hot concrete.*

Typhoon Lagoon won over a Texas family:

> *The water parks were great! Our favorite for the whole family was Typhoon Lagoon. There was a lot of shade if you wanted, the river around was better [than at Blizzard Beach], and the surf pool was great.*

WHEN TO GO

The best way to avoid standing in lines is to visit the water parks when they're less crowded. Because the parks are popular among locals, weekends can be tough. We recommend going on a Monday or Tuesday, when most other tourists will be visiting the Magic Kingdom, Epcot, the Animal Kingdom, or Disney-MGM Studios and locals will be at work or school. Fridays are good because people traveling by car commonly use this day to start home. Sunday morning also has lighter crowds. During summer and holiday periods, Typhoon Lagoon and Blizzard Beach fill to capacity and close their gates before 11 a.m.

A reader from Newbury Park, California, gives an idea of what "crowded" means:

> The only disappointment we had at WDW was Typhoon Lagoon. While WDW was quite uncrowded, Typhoon Lagoon seemed choked with people. I'd hate to see it on a really crowded day. Even the small slides had lines greater than 30 minutes. They weren't worth half the wait. Castaway Creek might have been relaxing, but I found it to be a continuous traffic jam. I [also] would have enjoyed the snorkeling area except we were forced to go through at warp speed. After half a day we returned to the Yacht Club where Stormalong Bay provided much more pleasant water recreation.

A mom from Manlius, New York, writes:

> Because we had the 5-Day Park-Hopper, we also visited Typhoon Lagoon, arriving before opening so we could stake out a shady spot. The kids loved it until the lines got long (11 a.m. to noon), but I hated it. It made Coney Island seem like a deserted island in the Bahamas. Floating on Castaway Creek was really unpleasant. Whirling around in a chlorinated, concrete ditch with some stranger's feet in my face, periodically getting squirted by waterguns, passing under cascades of cold water, and getting hung up by the crowd is not at all relaxing for me. My husband and I then decided to "bob" in the surf pool. After about 10 minutes of being tossed around like corks in boiling water, he turned a little green around the gills and we sought the peace of our shady little territory which, in our absence, had become much, much smaller. We sat and read our books, elbow to elbow with other pleasure-seekers, until the kids had their fill. They, however, loved the body slides and the surf waves, commenting on how useful your "coach's tip" was.

A visitor from Middletown, New York, had a somewhat better experience:

> *On our second trip [to Typhoon Lagoon], we dispensed with the locker rental (having planned to stay for only the morning when it was least crowded), and at park's opening just took right off for the Storm Slides before the masses arrived—it was perfect! We must have ridden the slides at least five times before any kind of line built up, and then we were also able to ride the tube and raft rides (Keelhaul and Mayday Falls) in a similar uncrowded, quick fashion because everyone else was busy getting their lockers! We also experienced the Shark Reef snorkeling three times with minimal crowds that day, because, I think, most people overlook this attraction. Shark Reef is lots of fun and a great way to cool off since their water temp is well below the wave pool's.*

If your schedule is flexible, a good time to visit the swimming parks is midafternoon to late in the day when the weather has cleared after a storm. The parks usually close during bad weather. If the storm is prolonged, most guests leave for their hotels. When Typhoon Lagoon, Blizzard Beach, or River Country reopen after inclement weather has passed, you almost have a whole park to yourself.

PLANNING YOUR DAY AT DISNEY WATER PARKS

Disney swimming theme parks are almost as large and elaborate as the major theme parks. You must be prepared for a lot of walking, exercise, sun, and jostling crowds. If your group really loves the water, schedule your visit early in your vacation. For many families, a visit to a water park is the highlight of their trip. If you go at the beginning of your stay, you'll have more flexibility if you want to return.

To have a great day and beat the crowd at any of the Disney water parks, consider:

1. *Getting Information.* Call (407) 824-4321 the night before you go to ask when your chosen park opens.

2. *To Picnic or Not to Picnic.* Decide whether you want to carry a picnic lunch. Guests are permitted to take lunches and beverage coolers into the parks. No alcoholic beverages are allowed. Glass containers of any kind (including mayonnaise, mustard, peanut butter, and pickle jars) are likewise forbidden.

3. *Getting Started.* If you are going to Blizzard Beach or Typhoon Lagoon, get up early, have breakfast, and arrive at the park 40 minutes before opening. If you have a car, drive instead of taking a Disney bus. If you're going to River Country, you don't have to get there so early.

4. *Attire.* Wear your bathing suit under shorts and a T-shirt so you don't need to use lockers or dressing rooms. Wear shoes. Paths are relatively easy on bare feet, but there's a lot of ground to cover. If you have tender feet, wear your shoes as you move around the park, removing them when you raft, slide, or go into the water. Shops in the parks sell sandals, "Reef Runners," and other protective footwear that can be worn in and out of the water.

5. *What to Bring.* You will need a towel, suntan lotion, and money. Since wallets and purses get in the way, lock them in your car's trunk or leave them at your hotel. Carry enough money for the day and your Disney resort I.D. (if you have one) in a plastic bag or Tupperware container. Though nowhere is completely safe, we felt very comfortable hiding our plastic money bags in our cooler. Nobody disturbed our stuff, and our cash was much easier to reach than if we'd stashed it in a locker across the park. If you're carrying a wad or you worry about money anyway, rent the locker.

6. *What Not to Bring.* Personal swim gear (fins, masks, rafts, etc.) aren't allowed. Everything you need is either provided or available to rent. If you forget your towel, you can rent one (cheap!). If you forget your swimsuit or lotion, they're for sale. Personal flotation devices (life jackets) are available free of charge, but you must leave a credit card number or a driver's license as a deposit (held until the equipment is returned).

7. *Admissions.* Purchase your admission in advance or about 45 minutes before official opening time. If you're staying at a Disney property, you may be entitled to an admission discount; bring your hotel or campground I.D. Combination passes that include both River Country and Discovery Island represent the best buy for anyone interested in these two minor theme parks. Guests staying five or more days should consider the 5-Day Park-Hopper Pass or All-in-One Passes, which include admission to all Disney swimming parks.

8. *Lockers.* Rental lockers come in small and large sizes for $5 or $7 per day, of which $2 is refunded when you return your key. Lockers are roomy enough for one person or a couple, but are a stretch for an entire family. Though you can access your locker freely all day, not all lockers are conveniently located.

Getting a locker at Blizzard Beach or Typhoon Lagoon is truly competitive. When the gates open, guests race to the locker rental desk. Once there, the rental procedure is somewhat slow. If you aren't among the first in line, you can waste a lot of time waiting to be served. We recommend you skip the locker. Carry only as much cash as you will need for the day in a watertight container you can stash in your cooler. Ditto for personal items including watches and eyeglasses. With planning, you can manage nicely without the locker and save time and hassle in the bargain.

9. *Tubes.* Tubes for bobbing on the waves, floating in the creeks, and riding the tube slides are available for free.

10. *Getting Settled.* Establish your base for the day. There are many beautiful sunning and lounging spots scattered throughout all Disney swimming parks. Arrive early, and you can almost have your pick. The breeze is best along the beaches of the surf pools at Blizzard Bay and Typhoon Lagoon. At River Country, pick a spot that fronts Bay Lake. At Typhoon Lagoon, if there are children younger than six in your party, choose an area to the left of Mount Mayday (ship on top) near the children's swimming area.

Available are flat lounges (unadjustable) and chairs (better for reading), shelters for guests who prefer shade, picnic tables, and a few hammocks.

The best spectator sport at Typhoon Lagoon is the bodysurfing in the surf pool. It's second only to being out there yourself. With this in mind, position yourself to have an unobstructed view of the waves.

11. *A Word about the Slides.* Water slides come in many shapes and sizes. Some are steep and vertical, some long and undulating. Some resemble corkscrews; others imitate the pool-and-drop nature of whitewater streams. Depending on which slide, swimmers ride mats, inner tubes, or rafts. On body slides, swimmers slosh to the bottom on the seat of their pants.

Modern traffic engineering bows to old-fashioned queuing. At water slides, it's one person, one raft (or tube) at a time, and the swimmer on deck can't go until the person preceding him is safely out of the way. Thus, the slide's hourly capacity is limited, compared to the continuously loading rides in the major theme parks. Because a certain interval between swimmers is required for safety, the only way to increase capacity is to increase the number of slides and rapids rides.

Though Typhoon Lagoon and Blizzard Beach are huge parks with many slides, they're overwhelmed almost daily by armies of guests. If your main reason for going to Typhoon Lagoon or Blizzard Beach is the slides and you hate long lines, be among the first guests to enter the park. Go directly to the slides and ride as many times as you can before the park fills. When lines for the slides become intolerable, head for the surf or wave pool, or the tube-floating streams.

For maximum speed on a body slide, cross your legs at the ankles and cross your arms over your chest. When you take off, arch your back so that almost all of your weight is on your shoulder blades and heels (the less contact with the surface, the less resistance). Steer by shifting most of your upper-body weight onto one shoulder blade. For top speed on turns, weight the shoulder blade on the outside of each curve. If you want to go slow (what's the point?), distribute your weight equally as if you were lying on your back in bed. For all curving slides, maximize speed by hitting the entrance to each curve high and exiting the curve low.

Some slides and rapids have a minimum height requirement. Riders for Humunga Kowabunga at Typhoon Lagoon and for Slush Gusher and Summit Plummet at Blizzard Beach, for example, must be four feet tall. Pregnant women and persons with back problems or other health difficulties shouldn't ride.

12. *Floating Streams.* Disney's Blizzard Beach and Typhoon Lagoon and the independent Water Mania and Wet 'n Wild offer mellow floating streams. A great idea, the floating streams are long, tranquil, inner-tube rides that give you the illusion that you're doing something though you're being sedentary. For wimps, wussies, and exhausted people of all ages, floating streams are an answered prayer.

    Disney's streams flow ever so slowly around the entire park, through caves and beneath waterfalls, past gardens, and under bridges. They offer a relaxing alternative to touring a park on foot.

    Floating streams can be reached from several put-in and take-out points. There never are lines; just wade into the creek and plop into one of the inner tubes floating by. Ride the gentle current all the way around or get out at any exit. If you lie back and go with the flow, it will take 30–35 minutes to float the full circuit.

    Predictably, there will be guests on whom the subtlety of floating streams is lost. They will be racing, screaming, and splashing. Let them pass, stopping a few moments, if necessary, to distance yourself from them.

13. *Lunch.* If you didn't bring a picnic, you can buy food. Portions are adequate to generous; quality is comparable to fast-food chains; and prices (as you would expect) are a bit high.

14. *More Options.* If you really are a water puppy, consider returning to your hotel for a heat-of-the-day nap and coming back to the water park for some early-evening swimming. Special lighting after dusk makes Typhoon Lagoon and Blizzard Beach enchanting. Crowds tend to be lighter in the evening. If you leave the park and want to return, be sure to keep your admission ticket and have your hand stamped. If you're staying in a hotel served by Disney buses, older children can return on their own to the water parks, giving Mom and Dad a little private quiet time.

15. *Bad Weather.* Thunderstorms are common in Florida. During summer afternoons, such storms can be a daily occurrence. Swimming parks close during a storm. Most storms, however, are short lived, allowing the swimming park to resume normal operations. If a storm is severe and prolonged, it can cause a great deal of inconvenience. In addition to the park's closing, guests compete aggressively for shelter, and Disney resort guests may have to compete for seats on a bus back to the hotel.

    We recommend you monitor the local weather forecast the day before you go, checking again in the morning before leaving for the swimming park. Scattered thundershowers are to be expected, but moving storm fronts are to be avoided. Because Florida is so flat, approaching weather can be seen from atop the slide platforms at the swimming parks. Particularly if you're dependent on Disney buses, leave the park earlier, rather than later, when you see a storm moving in.

16. *Endurance.* The water parks are large and require almost as much walking as one of the theme parks. Add to this wave surfing, swimming, and all the climbing required to reach the slides, and you'll be pooped by day's end. Unless you spend your hours like a lizard on a rock, don't expect to return to the hotel relaxed and refreshed. Consider something low-key for the evening. You probably will want to hit the hay early.

17. *Lost Children & Lost Adults.* It's as easy to lose a child or become separated from your party at one of the water parks as it is at a major theme park. Upon arrival, pick a very specific place to meet in the event you are separated. If you split up on purpose, set times for checking in. Lost-children stations at the water parks are so out of the way that neither you nor your lost child will find them without help from a Disney employee. Explain to your children how to recognize a Disney employee (by their distinctive name tags) and how to ask for help.

Part Fourteen

Beyond the Parks

Downtown Disney

Downtown Disney is a shopping, dining, and entertainment development strung out along the banks of the Buena Vista Lagoon. On the far right is the Downtown Disney Marketplace (formerly known as the Disney Village Marketplace). In the middle is the gated (admission-required) Pleasure Island nighttime entertainment, and on the far left is Disney's West Side.

Marketplace   Although the Marketplace offers interactive fountains, a couple of playgrounds, a Lagoon-side amphitheater, and watercraft rentals, it is primarily a shopping and dining venue. The centerpiece of shopping is the World of Disney, the largest Disney trademark merchandise store in the world. If you can't find what you are looking for in this 38,000-square-foot Noah's Ark of Disney stuff, it probably doesn't exist. Another noteworthy retailer is the LEGO Imagination Center, showcasing a number of huge and unbelievable sculptures made entirely of LEGO "bricks." Almost worthy of a special trip, spaceships, sea serpents, sleeping tourists, and dinosaurs are just a few of the sculptures on display. Rounding out the selection are stores specializing in resort wear, athletic attire and gear, Christmas decorations, Barbie dolls, Disney art and collectibles, and handmade craft items. Also located in the Marketplace is Studio M, where guests can have a professional photograph taken with Mickey. Most retail establishments are open from 9:30 a.m. until 11:30 p.m.

Rainforest Cafe is the headliner restaurant at the Marketplace. There is also Cap'n Jack's Oyster Bar, Wolfgang Puck pizza kitchen, a soda fountain, a deli and bakery, and a McDonalds. Full-service restaurants are profiled in Part 8, "Dining in and around Walt Disney World."

Pleasure Island   Pleasure Island is a nighttime entertainment complex. Though admission is charged after 7 p.m., shops and restaurants are open with no admission required during the day. Detailed coverage of the nightspots is provided in Part 15, "Nightlife in and out of Walt Disney World." Pleasure Island's shops offer more Disney art, casual fashions, Disney character merchandise, movie collectibles, and music memorabilia. Superstar Studios is a recording studio where you can make your own music video. There are four full-service restaurants at Pleasure Island. Fulton's Crab House and the Portobello Yacht Club can be accessed at any time without paying admission to Pleasure Island. The Wild Horse Saloon, a country music club and barbecue restaurant, and Pleasure Island Jazz Company are within the gated part of Pleasure Island.

Disney's West Side   The West Side is the newest addition to Downtown Disney and offers a broad range of entertainment, dining, and shopping. Restaurants include the House of Blues, which serves Cajun specialties as well as prime rib; Planet Hollywood, offering movie memorabilia and basic American fare; Bongo's Cuban Cafe, serving Cuban favorites; and Wolfgang Puck Cafe, featuring California cuisine. All four West Side restaurants are profiled in Part 8, "Dining in and around Walt Disney World."

West Side shopping is some of the most interesting in Walt Disney World. For starters, there's a Virgin (records and books) Megastore. Across the street is the Guitar Gallery by George's Music, specializing in custom, collector, rare, and unique guitars. Other specialty shops include a David Copperfield magic store, a cigar shop, a rock-and-roll and movie memorabilia store, and a western apparel boutique.

In the entertainment department, there is DisneyQuest, an interactive theme park contained in a building; the House of Blues, a concert and dining venue; and a 24-screen AMC movie theater. The West Side is also home to *Cirque du Soleil*, a not-to-be-missed production show with a cast of almost 100 performers and musicians. The House of Blues concert hall and *Cirque du Soleil* are described in Part 15, "Nightlife in and out of Walt Disney World." DisneyQuest is described in detail below.

DISNEYQUEST

For more than a decade, major theme parks have experimented with attractions based on motion-simulation and virtual reality technologies. Among other things, these technologies have allowed thrill rides with the punch of a roller coaster to be engineered and operated in spaces as small as a one-car garage. Analogous to the computer industry, where the power of a bulky mainframe is now available in a laptop, Disney is pioneering the concept of a theme park in a box, or in the case of DisneyQuest, a modest five-story building.

Opened in the summer of 1998 in the West Side area of Downtown Disney, DisneyQuest contains all the elements of the larger Disney theme parks. There is an entrance area that facilitates your transition into the park environment and leads to the gateways of four distinct themed lands, here referred to as zones. At other Disney parks, everything is included in the price of your admission, but at DisneyQuest, all attractions are à la carte, or "pay-for-play" as the amusement industry puts it.

It takes about two to three hours to experience DisneyQuest, once you get it. Disney limits the number of guests admitted to ensure that queues are manageable and that guests have a positive experience. Once DisneyQuest hits capacity, newly arriving guests are lined up outside to wait until departing guests make some room. Weekday mornings are the least crowded times to visit.

DisneyQuest, in concept and attraction mix, is aimed at a youthful audience, say 8–35 years of age, though younger and older patrons will enjoy much of what it offers. The feel is dynamic, bustling, and noisy. Those who haunt the electronic games arcades at shopping malls will feel most at home at DisneyQuest.

You begin your experience in the Departure Lobby, where you purchase a DisneyQuest Card. Cards are available in three preset amounts, so you can determine how much you want to spend. Each time you experience an attraction, an amount is deducted from the credit balance on your card. If you use up all your prepaid credit and wish to experience more attractions, you can buy additional credit at recharge kiosks located in the respective zones. Our recommendation is to buy the smallest amount of credit to start and then to add credit later if you want. There is no refund for unused credit.

From the Departure Lobby you enter a "Cyberlator," a sort of "transitional attraction" (read elevator) hosted by the genie from *Aladdin,* that delivers you to an entrance plaza called Ventureport. From here you can enter the four zones. Like in the larger parks, each zone is distinctively themed. Some zones cover more than one floor, so, looking around, you can see things going on both above and below you. The four zones, in no particular order, are Explore Zone, Score Zone, Create Zone, and Replay Zone. In addition to the zones, DisneyQuest offers two restaurants and the inevitable gift shop.

Explore Zone   The gateway to Explore Zone is the tiger's-head cave from *Aladdin.* You can descend to the attractions area on a 150-foot corkscrew slide or use more traditional means like elevators or ramps. The headline attraction in Explore Zone is the Virtual Jungle Cruise, where you paddle a six-person raft. The raft is a motion simulator perched on top of blue air bags that replicate the motion of water. Responding to the film of the river projected before you, you can choose several routes through the rapids.

The motion simulator responds to sensors on your paddle, so the ride you experience simulates the course you choose. As if navigating the river isn't enough, man-eating dinosaurs and a cataclysmic comet are tossed in for good measure. Another Explore Zone attraction, Aladdin's Magic Carpet Ride, has you seated on a motorcycle-shaped simulator. Here you are fitted with a head-mounted virtual reality display. Leaning left and right on your faux motorcycle allows you to navigate your magic carpet through the streets of Agraba.

Score Zone   Here you pass through a slash in a giant comic book to enter a theme area based on comic book characters and competition. The big deal here are enlarged, high-tech versions of electronic and video games where you pit your skill and reflexes against other players. The headliner is Mighty Ducks Pinball Slam, where you stand atop a mammoth hockey puck. By manipulating a joystick, you control the motion of your puck as it bounces around a virtual reality pinball machine. In Ride the Comix, you once again don virtual reality headgear to ride off into comic book scenes and do battle with archvillains.

Create Zone   A digital artist's palette serves as the entrance to Create Zone. Featured here is CyberSpace Mountain, an attraction where you can design your own roller coaster, including 360° loops, and then take a virtual reality–motion simulator ride on your creation. Also in the Create Zone is Sid's Make-a-Toy, where you can design a toy and receive the parts to actually construct it at home. Other creative attractions include virtual beauty salon makeovers and painting on an electronic canvas.

Replay Zone   Replay Zone draws its theme from a 1950s view of the future. Basically, it's three levels of classic midway games with a few futuristic twists. The balls on the Skeeball games, for example, glow in the dark. Winners of the various games earn redemption tickets, which can be redeemed for midway-type prizes. The pièce de résistance of Replay Zone is Buzz Lightyear's Astro Blasters, a fancy version of bumper cars. Here guests pilot two-person bumper-bubbles that suck up grapefruit-sized balls from the floor and fire them from an air cannon at other vehicles. Direct hits cause the other vehicles to spin momentarily out of control.

The Disney Institute

In 1996 Disney launched the Disney Institute, an ambitious alternative to the typical Disney World vacation. The institute, situated on its own campus in the Villas of the Disney Institute, offers a variety of educational and life-enriching courses and programs.

Participants enroll by the day for a fixed tuition. They choose among four dozen programs in the areas of culinary arts, design arts, entertainment arts, environment, lifestyles, story arts, youth programs, and sports and fitness. Students typically take a class in the morning and another in the afternoon, filling any remaining time with sports and fitness offerings. In the evenings there are concerts, lectures, films, and storytelling.

The campus is self-contained with lodging, a restaurant, classrooms, studios, and recreational facilities that include a championship 18-hole golf course. The institute is also the site of Walt Disney World's most comprehensive spa and fitness facility.

For most of its first three years, the Disney Institute struggled to hit its stride. Travel agents didn't understand the concept, and neither did the traveling public. The notion of an educational vacation is foreign to most, but the idea of spending four or five days at Walt Disney World without visiting the theme parks seemed like lunacy. Disney finally figured out that the institute was more likely to succeed as part of a guest's Disney World vacation than as the whole enchilada.

Most courses are without prerequisite. This means that the instructors can't make any assumptions about the student's knowledge of the topic. Our "Wine, Wonders, and Song" class, for example, included wine initiates and others who possessed extensive knowledge of wine. The course was too advanced for the former and too basic for the latter.

At present, you don't have to lodge at the Disney Institute or even at Walt Disney World to participate. What's more, if you take courses at the institute, you're eligible to use the extraordinary recreational facilities (except golf) as part of your tuition.

Before signing up, ask pointed questions about the courses that interest you. By our experience, most reservationists know their product and should be able to steer you to appropriate programs.

You can make reservations for courses with your credit card by calling (407) 827-4800 or (407) 827-1100, or by visiting the Institute Welcome Center in person. You will be required to arrive on the day of your course 45 minutes in advance to actually pay for and receive your course admission tickets, a process not appreciated by a dentist from Conyers, Georgia:

> *Our second surprise was associated with the Disney Institute. Since we were unable to obtain any specific program information from the Institute by phone before leaving home, we visited the Institute's Welcome Center for on-site registration. What we learned after two very frustrating hours was that the registration process is phenomenally inefficient! Once our courses were selected and reserved by credit card, we learned we still had to stand in line each day to "purchase our*

tickets" for that day's class! Although we were in line at 7:40 a.m. for 8:30 a.m. classes, we didn't make the classes on time! Five people in line ahead of us were registered for 8 a.m. classes. When they complained they were missing their program, the Disney employee snapped back that they "should have been here earlier!" WOW!

In defense of their registration process, the Disney Institute explains that the current system eliminates refunds and confusion when outdoor courses must be cancelled because of bad weather. Disney additionally claims that participants forget their course admission tickets when tickets are issued prior to the day of the course.

Disney's Wide World of Sports

Disney's Wide World of Sports complex is a 200-acre, state-of-the-art competition and training complex consisting of a 7,500-seat ballpark, a fieldhouse, and dedicated venues for baseball, softball, tennis, track and field, beach volleyball, and 27 other sports. From Little League Baseball to rugby to beach volleyball, the complex hosts a mind-boggling calendar of professional and amateur competitions, with one or more events scheduled nearly every day.

During late winter and early spring, the complex is the spring training home of the Atlanta Braves. Although Disney guests are welcome at the sports complex as paid spectators (prices vary according to event), none of the facilities are available for guests' use unless they are participants in a scheduled organized competition. To learn what events are scheduled during your visit, call (407) 363-6600.

In addition to scheduled competitive events, a program called the NFL Experience is operated daily from 10 a.m. until about 5 p.m. Appealing primarily to school-age boys, the NFL Experience is a supervised activity that allows kids to kick field goals, catch and throw passes, catch punts, and run through a small obstacle course, among other things. Though the NFL Experience is sometimes the only thing going on at the Wide World of Sports complex, Disney nevertheless charges full admission. Our advice is to pass on the Wide World of Sports unless there is a specific event you want to see. Call the sports complex directly to confirm event times and venues (as opposed to trusting Disney guest relations personnel at the theme parks or hotels).

Counter-service and full-service dining are available at the sports complex, but there's no on-site lodging. Disney's Wide World of Sports is off Osceola Parkway, between World Drive and where the parkway crosses I-4 (no interstate access). The complex has its own parking lot and is accessible via the Disney Transportation System.

Walt Disney World Speedway

Adjacent to the Transportation and Ticket Center parking lot, the one-mile tri-oval course is host to several races each year. Between competitions, it's home to the Richard Petty Driving Experience, where you can ride in a two-seater stock car for $106 or learn to drive one. Courses are by reservation only and cost between $424 (8 laps) and $1,378 (30 laps). For information, call (800) 237-3889.

Discovery Island

Discovery Island, located in Bay Lake near the Magic Kingdom, is a small, tropically landscaped zoological park primarily featuring birds. Intimate trails wind through the exotic foliage, in contrast to the broad thoroughfares of the major theme parks. Plants and trees are marked for easy identification, and the island has an enormous walk-through aviary, so cleverly engineered that you're barely aware of the confining net.

In the best traditions of small-attraction Florida tourism, Discovery Island offers two shows called Animal Encounters. *Feathered Friends* features cockatoos and macaws in natural and not-so-natural behaviors, with owls, hawks, vultures, and the like (most of them disabled birds convalescing at Discovery Island) for contrast. The second show, *Reptile Relations*, introduces guests to alligators, snakes, and other scaly species indigenous to Florida. Informative, interesting, and well presented, the Encounters are staged in natural surroundings with few props. Seating is in-the-round on benches, not unlike what you might expect at camp. Show times, four for each Encounter, are scheduled between 11 a.m. and 4 p.m., ensuring that guests will be in the company of "mad dogs and Englishmen" as they sit through presentations during the hottest time of day.

A trip to Discovery Island is fairly expensive (about $13 for adults and $7 for kids) for two shows, a few birds and animals, and a stroll through the woods. Children enjoy the island if allowed to explore but become bored and restless touring under the thumb of their elders. Probably the best deals for guests spending six or more days at Disney World are the All-in-One passes that provide admission to the major parks and to Typhoon Lagoon, River Country, Blizzard Beach, Pleasure Island, and Discovery Island. Don't buy the All-in-One passes unless you intend to take advantage of their features.

Discovery Island offers no lodging, but food is available. For anyone on an All-in-One pass, it's fun to break from touring the Magic Kingdom and cruise to Discovery Island for lunch. The boat ride is pleasant, the island serene. Best, there are no crowds. Food is simple but on the whole pretty good.

Access to Discovery Island is exclusively by boat from the main Bay Lake docks (Magic Kingdom dock, Fort Wilderness Landing, and resort docks). Boats run about every 15–20 minutes. Dock to dock, it takes about 12 minutes to cover the distance from the Magic Kingdom to Discovery Island. The last boat of the day leaves the Magic Kingdom dock at 3:34 p.m. While you could spend up to three hours on Discovery Island, most folks are ready to leave in an hour or so.

Reader reaction to Discovery Island is decidedly mixed. A father of two from Manning, South Carolina, writes:

> *The bad news is that you overestimated Discovery Island. Although you made it sound dreary and a bit dull, that is giving it too much credit. You would have to be a bird fanatic to really enjoy Discovery Island, in our opinion. It was a complete waste of time, and we spent more time waiting on boats than on seeing the island.*

A father from Bethesda, Maryland, disagrees:

> *It's probably their love of animals that caused our kids to flip out over Discovery Island. Despite our repeated earlier trips to WDW, I had personally always escaped going to this attraction. My kids enjoyed every moment of our excursion one sunny afternoon, and it really served to take the edge off an otherwise hectic day.*

Walt Disney World Recreation

Most Walt Disney World guests never make it beyond the theme parks, the water parks, and Downtown Disney. Those who do, however, discover an extraordinary selection of recreational opportunities ranging from guided fishing expeditions and water skiing outings to hay rides, horseback riding, fitness center workouts, and miniature golf. If it's something you can do at a resort, it's probably available at Walt Disney World.

Boat, bike, and fishing equipment rentals are handled on an hourly basis. Just show up at the rental office during operating hours and they'll fix you up. The same goes for various fitness centers in the resort hotels. Golf, tennis, fishing expeditions, water ski excursions, hayrides, trail rides, and most spa services must be scheduled in advance. Though every resort features an extensive selection of recreational options, those resorts located on a navigable body of water offer the greatest variety. Also, the more upscale a resort, the more likely it is to have such amenities as a fitness center and spa. In addition to the resorts, guests can rent boats and other recreational equipment at the Marketplace in Downtown Disney.

Recreational Services Covered	Recreational Services Not Covered
Use of bicycles	Game arcades
Use of Water Mouse Boats	Fireworks cruises
Use of canoes	Golf or tennis lessons
Use of rowboats	Spa services
Use of pedal boats	Water theme park admission
Use of pontoon boats	
Use of sailboats (Sunfish)	
Use of canopy boats	
Use of jet boats	
Water skiing	
Golf (for tee times after 1 p.m.; greens fees and cart included)	
Fantasia Gardens Miniature Golf	
Horseback trail rides (45 minutes)	
Pony rides	
Hayrides	
Tennis	
Cane-pole fishing	
Fishing excursions	
Health club admission	

DISNEY'S WORLD OF RECREATION

The new Disney's World of Recreation plan includes unlimited use of selected recreation activities and facilities at a cost of $33 per adult and $23 per child per night. At first, the recreation plan was sold exclusively as an "add-on" to the dining plan. In other words, you were only eligible to purchase the recreation plan if you were signed up for the dining plan. Subsequently, however, Disney began selling both plans as "stand-alones." If you're interested in the recreation plan, we suggest calling in advance to determine whether recreation is presently bundled with, or separate from, the dining program.

In the recreation plan, there's no account balance to worry about. Your daily charge covers unlimited use of the plan's eligible activities and facilities. All you do is present your plan card. Many recreational offerings are on an "unlimited hourly use" basis, while others, like golf, involve some schedule restrictions. If you check out a canoe or bike, for example, you'll have to return it after one hour. Then, subject to availability, you can check it out again or check out something else. Charges for recreational services not covered by the plan must be handled separately.

The plan is a good deal for golfers, but you'll have to play at least every other day (subject to tee time availability) to really come out ahead. For golf, fishing excursions, and water skiing, reservations are required, the further in advance the better.

Walt Disney World Golf

Walt Disney World has six golf courses, all expertly designed and meticulously maintained. The Magnolia, the Palm, and the Oak Trail are across Floridian Way from the Polynesian Resort. They envelop the Shades of Green recreational complex, and the pro shops and support facilities adjoin the Shades of Green hotel (for military personnel and retirees only). Lake Buena Vista Golf Course is at the Disney Institute, near Walt Disney World Village and across the lake from Pleasure Island. The Osprey Ridge and Eagle Pines courses are part of the Bonnet Creek Golf Club near the Fort Wilderness Campground. In addition to the golf courses, there are driving ranges and putting greens at each location.

Oak Trail is a nine-hole course for beginners. The other five courses are designed for the mid-handicap player and, while interesting, are quite forgiving. All courses are popular, with morning tee times at a premium, especially January through April. To avoid the crowds, play on a Monday, Tuesday, or Wednesday, and sign up for a late-afternoon tee time.

Peak season for all of the courses is September through April; off-season is May through August. Afternoon twilight rates are available. Carts are required (except at Oak Trail) and are included in the greens fee. Tee times may be reserved 60 days in advance by Disney resort guests, 30 days in advance for day guests with a credit card, and 7 days in advance without guarantee. Proper golf attire is required: collared shirt and Bermuda-length shorts or slacks.

Lake Buena Vista Golf Course

Established: 1971

Designer: Joe Lee

Address: 2200 Club Lake Drive, Lake Buena Vista, FL 32830

Phone: (407) WDW-GOLF

Status: Resort

Tees:

> *Blue:* 6,819 yards, par 72, USGA 72.7, slope 125
> *White:* 6,268 yards, par 72, USGA 70.1, slope 123
> *Gold:* 5,919 yards, par 72, USGA 68.2, slope 120

Red: 5,191 yards, par 72, USGA 69.4, slope 120

Fees: Seasonal. Call for current rates.

Facilities: Pro shop, driving range, practice green, locker rooms, snack bar, beverage cart, and club and shoe rentals

Comments This Joe Lee design is styled in a classic country club setting, with narrow fairways meandering through dense forest and resort residential areas. Small, elevated, well-bunkered greens require accurate shotmaking. The course hosts the first three rounds of the Disney/Oldsmobile Golf Classic PGA Tour Event and the Healthsouth Inaugural Classic LPGA Tour Event.

Osprey Ridge Golf Course

Established: 1992

Designer: Tom Fazio

Address: 3451 Golf View Drive, Lake Buena Vista, FL 32830

Phone: (407) WDW-GOLF

Status: Resort

Tees:

  Black: 7,101 yards, par 72, USGA 73.9, slope 135
  Silver: 6,680 yards, par 72, USGA 71.8, slope 128
  Gold: 6,103 yards, par 72, USGA 68.9, slope 121
  Red: 5,402 yards, par 72, USGA 70.5, slope 122

Fees: Seasonal. Call for current rates.

Facilities: Pro shop, driving range, practice green, locker rooms, Sand Trap Bar and Grill, beverage cart, and club and shoe rentals

Comments Dramatically elevated tees and greens distinguish this Tom Fazio–designed course. Rolling fairways cut through tropical wilderness, while high mounds frame the medium-to-large greens.

Eagle Pines Golf Course

Established: 1992

Designer: Pete Dye

Address: 3451 Golf View Drive, Lake Buena Vista, FL 32830

Phone: (407) WDW-GOLF

Status: Resort

Tees:

  Black: 6,722 yards, par 72, USGA 72.3, slope 131

Silver: 6,309 yards, par 72, USGA 69.9, slope 125
Gold: 5,520 yards, par 72, USGA 66.3, slope 115
Red: 4,838 yards, par 72, USGA 68, slope 111

Fees: Seasonal. Call for current rates.

Facilities: Pro shop, driving range, practice green, locker rooms, Sand
Trap Bar and Grill, beverage cart, banquet facilities, and club and shoe
rentals

Comments Low, dish-shaped fairways lend a unique look and challenge
to the course. This Pete Dye design requires well-targeted shots to the
appropriate transition areas and avoiding the water that dots 16 of the 18
holes. Medium-sized, undulating greens are guarded by St. Augustine grass
bunkers.

Palm Golf Course

Established: 1970

Designer: Joe Lee

Address: 1950 West Magnolia/Palm Drive, Lake Buena Vista, FL 32830

Phone: (407) WDW-GOLF

Status: Resort

Tees:

Blue: 6,957 yards, par 72, USGA 73.0, slope 133
White: 6,461 yards, par 72, USGA 70.7, slope 129
Gold: 6,029 yards, par 72, USGA 68.7, slope 124
Red: 5,311 yards, par 72, USGA 70.4, slope 124

Fees: Seasonal. Call for current rates.

Facilities: Pro shop, driving range, practice green, locker rooms, snack
bar, beverage cart, and club and shoe rentals

Comments This Joe Lee–designed course offers many tree-lined fairways
and elevated greens, and boasts 9 water holes and 94 bunkers. Considered
the most difficult tournament course, the Palm hosts the Disney/
Oldsmobile Classic PGA Tour Event.

Magnolia Golf Course

Established: 1970

Designer: Joe Lee

Address: 1950 West Magnolia/Palm Drive, Lake Buena Vista, FL 32830

Phone: (407) WDW-GOLF

Status: Resort

Tees:

    Blue: 7,190 yards, par 72, USGA 73.9, slope 133
    White: 6,642 yards, par 72, USGA 71.6, slope 128
    Gold: 6,091 yards, par 72, USGA 69.1, slope 123
    Red: 5,253 yards, par 72, USGA 70.5, slope 123

Fees: Seasonal. Call for current rates.

Facilities: Pro shop, driving range, practice green, locker rooms, sports bar, beverage cart, and club and shoe rentals

Comments   This is the longest of Disney's courses. Wide fairways invite you to hit the ball hard, but beware of the 97 bunkers, including the one shaped like Mickey Mouse that guards the sixth green. The championship round of the Disney/Oldsmobile Golf Classic is played here.

Oak Trail Golf Course

Designer: Ron Garl

Address: 1950 West Magnolia/Palm Drive, Lake Buena Vista, FL 32830

Phone: (407) WDW-GOLF

Status: Resort

Tees:

    White: 2,913 yards, par 36
    Red: 2,532 yards, par 36

Fees: Adult, $32; child, $20. Includes use of a pull cart (course is walking only). To replay the course costs an additional $16 for adults and $10 for children.

Facilities: Pro shop, driving range, practice green, locker rooms, sports bar, beverage cart, and club and shoe rentals

Comments   This nine-hole walking course is nestled within the back nine of the Magnolia Course.

Fantasia Gardens Miniature Golf

A couple of years ago, the Disney Intelligence Patrol (DIP) noticed that as many as 113 guests a day were sneaking out of Walt Disney World to play Goofy Golf. Applying the logic of the boy who jammed his finger in the dike, Disney feared a hemorrhage of patrons from the theme parks. The thought of those AWOL guests making instant millionaires of miniature golf entrepreneurs on International Drive was enough to give a fat mouse ulcers.

The response to this assault on Disney's market share is Fantasia Gardens Miniature Golf, an 11-acre complex with two 18-hole dink-and-putt golf courses. One course is an "adventure" course, themed after Disney's animated film *Fantasia*. The other course, geared more toward older children and adults, is an innovative approach-and-putt course with sand traps and water hazards.

Fantasia Gardens is beautifully landscaped and creatively executed. There are fountains, animated statues, topiaries, flower beds, and a multitude of other imponderables that you're unlikely to find at most putt-putt courses.

Fantasia Gardens is on Epcot Resort Boulevard, across the street from the Walt Disney World Swan. To reach Fantasia Gardens via Disney transportation, take a bus or boat to the Swan resort.

The cost to putt at this course is $9 for adults and $8 for children. If you arrive hungry or naked, Fantasia Gardens has a snack bar and gift shop.

Part Fifteen

Nightlife in and out of Walt Disney World

Walt Disney World at Night

Disney so cleverly contrives to exhaust you during the day that the thought of night activity sends most visitors into shock. Walt Disney World, however, offers much for the hearty and the nocturnal to do in the evenings.

In the Parks

Epcot's major evening event is *IllumiNations,* a laser and fireworks show at World Showcase Lagoon. Show time is listed in the daily entertainment schedule.

In the Magic Kingdom are the popular evening parade(s) and *Fantasy in the Sky* fireworks. Consult the daily entertainment schedule for performances.

On nights when the park is open late, Disney-MGM Studios features a fireworks presentation called Sorcery in the Sky and *Fantasmic!*, a laser, special effects water spectacular. The daily entertainment schedule lists times.

At present there is no nighttime entertainment at the Animal Kingdom.

At the Hotels

The Floating Electrical Pageant is a sort of Main Street Electrical Parade on barges. Starring King Neptune and creatures of the sea, the nightly pageant (backed by Handel played on a doozie of a synthesizer), is one of our favorite Disney productions. The first performance of the short but captivating show is at 9 p.m. off the Polynesian Resort docks. From there, it circles around and repeats at the Grand Floridian at 9:15 p.m., heading afterward to Fort Wilderness Campground, Wilderness Lodge, and the Contemporary Resort.

For something more elaborate, consider a dinner theater. If you want to go honky-tonkin', many lodgings at the Disney Village Hotel Plaza have lively bars.

At Fort Wilderness Campground

The nightly campfire program at Fort Wilderness Campground begins with a sing-along led by Disney characters Chip 'n' Dale and progresses to cartoons and a Disney movie. Only Disney lodging guests may attend. There's no charge.

At Disney's BoardWalk

Jellyrolls at the BoardWalk features dueling pianos and sing-alongs in the image of New Orleans' Pat O' Brien's. The BoardWalk has Disney's first and only brew pub. A sports bar and several restaurants complete the Board-Walk's entertainment mix. Access is by foot from Epcot, by launch from Disney-MGM Studios, and by bus from other Disney World locations.

At Downtown Disney

Pleasure Island Pleasure Island, Walt Disney World's nighttime entertainment complex, offers eight nightclubs for one admission price. Dance to rock, soul, or country; take in a comedy show; or listen to some jazz. Pleasure Island is in Downtown Disney next to Downtown Disney Marketplace and is accessible from the theme parks and the Transportation and Ticket Center by shuttle bus. For details on Pleasure Island and a touring plan, see pages 645–652.

Downtown Disney Marketplace It's flog your wallet each night at the Marketplace with shops open until 11:30 pm.

Disney's West Side   Disney's West Side is a 70-acre shopping, restaurant, and nightlife complex situated to the left of Pleasure Island. Not to be confused with the West End Stage at nearby Pleasure Island, this latest addition to Downtown Disney features a 24-screen AMC movie complex, the DisneyQuest pay-for-play indoor theme park (see pages 618–620), a permanent home for the extraordinary *Cirque du Soleil,* and a 2,000-capacity House of Blues concert hall. Dining options include Planet Hollywood, a 450-seat Cajun restaurant at House of Blues, Wolfgang Puck Cafe (serving gourmet pizza and California fare), and Bongo's (Cuban cuisine), owned by Gloria and Emilio Estefan. The complex can be accessed via Disney buses from most Disney World locations.

House of Blues

Type of Show: Live concerts with an emphasis on rock and blues

Tickets and Information: (407) 934-2222

Admission Cost with Taxes: $8–50, depending on who is performing

Nights of Lowest Attendance: Monday and Tuesday

Usual Show Times: Monday–Thursday, 8:30; Friday and Saturday, 9:30;
   Dark: Sunday

Description and Comments   The House of Blues, developed by original Blues Brother Dan Akroyd, features a restaurant and Blues Bar, as well as the concert hall. The restaurant serves from 11 a.m. until 2 a.m., making it one of the few late-night dining options in Walt Disney World. Live music cranks up nightly at 11 p.m. in the restaurant/Blues Bar, but even before then, the joint is way beyond ten decibels. The Music Hall next door features concerts by an eclectic array of musicians and groups. During our last visit, the showbill listed gospel, blues, funk, ska, dance, salsa, rap, zydeco, hard rock, groove rock, and reggae groups over a two-week period.

Touring Tips   Prices vary from night to night according to the fame and drawing power of the featured band. Tickets ranged from $7–30 during our visits but go higher when a really big name is scheduled.

   The Music Hall is set up like a nightclub, with tables and bar stools for only about 150 people and standing room for a whopping 1,850 people. Folks dance when there's room and sometimes when there isn't. The tables and stools are first-come, first-served, with doors opening an hour before show time on weekdays and 90 minutes before show time on weekends. Acoustics are good, and the showroom is small enough to provide a relatively intimate concert experience. All shows are all ages unless otherwise indicated.

Cirque du Soleil

Type of Show: Circus as theater

Tickets and Information: (407) 939-7600

Admission Cost with Taxes: $56.50; $44 ages 3–9

Cast Size: 72

Night of Lowest Attendance: Thursday

Usual Show Times: 7:30 and 10:30 p.m. *Dark:* Monday and Tuesday

Special Comments: No table service (no tables!)

Smoking Allowed: No

Author's Rating: ★★★★½

Overall Appeal by Age Group:

Under 21 21–37   38–50   51 and older

★★★★   ★★★★★   ★★★★★   ★★★★½

Duration of Presentation: An hour and a half (no intermission)

Description and Comments   *Cirque du Soleil* is a far cry from a traditional circus but retains all the fun and excitement. It is whimsical, mystical, and sophisticated, yet pleasing to all ages. The action takes place on an elaborate stage that incorporates almost every part of the theater. The original musical score is exotic, like the show.

Note: In the following paragraph, I get into how the show *feels* and why it's special. If you don't care how it feels, or if you are not up to slogging through a boxcar of adjectives, the bottom line is simple: *Cirque du Soleil* is great. See it.

Cirque du Soleil is a most difficult show to describe. To categorize it as a circus does not begin to cover its depth, though its performers could perform with distinction in any circus on earth. *Cirque du Soleil* is more, much more, than a circus. It combines elements of Classical Greek theater, mime, the English morality play, Dali surrealism, Fellini characterization, and Chaplin comedy. *Cirque du Soleil* is at once an odyssey, a symphony, and an exploration of human emotions. The show pivots on its humor, which is sometimes black, and engages the audience with its unforgettable characters. Though light and uplifting, it is also poignant and dark. Simple in its presentation, it is at the same time extraordinarily intricate, always operating on multiple levels of meaning. As you laugh and watch the amazingly talented cast, you become aware that your mind has entered a dimension seldom encountered in a waking state. The presentation begins to register in your consciousness more as a seamless dream than as a stage production. You are moved, lulled, and soothed as well as excited and entertained. The sensitive, the imaginative, the literate, and those who love good theater and art will find nothing in all of Walt Disney World that compares with *Cirque du Soleil*.

Touring Tips   Be forewarned that the audience is an integral part of *Cirque du Soleil* and that at almost any time you might be plucked from your seat to participate. Our advice is to loosen up and roll with it. If you are too rigid, repressed, hungover, or whatever to get involved, politely but firmly decline to be conscripted.

Because *Cirque du Soleil* is presented in its own customized showroom, there are no tables and, consequently, no drink service. In keeping with the show's circus theme, however, spectators can purchase refreshments at nearby concession stands. Tickets for reserved seats can be purchased eight days in advance at the *Cirque's* box office or over the phone using your credit card.

WALT DISNEY WORLD DINNER THEATERS

Several dinner theater shows play each night at Walt Disney World, and unlike other Disney dining venues, they make hard reservations instead of priority seatings. You must guarantee advance dinner-show reservations with a credit card. You will receive a confirmation number and be told to pick up your tickets at a Disney hotel Guest Services desk. Unless you cancel your tickets at least 48 hours before your reservation time, your credit card will still be charged the full amount. Dinner-show reservations can be made up to two years in advance; call (407) 939-3463. While getting reservations for the *Polynesian Luau* isn't too tough, booking the *Hoop-Dee-Doo Revue* is a trick of the first order. Call as soon as you're certain of the dates of your visit. The earlier you call, the better your seats will be.

A couple from Bismarck, North Dakota, explains:

> *I'm glad we made our reservations so early (a year in advance). I was able to reserve space for us at the* Luau *at the Polynesian and the* Hoop-Dee-Doo Revue. *At both of these, they seat you according to when you made your reservation. At the* Hoop-Dee-Doo Revue, *we had a front center table. We were so close to the stage, we could see how many cavities the performers had!*

If you can't get reservations and want to see one of the shows:

1. Call (407) 939-3463 at 9 a.m. each morning while you're at Disney World to make a same-day reservation. There are three performances each night, and for all three combined, only 3 to 24 people total will be admitted with same-day reservations.

2. Arrive at the show of your choice 45 minutes before show time (early and late shows are your best bets) and put your name on the standby list. If someone with reservations fails to show, you may be admitted.

Hoop-Dee-Doo Revue

Address: Pioneer Hall, Fort Wilderness Campground

Phone: (407) 939-3463

Show Times: 5, 7:15, and 9:30 p.m. nightly

Cost: $38; $20 ages 3–11.

Discounts: Seasonal; American Express discount at 9:30 show only

Type of Seating: Tables of various sizes to fit the number in each party, set in an Old West–style dance hall

Menu: All-you-can-eat barbecue ribs, fried chicken, corn-on-the-cob, and strawberry shortcake

Vegetarian Alternative: On request

Beverages: Unlimited beer, wine, sangria, and soft drinks

Description and Comments   Six Wild West performers arrive by stagecoach (sound effects only) to entertain the crowd inside Pioneer Hall. There isn't much plot, just corny jokes interspersed with song or dance.

Given Disney's technical resources and its pool of talented entertainers, the *Hoop-Dee-Doo Revue* is rather amateurish, with decidedly low entertainment value. Jokes are lame and tend to dwell on puns. One marathon of puns using the word "bear" even prompted a six-year-old sitting nearby to shout in exasperation, "Stop saying 'bear.'" Audience participation includes sing-alongs, hand-clapping, and a finale that uses volunteers to play parts onstage. Performers are accompanied by a banjo player and pianist who provide quiet accompaniment while the food is being served.

The fried chicken and corn-on-the-cob are good, but the ribs are a bit tough. With the all-you-can-eat policy, at least you can get your money's worth by stuffing yourself silly. There isn't much value in the show.

While the *Hoop-Dee-Doo Revue* is far from being the best dinner show in the Disney World/Orlando area, traveling to Fort Wilderness and absorbing the rustic atmosphere of Pioneer Hall augments the adventure. For repeat Disney World visitors, an annual visit to the revue is a tradition of sorts. Plus, good or not, the revue is all Disney, and for some folks that's enough. The fact that performances sell out far in advance give the experience a special (if undeserved) aura.

Most of our readers enjoy the *Hoop-Dee-Doo Revue,* but not all. The thoughts of a Texas family are typical:

> *What is all the hoop-dee-doo with the* Hoop-Dee-Doo Revue?
> *The food was okay, if "gut-busting" fare is your idea of a fine night out, and the entertainment was pleasant. As a dinner theater, however, our family of three found it unexceptional in every respect but its cost.*

Had your review of the Revue *tempered its enthusiasm (much as you present its Polynesian counterpart), we probably would have canceled our reservation, pocketed the $100 and spent the evening joyously stunned by another glorious light-and-fireworks spectacle.*

An alternative to the *Hoop-Dee-Doo Revue* is the Fort Liberty show, a non-Disney attraction on FL 192.

If you go to the *Hoop-Dee-Doo Revue,* allow plenty of time to get there. The experience of a reader from Houston, Texas, makes the point:

We had 7:30 p.m. reservations for the Hoop-Dee-Doo Revue, *so we left [Disney-]MGM just before 7 and drove directly to Fort Wilderness. Two important things to note: First, the road direction signs at WDW are terrible. I would recommend a daylight orientation drive upon arrival, except that there are so many ways to get confused that one might be lulled into a false sense of security. Second, when we got to Fort Wilderness, we had great difficulty determining where Pioneer Hall was and how to get there. I accosted several people and found a man who could tell us where we were on the map, and that a bus was the only way to get to Pioneer Hall. I would recommend leaving for Pioneer Hall one hour before your show reservations. Boredom is not nearly so painful as anxiety (reservations are held until 15 minutes after the stated time).*

A California dad suggests:

To go to the Hoop-Dee-Doo Revue *at Fort Wilderness, take the boat from the Magic Kingdom rather than any bus. This [is] contrary to the "official" directions. The boat dock is a short walk from Pioneer Hall [in Fort Wilderness], while the bus goes to the [main] Fort Wilderness parking lot where one has to transfer to another bus to Pioneer Hall.*

Polynesian Luau

Address: Disney's Polynesian Resort

Phone: (407) 939-3463

Show Times: 6:45 and 9:30 p.m. nightly

Cost: $38; $20 ages 3–11

Discounts: Seasonal; American Express discount for all shows

Type of Seating: Long rows of tables, with some separation between individual parties. The show is performed on an outdoor stage, but all seating is covered. Ceiling fans provide some air movement, but it can get warm, especially at the early show.

Menu: Tropical fruit, roasted chicken, island pork, fresh catch, mixed vegetables, rice, and pineapple cake

Vegetarian Alternative: On request

Beverages: Beer, wine, and soft drinks

Description and Comments South Sea–island native dancing follows a "Polynesian-style," all-you-can-eat meal. The dancing is interesting and largely authentic, and dancers are attractive though definitely PG in the Disney tradition. We think the show has its moments and the meal is adequate, but neither is particularly special.

The *Polynesian Luau* suffers from excruciatingly slow pacing, with long periods with nothing but recorded background music. The first part is little more than a fashion show. After a long intermission, there is a demonstration of island dances preceding a performance by a dancer twirling flaming batons. All the dancers perform well, but this show becomes a snoozer really early. The show has more value as a history lesson and is about as interesting. Audience participation includes learning the hula and yelling "a-LOHHH-ha" a lot.

A well-traveled, married couple from Fond du Lac, Wisconsin, describes the *Polynesian Luau:*

> *The* Polynesian [Luau] *was a beautiful presentation, better than some shows we have seen in Hawaii! The food, however, lacked in all areas. Better food has come out of Disney kitchens. During our visit, the fruit platter was chintzy; the honey-roasted chicken was a bit fatty; and the pineapple cake was dry.*

Also at the Polynesian Resort's Luau Cove is *Mickey's Tropical Luau,* at which Disney characters are added to the regular show. This performance starts at 4:30 p.m., when it is too early to be hungry and too hot to be sitting outdoors. Cost is about $33 for adults and $16 for children ages 3–11.

OTHER AREA DINNER THEATERS

Central Florida probably has more dinner attractions than anywhere else on earth. The name dinner attraction is something of a misnomer, because dinner is rarely the attraction. These are audience-participation shows or events with food served along the way. They range from extravagant productions where guests sit in arenas at long tables, to intimate settings at individual tables. Don't expect terrific food, but if you're looking for something entertaining outside Walt Disney World, consider one of these.

If you decide to try a non-Disney dinner show, scavenge local tourist magazines from brochure racks and hotel desks outside the World. These free publications usually have discount coupons for area shows.

Arabian Nights

Address: 6225 West Irlo Bronson Highway, Kissimmee (US 192 just east of I-4)

Phone: (407) 239-9223

Show Times: Nightly at varying times; currently at 7:30 or 8:30 p.m.; one show only

Cost: $36.95; $23.95 ages 3–11

Discounts: Dollars-off coupons in local visitor magazines, AAA, seniors

Type of Seating: Long rows of benches at tables flanking either side of a large riding arena. All seats face the action.

Menu: Minestrone, prime rib, mixed vegetables, new potatoes, and sheet cake

Vegetarian Alternative: Lasagna

Beverages: Unlimited beer, wine, tea, coffee, and soft drinks

Description and Comments   Horses and riders present equestrian skills and trick riding with costumes, music, and theatrical lighting. The loose story line involves a princess who spots a handsome prince who then disappears. A genie appears to grant her three wishes, which, of course, she uses to try to find the stud on the steed. For some reason, she doesn't just tell the genie to produce the guy front and center. They travel the world over—and back in time—to look for him. The search takes them anywhere you might find horses: the circus, the Wild West, the set of *Ben Hur*. In all, horses perform to musical accompaniment.

If you are an unbridled horse fan, you're going to think you've died and gone to heaven. Fifty horses, including Lipizzans, palominos, quarter horses, and Arabians, perform 22 acts. The stunts are impressive, and a great deal of skill and timing is employed to pull them off. But after awhile the tricks start to look the same, only the costumes and the music are different. The whole thing ends in a patriotic ploy.

Arabian Nights' food is distinguished in that it's the only dinner-show fare that doesn't include chicken. The prime rib is edible, and the lasagna alternative is fine. The salad is unappealing, as is the dessert.

American Gladiators Orlando Live

Address: 5515 West US 192, Kissimmee

Phone: (407) 390-0000

Show Times: 7:30 p.m. nightly

Cost: $35, $22 ages 3–12

Discounts: Discounts for AAA members, seniors, military, and Florida residents

Type of Seating: Arena-style

Menu: Tossed salad; choice of prime rib, stuffed chicken, or lasagne; new potatoes; glazed carrots; and dessert. Children's alternative is chicken fingers.

Vegetarian Alternative: Lasagna

Beverages: Unlimited beer, wine, and soda

Description and Comments This is a competition between two teams—red and blue—each consisting of a man and woman, based on the ESPN television show. They vie for points by engaging in games that pit them against members of the American Gladiators. Games include wall climbing, a joust where contenders and Gladiators use pugil sticks to try to knock each other off a eight-foot-high platform, and an event where contenders try to hit a target with a crossbow and arrow while a Gladiator fires tennis balls at them at 120 miles per hour. The action takes place on the arena floor or the large stage at one end.

The audience is divided and assigned to cheer for either the red or blue team. Audience members for the winning team are told they'll win a prize. It turns out to be a coupon that allows children to eat free at a seafood restaurant next door. At some point, emcees announce that everyone will receive a coupon.

American Gladiators Orlando Live is high-energy and glitzy, with pulsating music, flashing lights, lasers, and fog machines. All the men and women are gorgeous, with the kinds of bodies Spandex was intended for. Gladiators mingle with the audience and pose for photos. The games are exciting, and the equipment and platforms, which rise from the stage and are lowered from the rafters, are first-rate. The food here is some of the better served at the dinner attractions.

Medieval Times Dinner & Tournament

Address: 4510 East US Highway 192, Kissimmee

Phone: (800) 229-8300

Show Times: Vary according to season and nights

Cost: $41; $25 ages 3–12

Discounts: Seniors, military, AAA, hotel employees, travel agents. You get free admission on your birthday.

Type of Seating: Arena-style, in long rows that face the riding floor

Menu: Vegetable soup, whole roasted chicken, spare ribs, herb-basted potatoes, and strudel. Everything is eaten with the hands; no utensils are provided.

Vegetarian Alternative: Lasagna

Beverages: Two rounds of beer, wine, or soft drinks; cash bar available

Description and Comments   A tournament set 900 years in the past pits six knights against each other. Audience members are seated in areas corresponding to the color of the knights' pennants and are encouraged to cheer for their knight and to boo his opponents. Part of the tournament is actual competition. The knights perform stunts, including hitting a target with a lance or collecting rings on a lance while riding horseback. After each event, successful knights receive carnations from the queen to toss to young ladies in their sections.

After a while, the tournament takes on a choreographed feel—and with good reason. It comes down to a fight to the finish until only one knight is left standing. There are cheating knights who pull others off their horses and hand-to-hand combat with maces, battle-axes, and swords. The winning knight selects a fair maiden from the audience to be his princess.

The food is remarkable only in that you eat it with your hands, including a whole chicken you must pull apart. The chicken is good, the ribs a little tough. The appetizer (surely you jest) is a hamburger bun, either top or bottom, slathered with tomato sauce and melted cheese. Very cheesy, indeed.

The show is good, and the knights put out 100% (the bruises these guys must get!). The sword fights are so realistic that sparks fly off the metal blades. Audience participation reaches a fever pitch, with each section cheering for its knight and calling for the death of the dastardly opponents. It's amazing how bloodthirsty people can be after they've ripped a chicken apart with their bare hands.

With all the horses, jousting, and fighting, children shouldn't be bored, though parents of very young children might be concerned about the violence.

Capone's Dinner & Show

Address: 4740 West US 192, Kissimmee

Phone: (407) 397-2378

Show Times: 8 p.m. nightly; changes seasonally

Cost: $35.99, including tax and gratuity; $18 ages 4–12

Discounts: Florida residents, AAA, seniors, military, hospitality workers

Type of Seating: Long tables with large groupings facing an elevated stage; some smaller tables for parties of two to six

Menu: Buffet with lasagna, baked ziti, Italian sausage, spaghetti, baked chicken, baked ham, boiled potatoes, tossed salad, and brownies

Vegetarian Alternative: Spaghetti, ziti

Beverages: Unlimited beer, wine, sangria, and soft drinks

Description and Comments   The audience, attending a celebration for mobster Al Capone at a '30s speakeasy in Chicago, enters through a secret door using a password. The show is a musical of sorts, with most songs from other sources sung by cast members to recorded accompaniment. The story revolves around Miss Jewel—the speakeasy's hostess, who loves Detective Marvel, the only cop in Chicago that Capone can't buy—and one of the show's floozies and her gambling boyfriend. (Can you say, *Guys and Dolls?*)

The audience parades through the buffet line before the show; seconds are invited. The food is good for buffet fare. The lasagna is tasty, and it is nice to see variety on the line.

For a musical, this show employs a lot of nonsingers. Even the dancing is second-rate. The waiters—who speak with tough-guy accents and kid around with guests—did more to entertain the children than at any other show. Still, the theme is a bit too adult.

Wild Bill's Wild West Dinner Extravaganza

Address: 5260 US Highway 192, Kissimmee

Phone: 407) 351-5151

Show Times: Vary; usually at 7 and 9:30 p.m. nightly

Cost: $37; $23 ages 3–11

Discounts: Florida residents, AAA, military, AARP; coupons in most tourist publications

Type of Seating: Long tables surround a stage where acts are performed in-the-round. The room has the look of a mess hall at an Old West fort.

Menu: Stew, salad, barbecue ribs, fried chicken, vegetables, baked potato, corn, and ice cream cake

Vegetarian Alternative: Tortellini

Beverages: Unlimited beer, wine, and soft drinks

Description and Comments It's 1876 and Wild Bill and his co-host, Miss Kitty, are celebrating America's centennial with a show right out of the Wild West. Featured are knife throwers, archery demonstrations, rope tricks, saloon-hall dancers, and Native Americans.

Wild Bill's is a lot of fun, and the acts are first-rate. The Native American who performs a traditional hoop dance is fascinating. The room is divided, with half of the audience ranchers (lots of mooing) and the other half sheepherders (lots of baaing). There's plenty to keep the kids entertained. Whoever sits at the front of the table has the dubious task of serving much of the food to others at the table.

King Henry's Feast

Address: 8984 International Drive, Orlando

Phone: (407) 351-5151

Show Times: Vary; usually two shows nightly at 7 and 9:30 p.m.

Cost: $37; $23 ages 3–11

Discounts: Florida residents, AAA, military, AARP; coupons in most tourist publications

Type of Seating: Long tables encircle a stage where acts perform in-the-round.

Menu: Leek and potato soup, salad, baked chicken, barbecue pork, baked potato, vegetables, cake, and ice cream

Vegetarian Alternative: Lasagna or white fish entree with advance request

Beverages: Unlimited beer, wine, and soft drinks

Description and Comments   It's King Henry's birthday, and the celebration in his summer castle includes a show that would have made Ed Sullivan proud. The monarch and his jester are hosts, introducing such acts as a trapeze aerialist, a juggler, and a sword swallower who will make your throat throb. There's also lots of singing and a lame sword fight.

Most acts are impressive, but the main characters—the king, his jester, and a woman who helps them sing the food into the hall—seem bored and they more or less walk through the evening.

The food is neither bad nor good. Each course, or "remove" as it's called, is paraded in by serving wenches, who plop the containers onto the table for the poor dope sitting on the end to dish up and pass down the way.

Kids will find the acts entertaining, but they may get bored with the traditional English folk songs, even when the audience is encouraged to sing along.

Pirates at Colossal Studios

Address: 6400 Carrier Drive, Orlando

Phone: (407) 248-0590

Show Times: 7:45 p.m. Tuesday–Sunday

Cost: $37; $22 ages 3–11 (includes tax and tip)

Discounts: Florida residents, AAA, AARP, military

Type of Seating: Arena-style

Menu: Caribbean rice with pineapple, pork, beef, and chicken; ice cream and apple cobbler

Vegetarian Alternative: Lasagna

Beverages: Unlimited beer, wine, and soft drinks

Description and Comments   Setting is an old B-movie studio that used to make adventure movies. The audience sits in a lounge to watch a rehearsal for a new movie about pirates. Barrels fall off the wall, revealing the entrance to an old movie set. This is the dining area, centered by a life-size pirate ship surrounded by water. The crew begins filming on the newly discovered set.

The set is impressive, and during the evening pirates swoop from overhead, race around the ship on water scooters, toss balls into a net with the help of audience volunteers, and bounce on a trampoline that's part of the ship. What's mystifying is that there doesn't seem to be a reason for any of this. My companion and I were completely lost as to what was going on and why.

The audience sits in color-coded sections and is encouraged to cheer for the pirate wearing their color as they compete against each other.

There's plenty to interest kids. Adults might be interested, too, if the story were easier to follow. After the show, guests are invited into a disco for dancing.

Aloha! Polynesian Luau

Address: Sea World, 7007 Sea World Drive, Orlando

Phone: (407) 351-3600

Show Times: 6:15 p.m. nightly

Cost: $36; $26 ages 8–12, $16 ages 3–7

Discounts: Discounts seasonally

Type of Seating: Long tables with no separation from other parties

Menu: Fruit "pu pu" platter, salad, mahimahi in piña colada sauce, sweet-and-sour chicken, smoked pork loin, rice, vegetables, and hula pie (cheesecake)

Vegetarian Alternative: Mixed vegetables, sticky rice

Beverages: One complimentary mai tai; full cash bar. This is the only show to offer just one cocktail, an odd thing considering the park is owned by Anheuser-Busch, which owns practically all the beer in the world.

Description and Comments   *Aloha! Polynesian Luau* has the appearance of a touring lounge act that might play the Ramada Inn circuit in the Midwest. Even the venue, a large, dark room with a very low ceiling, looks like a motel lounge. In this musical revue featuring singers, dancers, and fire twirlers, a Don Ho–esque singer is given way too much time. The dancers perform well, and the fire twirler who ends the show is impressive, but there is otherwise little excitement.

The food is more varied than at many other shows. The mahimahi is good, but the fruit platter is uninteresting. The food is served family-style, and you may share a platter with someone else's family.

The service is not very attentive. Audience participation is minimal, and children probably will be bored.

Sleuths Mystery Show

Address: Republic Square, 7508 Republic Drive, Orlando

Phone: (407) 363-1985

Show Times: Vary nightly; 6, 7:30, or 9 p.m.

Cost: $33.95; $22.95 ages 3–11

Discounts: Coupon for Florida residents, AAA, seniors, students, Disney employees, travel agents, military, hospitality employees, full-blooded Chippewa Indians

Type of Seating: Large round tables that seat 8 to 10; some smaller tables

Menu: Cheese spread and crackers; tossed salad; choice of Cornish hen, prime rib, or lasagna

Vegetarian Alternative: Lasagna

Beverages: Unlimited beer, wine, or soft drinks

Description and Comments Sleuths perform a repertory of murder mysteries the audience must solve. Audience participation is key to the enjoyment. Guests are part of the show from the moment they enter the theater. Actors in character direct seating and try to drop clues as to who and what their parts are in the play. Although they work from a script, much of the show is ad-libbed. Unfortunately, the cast tends to be of limited talent and incapable of ad-libbing well. Each table must choose a spokesman and prepare a question for the actors as they try to solve the murder. Unless you come with a large group, you probably will find yourself interacting with strangers.

The cheese spread and crackers—one crock and one basket for the entire table—is about as cheesy an appetizer as you'll find. The salad is a bigger joke than any of the actors produced. The prime rib was tough during our visit, and the Cornish game hen offered little meat.

You'll probably have more fun if you go with a large group and occupy your own table. Older children might find the show interesting, but younger ones will probably be bored.

Pleasure Island

Pleasure Island is a six-acre nighttime entertainment complex on a manmade island in Downtown Disney. It consists of eight nightclubs, restaurants, and shops. While some restaurants and shops are open during the day, Pleasure Island doesn't really come alive until after 7 p.m., when the nightclubs open.

Admission Options One admission (about $20) entitles a guest to enjoy all eight nightclubs. Guests younger than 18 must be accompanied by a parent after 7 p.m. Unlimited eight-day admission to Pleasure Island is included in All-in-One passes.

Alcoholic Beverages Guests not recognizably older than 21 must provide proof of their age if they wish to buy alcoholic beverages. To avoid repeated checking as the patron club-hops, a color-coded wristband indicates eligibility. All nightclubs serve alcohol. Those under 21, while allowed in all clubs except Mannequins, aren't allowed to buy alcoholic beverages. Finally, and gratefully, you don't have to order drinks at all. You can enjoy the entertainment at any club and never buy that first beer. No server will hassle you.

Dress Code Casual is in, but shirts and shoes are required.

New Variations on an Old Theme The single-admission nightclub complex was originated in Florida at Orlando's Church Street Station, still very much alive in historic downtown Orlando. Starting fresh, Disney eliminated some problems that haunted Church Street Station and other nightspots over the years.

Good News for the Early-to-Bed Crowd If you aren't nocturnal or you're tired from a long day in the theme parks, you don't have to wait until 11 p.m. or midnight for Pleasure Island to hit its stride. All bands, dancers, comedians, and showmen come on like gangbusters from the very beginning of the evening. Later in the evening as the crowd builds and becomes more lubricated, Pleasure Island assumes the character of a real adult nightspot. During the transition (i.e., in the early evening), however, it is not unusual to see a lot of kids in the clubs.

It's Possible to Visit All the Clubs in One Night Whereas performances in nightclubs elsewhere might be an hour or more in duration, at Pleasure Island shows are shorter but more frequent. This allows guests to move among clubs without missing much. Since you can catch the essence of a club pretty quickly, there's no need to hang around for two or three drinks to see what's going on. This format enables guests to have a complete and satisfying experience in a brief time, then move to another club if they want.

The music clubs (Rock n Roll Beach Club, 8TRAX, Wildhorse Saloon, BET Soundstage Club, Mannequins Dance Palace, and the Pleasure Island Jazz Company) go nonstop. Sometimes, there are special performances within the ongoing club entertainment. The Adventurers Club and the Comedy Warehouse offer scheduled shows.

We are very high on Pleasure Island. The cover is a little pricey and the drinks aren't cheap, but the entertainment is absolutely top-notch. And if you arrive before 9 p.m., you'll have time to sample all of the clubs.

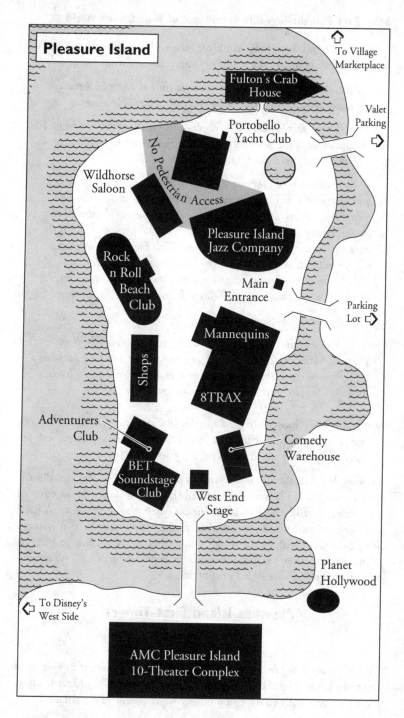

Pleasure Island

To Village Marketplace

Fulton's Crab House

Valet Parking

Portobello Yacht Club

No Pedestrian Access

Wildhorse Saloon

Pleasure Island Jazz Company

Rock n Roll Beach Club

Main Entrance

Parking Lot

Mannequins

Shops

8TRAX

Adventurers Club

Comedy Warehouse

BET Soundstage Club

West End Stage

Planet Hollywood

To Disney's West Side

AMC Pleasure Island 10-Theater Complex

A reader reminds us that "sampling" the clubs, as we suggest, isn't the same as spending some time and really appreciating them:

> *Pleasure Island clubs take much more time to appreciate than you allow. We spent two evenings and only got to four places.*

We get considerable mail from couples in their 30s and 40s arguing Pleasure Island's merits (or lack thereof). These quotes are representative. A reader from Bettendorf, Iowa, writes:

> *I would not spend the money to go to Pleasure Island again. It is quite obvious that Disney is interested in the 21- to 30-year-old crowd here. There were many people our age (38) and older looking for something to do and not finding it. The Adventurers Club is the only real Disney creation on the island. Walt Disney World crosses all age brackets, and I expected the same from Pleasure Island. What a disappointment! I think you need to go back to the drawing board on your evaluation of Pleasure Island (and so does Disney).*

A central Texas couple disagrees:

> *Your description, even with the statement that you are high on Pleasure Island, didn't prepare my wife and me for what a great place it is. Perhaps our expectations were moderate, but we thought it was an absolute blast, and we are neither under 40 nor club hounds.*

Sorry, Invited Guests Only   Occasionally, particularly before 9 p.m., certain Pleasure Island clubs are reserved for private parties and are declared temporarily off-limits to paying guests.

Parking Is a Hassle   Pleasure Island's parking lot often fills up. On the bright side, the lot is now well marked. If you jot down the location of your space, you'll be able to find your car when it's time to leave. A good strategy is to park in the lot adjacent to the movie theaters and Disney's West Side and enter via the bridge connecting the West Side to Pleasure Island. Because there's an admission booth at the bridge, there's no need to enter through Pleasure Island's main gate.

Pleasure Island First-Timers' Touring Plan

This itinerary is for first-timers at Pleasure Island who want to visit all of the clubs in one night. It provides a taste of each venue. If you settle someplace that you really enjoy, you probably won't complete the circuit.

1. Arrive by 6:30 or 7 p.m. if you intend to eat at a Pleasure Island restaurant. If you eat before you go, arrive at about 8 p.m.

2. Buy your admission.

3. **Comedy Warehouse** Go left from the admission windows at the main entrance to the Comedy Warehouse. This is Pleasure Island's toughest ticket. There are normally five shows nightly, with the two earlier shows (usually 7:30 and 8:25 p.m.) easiest to get into. If a show begins within 30 minutes, hop in line. If show time is more than 30 minutes away, check out the country and bluegrass music at the Neon Armadillo across the street. Use your judgment about whether you have time to buy a drink. Return to the Comedy Warehouse 30 minutes before show time. If you don't arrive at Pleasure Island in time to catch either of the first two shows, plan to queue at least 35 minutes before show time for subsequent performances.

4. **Adventurers Club** After the show at the Comedy Warehouse, cross the street to the Adventurers Club. Patterned after a stuffy English gentlemen's club, the Adventurers Club is a two-story, turn-of-the-century affair with big armchairs, walls covered with animal heads (some of which talk), and other artifacts.

   Many guests will stroll through the club, inspect the ridiculous decor, and leave, not realizing they missed the main attraction: a show in the club's library. About once every 30 or 40 minutes, all guests will be ushered into the library for a performance. Nobody tells guests a show is upcoming; they must either hang around long enough to be invited in or intuit that, with Disney, what you see isn't what you get.

   When you arrive at the Adventurers Club, ask an attendant when the next show in the library will begin. If it's in 20 minutes or less, go in and have a drink. If it's a long while, the Neon Armadillo is next door.

5. **BET Soundstage Club** Opened in 1998 in partnership with Black Entertainment Television, this club features soul and R&B.

6. **8TRAX** When Pleasure Island opened, this was an under-21 club called Videopolis East. For various reasons (fights and teenage gang conflicts), it was closed and reopened as Cage, which targeted older (over-21) rockers but never achieved much of an identity. Now it's 8TRAX, a '70s disco featuring the music of K. C. and the Sunshine Band, the Bee Gees, and Donna Summer. Though the decor during our last visit was the same steel

beams, catwalks, and metal mesh that imbued the club's previous incarnations with such charm, it was clear that the '70s concept had taken root. The place was rocking.

7. **Mannequins Dance Palace** Backtrack toward Pleasure Island's front entrance to Mannequins, a ritzy, techno-pop, rock dance club with a revolving dance floor, incredible lighting, and wild special effects. The dance music is recorded, but the sound system is superb (and very, very loud). There is often a line waiting to enter. This has less to do with the club's popularity than with the fact that Disney prefers guests to enter via an elevator to the second floor. The elevator helps distribute guests throughout the club, but there's a perfectly good entrance on the first floor. For some reason, cast members at the entrance will often invite 40-something (and older) guests to enter directly, without being subjected to the elevator. Patrons younger than 21 aren't allowed in Mannequins through either entrance.

8. **Pleasure Island Jazz Company** Cross the walkway from the Mannequins' entrance to the next nightspot on the touring plan. The Jazz Company occupies space previously used as a food court and private party room. The club features live jazz and blues and hosts jam sessions with local musicians. The crowd, more diverse in age and appearance than at other clubs, sits at tables flanking the stage on three sides.

9. **Rock n Roll Beach Club** Proceed to the Beach Club, featuring oldies and current rock. Bands here are always first-rate, and they raise the roof beginning early in the evening. Electronic games and pool are available for those who don't wish to dance.

10. **Wildhorse Saloon** Last on the club list is this newly opened nightspot featuring country music, line dancing, and barbecue.

11. **West End Stage** Continue to the West End Stage. It isn't a club, but it's the most happening place on Pleasure Island. Live rock bands perform under the stars in the plaza, with the BET Soundstage Club and Adventurers Club on one side and Comedy Warehouse on the other. Bands, without exception, are super, as are lighting and sound systems. The high stage provides excellent visibility. Performances usually occur four times each night, with a grand finale at 11:45 p.m., accompanied by fireworks, showers of confetti, and blazing searchlights. Street vendors sell drinks.

12. **Pleasure Island Restaurants** Dining at Pleasure Island has improved in the past year or so. Though still noisy, crowded, and

expensive, restaurants here offer a variety of creative and well-prepared dishes. For detailed profiles of Pleasure Island restaurants, see Part 8, "Dining in and around Walt Disney World" (page 239).

The Island's new headliner restaurant is the Wildhorse Saloon, replacing the Fireworks Factory as the barbecue capital of Walt Disney World. Other restaurants include Fulton's Crab House, on the *Empress Lilly* riverboat, specializing in shellfish and fresh Florida seafood, and the Portobello Yacht Club, serving seafood, pasta, and pizza. Casual yet stylish, the Portobello does a creditable job with its varied Italian fare.

Another big player on Pleasure Island is Planet Hollywood, at the entrance to Disney's West Side. While the food is pretty good and the servings large, the main draw is the Hollywood memorabilia decorating the restaurant. Unless you eat at strange times, expect long waits for a table.

Our researchers half-jokingly refer to Planet Hollywood as the restaurant with an attitude. A reader from Bartlesville, Oklahoma, agrees:

> *Planet Hollywood was NOT a pleasant experience. We arrived at 5 p.m. and still had to wait an hour [to be seated]. I had the feeling of being herded like cattle. I also felt the staff manipulated things so there was always a line (i.e., there were several tables that stayed empty during the time we were waiting). The hosts on duty were rude. By the time we were seated, our waiter was friendly and the food was good, but I was too stressed out to care . . . this was the only time at Disney World that we were treated rudely. I understand Planet Hollywood is not owned or operated by Disney, and the contrast in attitude was quite apparent.*

Priority seating is strongly recommended for all full-service restaurants. If you don't have one, arrive by 6 p.m. or eat after 10 p.m. An alternative is to eat sandwiches and snacks in the clubs. It isn't necessary to buy club admission to eat at the restaurants. Most are also open during the day.

If no Pleasure Island restaurant lights your candle, a number of themed and nonthemed restaurants are within easy walking distance at the Downtown Disney Marketplace and at Disney's West Side. Again, priority seating is advised for the full-service restaurants.

13. **Pleasure Island Shopping** Some shops on the Island are attractions in themselves. At Cover Story, guests dress up before being photographed for the mock cover of a major magazine. Want to

see yourself on *Cosmo?* Here's the place. Similarly, Superstar Studio lets you star in your own music video. Props include keyboard, drums, and guitar. Video technicians record your lip-syncing (or you can actually sing); varying camera angles make you look good. Post-production adds realism to your tape. Work alone or with a group of your friends. If you don't want your own magazine cover or rock video, watch others make them. It's a hoot!

It isn't necessary to pay admission to shop at Pleasure Island during the day. In the evening, all of the Island except the restaurants is gated.

The regular crowd settles in at Pleasure Island.

Appendix

Readers' Questions to the Author

Following are questions and comments from *Unofficial Guide* readers. Some frequently asked questions are addressed in every edition of the *Unofficial Guide*.

Q: When you do your research, are you admitted to the parks free? Do the Disney people know you are there?
A: We pay the regular admission and usually the Disney people do not know we are on-site. Similarly, both in and out of Walt Disney World, we pay for our own meals and lodging.

Q: How often is the Unofficial Guide *revised?*
A: We publish a new edition once a year, but we make minor corrections every time we go to press, usually about three times a year.

Q: Do you write each new edition from scratch?
A: We do not. With a destination the size of Walt Disney World it's hard enough keeping up with what's new. Moreover, we put great effort into communicating the most salient, useful information in the clearest possible language. If an attraction or hotel has not changed, we are very reluctant to tinker with its coverage for the sake of freshening up the writing.

Q: I have an old edition of the Unofficial Guide. *How much of the information [in it] is still correct?*
A: Veteran travel writers will acknowledge that 5–8% of the information in a guidebook is out of date by the time it comes off the press! Walt Disney World is always changing. If you are using an old edition of the *Unofficial Guide,* descriptions of attractions still existing should be generally accurate. However, many other things change with every edition, particularly the touring plans and the hotel and restaurant reviews. Finally, and obviously, older editions of the *Unofficial Guide* do not include new attractions or developments.

Q: How many people have you surveyed for your "age group ratings" on the attractions?
A: Since the publication of the first edition of the *Unofficial Guide* in 1985, we have interviewed or surveyed just under 16,000 Walt Disney World patrons. Even with such a large survey population, however, we continue to have difficulty with certain age groups. Specifically, we love to hear from seniors about their experiences with Splash Mountain, Big Thunder Mountain Railroad, Space Mountain, *Alien Encounter,* Star Tours, Tower of Terror, Body Wars, Test Track, and Countdown to Extinction.

Q: Do you stay in Walt Disney World? If not, where do you stay?
A: We do stay at Walt Disney World lodging properties from time to time, usually when a new hotel opens. Since we began writing about Walt Disney World in 1982, we have stayed in over 50 different properties in various locations around Orlando, Lake Buena Vista, and Kissimmee. During our last visit we stayed at the BoardWalk Resort and liked it very much.

Q: Why are there no photographs of the theme parks in the Unofficial Guide?
A: Disney has copyrighted many identifiable buildings and structures in Walt Disney World. Any recognizable photo of Walt Disney World that we publish without Disney's permission, even if we take the picture with our own camera, could constitute copyright infringement, according to Disney's legal representatives. Walt Disney World will not grant the *Unofficial Guide* permission to publish photographs because of its relationship with the *Official Guide to Walt Disney World.*

Q: What can we expect in terms of new developments over the next couple of years at Walt Disney World?
A: The Animal Kingdom is scheduled to add Asia to the lineup in 1999. Headliner attractions will include a whitewater raft ride and an exploration trail populated with tigers and other Asian animals. Another land based on mythical beasts has been a long time getting off the drawing board and may be postponed. Two proposed themed hotels adjacent to the Animal Kingdom had not broken ground at press time. Ditto for the proposed Wilderness Junction Resort, to be modeled on a Wild-West boomtown theme, and the Mediterranean Resort, to be located on the Seven Seas Lagoon between the TTC and the Contemporary Resort.

Q: What is your favorite Florida attraction?
A: What attracts me (as opposed to my favorite attraction) is Juniper Springs, a stunningly beautiful stream about an hour north of Orlando in the Ocala National Forest. Originating as a limestone aquifer, crystal clear water erupts from the ground and begins a ten-mile journey to the creek's

mouth at Lake George. Winding through palm, cypress, and live oak, the stream is more exotic than the Jungle Cruise, and alive with birds, animals, turtles, and alligators. Put in at the Juniper Springs Recreation Area on FL 40, 36 miles east of Ocala. The seven-mile trip to the FL 19 bridge takes about four and a half hours. Canoe rentals and shuttle service are available at the recreation area. Phone (352) 625-2808 for information.

Readers' Comments

According to this reader, priority seating posed no inconvenience:

> *You and your readers complained about priority seating for Disney restaurants. We used it twice and had no problem and saw no one else with a problem—and the parks were jammed and the restaurants busy. Both times, we were seated within five minutes of the appointed time. Disney can't control how long parties will stay at their tables after finishing their meals, or reduce no-shows without charging a deposit, so I thought the priority seating system was fair to all. The reservations policy is now carefully explained by operators and signs at restaurants. Maybe priority seating was a problem at first that they've fixed by better predicting guest behavior.*

A father from Longmeadow, Massachusetts, wilted at the World, writing:

> *You should prepare us Northerners (I am assuming you actually live in Alabama) for the incredible heat and humidity if you go to Disney World in the summer. It was at times overwhelming for us. Light-colored clothing, hats, and water bottles are an absolute must. [Speaking of water], you prepared us well for the expensive food, but $2.50 for 12 ounces of cold water is a hell of a lot to pay without a couple of shots of good scotch wrapped around it.*

A Hampton, Connecticut, dad passes on this tip about preregistration at Disney resorts:

> *I called ahead of time to get their preregistration policy because we would be arriving early Monday morning. This proved to be a great move. We arrived at the resort at 7:30 a.m. We were able to preregister and obtain our Length of Stay passes (two days, one night), and it only took us 15 minutes. We could not go to our rooms until after 3 p.m., but by preregistering early, we were able to use all the resort facilities and the Disney transportation.*

A couple from Milwaukee writes:

> *We have been to WDW many times. Seeing it, however, this time with our 4½-year-old, we were struck by how extremely loud everything is. [One show] was so loud, we were afraid it would do permanent damage to all of our ears—especially our 4½-year-old's. Does anyone check the decibel levels?*

On another subject, a mother from Savannah, Georgia, submits this opinion:

> *The final point I would like to address is babies and small children; nothing adds to the stress of a long, hot day like the sound of crying and screaming. Even our four-year-old noticed that "those babies don't like it here." If for some reason this is the only time you will ever be able to come to Walt Disney World, I guess there is no getting around it, but in reality it would be a good idea to wait until the kids are old enough to handle the place. There is a lot more to consider than the idea that the baby would like seeing Mickey Mouse.*

A woman from Pasadena, California, expresses similar thoughts:

> *My husband and I do not have children and were acutely aware of the masses of crying and screaming kids at every park. Be warned that at least one screaming child will be on every bus, in every line, on every ride, and in every restaurant.*

But a mother of two, from Columbus, Ohio, disagreed, writing:

> *While it is an exhausting vacation to take with young children, I think your guidebook underestimates the value of taking them when they are still young and so into the characters and the fantasy.*

A couple from Bloomington, Indiana, has this to say:

> *My wife and I are 42 years old. We took your advice on taking an afternoon break. That two–three hours' rest time back at the [hotel] kept us refreshed for our entire stay. I think without the afternoon breaks we would have missed more and enjoyed less.*

Similarly, a Michigan woman states:

> *We were so glad we took the nap advice. At first we thought no way, but then thought about it and it was such good advice. I think the adults needed it more than the kids. We were all ready and willing for our afternoon naps, and had a great time when we returned [to the theme park].*

A 12-year-old girl from Louisville, however, thought we had overstated the case, writing:

> *I do not understand why you are convinced that people cannot make it through the day without stopping to take a nap. I could probably make it through two days without stopping for a nap.*

A dad from Kirkland, Washington, describes how he kept track of his teenage daughter:

> *We found WDW to be a relatively safe environment for all. My daughter, who is 14, got around just fine by herself with no problems. I would recommend giving your teenagers some space, and [allow them to] be by themselves. We rented pagers from the Port Orleans guest services, and if we needed to get in touch with each other we just called the other's pager. The cost is very minimal for the peace of mind [the pagers] give you.*

A mom from Wilmington, Delaware, thinks we seriously overrate Disney thrill rides:

> *You are much too "wussie" when it comes to coasters. I kept waiting for Space Mountain to get scary. Big Thunder was just plain fun, and Splash Mountain didn't get me wet enough to do any good. I can't imagine Star Tours, Body Wars, and especially the tea cups getting anyone the least bit sick (well, maybe Body Wars!). I hope I'm never on the Tower of Terror with you!*

A dad from Claremont, New Hampshire, tested an *Unofficial Guide* claim and writes:

> *You hit it on the head when you said kids remember the pool at their motel. I waited a week before asking my five-year-old son what he remembered about his vacation: answer 1. the sandbox at the Disney Vacation Club. Last time I checked he had a sandbox in the backyard. . . . Must have been the Florida sun!*

On the subject of children's responses, a man from Plano, Texas, contributes this advice:

> *While on the subject, some parents might benefit from two other things that we learned. First, from our use in conversation of your terms "switching off" or "baby swapping," our daughter quickly caught on to the fact that she was standing in line for a ride that was potentially terrifying for her. As a result, her own imagination-*

driven panic sometimes led to messy scenes in the anterooms of rides (like Body Wars) that Mom and Dad took turns experiencing but had no intention of forcing on her. Second, and more happily, it occurred to us that Dumbo, the Mad Tea Party, and the delightful Cranium Command (all of which we experienced multiple times) were, in effect, "thrill rides" for our five-year-old. If a flying elephant can give a small child the same gleeful exhilaration that her parents enjoy on Star Tours, then the wait in line is justified in both cases.

Though this woman from Herndon, Virginia, didn't use the *Unofficial Guide* touring plans, she clearly got the main point of the book:

In all honesty, we didn't use any of your touring plans. After reading them I thought to myself, "you have to be kidding." Your plans did offer us hours of entertainment, though. We imagined ourselves following them, and all that went through our minds was that we had to go, go, go. We can't stop. We have to run, jump, push, and shove to get to Space Mountain by 7:10 am! Your plans are a great idea, but I'd rather go in the off-season and take my time.

In contrast, a woman from Baltimore, Ohio, elevated planning to new heights, reporting:

I made up little laminated pocket-size cards to take with me to help pinpoint items of interest and where to find them. (My co-workers thought I was nuts when they saw my cards—but they were very handy!) I also had day-to-day plans (that matched the laminated cards) typed out and taped to the wall of my hotel room to check every night for the next day, i.e., phone numbers to call for lunch/dinner reservations, questions to ask, etc. Am I too organized?

And a woman from Milford, Connecticut, learned something about letting the "tail wag the dog":

The plans we used for touring Epcot didn't work out perfectly mainly because I am one of those compulsive agenda followers and my husband was the complete opposite (wanted to do what he wanted to do, when he wanted to do it). Our second day at WDW was the make-it-or-break-it day for us. I learned to lighten up a bit with the plans, my husband decided to give the plans a chance, and we decided to do a vote as a family on certain attractions, whether to see them or not. Everything was great after that!

A woman from Readsboro, Vermont, shares this tip for beating the crowds when Epcot or the Magic Kingdom close early:

> *Here's a tip for anyone who wants to avoid the crush of cars leaving any park after closing (when the parks close early). Choose ahead of time a restaurant close to the park you are visiting for the day. For instance, we decided to eat at the Big River Grille & Brewing Works on the BoardWalk after spending the day at World Showcase. We drove to the BoardWalk parking lot and then walked into Epcot from there. We stayed to watch IllumiNations from the bridge near the International Gateway. We then walked to the restaurant and left after dinner into little traffic. This will also work in the Magic Kingdom if you have dinner at one of the resorts on the monorail, as the line for the express monorail back to the TTC is much longer than the monorail to the resorts.*

On things out-of-the-world, an English family took a day to visit the Kennedy Space Center, and they relate their experience as follows:

> *We also had a day at NASA, which I appreciate is difficult for you to include in your book. My friend had told me about having to buy tickets for the IMAX presentations and the bus tour. When she went several years ago, however, they had been given [departure] times for their bus tour. [During our visit], we were simply told that buses departed every 15 minutes. The queue was HORRENDOUS. In fact, the queues to buy tickets in the first place were horrendous too, and the whole place felt very badly organized in comparison to Disney.*

And finally, a father of two from Winnipeg, Manitoba, learned the quintessential Walt Disney World mantra from his young daughter:

> *Our six-year-old asks the same three questions about every attraction: Is it real? Will it eat me? and Can we go again?*

And so it goes.

Index

Magic Kingdom
Recommended Attraction Visitation Times

If you tour on an early-entry day, move all recommended attraction visitation times up one hour. It is best to see attractions with visitation times listed as "anytime" during the more crowded middle part of the day (noon to 4 p.m.).

1. *Alien Encounter:* Before 10 a.m., during parades, or after 6 p.m.
2. Ariel's Grotto: Before 10 a.m./after 9 p.m.
3. Astro Orbiter: Before 11 a.m./late p.m.
4. Barnstormer: Before 10:30 a.m., during events, or just before closing
5. Big Thunder Mountain Railroad: Before 10 a.m./hour before closing
6. Buzz Lightyear's Space Ranger Station: Anytime
7. Cinderella's Golden Carrousel: Before 11 a.m./after 8 p.m.
8. *Country Bear Jamboree:* Before 11:30 a.m., during parades, 2 hours before closing
9. *The Diamond Horseshoe Saloon Revue:* Per entertainment schedule
10. Donald's Boat: Anytime
11. Dumbo: Before 10 a.m./after 9 p.m.
12. Frontierland Shootin' Arcade: Anytime
13. *The Hall of Presidents:* Anytime
14. The Haunted Mansion: Before 11:30 a.m./after 8 p.m.
15. It's a Small World: Anytime
16. Jungle Cruise: Before 10 a.m./2 hours before closing
17. *Legend of the Lion King:* Before 11 a.m./during parades
18. *Liberty Belle* Riverboat: Anytime
19. Mad Tea Party: Before 11 a.m./after 5 p.m.

—continued on other side—

Magic Kingdom

Magic Kingdom
Recommended Attraction Visitation Times

If you tour on an early-entry day, move all recommended attraction visitation times up one hour. It is best to see attractions with visitation times listed as "anytime" during the more crowded middle part of the day (noon to 4 p.m.).

—continued from other side—

20. Main Street Cinema: Anytime
21. Mickey's and Minnie's Country Houses: Before 11:30 a.m./after 4:30 p.m.
22. Mike Fink Keelboats: Before 11:30 a.m./after 5 p.m. (closes at dusk)
23. Mr. Toad's Wild Ride: Before 11 a.m./after 6 p.m.
24. Peter Pan's Flight: Before 10 a.m./after 6 p.m.
25. Pirates of the Caribbean: Before noon/after 5 p.m.
26. Skyway: Before noon/during special events
27. Snow White's Adventures: Before 11 a.m./after 6 p.m.
28. Space Mountain: Park opening, between 6 and 7 p.m., or hour before closing
29. Splash Mountain: Park opening, during parades, or just before closing
30. Swiss Family Treehouse: Before 11:30 a.m./after 5 p.m.
31. *The Timekeeper:* Anytime
32. Tom Sawyer Island: Midmorning thru late afternoon (closes at dusk)
33. Tomorrowland Speedway: Before 11 a.m./after 5 p.m.
34. Tomorrowland Transit Authority: Anytime
35. Toontown Hall of Fame: Before 10:30 a.m./after 5:30 p.m.
36. *Tropical Serenade:* Before 11 a.m./after 3:30 p.m.
37. *Walt Disney's Carousel of Progress:* Anytime
38. Walt Disney World Railroad: Anytime

Magic Kingdom

Magic Kingdom
One-Day Touring Plan for Adults
Pocket Outline Version

For the detailed version of this touring plan, see page 421.

1. Arrive at TTC 50 min. prior to opening.
2. Go to City Hall for park maps containing the daily entertainment schedule.
3. As soon as Tomorrowland opens, experience *Alien Encounter.*
4. Ride Space Mountain.
5. Ride Splash Mountain.
6. Ride Big Thunder Mountain Railroad.
7. See the *Country Bear Jamboree.*
8. See The Haunted Mansion.
9. Eat lunch.
10. Ride Pirates of the Caribbean.
11. Take the train to Mickey's Toontown Fair.
12. Tour the Fair, then go to Tomorrowland.
13. Ride the Tomorrowland Transit Authority.

14. See *Walt Disney's Carousel of Progress.*
15. Ride Buzz Lightyear.
16. Experience *The Timekeeper.*
17. Experience *The Hall of Presidents* and the *Liberty Belle* Riverboat.
18. Return to Fantasyland and see *Legend of the Lion King.*
19. Ride It's a Small World.
20. Ride Peter Pan's Flight.
21. Back in Adventureland, ride the Jungle Cruise.
22. Explore the Swiss Family Treehouse.
23. Pick up any attractions you might have missed.
24. Browse Main Street.

Magic Kingdom

Magic Kingdom
Author's Selective One-Day Touring Plan for Adults
Pocket Outline Version

For the detailed version of this touring plan, see page 424.

1. Arrive at TTC 50 min. prior to opening.
2. Go to City Hall for park maps containing the daily entertainment schedule.
3. As soon as Tomorrowland opens, experience *Alien Encounter*.
4. Ride Space Mountain.
5. Ride Splash Mountain.
6. Ride Big Thunder Mountain Railroad.
7. See The Haunted Mansion.
8. See *Legend of the Lion King*.
9. Eat lunch.
10. Ride Pirates of the Caribbean.
11. Take the railroad from Frontierland to Mickey's Toontown Fair.
12. Tour the Fair, then go to Tomorrowland.
13. Ride the Tomorrowland Transit Authority.
14. See *Walt Disney's Carousel of Progress*.
15. Experience *The Timekeeper*.
16. See *The Hall of Presidents*.
17. Ride It's a Small World.
18. Ride Peter Pan's Flight.
19. See the *Country Bear Jamboree*.
20. Visit the Swiss Family Treehouse.
21. Take the Jungle Cruise.
22. Pick up any attractions you might have missed.
23. Browse Main Street.

Magic Kingdom

Magic Kingdom
One-Day Touring Plan for Parents with Young Children
Pocket Outline Version

For the detailed version of this touring plan, see page 426.
Review the Small Child Fright Potential Chart on pages 157–161.

1. Arrive at TTC 50 min. prior to opening.
2. Go to City Hall for park maps containing the daily entertainment schedule.
3. Rent strollers (if necessary).
4. Ride Dumbo the Flying Elephant.
5. Ride Peter Pan's Flight.
6. See *Legend of the Lion King*.
7. Go to The Haunted Mansion.
8. See the *Country Bear Jamboree*.
9. Ride Pirates of the Caribbean.
10. Take the train to Mickey's Toontown Fair.
11. Visit Mickey's Toontown Fair.
12. Return to the hotel for lunch and a nap.
13. Return to the Magic Kingdom and visit Tom Sawyer Island in Frontierland.
14. Ride It's a Small World.
15. Ride Buzz Lightyear.
16. Ride the Tomorrowland Transit Authority.
17. Try *The Timekeeper*.
18. Check the entertainment schedule for live performances, parades, fireworks, etc., or try any attractions you missed.
19. Tour Main Street.

Magic Kingdom

Magic Kingdom
Dumbo-or-Die-in-a-Day Touring Plan
for Parents with Young Children
Pocket Outline Version

For the detailed version of this touring plan, see page 429.
Review the Small Child Fright Potential Chart on pages 157–161.
(Interrupt the touring plan for lunch, rest, and dinner.)

1. Arrive at TTC 50 min. prior to opening.
2. Go to City Hall for park maps containing the daily entertainment schedule.
3. Rent a stroller (if needed).
4. Go to Cinderella's Castle.
5. Make dinner reservation at the castle.
6. Ride Dumbo the Flying Elephant.
7. Ride Dumbo again.
8. Ride Mr. Toad's Wild Ride.
9. Ride Peter Pan's Flight.
10. Ride Cinderella's Golden Carrousel.
11. See *Legend of the Lion King*.
12. Go to Tomorrowland.
13. Ride the Tomorrowland Speedway.
14. Ride the Astro Orbiter.
15. Ride Buzz Lightyear.
16. Return to the hotel for lunch and a nap.
17. Return to the Magic Kingdom. Go to Frontierland.
18. Go to Tom Sawyer Island.
19. See the *Country Bear Jamboree*.
20. Take the train to Mickey's Toontown Fair.
21. Walk through Mickey's and Minnie's Country Houses and play on Donald's Boat.
22. If you have time before dinner, ride It's a Small World.
23. Eat, then see The Haunted Mansion.
24. Watch the evening parade.
25. Ride the Jungle Cruise.
26. Repeat favorite attractions.
27. Depart Magic Kingdom.

Magic Kingdom
Two-Day Touring Plan
Pocket Outline Version

For the detailed version of this touring plan, see page 432.

Day One

1. Arrive at TTC 50 min. prior to opening.
2. Go to City Hall for park maps containing the daily entertainment schedule.
3. As soon as Tomorrowland opens, experience *Alien Encounter.*
4. Ride Space Mountain.
5. Ride Peter Pan's Flight.
6. See *Legend of the Lion King.*
7. Ride It's a Small World.
8. Experience The Haunted Mansion.
9. See *The Hall of Presidents* .
10. Eat lunch.
11. Ride the *Liberty Belle* Riverboat.
12. In Frontierland, explore Tom Sawyer Island.
13. See the *Country Bear Jamboree.*
14. Enjoy the shops, see some live entertainment, or revisit favorite attractions.

Magic Kingdom

Magic Kingdom
Two-Day Touring Plan
Pocket Outline Version

For the detailed version of this touring plan, see page 434.

Day Two

1. Arrive at TTC 50 min. prior to opening.
2. Go to City Hall for park maps containing the daily entertainment schedule.
3. In Frontierland, ride Splash Mountain.
4. Ride Big Thunder Mountain Railroad.
5. In Adventureland, ride the Jungle Cruise.
6. See the *Tropical Serenade (Enchanted Tiki Birds)*.
7. Walk through the Swiss Family Treehouse.
8. Enjoy Pirates of the Caribbean.
9. Eat lunch.
10. Take the Walt Disney World Railroad to Mickey's Toontown Fair.

11. Tour Mickey's Toontown Fair.
12. Go to Tomorrowland.
13. If you haven't eaten yet, try Cosmic Ray's Starlight Cafe or the Plaza Pavilion.
14. Ride the Tomorrowland Transit Authority.
15. See *Walt Disney's Carousel of Progress*.
16. Ride Buzz Lightyear.
17. Experience *The Timekeeper*.
18. Enjoy the shops, see some live entertainment, or revisit favorite attractions.

Disney-MGM Studios
Recommended Attraction Visitation Times

If you tour on an early-entry day, move all recommended attraction visitation times up one hour. It is best to see attractions with visitation times listed as "anytime" during the more crowded middle part of the day (noon to 4 p.m.).

1. The Magic of Disney Animation: Before 11 a.m./after 5 p.m.
2. The Great Movie Ride: Before 10 a.m./after 5 p.m.
3. Honey, I Shrunk the Kids playground: Before 10 a.m./after dark
4. *Indiana Jones Epic Stunt Spectacular:* First three morning or last evening show
5. *The Making of Disney's Latest Feature Film:* Anytime
6. ABC Sound Studio: Before 11 a.m./after 5 p.m.
7. *MuppetVision 4D:* Before 11 a.m./after 4 p.m.
8. New York Street Back Lot: Anytime
9. Star Tours: First hour and a half after opening
10. *SuperStar Television:* After 10 a.m.
11. *Theater of the Stars:* Evening
12. Tower of Terror: Before 10 a.m./after 5 p.m.
13. *Voyage of the Little Mermaid:* Before 9:30 a.m./just before closing
14. Fantasmic!: Evening
15. *Backlot Theater:* First show/evening
16. Disney-MGM Studios Backlot Tour: Anytime

Disney-MGM Studios

Disney-MGM Studios
One-Day Touring Plan
Pocket Outline Version

For the detailed version of this touring plan, see page 555.
(Before you go, check detailed itinerary for park opening procedures.)

1. Arrive 40 minutes before official opening time.
2. Pick up a handout guidemap containing the daily entertainment schedule. Ride the Tower of Terror.
3. Ride The Great Movie Ride (3a) and Star Tours (3b) and see *Voyage of the Little Mermaid* (3c) and *Indiana Jones Epic Stunt Spectacular* (3d).
4. See *MuppetVision 4D*.
5. Take The Magic of Disney Animation Tour.
6. Now is a good time to eat lunch.
7. Take the Disney-MGM Studios Backlot Tour.
8. Take the soundstage tour.
9. See *The Making of Disney's Latest Feature Film*.
10. Work live shows into the touring plan.
11. Visit the ABC Sound Studio (11a) and *SuperStar Television* (11b).
12. Explore the New York Street set.
13. Tour Hollywood and Sunset Boulevards. Enjoy *Fantasmic!*
14. Depart the Studios.

Universal Studios Florida
Recommended Attraction Visitation Times

It is best to see attractions with visitation times listed as "anytime" during the more crowded middle part of the day (noon to 4 p.m.).

1. "Alfred Hitchcock: The Art of Making Movies": After 3:30 p.m.
2. *Animal Actors Stage:* After experiencing all rides
3. Back to the Future—The Ride: First thing after park opens
4. *Beetlejuice's Rock 'n Roll Graveyard Revue:* At your convenience
5. *A Day in the Park with Barney:* Anytime
6. *Dynamite Nights Stuntacular:* Evening
7. Earthquake—The Big One: In morning, after Kongfrontation
8. E.T. Adventure: Before 10 a.m.
9. *Fievel's Playland:* Anytime
10. The Funtastic World of Hanna-Barbera: Before 11 a.m.
11. *The Gory Gruesome & Grotesque Horror Make-Up Show:* After experiencing all rides
12. *Hercules and Xena:* After experiencing all rides
13. Jaws: Before 11 a.m.
14. Kongfrontation: Before 11 a.m.
15. Lucy, a Tribute: Anytime
16. Nickelodeon Studios Walking Tour: When shows are in production
17. Street Scenes: Anytime
18. *Terminator 2: 3-D:* After 3:30 p.m.
19. *Twister:* First show after experiencing all rides
20. *The Wild, Wild, Wild West Stunt Show:* After experiencing all rides

Universal Studios
One-Day Touring Plan
Pocket Outline Version

For the detailed version of this touring plan, see page 581.

1. Call (407) 363-8000 the day before your visit for the official opening time.
2. Arrive 50 minutes before opening time and pick up a map and daily entertainment schedule.
3. Line up at the turnstile. Ask if any rides are closed and adjust touring plan accordingly.
4. Ride Back to the Future.
5. Ride E.T. Adventure.
6. Ride Jaws.
7. Ride Kongfrontation.
8. Ride Earthquake—The Big One.
9. Ride The Funtastic World of Hanna-Barbera.
10. See *Twister*.
11. This is a good time for lunch.
12. See the *Animal Actors Stage* (12a), *Beetlejuice's Rock 'n Roll Graveyard Revue* (12b), *Dynamite Nights Stuntacular* (12c), and *The Wild, Wild, Wild West Stunt Show* (12d) as convenient, according to the daily entertainment schedule. As time permits, work *The Gory Gruesome & Grotesque Horror Make-Up Show* (12e) and *Hercules and Xena* (12f), which run continuously, into your schedule. See *Terminator 2: 3-D* (12g) after 3:30 p.m. See "Alfred Hitchcock: The Art of Making Movies" (12h) last.
13. Take school-age children on the Nickelodeon tour in late afternoon and preschoolers to see Barney after riding E.T.
14. Revisit favorite rides and shows. See any live performances you may have missed.

1999 *Unofficial Guide* Reader Survey

If you would like to express your opinion about Walt Disney World or this guidebook, complete the following survey and mail it to:

> *Unofficial Guide* Reader Survey
> P.O. Box 43059
> Birmingham, AL 35243

Inclusive dates of your visit _____

Members of your party: Person 1   Person 2   Person 3   Person 4   Person 5

Gender (M or F)   _____   _____   _____   _____   _____
Age   _____   _____   _____   _____   _____

How many times have you been to Walt Disney World? _____
On your most recent trip, where did you stay? _____

Concerning accommodations, on a scale with 100 best and 0 worst, how would you rate:

The quality of your room? _____   The value for the money? _____
The quietness of your room? _____   Check-in/checkout efficiency? _____
Shuttle service to the parks? _____   Swimming pool facilities? _____

Did you rent a car? _____   From whom? _____

Concerning your rental car, on a scale with 100 best and 0 worst, how would you rate:

Pickup processing efficiency? _____   Return processing efficiency? _____
Condition of the car? _____   Cleanliness of the car? _____
Airport shuttle efficiency? _____

Concerning your touring:

Who in your party was most responsible for planning the itinerary? _____
What time did you normally get started in the morning? _____
Did you usually arrive at the theme parks prior to opening? _____
Did you return to your hotel for rest during the day? _____
What time did you normally go to bed at night? _____
If a Disney Resort guest, did you participate in early entry? _____

On a scale with 100 best and 0 worst, rate how the touring plans worked:

Park	*Name of Plan*	*Rating*
Magic Kingdom	_____	_____
EPCOT	_____	_____
Disney-MGM	_____	_____
Animal Kingdom	_____	_____
Universal	_____	_____

Concerning your dining experiences (also see WDW Restaurant Survey on following pages):

How many restaurant meals (including fast food) did you average per day? _____

How much (approximately) did your party spend on meals per day? _____

Favorite restaurant outside of Walt Disney World? _____

Did you buy this guide: Before leaving? _____ While on your trip? _____

How did you hear about this guide?

Loaned or recommended by a friend _____   Radio or TV _____

Newspaper or magazine _____   Bookstore salesperson _____

Just picked it out on my own _____   Library _____

Internet _____

What other guidebooks did you use on this trip? _____

_____

On the 100 best and 0 worst scale, how would you rate them? _____

_____

Using the same scale, how would you rate the *Unofficial Guide?* _____

Are *Unofficial Guides* readily available in bookstores in your area? _____

Have you used other *Unofficial Guides?* _____ Which one(s)? _____

Comments about your Walt Disney World vacation or about the *Unofficial Guide:* _____

_____

_____

_____

_____

_____

_____

_____

_____

Walt Disney World Restaurant Survey

Tell us about your Walt Disney World dining experiences. Listed below are the full-service restaurants. Beside each restaurant is a thumbs-up and thumbs-down symbol. If you enjoyed the restaurant enough that you would like to eat there again, circle the thumbs-up symbol. If not, circle the thumbs-down symbol.

Walt Disney World Full-Service Restaurants (in alphabetical order):

Restaurant	Location		
Arthur's 27	Buena Vista Palace	👍	👎
Artist Point	Wilderness Lodge Resort	👍	👎
Baskervilles	Grosvenor Resort	👍	👎
Benihana	Hilton	👍	👎
Biergarten	Germany: Epcot	👍	👎
Big River Grille & Brewing Works	Disney's BoardWalk	👍	👎
Boatwright's Dining Hall	Dixie Landings Resort	👍	👎
Bonfamille's Cafe	Port Orleans Resort	👍	👎
Bongo's Cuban Cafe	Disney's West Side	👍	👎
California Grill	Contemporary Resort	👍	👎
Cape May Cafe	Beach Club Resort	👍	👎
Cap'n Jack's Oyster Bar	Downtown Disney	👍	👎
Captain's Tavern	Caribbean Beach Resort	👍	👎
Le Cellier Steakhouse	Canada: Epcot	👍	👎
Chef Mickey's	Contemporary Resort	👍	👎
Chefs de France	France: Epcot	👍	👎
Cinderella's Royal Table	Magic Kingdom	👍	👎
Citricos	Grand Floridian Resort	👍	👎
Concourse Steakhouse	Contemporary Resort	👍	👎
Coral Cafe	WDW Dolphin	👍	👎
Coral Isle Cafe	Polynesian Resort	👍	👎
Coral Reef	Living Seas: Epcot	👍	👎
Crystal Palace	Magic Kingdom	👍	👎
ESPN Club	Disney's BoardWalk	👍	👎
50's Prime Time Cafe	Disney-MGM Studios	👍	👎
Finn's Grill	Hilton	👍	👎
Flying Fish Cafe	Disney's BoardWalk	👍	👎
Fulton's Crab House	Pleasure Island	👍	👎
The Garden Grill	Land Pavilion: Epcot	👍	👎
Grand Floridian Cafe	Grand Floridian Resort	👍	👎
Gulliver's Grill at Garden Grove	WDW Swan	👍	👎

Walt Disney World Full-Service Restaurants
(in alphabetical order): *(Continued)*

Harry's Safari Bar and Grill	WDW Dolphin	👍 👎
Hollywood & Vine	Disney-MGM Studios	👍 👎
Hollywood Brown Derby	Disney-MGM Studios	👍 👎
House of Blues	Disney's West Side	👍 👎
Juan & Only's Bar & Jail	WDW Dolphin	👍 👎
Kimonos	WDW Swan	👍 👎
Liberty Tree Tavern	Magic Kingdom	👍 👎
Mama Melrose's Ristorante	Disney-MGM Studios	👍 👎
Maya Grill	Coronado Springs Resort	👍 👎
Narcoossee's	Grand Floridian Resort	👍 👎
Nine Dragons Restaurant	China: Epcot	👍 👎
Official All-Star Cafe	Disney's Wide World of Sports	👍 👎
'Ohana	Polynesian Resort	👍 👎
Olivia's Cafe	Old Key West Resort	👍 👎
L'Originale Alfredo di Roma Ristorante	Italy: Epcot	👍 👎
The Outback	Buena Vista Palace	👍 👎
Palio	WDW Swan	👍 👎
Planet Hollywood	Pleasure Island	👍 👎
Pleasure Island Jazz Company	Pleasure Island	👍 👎
Portobello Yacht Club	Pleasure Island	👍 👎
Rainforest Cafe	Downtown Disney and Animal Kingdom	👍 👎
Restaurant Akershus	Norway: Epcot	👍 👎
Restaurant Marrakesh	Morocco: Epcot	👍 👎
Rose & Crown Dining Room	United Kingdom: Epcot	👍 👎
San Angel Inn	Mexico: Epcot	👍 👎
Sci-Fi Dine-In Theater Restaurant	Disney-MGM Studios	👍 👎
Seasons Dining Room	Disney Institute	👍 👎
Spoodles	Disney's BoardWalk	👍 👎
Tempura Kiku	Japan: Epcot	👍 👎
Teppanyaki Dining Rooms	Japan: Epcot	👍 👎
Tony's Town Square Restaurant	Magic Kingdom	👍 👎
Victoria and Albert's	Grand Floridian Resort	👍 👎
Whispering Canyon Cafe	Wilderness Lodge Resort	👍 👎
Wolfgang Puck Cafe	Disney's West Side	👍 👎
Yacht Club Galley	Yacht Club Resort	👍 👎
Yachtsman Steakhouse	Yacht Club Resort	👍 👎